UP TO A POINT

In search of pyramids in Britain and Ireland

David Winpenny

CONTENTS

Design and layout by David Winpenny

First published in 2009
by Sessions of York, Huntington Road, York YO31 9HS

ISBN: 978-1-85072-398-1

PREFACE

There are 225 individual pyramids listed in this book. They are found in 179 locations throughout England, Wales, Scotland and Ireland.

Pyramids are found almost everywhere, but there are particular concentrations in Yorkshire, which has 24, Gloucestershire (9) and southwest Scotland (16). Wales, though, musters only 10, and there are none that we have dicovered in Wiltshire or Cambridgeshire, for example. Ireland has plenty, though, some of them especially impressive.

What makes a pyramid - and how we chose them for inclusion

Essentially, a pyramid is four (sometimes three) triangular sides that join together to make a solid. That sounds simple enough, but the British and Irish pyramids vary enormously, as the pihotographs in this book show - some are the traditional Egyptian shape, others are taller and thinner. There are some set on plinths; some are stepped. The criteria used to include or exclude certain pyramids from this book are somewhat elastic, but in general we have excluded pyramid roofs, unless the roof comes to, or nearly to, ground level. There will be disagreement about our choices - sometimes we have included marginal examples with good stories - and there will no doubt be good pyramids that we have missed. We should be grateful to know of them.

How this book is organised

After the introduction, nine 'tours' visit all the pyramids. They radiate from our base in North Yorkshire, though the tours to Wales and to the western side of Scotland follow on from the tours before them without a 'return to base'. The Irish tour starts in Larne and goes generally anti-clockwise around the island.

Visiting the pyramids

Some of the pyramids are in churchyards or in gardens that are open to the public. Others are public buildings, or can be easily viewed from the road or public footpaths. Please bear in mind, however, that many are on private property. We received generous permission from owners to visit their pyramids (and, from many, lots of information about them, too). **Please respect their privacy by remembering to ask permission if you want to see pyramids that are not publicly accessible.**

David Winpenny
April 2009

INTRODUCTION

WHEN QUEEN VICTORIA ascended Creag-an-Lurachain by pony carriage in August 1862 to lay the foundation stone of a pyramid to her beloved Albert, it is unlikely that she knew she was following in a long line of emperors, living gods, medieval monks, Knights Templar, opera composers, landscape gardeners and freemasons.

Overcome with grief, her purpose was to commemorate the Prince Consort in a monument that was both intensely private and very public. The pyramid is on her own favourite estate of Balmoral, and was in part constructed by herself and her children, yet it is in a very visible position on the hillside - an implacable granite triangle keeping watch over the affairs of royalty and commoners on Deeside.

The pyramid shape Victoria chose to commemorate is the most ancient of all memorials. The pyramids of Egypt are the only one of the Seven Wonders of the World to have survived to today. And they have held a powerful sway over all ages and over people of widely-differing ideas.

Sacred mountains

The first pyramids were probably no more than heaps of rock piled over the graves of important men. They developed gradually into rectangular platforms with sloping sides, then into step-pyramids. One of the earliest of these was built for the Pharaoh Zoser (or Djoser) at Sakkara, south of Cairo. It dates from around 2600 BC.

What were these pyramid builders trying to do by building higher and higher? One idea was the 'sacred mountain' that held the body of the dead ruler and brought him closer to the abode of the gods up above. This seems to have been an almost-universal concept; there are pyramid-shaped structures right around the world, including Tibet, Australia, North America and Indonesia. The Aztec and Mayan peoples of Central and South America built their own versions of pyramids. In Africa there are pyramid-shaped structures, too - the great mosque in Timbuktu is pyramidal. In Germany, Italy and Greece there are hillsides reshaped into pyramids, and a huge one was tentatively identified in Bosnia in 2006. Even in England prehistoric people got in on the act - Silbury Hill in Wiltshire, the tallest prehistoric man-made structure in Europe, is thought by many experts to have been a version of a pyramid.

It was the Egyptian pyramids, though, that caught the imagination of the West throughout the centuries. The step pyramid was developed into the smooth-sided pyramid. The best-known examples are, and always have been, those at Giza. The greatest of them is the pyramid of Kheops or Khufu. Said to have been started around 2560 BC, today it rises 449 feet above the sands. When it had its original brilliant white limestone casing, it was another 32 feet high.

The Greeks seem to have ignored the pyramids - except possibly to give them a humorous, or diminishing, name; the word pyramid may derive from the Greek word for a small cake.

Step pyramid at Sakkara, Egypt

OPPOSITE:
Pyramid to the memory of Prince Albert, Balmoral

1

The pyramids at Gizeh, by Louis Haghe, c1846

Nevertheless, when the Romans conquered Egypt in 30 BC the pyramids had already been famous for centuries. In 332 BC Alexander the Great had taken the country from the grip of the Persian empire and had founded the city of Alexandria on the coast of Egypt the following year. On Alexander's death his empire was divided; Ptolemy, one of his generals, became ruler of Egypt. It was Ptolemy's descendent Cleopatra who finally lost her empire to the Romans.

The Cestius angle

The Romans might have been in charge in Egypt, but Egypt had a marked effect on them. The Romans absorbed the Egyptian gods into their culture, and worship of Isis and Osiris became very widespread. It was inevitable that the Romans would begin to imitate the pyramids in the monuments.

There were several pyramids known to have been constructed in imperial Rome, including one on the Vatican Hill demolished in the 15th century, but only one remains today - the pyramid of Cestius. It is an impressive work - 100 Roman feet (about 96 modern feet) high and made with a brick-faced concrete core covered in white marble. It occupies a prominent position at the point where the Via Ostiensis and the street along the slopes of the Aventine Hill meet. It was one of the landmarks that visitors entering Rome from the port at Ostia knew to look for. In the 18th and 19th centuries the cemetery for Rome's non-Catholic residents was laid out around the pyramid; both Keats and Shelley are buried there.

And who was Cestius? The inscription on his pyramid says that he was Caius Cestius Epulo, son of Lucius, and that he came from the Pobilian line. He is described as praetor, tribune and official of the public banquets. So he was an aristocrat, but not of the imperial family. When he died, somewhere around 12 BC, he left his estate to two heirs, who followed his demands that he had a pyramid built in his memory; the inscription says it took 330 days.

Cestius' pyramid was hugely influential for more than one and a half millennia. It is unlike the Great Pyramid at Giza because the base angles are not the 52 degrees the Egyptians used but about 70 degrees. This gives the pyramid a more-pointed profile. Its shape was copied by many of the 18th-century pyramid builders in the West - the twin pyramids at Naas in Ireland (see page 343) are good examples, but the shape occurs, too, at places as far apart as Falmouth (see page 157) and Kilmuir on Skye (see page 268). There are other examples in France, Germany and Sweden.

Pilgrims, Mummies and Venice Treacle

It is unsurprising that it was the Cestius pyramid and not the Egyptian originals that first influenced new pyramid builders. Egypt was for centuries largely unvisited. The few intrepid travellers who reached Giza were, of course, impressed - but confused. The early 7th-century Bishop Isidore of Seville reported correctly that the pyramids were tombs, though he had not been to see them. But in the 14th century the Anglo-Irish monk Symon Semeonis thought the pyramids were 'those granaries made by Joseph' that are mentioned in the *Book of Genesis*.

Sometimes medieval pilgrims visited Egypt as part of a pilgrimage to the Holy Land - there were special itineraries for them, showing them the site of the Burning Bush and the house where Jesus lived as a young child. There was also interest in Egyptian burials, but for a rather macabre reason; the preparation of drugs. Superstition said that by including pieces of mummy in potions their efficacy was increased. This notion was popularised by the

Galen

Greek-born physician Galen as early as the 2nd century AD. He advocated a brew called theriac, said to be sovereign against poisoning. Its 64 'active' ingredients included not only mummy but also goat dung and the heads of adders. An interesting footnote to this is that theriac was said to have been invented by Mithridate, King of Pontus - about whom the 14-year-old Mozart, later a freemason, wrote one of his early operas. Theriac was also known as Venice Treacle, and was a remedy much taken even in the 17th and 18th centuries, including by Samuel Pepys.

Star y-pointing

The Romans also copied another sort of pyramid - the sort built for people less exalted than the Pharaohs. By the 12th century BC the Egyptians began to build bijou pyramids, often sitting them on cubes of masonry - there are good examples at Deir-el-Medineh near Thebes. This style of pyramid monument continued beyond the end of the Roman empire, and far from Rome; there are examples in Syria, built by 5th-century Christians. One of Britain's earliest pyramids, the mausoleum at Penicuik in Scotland, which dates from 1683, employs the same plinth-and-pyramid form.

Much of this knowledge of early pyramids became known to a wide audience only in the 17th century, when publications explaining the wonders of the ancient world began to appear. There had been some decorative use of pyramids and obelisks in monuments in the late 16th century, but there were no free-standing pyramids. Milton wrote in his *Epitaph on Shakespeare*:

What needs my Shakspeare for his honoured bones
The labour of an age in piled stones,
Or that his hallowed reliques should be hid
Under a star y-pointing pyramid?

Until the late 18th century the pyramid remained a dark, shadowy outline shape that often appeared behind monumental groups of sculpted figures - there are some good examples in Westminster Abbey, as well as in many more humble churches across Britain and Ireland. The designers and makers of them are following the lead of great sculptors like Raphael, Bernini and Canova, who also used the pyramid background to their funerary monuments.

The first proper survey of Khufu's Great Pyramid, with drawings of the exterior and interior, was made by John Greaves of Merton College, Oxford. It was published in 1646 as *Pyramidographia*. Further publications about the pyramids followed - but they might have remained of interest only to a few historians, had it not been for the growth of Freemasonry in the 18th century.

Templars, Rosicrucians and the Esoteric

The history of Freemasonry is complicated - and confusing. It is very hard to separate myth from fact. We know that in the Middle Ages the top stonemasons, who worked on great cathedrals and castles, were organised into Lodges. They were freemasons in the sense that they were not tied to a particular job, but were free to travel wherever their skills were needed. The masons zealously guarded the secrets of their craft and admission to it.

The involvement of two other groups - the Knights Templar and the Rosicrucians - confuses the picture. As readers of the best-selling fantasy novel *The Da Vinci Code* know, the Knights Templar were an odd lot. Founded in 1118 to protect pilgrims to the Holy Land, their beliefs have been the subject of much speculation; they professed allegiance to the Pope and to the Catholic Church, but also followed esoteric paths, researching sacred geometry and, like the later Freemasons, viewing God as the Great Universal Architect.

The Templars were not committed to poverty; their great wealth made King Philip IV of France decide he wanted it for himself. He accused them of immorality, devil worship and abhorrence of Christian symbols. With the aid of the Pope, he had the Templars suppressed early in the 14th century.

Was that the end of the Knights Templar? Some say not, but claim that the order went underground, preserving its esoteric knowledge and beliefs, only to re-emerge centuries later - by which time it was inextricably linked with other mystical ideas, some of which were adapted by the Rosicrucians. Taking their name from books supposedly by a 15th-century alchemist 'Christian Rosenkreutz' published in the second decade of the 17th century, the Rosicrucians claimed to have occult powers and skills derived from Paracelsus. They mixed their mystical ideas with the genuine exchange of scientific knowledge.

Scots, Egyptians, Greeks and Romans

The strands of ancient arcane knowledge came together in modern Freemasonry. The first freemasons' lodges as they are recognised today were founded in Scotland around 1600. Over the following century their ideas were gradually formalised into a set of beliefs and rituals that had many Egyptian overtones.

There were, in particular, the notion of God as the Great Architect of the Universe and the secrets of the Temple of Solomon. The building of the Temple is detailed in the biblical *First Book of Kings*; it mentions Hiram of Tyre who set up two bronze pillars at the entrance to the Sanctuary. The pillars were called Jachin (on the right hand side) and Boaz. Hiram is said to have inscribed the pillars of the Temple with the secrets of divine geometry, learned from masters in Egypt. Representations of the Jachin and Boaz columns, usually depicted as having spiral twists, are central to Masonic ritual, and influenced later architecture; the so-called 'Apprentice Pillar' in Rosslyn Chapel in Scotland and the baldaccino designed by Bernini over the high altar at St Peter's in Rome have the same spirals, for example.

The other great name associated with the Temple is Hermes Trismegistus. Hermes is a shadowy but very influential figure. Said to have been Solomon's master-mason, Hermes has mystical origins in Egypt - some sources say he was the god Thoth (see page 208), others that he emerged from the lost city of Atlantis and that he directed the construction of the pyramids in Egypt.

Whatever his beginnings, Hermes is said to have given the secrets of geometry to the Greeks, and also to have compiled mystical treatises - the Hermetic writings - that have been the basis of much western occult thinking and many exclusive, secretive societies.

So early 17th century Scottish freemasonry had a complex background - and it rapidly grew. The Freemasons set up lodges and a hierarchy based on the progress from apprentice to master-mason. They looked not only to the distant past of Hermes Trismegistus and the pyramid-builders, but also to the Roman

Hermes Trismegistus

architect Marcus Vitruvius Pollio, whose ten-volume treatise *De Architectura* was the only complete work on architectural practice to have survived from antiquity. In fact, Vitruvius was a very minor architect. His writings are confused and obscure in meaning; a very useful attribute for anyone who wanted to prove their own theories of the mystical origins of building.

Pyramids as symbols

Gradually a consensus developed as to the symbolic meaning of pyramids. The square base symbolises the base nature of mankind; we are made up of four elements - either earth, air, fire and water or our physical, astral, etheric and lower minds - which return to the earth on our death. More happily for the Christians who wanted to adopt the pyramid as a piece of useful symbolism, the triangular sides can represent the Trinity - Father, Son and Holy Spirit - or they can be thought of as the higher elements of mankind - mind, soul and spirit. There are two British pyramids that take the Trinitarian idea a stage further by having not just triangular sides but also a triangular base. The pyramid at Woodchester (see page 134) is specifically inscribed with Trinitarian texts. The Spetisbury pyramid (see page 143) was erected by a clergyman, Thomas Rackett, whom we can imagine considered the question deeply before commissioning it as a monument to his wife. And in Ireland the pyramid to the Swife family at Castlerickard in Co Meath has a triangular base, too.

Even the construction of the pyramid is said to be symbolic; we build the base on the earth, representing our grosser nature, then raise the sides, aspiring to the eternal. As we reach the summit, our different natures converge to oneness with - well, with God, or with whatever we believe in. Templars, Freemasons, Rosicrucians and New Age disciples have all believed their own versions of these ideas.

Gentlemen architects and the Temple

A knowledge of architecture, as well as of other arts and sciences, came to be seen as one of the marks of a gentleman. Books that included illustrations of pyramids as well as of classical architecture, like Roland Fréart's *Parallel of the Antient Architecture with the Modern*, in its English translation by John Evelyn published in 1664, became famous. And as gentlemen read, so they wished to discuss their reading; and where better than in their Freemasons' Lodges? It was inevitable that many of the best architects and scientists in England became Masons - Sir Christopher Wren, Sir John Vanbrugh, Robert Hooke and Nicholas Hawksmoor among them.

Wren, as far as we know, built no pyramids. He wrote that only statues are 'worthy enough to appear in the Air [that is, on the parapet or the pediment of a building]. Pyramids are Gothick' - by which he meant barbarous and uncouth. There are, though, a couple of representations of pyramids in the carved reliefs by Francis Bird on the west front of St Paul's Cathedral. One appears in the background as the Apostle Paul undergoes his Conversion on the Damascus Road; the other as Paul is preaching. Wren's Masonic interests emerge mainly, however, in his studies of the Temple of Solomon. This was a hot topic in the late 17th century; much ingenuity was spent attempting to reconcile the classical orders of architecture with the biblical descriptions of the Temple, so that architects could claim that to build in a classical style was to build religiously.

Hawksmoor took enquiries into the Temple much further. It is possible that he produced plans and elevations for a complete reconstruction of the Temple; if he did it has been lost. The Temple certainly influenced some of his surviving buildings. The supposed cubic form of Solomon's Temple (the celestial Temple mentioned in the *Book of the Revelation* is described as being a cube, too) was the basis for at least one of Hawksmoor's churches; St Mary Woolnoth in the City of London is a cube - with a tower on its west front.

How does all this relate to pyramids? Solomonic Temples and Egyptology were, to the Freemasons, all part of the same esoteric language. Vanbrugh and Hawksmoor would find our compartmentalism of knowledge mystifying. To them, all knowledge worked towards a single end, that of opening the secrets of the universe as wide as possible. Alongside the Temple and the pyramids architects studied other ancient wonders, not least the Mausoleum at Halicarnassus; Hawksmoor drew conjectural reconstructions of that, too - and built a version of it as the spire of St George's, Bloomsbury.

India, stage setting and The Wisdom of Solomon

From the mid-17th century onwards pyramids had symbolic value. They provided gravity in a landscape, allowed thoughts of mortality and the inevitability of death, and linked the present time with a purer past, when true knowledge was abroad in the world and could be united in what today we might call the Theory of Everything. And these interests were not limited to the area around the Mediterranean; it is interesting to note that Vanbrugh spent 15 months in India, working for the East India Company, between 1683 and 1685. He was based in Surat, north of Mumbai (then Bombay). There he saw the cemetery, which contained domed buildings, a column, a tower - and a number of pyramids. The sketch he made of it - done only in 1711, when he'd 'hugely turned to architecture' (as Swift wrote) - shows the pyramids clustered together with the other buildings amid trees, all behind a row of railings that ends with heavily-rusticated pyramids on bases. That these corner pyramids so closely resemble the pyramid in Pretty Wood at Castle Howard (see page 31) cannot be mere chance; but were they really there in India, or did Vanbrugh project thoughts of his current work on his memories from 26 years before?

It was certainly Vanbrugh who began the taste for placing pyramids in landscape gardens. At Castle Howard his Pyramid Gate

Vanbrugh's drawing of Surat, India, with pyramids, drawn more than a quarter of a century after he was there.

(see page 28) led the way, to be followed by two others, the Great Pyramid (see page 29) and the Pretty Wood pyramid, both undoubtedly inspired by Vanbrugh if actually designed by Hawksmoor. Vanbrugh also designed a pyramid at Stowe, an impressive 60 feet high and, if the illustrations are accurate, taller and thinner than his Castle Howard examples (see page 93). Vanbrugh died in 1726, not long after its construction; in a Latin inscription on the pyramid Lord Cobham, Vanbrugh's client at Stowe, dedicated it to his memory. Viscount Perceval, visiting the Stowe garden in 1724 noted, inaccurately, 'The Pyramid at the End of one of the walks is a copy in miniature of the most famous one in Egypt, and the only thing of its kind I think in England.' The Stowe pyramid is long gone; so is another at the Studley Royal estate, Yorkshire home of the South Sea Bubble Chancellor of the Exchequer John Aislabie (see page 47).

One has a suspicion that Vanbrugh used his pyramids as much as stage setting (he was, after all, a former playwright) as a serious aid to the contemplation of mortality or of Masonic mysteries. His Gothick buildings have a similar theatrical air, as if made of wood and canvas. Hawksmoor was much more cerebral in his approach. His pyramids speak of high seriousness and were used not to add exotic glamour to a building or a landscape but to make a symbolic point. Unfortunately, it is not always clear what that point is. His pyramid in the churchyard at St George-in-the-East (see page 73) for example, is divided into five segments (a Masonic trait) and inscribed with the words 'The Wisdom of Solomon'. Why? The reference is again Masonic, and connected to his ideas about the Temple. But was St George's particularly associated in his mind with the Temple? Perhaps, but why this more than any of his other buildings? There are no answers.

Leaping the fence - mostly paper pyramids from Kent

In many ways Hawksmoor was plodding a lonely trail in the sands of Egyptianism. Future pyramids would - mostly - fall into one of two categories; monuments or landscape ornaments. Sometimes they were both.

Perhaps no one illustrates the contrast between Hawksmoor's seriousness and the decorative aspects of using pyramids better than William Kent. Kent was never an out-and-out follower of the fashionable classical style based on the work of Palladio that his patron Lord Burlington tried to impose upon Britain. Kent was an eclectic, by turns baroque, rococo, Gothick and pure classical. And he loved pyramids.

For Kent, the place for a pyramid was not stuck on a church or in a churchyard but in a carefully-considered landscape. In this, he was following Vanbrugh. But Kent's pyramids are not free-standing objects - only the Congreve Monument at Stowe (see page 96) finds an isolated spot for itself. They were planned to crown garden gateways, as at Holkham Hall in Norfolk; temples, as at Chatsworth in Derbyshire; a belvedere, as at Claremont in Surrey; and curving exedrae, as at Chiswick in Middlesex. In his imagination - and in his sketches - they rise, often rusticated, above their classical bases, surrounded by spindly pines and with diminutive figures in the high fashion of the early 18th century sporting in front of them, while little dogs misbehave behind their backs.

And on paper is where they stayed. No pyramids were built at Holkham or at Chatsworth, at Claremont or at Chiswick. For all

the delightful eccentricity they convey, the pyramids failed to convince Kent's noble patrons.

Yet there are some Kentian pyramids. As well as the Congreve Monument, there is the pyramid crowning the Temple of British Worthies in the Elysian Fields at Stowe (see page 94). This is the Chiswick exedra all over again, the drawing reused in a different context. Best of all is the use Kent made of two pyramids - just like those removed from his Holkham gateway design by a stroke of his client Thomas Coke's pen - on his greatest building, the Worcester Lodge at Badminton in Gloucestershire (see page 137) for the Duke of Beaufort.

Not an obelisque - British pyramids lead European fashion

All this pyramidal activity in Britain was ahead of fashion elsewhere. Pyramids became engrained early in the British imagination. They were the ornament for a gentleman's park; Alexander Pope, a friend of Kent, advised his friends to have them - writing to Lord Bathurst (probably tongue in cheek) about Cirencester Park in September 1728 he says, 'I would not advise you to an obelisque . . . but rather to a solid Pyramid of 100 ft square, to the end there may be Something solid and Lasting in your works.' What a sight that would have been!

This desire for pyramids led to the many tombs and monuments of pyramid form throughout the British Isles. From Lord Fraser of Lovat's's monument in Skye (see page 268) to James Burton's at St Leonard's in Sussex (see page 66), from the great Blickling pyramid in Norfolk (see page 53) to the O'Donovan pyramid at Myross in County Cork in the south-west of Ireland (see page 325), there are pyramids of all sizes. Perhaps the most impressive are the Darnley Mausoleum at Cobham in Kent (see page 62), based on a building in a Poussin painting, and the Wemyss Mausoleum at Gosford House, Aberlady (see page 235). On a smaller scale there is, for example, the pyramid to Dr Douce at Nether Wallop (see page 105) of 1760. In Ireland, too, the spirit moved them to build pyramids - in the 1740s at Killiney (see page 337), in 1750 at The Neale (see page 317), at Caledon in 1796 (see page 309), in 1785 at Arklow (see page 334).

The trend also appeared in the literature of the time. Even Robert Blair, who is often thought of as the archetypal Gothick poet, was happy to use the pyramids as symbols of a Gothick Götterdämmerung:

> The tap'ring Pyramid! th' Egyptian's Pride,
> And Wonder of the World! whose spiky Top
> Has wounded the thick Cloud, and long out-liv'd
> The angry Shaking of the Winter's Storm;
> Yet spent at last by th' Injuries of Heav'n,
> Shatter'd with Age, and furrow'd o'er with Years,
> The mystick Cone, with Hieroglyphicks crusted,
> Gives Way. Oh! lamentable Sight! at once
> The Labour of whole Ages lumbers down;
> A hideous and misshapen Length of Ruins.

By 1822 Thomas de Quincey's opium-induced visions included Egyptian elements: 'I suddenly came upon Isis and Osiris: I had done a deed, they said, which the ibis and the crocodile trembled at. I was buried for a thousand years, in stone coffins, with mummies and sphinxes, in narrow chambers at the heart of eternal pyramids. I was kissed, with cancerous kisses, by crocodiles; and laid, confounded with all unutterable slimy things, amongst reeds and Nilotic mud.'

The continent of Europe took a while to catch up with Britain's pyramid tastes, but by the later part of the 18th century pyramids were springing up everywhere, particularly in France and Germany, and with others from Russia to Spain. This was the time of the greatest interest in things Egyptian.

Additional impetus was given by artists, who began adding Egyptian elements to their work - Piranese, especially, often included pyramids, sphinxes and obelisks in his engravings. He was responsible, too, for his decoration of the interior of a famous café in the Piazza di Spagna in Rome, where he painted the walls with a fantastic agglomeration of Egyptian motifs, including pyramids. Was it significant that the building was the Caffè degl'Inglesi - the English café?

Cagliostro and Mozart

The links between pyramids and freemasonry were strengthened in the third quarter of the 18th century by the activities of the alchemist and rogue Count Cagliostro. He criss-crossed Europe hoaxing its crowned heads. He was involved in murders and spent time imprisoned in both the Bastille and the Castel Sant'Angelo. He was sentenced to death (commuted to life imprisonment) by the Inquisition. He also travelled further

Count Cagliostro

afield, visiting Greece, Persia, India, Ethiopia and Egypt - which is where he seems to have formulated new 'Egyptian' rites for freemasonry. These were quickly taken up in France (where for a time Cagliostro was Grand Master in Paris), in Germany and particularly in Vienna - though the English were very suspicious and for many years regarded the new rites as a fraud.

From Vienna the new Egyptian freemasonry affected composers. Both Haydn and Mozart were Masons. Mozart, who was admitted as a Mason in 1784, wrote music on Masonic themes from as early as 1773, with incidental music to *Thamos, König in Ägypten*, a Masonic play by Gebler. Other Masonic works include the *Mauerische Trauermusik*, probably written for the installation of the Master of his Lodge. Best known of all his Freemasonry-influenced works is, of course, the opera *Die Zauberflöte* of 1791. With a text by a fellow-Mason, Schikaneder, *The Magic Flute* mirrors the stages of Masonic initiation and the mysteries of the craft. Within much of the music, too, there is Masonic symbolism - the key of E-flat, with its three flats in the key signature, represents the perfect three of the Masonic initiation rite (and the triangular shape of the pyramid). There are other groups of three, including the three 'Masonic Knocks' at the start of the overture to *Die Zauberflöte*.

Other composers, too, including Porpora, Gasparini, Capelli, Graun and Alessando Scarlatti wrote operas with an Egyptian background. And there was a 'heroic-comic opera' called *Babylons Pyramiden* with music by Johann Mederitsch. Like *Die Zauberflöte* its libretto was by Schikaneder and it was also first performed in Vienna's Freihaus-Theater auf der Wieden - seven years after Mozart's death.

These exotic productions required exotic sets, and there were famous Egyptian set designs from the last part of the 18th and the early 19th centuries - many of them, like those by Quaglio, Mauer and especially Schinkel, using pyramids, sphinxes, obelisks and sarcophagi with particular inventiveness. Later set designers, too, have made play with pyramids, among them David Hockney's famous sets for a Glyndebourne Festival Opera production of *The Magic Flute* in 1978, which include a dramatic pyramid flanked by obelisks and Ozymandean heads. And, of course, in 1871 Verdi captured his own Egyptian theme in *Aida*.

Freemasonry was influential in America, too. The last quarter of the 18th century was momentous for the new nation. The Declaration of Independence of 1776 was signed by many Freemasons, including George Washington and Benjamin Franklin. As they agreed the design of the country's new Great Seal, they adopted Masonic symbolism, including, on the reverse, an unfinished stepped pyramid with 13 steps, below a equilateral triangle bearing the all-seeing eye of God. As with most things Masonic there has been argument as to whether this is an overt reference to Freemasonry or not, but certainly the new nation was using symbolism that was very fashionable at the time - and even today American citizens spending their dollar bills pay with money that includes the representation of a pyramid.

Karl Friedrich Schinkel's set for the last act of Mozart's Die Zauberflöte

Revolution and Napoleon

The end of the 18th century was a fertile time for anyone inspired by Egypt's architecture. Designs for pyramids sprang up like a rash across the British Isles - though few of them were built. One that was, Robert Adam's pyramid-shaped gateway at Nostell Priory (see page 34), dates from 1776. There were plans else-

Drawing of the Sphinx and pyramid by Denon, made during Napoleon's Egyptian campaign

where for a pyramidal dairy by John Carter, dated 1777, and for a garden temple by Sir John Soane from the following year. Neither was built.

In France the influence was even more marked. In the early 1780s Etienne-Louis Bouleé designed a gigantic pyramid. Claude-Nicholas Ledoux, royal architect from 1773, designed a gun-foundry with four pyramid-shaped forges. There is a pyramid in the Wilhelmshöhe Park in Kassel, Germany, designed in 1775, and another in the 'Jardin Anglais' of Parc Monceau in Paris, built in 1779. Back in Germany, the Staatspark Wilhelmsbad in Hanau, Hessen, has a pyramid dating from 1784.

All this happened dangerously close to the French Revolution. The Revolutionaries were themselves influenced by Egyptomania. Celebrating the third anniversary of the storming of the Bastille, the authorities erected a temporary pyramid of wood and black serge on the Champ-de-Mars to add monumentalism to the ceremonies - an exercise they repeated the following month in the Tuileries with a pyramid inscribed 'Silence, they rest', where civic dignitaries placed wreaths. It cannot have been far from where Europe's most famous modern example - I M Pei's glass Louvre pyramid - now stands.

And then came Napoleon. Inspired by visions of pharaonic grandeur as much as by a determination to show his strength to the British, he invaded Egypt in 1798 with 34,000 men. At the Battle of the Pyramids on 21 July the French ended the rule of the

Mamelukes, who had been ruling Egypt for the Turkish Sultan for almost seven centuries. Before the battle Napoleon addressed his men with the words, 'Soldiers, from the summit of yonder pyramids forty centuries behold your actions'. A fortnight later came disaster for the French; Nelson's fleet soundly trounced them at the Battle of the Nile - a British victory commemorated by the pyramid at Perlethorpe in Nottinghamshire (see page 114), raised to Nelson's greatness by a captain who served under him. That was really the end of Napoleon's Egyptian venture - though part of his army stayed on the banks of the Nile until 1801.

It was not the military outcome of the campaign that proved of lasting importance, but rather its artistic results. With the French invading army came artists, archaeologists, architects, scientists and historians, charged by Napoleon with the task of recording as much of Egypt's history and architecture as possible. This was a mammoth undertaking, and the result was a mammoth publication - nine volumes of scholarly text and eleven of beautifully-drawn folio-size plates. It was the *Description de l'Egypt . . . publié par les ordres de sa Majesté l'empereur Napoléon le Grande*. The first volume came out in 1809 and the last, long after Napoleon's departure, in 1828.

Even before the first volume of *Description* was published, accurate and well-informed descriptions of Egypt, gathered during Napoleon's campaign, began to appear. The first and most influential was Baron Dominique Vivan Denon's *Voyage dans la Basse et la Haute Egypte pendant les campagnes du général Bonaparte*, published in 1802, with an English translation in 1803. Its success was sensational. Until its appearance Egyptian-style buildings, including pyramids, were playing with the genre - they were like the Strawberry Hill Gothick of not many years before; fun, but inaccurate and unscholarly. Denon's *Voyages* was as much a wake-up call as, 30 years later, was Augustus Welby Pugin's seminal work on Gothic, *Contrasts*.

Egypt indoors - riding on a sphinx

The influence of Deneon's *Voyage* was felt first in interior decoration. There had been an early example, in 1793 at Cairnes House near Aberdeen, where James Playfair decorated the Billiard Room in a simple Egyptian design taken from a Piranese engraving. The full-blown Egyptian style, though, is typified by the interiors that Thomas Hope designed for his own house in Duchess Street, just off Portland Place in London. He transformed the main rooms of the house into an Egyptian jewel-case - friezes of Egyptian figures, furniture with sphinxes, fireplaces with winged solar discs, free-standing figures of gods . . .

Hope was jumping on an already-moving bandwagon. He steered the development of Egyptianism with success - just as he did with both Gothic and Italian Renaissance styles in the years to come. In 1807 he published his Duchess Street designs in *Household Furniture and Interior Decoration, Executed from designs by Thomas Hope*. Some of the furniture from the house is now in the Royal Pavilion in Brighton.

The first quarter of the 19th century was the heyday of the Egyptian style. It insinuated itself into every facet of polite society. In 1805 'Priscilla Plainstitch' (really the author Charles Lamb in satirical mode) wrote to the *Morning Chronicle*: 'Since this accursed Egyptian style came into fashion my eldest boy rides on a sphinx instead of a rocking-horse, my youngest has a

'Modern Antiques' by Rowlandson, a cartoon of 1806

papboat in the shape of a crocodile, and my husband has built a watercloset in the shape of a pyramid, and has his shirts marked with a lotus.'

The following year satirist Thomas Rowlandson produced a cartoon entitled *Modern Antiques* showing a room crammed with Egyptian statues and mummies. A military man, plumed hat in hand, is being kissed by his lady as he emerges from an upright, open mummy-case that serves as the front door of their house. This was exactly what the poet Robert Southey, in his *Letters from England*, published in 1807, noted: 'Everything must now be Egyptian: the ladies wear crocodile ornaments, and you sit upon a sphinx in a room hung round with mummies, and the long black lean-armed hieroglyph men, who are enough to make the children afraid to go to bed.'

Josiah Wedgwood, never a slouch when it came to following fashion, fired up his kilns to produce black basalt ware with Egyptian motifs, including sphinxes and lions and a mould for blancmange in the form of a canopic jar - a less gruesome use than the origin of the jars, which was to hold internal organs removed during mummification. Other potteries followed suit - there is, for example, a Sèvres porcelain dinner service painted with Egyptian scenes and pretend hieroglyphics, accompanied by a centre-piece based on the temple at Edfu, complete with seated figures of pharaohs and sacred rams.

The Egyptian House in Chapel Street, Penzance

In 1812 one of Britain's most public of the Egyptian buildings appeared, in Piccadilly in London. Called the Egyptian Hall, it was designed by Peter Frederick Robinson 'from drawings by Denon'. It was really a hotchpotch of Egyptian motifs - sphinxes, solar discs, scarabs, columns with lotus capitals, even life-size statues purporting to be Isis and Osiris - plastered on to a quirky façade, intended to attract the people to the museum inside. Though long-vanished, it spawned at least two extant copies. One, the Egyptian Library in Ker Street in Devonport, was designed by John Foulston in 1823 as part of a civic centre that included a Grecian Town Hall and a 'Hindoo-style' chapel. A closer copy, the Egyptian House in Chapel Street, Penzance, probably from about 1835, is also by Foulston. There were other Egyptian frontages in Exeter and Hereford. Even the great Isambard Kingdom Brunel was not immune to the Egyptian influence. In his original design for the Clifton Suspension Bridge in Bristol he intended the great brick piers on each bank to be crowned with sphinxes and decorated with winged solar discs and Egyptian figures.

Much of this is *jeux d'esprit*, Egyptian witticisms - the sphinx rocking-horses and crocodile papboats of architecture - that were in keeping with the time. But a more serious wind was blowing from the Nile - a wind that brought the pyramid as a funerary monument back into style.

A return to death

Even as the craze for Egyptian decoration ran its course, architects were planning monuments. A funerary pyramid with attached columned porches was designed for Berlin in about 1797. In France, Durand followed Boulée's example in 1805 with a design for what seems to be a crematorium, with a tall chimney dwarfed by an even taller pyramid for holding urns of ashes. In Kazan, on the River Volga, a truncated pyramid was erected by Alferov in 1823 to commemorate the defeat of the Tartars. Benjamin Latrobe, a Yorkshireman who became America's greatest architect, devised a pyramidal monument, possibly for Richmond, Virginia, that has affinity with both the Wemyss mausoleum at Gosford (see page 235) and the mausoleum at Kilbixy, County Westmeath (see page 354). A particularly visionary design was for a cenotaph for Isaac Newton, submitted by Joseph-Jean-Pascal Gay as an entry for the French Academy of Architecture prize in 1800. His enormous stepped pyramid rises from a terrace planted with pines. Deep within the structure is a vast celestial globe. What would Newton have thought?

We may especially regret that two of the Wyatt clan, sculptor Matthew Coates Wyatt and architect Philip Wyatt, failed in their attempt at a London pyramid. After the Battle of Waterloo the Government invited artists to suggest a suitable monument to celebrate British victory. The two Wyatts proposed a 360-foot stepped pyramid with 22 tiers, one for each year of the recent war. There would be bronze reliefs along the tiers - a colossal undertaking just by itself. On top was to have been a columned rotunda with a dome, under which was a statue of George III. And in what appropriately wide-open space did these Wyatts propose their Brobdingnagian pyramid should go? Their chosen site was at Charing Cross, next to St Martin-in-the Fields. It would have occupied the site (and more) where the rather more timid National Gallery now stands.

The mammoth National Memorial to the Battle of Waterloo as proposed by MC and P Wyatt for Charing Cross

The example of the Wyatts seems to have inspired Thomas Willson to propose, in 1824, Britain's biggest unbuilt pyramid. His 'General Metropolitan Cemetery' was planned for a site 'in the vicinity of Primrose Hill.' It would have been vast - a base 635 feet square (almost the distance from Cleopatra's Needle to Trafalgar Square) and a height nearly 300 feet higher that St Paul's Cathedral. It was to have been of granite-faced brick and, as Willson wrote, it would be 'practical, economical and remunerative' - practical, as it was to 'contain Five Millions of Individuals' in its 94 levels of catacomb; economical, in that the whole thing could be built for a mere £2,583,552; remunerative, in that by selling freehold spaces at between £100 and £500, and letting out vaults, a profit of £10,784,800 could be realised. If it had been built, it would have certainly lived up to Willson's description of it as 'The Glory of London'.

Smaller pyramids continued to be built, seemingly oblivious of the ebb and flow of fashion and history. There is a fine slate pyramid to Benjamin Wyatt (stay-at-home brother of James, architect of the Darnley Mausoleum at Cobham, see page 62) at Llandegai in North Wales (see page 227), dating from 1818. A little earlier is the memorial to the 4th Duke of Dorset at Ballybrack, County Dublin (see page 339). The Rev'd Thomas Rackett's three-sided pyramid at Spetisbury in Dorset (see page 143), was put up in the 1830s. The pyramid 'To please the pigs' at Bishops Wood in Staffordshire (see page 210) appeared in about 1818, and its sister, the Egyptian Hen House at nearby Tong in Shropshire (see page 210), in 1842. The yew pyramid in the garden at Biddulph Grange (see page 205), also in Staffordshire, was planted in the same decade.

As the 19th century progressed, though, Egyptian styles gradually slipped from favour. There are unexpected delights in the style, like Temple Mill in Water Lane, Leeds; its offices are based on the Temple of Horus at Edfu and the street elevation of the flax mill from the Temple of Hathor at Dendra. Sheep once grazed on

A W N Pugin's satire on the Egyptian style for cemeteries, from his 'Apology' of 1843

the mill's roof, until one fell through a skylight on to a machine below. The mill was designed by Joseph Bonomi, Junior, son of the designer of the fine pyramid of 1794 at Blickling Hall in Norfolk (see page 53). But the Egyptian style was by then mainly back to where it began, a style for funeral monuments and cemeteries.

There is a spirited polemic on the trend from arch-Gothic architect Pugin. Writing in his *Apology for the Revival of Christian Architecture* of 1843 he castigates 'the new Cemetery Companies [who] have perpetrated the grossest absurdities in the buildings they have erected . . . nearly opposite the Green Man and Dog public house, in the centre of a dead wall (which serves as a cheap medium of advertising for blacking and shaving strop manufacturers) a cement caricature of an Egyptian temple, 2½ inches to the foot . . . surmounted by a huge representation of the winged Osiris bearing a gas-lamp.' The accompanying plate is even more telling than his prose. Here is the Egyptian gateway, with pylon-shaped 'convenient lodges for the policeman and his wife', with animal-headed gods set into the cracked stucco render. Between the lodges are two lotus-capped columns, bearing a frieze inscribed 'NEW GENERAL CEMETERY FOR ALL DENOMINATIONS', supporting a winged solar disc and serpents with the gas-light on top. It is cruel, but pretty accurate.

Pyramidiots, mystics and painters

Early explorers of the pyramids in Egypt were content with recording and measuring the monuments inside and out. It was not until the middle of the 19th century that interested observers started to draw conclusions from them. These are the people whom Sir Flinders Petrie dubbed 'Pyramidiots' - men like John Taylor, whose book *The Great Pyramid. Why was it Built? & Who Built it?* was among the first to find significance in the layout and measurements of the Great Pyramid. His friend Charles Piazzi Smyth, Astronomer Royal for Scotland, devoted much of his time to producing books and papers 'proving' that the pyramids were built by the High Priest Melchisedech and that all the measurements they are based on were the same as British Imperial lengths and weights and totally unlike that foreign upstart, metrication.

Smyth ended up under his own small pyramid in a Yorkshire churchyard in 1900 (see page 23); another pyramidiot, Melancthon William Henry Lombe Brooke, who also wrote on the subject of mensuration and the Great Pyramid, was also buried under a pyramid, this time in Norfolk (see page 56). Their spiritual progeny live on. Pyramids are still thought to possess mystical powers - they help you develop psychic powers, heal damaged limbs, purify the air, improve sleep. There are many people who swear that placing a blade under a pyramid will re-sharpen it - a belief alluded to by sculptor Richard Farrington in a work called 'Pyramid', now in a private garden at Alton in Hampshire, which shows a small black pyramid with an oversized safety-razor blade slicing into the top of it. Some believe that sitting inside a pyramid of wood or even blue polythene will spiritually energise them, or that putting a selection of small pyramids under a bed will promote restful sleep.

By the end of the 19th century the Egyptian impulse had largely moved from buildings to painting. Artists were inspired particularly by the Egyptian Court at the Crystal Palace in Sydenham, which opened in 1854. Joseph Bonomi the younger, a noted prac-

Richard Farrington's Blade sculpture, in a private garden at Alton, Hampshire, plays with ideas about the power of pyramids

tical Egyptologist who spent much time in the country on archaeological work, had already organised the British Museum's display of Egyptian treasures, in association with design guru Owen Jones. Bonomi was the natural choice for the Crystal Palace. Under his guidance the Egyptian Court sprang to colourful existence. Accurate, though scaled-down, models of Egyptian buildings crowded together beneath the curving glass roof - chief among them seated statues of Rameses the Great from the Abu Simbel temple. What was revelatory was the colouring of the exhibits. Rameses appeared in his full glory of lapis blue and gold leaf, red, yellow and ochre. Lotus capitals and solar discs were decorated with painted figures. And hidden away in the decoration were academic jokes - the names of Queen Victoria and Prince Albert were written in hieroglyphics - and so, of course, were the names of the directors of the Crystal Palace Company.

Such a feast of colour set painters alight. There had already been some interest in Egypt as a subject - especially John Martin's huge paintings of the *Plagues of Egypt*, dating from the 1820s. Here are vast vistas of temples and obelisks, with a good number of pyramids providing stage scenery in the background. They are archaeologically as correct as scholarship of the time allowed -

Pyramids in the background of The Seventh Plague of Egypt' by John Martin

unsurprisingly, because Martin was Joseph Bonomi's brother-in-law. What they lack, though, are the vibrant colours that Bonomi revealed at Sydenham.

The Egyptian Court's influence is seen in several paintings of the next 15 years. Alma-Tadema's *Pastimes in Ancient Egypt* of 1863 shows a dancer cavorting for nobles in front of lotus-capped columns - the picture has sometimes confusingly and ludicrously been called *An Evening Party at Nineveh*. E J Poynter's *Israel in Egypt* of 1867 shows slaves labouring to drag a huge seated lion to a brightly-painted temple; inevitably there is a pyramid in the background - in case of doubt, perhaps.

Into the 20th century - with no pyramids

By the mid-19th century pyramid building in Britain was moribund. There are isolated examples - William Mackenzie's Liverpool pyramid of 1851 (see page 199), John Mowlem's at Swanage of 1854 (see page 146), the curious cast-iron stepped pyramid at Hampton Norreys of 1855 (see page 102), the Star Pyramid in Stirling (see page 251), from 1863, and of course, Prince Albert's pyramid of 1862 (see page 260). The last quarter of the 19th century was not given to Egyptian excesses; nor were the first two of the 20th century. Only Colonel Elwes's rough-hewn pyramidal tribute to his horse at Leckhampton (see page 128) of 1902 breaks the silence.

Despite its obvious funerary associations, the pyramid (unlike the obelisk) does not seem to have been considered suitable as a memorial to the fallen of the Great War. There were ideas by Sir Frank Baines for a National War Memorial at Hyde Park Corner in London in the Egyptian style. It would have been a gigantic twin-columned pylon with temples at each side. Some liked it, including the influential *Builder* magazine, which wrote that it would 'embody one great idea - that of sacrifice' - though it was not quite clear why. Correspondents to its letter columns disagreed; 'Of all the styles suited to London the Egyptian is the most unfit and alien; and the bigger it might be, the more vulgar it would be. It is heavy, passive, sulky; it is the style of a caste-ridden people; it requires sunlight and the desert; it would show the dirt; it proclaims complete indifference to the hard estate of the poor' - comments that may say more about the writer than about the proposed monument. And there were no pyramids, except the one marking the Chilwell disaster of 1918 (see page 112) and the rough pyramid at Carsphairn (see page 285); perhaps the associations that pyramids conveyed were not considered to be serious enough. It was left to the first years of the 21st century to mark military events with pyramids - the pyramids at Alrewas in Staffordshire (see page 176) mark the Suez Crisis and the loss of *HMS Neptune*; that at Torquay (see page 152) is to Home Guard members; and at Saxton in Yorkshire (see page 32) the new pyramid marks an old conflict, the Battle of Towton in 1461.

Melancthon Brooke's 1928 pyramid at Attleborough (see page 56) seems to be the sole representative of the 1920s, though the Egyptian style was now back, influenced by the treasures unearthed in 1922 when Tutankhamun's tomb was opened. Egyptian motifs engulfed cinemas with lotus columns, sphinxes and scarabs - but no three-dimensional pyramids. The appropriately-named *Luxor* in Twickenham was typical of the style. Egyptian was used for factories, too - the Firestone tyre factory in Brentford (demolished in 1971), the Pyrene Building, also in

Sir Frank Baines's proposal for an Egyptian-style National War Memorial at Hyde Park Corner, 1920

One of the pyramids at the Cathedral of Christ the King in Liverpool, by Gibberd, 1962, sitting on the crypt of Lutyens' unfinished pre-war cathedral

Brentford, and the Hoover Factory in Greenford (both still standing) show the style slipping easily into Art Deco. Similar Egyptianising motifs can be found on the entrances to the Mersey Tunnel, which opened in December 1933.

Where are the British pyramids of the 1940s and 1950s? If they exist they are keeping a low profile. Only in the 1960s is there the beginning of a resurgence. It may have been prompted by two pyramid roofs outside Liverpool Metropolitan Cathedral. They sit at one end of the platform constructed by Frederick Gibberd to cover the crypt of Lutyens's unfinished cathedral, abandoned when World War II began. Part of Gibberd's 1962 designs for the new Cathedral, the pyramids were in place by the time the building was finished in 1967.

An Egyptian renaissance

Whether Gibberd's pyramids were the spur for a renaissance of interest in the pyramid shape is unclear, but new ones began to appear. The dominating pyramid roof of Wolfson Hall in Glasgow (see page 274) was finished in 1965, its near neighbour Anderston Kelvingrove Church (see page 275) more than a decade later. There are vast stepped-pyramid structures - really more ziggurats that pyramids, at the University of East Anglia in Norwich, designed by brutalist architect Sir Denys Lasdun. Sir Basil Spence, who presumably kept an eye on cathedral building in Britain after his Coventry Cathedral commission, designed the art gallery-cum-boathouse at Mongewell in Oxfordshire (see page 98) as a neo-brutalist pyramid in 1969.

Leisure centres saw the advantages of a pyramid shape (ease of building, less volume to heat, greater floor space, distinctive shape to attract customers) in the 1970s. Earliest on the scene was Bletchley (see page 90); Bedford's swimming pool (see page 85) followed in the early 1980s and Bexhill (see page 67) in 1987. Other leisure activities, too, adopted the shape - The Point at Milton Keynes (see page 89) in skeletal form in 1985, The Pyramids at Southsea (see page 109) in 1988, the Sea Life Centre in Scarborough (see page 26) in 1991 and Fantasy Island at Ingoldmells (see page 50) later in the decade.

Other enterprises also took on the idea, notably Britain's biggest pyramid, an office block in Stockport (see page 204), now the headquarters of the Cooperative Bank, finished in 1986. The truncated pyramid of the Irish Meteorological Office in Dublin (see page 361) is of much the same date. In 1990 Plantasia in Swansea (see page 219) opened its slightly-lopsided glass pyramid. Most recent are the Visitor Centre at Ceide Fields in County Mayo (see page 315), opened in 1993 and Hills Electrical and Mechanical pyramid in Bilston Glen near Edinburgh (see page 243), only a stone's throw from Rosslyn Chapel (see page 5) with its Templar, Freemasonry and Rosicrucian links.

Pyramids as sculpture seem to have lost their memorial function for most of the 20th century. When they were designed it was as public works of art - the modern equivalent of the follies in 18th-century gardens. Derek Linstrum's pyramid at Bretton Hall near Wakefield (see page 42) of 1963 is an early example (though this had a practical purpose, too). Dundee's laminate pyramid (see page 259) of the 1970s and the pyramid in Salford (see page 202) of 1992 are later examples. Some, like the Millennium *Time and Tide* pyramid at Gosport (see page 110) and the Geoneedle at Exmouth (see page 150), unveiled in 2002, have an educational function; others, like the Tetra Trellis at West Drayton (see page 81) act as a focal point for a planned development. In Wales, the pyramid of road signs in Cardiff (see page 218) adds a note of frivolity to an otherwise dull roundabout.

In Ireland there seems to have been a particular fondness for the pyramid shape; James Scanlon's *The Way the Fairies Went* at Sneem (see page 321), with its varied pyramids, dates from 1989; *The Pyre* by Julie Kelleher in Boyne Crescent, Cork (see page 327), from 1996, and the fine stepped pyramid at Lough Boora in County Offaly (see page 352) from 2002. In Scotland Ian Hamilton Finlay's small pyramid at Little Sparta (see page 246) adds its own symbolic resonance. Two pyramids in private gardens for disparate 'celebrities' also highlight contrasting modern uses; the Prince of Wales has a pyramid-shaped fernery in his private garden at Highgrove in Gloucestershire (see page 137), while psychic spoon-bender Uri Geller has added a glazed 'well-being' pyramid to his house at Sonning in Berkshire to serve as a media centre where he can give his many interviews.

Perhaps the most endearing modern pyramid is that at Clearbeck House in the Pennines at Tatham in Lancashire (see page 195). It seems to draw together many of the strands of pyramid history: its shape is like that of the Egyptian pyramids; a passage through it is symbolic of a journey through death that would no doubt have pleased the early Freemasons; it is one of the focal points of a fine landscape garden in best 18th-century tradition. And, most pleasingly, it was made (from the remains of an old coal bunker and with the use of garden string) in the 1990s for the sheer enjoyment of the shape. Despite the great endeavours of everyone from Pythagoras to the latest of New Age devotees, that seems to be the best of all possible reasons.

Tour 1

YORKSHIRE

IN A SHADY corner of the churchyard at **Sharow**, a village just across the River Ure from the city of Ripon, is the small pyramid that Charles Piazzi Smyth erected in 1896 to his wife Jessie. The pyramid, which mirrors Smyth's preoccupation with the Great Pyramid of Khufu, became his own memorial four years later.

Smyth was one of the most eminent scientists of the 19th century. Born in Naples, where his father, a naval officer, was based, he was named after a renowned Sicilian astronomer, Giuseppe Piazzi. Educated at Bedford Grammar School (they have now, fittingly, named their modern observatory after him), he was given an apprenticeship at the Royal Observatory at the Cape of Good Hope - it was his good fortune to be there in 1836 when Halley's Comet put in one of its appearances.

His progress was so rapid - astronomical, even - that in 1845, aged just 26, he was appointed Astronomer Royal for Scotland and Professor of Practical Astronomy at Edinburgh University. He stayed for 43 years, even though he mostly had a hard time of it. He spent a great deal of energy - and he had prodigious amounts of it - in repeatedly-thwarted attempts to persuade the Home Office to spend money improving the equipment at the Observatory on Calton Hill. He did, though, have time to undertake some important scientific work. He was a pioneer in spectroscopy and he introduced the 'rain-band' method to aid weather forecasting (there is a dark band in the solar spectrum that is caused by water vapour in the earth's atmosphere; vital to know about if you are a meteorologist). He observed the total solar eclipse in 1851.

He was also responsible for initiating the one o'clock gun that is still fired every day at Edinburgh Castle, to the continual annoyance of the pigeons and the delight of the tourists. At the same moment a red time-ball falls on a pole Smyth ordered for the summit of the Nelson Monument on Calton Hill. The purpose of all this was to give an accurate time signal to the fleet when it was in Leith Harbour, so the ships' officers could set their chronometers and check their longitude when at sea.

Smyth's achievements were many. In June 1856 he sailed (in railway engineer Robert Stephenson's yacht *Titania*) to Tenerife. Here he made the first experiments with a telescope placed on a mountain top. He had had this original idea as early as 1845; 'The atmosphere . . . being so determined an opponent, every effort should be made to eliminate its effects as far as possible; and this can only be accomplished by rising above its grosser parts.' With his seven-and-a-half inch telescope set up at Alta Vista on Tenerife, 10,700 feet above sea level, he was able to view the heavens with hugely-increased clarity. His drawings of Jupiter were described as 'revelations.' Not content with this, he also took stereoscopic photographs of his expedition. His book *Tenerife, an Astronomer's Experiments* was the first to be illustrated with 3D pictures (though it was perhaps a cul-de-sac in publishing).

OPPOSITE:
Pyramid in the churchyard at Sharow near Ripon to astronomer and pyramidologist Charles Piazzi Smyth

His photographic experiments also included perfecting a new type of high-quality miniature image, only an inch square, which could be enlarged without loss of quality. This was important to him in his other passion - the Great Pyramid.

Piazzi Smyth - one of Flinders Petrie's 'pyramidiots' (see page 17) was obsessed by the Pyramid. He was convinced it held the secrets of the universe. He described it as 'the primeval Great Pyramid, standing in Egypt, but supposed now, according to an increasing body of evidence, to have been erected there under the eye of Melchizadek, and according to a design furnished to him by Divine Inspiration.'

Accompanied by his wife Jessie (whom he had also dragged up the mountain in Tenerife), he measured every inch, and studied every angle. He 'discovered' that the pyramid was constructed on the 'pyramid inch' measure - only 0.001 per cent away from the imperial inch (he hated metric measurements). He 'proved' that the relationship of the Pyramid's height to twice its base is equivalent to *pi*, and that one pound's weight of the Pyramid is the same as five cubic pyramid inches of the earth's mean density.

He took the first photographs - his miniature images - in the chambers of the Great Pyramid, using coils of magnesium wire to create a bright light. These coils apparently once featured in one of Arthur C Clarke books of *Mysteries* as proof that the Ancient Egyptians used magnesium wire as they were building the pyramids; the claim now seems to have disappeared - Google proclaims ignorance of it. Among the pictures that Smyth took is one of Jessie in the King's Chamber, dressed in voluminous tartan skirts and looking intently into the so-called Coffer which may once have held a Pharaoh.

Alas, Smyth's book about his pyramidology, *Our Inheritance in the Great Pyramid*, was largely ridiculed by his contemporaries. He submitted a paper on the subject to the Royal Society. In it, he refuted an earlier publication by the Society of a paper by Sir Henry James of the Royal Engineers about measuring the sides of the Great Pyramid. The Society rejected Smyth's paper, saying that 'it is not of a nature suited for public reading before the Society'. They were quite right - most of it was just a diatribe against James's sloppy methods. Hurt, Smyth published his vituperative correspondence with the President of the Royal Society, Sir Joseph Hooker, and resigned his Fellowship. He then resumed his other scientific work until, in August 1888, he left the Royal Scottish Observatory for the last time, and retired to Ripon - probably so that Jessie, who was unwell, could benefit from the beneficial climate in the lee of the Pennines, but also because nearby York gave easy access to both London and Edinburgh. Another advantage was that York was the base of Smyth's favourite scientific instrument maker, Thomas Cooke.

Jessie died in 1896. Piazzi (he was never 'Charles' to his friends and colleagues) designed the pyramid-shaped tombstone topped with a cross that is now Sharow churchyard's most unusual sight. The plaque he placed on it describes his wife as 'his faithful and sympathetic friend and companion through 40 years of varied scientific experiences by land and sea, abroad as well as at home, at 12,000 feet up in the atmosphere on the wind-swept Peak of Tenerife, as well as underneath and upon the GREAT PYRAMID of EGYPT.' Four years later, he was buried there, too. His inscription calls him 'a Bright Star in the Firmament of Ardent Explorers of the Works of their Creator'. One of the Bright Star's last acts was to order a camera from Cooke in York that would be strong enough to survive the Last Judgement. Perhaps he wanted to sell picture postcards to the Redeemed.

Piazzi Smyth in retirement in Ripon

THE TINY VILLAGE of **Bolton-on-Swale**, just a few furlongs across the River Swale from Catterick racecourse, clusters round its pink sandstone church.

Just west of the church tower stands the pyramid, 'Erected', as the inscription says, 'By CONTRIBUTION In ye year 1743 to ye memory of HENRY JENKINS. The inscription is an amateur - and quite endearing - job; the lines aren't quite straight, and the carver ran out of room on the second line, so that the final word reads CONTRIBUTIO, and the last N floats free above the terminal O.

It was obviously worth the effort of the Bolton villagers to go to the trouble of putting up this handsome pyramid, on its tall base and with a splayed point, to local hero Mr Jenkins. But what had he done to deserve it?

Jenkins holds the record for being the oldest-recorded British person. He was born in 1501 in the neighbouring village of Ellerton-on-Swale and lived in the immediate area until his death in 1670 - an astonishing (unbelievable?) 169 years later.

Were the 18th-century contributors to the pyramid merely simple and trusting peasants who foolishly believed the stories their parents had told them about the village's most famous inhabitant? Or did Henry really live so long? There is certainly evidence that he was famous for his longevity in his own lifetime. One story says that a local official, wanting to check on exactly where a boundary ran, decided that one of the old folk in the village would probably know. Seeing a very old man sitting at his door, he asked about the boundary. 'Nay, lad, I don't knaw, but if tha goes inside tha can ask me fayther; he'd likely tell thee.' Inside was an even older man. The official asked his question again. 'It is not summat I knaw,' he replied. 'Tha'd best ask me fayther - he's out back chopping wood.' And in the yard he found Henry Jenkins, swinging an axe.

During his long life Henry worked as a thatcher, a salmon-fisher and on the land. He also served for some time as butler to Lord Conyers at Hornby Castle. One of the visitors he served there, he recalled, was the affable Abbot of Fountains Abbey; King Henry VIII closed the abbey in 1539. Henry Jenkins also told anyone who would listen that he had talked to the men from Bolton about their experiences fighting the army of the Scots king James IV at the Battle of Floddon Field in 1513. In fact, he remembered that he played a very small role in preparing them; 'I was sent to Northallerton with a horse-load of arrows, but they sent a bigger boy from thence to the army with them.'

Much of his life seems to have been uneventful; Robinson's *Guide to Richmond* of 1833 ascribed Jenkins' survival to 'the regularity of his habits and the absence of exciting vicissitudes in his condition'. He retained both his vigour and his keen eyesight to the end of his life. Aged over a hundred he regularly swam across the Swale (the fastest flowing river in England) and two years before he died was still tying fishing flies.

There was some excitement in his life, though. When he was 161 he walked to London to see Charles II - the eighth monarch in whose reign he had lived, not counting Cromwell's Commonwealth. He was obviously an object of some curiosity. The newly-married queen, Catherine of Braganza, said to him, "Well, my good man, may I ask of you what you have done during the long period of life granted to you, more than any other man of shorter longevity?' Henry's reply was frank. 'Indeed, Madam, I know of nothing greater than becoming a father when I was over a hundred years old.'

Monument to Henry Jenkins, (below) who died aged 169 in 1670, at Bolton-on-Swale

By the end of his life Jenkins was described, unsurprisingly, as 'a very aged and poore man' who had to beg for his food. Nothing seems to have been done to mark his death, except an entry in the parish register at Bolton. It took more than sixty years for the locals to raise the funds for the pyramid, and for the marble plaque inside the church that reads:

> Blush not marble to rescue from oblivion the memory of HENRY JENKINS, a person obscure in birth, but of a life truly memorable; for he was enriched with the goods of nature if not of fortune; and happy in the duration, if not the variety of his enjoyments; and though the partial world despised and disregarded his low and humble state, the equal eye of providence beheld and blessed it with a patriarch's health and length of days; to teach mistaken man these blessings are entailed on temperance, a life of labour, and a mind at ease.

It has been calculated that the odds of anyone else surviving as long as Henry Jenkins are 1,400,000,000,000,000 to one.

The 'truncated pyramid' of Fylingdales Early Warning System on the North York Moors

STRATEGICALLY PLACED ON a ridge in the North York Moors, just a few miles from the coast, is what's often called a truncated pyramid - the **Fylingdales** Early Warning System.

Really, it only resembles a pyramid if you stand at a certain angle to it with your eyes half closed. It is more like a triangular sand-castle on a gigantic scale - or perhaps like an early radio. The whole site - and several thousand surrounding acres of moorland that glow with the imperial purple of heather in the late summer - is heavily fenced and severe notices warn of the penalties for trespass and the importance of the Official Secrets Act.

Once, the Fylingdales early warning equipment was housed in three huge 'golf-ball' structures of an attractive pale blue; perfect spheres in a rugged landscape. The aesthetics of their 1980s replacement are not so attractive. The 'pyramid' is almost 40 metres high and the same across. Inside are 2,560 aerials; together they give out an average transmitter power of 2.5 Megawatts. For years it has been the focus of anti-war, anti-American demonstrations; temporary encampments of peace protesters huddle as close to the gates as they are allowed by the North Yorkshire police. And now that the US has asked the British government for permission to upgrade Fylingdales to become part of the National Missile Defence (or possibly Defense) system to help protect the US mainland from attack, the protests have increased. North Yorkshire people, who host both Fylingdales and the US listening station at Menwith Hill near Harrogate, feel uncomfortable about being in the front line.

SCARBOROUGH - 'QUEEN OF the Yorkshire Coast' - boasts many attractions. At Scalby Mills, the end of the line for the North Bay miniature railway, is the Scarborough Sea Life Centre.

It is housed in three large, gleaming white pyramids that overlook the North Sea and the headland that divides Scarborough's north and south bays. This is one of the most exposed parts of the coast, and the pyramids are a good shape to withstand the severe easterly gales that often batter their insulated metal roofs.

We asked Mike Stevenson from Merlin Aquarium Projects, which runs the Sea Life Centre, about the building. 'David Newman was the architect, and it is a very clever design. The biggest of the pyramids is about 25 metres high, and interlocks

with the other two. That way, he's given us a total area of almost
two-and-a-half thousand square metres. And by glazing the point
of each of the pyramids, light floods into the public areas inside.'

The Sea Life Centre opened in June 1991 after nine months of
construction and is now one of Scarborough's most popular
attractions. Certainly, the children visiting on the day we were
there were keen. 'I like the giant octopus best,' one lad said. 'It
is huge and has lots of suckers.' Others voted for the underwater
Ocean Tunnel: 'It is like you're right underneath, and the sharks
and turtles and things swim up to you and look at you.' Smaller
children liked the touch pool where they could get their hands
wet and touch some of the smaller creatures. And everyone was
pleased with the penguins, otters and seals - though the jelly fish
caused a mixed reaction.

The Centre is not just for entertainment, though - there is a lot
of serious scientific conservation and research work going on,
too, including pioneering breeding programmes, bringing attention to global marine issues and promoting education - all housed
in these three white pyramids.

WHEN HORACE WALPOLE, the eighteenth-century writer,
collector and antiquarian, was taken to see **Castle Howard**, he
said in a famous letter that 'Nobody had informed me at one view
I should see a palace, a town, a fortified city, temples on high
places, woods worthy of being each a metropolis of the Druids,
the noblest lawn in the world fenced by half the horizon, and a
mausoleum that would tempt one to be buried alive; in short, I
have seen gigantic places before, but never a sublime one'. Spot
on, Horace, except for the curious fact that you've overlooked the
pyramids. Castle Howard has three of them, and they are among
Britain's earliest.

*The Pyramid Gate
at Castle Howard*

Approaching from the A64 Scarborough to York road there is a wonderful glimpse of the honey-coloured mausoleum. Then the road winds up a ridge and passes a mid-nineteenth-century column to the seventh Earl of Carlisle, a colossal affair, now restored to its former glory after years of decay. Perched on top is a gilded tripod and bowl, while four huge stone helmets guard each corner of the base. The column marks the beginning of the succession of surprises dished up by the estate.

The ruler-straight drive that is the main axis of the carefully-controlled landscape around the great house takes visitors through the woods and passes through the Carrmire Gate, a flight of fancy of about 1730 by Nicholas Hawksmoor, one of the architects employed by the third Earl who instigated all this pomp. The gate is made up of a line of battlemented walling, punctured by an arch with a big triangular pediment over it, pepper-pot turrets with loopholes at each end and fat obelisks (or are they very thin pyramids?) clustering around the gate.

As a barrier to trespassers, it is useless; even if the gate was closed they could walk round the end. As part of the huge stage set that is the Castle Howard estate, though, it is tremendous; and it prepares visitors for the first of the proper pyramids, the Pyramid Gate.

If you were writing an architectural recipe book, the instructions for the Pyramid Gate would be simple. 'Take one cube of stone. Pierce back to front with a round-headed arch. Place a pyramid with the same base area as the cube on top. Decorate with a few mouldings and serve.' Once the gate stood stark and alone. No well-trimmed hedges led to it. There were no wings at each side. Just the cube and the pyramid. Imagine, in the eighteenth century, arriving in a bumpy coach from York and struggling slowly uphill on a road deep with mud. Suddenly, you are confronted with, first, a medievalising, crenallated wall, then, approached from below, this massive, almost aggressive, gesture in stone.

Just so you know to whom you owe this vision, there is the third Earl's coat of arms and the inscription 'CAROLUS HOWARD COMES CARLEOLENSIS CONDIDIT ANNO DNI MDCCXIX'. (Charles Howard, Earl of Carlisle, built this in the year of Our Lord 1719) above the arch. But as well as introducing us to the Earl, the Pyramid Gate serves as the calling card of Castle Howard's main architect, John Vanbrugh.

Vanbrugh was given the job of designing the Earl of Carlisle's country house in 1699, after his lordship had quarrelled with his original appointee, William Talman. Vanbrugh was not the obvious choice. The son of a Flemish sugar-baker, he was a career soldier, and spent more than four years in prison in Paris - part of the time in the Bastille - for proclaiming his support for William of Orange. On his release he spent five months in Paris where, mostly subconsciously, he was absorbing the city's new architecture. This was his only architectural qualification before he started on his building career at Castle Howard.

That career, however, lay some years ahead. Back in London, he needed something to occupy him. Instead of applying for a steady, quiet job in Whitehall, he decided to become a playwright, believing he could write better plays than those currently on stage. His contemporaries decided that he was right; *The Relapse* and *The Provok'd Wife* were huge successes, and are still regularly staged.

But why did Vanbrugh's career as a soldier and a playwright make the Earl of Carlisle decide he was the right man to design Castle Howard? We have no real idea - neither man left us any clues. Vanbrugh was probably just in the right place at the right time. Like Howard, he was a member of the Kit-Kat Club. When Howard argued with Talman, Vanbrugh used his gift of persuasion as a successful dramatist to persuade the Earl to let him have a crack at something different. But really, as the Earl of Ailesbury remarked at the time, it was just as likely that Sir Christopher Wren would be made Poet Laureate. Jonathan Swift wrote that

> Van's genius, without thought or lecture,
> Is hugely turned to architecture.

For all the doubt they might have expressed, Vanbrugh proved them wrong. He may not have had the technical skills that a man brought up through the trade may have had. But he brought an eye for what looked right, and an imagination that soared. In his architecture he used his experience of the theatre to create dramatic 'stage-set' designs - though some said that his design skill came from his parentage; his buildings were supposed to look like the confections his father had baked. Wherever it came from, 'Van's genius' was successful; after Castle Howard, Vanbrugh went on to design other houses, including Seaton Delaval in County Durham and the vast Blenheim Palace in Oxfordshire, the nation's tribute to the victorious Duke of Marlborough.

When the wings were added to the Pyramid Gate in 1756 for the 4th Earl, the pyramid was put to practical use. Conveniently, it is hollow, so it was used to house the water tank for the buildings to each side. And the top part of the archway was hollowed out to make a passageway between the wings. For some time the whole building was used as a temperance inn, with all the comforts of a local hostelry except the strong drink - there are now plans to return it to use as an hotel. Beyond the wings, ruined 'medieval' walls with turrets straggle along the ridge. They are another example of Vanbrugh building in an ancient style to underline the Earl's lineage.

After the Pyramid Gate is the huge, 100-foot-high obelisk dedicated to the Duke of Marlborough, where there is a right turn to the house itself. It all looks very familiar to those of us who've watched *Brideshead Revisited*. From the south front, where the sun casts wonderful shadows with Vanbrugh's Corinthian pilasters, you can look out over the carefully-tended gardens and beyond the grandiose Atlas Fountain by Prince Albert's favourite sculptor John Thomas, into the wider landscape. And there on the ridge is Castle Howard's Great Pyramid.

It is not easy to get at. There is a public footpath along the road, and the Pyramid is conspicuous from many other parts of the estate, but it is enclosed by barbed wire fences and often-

The Great Pyramid and Vanbrugh's turret at the end of his fake 'Ruined Wall' at Castle Howard

impenetrable crops. Built of carefully-cut stone, it has eight baroque stone lanterns set around it. They were designed by Hawksmoor, whom Vanbrugh had drafted in as his assistant in either 1700 or 1701. Hawksmoor provided the expertise in handling the practical aspects of building that Vanbrugh so conspicuously lacked. His work was invaluable, and after Vanbrugh's death Hawksmoor continued to work for the Earl of Carlisle.

The Great Pyramid, built in 1728, was part of a new phase of landscaping at Castle Howard - placing buildings further from the house to form specially-created vistas. It seems to have a special spatial relationship with the Mausoleum and the Palladian Bridge over the river - though for some reason it is placed at an angle to the house, as if the underlying rhythm of the landscape is different here from nearer the main building.

The inside is accessible only on specially-conducted tours. The small, low wooden door in the south side of the plinth means you have to stoop to get in. Inside, all is gloom until your eyes become accustomed to the change of light. Suddenly, looming over you, you see a monster bust of the third Earl's great-great-grandfather staring down at you. It is so large that it cannot have come through the door, so the wonderfully beehive-shaped vault must have been built around it. With its womb-like curves, it is a great contrast to the geometrical perfection of the outside.

The monster bust, which looks away from the house into the wider landscape, is of Lord William Howard, Elizabethan founder of the Howard family's fortunes - 'that noble and Beneficent Parent' as the inscription says. As well as inheriting a fortune, the 18th-century Howards seem to have developed a poetic streak. The third Earl wrote a verse to the bust, which he caused to be carved in the plinth on the north side. It says:

To thee, O venerable shade
Who long hast in oblivion laid
This pile I here erect;
A tribute small for what thou'st done,
Deign to accept this mean return,
Pardon the long neglect.

And the Earl's daughter, Viscountess Irwin, wrote of the pyramid:

East from the House a beaut'ous Down there lies,
Where Art with Nature emulating vies. . . .
Upon this Plain a Monument appears,
Sacred to Piety and filial Tears.
Here to his sire did grateful Carlisle raise
A certain record a more lasting Praise,
Than Volumes writ in honour to his Name:
These often die, being made the Sport of Fame:
The Moth the Worm, and Envy them annoy,
But Time can only Pyramids destroy.

The Great Pyramid has a geometric relationship with the Temple of the Four Winds on the edge of the formal garden and the great Mausoleum to the east: the main shape of the pyramid is a triangle; the plan of temple is a square (and the shape is a domed cube) and the mausoleum has a circle as its plan and a hemispeherical dome. The three buildings also represent three different styles of ancient buildings - Egyptian, Greek (the mausoleum) and Roman (the temple) - which in the eyes of Vanbrugh and Hawksmoor were direct links to ancient glory and so suitable to laud their patron, the Earl. And given that three is a significant number in Freemasonry, that Lord Carlisle was a Mason and that Hawksmoor is very likely to have been one, these combinations of three may have had mystic roots as well.

And there are three pyramids at Castle Howard, too. It is a bit of a walk from the Great Pyramid to the third of them in Pretty Wood, to the east of the house. It is in a private area of the woodland, so you need permission to see it - permission not likely to be given in the nesting season for game birds. When we first saw it some years ago, it was in a sorry state - the point was missing, many of the blocks of stone, with their deep grooves, were out of true, and a small tree was growing out of it.

Today, though, it is a much happier story. Money has been spent on putting it all to rights, and now, standing among Pretty Wood's bluebells, it looks much as it must have done when it was built, to designs by Hawksmoor in the 1720s - before the Great Pyramid. It has no inscription, so it is not clear exactly what its purpose is, though the Earl of Carlisle and Hawksmoor will have decided on its style and location with precise ideas in mind. If they were inspired by Egyptian influences on Freemasonry, the proliferation of pyramids at Castle Howard must have pleased their fellow Masons.

FROM MYSTICISM AND bluebells at Castle Howard to more straightforward influences among the lavender in the Howardian Hills. We called for tea at Yorkshire Lavender, outside **Terrington**, three miles from Castle Howard. We had been there a couple of times before, and enjoyed their lavender-flavoured scones in the tea-room. It looks south from the ridge across the valley towards Sheriff Hutton Castle. This wasn't a pyramid stop, just a break for refreshments.

As we were leaving we noticed that, since our last visit a few months before, four pyramids had appeared in the field next to

Hawksmoor's pyramid in Pretty Wood, Castle Howard

OPPOSITE
Top:
Castle Howard's Great Pyramid, with the dome of the house appearing over the ridge

Below:
The giant bust inside the Great Pyramid at Castle Howard

31

The four lavender-coloured pyramids of the Goodwill family at Yorkshire Lavender, Terrington

The fifth pyramid at Yorkshire Lavender, Terrington, at the centre of the new maze

the car park. They were of different heights and made of lavender-painted steel. Why were they here?

We went back into the building that houses the tearoom and lavender shop. 'Tell us about the pyramids.' Without looking too taken aback, Nigel Goodwill, founder of Yorkshire Lavender, explained.

'It is a memorial to my wife, Lynne, who died in 1993 when she was only 38. I wanted to put up something to commemorate her, and the idea of the pyramids came out of a doodle I was doing.'

'And why are there four of them?'

'They represent the family - the largest is me, then Lynne, with the two smaller ones our two children. We all worked hard together to set up Yorkshire Lavender and make it a success.'

On a later visit we found that the four pyramids had been joined by another, lower version on the other side of the garden, in the middle of a nascent lavender maze.

The lavender fields of Terrington are a good place to visit, especially when the plants are in flower. The scent of lavender in its many different varieties floats on the air, and the bees are in heaven, busily buzzing from plant to plant. And as you enjoy your tea or buy that pot of lavender jam, you'll suddenly find yourselves being stared at from the adjoining field by a Highland cow or shyly observed from the bushes by a group of roe deer.

AT **SAXTON**, SOUTH of Tadcaster, we were due at the unveiling of a new pyramid to mark an old event.

The Battle of Towton was fought on undulating pastureland between Saxton and the neighbouring village of Towton. A decisive battle of the Wars of the Roses, it was the bloodiest ever fought on English soil. On Palm Sunday, 29 March, 1461 the Yorkist and the Lancastrian forces fought in freezing temperatures and in the face of bitter blizzards. After more than 12 hours of fighting the Lancastrians had been routed, and the landscape was littered with bodies. The estimate is that at least 28,000 men were killed, and the Cock Beck, which flows through the battlefield, ran red with blood for three days.

The pyramid to the Battle of Towton is unveiled, 23 April 2003

The Yorkist victory placed Edward IV firmly on the throne, but left thousands of widows and fatherless children throughout the north of England. The bodies of the dead were mostly buried near the battle's site, and in 1996 40 skeletons were unearthed near Towton Hall. They were reburied in Saxton churchyard, and the Towton Battlefield Society raised funds for a permanent memorial - a pyramid carved with representations of the minutes before the battle began.

We were invited to its unveiling on St George's Day, 23 April, in 2005. It was a splendidly sombre occasion. Archers and soldiers in 15th-century dress lined the churchyard, and fluttering in the breeze were banners with the coats of arms of the knights who had fought. Children from the village primary school read passages about the battle, and the pyramid was unveiled and then dedicated.

The sculptor, Steve Hines, chose the triangular, pyramid shape because it reminded him of an arrowhead; flights of arrows

33

Detail of the pyramid to the Battle of Towton at Saxton

marked the start of the battle. 'I started with a rectangular block and I could see the arrow shape straight away. I've never worked a triangular shape before, ever, but on this one I could see the triangle, and I'd heard people talk about the power of the triangle, but until you're actually doing one you don't realise it - and it is strong, a very strong symbol. The other thing for me as a sculptor, working by hand, is that it's the triangle of the mind, the heart and the hands all working together. It wasn't until I was half way through that that I realised this is how I think, as well.'

The pyramid is narrow - narrower at one edge than the other. On the north face Steve depicted the soldiers waiting for the battle to begin, Yorkists on the right, Lancastrians on the left. There is also a woman spinning with her distaff, to commemorate the women who were present on the battlefield, supporting and tending the men. On the opposite side is the inscription, which is symbolic in two ways. The top text, about the skeletons buried there, is tightly carved in the top point of the pyramid, to represent the thin wedge into which the Lancastrians were forced before they were killed. Two different scripts represent the opposing forces. There is a palm cross - for Palm Sunday - and a sprig of broom, the *planta genista*, symbol of the Plantagenet dynasty that was divided against itself in the battle.

Steve Hines chose stone from Yorkshire - Morley Blue sandstone, which has not been quarried for more than a century. 'It's absolutely pure,' Steve said. 'Michelangelo could have worked that. It's a beautiful stone, not a flaw.'

Right next to the new pyramid is the 15th-century tomb of Lord Dacre, who led part of the Lancastrian army. Local tradition says that he is buried upright, along with his horse. As Steve Hines put it, 'Now Lord Dacre's got some of his own men around him. And the delicious irony is that we've all grown up with this Lancashire/Yorkshire conflict, but in fact the Yorkist side were more likely to be southern troops, and the Lancastrian side would be a combination of Yorkshire and Lancashire men. It was the way the levy was called. There was no choice.'

FROM THE BATTLEFIELD at Towton we travelled south west to **Nostell Priory**. It lies east of Wakefield and south-west of Pontefract in a landscape that bears the scars of industry. It was probably very different - and much more rural - when Sir Roland Winn, 4th Baronet (or possibly Wynn, or even Wynne - spelling seems never to have worried the family too much) started to build a new house near the remains of the medieval Augustinian priory.

The great Palladian house designed by James Paine sits - rather dumpily - at the top of a short rise, surrounded by grassland and trees. Its main front has been unbalanced by a large wing designed by Robert Adam, who replaced Paine when the 5th Baronet, also imaginatively named Sir Roland Winn (or Wynn or Wynne) succeeded to the estate. Adam's plan for three more wings in the same style failed to materialise.

Nostell has great interiors by Adam, as well as superb furniture by Chippendale, but we were here to look at something else by Adam - what's known as the Obelisk Lodge.

We had seen the Nostell Lodge before, and we knew it was definitely a pyramid - and designed by Robert Adam. There was even a photograph of it in the National Trust's handbook for 2004. This was a bit misleading, because in 2004 it wasn't really visible, as it was fenced off and scaffolded. Repair began in 2005, and by 2007 it was back in its pristine state.

*Robert Adam's
Obelisk Lodge
or Pyramid Gate
at Nostell Priory*

The Obelisk Lodge at Nostell Priory before restoration

It had certainly needed work. When we saw it some fifteen years ago it wasn't in good shape. The stonework was crumbling, the pointed top was missing and the iron gateways bent and rusted. It was all a far cry from Adam's original vision - and, wonderfully, his designs still exist at the house. The drawings are inscribed 'Design of a Gateway for the Park at Nostell, One of the Seats of Sir Roland Winn Bart, to be situated at the approach to the House from the York & Pontefract roads.'

These days the lodge is stranded on the edge of the park, approached by a grassy track that must once have been one of the main approaches to the Priory. It seems likely that Adam was inspired by the Pyramid Gate at Castle Howard (see page 28). What he gives us here, though, is more direct, though perhaps not quite as impressive. He has planted the pyramid firmly on the ground, not on a cube as Vanbrugh did. And then he has punched the gateway straight through the middle, and given it a sturdy Tuscan surround, complete with columns and pediment. It is not in Adam's usual refined style - here's something much more basic, even crude.

Adam does have something in common with Vanbrugh, though. This is stage scenery, designed to impress as you approach and leave the park. So he has not bothered about archaeological accuracy. Instead of being on a square base, like any self-respecting pyramid, the Lodge is rectangular in plan - in fact, viewed from the side, it is certainly more obelisk-like.

Adam designed the pyramid, and its flanking walls that were intended to be terminated with sphinxes, in 1776. It was built in the same year by stonemason Cosmo Wallace. There are some practical aspects to it; Adam provided tiny rooms to each side of the arch where the gate-opener could loiter until, like a figure from a weather house, he would emerge to fling open the gates for the Baronet and his guests. Adam thoughtfully supplied a fireplace at each side, too, to try to keep the unfortunate servant warm; the flues are ingeniously carried up inside the pyramid to emerge unnoticed at its summit.

From very early in its life the Obelisk Lodge acquired another nick-name; the Needle's Eye. We were now on our way to another Needle's Eye, at Wentworth Woodhouse near Rotherham (see page 37). And that was inspired by a now-vanished rival pyramid at Wentworth Castle. Adam's Needle's Eye is supposed to have been named after the Wentworth Woodhouse one, which was built in the first two decades of the 18th century and in turn was inspired by Castle Howard's gateway. The gentry of Yorkshire were keen to rival each other, even when it came to pyramids.

SAY **BADSWORTH** IS set between Pontefract and Doncaster, a couple of miles from the A1, and you would probably imagine a downtrodden, grimy pit village - the sort of place where *Brassed Off* might have been filmed if they had not decided instead to build a special set at Elsecar Heritage Centre near Barnsley. You would be wrong. This south-eastern part of West Yorkshire, near the borders of both South and North Yorkshire, is much more 'County'. There are large, prosperous-looking farms, paddocks with jumps for ponies, bridleways shooting off in all directions, and 4x4s in the drives of houses that wouldn't come cheap.

Badsworth village itself is leafy, and the churchyard, where the pyramid stands, is shaded by fine beech trees. So it comes as a shock to find that the pyramid is not a memorial to a local Master of Foxhounds or the châtelaine of the local manor, but to an

Indian boy known as Osmond Alexander. What was this lad (whose original name was no doubt very different) doing buried under a pyramid in Yorkshire, so far from the heat, noise and dust of his native land?

The inscription on the pyramid says: 'In memory of Osmond Alexander a native from the capital of Hindustan. He departed this life on 18th July 1788. In years a stripling, in person handsome, a temper and disposition most amiable, an honest lad and a faithful servant. This stone is erected by direction of his master Colonel Edward Rawstorne. In memory of his adoration and regard.'

We were only a little further forward. Colonel Edward Rawstorne lived at nearby Rogerthorpe Manor. He may have served in India, possibly in the East India Company, and brought Osmond back with him on his return. But what was Osmond's role in the Rawstorne household? Was he that then-fashionable accessory for the lady of the manor, a black pageboy?

And is there any connection between his death from what the parish register called 'decline' and that of Colonel Rawstorne's daughter Elizabeth? She died of consumption - tuberculosis - just six weeks after Osmond. She, too, was 14 years old.

Perhaps there is still some folk memory of this exotic lad around in the area. Apparently, in the 19th century, one of the local residents told us, the local children believed that if they ran round the pyramid seven times without stopping, Osmond Alexander himself would appear to them. But, she said, none of them ever did it - though she wasn't at all sure whether it was breathlessness or fear of the consequences that stopped them completing their seventh circuit.

Osmond Alexander's monument in Badsworth churchyard

AND NOW FOR the Needle's Eye itself - the real one. **Wentworth Woodhouse** is the most palatial back-to-back in the country. Two huge eighteenth-century houses sit, joined uncomfortably and slightly out of true, in a vast park that was landscaped, in part, by Humphrey Repton. Each house has a stunning façade - the west front, finished about 1735, is baroque. The east front, from 15 years later, is in a purer, Palladian style - and at 600 feet is the widest country house in Britain.

The house - or houses - went through many trials and tribulations. There was a more modest structure on the site from about 1630, built for Sir Thomas Wentworth, Earl of Strafford, who was beheaded in 1641. Strafford's great nephew, another Thomas, who was later created Marquess of Rockingham, was responsible for building both the houses - and the eastern one was started even before the western one was finished. There is no rational explanation for this - perhaps he fell out with his relatives, perhaps he wanted to keep up with the latest fashion - or maybe he just liked building.

The house was in the family's hands until after World War II. Then they let the east part to the Local Education Authority and it became Lady Mabel Teacher Training College. The young ladies who studied Physical Education at the college had use of some of the most sumptuous interiors, including the Marble Saloon, where they played badminton - fantastically impressive, if rather chilly. They stayed until 1986, after which the house reverted to the estate, which had plans to turn it into that most go-ahead of uses for a country house, a conference centre. But the plans fell through and in 1989 the place was sold for development as a

*The Needle's Eye
at Wentworth
Woodhouse*

residence - and then the developer ran out of money . . . The Grade I listed building is now once again in private ownership, and is not open to the public.

In the western part of the house used to hang one of its greatest treasures, George Stubb's massive painting of the 2nd Marquess of Rockingham's horse Whistlejacket. After some wanderings to other homes, the picture, which shows the chestnut horse rearing against a plain, buff background, is now in the National Gallery.

Whistlejacket, foaled in 1749, is buried near the Wentworth Woodhouse stables. He was the Marquess's most famous and valuable horse. His greatest victory seems to have been in a four-mile race at York in August 1759 for a prize of 2000 guineas (around a quarter of a million today) - though some say that he actually lost to his rival Brutus. If he didn't win, the Marquess would not have been pleased, for he was a man who liked a bet.

He once placed £500 on the outcome of a race from London to Norwich by five geese and five turkeys. And the Needle's Eye is also said to be the result of one of his drunken wagers. As the bottles were emptied, the boasts of the Marquess and his friends became wilder - and just as young men today might brag about their cars and their driving, so the drinkers made inflated claims about their abilities to handle a coach and four.

Eventually, the story goes, Rockingham boasted that he could drive through the eye of a needle. 'Bet you can't!' the cronies chorused. 'Bet I can!' the Marquess retorted. And, perhaps as dawn broke, they settled on a compromise; he would build a special Needle's Eye and the coach and four would drive through that. Is this story true? Who knows? The locals insist on it, and it is been around for a long time, so it may be. In the early 20th century the 7th Earl Fitzwilliam recreated the supposed feat by taking a gun carriage through the Eye.

Whoever did the original driving (if they did it at all), it was not the 2nd Marquess of Rockingham. He was born in 1730 - and an engraving of the estate in 1723 shows the Needle's Eye to be already there. So it was probably built by Thomas, Lord Malton. And as the Pyramid Gate at Castle Howard (see page 28) was built in 1719, it is very likely that it provided the impetus for his work. Close to home, there was another pyramid at the rival Wentworth Castle estate. Called the Flat Iron, it was built before the Needle's Eye, which must have been constructed as a riposte. The Flat Iron was demolished in the 19th century.

When we went and inspected the Needle's Eye - it is about half a mile north of the mansion, off the lane to Brampton - we could get some idea of the Marquess's supposed carriage-driving skill. It is a tall pyramid, pierced with an ogee - double curved - archway. It sits on top of a ridge with a steepish drop to the south. Like much of South Yorkshire, the land beneath is riddled with old mines, so the eastern side of the Needle's Eye has sunk a few inches.

You still get a sense of how tricky the drive must have been - if he actually did it. Whichever side he approached from - and it would be much easier from the north - he would have had to have been pretty good at handling the horses. The archway is only eight feet, nine inches wide. But actually the space for the wheels to pass is restricted by kerb stones at each corner, so the real width is less than seven feet. Coupled with that is the limited height - about eleven feet of straight wall, then another five and a half of curved arch to the top.

To get four horses through it would be no mean feat - especially going at any speed - and no doubt the driver would want to go as fast as possible just to show off. And then there is that steep hill to contend with . . .

So was it really all built for a bet? Maybe, but there are other explanations. Assiduous measurers have come up with some interesting facts about the Needle's Eye. Every measurement in the structure can be divided exactly by seven. This is a mystical number, of significance especially to Freemasons. Add to that the flaming urn that crowns the pyramid, as symbol of light and life, and it may be that the pyramid was built as a sign of Masonic beliefs.

We could not leave the Wentworth Woodhouse estate without seeing the 1st Marquess of Rockingham's monument to the defeat of Bonnie Prince Charlie at Culloden, the wonderfully-named Hoober Stand.

It is a tall, triangular structure with rounded corners, tapering dramatically to a platform with a small turret on the top. Now smoke-blackened from years of local industrial activity, it stands on the same ridge as the Needle's Eye, but a little to the east. For years it was in a bad way; the door and windows were bricked up, the iron balcony rusted and warped and the turret rotting. Now, all has been transformed. Money has been spent repairing and restoring it, and you can once more ascend the winding stairs and see the panoramic view from the top, which takes in the Rockingham mausoleum nearby and the tall Doric column the Marquess erected to celebrate the acquittal at Court Martial of his friend Admiral Keppel.

Hoober Stand has had restoration work on the inscription over the doorway, too, which used to be unreadable. It now says clearly: *This pyramidall building was erected by his Majestys most dutiful subject Thomas Marquess of Rockingham in grateful respect to the preserver of our religious laws and libertys King George the Second who, by the blessing of God having subdued a most unnatural rebellion in Britain anno 1746 maintains the balance of power and settles a just and honourable peace in Europe 1748.*

Hoober Stand is hardly a 'pyramidall building', even within our rather loose definition, but it is fun. It is likely it was designed by the man who was also responsible for the lengthy east front of the great house. He was Henry Flitcroft, an assistant to the arch-Palladian architect Lord Burlington. But the look of Hoober Stand would probably have given the very-correct Lord B a fit of the vapours.

Despite the loyal and dutiful inscription, it was probably built to show off to the locals that Thomas Wentworth had just been created a Marquess. And the name? What are the exotic origins of the magical words Hoober Stand? What is a Hoober? And why did it stand? Sorry - it is not romantic at all. Rather boring, in fact. A stand is a place from which you could go to watch the hunting across the estate below you. And Hoober is the name of the hamlet in which it sits. It means a mud house.

'This pyramidall building' - Hoober Stand at Wentworth Woodhouse.

SILKSTONE IS A prosperous-looking village a few miles west of Barnsley. In 1838 it was at the heart of a mining community - a community that was reeling from a dreadful accident that shocked the nation as much as the tragedy at Aberfan was to do 126 years later.

We drove into the centre of the village as the blue-dialled clock on the tall tower of the parish church struck a quarter to six. The pyramid is immediately next to the churchyard wall, west of the tower. It is tall and narrow, built of reddish sandstone and surrounded by a cluster of small gables. Below is a tall pedestal, carved with the story of the disaster it commemorates and the names of the many victims. It is one of the most poignant churchyard monuments to be found anywhere.

The story it tells is of the drowning of twenty-six local children on 4 July 1838. It was a fine summer's day but they were not out enjoying it; they were hard at work underground in Huskar Colliery near Silkstone Common. Suddenly, at three o'clock in the afternoon, out of the clear blue skies, came a torrential thunderstorm. In a very short time it dumped two-and-a-half inches of rain in the area.

People working at the surface saw water running down into the pit shaft. They raised the alarm and tried to get the miners and their forty young helpers to the surface, but the deluge had put the engine that drove the winding mechanism out of action. When everyone underground assembled at the foot of the shaft they were unable to ascend to the surface.

There was no immediate danger at this point. But the children had already spent nine hours underground, and understandably became restless as they waited for something to be sorted out. So they asked their supervisor if they could make their way out along a ventilation drift. At first he refused, but they were so persistent he eventually told them to do as they wanted.

They set off along the drift, passing through a set of doors on the way. Suddenly a surface stream overflowed and swept into the drift, forcing the doors closed and rapidly filling the confined space. Of the forty children, only fourteen escaped; two of them were pulled out by their hair by rescuers.

When the waters had subsided the bodies were taken to nearby Throstle Hall Farm, where their faces were washed and identifications were made - fifteen boys and eleven girls, the youngest of them just eight, the oldest seventeen. There were two sets of brothers, and a brother and sister, among the dead. The average age of the victims was just over ten.

An inquest was held at the Red Lion Inn at Silkstone on 12 July. Some of the surviving children gave evidence. One, William Lamb, said 'We didn't know what we were going out for. We thought it was a fire. The water washed the children down the day hole against a door, through which we'd just come, and they were all drowned. If we'd stopped at the pit bottom we'd have been saved.'

The disaster caused an outcry in the country; Queen Victoria herself took an interest and ordered a Royal Commission under Lord Ashley (later the Earl of Shaftesbury) that eventually led to a ban on children and women working underground in mines.

The pyramid monument was erected soon after the disaster. Its main inscription reads:

> THIS MONUMENT was erected to perpetuate the
> remembrance of an awful visitation of the Almighty
> which took place in this Parish on the 4th day of July
> 1838. On that eventful day the Lord sent forth His
> Thunder; Lightning, Hail and Rain, carrying
> devastation before them, and by a sudden irruption of
> Water into the Coalpits of R.C.Clarke Esqr
> twenty six human beings whose names are
> recorded here were suddenly Summon'd to
> appear before their Maker.
> READER REMEMBER! Every neglected call of God,
> will appear against Thee at the Day of Judgment.
> Let this Solemn Warning then sink deep into thy

Silkstone Church and the Huskar Pit Disaster Memorial

hearts & so prepare thee that the Lord when He
cometh may find thee WATCHING.

Lists of the dead children - boys on one side, girls on the other, are
carved on other faces of the monument, and there are also four appropriate texts:

'There is but a step between me and death'
'Boats [sic - for *boast*] not thyself of tomorrow'
'Therefore be ye also ready'
'Take heed watch and pray for ye know not when the time is.'

There are other monuments to the disaster elsewhere in the
area, including a modern sculpted stone by Tony Slater showing
the inundation, a child's head and a pair of supplicating hands.
There is also a memorial on the site of the disaster itself, put up
on its 150th anniversary in 1988. And to show that the memory
of the drowned children lives on, in November 2004, local children planted twenty-six trees, one for each victim, to form an
avenue up to the site memorial in Nabs Wood.

FROM THE POIGNANCY of the Huskar monument, it is a
short distance in miles, but a long way in ethos, to the pyramid at
Bretton Hall near Wakefield.

For many years Bretton Hall was a College of Education, and
then served as the Performance Centre for the University of
Leeds. It closed in 2007 and was leased for transformation as a
luxury hotel. In its grounds is the Yorkshire Sculpture Park. We
turned up there, called at the Park's information desk and said
confidently to the assistant, 'We've really come to see the pyramid.'

'What pyramid?' she asked, puzzled.

'The pyramid near the lake.'

'I don't think we've got one of those. Lots of Henry Moore and
Barbara Hepworth, though.'

So we were left to find it for ourselves. Fortunately, we had
some help - from the man who designed it. In the *Yorkshire Post* in
November 1982 Derek Linstrum reviewed a book about the
Egyptian Revival. 'Only 20 years ago,' he wrote, 'I myself
designed and built a pyramid in Yorkshire. It may be found by the
side of the lake at Bretton Hall, a picturesque little object that is
acquiring the patina of age, and I like to imagine it as a modest
echo of the greater garden buildings of the 18th century as well as
a distant echo of old Nile.'

We scoured the grounds and sure enough, there it was, hidden
behind silver birches, which have been planted as close as possible
to the sides to screen it. No wonder the information desk people
knew nothing about it.

We telephoned Professor Linstrum at his home in Leeds. 'How
very odd to be reminded of it after all these years!' he said. 'I
designed it at the beginning of the 1960s. The College had no
mains water at the time, and the pyramid held pumping equipment that drew water from the lake to a filtration and purification
plant. But almost as soon as it was ready, mains water arrived, so
it was redundant.

'It wasn't difficult to build. The drawings were done by the
structural engineer at the County Council - I can't remember his
name after so long - and once the forms were made it was
straightforward. It is certainly well-constructed, with good concrete. My inspiration was eighteenth-century garden buildings. I
think perhaps it was too small, but it looked well if you viewed it

*Derek Linstrum's
1963 pyramid at
Bretton Hall, now
closely screened
by trees in the
Yorkshire
Sculpture Park*

from the edge of the lake. But they didn't like it at the College, so they tried to hide it with the trees.'

It is a pity that, more than forty years on, Professor Linstrum's pyramid is almost totally forgotten - even he was surprised to be reminded of it. There should be a concerted effort to clear it of the encircling trees and shrubs, and let it once again evoke 'a distant echo of old Nile'.

IN THE CHURCHYARD at **Adel**, just north of Leeds, is a pyramid with echoes of Norman England. The small parish church of St John the Baptist at Adel is the best Norman church in Yorkshire. It was built between 1150 and 1170, and has changed remarkably little since. It has an ornate chancel arch and a south doorway that has plenty of chevron mouldings, as well as sculptures of Christ in majesty and groups of beasts and serpents, now badly worn. On the south door is a replica of its ancient sanctuary ring - the original was stolen in 2002. It is in the shape of a fearsome animal (lion? boar?) devouring an understandably glum-looking bearded man.

When John Wormald of Cookridge Hall, a short distance from Adel, came to order a memorial for his late wife Zinai in 1846 it was perhaps inevitable that he chose the Norman style. He may have commissioned Leeds architect Robert Dennis Chantrell, who designed the Gothic Leeds Parish Church, to provide drawings for it. Chantrell restored St John's at Adel in 1844, when he rebuilt the chancel roof to its original Norman line. If Chantrell did design the memorial, it was one of his last Yorkshire works, as he moved to London in 1846.

What Wormald got for his money was a memorial about six feet tall. The lower part consists of four arched openings, surrounded by chevron mouldings like the church doorway. At each corner are small columns, topped with Norman-style capitals carved with interlacing patterns that are derived from carvings on the chancel arch. Above the arches is an undulating frieze, like one found below a line of battlements in a Norman castle, and over that a patterned frieze carved with diamond shapes. On top of this is a pyramidal cap, divided into three sections. The top section is decorated with more undulating patterns, and there is a finial with two crosses on top.

It is an odd structure, reminiscent of the neo-Norman castles that were being built about this date, like Penrhyn in North Wales (see page 227). Unfortunately, it also looks like some mid-Victorian fire surrounds - it is as if four had been brought together and topped not with a mantelshelf but with the pyramid-shaped top of a gatepost, enlarged to fit. It is not a successful composition, though it is individual.

The inscription, beneath one of the arches, is in Gothic rather than Norman lettering. It reads 'Here lie the remains of Zinai wife of John Wormald Esqr of Cookridge Hall who died June iii mdcccxlvi'. Zinai remains a mysterious figure. Even her first name is unknown to Google; the only other Zinai to be found on the internet seems to have been a later relation. In the 1868 will of William Wormald Mason, who lived at Caunton in Nottinghamshire, there is a specific clause that excludes his sister Mary Zinai Mason from benefiting from his estate. It is not even clear which John Wormald the original Zinai was married to: it was probably John William, who died in Leeds in 1859. He was either the son or the nephew of John Wormald, Lord

The 19th-century monument to Zinai Wormald in the churchyard at Adel

Mayor of Leeds in 1776. Lord Mayor Wormald was in business for a time with one of the city's most progressive mill-owners, Benjamin Gott.

Wormald, Fountaine and Gott built the first steam-powered mill in Leeds - it was known as Bean Ing - and produced some of the country's earliest twill cloth. Opened in 1793, the mill was demolished in 1965, and the site is now occupied by the ugly 1970 building housing the *Yorkshire Post* newspaper. John Wormald and his partner Joseph Fountaine were cloth merchants - one of the biggest firms in the city - and Gott was originally apprenticed to them. In 1785, aged 23, Gott became a junior partner in the company, and soon took over sole control, as John Wormald Junior was too young to do so. From 1816 the Wormalds no longer took a part in the company, though they intermarried with the Gotts, and as the Wormalds had a tendency to call their sons John, the succession becomes unclear.

Young John seems to have lived the life of a gentleman at Cookridge Hall, while his brother Henry lived at Sawley Hall near Ripon. They jointly leased property at Kilnsey and Threshfield in Wharfedale from Benjamin Gott, and in the 1840s John was fighting the Leeds and Thirsk Railway for compensation for loss of streams and springs on the Cookridge Hall estate before allowing the company to build the line; the land taken for the railway was valued in 1850 at £2226 10s 0d - several hundred thousand in today's values.

From these snapshots of the Wormald family we can build up a picture of a generation of hard-working mill-owners, succeeded by a generation that used the money made by their fathers to move up the social scale - in a typical Victorian fashion. Against this background Zinai lived and died, presumably loved by her husband, but leaving little mark on history. Only her neo-Norman pyramid in Adel churchyard and the mystery of her name stand as her memorial.

'The Inspire' office block in Harrogate

THE PENULTIMATE PYRAMID on our round-Yorkshire journey is a new structure in a business park in **Harrogate**. Chris Bentley, an engineer, went on a business trip to San Francisco, where he was fascinated by the famous Transamerica Pyramid. While he was in California he sketched a pyramid of his own, and decided there and then that it was just what Harrogate needed.

On his return he set about his task. On a site in Hornbeam Park he started to build The Inspire. A thinnish pyramid (though not as thin as its Transamerica inspiration), it has four floors clad in blue-tinted, solar-reflective glass, providing almost 1,800 square metres of office space. The top half of the pyramid is open, showing the stainless steel structure. There is a terrace beneath the point and a roof garden was planned.

Mr Bentley has said that his aim is to make The Inspire more famous than *The Angel of the North*. There is nothing like having ambition - though the *Angel* does have the advantage of the A1 channelling thousands of motorists past it each day . . . .

When we first saw it, The Inspire was unfinished, and a cylindrical tower, to be called The Round, intended as a counterbalance to the spikiness of the pyramid, was not started. Now complete, The Inspire remains empty, thanks in part to leaky glazing and problems with the foundations. Even so, it is a fine, though rather startling, sight on the edge of so staid a town as Harrogate.

WHILE THE LEISURE industry took up the pyramid with some enthusiasm from the 1970s onwards - for example at Bletchley (see page 90) and Bexhill (see page 67) - the Church did not. There are a few churches with pyramid-shaped roofs, but the church of Our Lady of Dolours at Glasnevin in Dublin (see page 362) and St Margaret Clitherow in **Threshfield** in the Yorkshire Dales have a proper pyramidal shape.

Margaret Clitherow was proclaimed a saint by Pope Paul VI on 26 October 1970. Threshfield's Catholic Church of St Margaret Clitherow was dedicated less than three years later, on 2 October 1973. A York woman, Margaret Middleton was born in 1556 and brought up as a Protestant. Her father was Sheriff of York, and her stepfather was later Lord Mayor of the city. In 1571 Margaret married John Clitherow, a butcher who lived in York's street of butchers, Shambles - their house, though heavily restored, is still there and is now a shrine. Soon after her marriage Margaret converted to Catholicism, apparently with her husband's agreement, though he remained ostensibly Protestant. She was ardent in her new religion - to a dangerous extent.

As well as helping the poor and visiting the sick (her first biographer and spiritual director, Fr John Mush, wrote that 'she collected as a honey-bee, of every flower, some honey both for her own store and her neighbour's.') she tended fellow Catholics in prison - and it was not long before Margaret herself was in prison. She regularly harboured Catholic priests in her house, and Mass was frequently said there. The house was searched while her husband was away. The Clitherow's children refused to help the searchers, but a young Flemish boy who lived with the family showed them a priest hole, Mass vestments and altar breads ready for Mass. Margaret was arrested. Despite the apparently damning discovery in the house, the prosecution had great difficulty in producing people to testify against her, because she was greatly loved in York. When she eventually appeared in court, and was asked to plead to the charge, she replied 'I know of no offence whereof I should confess myself guilty'.

Inevitably she was found guilty and was sentenced to death by 'peine forte et dure'. Her last weeks in prison before her death were spent making a simple linen shift for her execution. On 25 March 1586, aged just 30, she was taken to an underground cell near Ouse Bridge in York. When she was told that she must pray before her death, her prayer was not for herself but for the Queen to be turned to the Catholic faith. Then she was laid on the floor and a wooden door placed on top of her. Heavy weights were placed on the door, not by the executioners, who refused the task, but by four beggars bribed with gold. Her last words, as the weights were piled, were 'Jesu, Jesu, Jesu, have mercy on me.' Her body was buried by the authorities in 'a filthy dunghill' but six weeks later was dug up by loyal Catholics and reburied (the site of her grave is lost) - all except one hand, which is now one of the treasures of the Bar Convent in York.

The canonisation of St Margaret Clitherow, one of the Forty Martyrs of England and Wales who died for their Catholic faith in Protestant England between 1535 and 1679, was an important moment for Yorkshire Catholics. Several churches and schools were named after her, but the church at Threshfield was the first to be consecrated. It was designed by Bradford architect Peter Langtry-Langton, who was inspired for the pyramid shape by a simple church constructed of poles, wattle and palm leaves he had seen in Africa. 'It was a long time ago,' he says, 'and I can't even remember which country it was in. But I thought that it was very

St Margaret Clitherow

*St Margaret
Clitherow
Catholic Church
at Threshfield*

simple and effective - especially as the altar was put into one of the corners of the square, with the congregation in a semicircle around it. So that's what I did here.' He is clear that simple geometric shapes make good architecture; 'They have a devotional quality to them - think of the greatest churches, like the former St Sophia in Istanbul, which is a work by a mathematical genius.'

There was some local opposition to the new 'modern' church at Threshfield, which led to a public inquiry run by an inspector whom Peter Langtry-Langton called 'an old-fashioned civil servant, of the type you don't see today. He recognised local prejudice, listened quietly and courteously to everyone - and in his summing up was just and kind to everyone.'

For his church design the architect used zinc-clad buttresses that form ridges from the apex to the ground in place of the African church-builder's poles. The buttresses are anchored in low walls of local stone. The body of the church is also stone-built, and has a wedge-shaped zinc-covered skylight over the altar - a typical 1970s touch in church design. Inside, the most notable feature is the stained glass windows at each side of the altar. They are of swirling geometrical forms and were designed by Jane Duff. The church has the local nick-name of Paddy's Wigwam - a title it shares with Liverpool's Catholic Cathedral.

THERE IS A postscript to the Yorkshire pyramids - one that probably used to exist but has long since vanished. On the western edge of Ripon is the World Heritage Site of Fountains Abbey and **Studley Royal**. Most of the visitors to the site, with its early-18th-century water gardens and the stupendous ruins of the Cistercian abbey, are directed to the new visitor centre high above the ruins, but for the Aislabie family who laid out the estate the main approach from Ripon was along the long, ramrod-straight avenue aligned on Ripon Cathedral's towers. After passing under a delicate Adam-style arch the avenue rises to the highest point of the park. Today the height is occupied by the Victorian St Mary's

Church, one of the masterpieces of the architect William Burges; but behind it is an early 19th-century obelisk, standing on the site of one of Yorkshire's lost pyramids.

The pyramid was built as a memorial to John Aislabie, founder of the family fortunes and speculator with the nation's money. Born in 1670, Aislabie was elected as an MP (for Ripon for most of his career) and rose to be Chancellor of the Exchequer, a post he achieved in March 1718. It must have seemed a great opportunity. The speculation on the fortunes of the South Sea Company, launched 1711, was at the height of its fame. Aislabie, probably inspired by large bribes from Sir John Blunt, the Company's promoter, was active in its promotion, and in the eventually-disastrous plan to reduce the National Debt by allying its fortune to the South Sea's rise. By July 1720 £100-worth of South Sea Stock was worth £1000. It was the Dot Com miracle of the age.

And like the Dot Com boom, it bust. Two months later it was barely a quarter of the price, and it continued to plummet. Thousands of investors - both those with large holdings and people like the country clergy and innkeepers with little - lost heavily. Heads had to roll - and chief among them was Aislabie, as Chancellor. The House of Commons investigated his part in the disaster and he was forced to resign in June 1721. For a time he was confined to the Tower of London, and a parliamentary report castigated him for 'most notorious, dangerous and infamous corruption.'

Before his fall Aislabie had amassed a fortune of £164,000. Would he, like others, lose it all? A behind-the-scenes deal seems to have been done. An apparently arbitrary date of 20 October 1718 - seven months into his Chancellorship - was chosen; he could keep everything he had before then. Conveniently for Aislabie, he was already rich in 1718, so he retained £119,000 (more than £15 million in today's values), an ample amount on which to retire and cultivate his garden at Studley Royal.

His gardening leave lasted 21 years. When he died on 18 June 1742 a pyramid nearly 50 feet high was planned as a memorial. It was based on the pyramid by Vanbrugh at Stowe (see page 93), which was erected in 1726. It had the same form - a tall, narrow, stepped pyramid on a square base. Inside was an oval room with niches, accessed by a heavily-rusticated door. Unlike the Vanbrugh pyramid it had, so far as we know, no lettered inscription around it, though there must have been some indication of its purpose on a plaque. Like the Vanbrugh example it did not last long.

In fact, there is some doubt about whether it was actually built. There are estimates and a design in the estate papers, but visitors to Studley (even in the 18th-century, without the National Trust to care for and promote it, it was a great attraction to 'persons of taste and discrimination') never mentioned it - odd, if it dominated the main drive with its imposing height and its elevated situation. If it was constructed, there may have been structural problems early on - perhaps because of unstable ground - leading to its early demolition.

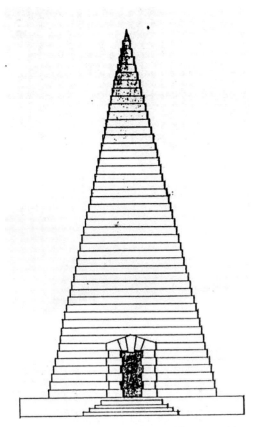

The pyramid at Studley Royal near Ripon - demolished (or unbuilt)

Tour 2

EAST AND
SOUTHEAST ENGLAND

CROWLE IS NEAR the only completely empty square on the Ordnance Survey's Landranger maps. It's in the top left corner of Lincolnshire, south of Goole and west of Scunthorpe, and the landscape really is pretty featureless. And even Crowle's villagers would be hard-pressed to say that it is ever likely to win the Best Kept Village competition. It has the slightly-depressed air that goes with largely-agricultural communities that have to fight hard to make a living off the land.

Flat farmland surrounds it, criss-crossed with drainage ditches large and small - Pauper's Drain, Warping Drain, Swinefleet Warping Drain. Immediately west of the village is Crowle Waste. Three miles south is the Isle of Axholme, where there's an 18th-century brick Egyptian-style obelisk put up by Squire Bellwood of Temple Bellwood in memory of his favourite horse and his hounds.

We were looking for other Egyptian inspiration, though - the pyramid to the Stovins of Crowle. We'd had difficulty finding out just where in Crowle the Stovin pyramid is. The official listing (it's Grade II) said 'approximately 50 metres north of Tetley Hall'. A call to the post office in Crowle produced bafflement. 'Pyramid? I don't know about any pyramids. I can tell you where Tetley Hall is, but I'm not sure they'd let you go there . . .' Later we tried the public library, where Mrs Andrew was much more helpful. She didn't know about the pyramid, but knew who lived in Tetley Hall - and provided the phone number. Mr Ramsden there said he'd be very happy for us to visit the pyramid and take photographs 'Just come down the drive, nearly to the end. The pyramid's just to the right, in the trees.'

In all about four feet high, there is a two-course stone plinth topped by a low pyramid of stone slates. Many of them have slipped and are in danger of collapsing into the hollow centre of the structure. The pyramid may once have had a more elaborate cornice to the plinth, but that has largely been lost. It's covered in moss and so encompassed by evergreens that it has an air of dankness and decay even on a sunny day.

The pyramid has no inscription, but just beside it is a tiny walled graveyard with narrow slabs over the graves of a number of 18th-century Stovins. They were a prominent family in the area, and many of them were Quakers. One, though, George Stovin, was influenced by the preaching of John Wesley, who was born in nearby Epworth. Wesley's journal for 20 July 1774 mentions 'Mr. George Stovin, formerly a Justice of the Peace near Epworth, now as teachable as a little child, and determined to know nothing save Christ crucified'. Stovin would have been approaching the age of 80.

It's probably the same George Stovin who compiled a local history from now-vanished manuscripts and who, a few years earlier, had helped dig out of the local peat the beautifully-preserved body of a medieval woman, dated from the style of her sandals to

The Stovin pyramid at Tetley Hall, Crowle, Lincolnshire

OPPOSITE:
*Leonard Manasseh's pyramid at King Solomon Academy, Marylebone, London
(see page 76)*

somewhere between the early 13th and mid-15th centuries. *The Gentleman's Magazine* says that Stovin 'found the skin and thigh bones, which measured eighteen inches, then the skin of the lower parts of the body, which distinguished it to be a woman, afterwards the skin of the arm, which, when the bones were shaken out, was like the top of a muff; likewise a hand, with the nails as fresh as when alive, though they shrank on being exposed to the air.'

A later member of the family was Frederick Stovin, a distinguished army officer who joined the infantry at the age of 17, served in France, in Denmark (where he was at the capture of Copenhagen) and in Spain with Sir John Moore during the Corunna campaign. He also served as deputy adjutant-general when the British attacked New Orleans in 1814. He had commands in Jamaica and the Ionian Islands before returning to England to become a groom of the bedchamber to Queen Victoria and a knight of the Order of the Bath. General Sir Frederick Stovin died at St James's Palace in 1865.

IF THE CROWLE pyramid is hardly known, even in its home village, our next one is much more public. Fantasy Island is at **Ingoldmells** on the Lincolnshire coast, and is billed as 'Lincolnshire's number one tourist attraction'. It is just north of the village centre and dominates a wasteland littered with huge concrete drainpipes. It is a fantasy indeed - a huge Ferris wheel, the high curve of a roller coaster and what appears to be a tangle of red, yellow and grey noodles, which form the Millennium Coaster and the Jubilee Odyssey. And behind them, rather more substantial in comparison, is the Fantasy Island pyramid.

If we could have looked at it objectively, without the fairground

Fantasy Island, Ingoldmells, Lincolnshire

surroundings, we would have been impressed, perhaps. It's a fine pyramid, well-proportioned, and an unassuming grey colour. There are glazed panels down each side, and on top what on a Burmese pagoda would be called a *hti* - a decorative finial. But look closer; the *hti* is an oversized Coca-Cola bottle (see Lough Boora, Co Offaly, page 352, for another bottle-topped pyramid).

Inside the pyramid, says the Fantasy Island website, there are 'themed rides', and the site boasts 'every type of attraction from white-knuckle rides, roller coasters and water rides down to small children's roundabouts . . . the themed central pyramid structure sets the tone for the rest of the park, making it an award-winning family attraction.' It's good to know that the pyramid is so influential.

Much of this stretch of the Lincolnshire coast is given over to caravan parks - it has the largest concentration of caravans in Europe. Curiously, at Ingoldmells they have no view of the sea - a large bank comes between them and the beach. The low-lying land is prone to flooding - without the bank, there would be no pyramid and no Fantasy Island. It made us think of the poem *The High Tide on the Coast of Lincolnshire* by Jean Ingelow, born in nearby Boston: the narrator's son rushes to his mother:

> 'The olde sea wall,' (he cried) 'is downe,
> The rising tide comes on apace,
> And boats adrift in yonder towne
> Go sailing uppe the marketplace.' . . .
> Then bankes came downe with ruin and rout -
> Then beaten foam flew round about -
> Then all the mighty floods were out . . .
> The feet had hardly time to flee
> Before it brake against the knee
> And all the world was in the sea.

Ingoldmells is a bleak place in winter, as winds from the Urals lash the sea against the bank and drench the holiday homes in spray. But there's obviously plenty to do in Ingoldmells for the summer without needing to visit the beach; which accounts for its huge popularity.

Nikolaus Pevsner, writing about the nearby Butlin's Holiday Camp more than 40 years ago in *The Buildings of England; Lincolnshire*, says, 'This is, of course, the chief attraction of Ingoldmells . . . but it is a social not an architectural attraction.' A fair comment; but then he spoils his lofty aesthetic stance with a snobbish aside: '. . . there is a sea of caravans which makes the real sea twice a day retire far out in shame.'

DOWN THROUGH LINCOLNSHIRE and into north-west Norfolk. In the flatness of the Fens, **Downham Market** sits on a small ridge above the River Great Ouse. It was once known as 'The Gingerbread Town' because many of the buildings were made of thin stones the shape, colour and texture (though not, fortunately, the porosity) of gingerbread; they can still be seen in the walls of the Town Hall.

Next to the Town Hall is the Town Square. Until 1835 it was much smaller; there was a row of thin houses along its centre. Now it is a proper square, dominated since 1878 by the splendid black-and-white-painted Gothic cast-iron clock, symbol of the town.

Nearby are the latest additions to the Square - the Carved Wall and the Town Pump. The wall has carved pictures and texts on it, provided by children aged from 6 to 16 at three local schools.

Detail of the Carved Wall at Downham Market

*The Town Pump,
Downham
Market, Norfolk*

They were asked what inspired them about the town and about the square as a place to meet. The texts include 'When I meet my friend I punch him on the shoulder. He punches me back' and 'Mischievous Adventures Enjoying Giggling Swimming Together'.

Between the wall and the clock tower is the pyramid we had come to Downham to see. On a plinth of the same York stone as the wall is a thin, copper-capped pyramid of greenish glass, which lights up at night. This is the 2003 version of the Downham Market Town Pump, which stood on the site until 1933.

Designed by landscape architects Sheils Flynn, it was constructed by Smith of Derby - who also made the pyramid at Gosport (see page 110). At the front is a stainless steel drinking fountain, with the inscription 'The Town Pump'. When we were there a local wit had added his own graffito comment - 'Don't drink the water'.

There is a local legend that the gutter that took the waste water from one of the new pump's predecessors was a favourite place for small boys to sail their paper boats. One young lad, at school in the town, was supposed to have been particularly influenced by this pastime - he grew up to be Lord Nelson. Unfortunately there is no evidence that young Horatio was ever at school in Downham Market, 30 miles from his home in Burnham Thorpe near the coast. It is said that the story comes from confusion with 'another child of the same name.' Just how many boys were there called Horatio Nelson in west Norfolk in the 1760s?

A BEAR WAS next - a bear on a pyramid. We're in the village of **Briningham** in rural north Norfolk. Despite Noel Coward's 'Very flat, Norfolk,' this is gently-undulating Norfolk, and the village sits in a slight fold in the hills. In St Maurice's churchyard, to the east of the church, is the pyramid - a monument about seven feet high, topped with a rope-moulded plinth on top of which sits the muzzled head of a bear - the crest of the Brereton family.

The history of the Breretons is like that of many families; a few outstanding individuals, and a lot of also-rans. Two (or maybe three) Breretons stand out. One was John Brereton, a clergyman from Lawshall, south of Bury St Edmunds in Suffolk. He set out from Falmouth in March 1602, with thirty others, in the vessel *Concord*, captained by Bartholomew Gosnold. The voyage of exploration was sponsored by Henry Wriothesley, third Earl of Southampton - the man to whom William Shakespeare dedicated his poems *Venus and Adonis* in 1593 and *The Rape of Lucrece* in 1594, and who may be the patron addressed in the *Sonnets*.

The *Concord* made it to the coast of Maine. The adventurers didn't stay long, returning to England in September 1602, but they were the first Englishmen into Massachusetts Bay, and they gave Cape Cod its name. On their return home, John Brereton wrote *A Briefe and True Relation of the Discoverie of the North Part of Virginia*; he dedicated it to Sir Walter Ralegh. Brereton describes the voyage ('by chance the winde favoured us not at first as we had wished, but inforced us to farre to the Southward, as we fell with St Marie, one of the islands of the Açores (which was not much out of our way) . . we made our journey shorter (than hitherto accustomed) by the better part of a thousand leagues . . ') and their adventures in the New World. It is the American link that draws US visitors to this quiet corner of Norfolk.

As far as the pyramid is concerned, however, it's a different story. Though the monument seems to be from the nineteenth century, the muzzled-bear crest of the family is much earlier - though how much earlier is open to question. So is the reason for it. Two stories exist. In one, Sir William Brereton kills his valet for interrupting him at dinner. He goes to the king (which king is not recorded) to ask for mercy. The king gives him a sporting chance. In three day's time he will come face to face with a bear. If by then he can invent a practical muzzle for the beast, he will be pardoned.

Sir William spends the three days in the Tower of London, working on his invention - the materials he has to hand are unspecified - perhaps he uses his belt, or a handy length of rope. On the third day the bear is let in. Can he get his muzzle over the bear's snout? Not a chance; the beast is almost twice his size. But with low cunning he distracts the bear by throwing the muzzle over its head - and runs away. The king is apparently satisfied with this wriggling out of his edict; Sir William is spared, and the muzzled bear becomes the crest of the Breretons.

Or . . . An eager young cavalry officer called Brereton jumps the gun in battle and leads his men in a charge before the king is ready (again, which king?). Instead of bawling him out, the monarch merely remarks 'Let the bear be muzzled', and no doubt his aides-de-camp laugh uproariously at the royal pun on the officer's name.

Whatever the truth (and it's probably neither of these stories) the pyramid itself is enjoyable. Sadly, the official listing tells us that it shows 'at the apex the family crest: a muzzled dog.' The man with the clipboard must have been in a hurry when he visited Briningham in 1984 to prepare the list.

A FEW MILES further east, in **Blickling** Park, is the pyramid mausoleum to the 2nd Earl of Buckinghamshire. It's about three-quarters of a mile west of Blickling Hall, the great Jacobean house of the Hobart family, and set deep in the remains of a medieval forest, now known as Great Wood.

We approached the pyramid from the north, from the car park at Itteringham Common, though it's also possible to reach it from the house on a pleasant route that takes you beside the lake. We were in rather a hurry (driving through Norfolk always takes longer than we think) so we needed directions. There were plenty of local people walking their dogs in the woodland, who were keen to set us on the right route. 'Just to the end of this ride, then turn left by the trees, and you're there.'

The pyramid is set at the end of a grassy glade bounded by yew trees. It is an impressive 45 feet high and set on a base 45 feet square, so it is about half the height of its inspiration, the pyramid of Cestius in Rome (see page 2). Each face has shallow projecting classical porticos. On the eastern and western faces they have iron grills to allow light into the interior. To the south are two grey-painted panel doors, through which the coffins of the deceased could be taken, while to the north is an inscription on a slab of red-tinted stone, now spotted with lichen.

It is all very severe and perfect - except that above the doors there is sculpted the coat of arms of the Earls of Buckinghamshire, supported by a stag with impressive antlers and a very superior-looking talbot dog. And above the inscription on the north side is an even more magnificent beast, a spiritedly-carved bull, the crest of the Hobart family.

Bear-topped Brereton pyramid, Briningham, Norfolk

53

Bonomi's
pyramid for the
Earl and
Countesses of
Buckinghamshire,
Blickling, Norfolk

Who was all this Egyptian splendour for? It commemorates John Hobart, the 2nd Earl, who was born in 1723. His was an interesting family. His grandfather, Sir Henry, died in a duel with a neighbour who had been spreading rumours about Sir Henry's supposedly cowardly behaviour at the Battle of the Boyne, where he was an equerry to King William III. John's father, also called John, is said to have been raised to his peerage through the influence of his sister Henrietta. She married Charles Howard, Earl of Suffolk, but more importantly was a Lady of the Bedchamber to Queen Caroline, and mistress of King George II.

The younger John - the 2nd Earl - had a mixed career; he was Ambassador to the court of Catherine the Great in Russia, where he seems to have been a success, though on his appointment the waspish Horace Walpole called him 'the clearcake; fat, fair, sweet and seen through in a moment'; on his return to Blickling John brought with him a huge tapestry of Peter the Great at the Battle of Poltawa. It was so big a room had to be made to fit it, and it's still in the house. Then, from 1776, he was Lord Lieutenant of Ireland. It was said of him there that 'he was hardly equal to the exceptional difficulties with which he had to deal,' and he wrote on relinquishing his post that he was 'a man whose mind has been ulcerated with a variety of embarrassments for thirty weary months.'

Despite a busy life, the Earl managed to marry twice. His first wife was Mary Anne Drury, with whom he had three daughters. One of them, Henrietta Hobart, was married for a short time to Armar Lowry Corry, later Lord Belmore, of Castle Coole in Co Fermanagh; the Lowry Corry's pyramid at Caledon (see page 308) may have inspired the Blickling pyramid. Lord Buckinghamshire's second wife was Caroline Conolly, who also produced a daughter but no surviving sons. When Buckinghamshire died in 1793 (the result of sticking a gouty foot in a pail of ice water) the title went to his brother and the Blickling estate to his second daughter, Caroline, and her husband William Harbord, who commissioned the pyramid.

Its architect was Joseph Bonomi, a Roman who came to Britain in 1767 at the age of 28 at the suggestion of Robert Adam. He became a fashionable architect, designing and altering country houses and building an undoubted masterpiece, the austere church of St James, Great Packington, in Warwickshire - for which, Pevsner says, he 'deserves to be a household word of English architecture.' St James is in the Greek style, but his versatility is shown by his equal facility in the then fashionable Egyptian style here at Blickling. Something of his Egyptian interest rubbed off on his sons; Ignatius designed a flax mill in Leeds like a pharaonic temple (see page 16), while Joseph Junior was a renowned Egyptologist who worked on the design of the Egyptian Court at the Crystal Palace exhibition erected in 1854 (see page 17).

Bonomi's first design for the pyramid was made at the beginning of 1794 - his estimate for its building, at £1,850, came in March that year. It was for a two-storey pyramid-cum-obelisk of the sort at Desertcreat in Co Tyrone (page 306), at Staverton in Gloucestershire (see page 127) and at Cheshunt in Hertfordshire (see page 84), for example. This was gradually modified into the purer pyramidal form eventually built. The contract was given to a London builder with Norfolk connections, Henry Wood. Among his jobs was the construction of a brick kiln at Blickling to burn 190,000 bricks, 17,000 of them special bevelled-shaped ones for the brick cone that forms the interior structure of the pyramid.

The Hobarts' crest, the bull, on the Blickling pyramid

Wood was dilatory, and Bonomi had to make surprise visits to his London workshop to get him to complete the work on the Earl's sarcophagus and the marble pavement. Both were big jobs - the sarcophagus cost £60.00 (with the second sarcophagus it was sent by water from London to Yarmouth and then by cart to Blickling at an extra cost of £16 2s 6d) and the estimate for the pavement was £135 4s 6d. Although Bonomi had set a completion date of August 1795, it was not until October 1797 that the new mausoleum was consecrated and the bodies of the Earl and his first Countess were moved in. Funding for the pyramid, it is said, was provided by selling the Countess's emeralds, which Lady Caroline must have inherited along with the estate. The total cost was £2270 4s 6d - getting on for £200,000 today.

Through the grilles we could see the sarcophaguses of the second Earl and his two countesses. Despite its roominess, the pyramid holds only the three of them. Like other mausoleums we've visited - Cobham (see page 62) and Gosford (see page 235), for example - it seems to obey the rule that the grander the concept, the fewer are those who end up inside it.

AT OUR NEXT stop we left the ranks of the aristocracy and came face to face with the middle classes. **Attleborough**, between Norwich and Thetford, is a pretty market town, set around its church. One of its few claims to fame, apart from the

The 1928 pyramid to Melancthon William Henry Lombe Brooke at Attleborough, Norfolk

pyramid we had come to see, is that about a century ago it held the biggest market for Christmas turkeys in the country.

In the cemetery just north of the centre of Attleborough is the small, white pyramid to the euphoniously-named Melancthon William Henry Lombe Brooke, solicitor and commissioner for oaths.

'Lawyer Brooke', as he was known, died in his 90th year on 15 September 1929. He is remembered in Attleborough today (if he's remembered at all) by a plaque in the town's library; a photograph of him that used to be there has disappeared. It was thanks to a bequest from Brooke that the library was built - though not until 30 years after his death. He left his home, Point Cottage near the church, first to his sister Lucy and, on her death, to the town 'to be for ever hereafter used by the inhabitants of Attleborough as a library reading room and pleasure grounds together with my said books, picture and garden effects'.

When the building came to the town on Lucy's death it proved inadequate as a library so it was sold. The money was invested and eventually there was enough to build the library. Among the books it should contain - but it doesn't - is *The Great Pyramid of Gizeh: Its Riddle Read, Its Secret Metrology Fully Revealed as the Origin of British Measure. Interpreted from the Measures by Professor C. Piazzi Smyth and Professor W. M. Flinders Petrie* by Melancthon William Henry Lombe Brooke. For Brooke was a pyramidologist ('Pyramidiot' in Flinders Petrie's terminology - see page 17) in the mould of Piazzi Smyth (see page 23). Like Smyth, Brooke was convinced that the 'pyramid inch' which the ancient Egyptians used for their building showed the superiority of British imperial measures to the foreign metric usurper.

It was this interest that resulted in his final resting place being marked by a pyramid. His will of 28 April 1927, as befits a lawyer, is very specific. 'I desire that my body may be buried in the Cemetery at Attleborough aforesaid and I DIRECT my Trustees at the expense of my estate to erect over my grave a Monument or Pyramid in White Lime Stone to my memory of the following dimensions:- Base 91" square and Pyramid from top of base to apex 58" in height.' He did not specify pyramid inches, but his instructions were obeyed, giving him a memorial of the same proportions as (though a great deal smaller than) the Great Pyramid.

The rest of his will also made interesting reading for the curious of the village. As well as the instructions about his pyramid and the library, there were some odd clauses (no doubt carefully drafted by the wily solicitor himself) referring to his old housekeeper, Florence Curtis. For a moment a veil is lifted from the household of an early-20th-century bachelor. In a codicil from July 1928 he leaves Florence 'the sum of £20 free of legacy duty' - reasonable, but not over-generous. Then he adds, 'This legacy would have been £100 if she had complied with my wishes and continued to wear for service the white cap and apron which became her so well.' On 28 May the following year he changed the bequest to £50.

His servant Jon Dagless received 'all my wearing apparel' and a legacy of £10. He was obviously a less argumentative character than Florence, for Brook described him as 'a man of absolute honesty, a conscientious worker and one who never contradicted or disputed his master's orders'.

Six weeks after Brooke's death his will was proved in the sum of £4565 10s 5d. Once the pyramid had been paid for and the bequests paid, it was not a large amount for a man who had been a pillar - even if an eccentric one - of the Attleborough community.

PORTRAIT AND PLAQUE TRIBUTE TO LAWYER

A PORTRAIT of Mr. Melancthon Henry Lombe Brooke, together with a plaque has recently been mounted in the entrance hall wall of the Attleborough Public Library, by the Norfolk County Council, at the request of the Parish Council and townsfolk.

Mr. Lombe Brooke, an important resident of Attleborough at the turn of the century, lived for many years at Point Cottage, Church Corner. He died in September 1929, at the age of 90.

In his will he left the cottage to the town, as a library. It was realised by the Parish Fathers that the structure was unsuitable for this purpose and they wisely sold the property and invested the money.

Over the years the money accumulated interest and reached a total of £4470. By adding about £2000 the Norfolk County Council was able to buy land in Connaught Road and to build the up to date and fully stocked library that has now become an important amenity in the towns' life.

The number of adult and juvenile registered readers is now well over a thousand.

Mr. Lombe Brooke came from a well-known Norfolk family, and was the author of a publication dealing with the Pyramids, and his tomb in Attleborough cemetery is in that shape.

He practised as a lawyer in the town, and many stories are still told by the older inhabitants of his quick wit and eccentricities.

A newspaper cutting from 9 July 1959, when Lawyer Brooke's photograph and a plaque were put up in Attleborough Library. The photograph has since disappeared.

WE HAD DRIVEN through the vast interiors of Lincolnshire and Norfolk, through tedious traffic around Boston and King's Lynn. Negotiating Norwich had put us well behind our planned schedule, so we were running late - very late - for the last visit on our schedule for that day, **Great Bealings** near Ipswich. The February light was fading and becoming hopeless for photographs, so we had to telephone to reschedule our appointment; fortunately Jonathan Peto at Bealings House was very understanding, and happy to rearrange for the following morning.

When we arrived at the mellow eighteenth-century brick mansion we went (of course) to the tradesmen's entrance, where Mr Peto welcomed us generously, led us through the house and out of the front door. The pyramid was away to the left, set by itself in a field. He set us on our way, and said he would join us in a moment.

This is the British Isles' only Hindu pyramid. Carefully protected from the local sheep by a rusting iron fence, it stands about ten feet high and is crowned with an unlikely sight - a three-faced sculpture of the head of the Indian God Shiva. On one of the sides is another carving, of Brahma, with three faces and four arms.

Why this amalgam of Egypt and India? In the 1820s Bealings House was the home of the eccentric Major Edward Moor, who walked around the neighbourhood wearing an oversized-hat and wielding a massive cane. Beneath this odd exterior, however, lay a scholar - especially of India and its gods. At the age of 12 he joined the army as a cadet and was sent to India. By 17 he was a lieutenant stationed in Bombay (Mumbai) - and had already made

Edward Moor's 'Hindu' pyramid, Great Bealings, Suffolk Norfolk

OPPOSITE:
Sculptures of Shiva and (below) Brahma on the pyramid

himself an expert on Indian language and law.

He was wounded in the Third Mysore War of 1791, but after a spell back in England to recover he returned to India, where he threw himself into studying the local gods and collecting images of them. He returned to England in 1806 with a collection of more than 1,000 objects, many of which he used to illustrate his book *The Hindu Pantheon*, which was a pioneering study of the subject. Moor influenced Edward Fitzgerald, translator of the *Rubaiyat of Omar Khayyam* and, through another publication, *Suffolk Words and Phrases*, Charles Dickens. Peggoty in *David Copperfield* speaks words that Dickens borrowed from Moor's work.

Moor's collection is now dispersed, except for the two sculptures on his pyramid. Both come from Bombay's Malabar Point, opposite the famous island of Elephanta. On Elephanta is a great cave, made into a temple and dominated by a statue, monumentally carved into the rock, of three-faced Shiva. Moor, excavating at Malabar Point among the ruins of a temple blown up by, as he wrote, 'the pious zeal of the idol-hating Portuguese', found the stone head that is now on his pyramid at Bealings - 'a fine specimen of the mythiarchaeology of India . . . more than two feet high and nearly as broad . . . weighing over a ton.' Nearby he found the four-armed Brahma.

Experts say that both sculptures date from the 11th century - 500 years later than the Elephanta sculptures, but old enough to make us wonder that they still remain on Major Moor's pyramids, accepting the rain and the east winds of Suffolk.

The three-faced Shiva is often referred to as the 'Trimurti' - and the name has been applied to the pyramid, too. All this seems to have been too much for the local people, who voiced their suspicions of the Major, and spread a rumour that Moor not only was a heathen himself but had interred his collection of idols in the pyramid so that they came to no harm.

We had finished examining and photographing the pyramid when Mr Peto arrived to meet us, dressed in a checked, caped ulster and leading two black labradors. Courteously, he showed us back to the house and discussed the pyramid with us. His pride in it was undoubted, and he was pleased that we had come to see it. Unfortunately we couldn't stay to chat for too long, as our itinerary for the day was very full.

NOW IT WAS off to Chelmsford where we were to inspect the first of two Essex pyramids. Our destination was **Widford**, a Chelmsford suburb, and the pyramid to Sarah, Viscountess Falkland.

This may have been a fine pyramid - but it has been so shamefully neglected that it is all but swamped by ivy. As far as it is possible to tell, there is a three-stepped square base supporting a shaped upper section, which may be in the shape of a Greek cross. On top of this sits the pyramid. There seems to be an oval cartouche on the eastern side, with an inscription that is now unreadable. There are perhaps similar shapes on the other faces, too. It is possible that there is some sort of sculpture on the pyramid's apex - an urn or a crest, perhaps - but it could just be an extra-thick tangle of ivy. All this is to commemorate a woman about whom history says little. Sarah Inwen, whose father Thomas was MP for Southwark, made two good marriages. Her first husband was Henry Howard, 10th Earl of Suffolk - a relation of the Earls of Carlisle at Castle Howard (see page 27). He was

The pyramid specified in her willl by Viscountess Falkland at Widford, Essex

29 when they married; we don't know how old she was, but as she died in 1776 she was probably much the same age. Henry's mother was Henrietta Hobart, mistress of George II and the 1st Earl of Buckinghamshire's sister. It may have been the Buckinghamshire's Blickling pyramid (see page 53) that influenced the Widford version.

Sarah and Henry married in May 1735. Less than ten years later he was dead - and the couple left no children. So a distant relation, the 4th Earl of Berkshire, became also the 11th Earl of Suffolk. How did the new earl treat Sarah, the new Countess Dowager - who was younger than he was? No information has come down to us. But it may have been a relief when in 1752, she married Lucius Charles Cary, 7th Viscount Falkland, who was considerably younger than she was - he was born a year before her first marriage. He lived nine years longer than her, dying in 1785.

It was her idea to have a pyramid. In a very rare example of a pyramid being mentioned in a will - the only other examples we have found are those of the third Earl of Darnley at Cobham (see page 62), Dr Douce at Nether Wallop (see page 105) and Lawyer Brooke at Attleborough (see page 56) - she left 'the sum of one hundred and fifty pounds to my Executors hereafter named in Trust to apply the said Sum in Building a Vault and . . . an Egyptian Pyramid to the East front in the Church Yard of the Parish of Widford in the County of Essex for the Interment of my body the model for the aforesaid Pyramid to be taken from the late Mr Blackwell that now is in the churchyard of Lewisham in Kent and also order that an Inscription that I shall leave among my papers be engraved on the aforesaid pyramid.' This instruction is curious. There is still a Blackwell monument in Lewisham churchyard, but it is not a pyramid but an obelisk, much taller and thinner than the Viscountess's monument. Either the Lewisham monument has been rebuilt since the mid-18th century, or the executors of Lady Falkland's will amended the design so it was more pyramidal.

The Viscountess also left £200 to institute a weekly bread dole for the poor of Widford, and all her books and four pictures to the Rectory of Widford as a parish library to edify the local people. Many of the books still exist, but you now have to go to the library of Chelmsford Cathedral to see them. The pyramid was designed by George Gibson (probably Gibson Senior, who designed many monuments in the south-east, including the fine Raikes mausoleum at Woodford). The sculptural decoration, now cruelly swamped in vegetation, is a mystery. The references, including the official National Monuments Record listing, say it's by Edward Pierce. This can't be the famous baroque sculptor who worked for Wren and died in 1695. Was it his son? There's no record of the maker of the fine eighteenth-century iron railings around the monument; they, too, need caring for.

FROM WIDFORD WE headed for **Orsett**, an Essex village that still manages to maintain its rural feel despite the closeness of the A13 and the ever-growing suburbs of Grays.

It was once an important place. In the middle ages it was the local administrative centre, and the Bishop of London had a palace north west of the village - its earthworks remain.

Orsett's pyramid is in the churchyard in the middle of the village. It is an eccentric design, with a square base supporting a curvaceous, sarcophagus-like section on somewhat shapeless feet. Then comes the pyramid, a rather emaciated affair pierced at the base with semicircular openings. The whole structure stands about 10 feet high. Inset into the base are marble rectangles, one of them carved with an inscription to Captain Samuel Bonham.

There is little information about Bonham beyond the meagre facts recorded by the inscription - that he was 'late of the parish of St Dunstan's Stepney', that he died on 28 February 1745 aged 68 and that his wife, who died in 1771, was called Jane. His will details many investments (including in the 'Pensilvania Land Compy') and indicates that he had difficulties with his family: ' . . . if my son William gives his Brother or Sister or their Heirs any trouble in law . . . he shall forfeit to his Elder Brother not only the House at Heppell Side but the five hundred pounds left him by this Will.' His other children were Samuel, Henry and Jane.

Bonham lived in Orsett House, which was built for him in 1740 on his retirement. And from what did he retire? Locally he is always referred to as 'the slave trader' - and there is some evidence that this was true - certainly his son Henry was a trader in black slaves from Africa.

In the first half of the 18th century enterprising men could make vast sums from transporting human cargo across the Atlantic. Slaving had originally been a trade for aristocrats, but their monopoly on the trade, claimed through the Royal African Company from 1672, was quickly undermined by 'interlopers' - middle-class entrepreneurs who saw the profits available. Men like Samuel Bonham refused to pay the duty demanded by the Company, and circumvented its protectionist Acts of Parliament. In any case, the Royal African Company could not meet the demands of the slave-owning colonies in America and the West Indies - at least 25,000 slaves were wanted each year for English colonies in the first decade of the 18th century. More than 500 ships constantly ran between the west coast of Africa, the West Indies and the east coast of America - and the Bonhams were among the captains who made the voyage. One day in 1750, for example the *Maryland Gazette* noted: 'Thursday last arrived in Patuxent [south of Washington], from Guiney, but last from St Kitts, the Ship *Kouli Kan*, Captain Henry Bonham, with a very large cargo of choice slaves.'

Samuel and Henry Bonham were probably minor players in slaving - yet it was a very profitable business for them; Orsett House is a large and handsome property, and the family were rapidly accepted as wealthy country gentlemen.

The parish of St Dunstan, Stepney, where Samuel had previously lived, was a magnet for seamen; forty-four of them were buried in the churchyard in 1749. Less than a mile and a half away is a possible inspiration for the design of Bonham's monument. The pyramid in the churchyard of Hawksmoor's Christ Church, Spitalfields (see page 75), which may have been put up in the 1720s, has striking similarities - the square, panelled base and the pyramid have much the same spirit, and the feet on which the pyramid rests are similar, too, though Bonham's designer has added the sarcophagus. Perhaps Bonham knew either the Spitalfields pyramid or the somewhat similar Raine Monument in the churchyard of another Hawksmoor church, St George-in-the-East (see page 73), also not far from his Stepney home.

Samuel Bonham's great-granddaughter Isabella also had pyramid links; she married George Canning, who built the pyramid at Garvagh in Co Londonderry (see page 304). And Samuel has another claim to fame; he was the great-great-great-great-grandfather of Camilla, Duchess of Cornwall.

The monument to 'slave trader' Samuel Bonham, Orsett, Essex

WE ENCOUNTERED MORE pyramidal influences at **Cobham** in Kent. The Darnley pyramid there is one of the most architecturally significant of the British pyramids - and for years it has been one of the most threatened.

To gain access to the mausoleum we had arranged to meet Alison Nailer from Cobham Ashenbank Management Scheme (CAMS) on a lane just beyond the war memorial in Cobham village, near the A2 between Gravesend and Rochester. We transferred to Alison's car, which then jolted and shuddered along an incredibly bumpy track for what seemed like hours, but was really about five minutes. When we could bump no further we braced ourselves against the bitter wind and with an eye on the threatening sky we walked uphill on a winding path through woodland to the mausoleum.

We'd seen pictures of it, and it has featured in BBC television's *Restoration* series, but it was still a moving sight. Like a duchess compelled to don overalls and get down to scrubbing her own floors, the Darnley Mausoleum retains an aura of magnificence amid its now-degraded surroundings. It had already suffered disastrous vandalism; now it was surrounded by an eight-foot-high metal fence to try to deter further indignities.

Alison unlocked the gate in the fence and let us look closely at both the outside and inside of the building. The basic exterior structure of the mausoleum is intact - there's a cubic base with protruding, canted corners, topped by a plain and austere pyramid. Above each of the corners is a Greek sarcophagus, and over the entablature on each of the sides, above the Doric columns, are semicircular lunettes, from which the original carvings have disappeared. The spaces are now filled with brick.

All this appeared to be in not too bad a condition - but inside was a very different story. There were originally two floors - the burial chamber, with its 32 coffin-niches on the lower level, and a circular chapel above it decorated with red marble columns. Much of this (though not the red marble, which was mostly hacked off) survived until 5 November - Bonfire Night - in 1980. To celebrate Guy Fawkes, or just from wanton vandalism, a group of youths piled car tyres high inside the burial chamber, and set fire to them. The resulting high-intensity blaze brought the chapel floor crashing into the crypt, destroyed the outer staircase and calcined much of the stonework.

When we visited the interior was a tumbled mess of stone and brick. Most of the coffin niches were still sound, but the once-paved floor was uneven. Looking up through the jagged hole that was once the floor of the chapel, we could see graffiti sprayed on most available surfaces. It was a depressing place - but there is still evidence of a masterly architectural hand.

That hand belonged to James Wyatt, who designed the mausoleum in 1783 to receive the body of John Bligh, third Earl of Darnley. The Bligh family lived at nearby Cobham Hall, a magnificent Elizabethan mansion, and the new mausoleum was built on an eminence within sight of the house. The third Earl left detailed instructions in his will about the building; it is thought that he was influenced by a detail from a painting by Poussin called The Sacrament of Ordination (now in the National Gallery of Scotland), which shows a strikingly-similar building. Within the tight limits that the Earl set out, Wyatt produced a masterpiece.

As one of the late 18th century's most fashionable architects, Wyatt left the construction to others. He was fortunate that he could rely on George Dance, Junior, himself an eminent architect whose designs included the innovative Newgate Prison in

*James Wyatt's
great pyramid
mausoleum for
Lord Darnley,
at Cobham in
Kent, before
restoration
work began*

London, demolished in 1902. Dance interpreted Wyatt's design with great fidelity and a rigorous insistence on top-quality workmanship - which, despite the depredations of time, neglect and willful damage, has ensured the mausoleum's endurance.

It has been a chequered survival. The western niche of the burial chamber, with a stone table awaiting the coffin of the third Earl, remained empty; it is likely that there was an argument with the Bishop of Rochester, who refused to consecrate the building and prevented any burials there. All the other niches were unoccupied, too. The mausoleum remained an ornament in the park, but in the early 20th century its condition was already giving cause for concern. Money was short, and in 1957 the family sold Cobham Hall and much of the estate (though not the mausoleum and its woodland) to the government; the Hall has housed an independent school since 1962. The mausoleum and the surrounding woodland became a magnet to the vandals - in a recent clear-out, 98 burned-out cars were found hidden in the woods and more may be still lurking. There have been even stranger goings-on, too; black masses and porn-filming among them.

Although permission was given in 1985 to turn it into a sumptuous home, the prospective developer became bankrupt and the mausoleum became one of the odder possessions of the Official Receiver. At last, in 2001, CAMS raised £150,000 so that Gravesham Borough Council could buy the mausoleum and woodland. CAMS is a consortium of the Council, the National Trust, English Heritage, the Woodland Trust and Union Railways - the last because some money for the work comes from compensation for loss of land as the Channel Tunnel rail link passes through the park. Nearly £5 million from the Heritage Lottery Fund is in place to restore the mausoleum and the historic parkland.

So restoration is underway. This Grade 1 building will be brought back from the brink of destruction, and will once again shine in its beauty. The National Trust will eventually take over the mausoleum and it will be open to the public. And its progeny, including the mausoleums at Gosford House in Scotland (see page 235), and at Kilbixy (see page 354) and Arklow in Ireland (see page 334) will be able to acknowledge the dowager from whom they are descended.

WE LEFT THE grandeur of Cobham to visit a pyramid on a much smaller scale. At **Nonington** near Canterbury we had been given permission to visit the Beech Grove Bruderhof Community, which has a pyramid in its garden. As so often, we did not know what to expect. We found the place easily, and drew up in front of what seemed to be workshops. In the office were two women dressed in gathered skirts and headscarves. They were our first - and very helpful - introduction to Bruderhof. They called for Fritz Kleiner to show us to the pyramid. Fritz, who was probably in his 70s, wore the men's outfit of the Community - dark trousers, check shirt and braces.

A generous and gracious guide, Fritz led us through the workshops where the Community makes wooden play equipment - there was a smell of sawn wood and glue - and out to the Peace Garden where the pyramid was. The garden, dedicated to children around the world, was created in 1997 by the Community's children, who wrote hundreds of letters to people throughout the world asking what the recipients believed peace to be. From the answers they were inspired to plant the garden and to create

The pyramid in the Peace Garden at the Bruderhof Community, Nonington, Kent

sculptures - there are corners of the garden for, among others, Northern Ireland, for the children of Dunblane and for the Arab-Israeli conflicts, as well as a memorial to the victims of the World Trade Center attack on 11 September 2001.

In the middle is the pyramid, which has been there much longer than the garden. In 1875 work was being carried out to build St Alban's Court, the main house that is now home to the Community, to designs by George Devey. During the work 15 skeletons were discovered. One of them had a bronze ring around its forearm. That and other grave goods suggested that this was a Saxon burial ground. There was, though, a story that the bones were of medieval nuns who once had a convent on the site; in the 1970s students who used the house when it was a College of Physical Education claimed to have seen the ghost of a headless nun.

The bones were reburied in the garden under a small pyramid, with an appropriate - though somewhat flowery - Latin inscription. In translation it reads 'These remains, recently uprooted by a barbarian hand, which until now the earth held firm in the sacred peace of the tomb, a stranger has restored to the safety of this mound, AD 1876. Whether perchance Romans for Caesar's empire, whether Britons for hearth and home, whether Saxons amongst their flocks - whoever, yet after as many as fourteen centuries, they await the Judgment Day.'

Although we had come to see the pyramid, it seemed perhaps the least affecting of the many objects in the Peace Garden. On our way back to the entrance we met some of the children, who greeted us happily. Fritz Kleiner told us something of his life before coming to Beech Grove. His family had joined the Community in Germany before the War; the first Bruderhof Community was started in 1920 in the Rhön Mountains by Eberhard and Emmy Arnold. The aims were - and remain - to live the way Jesus wanted; not worrying about food, clothing or possessions, loving one's enemies and promoting peace and harmony. This was not a message likely to endear them to the rising Nazi party; the Gestapo forced the Community to close and briefly imprisoned three of its members.

Community members - including Fritz - were forced to flee Germany. Some went to England, but as Germans they were threatened with internment as enemy aliens. 'So we went to Paraguay,' said Fritz. 'It was hard at first, but we managed to establish ourselves. After the War some of us went to America and Canada, and some back to England.'

He led us back through the workshop and we said our farewells. It was one of the most fascinating of all our pyramid visits - a window into an alternative way of living.

IN THE 1800s the builder and contractor James Burton laid out new squares and streets in London's Bloomsbury for the fifth Duke of Bedford. Russell Square, Bedford Place and Montague Street - described as 'absolutely plain, decently proportioned' - were his, and he was the architect John Nash's favoured contractor for his great London schemes, including Regent Street and the sumptuous Regent's Park terraces.

Rubbing shoulders with the aristocracy gave Burton an idea. The popularity of Brighton, especially under the Prince Regent, suggested to him (in a dream, it is said) that he should develop a seaside resort himself. In 1828 he bought two-thirds of a mile of seafront just to the west of Hastings, where he began to lay out his garden village - **St Leonards**, named from the dedication of a ruined chapel on the site. On the seafront he built Crown House for himself. There were - and still are - public gardens, an Assembly Room and Grecian and Gothic villas. There was a tradesmen's area, which he named *Mercatoria*, and a place for the laundresses, called *Lavatoria*.

In 1834 Burton gave Crown House to Princess Victoria, the heir to the throne; his new venture was already a success. He built the parish church - St Leonard's, of course - on the seafront below the steeply-rising ground where most of the development was situated. The church was destroyed in World War II and was replaced in the 1950s. The development of St Leonards was continued after James Burton's death in 1837 by his more-famous son Decimus (he was the tenth son), architect of the Camel and Giraffe Houses at London Zoo, of the Atheneum Club and of the Palm House at Kew.

James Burton's tomb at St Leonard's, the town he founded, with the tower of St Leonard's Church

James Burton was buried not inside his own church of St Leonard but beneath a pyramid in a small graveyard on the hill above, with wide views of the sea. He is justly described on one of the four white, sarcophagus-shaped niches on the pyramid as 'Founder of St Leonards'. The pyramid later served as the memorial to other members of the Burton family, including Decimus. It is Grade II listed and was restored in 1973 by the local Burton's St Leonards Society.

And why did James Burton, who favoured the Greek, Renaissance and Gothic styles, choose a pyramid for his tomb? One reason may be that one of his sons, another James (who reverted to the family's orginal name of Haliburton), was an Egyptologist of some note. It is also likely that James Burton was a Freemason, which influenced his choice of monument.

There is a third possibility, too; a Burton family tradition maintains that the pyramid shape was chosen to evade an ancient curse from the east - 'May jackasses sit upon your tomb'.

Bexhill Leisure Pool

LEAVING ST LEONARDS we drove through **Bexhill**. We passed the De La Warre Pavilion, the great modernist building designed by Mendelsohn and Chermayeff in 1933, with its sweeping lines and curves. Then, as we were looking forward to visiting one of Britain's most famous pyramids, we noticed another - Bexhill Leisure Pool. Designed by John Gill Associates of Eltham Hill in London, it opened in April 1990. Its heated pool has a flume, a wave machine and a 'beach' area, all within a top-glazed pyramid clad in two tones of corrugated metal.

Bexhill's pyramid didn't detain us for long. We were on our way to see Mad Jack Fuller in his pyramid at Brightling, a few miles north-west of Battle.

Mad Jack Fuller's famous pyramid in the churchyard at Brightling, East Sussex

IF YOU LOOK up English pyramids in any book about follies, or do an internet search for them, you're more likely to come across Mad Jack Fuller's than any other. Its fame is wide - it has even appeared on a set of collectable cards in the packets of PG Tips tea. Why should this be - what makes Jack's pyramid famous, when others languish unknown?

First, the pyramid, at 25 feet high, is quite big - it certainly dominates the churchyard at **Brightling**, as Fuller intended. It was probably designed by Fuller himself with technical help from one of his friends, the architect Sir Robert Smirke, designer of the British Museum.

Next, it is in good company, as Fuller built a number of follies on his Rose Hill estate. They include the Brightling Needle, an obelisk that marks either the victory of Nelson at Trafalgar or (more likely) that of Wellington at Waterloo. Then there's the domed Observatory, designed, like the Needle, by Smirke and suggested to Fuller by another friend, the astronomer and discoverer of Uranus Sir William Herschel. Another building, a Grecian-style Rotunda Temple seems, in comparison to the other follies, quite ordinary, but attached to it are stories that Fuller, who never married, entertained ladies of the night there.

Many of the buildings, which also include towers and a four-mile-long estate wall, were projects devised by Fuller to provide employment for local men. Over seven years he paid out £10,000 - almost half a million in today's values. It was a good bargain; he paid only half the normal rate to get the work done.

Another Fuller folly, which attracts almost as much attention as the pyramid, is the Sugar Loaf. A white cone on the south-west side of the park, it looks like the top of a church spire - indeed, like the top of nearby Dallington church's spire. And, supposedly, for good reason. One night, the story goes, when in London, Fuller bet his cronies that Dallington church spire was visible from Rose

Hill. When he reached home he found it was not true; he had the Sugar Loaf erected overnight so that when his friends looked out in the morning they'd be fooled.

But it is the pyramid that has the best stories. Fuller started to plan it in 1810. He got the vicar to agree to its being sited in the churchyard in return for a new wall and gates. He then persuaded Smirke to help with the design, and the pyramid was built between 15 November 1810 and 15 June 1811. For the remaining 23 years of Fuller's life he could see it from the windows of Rose Hill.

After he had died and had occupied the long-awaiting mausoleum, Fuller's entombment attracted stories. He was said to have been placed in the pyramid dressed for dinner - complete with top hat - sitting on an iron chair at a table on which a complete meal, including his best claret, was laid out. Not only that, but around him was a circle of broken glass that would get caught in the Devil's hoofs if he came, as expected, to claim Fuller as his own.

What a pity that it's not true! When the pyramid was opened in 1982 there was no table, no chair, no glass. And the bones of Jack Fuller weren't lying on the floor but were decently buried under it. It's now possible to see through an iron grille to the inside of the pyramid. You can just make out a stanza from *Gray's Elegy in a Country Churchyard* engraved on the wall:

> The boast of heraldry, the pomp of pow'r
> And all that beauty, all that wealth e'er gave
> Await alike th'inevitable hour
> The paths of glory lead but to the grave.

While Jack Fuller didn't have beauty, he could lay claim to wealth (from the family iron foundry at Heathfield) - and to heraldry (the Fuller coat of arms has the motto 'Carbone et Forcipibus', meaning 'By charcoal and tongs'). He also had something of the 'pomp of pow'r', for he was MP for East Sussex from 1801 to 1810.

Fuller was a controversial parliamentarian. He opposed the abolition of slavery (unsurprisingly, for some of the family's money came from West Indian sugar plantations) and the granting of civil rights to Catholics. A large man (he weighed 22 stones) and with a voice to match, it was difficult to make him be quiet in the House of Commons. He once called the Speaker the 'insignificant little man in the wig'. William Pitt the Younger, probably desperate to muzzle this loose cannon of an MP, offered him a peerage, but Fuller refused, saying 'I was born Jack Fuller and Jack Fuller I'll die.' His career as an MP ended in uproar when he intemperately denounced almost everyone in the government after a failed military expedition in the Low Countries. He was arrested by the Sergeant at Arms and threatened with imprisonment in the Tower of London.

Despite his volatile nature, Fuller was loved by locals, and made friends among the famous, too. As well as his friendship with Smirke and Herschel, he was close to the painter Turner, who produced watercolours and oils of a number of local scenes, including *Brightling Observatory from Rose Hill*. Fuller also saved Bodiam Castle from threatened demolition by purchasing it. He was a founder member of the Royal Institution, and endowed two professorships there. The scientist Michael Faraday was the first Fullerian Professor of Chemistry, and Dr Paul Roget (of Roget's *Thesaurus*) was the first Fullerian Professor of Physiology. There are still Fullerian Professors.

Bust of Jack Fuller in Brightling Church

FROM THE QUIET of Brightling, enfolded in the Sussex Downs, we went into Surrey, to busy **Reigate** ('a characterless little town in the middle of the county' says Nairn and Pevsner's Surrey volume of *The Buildings of England*; Redhill is 'Reigate's plebeian twin') to answer the question 'What's the connection between a pyramid and Magna Carta?'

To find out, we were directed to Reigate Castle, plumb in the middle of the town. What we discovered was the mound - the motte - of the castle founded around 1088 by William de Warenne, second Earl of Surrey. There are no remains of any buildings; only a pretend-castle gatehouse cobbled together in 1777 ('a poor little ivy-covered affair' - *The Buildings of England* condemning Reigate again.)

Bang in the middle of the motte (and beneath the notice of Nairn and Pevsner) is the pyramid - about eight feet high and probably constructed at much the same time as the sham gatehouse. It is made of roughly-cemented, irregular stones, and patched with somewhat smoother blocks. On one side is a grille, behind which steps descend into the subterranean gloom. The steps lead to perhaps the most interesting feature of Reigate, the Barons' Cave.

Down the steps there is a brick-vaulted chamber beneath the motte, then a stone-lined passage that runs to a tunnel, carved through the soft stone, to the bottom of the castle's dry moat. How old is the system? It was certainly there in 1586, when the Elizabethan antiquary William Camden noted 'an extraordinary passage with a vaulted roof hewn with great labour out of the soft stone.' It has been said that the slightly-Gothic cross-section of parts of the cave are consistent with a date of the early 12th century - was the warren of tunnels dug soon after de Warenne founded the castle?

The workmanship is good, and the hard work and skill needed to dig the cave suggests that it was of some special importance. It is unlikely that it was merely the castle dungeon. It may have been a secret escape tunnel from the castle in case of attack, but it certainly did not link the castle to Reigate Priory or to nearby Bletchingley or Betchworth castles as some have hopefully suggested. But from long past it has had the name of Barons' Cave, and attached to it the legend that the English Barons met there in 1215 to draw up Magna Carta before travelling to Runnymede and forcibly presenting it to King John.

Whatever its origins and history, the Barons' Cave has been a tourist attraction for many years - from the late 18th century people have descended through the pyramid to explore the darkness beneath their feet. In the World Wars the cave was a storage depot for ammunition and, after a time of neglect, was restored and opened to the public by Wealden Cave and Mine Society. They now open it, and the nearby Tunnel Road Caves, for guided tours on certain days each year.

THE EAST END of **London** is a significant contrast to the wealthy purlieus of Reigate. We had three churches by Nicholas Hawksmoor to visit, each with a pyramidal monument. The Docklands Light Railway swayed us above the streets from Bank station to Limehouse. We walked along the Commercial Road; until the late 17th century this was an area of pleasant fields, with Limehouse itself a village where sailors, shipbuilders and rope-makers lived and lime-makers slaked the chalk from Kent. Now the road, created only in 1802, passes grimy commercial buildings and flats where washing flutters on balconies between straggly geraniums.

This was the area that Clement Atlee represented in parliament, and his statue, complete with his characteristic round glasses, peered myopically at us from outside the Passmore Edwards Library. A little further along, after we had crossed Limehouse Cut that joins the Thames to the River Lea, was one of London's greatest churches, **St Anne Limehouse**.

Its white Portland stone shone, even on a day of grey cloud. Today it is surrounded by urban sprawl, but when Hawksmoor designed it in 1714 (it wasn't consecrated until 1740) it stood like a beacon amid the low brick houses and sheds of the local, river-orientated industries. It would have been as alien as a tank on a medieval battlefield - and as powerful a symbol.

Like St George-in-the-East and Christ Church Spitalfields, both founded in the same year as St Anne's, it was a Commissioners' Church - built under the control of the Commissioners of the New Churches Act of 1711. The Tory party had been returned to political power in 1710, and, because they were High Church, they wanted new churches in areas of growing population. Their fear was that the Dissenters (natural Whig supporters, they believed) would become too strong without a formidable High Church of England presence in the poorer areas of London. The new churches were to be paid for by a tax on coal.

Hawksmoor was appointed by the Commissioners (who included Sir Christopher Wren and Sir John Vanbrugh) as one of the two Surveyors, who were to find sites for 50 new churches and make sure the building campaign went smoothly. He was not asked to design them, but was obviously in a good position to get at least some of the commissions.

Nicholas Hawksmoor's 'Wisdom of Solomon' pyramid outside his church of St Anne Limehouse, London

In the end only twelve churches were built - the three in the East End of London were all by Hawksmoor, and all three are masterpieces. St Anne's, like St George's and Christ Church, has a magnificent tower, thrusting up above a semi-circular projection (there is a circular porch at the tower's base) and finishing with an octagonal turret, each pinnacle crowned with a small pyramid.

In the churchyard, near the north-west corner of the tower, is another, larger, pyramid. It is about ten feet high, quite slim, and each side has five panels. On one face it has the inscription *The Wisdom of Solomon* in English and Hebrew. There is also a very worn coat of arms, with little recognisable except a spirited lion rampant.

What does all this mean? Hawksmoor is likely to be the designer of the pyramid. Like the one in Pretty Wood at Castle Howard (see page 31) it has no immediately apparent purpose. The suggestion that it was intended for the top of the tower, above the lantern, is very unlikely. Hawksmoor's early drawings of the church show two pyramids at the other end of the building, on the roof above the east window, so it is just possible that it may be one of these. But then, why the inscription, where it could not be read, and the coat of arms, that would not be seen? The pyramid, which now sits directly on the ground, used to be on a substantial plinth, making it seem even less likely that it became redundant on the church roof and was then placed in the churchyard.

It is more likely that we need to look at Hawksmoor's links to Freemasonry and the arcane for an answer. He appears to have been closely associated with Masons from early in his career, and it seems that he was formally initiated into a Lodge soon after 1722. He was fascinated by many aspects of Freemasonry, in particular by the Temple of Solomon (he did conjectural reconstructions of it) and the Egyptian Masonic traditions that were used for building it.

Hawksmoor used the pyramid shape throughout his career, and based other buildings on Masonic ideals. So it is likely that the pyramid is a specifically Masonic symbol, proclaiming that the architect sees himself to be in a direct line from the ancients.

UNDER THE TOWERING presence of the Canary Wharf tower (itself topped with a pyramid, which has led ley-line fanatics and 'pyramidiots' to infer cosmological intervention) we walked to the next Hawksmoor church and the next pyramid.

Our route took us along Cable Street, where on 4 October 1936 Sir Oswald Mosley's Blackshirts, the British Unionist of Fascists, were defeated by a grouping of the Labour Party, Communists and the Trades Unionists. The Blackshirts had planned an anti-Semitic march through this area that was then predominantly Jewish. The Battle of Cable Street is marked by an appropriately red plaque. Now the area is peaceful, with Afro-Caribbean and Asian lads playing football together in the nearby streets.

The church of **St George-in-the-East** was burned out in 1941 during the Blitz. Now there is a smaller church within Hawksmoor's walls, so that the external vision remains pretty much in tact. Like St Anne's, its tower is topped by an octagonal lantern - perhaps it was a memory of churches like All Saints, Pavement in York, which Hawksmoor must have been familiar with from his many visits to Castle Howard.

There are no pyramids as part of the structure, but in the churchyard, square with the eastern apse of the church, is a pyramidal monument to the wife of local brewer and philan-

thropist Henry Raine.

The pyramid is a little the worse for wear. Its marble (there are two types, one with grey veins and another of the pure white from which statues are carved) is now stained and scuffed. It has not escaped the attentions of the desultory graffiti scrawlers. The reclining figure sculpted on one face of the pedestal has lost its head and most of an arm. The urn that once graced the top has vanished - though it may have not been an urn, but flames, like Dr Douce's pyramid (see page 105) - Raine's pyramid is sometimes called 'The Flare'.

But for all that, it remains a noble and imposing presence in a rather depressed area - and Henry Raine seems also to have been a noble and imposing figure. He was a Wapping brewer, born in 1679, who made a large fortune from beer. In 1724 he married Sarah Petrie at St Dunstan's church in Stepney, only to become a widower six months later. The pyramid was her monument.

Henry did not remarry. Instead, he devoted his time and his money to educating the poor children of the area. He was a trustee of the Wapping Charity School for some years before, in 1719, he began to fund it completely, taking an active interest in the appointment of the schoolmaster and mistress (for the school catered equally for boys and girls), in the curriculum, and in ensuring that his own High Church principles were taught.

The original school building still stands in what is now Raine Street in Wapping. It is the base for the Academy of St Martin-in-the-Fields. The entrance is beneath niches on the handsome Georgian brick front that hold statues of two of the children in their characteristic charity children's outfit - the boy in long blue coat and knee breeches, the girl with apron and cap. Fifty boys and fifty girls were educated between the ages of nine and twelve. The boys were then apprenticed to local tradesmen, and most of the girls were destined for a life of domestic service. Henry's school, underpinned by his money and his firm Anglican convictions, still survives today as Raine's Foundation School, now sited in Bethnal Green.

One curious feature of Henry's will, drawn up in 1736, was that each year six girls were given the chance to escape their life as servants at the age of 22. They had to be of good character (their employers had to testify to that effect), and be engaged to good, steady local men. Lots were then drawn by the six lucky 'contestants' and the two winners were provided out of Henry Raine's charity with a dowry of 100 guineas. The marriages (and the next draw) took place on either 1 May or 5 November, when the children from Henry's school accompanied the bridal parties to the church, the girls sang odes and £5 extra was provided for a decent wedding breakfast.

If Henry attended any of the weddings he must have been torn between happiness for the couples marrying and sadness at his own short married life. The inscription on the pyramid at St George-in-the-East does not speak of his philanthropic educational works. It says only: 'Here lies Near the Remains of his beloved Wife Mr Henry Raine of this Parish Brewer who died April 18th 1738 Aged 59'.

THE THIRD OF the trio of Hawksmoor's Commissioners' churches in the East End is **Christ Church, Spitalfields**, perhaps the greatest of the three. Like St Anne's and St George's, it was started in 1714. Like them it has suffered - the interiors of the other two were burned out; Christ Church survived fire and war, but was condemned as unsafe in 1958. Only in the 1970s did work begin to save it - work that was finished in 2004.

Now the church is back to its former glory as one of London's greatest buildings. Its spire dominates the area, especially when you approach it, as we did, from the west, along Brushfield Street. The huge portico - a Serlian opening of a great arch joined by two rectangles, was an afterthought, but it ties the whole building together.

The pyramid we had come to see was just to the south of the church; it, too, has been restored. It is a bit of a puzzle. Ostensibly it is a monument to the Nash family - William, who died in September 1835, his wife Elizabeth and other family members. That is all straightforward. What is odd, though, is the monument itself. Its form - a tall thin pyramid set on a base, with four squat feet and a flaming urn on the top - is not obviously 19th-century.

Did the Nashes commission the monument? Did they find an old one at the monumental masons and buy it for their own use? Or was the pyramid already a feature of the churchyard and they appropriated it to their own use? The similarity of the monument to 18th-century examples like the Bonham monument at Orset (see page 60) for example, suggests the last of these possibilities.

The Nash monument at Hawksmoor's Christ Church, Spitalfields

The other mystery is the identity of the Nash family. The monument gives no helpful description (not like Henry Raine's 'Brewer', for example. And Nash was quite a common name in 18th and 19th-century London. Despite extensive searches, we have been unable to pin William and his family down.

A William Nash was Lord Mayor of London in 1771-2, but he died the following year. Then there are other local Nashes, who are tradesmen of various sorts - sugar refiners, drapers, tea-dealers, upholsterers, stationers and coach-makers, but they seem unlikely candidates - the Christ Church Nashes seem to have been slightly higher-class. Even lower on the social scale are the members of the clan who appeared regularly at the Old Bailey for 'feloniously stealing'; we can probably discount them, too.

Whoever they were, the Nash family's monument has been well-restored. Now gleaming white, like the church itself, it has been provided with new railings to replace the ones that were removed in World War II. It is one of very few memorials that remain in the churchyard at Christ Church. Unknown to us otherwise, the Nashes should be pleased that their memory has been kept to this extent.

Concrete sculptures, including the pyramid, by Leonard Manasseh at King Solomon Academy, Marylebone, London (see also page 48)

A SHORT WAY north-west of Paddington Station and across the **Marylebone** flyover is one of the best-designed schools of the late 1950s. In its latest incarnation it is known as King Solomon Academy, and when we visited to see the pyramid in its grounds only two reception classes of four-and-five-year-old children were there, occupying a small part of the site. The idea is that over the years it will build into a school of 900, specialising in music and maths, for children from 3 to 19.

The main school building is a classic modernist block of pre-cast concrete, three storeys high and almost 100 yards long. The structure is given its rhythm by the tall, narrow concrete columns that divide the windows. On the roof are slate covered pyramids - one of them inverted to hold the water tanks. The building was designed in 1958 by the architect Leonard Manasseh.

Manasseh, who was born in 1916, served as a pilot in the Fleet Air Arm in World War II then joined Hertfordshire County Council Architects Department in 1948, where he had his first taste of designing schools. From 1948 to 1950 he was a senior architect to Stevenage Development Corporation and then set up his own practice. His professional breakthrough came in 1950 when he was invited to design a bar at the Festival of Britain - though such was the 'all-hands-on-deck' fervour of the Festival that he found himself designing toilet blocks first. Still, his *51 Bar* was eventually constructed. It was sited by the Thames next to Nelson Pier, between the stylish *Sea and Ships* pavilion designed by Basil Spence and the industrial-looking *Power and Production* pavilion by Grenfell Baines and Reifenberg. With a gull-wing roof and glass walls, the *51 Bar* announced its presence with a skeletal water-tower overlooking the roof-top terrace. Manasseh later said of the Festival, 'There really was a feeling around that we were creating a new Britain - things were going to be marvellous!'

By the end of the decade Manasseh's reputation as an architect was well established. The commission to design what was originally the Rutherford School for Boys in Marylebone included the interior design as well as sculpture for the grounds - and it was one of these sculptures that had brought us to Penfold Street, near Edgware Road Underground station.

The tiny children of King Solomon Academy were out at play when we arrived, but we were guided through from the rear of the building by the Site Manager, Tom McManus. He explained that several schools have been housed there since Rutherford School for Boys vacated it. They included, from 1980, North Westminster Community School and, for just a year while new accommodation was prepared, Westminster Academy. The detritus from the temporary use was still all around, and the unused interiors were very shabby. Still, the main entrance hall, with its Carrara marble walls and a purpose-made sculpture by Hubert Dalwood, was still impressive.

The sculptural group by Leonard Manasseh was just outside the main entrance. There are three elements, all of cast concrete, carefully placed around a series of pools. A tapered block is pierced with a circular hole through which the sun casts changing shapes on a solid wedge beside it - they have a startling resemblance to World War II anti-tank defences. A bowl with upright wings and a rounded pedestal spills water into one of the pools. And then there is a pyramid.

It is tall and thin - slightly taller and thinner than the pyramid at St Anne Limehouse (see page 71), which it resembles. It is constructed in six layers and sits in the centre of the largest of the pools. It is a strong, geometrical accent, especially when viewed against the grid of the school's main block and the translucent blue-green glass on the façade that is characteristic of its date. The sculpture also links visually to the pyramidal shape on the rooftop.

Leonard Manasseh has said that the school was one of his most successful works. Staff who have taught there say that the building works efficiently. Its value was recognised in 1998 when it was listed Grade II*. The three sculptures, including the pyramid, which are an important part of the design, are Grade II.

The pyramid and other concrete sculptures at King Solomon Academy

DEUCE! OUR NEXT pyramid was a tennis-ball-hit from the All England Lawn Tennis Club in **Wimbledon** - but the man it commemorates has links not with the grass of the courts but with a spectacular garden in Portugal.

The pyramid to Gerard de Visme near the north wall of St Mary's Church in Wimbledon is a fine amalgam of Egyptian and Greek architecture. On a plain base is set a rusticated pyramid, with de Visme's coat of arms and a brief inscription. At each corner is a Greek-style acroterion with honeysuckle decoration.

Gerard de Visme was a wealthy - sources say 'fabulously wealthy' - man who was descended from a Huguenot family. Details of his life are sketchy, but we know that he was the fifth son of Philippe de Visme (or de Vismes - the family seemed to spell it either way), who styled himself Count de Vismes. There was a dispute about whether the title was legitimate or assumed. Gerard's elder brother Louis was a British diplomat who served in Italy, Spain, Russia and Germany, dying, apparently in poverty, in Stockholm. In contrast Gerard, born in 1726, was a successful and wealthy timber merchant whose company was Purry, Mellish and De Visme. He was in Portugal for 40 years and 'held high office' in Lisbon; he was there at the time of the great Lisbon earthquake in 1755. He had a house in London's fashionable Grosvenor Square, as well as 'my lodge on Wimbledon Common'. This was Wimbledon Lodge, later renamed Murray Lodge by his daughter Emily, who married General Sir Henry Murray, son of the second Earl of Mansfield. It was designed in 1792 in the Greek style by Aaron Henry Hurst, who died aged 37 in 1799.

Gerard de Visme's pyramid at Wimbledon

Virtually all of his very few, very elegant buildings, including Wimbledon Lodge, have been demolished.

Emily (or Emilie) de Visme was Gerard's illegitimate daughter, and there is no reference to her mother in Gerard's will of 11 September 1795. Her illegitimacy didn't seem to bother the Earl of Mansfield, probably because Emily was a very rich heiress; her father left her the residue of his vast estate in trust for her, to be hers absolutely when she was 25 or on her marriage. Emily was naturalised as a British Citizen by private Act of Parliament in 1798.

Gerard's will left other bequests; to his nephew in Switzerland, to his clerks in Lisbon, and to Emily's governess, Miss Green.

There are also charitable bequests - one to Lisbon Hospital for repairs, another to set up a charitable trust for the poor in Lisbon, and an annual £10 to buy bread for the poor people in Wimbledon; the Wimbledon charity survived until 1930.

Gerard de Visme was famous or wealthy enough to commission the French portrait sculptor Jean-Louis Couasnon to make a bust of him in 1790, when de Visme was 64 years old. It was sold at auction in Paris in 2005. He was also a patron of other arts; among those he supported was a young poet, Henry Headley. Headley was sent to Portugal in 1787 to find relief from consumption but, as Thomas Campbell noted in his *Essay on English Poetry*, 'on landing in Lisbon, far from feeling any relief from the climate, he found himself oppressed by its sultriness; and in this forlorn state was on the point of expiring, when Mr De Vismes, to whom he had a letter of introduction from the late Mr Windham, conveyed him to his healthful villa at Cintra, allotted spacious apartments for his use, procured for him the ablest medical assistance, and treated him with every kindness and amusement that could console his sickly existence.'

De Visme's villa at Sintra (then usually spelled Cintra) is the reason why he is still known, and why an internet search will actually find him. In 1790 he rented from the Melo e Castro family an estate near Sintra, north west of Lisbon. At the time there was a ruined chapel, dedicated to Our Lady of Monserrate, on the land. Gerard de Visme decided to landscape the garden and build a new house in the Gothick style on top of the chapel site. First, though, he had the chapel ruins carefully demolished and rebuilt as a Romantic garden feature.

It was a good place to be planting a garden. The climate is very special, with just the correct mixture of rain and sunshine for a wide variety of plants to flourish. Robert Southey wrote of Sintra that it was 'the most blessed place in the whole of the inhabitable world.' Byron, in *Childe Harold's Pilgrimage*, was also enchanted:

Lo! Cintra's glorious Eden intervenes
In variegated maze of mount and glen.
Ah me! what hand can pencil guide, or pen,
To follow half on which the eye dilates
Through views more dazzling unto mortal ken
Than those whereof such things the bard relates,
Who to the awe-struck world unlocked Elysium's gates?

And in a letter he said, 'I must just observe that the village of Cintra in Estramadura is the most beautiful, perhaps in the world. I am very happy here, because I loves oranges and talk bad Latin to the monks . . . and I goes into society (with my pocket pistols) . . .'

Gerard de Visme must have loved it too, at least for a while, but in 1794 he let it to the great English eccentric William Beckford, who may have been impressed by the Gothick house, so like his own Fonthill Abbey. Over the next 14 years Beckford continued to develop the gardens, building an impressive waterfall from huge blocks of stone.

After Beckford's tenure, the garden slumbered. As John Claudius Loudon (see page 82) wrote in his Encyclopedia of Gardening, 'Monserrate near Cintra, seat of the late eminent merchant, Beckford, was formed at immense expense by a native of Cornwall for M de Vismes, and further improved by the former gentleman. It is laid out in the geometric style; abounds in inequalities, stairs, terraces, statues, and orange trees. Of late, we are informed, it has been much neglected.'

The garden was reawakened by more English people, textile

Detail of the Gothick chapel built by Gerard de Visme at his garden at Monserrate, Sintra, Portugal

Monserrate Palace, rebuilt by Francis Cook and landscaped with the help of William Colebrook Stockdale

The Greg pyramid at Hampton is in the same style as the nearby Wimbledon pyramid (see page 78)

millionaire Francis Cook and his family, in 1856. They rebuilt de Visme's house in a Moorish style and filled the garden with plants from across the world. They were helped in laying out the garden by William Colebrook Stockdale from Tiverton, whose family is commemorated by a pyramid there (see page 168). The Cook family looked after the Sintra garden until World War II, when they lost much of their fortune and sold Monserrate to the Portuguese government. Now, after many more years of neglect, it is being restored and is open to the public.

Gerard de Visme returned to England after disposing of his Sintra house. We do not know why a man at the forefront of the Gothic revival should choose a Graeco-Egyptian monument to himself - except to surmise that he was a man of fashion, and around the time of his death both the Greek and Egyptian styles were becoming *de ton*. But it obviously impressed someone, as it was surely the inspiration for the next pyramid we were to see.

A FEW HUNDRED yards from Hampton Court Palace stands St Mary's, the parish church of **Hampton**. Given the architectural splendours just down the road, we had expected the church to be of equal worth. But St Mary's was rebuilt in white brick in 1831 - 'nothing mysterious, nothing enthusiastic', says *The Buildings of England*. It must have been raining when the authors visited - they adopt a distinctly grumpy tone; one monument inside the church is dismissed as 'not very sensitive.' In the churchyard they note 'a clumsy bare pyramid to John Greg of Dominica' - the pyramid we had come to see.

It was certainly bare, probably as the result of recent over-enthusiastic restoration. And perhaps it is clumsy - but it is interesting, nonetheless. Its design is almost certainly taken from the pyramid to Gerard de Visme in Wimbledon (see page 77), just a few miles to the east. It has a similar base, the angle of the pyramid is the same and, most tellingly, it has the same honeysuckle anthemia - rather more crisply cut than on de Visme's, where they resemble broad-bean pods.

There seems to be no direct evidence that whoever designed the Hampton pyramid copied the Wimbledon example, but it seems likely. Gerard de Visme died in November 1797 in London, John Greg in June 1795 in Dominica. Given the length of time it would have taken to bring his body back from the Caribbean, Greg was probably buried after de Visme, and his monument built later. The Hampton pyramid was instigated by 'his affectionate wife Catherine.' It also contains the remains of their daughter who died in 1809, and of Catherine who died 'full of years and benevolence' aged 82 in 1819, so it is possible that the pyramid was not erected until the early part of the 19th century.

The Greg family was originally from Ayr, but John Greg's father had settled in Belfast in 1715. They had a long history in Dominica - and John was the first of the family to go there. For nearly two centuries the island was the subject of a tug of war between the British and the French. It was the last of the Caribbean islands to be taken over by Europeans, thanks to hard fighting from the native Caribs, but was conquered by the British in 1627. After 121 years the French forced the British to cede it to them, but the British got it back in 1763, lost it again in 1778 and eventually took undisputed possession in 1783.

In this welter of dates, it is 1763 that was important for John Greg. The Treaty of Paris, giving Dominica to Britain, set up a single government for Grenada, the Grenadines, St Vincent, Tobago and Dominica. A Governor of Dominica, Sir William Young, was appointed. He was responsible for having all the land surveyed before its sale to British investors. He arrived in Dominica in 1765 - and with him was John Greg, Government Commissioner for the sale of land. As well as overseeing the survey and sale, he managed to get two estates for himself, known officially as Hertford and Hillsborough (the Ulster influence coming out), but to the native workers just as 'Greg's'. The family managed to hang on to their land at Hillsborough through the disputes with the French, and finally left Dominica in 1928.

John Greg's brother Thomas also had Dominican estates (one actually called Belfast). In 1772 Thomas, in Britain, gave John power of attorney 'to enter upon and take possession of all and every Lands Houses Plantations Negroes Cattle Stock and Hereditaments whatsoever belonging to us in the said Island of Dominica'. Thomas's son Samuel founded Quarry Bank Cotton Mill in Styal, Cheshire, now owned by the National Trust.

We were getting lost in both the labyrinthine complexities of late 18th-century genealogy and the suburbs of west London. We escaped the first, at least, with our next visit - to a modern office park at West Drayton, near Heathrow Airport.

WEST DRAYTON'S **STOCKLEY** Business Park was only the third in the country. From 1985 a master-plan by Arup Associates transformed an area of scrubland and gravel pits into an impressive array of office buildings, surrounded by fine landscaping.

We arrived at the main gate. 'We've come to take photographs of the pyramid,' we said brightly.

The security guard looked confused.

'Pyramid?'

'The *Tetra Trellis*.'

'*Tetra Trellis?*'

'It's a fountain. Outside the headquarters of Tetra Pak,' we said. Light dawned. 'Just round here, on the right.' He waved us through.

The *Tetra Trellis* is a work by the UK's foremost water sculptor, William Pye. It is both sculpture and fountain - or should be. It stood dry and forlorn in its octagonal pool when we visited. No sparkling jets of water flowed from the nozzles along the inner surfaces of the three stainless steel legs that form the pyramid shape. There was no water-formed trellis.

William Pye has written that 'water shapes the concepts, directing the form and determining the fabric of the sculpture. It is often the smallest and most timeless of means by which water can be controlled, that enchant and obsess me.'

Without the water, the sculpture seems bereft, even soulless. The carefully-controlled jets of water should work as an animated, scintillating paraphrase of the metal strings used by Barbara Hepworth in some of her work.

Pye was born in 1938, and was inspired to use water by the ponds near his childhood home in Surrey. His water sculptures are found around the country, including works in London's Docklands, on Central Square in Cardiff, at Alnwick Castle in Northumberland, at Wilton House in Wiltshire and in the Prince of Wales's garden at Highgrove (see also page 137).

'The idea for *Tetra Trellis* was to create a sculpture of equilateral triangles', he told us. 'Using hydrostatic pressure I can get

William Pye's
'Tetra Trellis' at
Stockley Business
Park, West
Drayton,
Middlesex
Norfolk, now
without its
water jets

very constant jets of water that work with great precision *ad infinitum*. Tetra Trellis is one of a series of works I made in the early 1990s, and the jets impact on each other to create a moving shape.'

Tetra Trellis was commissioned by the Swedish packaging company Tetra Pak in 1993, as one of the main features outside the company's UK headquarters. But now Tetra Pak has relocated from Stockley Park to Wrexham in north Wales, and there is some doubt about the pyramid's future. 'I drove past fairly recently,' said William Pye, 'and it looked very sad, sitting in its dry pool with no jets. Perhaps I should ask Tetra Pak if they have plans to move it to their new headquarters.'

There is another water pyramid by William Pye that has suffered a similar - if not worse - fate. *Balla Frois* (pronounced Frosh) was constructed for the 1988 Glasgow Garden Festival, held on the site of the filled-in Prince's Dock in Govan. When the Festival was dismantled after it closed in September 1988 *Balla Frois* was bought by Clyde Port Authority. It has been in storage ever since, and enquiries about it to the Port Authority brought no reply.

FROM THE FUTURISTIC vision of Stockley we made our way to schizophrenic **Pinner**. Pinner was once a small, rural village, and its centre, near the church, still retains a village feel, with some decent old houses nearby. But all around is the apotheosis of the suburb - villas, semis, mock-Tudor, neo-Georgian. It's Jonah and the whale; the Jonah-ish village still struggles to live within the belly of the sprawl of London.

And whose fault is this sprawl? You could lay it at the door of John Claudius Loudon, the great publicist of new building, who was also responsible for the next pyramid.

Actually, this one is only loosely a pyramid, but it's so interesting that we couldn't leave it out. It's tall and triangular, with flat sides and semicircular, grill-covered openings at the base. Most surprisingly, though, it's pierced through, about 10 feet from the ground, by a stone sarcophagus.

Loudon designed this as a last resting place for his parents, William Loudon, who died in 1809, and Agnes, who survived him by 22 years. It wasn't the first thing John Claudius had designed for them. Just before his father's death the young JC remodelled Woodhall Farm, a decent 17th-century farmhouse being rented by the family, into his beau ideal of a suburban villa, with neat sash windows and whitewashed render.

His career had begun. He was an inveterate writer who wasn't short of an opinion on most things to do with architecture, agriculture and gardening. Of his many books (including encyclopaedias of gardening, plants, agriculture and trees and shrubs) by far the most influential was his *Encyclopaedia of Cottage, Farm, and Villa Architecture and Furniture*. Published in 1833, it went into many editions and was sold in many countries.

Throughout England, people started building cottages, farms and villas (some of them semi-detached, like Loudon's own home in Bayswater) to his basic patterns. Although he urged the users of his works 'never to mimic individual examples, but to imitate the general spirit of style and manner', he urged in vain. People with no architectural imagination could use his designs as patterns - and did so, relentlessly. The *Encyclopaedia* was a hit in Britain; in the United States it became almost holy writ. From it have flowed the millions of acres of today's suburbia.

SUBURBIA ALSO FEATURED in the next place we visited - Watford. It's recognisably both a London satellite (with the terminus of the Metropolitan underground line in the town) and the struggling rump of a distinctive country town in what used to be rural Hertfordshire.

There was enthusiastic mention on several websites of an 18th-century pyramid at The Grove, a large country house on the outskirts of **Watford**. It took quite a lot of additional digging around, and phone calls to several local history experts, before we discovered that the Pyramid, along with several other garden features such as the Ruined Tower and the unlikely Malayan Hut (even fewer of those than pyramids in Britain!) had long since disappeared. The Grove is now a smart hotel, with a collection of modern art both inside and on the estate, but the owners have not yet commissioned a replacement pyramid.

So what we were left with was, perhaps, something of a comedown; a furniture shop at the end of Watford's High Street. The street dips and turns at its southern end in an interesting way, and the pyramid terminates the view, coyly half-peering out as you approach it.

Close up, it turns out to be a parent-and-child pyramid - a large one for the shop floor, and a smaller one for the entrance. Of blue glass with a grey metal framework, the building is an attractive landmark for the town. Locals use it to give directions ('Turn left when you get to the Pyramid' often leaves visitors even more confused than they were before they stopped to ask the way).

In a phone call to the store to get more information Peter Fox said that it had changed its name since we visited it to take photographs.

'Aren't you Sofas-UK anymore?'

'No, it's Emporio Home,' he said, breaking off from serving a cus-

The eccentric pyramidal monument erected by John Claudius Loudon to his parents in the churchyard at Pinner in Middlesex

Little and large pyramids form an effective finale to the High Street in Watford, Hertfordshire

tomer to talk. 'We sell wooden furniture as well as sofas, so it was changed.'

Peter told us that the pyramid was built around 1994 ('When I was about 15,' he said), and that it started life as a Blockbuster Video store (important if you're 15). After various changes of use it was taken over by Sofas-UK a few years ago.

'What's it like to work in?'

'It's OK', said Peter, 'but we've had to put in a suspended ceiling as the whole place got too hot. The bottom part is now air-conditioned, and the top of the pyramid is empty, except perhaps for some rubbish. We can't store furniture up there as the staircase is too difficult.'

THE HEAT OF the pyramids in Watford gave way to a rather damp churchyard in **Cheshunt**. St Mary's Church is the heart of the old Cheshunt village - it certainly has a country feeling far removed from the acres of housing that mostly comprise the town. We were here to see what the official Grade II listing described as 'Late C18. Stone pyramid.'

What we found was one of those curious hybrids that are neither pyramid nor obelisk. It certainly rises from the tall base as if determined to grow up into a pyramid. But as it approaches the

84

point, it loses the courage of its convictions, takes a sharp inward turn and ends up topped by a pyramidion, like any self-respecting obelisk. It's not an unknown phenomenon - there are others, like, for example, the pair at Staverton in Gloucestershire (see page 127) and the large example at Desertcreat in County Tyrone (see page 306).

It's a monument to the Prescott family. Originally put up to commemorate 20-year-old Mary Prescott, who died in 1775, it later commemorated six other family members, all of whom lived at nearby Theobalds Park, a Georgian House built in the grounds of the demolished Theobalds, Lord Burghley's sumptuous house that King James I appropriated.

The 18th-century house was built in 1763 by banker and Member of Parliament George Prescott. It was George's daughter for whom the pyramid was constructed, and George and his wife are among those it commemorates. In 1766 George jointly founded a bank in Threadneedle Street called Prescott, Grote, Culverden and Hollingsworth. It survived mergers with other banks until it became simply Prescott's Bank in 1903, when it had 31 branches. Almost immediately after its final name change, it was swallowed up by Union of London & Smith's Bank, and is now part of the Royal Bank of Scotland.

When Prescott came to Hertfordshire from Cheshire, he also became Lord of the Manor of Cheshunt, and the family retained the title until 1955. They didn't keep Theobalds Park, though; in 1806 it was leased to the Meux family, who made their money from brewing. It was Sir Henry Meux who brought one of Cheshunt's most famous temporary residents to Theobalds Park - Temple Bar.

When Sir Christopher Wren's Temple Bar structure, which stood in The Strand at the entry to the city of London, was demolished in 1878, Sir Henry bought the numbered stones and had them transported to Theobalds, where he re-erected them over his carriage drive in 1888. Temple Bar remained there for the next 116 years. It gradually decayed until it became a dangerous and vandalised eyesore. But now, thanks to an heroic rescue, it is back in London though, controversially, not in its original position but as the southern entrance to Paternoster Square, beside St Paul's Cathedral.

And Prescott's house and grounds have a new role, too; Theobalds Park is now home to the Country Club for one of Britain's biggest employers - Tesco, whose headquarters are in Cheshunt. One other interesting fact emerged about Cheshunt; the patronage of the vicarage belonged to the Bishop of London from 1554 until 1660, when the bishop swapped it with Robert Cecil for one of his patronages - Orsett in Essex (see page 60).

TESCO CROPPED UP again at the next pyramid, in **Bedford**. We'd been told to look out for the Bedford Tesco so that we would be able to find the pyramid. The advice was ridiculous; the pyramid was far more obvious than the superstore. We found out about the pyramid first by its mention in a country walk from Sandy to Bedford, published on a website. Unsurprisingly, the walk uses the pyramid as a landmark. To find out more, we carried out another internet search for a pyramid in Bedford. This took us to the site for Club Soleil, a naturist organisation, which meets at the pyramid - for this is Bedford Oasis Beach Pool, 'Bedford's indoor tropical paradise'.

It's an impressive sight - a vast, grey-clad pyramid that seems

The Prescott monument at Cheshunt

Temple Bar (bottom left) and Paternoster Sqaure

*Bedford Oasis
Swimming Pool*

to have been cloven into two parts and reassembled with a section missing - like the church at Glasnevin, a Dublin suburb (see page 362). This design allows the larger cut side to be glazed, letting light flood the interior.

And around it cluster several more smaller pyramids, like ducklings round the mother duck. They house the machinery that keeps the temperature in the complex up to a steady 27 degrees ('80 degrees Fahrenheit' they say; it sounds hotter to the British) and that powers the flumes, jets, waves and fountains inside.

This is not a 'swim up and down in lanes or you're out' swimming pool. It's fun all the way for the citizens of Bedford, whether costumed or naked (perhaps we need to point out that the naturists book the centre privately, so non-naturist visitors in normal opening hours will not find themselves suddenly confronted by something unexpected). It has two of the best flumes in the business - *Yellow Screamer* is 55 metres of twisting, jaundiced tubing that delivers the swimmers - fast - into a deep pool. The *Flume of Doom*, though ten metres shorter, is even more exhilarating.

If you're less inclined to heart-pumping thrills, there's the *Lazy River* that gently circumnavigates the area - 'like a Mediterranean cruise', says the publicity - as well as shallow *Bubble Beds* for small children, spa treatments and Turkish baths.

Popular though the Oasis is, it has proved a talking point for locals. One spoof website - *St Neots Citizen* - ran a story about the grey cladding being marred by green mould, and Bedford Council running out of funds to clean it - so they were planning to solve the problem by painting the whole thing green.

And when we mentioned our visit to Bedford to a colleague she came up with another story - The Disappearing Pyramid. She said that when she was younger she lived in the town while the pyramid was being built.

'The first time we had fog, the pyramid vanished', Debs said. 'Because it's covered in light grey metal it just merged into the mist, even when you were very close and other things around it were visible. It was quite a talking point in Bedford, and the local newspaper had the story on its front page.'

THERE'S ANOTHER DISAPPEARING pyramid at **Welham** in Leicestershire - or perhaps not so much disappearing as moving. The Edwards monument once stood immediately to the east of St Andrew's church in this small Leicestershire village. Put up in 1728 to the memory of local landowner Francis Edwards, it stayed there for nearly a century, its finely-carved marble taking everything that the British weather could throw at it.

In 1809, though, the Edwards family had the whole thing taken apart and transported to Stamford for repair and cleaning by a marble mason, Mr Sparrow. They also asked him to build a new north transept for the church for it. When the cleaning, mending and building were finished, the pyramid (except for its surrounding railings) was moved inside. Mr Sparrow's transept fits it like a glove - a very tight glove, for the urn on the top scrapes the ceiling and there's hardly any room to stand back and admire the pyramid's design. Only from the nave of the church is it possible to see the thin pyramid on its tall base and steps - with the parted red velvet curtains, it looks like a very cramped early-19th-century stage, ready for a rather static production of *The Magic Flute*, perhaps.

The marble used by the unknown mason of the pyramid is finely veined in pale grey, and is deeply carved with flowers and acanthus leaves at the corners of the pedestal. Four large, free-standing urns are placed on the transept floor at the corners of the monument's steps - the same position they occupied outdoors.

The monument was commissioned, at a cost of £1,500 - around £145,000 today - by Francis Edwards' daughter Mary. Her name was later added to the pedestal, as were those of her son and grandson. The son, Gerard Anne Edwards, (his confusing middle name came from his mother's lover, the even-more-oddly-named Lord Anne Hamilton), married Jane Noel, second daughter of the 4th Earl of Gainsborough and took her surname. Their son was Sir Gerard Noel Noel, whose own son became Earl of Gainsborough when the title was revived after the 5th and 6th Earls died without heirs.

Francis Edwards had a huge effect on Welham - though not as big as he would have liked. When he bought the manor in 1717 he demolished the village, which was then south of the church, and built a new one to the north east. He rebuilt the church and, of course, constructed a new house for himself; this has now disappeared. But his plan to have the Leicester to London turnpike road run through Welham failed. It went via Market Harborough instead, so Welham stayed a tiny village, deep in the Leicestershire countryside.

The elaborate pyramid at Welham was an appropriate end to our eastern pyramid hunt. Now we had another trip to look forward to, this time right through the centre of England, as far south as Portsmouth and including Britain's only cast-iron pyramid and one by the architect of Coventry Cathedral. Pyramid-hunting is nothing if not varied!

Once outdoors, the Edwards monument at Welham in Leicestershire has been safely inside the parish church since 1809

The Edwards monument at Welham in its original position

Tour 3

CENTRAL AND SOUTHERN ENGLAND

BEGINNING A PYRAMID tour at **Milton Keynes** could be seen as perverse. After all, the town is not among the first to spring to mind when one considers either fine or quirky buildings. As a paper from the then Office of the Deputy Prime Minister, *Living places: urban renaissance in the South East*, put it, 'Milton Keynes has been the butt of jokes, and is still looked down on by some.'

You probably have to live there to appreciate it, and it must have something going for it; it is growing five times faster than anywhere else in the south-east of England. With a masterplan inspired by Los Angeles and a design that recognises that the car is king, it may be a fine example of mid-20th-century planning, but it's a bit of a shock for anyone used to conventional towns. It reminded us of some Swedish suburbs - all low rise buildings set in spacious landscaped grounds, but, seemingly, not made for intimate living.

We were heading for the centre of MK, as the locals call it. After a few false starts and several confusingly-signed roundabouts we managed to find what we were looking for - The Point. This was once the hub of MK's entertainment area, just off the central Midsummer Boulevard.

The Point is three receding storeys of rather uninteresting rectangular, glass-walled, red-framed buildings, forming a rudimentary ziggurat. This would hardly be worth the journey to this part of Buckinghamshire to see. But over the top is a red-painted pyramidal framework that gives interest to the building and a reason for its name. At night, red lights along each arm of the framework make The Point visible for miles.

The Point is set on a low plinth of four shallow steps, and the pyramid framework is balanced on small stainless steel pads. The framework swells into bulbs like overgrown turnips just above the pads, as if to emphasise the weight that they carry.

When it opened, on 29 November 1985, The Point was home to Britain's first multiplex cinema. Originally operated by American Multi Cinema, it had 10 auditoriums that between them seated more than 2000 people. It was later owned by UCI (and known as The Point 10) before it became another experiment for entrepreneur Sir Stelios Haji-Ioannou and his Easy Group.

The founder of airline firm easyJet took over the cinema and on 13 May 2003 opened the world's first (and only) easyCinema. Like his airline, it was Stelios's way of trying to ensure that seats were filled at less popular times by having various levels of prices, which change as the performance you want to go to draws nearer. Visitors to the 10 screens at The Point were encouraged to buy their tickets on-line - and with some judicious planning you could get a seat for as little as 30 pence, though you paid rather more for popular films in weekend evening slots.

Stelios had trouble from the first; the big movie distributors distrusted his ambitions and refused to let him show the latest

OPPOSITE:
The Point, Milton Keynes, Buckinghamshire

blockbusters at the same time as they released them to other cinemas. Agreement was eventually reached, but the easyCinema plan never really prospered. Plans to extend the idea, including one in London's West End, never materialised, and early in 2006 easyCinema was forced out of The Point by its owners and UCI took over the pyramid again. It is now, thanks to mergers, an Odeon cinema. For how long remains in doubt. There are rumours that The Point may be demolished, and MK will lose its pyramid.

NEARBY **BLETCHLEY** IS an enigma - appropriately, for it was at Bletchley Park that the German Enigma machine was decoded. It was an important railway town in the 19th century, and it has some old cottages near the church, but it's suffered both from years of neglect and then from the overwhelming influence of Milton Keynes, of which it is, apparently, 'a cornerstone'. In 1981 the *Shell Guide to Buckinghamshire* called it 'one of the least attractive places in the county'.

It seems to have been like that for decades. In 1974 John Smithie from Bletchley Urban District Council wrote that in the 1960s 'one frequently heard the cry "There is nothing to do in Bletchley".' Fortunately, Mr Smithie and his colleagues were there to solve the problem, so that he could continue his article with the words, 'If it was only partly true in the 60s, it certainly cannot be sustained in the 70s.'

And why not? Smithie's answer was a pyramid. In 1971 the Council commissioned the architects Faulkner-Brown, Hendy,

*Bletchley
Swimming Pool*

Watkinson and Stonor to design them a leisure centre, complete with pyramid-covered swimming pool.

They chose their architects wisely. Harry Faulkner-Brown and his team were, and remain, among the leading designers of leisure and sports buildings in the world. Faulkner-Brown, who died in 2008, was also an expert on library design, with many to his credit in universities around the world. The Bletchley pool was a global innovation - one of the first 'leisure pools' to be built, with a free-form pool, palm trees and pool-side relaxation areas. It is the precursor of all modern indoor-activity swimming pools, including Bedford Oasis (see page 85), which pays tribute to Bletchley in its pyramidal shape.

The whole complex, with its adjoining sports hall, a small theatre, cafeteria and squash courts was built between 1972 and 1974 and cost £2.5 million. Its official opening was on 10 February 1975, when the Chairman of the Sports Council of England, four-minute-miler Roger Bannister, got it off to a flying start.

The following year the pyramid was highly commended in the Steel Design Awards. The judges commented, 'The building was required to contribute to the holiday atmosphere, let in the maximum amount of filtered sunlight and create an open-air feeling. The tinted translucent glazed pyramid structure does all this and at the same time encloses a smaller volume than a traditional cuboid form. This is an exciting enclosure to the swimming pool which creates a slightly exotic and almost sub-tropical atmosphere entirely appropriate to leisure swimming.'

It might not seem 'slightly exotic' to us now, but it's still an attractive building. From the inside, it's possible to admire the diagonal lattice work of the frame, which is covered by hundreds of small, smoked-glass pyramids that when lit at night glow attractively.

Bletchley Urban District Council was, understandably, pleased with the result. Councillor Staniford wrote, 'We are proud of our architects, we are proud of our builders and we are proud of the men we have appointed to the staff of the leisure centre for their breadth of vision.' Sexist he may have been, but there's no denying that his glow of civic satisfaction matched the pyramid's own.

After many years of use, it was inevitable that the pyramid pool should begin to show its age. Milton Keynes Borough Council has passed plans for Bletchley Leisure Centre to relocate, with a new, more serious swimming pool and better sporting facilities - coincidentally releasing the existing site for 400 or more new houses. The pyramid is not a listed building (a recent application for listing has been turned down) and so is vulnerable in the redevelopment; the Council has voted to demolish it. It's a landmark in a town that really needs landmarks; the townspeople like it; and it even appears as part of the Leisure Centre's logo. It is a building that is both attractive and important historically, and it should be preserved.

GOING FROM A 1970s leisure centre to the symbolic elegance of **Rousham** Park near Bicester was a jolt. Rousham is one of the great gardens of Britain. It is a miraculous survival of the gardening style of the early 18th-century; since the death of General Dormer in 1741 it has hardly changed, despite the sweeps of gardening fashion that brought in the vast rolling vistas of 'Capability' Brown's landscapes, the swing back to ornate flower gardens under the Victorians and the 20th-century's desire to simplify and tidy. Rousham remains an idyllic vision - but possibly one with a rather libidinous underlying message.

Two military brothers were the prime movers of the changes that transformed the Rousham landscape from an unpromising slope on the banks of the sluggish River Cherwell to an Arcadian landscape. First on the scene was Colonel Robert Dormer, who served with Lillingstone's Regiment, the 6th of Foot. He was a close friend of Alexander Pope, and it was probably through the poet that he became interested in the design of gardens. Colonel Dormer employed the fashionable Charles Bridgeman to create the Rousham landscape.

In some ways Bridgeman was a revolutionary. Until he started work, landscape gardens were slaves to the ruler and the compasses. As Pope wrote:

> No pleasing Intricacies intervene,
> No artful Wilderness to perplex the scene.
> Grove nods at Grove, each Ally has a Brother,
> And half the Platform just reflects the other.

And within this geometrical framework were other oddities; Horace Walpole noted that Bridgeman's predecessors as royal gardeners, London and Wise, 'had stocked our gardens with giants, animals, monsters, coats of arms and mottoes in yew, box and holly.' Or, as a letter by Pope mocked, 'ADAM and Eve in Yew; Adam a little shattered by the falling of the Tree of Knowledge in the great Storm; Eve and the Serpent very flourishing . . . NOAH's Ark in Holly, standing on the Mount; the ribs a little damaged for want of Water . . . A Pair of Maidenheads in Firr, in great forwardness.'

Bridgeman did not do away with all this, but he loosened the stays somewhat and added serpentining paths and glades, carefully-placed vantage points and statues. Above all he 'called in' the wider landscape by the use of the sunken fence or 'ha-ha'. For Colonel Dormer, Bridgeman laid out a garden that combined the naturalistic and the formal; the ha-ha linked the garden with the fields and trees beyond. There were pools, cascades and a tiny turf amphitheatre, twisting walks and a wilderness. All this was complete by 1737. In that year Col Dormer died, and Rousham was inherited by his brother, General James.

James seems to have been a more robust character than Robert. He was wounded at the Battle of Blenheim and despite the many flaws in his character rose to become a Lieutenant General and, in 1740, Governor of Hull. It is unlikely he spent much time beside the Humber, but he brought William Kent, an East Yorkshire man, to Rousham to remodel the house in a Gothick style, and to take over the planning and planting of the garden.

Kent took Bridgeman's timid naturalism and shook it into sensuous beauty. 'At that moment appeared Kent, painter enough to taste the charms of landscape, bold and opinionated enough to dare and dictate, and born with genius to strike out a great system from the twilight of imperfect essays. He leaped the fence, and saw that all nature was a garden'. In this, his most famous, sentence, Walpole has neatly pinned down Kent's contribution to the English landscape garden. Naturalness was his aim - but naturalness controlled by artifice.

At Rousham he constructed a carefully-planned circuit to lead the visitor to specific viewpoints, to statues and temples that aid contemplation. The sensuous beauty of the garden might also have had a more basic sensuality. The bachelor General had an earthy liking for nude statues - the so-called Apollo may really be Antinous, the Emperor Hadrian's favourite boy. As a counterpoint there are statues of seductive goddesses, of goat-hoofed Pan, of a leering satyr. *A Dying Gladiator*, sculpted by Sheemakers,

Venus Vale, Rousham, designed by William Kent

tops the terrace over the arcaded gallery called Praeneste; on the axis of the house, seen across the bowling green, is a horse being dreadfully mauled by a savage lion. These are disturbing images in a place of such beauty, and during the General's time Rousham had a troubled reputation for louche behaviour, a place that moral neighbours shunned.

Disturbing, too, is the Pyramid, away from the main circuit in a dark glade below the house's walled kitchen garden. It is the roof that is aggressively pyramidal; the lower part of the building is a cube, with angled buttresses that add to the pyramid effect. The Pyramid's purpose seems to have been two-fold; it served as a place to contemplate death; inside it, Kent set busts and statues of some of the ancients who had died for what the General considered noble ends - Socrates, Julius Caesar and Marcus Aurelius among them; it is also beautifully placed to take in a view of the Cherwell. All seems natural, but the river banks were carefully moulded, with up to 70 workmen employed at one time to shovel the earth and turf the slopes

Despite the generosity of the General's giving him unstinting support in developing Bridgeman's stiff naturalism into a what today is recognised as a supreme work of art, Kent seems to have been on site remarkably little. There are plaintive notes from the General to his friend Lord Burlington, one coming in the last year of the General's life: 'If Kent can be persuaded to come I shall take it kindly.' But Kent did not come. Was it moral scruples that kept him away, or was he too much occupied with larger plans for more prestigious clients? During the years when he was advising James Dormer mostly by lwtter on is small-scale works at Rousham, he was also designing, less than a day's ride away, a much larger scheme at Stowe for a more noble patron, Lord Cobham.

The Pyramid, Rousham

THERE WAS ONCE a famous 60-foot-high pyramid at **Stowe**, designed by Vanbrugh (just before his death in 1726) for Viscount Cobham, for whom he was working on structures in the garden and possibly also on the mansion. On the architect's death, Cobham made the pyramid Vanbrugh's memorial. The pyramid was swept away by later changes in the garden; when the future American President Thomas Jefferson visited Stowe in 1786, while he was the US minister in France, he wrote 'the Egyptian pyramid is almost entirely taken down by the late Ld Temple, to erect a building there, in commemoration of mr. Pitt. But he died before beginning it and nothing is done to it yet.' But there are still pyramids, if smaller versions, at Stowe. Cobham lavished a fortune on his garden; Vanbrugh said that he 'spends all he has to spare' on his house and gardens. Like the Dormers at Rousham, employed Charles Bridgeman as the first of his garden planners, then from some time in the 1720s, William Kent came on the scene. He was first employed in redesigning the house, but from around 1725 he started work on the gardens, too.

Bridgeman had already introduced ha-has and winding 'wilderness' paths, but in the main he relied on straight avenues that led to regular features, like the Octagon Pond on the main axis of the mansion's garden front. Kent began to work as Lord Cobham's main landscaper around 1733, just when Cobham had finally fallen out with Sir Robert Walpole and the King over the imposition of Excise Duty. Bereft of his political career, Cobham diverted his energies to the garden - just as John Aislabie at Studley Royal (see page 46) had done in the aftermath of the South Sea Bubble debacle. Financial crises did wonders for English landscape gardens.

The first task that Kent undertook for Cobham was the creation of a new part of the garden, on a site that had until recently held the inconvenient village of Stowe. This was cleared away by Lord Cobham (all but the church, which was allowed to remain as a picturesque object) and the site given over to Kent. He laid out one of Stowe's finest creations, the Elysian Fields. Carefully-mown lawns gently slope amid trees to the Octagon Lake, itself made irregular and 'natural' by Kent.

Kent provided several important buildings in his paradisical grove. They add glorious punctuation to the scene and also provide Cobham's ironic comments on the politics of his day. The Ionic circular Temple of Ancient Virtue represented the Greeks who had upheld the type of liberal view that Cobham espoused. This was pointedly contrasted with the deliberately-ruined Temple of Modern Virtue. Inside it was a headless torso, believed to have been meant as Walpole. Only its foundations remain as a remonder of its existence.

Nearby is the first pyramid, on the Temple of British Worthies. Kent's design for the temple is an arc of pedimented niches, each containing a bust. In the centre is a stepped pyramid with an oval recess in it, which once held a statue of Mercury.

It sits perfectly in the Elysian Fields, mirrored in water and backed by dark foliage. Kent did not design it for this location, though, but for Lord Burlington's garden at Chiswick House. It

The Temple of British Worthies, Stowe, by William Kent

*The Temple of
British Worthies;
the near bust
is of Sir Thomas
Gresham, founder
of the Royal
Exchange*

was influenced by a number of Italian garden features - the Villa Mattei in Rome, the Villa D'Este in Tivoli and the Villa Brenzone at San Vigilio on Lake Garda are all likely candidates.

The British Worthies whose busts are displayed are another dig at Cobham's political enemies. Picking 16 people (only one of them a woman) must have been a good party game for his friends. They had to be divided into patriotic men of action and men of contemplation. And they had to have impeccable liberal (and if possible true Whig) credentials.

The list they came up with was, to modern eyes, somewhat eclectic: The active patriots are King Alfred, the Black Prince, Queen Elizabeth (action woman), Walter Ralegh, Francis Drake, John Hampden and King William III. The contemplatives comprise Inigo Jones (no doubt suggested by Kent), Shakespeare, Bacon, Milton, Locke, Newton and Sir Thomas Gresham (founder of the Royal Exchange in London and the beau ideal of 'the honourable profession of merchant'). They were joined by two living people - Alexander Pope and Sir John Barnard, Cobham's fellow MP and opponent of the Excise Bill, otherwise largely unknown to history.

They are represented on the temple by busts (by Rysbrack and Scheemakers), and there are laudatory verse inscriptions over the busts, probably written by Lord Cobham's friends and relations, including Pope and the amateur poet George Lyttleton. The inscriptions to Pope and Barnard were added in 1763.

This is stuff of high seriousness - even though there is something rather festive about Kent's architecture. But go round the back and there's another long inscription in a niche, this time in formal Italian, to someone who, though born in Italy, came to retire to England in his old age and stayed with a local clergyman. He was a faithful friend, an agreeable companion and a loving husband, says the inscription, probably written by Lyttleton. It's only when you've ploughed through the encomium that the last line reveals all - Signior Fido was a greyhound.

This joke, subverting the message of the monument, has been creditably ascribed to Kent, who was known for such japes. And his other pyramid at Stowe also carries a mixture of the serious and the amusing.

In 1736, on an island in part of the Octagon Lake - which was already being modified under Kent's direction - Cobham put up a pyramid to his old friend and drinking companion, the dramatist William Congreve. Congreve died in 1729, and was buried with great pomp in Westminster Abbey, despite public criticism during his lifetime for his representation of immorality and profaneness on the English stage and for his own string of mistresses, who included the actress Mrs Bracegirdle. As the author of the masterly play *The Way of the World* Congreve seems to have been forgiven much by the British public.

Kent's design for the monument begins as a conventional, if steep-sided, pyramid. On the front is carved a large urn, bearing comic masks, a bow and quiver of arrows and a set of pan pipes - perhaps to symbolise the sharpness of Congreve's penetrating wit and the clarity of his writing. So far, so conventional. But on the top of the pyramid squats a monkey. In its hands is a mirror in which it admires itself. Here is Kent making a joke - or is it a serious point? - about the role that Congreve played in reflecting the society in which he lived through his plays. The inscription on the pyramid underlines the message - 'Comedy is the imitation of life and the mirror of society.'

The monkey-topped pyramidal monument to William Congreve at Stowe

YOU WOULD PROBABLY recognise the Buckinghamshire village of **Hambleden**. The charm and old-fashioned look of the flint-and-brick cottages that cluster around the Stag & Huntsman pub and the church of St Mary the Virgin are perfect for filming period and rural dramas. It has appeared in *Chitty Chitty Bang Bang*, *One Hundred and One Dalmatians*, *Poirot* and *Midsomer Murders*, for example.

None of them has made use of the pyramid-topped monument in the churchyard. Set on three shallow steps and a square plinth, the pyramid holds aloft a small stone ball. It is a relatively sophisticated design for a small village, with plenty of emphatic mouldings to create interesting shadows and add gravitas to the structure. It is similar to some of the Gloucestershire pyramidal monuments, but where they have very shallow points, here we have a full-blown pyramid.

The family commemorated was of some consequence in the parish, and held some status in the county, but none of its members seems to have made a mark on the national scene - unlike Lord Cardigan, commander of the Light Brigade during its disastrous Charge and 'the most notorious officer in the entire British Army', who was born in Hambleden's Manor House, or the stationer W H Smith, who bought the nearby Greenlands estate in 1871. Smith was Financial Secretary to the Treasury, Secretary of State for War and First Lord of the Admiralty, but is remembered as being the original of Sir Joseph Porter in Gilbert & Sullivan's *HMS Pinafore*. Porter's song about being 'the Ruler of the Queen's Navy' stems from W H Smith's time as First Lord of the Admiralty, despite his having no naval experience at all.

There was no such fame for the Lane family of Hambleden. Four of them are commemorated on the pyramidal monument. The earliest is Richard Lane of Poynatts, 'who exchanged this life for a better' on 17 July 1739. Poynatts is a substantial farm a little to the north of Hambleden. Then there are two more Richard Lanes, both of 'Millend in this Parish' - Mill End is south of the village, beside the Thames at Hambleden Lock, where the mill was first built in the 14th century. One Richard Lane died in December 1785, aged 75, and was probably the son of the Richard who died in 1739. The other died just four years later, in December 1789, aged only 42, so he must have been the third generation. There is also Elizabeth Lane, 'Wife of Rd Lane Esq'. She was only 25 when she died in 1747 and must have been married to the second Richard.

This Richard seems to have been the only Lane to have held public office. He was High Sheriff of Buckinghamshire from 1757 to 1758. Otherwise they have left little mark of their existence except for the handsome pyramid at Hambleden. Keep a sharp eye out for it next time a period drama or a murder comes up on the television.

SOMETHING MORE ASSERTIVE was waiting at our next destination, **Mongewell** near Wallingford in Oxfordshire. On the banks of the Thames is a pyramid that houses a combined exhibition gallery and boathouse by one of the 20th century's best-known British architects, Sir Basil Spence.

From 1953 to 1997 Mongewell was the home to Carmel College, a Jewish public school founded in 1948 at Newbury by Rabbi Dr Kopul Rosen. The school took over a late-19th-century house, said to have been the original of Monkswell Manor Guest House in Agatha Christie's record-breaking play *The Mousetrap*. In the 1960s the school added many buildings to adapt the site for its new use. One of the best of the new structures is the wedge-shaped, glass-sided synagogue, with its adjoining sunken amphitheatre, designed in 1963 by Tom Hancock.

In 1970 one of the school's governors, Lieutenant Commander E J Gottlieb, gave money for a new building in memory of his father, Julius. Julius Gottlieb (1888 to 1961) was a designer in wood and a patron of the arts - 'A craftsman and lover of beauty' as the slate-cut inscription on the building says. The school needed two things - a gallery to display art, crafts and examples of engineering and industrial design, and a boathouse for the rowers.

The school commissioned Sir Basil Spence. They may have been expecting something in the style of his most famous work, Coventry Cathedral, consecrated in 1962. But by 1970, nearly 20 years after he had designed the cathedral, Spence's style had

Pyramid exhibition hall and boathouse at the former Carmel College, Mongewell, Oxfordshire, designed by Sir Basil Spence

moved on. He was exploring much more stark architecture, of reinforced, shuttered concrete and geometrical shapes punctured by simple openings. So for Carmel College he and his son John Urwin Spence came up with the pyramid, which housed the gallery, sitting on a low plinth that forms the boathouse. 'The pyramidal form was chosen,' according the official listing (it is Grade II*) 'as appropriate for a monument'. Writing about the building in 1970 *Concrete Review* says, 'The architects were asked for a building which would not only be an exhibition hall but would also serve as a memorial. With this in mind, they chose a pyramid as the best solution. For not only is this a shape traditionally connected with memorials; it also gives a feeling inside of great space and scale and is suitable for very tall exhibits.'

The plinth is a self-effacing structure of mellow brick. The pyramid is a different matter. It is Spence in his Brutalist phase - four great triangles of sprayed reinforced concrete, now marked with black bands and streaks, rise to meet each other in an almost-perfect pyramid, its sides still crisp and its point still sharp. Triangular openings are punched through the concrete on three sides - one side is left starkly blank. These 'windows' are painted in primary colours - yellow on the river side, blue and red on the others.

Only in one place is the perfection of the pyramid broken, with a glazed entrance. Nearby, on the terrace formed by the boathouse plinth, is a glazed skylight to provide illumination to the students taking out or returning their boats. It is in the form of half a pyramid, again painted a slightly sulphurous yellow.

The Buildings of England: Oxfordshire dislikes it. It accuses it of 'spoiling an excellent view of the river', of having a 'grim interior', of being 'not well-sited' and suggesting that it 'would have been more successful in a wide landscape setting.'

By the steps that lead up to the terrace is the dedication plaque. It names the building 'The Julius Gottlieb Exhibition Hall' and tells us that 'The Boathouse was erected with the help of the pupils and friends of the school.' It's not clear whether this means that they raised the funds for it, or that they dug the foundations, mixed the mortar and laid the bricks.

We should have liked to have been able to see inside the gallery, to see whether it is really 'grim' - *Concrete Review* says, 'Inside, finishes are of boardmarked concrete and white-painted brickwork which provides a good neutral background for exhibits' - but at the top of the steps to the terrace is a wooden barrier, preventing entrance. And, actually, we weren't at all sure that we should have been there at all, although a helpful local told us the way, past the ruined church. So we can only pass on the second-hand information that inside there is a raised platform area and concrete benches around the walls. The gallery is lit with spotlights set in shuttered concrete.

And why was none of this accessible? When Carmel College closed in 1997, as pupil numbers declined and costs rose, there was doubt about the future of the whole site - doubts still unresolved. After much discussion, the site is now run by the Exilarch's Foundation, a charitable organisation which was started by a London businessman, Naim Dangoor. The Foundation uses the college part-time for education programmes for young Sephardic Jews.

But this use has not solved the problem of the whole site. A master-plan was drawn up to open an international business school alongside the charitable users. The plans were, first, approved by South Oxfordshire District Council planning committee. They recognised that, even if the use did not fall within normal policy guidelines, it was a way to save an important site, with its listed buildings. Unfortunately, Council politics intervened, and the planning committee's approval was not endorsed by the full Council.

So now 'the utterly-unexpected pyramid of Carmel College', which the Listing describes as 'proto-post-modern for its classical geometry' is in limbo, awaiting a sensible solution to its dilemma. If nothing is done soon, Spence's pyramid will be yet another entry on the *Heritage at Risk Register*.

AT RISK, TOO, is the small pyramid at **Ipsden**, less than five miles away from Carmel College. It was difficult to find: what was marked on the Ordnance Survey map as 'Meml' turned out to be a different memorial, but, fortunately, Helen McRobbie who lived nearby put us right.

The pyramid, which is in a precarious state, is hidden in a small wood, by a tiny pond, beside the Icknield Way. It seems an odd place to have put a monument - it's not in a place where it would readily be seen, even if the trees were not there. Why not put it on the top of a nearby hill?

The answer is that it had to be there. It is a monument to John Thurlow Reade, the eldest son of John and Anna Maria Reade of nearby Ipsden House. John Thurlow was said to be the cleverest of the Reade children. He had been Head Boy at Rugby School before going, like many members of his family, to work in India - several of his brothers were in the Indian Army. He was a Collector in the Indian Civil Service - effectively a District

Magistrate, who not only collected revenue for the Crown but also administered the law and helped maintain order. He worked in Saharunpur on the Jumna River, north of Delhi in the foothills of the Himalayas.

As a dutiful son, John Thurlow Reade wrote very regular letters to his mother. The letters stopped suddenly towards the end of 1827. Anna Maria Reade was worried about this silence, and had an impulse that she must go down the road he would take if he were making his way home to Ipsden House. And at a secluded spot near an ancient trackway she met him. Or rather, she met his ghost, for John Thurlow Reade had died on 26 November 1827.

There was no news from India for some time, but so convinced was Anna Maria that her son was dead that she organized a memorial service in Ipsden church. The confirmation reached Ipsden the following day - John had died and had been buried by his servants in the jungle. Another son, Edward Anderton Reade, erected the pyramid to his memory on the spot where his mother had encountered John's spirit.

John Thurlow Reade was 30 when he died, and was unmarried. The inscription on the pyramid where his mother had her mystical encounter is worn and almost impossible to read. We know, though, that it says, 'John Thurlow Reade Esquire SCHAARUN-PORE November 26 1827 "Alas my brother"'.

Was it something in the air of Ipsden that made Anna Maria receptive to spirits, or was it hereditary? Certainly her forebears were an impressive bunch. Her mother, also Anna Maria, had married Major John Scott-Waring, agent to, and close friend of, the 1st Governor-General of India, Warren Hastings. Scott-Waring supported Hastings at his impeachment for his bad government of India - the charges included extortion, murder and massacre. The judge at the seven-year trial, which started in 1797 and which eventually acquitted Hastings, was another of Scott-Waring's friends, the Lord Chancellor Edward Thurlow - who was John Thurlow Reade's godfather.

Anna Maria and John Scott-Waring's daughter, Anna Maria Reade, seems to have had the family connections well engrained. Not only did she and her husband call their eldest son John Thurlow after the Lord Chancellor, they also named their youngest daughter Elinor Hastings. Anna Maria Reade was a formidable woman. Born in Madras (now Chennai), she spent her youth in London where she knew everyone from the Prince of Wales and his brothers downwards. Charles James Fox was a close friend, and she knew Sheridan so well that she was allowed to sit on the stage while he directed *The School for Scandal*.

Then, suddenly it seems, she fell in love with and married John Reade, whom she met at the Assize Ball in Oxford. He was intelligent and handsome, and clever enough to let her shine. His family was ancient. His forebears included at least one literary eccentric, Philip Edward Reade, who not only wrote erotic verse - now lost - but who also spent money searching at Ipsden for the Philosopher's Stone. In John's day, however, Anna Maria ruled at Ipsden. On their marriage the composer Haydn, from whom Anna Maria had had music lessons, gave her a picture of himself. On the reverse was written the rather worrying maxim 'Reckon not on Happiness'.

Anna Maria's new husband was happy to let her decide on the future of their sons. John Thurlow Reade was sent to his father's old school, Rugby, before joining the East India Company and making a new life on the sub-continent. As John Thurlow's

The pyramid at Ipsden, Oxfordshire, erected on the spot where Anna Maria Reade saw the ghost of her son

nephew wrote, when Anna Maria found that her husband was satisfied with his dogs and his guns, she 'centred all her hopes in her sons. Earnestly, almost oppressively, she sought to fire them with her vaulting ambition to be first among the first. The names of John Thurlow Reade and of Edward Anderton Reade still live in the memory of the dark-skinned inhabitants of the north-west provinces of India.'

It was Charles Reade, her youngest son, who most nearly fulfilled her wishes. He is best remembered today as the author of the historical romance *The Cloister and the Hearth*. In his day he was renowned as a dramatist and a journalist as well as a novelist, and many saw him as being the equal of Dickens and Trollope. He was also a great self-publicist and, according to the *Oxford Companion to English Literature*, 'cantankerous and perverse'. Throughout his life he frequently returned to his home village, though one of his biographers called it 'Ipsden, sedately shrouded in a correctness comparable only with "*Mansfield Park*" '. Reade called Ipsden 'the coldest house in Europe'.

Charles must have been aware that, when he was 13, his dead brother mysteriously appeared to his mother; he presumably attended the memorial service. It is strange, then, that he does not seem to have used this odd tale as the basis for one of his novels; perhaps it was too personal to be put before the public.

The only cast-iron pyramid, at Hampstead Norreys, Berkshire

IN THAT PART of Berkshire that remains unexpectedly rural - the western part of the county, north of the M4 - is **Hampstead Norreys**. Although it's only a mile from the motorway and about

15 miles from Reading, it feels remote. Clustered at the heart of the village are three important buildings - the church of St Mary, with a tower that's possibly Saxon; Hampstead Norreys Farm (or the Manor Farm); and an impressive tiled, weather-boarded tithe barn.

We stayed at Hampstead Norreys Farm in some splendour - a big room in the comfortable Georgian house. It was a good choice, because Pamela and Richard Betts, who own it, are descended from the family that built the pyramid we had come to see.

Just beside the church is Britain's only cast-iron pyramid. It was put up in the 1850s and has seven steps, each made of individual plates with names of the Lowsley family cast into them. On top is an eight-sided finial of gothic design, like the spire of a Breton parish church. Flanking the point are four studded spheres, like the business end of a medieval mace, from which spikes grow upwards, to break into four curls of iron around a central core. There's a similar, though un-studded, sphere and spike on top. The whole monument has rusted to an attractive orange-brown, as you'd expect of unpainted wrought iron.

The colour is also a tribute to the origins of the pyramid. 'After Job Lowsley's death in 1855,' Pamela Betts told us, 'the farmhands were sent round the whole of the Manor estate to gather up all the disused iron farm implements. They were then melted down and turned into the pyramid.'

There was some professionalism in the design - it's quite a complicated structure, with each panel cast separately and then bolted together. Many of the panels have inscriptions on them. It's not, though, a sophisticated effort - it could have been put together by a skilled local blacksmith.

As well as its interest as a unique cast-iron structure, the pyramid's inscriptions also illustrate the Lowsley family's love of obscure names. They start innocuously enough with Joseph Lowsley. 'The family bought Hampstead Norreys Farm at auction at the George and Pelican Inn in Speenhamland in 1817,' said Pamela Betts. 'Joseph built the house for his son Job, who was a great collector of books - he had around 20,000 of them, and a special wing was built to house them. It's still here, but the books have long gone.'

The pyramid was a monument to Job, but the family continued to add plaques for the rest of the 19th century. So we get Job's children and grandchildren, and their names (with a few honourable exceptions) seem to get more and more weird. Four of Job's children take their names from the *Acts of the Apostles* - Luke, Rhoda, Dorcas and Eunice. All of these are relatively common names. The other four, though, were names garnered from a thorough search of the more obscure corners of the Old Testament - two sons were called Barzillai and Oded, and two daughters Vashti and Adah.

When Luke came to name his children, the Biblical influence seemed to have been losing its grip - but he still had a penchant for the out-of-the-ordinary. His children were Lionel Dewe, Warin Ashbel, Gerald (who must have felt left out in this concatenation of oddness), Montague Marmion, Miriam Marie, Naomi Ella, Hubert Ivan and Conrad Offa.

There was obviously a strain of eccentricity lurking in this remote corner of rural Berkshire, what with an iron pyramid instead of a normal god-fearing tomb, and a hoard of children with peculiar names. Whatever did the neighbours think?

The pinnacle of the pyramid in the churchyard at Hampstead Norreys

FROM A TINY village in Berkshire we drove to one in Hampshire - **Wootton St Lawrence**, just four miles from Basingstoke. All that we knew was that there was a pyramid in the churchyard, but we had no further details.

It was easy to find - indeed it is the biggest thing in the churchyard. A step-pyramid with a pointed cap, it sits inside a square of iron railings just beside the church. Ivy is doing its best to smooth its outlines, but the silvery granite from which it is made is still holding its own.

It is a monument to the Poynder family - notably to Thomas Poynder, who died in 1750, though the pyramid is certainly later, the first half of the 19th century. Who were the Poynders? No doubt the local big-wigs, who thought so much of themselves that they needed to show off with this impressive memorial.

It seems not. In fact, it is difficult to find out much about them at all. Hampshire County Record Office has very little - a few signatures witnessing deeds, and that's about all. A later Thomas Poynder is listed in a tithe reckoning in 1846 as being a yeoman who was the sixth-largest landowner in Wootton St Lawrence, with a holding amounting to about 64 acres. And that's about it. It seems that the Poynders kept themselves to themselves except for this architectural statement that is passed every time the villagers go to church.

Wootton itself does not seem to have been much more forward. Apart from supplying 91 cartloads of oak to help build the nave of Winchester Cathedral in 1392, as well as three more big oak trees in 1459 to build the roof of Winchester's Prior's Hall, the village seems to have slumbered.

It might all have been very different, though, if a local landowner had married a lady from less than five miles away. He was 21-year-old Harris Bigg-Wither, who lived at Manydown Park in Wootton. She was a 26-year old spinster, Jane Austen.

Harris Bigg-Wither was the brother of two of Jane's friends, and he was taken with Miss Austen. One evening in 1802 he proposed marriage - and she accepted. By the next morning she had changed her mind, and told him so. As took place at Manydown, the situation was awkward, if not thoroughly embarrassing. Jane and her sister Cassandra rushed away to their brother James' house at Steventon, and demanded that he take them back to Bath, where they were now living.

So Jane Austen never became Mrs Harris Bigg-Wither. If she had, her novels might have been unwritten as she became immersed in the needs of husband and children and in maintaining their social position. But if she had managed still to write, Wootton St Lawrence would have been firmly on the literary map. American academics writing theses, literary groups from around the world, parties of bored schoolchildren, would all have made their way to this tiny village. The villagers are probably pleased that Harris and Jane did not marry, after all.

AFTER THE PYRAMID to Mad Jack Fuller (see page 68), that of Dr Douce of **Nether Wallop** is perhaps the most famous in Britain. Nether Wallop is a pretty village between Andover and Salisbury and has at least four other claims to fame - it was the estate of Lady Godiva before her marriage; it has the only Anglo-Saxon wall-painting in situ in Britain; it was the place where the best cricket bat willows grew (as always specified by Dr W G Grace); and here Leopold Stokowski, the conductor who famously shook hands with Mickey Mouse in Walt Disney's film *Fantasia*, died at the age of 95 in 1977, not long after having signed a new five-year recording contract.

We arrived at the village on Good Friday morning. The sun was shining, the daffodils were blooming, and the parishioners were making their way up the lane to the church, which sits on the side of a ridge. To reach the door they have to walk past Dr Douce's pyramid.

This was certainly deliberate. Francis Douce wanted people to remember him, and if they looked at his tomb every time they went to church, then they certainly would.

Dr Douce was a 'Doctor of Physick', as the worn inscription on the pyramid says, and he practised in Hackney. It is not clear what his connection was with Nether Wallop, but it is likely that he or his wife came from the village. The pyramid was built in 1748 as a memorial to him and his wife; that was the year she died, and she was interred beneath it.

It was another 12 years before Dr Douce joined her there. His will, in which he makes it clear how much he thought of his pyramid, was probably written in 1758. A deposition attached to it tells a sorry tale. The deponent was a relative of Douce's, Robert

Dr Francis Douce laid down strict instructions about the construction and care of his pyramid at Nether Wallop, Hampshire

Gosling, 'of the Parish of St Dunstan in the west of London, Banker': he 'deposeth and saith that on or about the 20th day of December 1758 one of the Servants of the said Francis Douce came to him the Deponent and Acquainted him that the said ffrancis Douce was taken extremely ill that he thereupon went immediately to the deceaseds abode at Hackney and there found the deceased greatly disordered he having had a paraletic ffit whereby his senses memory and understanding appeared to him to be greatly impaired.' Dr Douce did not recover from his 'ffit'; on 26 January 1759 he was 'found a Lunatick by a writ of Inquisition'.

The point of the deposition was to testify to the legality of Douce's will, which Robert Gosling discovered in the house - 'upon the Table the will or Testamentary schedule hereunto attached which was a single sheet and had then a black ribbon at the top thereof and was sealed with a black seal and was then torn at the bottom.' Despite being incomplete Douce's will was allowed to stand - and Robert Gosling to receive his £500 bequest from it.

Much of the will is taken up with instructions about the pyramid. 'I give to the parish of Lower Wallop provided they do not suffer my pyramid to be injured the interest of a thousand pounds as they stand now which I shall dye possessed of in South Sea Annuities at the South Sea House for ever, to be made use of for the following purposes, vid: to help support the men and women who are past their Labours and do dwell in that Parish of Lower Wallop to be distributed by twelve of the heads of the Parish or as the majority of the Jury meaning the twelve men and if they do not do Justice I cannot help that. I order that out of the said Interest money that the Boys and Girls of the said Parish are taught to read and write and cast an Account a little way especially those who cannot pay for their schooling or learning but they must not go too far least it makes them saucy and the Girls all want to be Chamber Maids and in a few years you will be in want of Cooks.'

Having delivered this little homily (was it tongue in cheek? Probably) Douce goes on to lay obligations on the parish. 'I Give this Charity provisionly that my Pyramid shall be kept in good Order and the Iron Rails painted every second year at the Charge of the Parish, and if the Parish boys do climb or injure it they shall not only be deprived of their learning but shall also be punished and if the Parish do not keep the Pyramid in good repair this Charity shall cease and be void and subsist no longer.' Painting the 'iron rails' every two years must eventually have proved too much for the parish. They are no longer there.

Unusually, we know a great deal about Douce's motivation for building the pyramid. He was anxious to have his body buried somewhere secure and away from the rest of the corpses in the churchyard, and he was also fascinated by embalming. He was a member of the Company of Surgeons, and in 1705 he subscribed to a book by a fellow member, Thomas Greenhill, called *Nekrokedeia or The Art of Embalming Wherein is Shewn the Right of Burials and Funeral Ceremonies, especially that of Preserving Bodies after the Egyptian Method together with An Account of the Egyptian Mummies, Pyramids, Subterranean Vaults, Lamps, and their Opinion of the Metempsychosis, the Cause of their Embalming.* Greenhill's work emphasised the physical decay of the unembalmed corpses and their vulnerability to violation, whether by animals or resurrection-men. He also wrote that a pyramid 'is the most durable structure that can be invented; being neither over-pressed with its own weight, nor to be undermined by the sinking in of rain as other buildings.'

The 'flare' on top of Dr Douce's Nether Wallop pyramid

Following Greenhill's direction, Douce had the architect John Blake of Winchester construct his secure resting place. A letter, probably from Blake, in the *London Evening Post* during January 1749, described the structure: 'The area of the vault, under a very strong arch, is curiously paved with stone: the walls being very substantial, are, by the Doctor's express order, rendered with fine mortar, and decently whitened so that it is a receptacle or Lodging Room fit for the remains of a Prince . . . The whole is joggled, cemented and cramped in the most workmanlike manner; and being enclosed in strong iron rails, the steel teeth of time will scarce ever be able to devour it; and the doctor's bones may sleep undisturbed "till the last day" '.

Douce's pyramid is a handsome creation. Its proportions are carefully based on the pyramid of Cestius (see page 2) - though it is much smaller. On the west side is Douce's coat of arms and the very worn inscription that may once have told of the Doctor's association with Nether Wallop. At the top of the pyramid is a finely-carved 'flare' - flames leaping up and representing eternal life, like those on top of the pyramids at Christ Church, Spitalfields (see page 75) and Wentworth Woodhouse (see page 37). They still retain traces of their original red paint. It is perhaps unfortunate that they make the whole monument look like a giant firework . . .

FRANCIS DOUCE WAS a relative of the wealthy Paulet family - as were Mad Jack Fuller (see page 68) and Sir Paulet St John, the builder of the next pyramid on our tour. It's strange that not only were they linked by family, but also by the fame of their pyramids - the most famous three in the country.

Paulet St John's pyramid is at **Farley Mount**, about 10 miles south east of Nether Wallop and five miles west of Winchester. The site is stunning, the highest point of Mount Down. Here Bronze Age people - or possibly people from the Iron Age - constructed a barrow. It commands a wide view - south towards Southampton Water and north over the Test Valley.

It was on this site that Paulet decided to build his pyramid. It was not to glorify himself or his family - it went up in about 1740, more than 30 years before he was created a Baronet after many years as MP for Winchester. It is, instead, a monument to a remarkable horse.

An inscription on two iron plates inside the pyramid tells the story:

> UNDERNEATH LIES BURIED A HORSE THE
> PROPERTY OF PAULET ST JOHN, ESQ THAT
> IN THE MONTH OF SEPTEMBER 1733
> LEAPED INTO A CHALK PIT TWENTY FIVE
> FEET DEEP A FOXHUNTING WITH HIS
> MASTER ON HIS BACK AND IN OCTOBER
> 1734 HE WON THE HUNTERS PLATE ON
> WORTHY DOWNS AND WAS RODE BY HIS
> OWNER AND ENTERED IN THE
> NAME OF "BEWARE CHALK PIT"

So Paulet St John had double reason for being grateful to his remarkable horse - it both saved his life by managing to remain on its feet after its unexpected dive into the pit, and won him money in a race - Worthy Down was the racecourse for Winchester.

It is not recorded whether the horse was grateful for being lumbered with a name even odder than those of most horses. The pyramid is a curious structure; a restoration completed in 2004 has left it gleaming white, with bright red pantiles over its four porches - only one of which is functional. It resembles a bathing pavilion from a 1930s lido. There's doubt about whether this was its original form. There is a print dating from around 1860 that shows Farley Mount as a square building with a pyramidal cap. Was this how it looked when Paulet St John built it? If so, when did it become a pyramid?

It may have been in 1870, when the two black iron plates with their white lettering were put up: beneath the story its says

> THE ABOVE BEING THE WORDS OF THE
> ORIGINAL INSCRIPTION WERE RESTORED
> BY THE RT. HON SIR WILLIAM
> HEATHCOTE BARONET SEP. A.D. 1870'.

Recent investigations have shown two things - that there is no horse skeleton in the mound, and that the pyramid was not built of mid-18th-century bricks, but ones of a later date.

There is just one more interesting fact about Sir Paulet St John to note. He married three times; his first and third wives had no children. His second wife, and the mother of their six sons and one daughter, was the widow of Sir Halswell Tynte, 3rd Baronet, the brother of the man who built another pyramid, at Halswell Park in Somerset (see page 172).

Farley Mount's pyramid to the horse oddly-named 'Beware Chalk Pit'

THE NEXT PYRAMID on our itinerary is a little too far away to see from Farley Mount - but only just. It is on **Southsea's** Clarence Esplanade, on Southsea Common and near the point on which Henry VIII's Southsea Castle stands. The Pyramids Centre is a leisure complex that follows the lead of pioneers such as the swimming pool at Bletchley (see page 90) - its pool also has

*The Pyramids,
Southsea*

flumes, including the 100-foot 'Sidewinder', described as 'one of the speediest superflumes you'll ever find'. A touch of Hawaii is added in the Wave Pool, where 'wicked crashing waves and white surf await you', while 'toddlers can play safe and sound in their own miniature pool with animal slides'. Elsewhere in the building are the Plaza Suite, for 'functions', a large hall for conference and exhibitions and a nightclub, imaginatively named 'The Glasshouse'.

And talking of names, 'The Pyramids' is a misnomer - there is only one pyramid, a blue-framed structure with blue-tinted glass that houses the pools. It rises through an angled canopy that runs round much of its periphery. The rest of the building is a more utilitarian structure of the same materials, resembling a shopping mall.

The Pyramids Centre was the result of a crisis in Portsmouth City Council. In 1982 it decided that it needed a more modern image to attract tourists. The slogan the council had used until then was 'Come to Sunny Southsea'. It was felt that Portsmouth's other attractions were being ignored. This change of mind coincided with the rise of the 'heritage' industry.

So the new selling point for Portsmouth became its naval traditions, and its new slogan 'Portsmouth: Flagship of Maritime England'. This, it was believed - and the belief has proved well-founded - would bring many more visitors to the city, rather than just those wanting a traditional seaside holiday. The bucket-and-spade brigade could not be ignored, though - nor could the accommodation providers, tourist attractions and shops of sunny Southsea be completely disregarded. And so the Pyramids Centre, rather grudgingly described as 'a wet weather facility' was given to the area.

The site chosen had been occupied for many years by the Rock Gardens Pavilion, which had seen better days. It was demolished, and the Pyramids was built. The design was by a firm from Yorkshire, Charles Smith Architects of Boston Spa, and the centre opened in July 1988.

It is certainly a dramatic sight on Southsea front, especially at night when the pyramid is lit internally, but it sits rather uneasily in its surroundings - the polite mid-Victorian houses across the grass on Clarence Parade and the massive strength of the castle. Such considerations, though, don't bother the families who enjoy the tropical temperatures within the pyramid, and sometimes glimpse the ships sailing past Spithead into the Dockyard or out into the wider sea.

NOW IT WAS time for us to take to the sea, remembering that time and tide wait for no man, on our way to **Gosport**. The ferry crossed the sunlit harbour, with *HMS Warrior*, the first ocean-going warship to have an iron hull, and Nelson's *HMS Victory* away to the right. Somewhere between the two, under a constant mist of water inside a specially built shed, are the remains of the *Mary Rose*, Henry VIII's favourite ship of war, which sank in 1545 in the waters beneath our ferry's keel.

We disembarked at Gosport. In 1967 David Lloyd in *The Buildings of England - Hampshire and the Isle of Wight*, wrote of the journey we had just taken, 'Gosport is reached from Portsmouth across the harbour mouth. It looks impressive as one approaches . . . when one lands there is an anticlimax, for in front is some distressingly banal recent development at the entrance to the High Street.'

This 'banal recent development', now more than 40 years old, is still there, but there is now no anticlimax, thanks to the development on the water's edge carried out to mark the Millennium. The pyramid we had come to see was set on the rocky shoreline of the Solent, in front of Gosport's impressive Millennium Promenade. Where there used to be lines of parked cars, a wide, paved walkway follows the curve of the estuary for nearly two miles, southwards from The Museum of Naval Firepower, (excitingly called *Explosion!*) at Priddy's Hard to the Royal Navy Submarine Museum.

The pyramid is part of this new-look Gosport, and is a short walk from the ferry terminus. Tall and thin, it consists of four stainless steel legs resting on tumbled rocks, with the upper portion filled with different shades of blue glass. Below the glass panels is a white-faced clock.

Called *Time and Tide*, its purpose is to mark the change in the tide; each of the blue glass panels lights up progressively as the tide flows, until at high tide they are all lit. The clock beneath shows both the time and the direction of the tide. On the walkway in front is a mosaic inscription, with the motto *Time and Tide Wait for No Man* and the words *Spring Tides and Neap Tides*. It also says that the pyramid was sponsored, appropriately, by the Gosport Ferry Company.

The setting is superb. *HMS Warrior* can be seen framed through the legs of the pyramid. *Victory* is visible to the north, while straight across the harbour is Portsmouth's newest landmark, the Spinnaker Tower, with its top viewing deck at 110 metres above the ground. The Tower was still under construction when we visited.

Time and Tide was constructed a long way from the sea - at the works of John Smith & Sons in Alfreton Road, Derby, founded in 1856. The firm's work is found around the world, including in Stuttgart (the Opera House clock based on Mozart's *The Magic Flute*), Shanghai, Mecca, Bahrain (a tall thin pyramid), Kampala, Madras (Chennai), Chicago and Barbados. Nearer home, Smith's built another pyramid at Downham Market in Norfolk in 2003 (see page 51).

Time and Tide
pyramid at
Gosport

THE PHYSICS BEHIND constructions like Gosport's 'Time and Tide' were beyond us - but probably not beyond the children inside the INTECH pyramid just east of **Winchester**. Billed as 'The South of England's hands-on interactive science and technology centre', INTECH sets out to explain, in simple terms, the way the world works.

INTECH, which is run by the Hampshire Technology Centre Trust, is housed in a big, top-lit pyramid - and the pyramid itself is an exhibit. From the outside you can see the big concrete buttresses that support the steel roof, but inside they are replaced by an innovative structure that uses steel ties that brace the roof, so that, as Gary Wood, director of the designers and engineers Gifford Wood says, it will 'give the impression of four triangular plates leaning on one another.'

Parties of schoolchildren roam the inside of the pyramid, trying out all the experiments and demonstrations that show the principles of physics. There was a crowd round the machine that showed how a tornado was created. They were taking it in turns to speed up and slow down the vortex created by the machine, and getting it to change shape and location.

'It's brilliant!' said one girl. 'And we've been to see how rubbish and recycling works, too, and we've been bending light.'

INTECH, the interactive science and technology centre outside Winchester

Her friends had been looking at how you can tell the viscosity of liquids, and seeing how the giant Newton's cradle demonstrates the conservation of energy and momentum. Earlier they'd been in the big dome attached to the pyramid, an auditorium where they'd heard a talk on light, so they were full of enthusiasm.

INTECH has a loan collection, so that schools can create the excitement of the centre in the classroom. Among the equipment available is a chicken brooder, a mini tensile testing machine (that may help to explain the pyramid's roof construction), a solar power kit, a giant model of teeth, a beam bending kit and a bag of bones.

THE LAST TWO pyramids of this tour were in Nottinghamshire. Both needed careful planning - one because it is set in a nationally-restricted area, the other as it is on a private estate. First came a visit to an Army camp, at **Chilwell** to the south-west of Nottingham. We had arranged with the Station Adjutant to visit the camp, the national mobilization centre for the Territorial Army and reservists, to see the only World War I pyramid in the country.

It is not a conventional war memorial that lists men who died in the trenches. Listed on the sides of the pyramid are the names of 109 men and 25 women who died on 1 July 1918 in the worst explosives disaster that ever happened in Britain.

What is now Chilwell Camp was, from 1916 to 1918, the National Shell Filling Factory. Until the middle of 1915 the site was farmland, but it took the eye of the 8th Viscount Chetwynd. A qualified civil engineer and a skilled businessman, he had been charged by Lloyd George with setting up a factory for the Ministry of Munitions. Chetwynd was a human dynamo. He received his commission as Chief Executive of the new factory on 20 August 1915. Four days later he had not only familiarised himself with the problems of shell manufacture and worked out a new and faster method of shell-filling; he had also picked Chilwell as the spot for the factory.

Its advantages were obvious to him - it was between the main places where shell casings were manufactured and the ports from which they were delivered to the Front; there was no large centre of population nearby, but there was a pool of labour - including nible-fingered women who had formerly worked in the lace industry; it was adjacent to a main railway line; and the lie of the land - a hill-surrounded hollow with trees - was ideal to fill and store shells, as it would contain and limit any possible explosion.

Chetwynd requisitioned the land; building the factory began on 13 September 1915. Over the next three months building went on at breakneck speed - 167,000 feet of drainpipes and

Pyramid
monument to the
134 people who
died as a result of
the explosion in
1918 at the
National Shell
Filling Factory,
Chilwell,
Nottinghamshire

1,650,000 feet of rails were laid, for example. Then there were 400,000 square feet of glass, 11,000 tons of timber and 40,000 tons of bricks and slabs. On 8 January 1916 the first shells were filled; by September the factory had filled 1,260,000. Nearly all the British shells fired at the Battle of the Somme in 1916 came from Chilwell.

Making shells was dangerous. The TNT, mixed with ammonium nitrate to make the Amatol that filled the shells, coated the workers with yellow dust and turned their hair green; the women workers became known as the Chilwell Canaries. Many workers suffered from lung diseases. There was the constant fear of raids by Zeppelins. And, of course, there was the danger of explosion.

By the middle of 1918, when the factory had already filled more than 18 million shells, there had been 17 small explosions, with the loss of three lives. On 1 July 1918, a day of great heat, came the big one. At 7.12 pm there was, with no warning, an explosion that was heard 30 miles away and devastated the factory. It instantly killed more than 100 workers; such was the force of the blast that very few of them were able to be identified. The cause was never properly determined - a hastily-commissioned official report failed to find a real reason for the explosion and then was marked Secret, so no one knew what it said anyway. Lord Chetwynd was convinced there had been sabotage by dis-

The aftermath of the explosion at Chilwell

contented workers. Others thought it was the work of German agents.

Even before the funerals were held and the remains of the unidentified bodies were buried in the churchyard at nearby Attenborough, the factory was at work again. It had to be - the British Army was about to begin its great final push against the enemy. By dawn on 3 July, 36 hours after the explosion, shells were being filled again. By 6.00 pm that day 27,800 had been completed for dispatch.

Constructing an official memorial to the disaster was, inevitably, postponed until after the Armistice was signed. As most of the men and women were laid off, some remained to build the obelisk-topped pyramid that stands on the site of the explosion. It was unveiled by the Duke of Portland, Lord Lieutenant of Nottinghamshire, on 13 March 1919. The plaque on its front emphasises the total number of shells filled by the factory - 19,359,000 - '50.8 per cent of the total output of high explosive shell . . . produced in Great Britain during the War'. The lists of names of the 134 people who died are to be found round the sides of the pyramid. Only in 1968, 50 years on, was another plaque unveiled on the front, paying tribute to 'the bravery and fortitude of the employees'.

Their bravery was unofficially recognised at the time of the explosion in a different way. In a speech on 9 July 1918 the Parliamentary Secretary to the Ministry of Munitions said, 'The French, who have a very sound instinct in matters of this kind, gave the highest military decoration to the citadel of Verdun, when it defeated the great German advance of 1917. I wonder why we should not emulate that example and give the Victoria Cross to this brave Factory.' Nothing official was ever done - the Parliamentary Secretary must have been going off on his own with the idea - but thereafter the National Shell Filling Factory was often known as 'The VC Factory'.

THE FINAL PYRAMID of the tour was another memorial to bravery - one built in honour of Horatio Nelson. Most Nelson monuments were built after his death in 1805 at the Battle of Trafalgar, but the pyramid on the Thoresby Estate at **Perlethorpe** in the Nottinghamshire Dukeries is different. It commemorates Rear Admiral Sir Horatio Nelson's earlier victory over the French at the Battle of Aboukir Bay - better known as the Battle of the Nile - on 1 August 1798. Nor was it a tribute by local people anxious to show their loyalty to the forces of the crown. This was a private hurrah from a former naval captain to Nelson's prowess. Its builder was Charles Pierrepont.

Charles joined the Navy as a midshipman in 1747, aged nine. Within ten years he was a post-captain in command of the 36-gun frigate *Shannon*. He served off both the European and American coasts. By spring 1761 he was captain of the 50-gun *Isis*. A few years later he resigned his commission on being made heir to the estates of his mother's brother, the Duke of Kingston. The Duke died in 1773, and there was a scandal about the will; it left a life interest in his estates to his wife Elizabeth. Unfortunately, Elizabeth had omitted to divorce her previous husband, the Earl of Bristol; she was tried in the House of Lords for bigamy and found guilty. By claiming benefit of peerage she was left without punishment and spent the rest of her life abroad.

So Charles Pierrepont inherited the Kingston property, which included the Thoresby estate, immediately. In 1796 he was created

Viscount Newark; his eldest son Evelyn was given the courtesy title of Baron Pierrepont. By this time his second son, Charles Herbert, had followed in his father's wake to become a naval officer. He joined the service as a midshipman at the (rather late) age of 16. He was promoted rapidly, rising to commander. His naval career ended suddenly in October 1801 when Evelyn died and Charles Herbert returned to Thoresby as heir to the estate and peerage.

With their seafaring background both father and son were keen to celebrate England's naval glory. There was already a naval tradition at Thoresby; in the early 1750s the Duke of Kingston had enlarged the lake so that he could stage mock naval battles with small-scale men-of-war, crewed by professional sailors and estate staff. Charles Pierrepont's vision was much grander. From the 1790s he set out to remodel the whole landscape as a tribute to some of the naval leaders, like Keppel, Bowsawen, Howe and Rodney, with whom he had served. Along the south side of the lake he planted clumps of trees named after them, and he built a number of monuments and a mock fort. And although his son Charles Herbert did not serve in the Battle of the Nile in 1796, Pierrepont was obviously impressed by Nelson's victory, and he built what is probably the first monument to Nelson in the country.

Nelson's Seat is a pyramid near the lake, and we had permission to visit it. We met George Clarke, who was to lead us to it, at the estate office in Perlethorpe. 'Follow me!' he said, and set off at a great lick in his Land Rover. We followed in our own car, trying to keep him in sight. He suddenly veered right over long grass; after that it we had to follow his tracks rather than his vehicle - he was well ahead. In and out of trees, with glimpses of water away to the right, across other drives - it seemed never-ending. At last we saw him ahead, and drew up alongside his vehicle. The pyramid was a few yards away.

It was a surprise. We'd seen only one picture of it before, and it was shown in a poor state, with brambles and ivy quietly overwhelming it, and the slates that covered it slipped or missing. Now it was transformed. Encroaching trees had been felled, and the pyramid looked to us much as it would have done when Charles Pierrepont had completed it.

It is an unusual structure, with a wooden frame that has been covered in grey slates. The old picture showed it with ridge tiles along each sloping edge, but these have been removed, leaving the edges sharp. The entrance, with its stumpy and rudimentary Doric columns standing like marines outside the Captain's stateroom, resembles a superior dormer window.

It is not immediately obvious, beyond its appropriately-Egyptian shape, what connection this pyramid has with the Battle of the Nile. The first clue comes over the doorway, where the words 'PALMAM QUI MERVIT FERAT' are inscribed. This is the motto of Nelson, granted as part of his coat of arms in 1797. It means 'Let him who has deserved it bear the palm'.

Inside the porch the details begin. In black text on a series of now-crumbling panels Pierrepont has listed all the ships that took part in the battle, both British and French. This is a thunderous roll-call - *Audacious, Minotaur, Leander, Bellerophon* . . . for the home side; *Conquérant, Timoleon, Tonnant, Heureux*. . . for the enemy. Captains are listed, including Troubridge, Perry, Louis, Westcott . . . and the number of guns - nearly all had 74, but the French flagship *Orient* mustered 120.

The British fleet was victorious, thanks to Nelson's daring strategy of sending his ships between the French and the coast. The

The entrance to the Perlethorpe pyramid

Celebrating Nelson's victory at the Battle of the Nile - the pyramid at Perlethorpe, Nottinghamshire

turning point was the exploding of the magazines on board *Orient* - the blast threw the huge ship's 15-tonne rudder nearly a mile, and killed Giocante, the young son of Casa Bianca, the French Flag Captain. The boy had refused to leave the body of his father, who had been killed earlier in the battle. Mrs Hemans' famous and much-parodied poem beginning

> The boy stood on the burning deck
> Whence all but he had fled

is about young Casa Bianca.

In his dispatch to the Admiralty reporting on the battle, Nelson, on board *Vanguard*, said, 'Almighty God has blessed His Majesty's Arms in the late Battle, by a great Victory over the Fleet of the Enemy, who I attacked at sunset on the 1st of August, off the Mouth of the Nile . . . nothing could withstand the Squadron Your Lordship did me the honour to place under my command . . . I was wounded in the head, and obliged to be carried off the deck; but the service suffered no loss by that event.' He concludes with a list of British sailors killed (213) and wounded (677) - a figure that compares with at least 1400 French killed and 600 wounded. It is not surprising that a British soldier described the result of the battle as 'an awful sight . . . the whole bay was covered with dead bodies, mangled, wounded and scorched, not a bit of clothes on them but their trousers.'

Hundreds of miles away, safely in England, Nelson's mistress Lady Hamilton could take a jauntier view. She wrote to him on 26 October 1798, 'If I was King of England I would make you the most noble puissant DUKE NELSON, MARQUIS NILE, EARL ALEXANDRIA, VISCOUNT PYRAMID, BARON CROCODILE and PRINCE VICTORY, that posterity might have you in all forms.'

Charles Pierrepont's celebration was more serious. To underscore his feelings, he added lines from a poem by William Lisle Bowles, *Song of the Battle of the Nile*, praising Nelson's overwhelming victory. Though much of it has now been lost, it originally read

> SHOUT! For the Lord hath triumph'd gloriously!
> Upon the shores of that renowned land,
> Where erst his mighty arm and outstretched hand
> He lifted high
> And dash'd, in pieces dash'd the enemy
> Upon that Ancient Coast,
> Where Pharaoh's Chariot and his host
> He cast into the Deep.

The inside of the pyramid is a simple cylinder with a saucer dome. Round the wall is a wooden bench on which visitors could sit and contemplate the 'hearts of oak' that helped Nelson win his Egyptian victory. And, not long after it was completed, they would no doubt sit to commemorate the Admiral who had been killed at the hour of his greatest victory at Trafalgar.

After we had contemplated our naval history, we expected to have to bump our way back to Perlethorpe, but George Clarke took pity on us and let us out through the back gate. It was, perhaps, a less-than-heroic end to our visit to Thoresby Park and the Nelson pyramid, and to all the central English pyramids. It had been a journey full of interest - from the modernism of Milton Keynes to the wooden walls of Nelson's navy - and another pyramid adventure was about to start.

Tour 4

SOUTHWEST ENGLAND

THE INSCRIPTION NEATLY places it:

> 6 miles
> To Shakspere's Town whose Name
> Is known throughout the Earth
> To Shipston 4 whose lesser Fame
> Boasts no such Poet's Birth.

The milestone in the Warwickshire village of **Newbold-on-Stour** was the herald of the first stop of the tour of southwest England's pyramids. It is a modest beginning, but with some illustrious names attached to it.

It is not your normal milestone. Placed where the A3400 (once the grander A34) is joined by a minor road from the hamlet of Crimscote, it consists of two pyramid-topped cubes, the smaller apparently jammed hard, at right angles, into the lower, larger one. As well as the poetic distance-giving, there are other texts - *Post tenebras lux, In luce spes, In obito pax* - and another, longer, inscription, which translates them:

> Crux mea lux
> After darkness LIGHT
> From light hope flows
> And Peace in death
> In CHRIST as sure repose
> Spes1871

What does all this mean, and who was responsible for it? The clues to a probable answer lie in the two coats of arms on the milestone - those of the Dukes of Cornwall, with twelve bezants or golden roundels, and of the Shirley Family of nearby Ettington Park.

In late autumn of 1871 Albert Edward, Prince of Wales and Duke of Cornwall - known as Bertie and later King Edward VII - contracted typhoid fever from polluted water at Londesborough Lodge in Scarborough. One fellow guest quickly died and there were fears for Bertie. Neither the timing nor the disease could have been worse; his father, Prince Albert, had died of typhoid on 14 December, exactly ten years before. Bertie's illness was at its worst on 13 December; recovery was not expected. It was of this illness that future Poet Laureate Alfred Austin wrote his most famous couplet:

> Flash'd from his bed, the electric tidings came,
> He is not better; he is much the same.

But on the anniversary of his father's death Bertie rallied, and by the 15th it was clear he would recover. There was national rejoicing. Early in 1872 there was a thanksgiving service at St Paul's Cathedral. Twenty-six thousand people attended a mammoth celebration in the Crystal Palace to hear a festive *Te Deum* specially written by Arthur Sullivan for soprano solo, chorus, symphony orchestra and organ, as well as a military band. And Evelyn Philip Shirley of Ettington Park put up his milestone.

Shirley was a scion of one of the few English families that can genuinely trace their ancestry back to before the Norman conquest - back to the Saxon Sewallis, who appears in the Domesday Book of 1086 as owning land at 'Etendone'. Shirleys fought

The pyramidal milestone at Newbold-on-Stour, Warwickshire

OPPOSITE:
*The pyramid at Stanway House, Gloucestershire
(see page 123)*

against the Scots and the Saracens and later for Henry Bolingbroke at the Battle of Shrewsbury - this was Sir Hugh Shirley, whose rebellion against King Richard II tested the family motto *Loyal je suis* but earned him immortality from 'Shakspere' in *Henry IV part 1*; he was one of the knights who dressed in royal armour to confuse the enemy, and was killed by Harry Hotspur; Prince Henry taunts the Earl of Douglas with

> Hold up thy head, vile Scot, or thou art like
> Never to hold it up again! the spirits
> Of valiant Shirley, Stafford, Blunt, are in my arms.

Shakespeare would have known Ettington - during his lifetime it was let by the Shirleys to the Underhill family, from whom Shakespeare bought New Place, his Stratford house, and he is thought to have hunted deer in the park.

In the 19th century the Shirleys built a huge house at Ettington. Evelyn Shirley inherited a 17th- and 18th-century house in 1856. An antiquarian and historian, the author of a number of books - titles like *The Noble and Gentle Men of England* and *English Deer Parks, with some notes on the management of deer* - as well as *Why is the Church of Ireland to be Robbed?* - give an idea of his interests. He was not a man to be satisfied with an ugly house. It must be rebuilt in a modern style - the muscular Gothic architecture praised by Ruskin in *The Stones of Venice*. Shirley asked one of the leading architects of the time, George Edmund Street, for plans, then rejected them because they looked like a rectory. Who, then, should design the new house?

The answer was near at hand. The euphoniously-named Reverend Richard Prichard was vicar of Newbold-on-Stour. His brother John was an architect. In 1844 John Prichard had begun restoring Llandaff Cathedral. Now Richard secured another commission for him, Ettington Park. Fortunately, John Prichard was a good and sensitive architect: the design Prichard prepared for Shirley was inspired by the Gothic of France and Italy. It has two towers, one square, one circular. Gables are varied in style. There are rounded and polygonal window bays. The windows have plate tracery. And most startling of all, the whole building is striped, like some French and Italian Gothic buildings, with stones of different colours - white, yellow, brown, blue.

Relations between client and architect were not always easy. Shirley complained of slow progress, mounting costs and Prichard's unauthorised changes. The stone-vaulted porch was added without Shirley's agreement, and an extra staircase suddenly appeared, to Shirley's annoyance. When in April 1863 Shirley threatened to replace him, Prichard complained, 'I am a Victim, yes that is now too clear . . . I am not a machine. I must work pleasantly with my client'. The relationship struggled on until 1865, when the chapel was completed. The final bill was almost £12,000 (nearly £7 million today), of which, Shirley noted, about £4,500 was a direct result of Prichard's second and third thoughts. Prichard's last letter reveals that he had had great hopes for his career as a result of the work at Ettington - hopes that were not realised; he said he no longer expected success, but 'a posthumous reputation, to deserve which I spare no pains'. Somehow, it seems unsurprising that his spirit is said to be one of the many ghosts that haunt Ettington Park.

Despite the difficult relationship between Evelyn Shirley and John Prichard, it is possible that the pyramidal tribute to The Prince of Wales is a very minor work of the Welsh architect. It certainly reflects aspects of Shirley's character - his love of Gothic, his antiquarianism, his high-churchmanship - and perhaps his desire to live up to the family's motto - *Loyal je suis*.

PRESERVING THE COUNTRY from the knavish tricks of its enemies has been a preoccupation of Britain throughout the centuries. And finding ways of giving warning of invasion did not begin with the massive technological might of Fylingdales (see page 26) or GCHQ in Cheltenham - nor even with Watson Watt's discovery of Radar. Before 'electric tidings' were flashed from north to south, from east to west, simpler methods were used - and the most famous is the chain of beacon fires on hill tops, by which news of a feared invasion could be relayed in a comparatively short time. The sites where these beacons sat are often still known and still used - these days at times of national rejoicing rather than of panic; coronations, jubilees, the Millennium . . . And a few are marked with pyramids - like those at Penrith in Cumbria (see page 192) and at Ashurst's Beacon near Skelmersdale in Lancashire (see page 197).

Undoubtedly the great-great-grandfather of them all, though - and the oldest pyramid we have found in the whole of Britain and Ireland - is **Compton Pike** in Warwickshire. An impressive 20 feet high or so, it has a slightly irregular taper and a twist towards the top, as if, after years of standing, the old man has developed a problem with his back. And he has stood a long time, for it seems that he was built to give warning of the approach of the Spanish Armada in 1588. As Drake finished his game of bowls on Plymouth Hoe, the villagers of Compton stood by on the hilltop overlooking their great house, a bundle of faggots attached to the hook on top of the Pike's ball finial and a flambeau at the ready to

The 16th-century Compton Pike, Warwickshire

ignite it when the gleam of the beacon of their neighbours to the south was visible.

Compton Pike played its part, too, in other national emergencies throughout the succeeding centuries, being ready to blaze away at the first hint of a foot being set on British soil by a Napoleonic Frenchman or a German Nazi. The call did not come, but the Pike blazed away for other, happier events - royal jubilees among them. And it played its part in the life of the great family who lived in the valley below - the Comptons. Comings-of-age and weddings were celebrated with a blazing beacon on the hill-top, while festivities were held in the great house of what was once known as 'Compton-in-the-Hole' and is these days more politely known as Compton Wynyates.

The house at Compton Wynyates was there even before the pyramid on the Pike was built. It was started at the very end of the 15th century by Sir Edward Compton - but even then the family had been living here for almost 200 years. Edward's house was built of brick, and probably fairly modest. When he died, in 1493, his young son William was made a ward of the crown and, aged 11, a page to young Prince Henry, then aged 2. They became friends - which was fortunate, as Henry unexpectedly became heir to the throne when his elder brother Arthur died, and became one of England's most famous monarchs, Henry VIII. The friendship of the king had direct consequences for Compton Wynyates. When he succeeded to the throne, Henry gave William Compton a dilapidated castle near Warwick, called Fulbroke, which William used as an architectural salvage yard. From it came the roof of the new Hall at Compton Wynyates, as well as a magnificent bay window, complete with heraldic stained glass.

After Sir William Compton's building campaign at the beginning of the 16th century, there were a few additions - wonderful twisty chimneys, a couple of timbered gables - through the succeeding decades. Then, in 1574 the house became neglected, as the Comptons turned their attention to their other home, Castle Ashby in Northamptonshire. Change at Compton Wynyates virtually ceased, and it became frozen in time; the moat was drained in the Civil War, the chapel was added at the Restoration, a new range was tacked on the back in the mid-19th century. But the house remains essentially a Tudor building. As the author Oliver Wendell Holmes noted in his visit in 1886, 'It is the place of all others to be the scene of a romantic story . . . The great hall, with its gallery, and its hangings, and the long table made from the trunk of a single tree, carries one back into the past centuries'. The effect was heightened by the famous topiary garden, to the south of the house, planted in 1895 to replace labour-intensive bedding schemes. The contrast of the mellow pink Tudor brick and the dark green of shaped yew and box was much-photographed.

The Comptons hosted royalty at Compton Wynyates - Henry VIII, of course, then Elizabeth and in 1617 James I & VI. Twelve years later James created the Earldom of Northampton for them. The Second Earl, Spencer Compton, entertained his friend Charles I at the house, and died for him in the Civil War, when Compton Wynyates was taken by the Parliamentary troops. By the 18th century the family was in financial straits, and the order was given to demolish Compton Wynyates. It was ignored by the Land Agent, and no one came to check. In 1812 the Earls of Northampton went up a rung of the peerage, and it was the Fourth Marquess who restored Compton Wynyates as a wedding present for his son. When the Sixth Marquess died in 1978 the family decided that they should open their Castle Ashby home as a tourist attraction. The Seventh Marquess ('Britain's wealthiest Buddhist') moved back to Compton Wynyates, which is now a zealously-guarded private house and estate.

A prominent Freemason, the Marquess has been at the centre of controversy. First, he was heavily criticised in 1983 when he brought in heavy machinery to grub up the 90-year-old and much-loved topiary at Compton Wynyates. More recently, he has been involved in disputes over the ownership of a mysterious and important hoard of late-Roman silver, called the Sevso Treasure, still the subject of dispute by three governments - those of Lebanon, Hungary and Croatia. There are million of pounds at stake on the outcome.

Meanwhile, Compton Pike sits calmly on its hill above the old house in the centre of rural Warwickshire, surveying succeeding generations of Comptons.

ODDLY, THE STORY of **Stanway** House in Gloucestershire, the location of the next pyramid we visited, is another example of a Sleeping Beauty country house that was ignored and then re-awoken by a nobleman. And like the Shirley family at Ettington Park (see page 119), the owners can trace descent from before the Norman conquest.

Stanway lies at the foot of the Cotswolds, overlooking the Vale of Evesham. It sounds idyllic - and it is. The house - low and spreading - is built of golden Cotswold stone. A beautifully-detailed gatehouse with mullioned windows and wonderfully-curly gables protects the house from the eyes of curious passers-by. Stanway has been one of the homes of the Earls of Wemyss and March since 1817 - and of family members since 1533, when they bought the estate from Tewkesbury Abbey. The family tree is very impressive. It includes four kings of England (Richard I and Richard II, Aethelred the Unready and Edward the Confessor); a French King (Pippin the Younger); two Holy Roman Emperors (Louis the Pious and Charlemagne); and a saint, Arnulf of Metz, who died in 640 AD. It also includes one of the knights responsible for killing Thomas Becket in Canterbury Cathedral.

The gatehouse at Stanway

It was not the illustrious pedigree that brought us to Stanway, however, nor the beauty of the house. We had come to see the pyramid on the hillside above the house. Lord Neidpath, then the Earl's heir, welcomed us and pointed us in its direction. Actually, we had been here before, 20 years earlier, when we saw the pyramid from the bridleway that runs to the east of it. Then it was perched in isolation on the hillside, with a grassy slope leading down towards the house. A depression in the ground may once have been a pond. On this official visit, though, things had changed.

Now the pyramid has been restored, and is again one of the focal points of a remarkable garden. The depression has been cleared and is now a circular pool that reflects the pyramid. Excavations on the grassy slope below have uncovered a great rarity, the remains of a cascade with, at its foot, a rectangular canal 500 feet long on a terrace above the house. When restoration is complete, water from the circular pool will run under the pyramid and gush down the cascade into the canal. The effect will be like the cascade at Chatsworth - but at 623 feet long it outdoes Chatsworth.

The cascade and canal were part of the design for the Stanway garden carried out in the 1720s for John Tracey, who owned the

The pyramid, fountain and canal at Stanway, with the cascade under restoration

estate from 1682 to 1735. It is likely, though not proved, that the plans were drawn up by Charles Bridgeman; John's daughter Anne wrote in her diary for 18 May 1728 that her father had visited the garden at Rousham (see page 91); he reported, she noted, 'his Garden Beautiful his Cascade surprizingly fine'. Bridgeman was responsible for the Rousham garden at that point, and Tracey probably employed Bridgeman for his new design. It is certainly a 'Bridgemannick' design; the canal, the cascade and the shaped turf banks are typical of his style.

Gardening fashions change, so the cascade and canal could have disappeared under a 'Capability' Brown-style 'makeover' by John's son Robert Tracey. Instead, he preserved it, and added something of his own - the pyramid, a monument to the taste of his father. The architect was Thomas Wright. As a garden designer Wright published two volumes of *Universal Architecture*, which contained plans for arbours and grottoes, as well as providing individual buildings; as well as the Stanway pyramid he designed the pyramid at Tollymore in Co Down (see page 365) and its associated follies. Wright was also famous as an astronomer; he was the first to identify the Milky Way as the galaxy to which the earth belongs, and suggested its flattened shape. For Richard Tracey, Wright produced an elegant structure - a cube pierced with arches, topped by the tall pyramid, and with urns at the corners. Inside there are niches, with shells at their heads, which make the square plan of the base into an octagon. Soaring above is the interior of the pyramid, a beautifully-built cone - though it used to be hidden by an ornate plaster ceiling. The Tracey ladies would take their tea in the pyramid, looking over the elegant balustrade and the cascade to the Welsh mountains.

On the side of the pyramid facing the cascade is a long Latin inscription dedicating it to John Tracey 'viri sanquine quamvis avito facile clari virtutibis tamen quam genere clarioris' - 'a man who, although easily distinguished by his ancient lineage, was yet by his own virtues even more distinguished than his race'. The pyramid was erected 'anno salutis humanae' 1750.

Robert Tracey had no male heirs, and it was through his niece Susan that Stanway passed to the Earls of Wemyss in 1817 - though it had not been a family home since Robert's death 50 years earlier. The Wemyss' family home was at Gosford House in Lothian (see page 235), and their visits to Stanway were infrequent. In 1824 the cascade and the canal were filled in when a publican's wife drowned there, and 'Stanway was left to caretakers and the tender mercies of rats, bats, moths, cockroaches and ghosts, who roamed at will through the deserted rooms' - the description is by the woman who was to revive it. She was Mary, wife of Hugo, Lord Elcho (later 11th Earl of Wemyss). The Elchos were given Stanway as a wedding present in 1884, and brought it back to life. Hugo's great-grandson Lord Neidpath (now 13th Earl of Wemyss - see page 236) now lives there, and, following in his ancestors' traditions, he has been responsible for Stanway's latest water feature - the world's tallest gravity-fed fountain.

It came about largely as the result of an unfortunate incident. James Neidpath and his landscape architect Paul Edwards had the idea of a small fountain, fed from the Pyramid pond, which was to emerge from a re-dug canal. They achieved this in 1998, the water gushing 70 feet into the air. In the meantime, unknown to them, an incontinent sheep was helping them. In 1997 it contaminated the water of Lidcombe reservoir, on the hillside above Stanway, with the parasite *cryptosporidium parvum*. Severn Trent Water, fearful of an outbreak of diarrhoea among its customers, immediately shut the reservoir. It seemed too good an opportunity to miss; 88,000 gallons of water on the hillside 235 feet above the canal that could be harnessed to power a bigger and better fountain. But in March 1999 Severn Trent said it planned to build a new reservoir on the site of the old - plans that were eventually abandoned in 2001.

With the help of David Bracey of the Fountain Workshop Limited, Lord Neidpath gained permission to use the water and was granted a water abstraction licence. With more than a mile of 12-inch polythene pipe laid from the reservoir and a 2½-inch nozzle emerging from the canal, the new, improved fountain was opened in June 2003. It had a working height of 165 feet. That was ten feet higher than its closest British rival, at Witley Court in Worcestershire. Such an achievement would have been enough for most people, but James Neidpath was not satisfied. Although he once remarked that playing with waterworks is the quickest way to go bankrupt, he decided that he wanted to go higher. In 2005 a new reservoir was constructed higher up the hillside - 100,000 gallons of water can be pumped to it from the Lidcombe reservoir. Another half-mile of polythene pipe links the two reservoirs. The resulting head of water gives such force that the fountain can now rise to 350 feet, though its normal working height is 300 feet. Only a few fountains are higher - those in Jeddah in Saudi Arabia, in Sharjah in the UAE, in Arizona, and the Jet d'Eau on Lake Geneva - but these are all pumped fountains, using turbines to achieve their height.

And is the 13th Earl now satisfied? Not entirely. He has set his sights on another achievement. Although his cascade - rediscovered when a very short section of the kerb was laid bare by a motor mower in 1987 - is of spectacular length, it is only part of the original concept. On the hillside behind the pyramid there was another cascade, narrower, but considerably longer - 1,150 feet. He plans to reinstate it; it will be a spectacle even more wonderful than his magical fountain.

The Dyer pyramid at Prestbury, Gloucestershire

PRESTBURY, TOO, IS a Cotswold-foot village, but unlike Stanway, it is a suburban settlement, a well-heeled satellite of Cheltenham. The Gold Cup racecourse is just north west of the village. The High Street has Georgian buildings that would be just as happy in the centre of its bigger neighbour. Only around the church of St Mary does the former village character assert itself. The church was owned by Lanthony Priory in Gloucester, and the remains of the Prior's house are next to the churchyard.

The pyramid in Prestbury is on the south side of St Mary's. About five feet high, it is built of green sandstone, with two simple plaques on it in contrasting red sandstone. It commemorates a brother and sister, William and Ann Newman, and was probably designed by Ann's husband, Gloucestershire architect Nathaniel Dyer. William Newman, about whom we have little information, died in 1781. Ann, according to the inscription, 'Left this Life Feby 2: 1796 Aged 59 Years'. Because the inscription to Ann says the pyramid was erected to her memory, it is likely that it dates from the time of her death rather than of William's.

Ann Newman married Nathaniel Dyer at King's Stanley near Nailsworth on 6 December 1781. Dyer was described as being from Avening, south-east of Nailsworth. The Newman and Dyer families were long-established in the deep valleys south and west of Stroud. Unlike his farming forebears, Nathaniel took up a profession. His was never a nationally-known name, but he was of sufficient local eminence as an architect that he raised his status to that of 'gentleman'. So it is sad to relate that the pyramid to his wife and brother-in-law is one of possibly only two surviving works.

Much of his fame seems to have rested on his 1793 designs for Nailsworth Episcopal Chapel. Nailsworth had had no church since the Reformation - and even before that it was only a subsidiary chapel to Avening. By the late 18th century this had become something of a local scandal, so a group of locals raised a subscription and approached Nathaniel Dyer to produce a design for their new place of worship. This in itself was a little odd; in 1788 he was described as 'a carpenter with Nonconformist connections.' Yet five years later here he was, a respected architect and apparently a stalwart member of the Church of England.

Whether this was through conviction or Vicar-of-Bray-like expediency, we do not know. Dyer was commissioned and produced a simple classical box, with a curved apse for the altar and a tower with a pepper-pot turret. He did not charge for his work. The curate of Avening was put in charge of the new chapel, but it was never officially consecrated, and the worshippers struggled to find a salary for their minister throughout the following century. Dyer's chapel was replaced by a new, properly-consecrated church in 1900.

We know that Dyer gave an estimate and produced a plan for rebuilding the south aisle of Woodchester church - the church was abandoned in about 1863 and little now remains except two arches and a window (see page 134). He also designed the new ceilings in the nave and aisles of the church at Wotton-under-Edge. They still exist and are described in *The Buildings of England - Gloucestershire: The Cotswolds* as being 'in a rather charming Early Gothic Revival style by the architect Nathaniel Dyer and the pargeter John Pike.' Dyer is also said to have built a number of local houses, though his work has not been positively identified.

It is possible that Dyer was a Freemason, which would help account for his choice of a pyramid to his wife Ann in 1796. Nathaniel outlived her by 37 years, dying in 1833. In his lengthy will (22 closely-written pages in the National Archives) he is described as 'Nathaniel Dyer of Bredon in the County of Worcestershire and of Nailsworth in the County of Gloucestershire, Esquire.' He leaves most of his estate to his nephew Nathaniel Dyer Ball. He also remembers the Episcopal Chapel in Nailsworth, bequeathing £100; any interest over one guinea is to be given to the minister to preach a sermon, with ten shillings to go to the chapel wardens to distribute bread to the poor of the parish.

Although Ann was buried in Prestbury, Nathaniel was interred at Nailsworth. It would have seemed logical for his grave to be at the Episcopal Chapel (where there was a plaque to him, now in the successor church). But in fact he was buried in a field behind his house, The Lawns, in Spring Hill in Nailsworth. The house, extensively rebuilt, was later owned by the Archer-Shee family - 17-year-old George Archer-Shee was accused in 1908 of stealing a five-shilling postal order when a cadet at Dartmouth. The subsequent case against the Admiralty was the basis of Terrence Rattigan's play *The Winslow Boy*. Nathaniel Dyer's links with the house are forgotten today; it is now Winslow House Residential Care Home.

STAVERTON, ON THE western side of Cheltenham, is known, if at all, as the location of a local airport. There are now aircraft component factories nearby, but in 1868 *The National Gazetteer* noted that 'the inhabitants are wholly agricultural'. There were, though, some gentry, among them the St Clairs of Staverton House and Staverton Court. Two of the family have an unusual pair of pyramids in the churchyard of St Catherine's.

David Latimer St Clair was a Royal Navy Captain but finished his days far inland on the family estates. The St Clairs were, as the inscription on his pyramid says, 'an ancient family' - more ancient even than the Shirleys at Ettington Park (see page 119) and the Comptons at Compton Wynyates (see page 121). The St Clairs trace their line back to Rognvald the Mighty, Jarl of Orkney and Earl of Moere and Romsdahal, born in 835, and they take their name from a treaty signed at the French village of St Clair-sur-

The twin St Clair monuments at Staverton, Gloucestershire

Epte between Paris and Rouen. They came over to Britain with William the Conqueror, and many moved north to Scotland. They served the Scottish kings, and in 1379 Henry St Clair was made Prince of Orkney. One of their principal seats was at Roslin, where in 1446 Sir William St Clair founded Rosslyn Chapel (see page 243).

The Staverton St Clairs were a cadet branch of the family, descended from Henry, 10th Lord Sinclair (family spellings varied). Henry's eldest son John, Master of Sinclair, chose the wrong side in the Old Pretender's Rising of 1715. In 1716 the Sinclair peerage was attainted - no one was allowed to inherit it, and John was barred from the succession. John's brother James did not help him, but left the family estate to the children of their sister Grizel instead. This meant that William, the third brother and the only one to have children of his own, had to make his own way in the world. He became a soldier, rising to be Colonel of the 25th Regiment of Foot, the King's Own Scottish Borderers. He married the daughter of the Governor of Minorca, and their second son, born 8 May 1784, was David Latimer St Clair.

David St Clair followed his father into the military but he became a captain in the Royal Navy. There seems to be little information about his career, beyond the facts that he was twice wounded on active service (presumably in the Napoleonic Wars) and was made a Knight of the Swedish Order of the Sword - the Svärdsorden - for his services. He married Elizabeth Isabella Farhill from Chichester (did he meet her while stationed at nearby Portsmouth; or were they old family friends? - both of them were born in Chichester) at St Marylebone church in 1819.

When Elizabeth died in 1855, aged 55, David St Clair ordered a pair of monuments from R Allen of Cheltenham. It was an odd commission; his-and-hers matching tombs were never common, and the form that he chose - a pyramid without a pedestal, that becomes obelisk-like at the top - is unique in Britain, though similar shapes with pedestals are found at, for example, Desertcreat in Co Tyrone(see page 306) and Cheshunt in Hertfordshire (see page 84). David's choice may have been influenced by Freemasonry; the St Clairs have for centuries been leading lights in the Brotherhood and they are related to the guardians of the Rosslyn Chapel. The pyramids are identical (though Elizabeth's has lost its very top) and are set on a single base, showing that they were put up at the same time. They were once surrounded by iron railings. Elizabeth's inscription notes only her name and who her husband was; that to David, who died in 1861, is slightly more forthcoming: 'He served his country in parts of the world under three Kings and one Queen' - George III, George IV, William IV and Victoria. And then there is the small note of pride: 'He was of an ancient family'.

GOOD BREEDING WAS something that Cecil Elwes of **Leckhampton** Court looked for in his horses. When he bought The Continental in 1896, the five-year-old had won 19 races over jumps, as well as a number of hunter chases and similar local events. Six years later The Continental died, and Elwes commemorated him with a rough stone pyramid on the Cotswold escarpment, not far from the Court.

Elwes was the sixth owner of The Continental - the first was Lord Shrewsbury, who then sold him to Mr Cottrell-Dormer of Rousham (see page 91). Mr Hudson, Mr Ward and Mr Gore followed as owners, before Elwes gave him stabling. Cecil Elwes had

A rough pyramid
marks the grave
of the horse
called
The Continental
at Leckhampton
in Gloucestershire

been master of Leckhampton Court the since 1901. On 10 July that year he married Edith Muriel Hargreaves at the Guards' Chapel in Wellington Barracks. Muriel's father John was a Wigan man, who had married the daughter of a wealthy manufacturer of machinery for cotton mills, from Oldham.

When he moved from industrial Lancashire in 1872 to be tenant of Leckhampton Court, John Hargreaves entered a new way of life into which he threw himself with enthusiasm. He hosted the local village fete, contributed to local causes and entertained lavishly at the Court. Among his guests were the Dukes of Wellington and of Beaufort, the Marquess of Worcester and the Earl of Dunmore. The Earl sometimes gave signed copies of his books instead of a tip to the staff. With titles like *The Panims - Being a narrative of a year's expedition on horseback and on foot through Kashmir, Western Tibet, Chinese Tartary and Russia and Central Asia* and *The Revelation of Christians and Other Christian Science Poems*, they were probably less-than-enthusiastically received; the servants would have rather have had the cash. The Prince of Wales, the future Edward VII, probably stayed at Leckhampton to hunt - and, it is rumoured, he brought Lillie Langtry with him.

In 1894 John Hargreaves was able to buy Leckhampton Court. Parts of it date back to the 14th century, but now he extended it in a comfortable late-19th-century style. It became a Red Cross hospital in World War I, had a Prisoner of War camp in the grounds during World War II, and is now a hospice. Hargreaves did not enjoy the house for long; when he died in 1900 he bequeathed it to his younger daughter Muriel. Her wedding the following year to Captain Elwes of the Scots Guards brought a connection, though admittedly somewhat tenuous, with Royalty - Elwes was descended from the dashing military commander Prince Rupert of the Rhine, nephew of Charles I, through his mistress, London actress Peg Hughes. Cecil's father, Henry John Elwes, was a noted plant collector and built up the most celebrated collection of snowdrops in the country at his estate at Colesbourne Park between Cheltenham and Cirencester. From the age of 17 Henry spent large parts of each year abroad, either collecting botanical specimens or big game hunting. It is likely, therefore, that Cecil saw little of his father as he grew up, and thus developed his own taste for country pursuits that were based around his home.

Cecil and Muriel Elwes seem to have been genuinely liked in Leckhampton. To celebrate their fifth wedding anniversary and the birth of their daughters they gave a huge party for the village, with 300 for tea and games and dancing on the lawns in the evening. Elwes was Chairman of the Parish Council and supported the parish church. He also hosted the flower show at Leckhampton Court 'to encourage good gardening, good poultry-keeping and the keeping of good horses.'

Good horses were certainly a passion with Cecil Elwes. He was a keen huntsman - he formed his own pack of hounds at Leckhampton Court, and before World War I was Master of the Burton Hunt in Lincolnshire. The Court had stabling for sixteen horses - and The Continental had pride of place. Described as 'a good steeple-chaser and a terrific jumper', its sire was Boulevard and its dam Fairhaven. It may have been foaled abroad. As Cecil Elwes' favourite mount, it could have been expected to have lived out its days, once the hunting was over, in comfort, even in equine luxury.

Fate had other ideas. In 1902 The Continental severed an artery in its leg by putting its foot into a metal manger. The injury was

Cecil and Muriel Elwes with their children and their dog

so bad that it had to be shot. Elwes was undoubtedly upset at this
bloody end. He organised the piling up of large stone blocks on
the hillside overlooking the Vale of Gloucester in the horse's
memory. Inscribed in the top stone are the words

     TO THE MEMORY OF THE CONTINENTAL
     BY BOULEVARD/FAIRHAVEN
     FOALED 1891 DIED 1902
     WINNER OF 25 STEEPLECHASES
     AND THE FAVOURITE HUNTER
     OF CECIL ELWES
     BY WHOM THESE STONES WERE ERECTED

*The pyramid to
the Bryan quarry
owners and
carvers is
surrounded by
the famous 99
yew trees of
Painswick
churchyard*

THE BRYAN FAMILY of **Painswick**, a little further south in
Gloucestershire, would have been a good source of stone for
Colonel Elwes, had he lived a century earlier. They were quarry
owners, and their Painswick stone was famous. It was used in
many of the town's 18th-century buildings, often with crisply-
carved decoration. The Bryan quarries also supplied stone in
1766 for the Shirley family at Ettington Park (see page 119). In
charge of the family business at that date was John Bryan, whose
remains lie under a pyramid in Painswick churchyard, surrounded by the 99 famous clipped yew trees.

John was born in 1719, son of Joseph Bryan. With his younger
brother Joseph, John was trained as both a quarryman and a
stonemason and carver. Their father died in 1730, and John and
his brother took on the business. Joseph soon went off to
Gloucester, where he set up a modest carving and masonry business. John remained in Painswick, living eventually at a house
called Selsdon in Brisley Street. There he acquired a significant
local reputation as the best carver of interesting monuments,
many of them using imported coloured marble. There are, of
course, many in and around Gloucestershire, but his work can be
found as far afield as Abergavenny and St David's.

As a stonemason John collaborated with his brother on a number of contracts. An important one was the new west tower of the Norman church at Great Witcombe, between Cheltenham and Stroud. The brothers sent in their estimate of £80 for the work (for which William Clark of Leonard Stanley was the carpenter), and the tower was complete by 1752, when they fixed the sundial in place. They were also probably responsible for the church's south porch. In 1776 John and Joseph proposed to rebuild the spire of St Nicholas' church in Gloucester, which had been hit by a cannon ball during the Civil War and was in a precarious state, a long way out of true. The citizens of Gloucester decided to live with the imminent danger of its possible collapse until 1783 when John (Joseph had died in 1779) was contracted to take off the top of the spire to reduce it nearly to half its original height. He capped it with a crown of stonework, pinnacles and a ball with a weathercock, making it one of the most recognisable of the city's churches.

Earlier, John had designed and constructed the elegant northeastern gateposts to the churchyard at Painswick, where his pyramid now stands. The monument was probably constructed by his nephew, also called John, who took over the Gloucester business of his father Joseph on his death and then his uncle John's as well. The younger John Bryan married his cousin Anne - his uncle John's daughter. It is possible that the Bryans were Freemasons as well as masons, which would account for the pyramidal shape of the monument. The older John Bryan had two other daughters, besides Anne - one who became Mrs Loveday, and Sarah, their eldest. Sarah died in June 1764, aged 20, and she is commemorated on the pyramid along with her mother, also Sarah, who died in May 1786, aged 66. John Bryan, the first named on the monument, died on 21 March 1786; he was 71. The inscription describes him as 'late of this town, Carver'.

IT IS POSSIBLE that the younger John Bryan was the carver of the next pyramid we visited, just down the valley in **Stonehouse**. It certainly has something of the delicacy of touch and sureness of design that marked his uncle's work. Its shape, too, is very similar to the Painswick pyramid, though here the sculptor has added a pedimented niche on each face, like little, low dormer windows. On one of the faces is a spirited carving of a memento mori - a skull, a crown and sceptre, a globe and what appears to be a fish. On all four sides, above the niches, there is a carved swag.

The pyramid is listed along with three other monuments in the churchyard of St Cyr's in Stonehouse. The listing for the pyramid says 'inscriptions illegible', but in fact they are reasonably easy to decipher. From it we know that the pyramid is a monument to 'Joseph Ellis who died greatly regretted September 8th 1771 aged 53 years at Spa in Germany and his remains lie interred there in the chancel of the Protestant Chapel of Olne in the adjacent Dutch Territory.'

Joseph Ellis was a Stonehouse bigwig - a textiles magnate who owned a mill in Ebley. He lived at Ebley House, which was rebuilt in 1874 and was for many years a children's home. His Ebley mill, a mile down the valley towards Stroud, was also altered in the 19th century by the great Victorian church architect G F Bodley. It is now the offices of Stroud District Council. As an upholder of law and order (he was a Justice of the Peace) Ellis would have approved of its new use. He was certainly keen on upholding his own rights to pay his weavers whatever wages he wished.

For many years he and his fellow textile magnates had fixed the sums they paid, and believed they had every right to do so. In fact, they had not. A two-hundred-year-old law, the Statute of Labour of 1563, said that it was the JPs who should fix wages. The law was revived in 1728, but it had no teeth - there were no sanctions against any mill owner who conveniently forgot to run his pay proposals past the Justices. As a consequence, wages became more and more depressed.

Matters came to a head in July 1755. Weavers in Horsley, nine miles south of Stonehouse, got up a petition to their local JPs, asking them to make the masters obey the law. The following month they put forward their own 'table or scheme of the rate for wages to be paid to the woollen broadcloth weavers' of the area. Surprisingly, as at least some of the JPs were also the mill-owners, they got their way. What happened next, though, was entirely predictable. The mill owners, Joseph Ellis among them, forced their workers to sign 'voluntary' agreements that they were quite happy with their current wages. This caused a huge rumpus. Letters threatening reprisals were sent from weavers to owners. At Ellis's mill the weavers went on strike, and he was forced into a humiliating climb-down. He had to visit the mill and tear up the enforced agreements before the workers' eyes.

That wasn't the end of the story. Argument continued for a year, with more than 70 of the most important owners petitioning the Justices against the ruling, and the workers rioting. In November 1756 a new table of wages was approved - but even that did not end the dispute. The owners succeeded in getting Parliament to repeal the Act - and won back the right to set the wages themselves.

Joseph Ellis does not come out of the episode very creditably - but he obviously had redeeming features - even if 'greatly regretted' was not a universal sentiment. He was a friend and encourager of Gloucester-born George Whitefield, founder of Calvinistic Methodism (see Adfa, page 222). Just four years older than Ellis, Whitefield deputised for the vicar of Stonehouse in spring 1736, when he was 22. On one occasion he was preaching when such a violent thunderstorm burst over the church that the congregation rushed out of St Cyr's, thinking the building was about to collapse about their ears. Unruffled, Whitefield continued to preach (at full volume, presumably) in the churchyard as the storm raged. In his journal he referred to Stonehouse as 'the pleasantest place I was ever in' - no doubt his friendship with the rich Ellis family made his stay there very comfortable. Whitefield soon left the Church of England (he once described the Archbishop of Canterbury as 'no more a Christian than was Mohammed') and preached his own Calvinistic ideas both in Britain and on the east coast of America. For many years associated with the chapels of the Countess of Huntingdon's Connexion, he regularly visited Ebley, preaching in a barn and renewing his acquaintance with Joseph Ellis and his wife, the appropriately-named Christian, who is also commemorated on the Stonehouse pyramid; she died on 28 March 1776, when she was 56. Whitefield died in Massachusetts in 1770, a year before Joseph Ellis's death.

Ellis seems never to have followed Whitefield into the evangelical movement - his burial at St Cyr's shows that he remained, at least nominally, a member of the Church of England. He gave

Monument to Joseph Ellis at Stonehouse, Gloucestershire

support to another clergyman, of a very different stamp from Whitefield, the scholarly Joseph White. White's father, Thomas, was a journeyman weaver around Stroud, and it was probably through working for Ellis that Thomas brought his clever young son, who was also destined to become a weaver, to the magnate's attention. Ellis recognised the spark of genius, and with Dr Jones, a Stroud physician, paid for young Joseph's further studies. In 1765, aged 19, Joseph went up to Wadham College, Oxford, where he studied Hebrew, Syriac, Arabic and Persian. By 1773 he was a Fellow of Wadham, and the following year was elected Laudian Professor of Arabic. His scholarly work included translations of early versions of the gospels and of the Old Testament. He left Oxford in 1787 to become rector of Melton in Suffolk, and, next year, became a prebendary of Gloucester Cathedral - a position that gave him considerable income. He was back in Oxford in 1807 as a Canon of Christ Church Cathedral and Regius Professor of Hebrew. He died in 1814, 43 years after his early benefactor Joseph Ellis.

William Leigh's unfinished bedroom at Woodchester Mansion

THERE ARE TWO things that **Woodchester**, two miles south east of Stonehouse and just south of Stroud, is famous for - and neither of them is its pyramid. One is Woodchester Park, an estate once known as Spring Park, which may have been landscaped by both 'Capability' Brown and Humphrey Repton (or possibly by neither). The mansion in the heart of the park is definitely by Benjamin Bucknall. He designed it for William Leigh. A Catholic convert who had moved to Woodchester from Staffordshire, Leigh had first commissioned the architect and designer Augustus Pugin, but because Leigh refused to commit enough money to the building, Pugin withdrew his plans.

Pugin was, as things turned out, probably wise, for Bucknall's house was never finished. Bucknall was a local man from Rodborough and in his very early 20s when he designed Woodchester. He was a great admirer of the French Gothic architect Viollet-le-Duc, who rebuilt both the château at Pierrefonds in Picardie and the city walls at Carcassonne in the Aude Département. Viollet insisted on real structural gothic - and so did Bucknall. Work went on at Woodchester for 14 years, with thick stone walls and beautifully-detailed stone vaults rising amid the woodlands. In fact, everything was stone - including the gutters and the bath. Suddenly, in the late 1860s, work stopped at a stroke. Workmen left their tools, form-work for the arches was abandoned, windows were left unglazed. A century of neglect followed. Woodchester Park became a Gormenghastian fantasy of hooting owls and scampering mice. But Bucknall's masterpiece did not decay. Now cared for by The Woodchester Mansion Trust and open to visitors, the partially-roofless house is still solid, its stonework crisp, the gargoyles not softened by weather or time.

Woodchester's other famous sight is seen rarely. The Orpheus Roman pavement is the largest mosaic ever discovered in Britain. It was known to be there in the 17th century, but it was first completely excavated at the end of the 18th. Although it has suffered considerable damage, the mosaic still retains its original bright colours. Near the centre the figure of Orpheus plays his lute while around him animals - a tigress, a leopard, a gryphon, and a stag among them - cavort. The mosaic formed part of a villa. It may have been the home of either the local Roman administrator or a native Romanised chief. It dates from the second-century reign of the Emperor Hadrian. Spectacular it may be - but it is

*The three-faced
Trinitarian
pyramid at
Woodchester in
Gloucestershire*

not visible. Although it has been occasionally uncovered - last in 1973, when 140,000 people came to see it - it is normally kept buried beneath turf. A full-size replica, with the missing parts restored, is now at nearby Prinknash Abbey. The replica is said to be worth more than £1,000,000. You can see where the original pavement is - a flat platform of grass beside the ruins of Woodchester's Norman church, which was abandoned when a new one was built in the village centre in 1863. And just beside the platform is the Woodchester pyramid.

Like the pyramid at Spetisbury in Dorset (see page 143) and the Swifte pyramid at Castlerickard in Co Meath (see page 358), the Woodchester pyramid is three-sided. There is a particular symbolism in the shape here. The three triangular sides of the pyramid represent the Holy Trinity. The circle on which the pyramid sits is Eternity; it is inscribed with the words 'TO THE GLORY OF THE EVER BLESSED, ETERNAL AND UNDIVIDED TRINITY.'

The pyramid is a memorial to the Dunn family. The inscriptions carved into the hexagonal plinth on which the circle and pyramid sit remember, first, Thomas Plummer Dunn, who 'fell asleep Novr 22nd 1867 aged 65. Forever with the Lord'. Thomas Dunn, originally from near Trowbridge in Wiltshire, came to the area when Stroud was at its height as a centre for the production of textiles, especially broadcloth. He was a wool merchant, and at one point he owned a dyehouse in Dudbridge, the next village upstream from Ebley (see page 132) and later ran Lightpill Mill, between Woodchester and Stroud. By 1861, when he was 58, he is described as a Woollen Flock Dealer. Flock is a by-product of the textile industry - short woollen fibres that are shredded and dyed. Originally applied to cloth, flock became fashionable when applied to wallpaper from the 1730s. Flock papers were very labour-intensive to make, and therefore expensive. Some, for the grandest houses, had huge damask patterns, based on the cut-velvet hangings that had preceded them; others were more modestly-scaled for people with smaller establishments. The fashion was long-lived; in the late 1840s Pugin specified (and designed) special flock wallpapers for the new Houses of Parliament. The craze for flock died out by the late 19th century. Modern imitations are made with rayon, applied with a spray gun.

Thomas Dunn was married twice. His first wife was Margaret Peach Wathen, the daughter of Obadiah Wathen, who owned Woodchester Mill; they married in Woodchester church, then lived in Hackney before moving back to Gloucestershire. Margaret is not remembered on the pyramid, but three of the couple's children are - daughters Ellen Hawtrey Dunn and Julia Peach Dunn. They both died of croup; Ellen was five and a half and Julia was one and a half, and both were buried on 19 September 1839. Their brother, Herbert Wathen Dunn, had been baptised the day before; he died, aged five months, in October. Another daughter, Amy Bateman Dunn, survived until 1873, dying aged 31, while Margaret died of asthma in October 1850. A year later Thomas married Margaret's cousin Grace Caruthers Wathen in Amberley church.

Grace was quite a wealthy woman, with money in trust for her from her family. It was just as well; in 1859 Thomas Plummer Dunn began a disastrous financial venture by taking a stake in the Maesteg Iron Company near Bridgend in Glamorgan, which had opened in 1828. He lost his money, and was declared bankrupt in 1860. It may have been Grace's wealth that saved him, along with some judicious renting of property rather than outright purchase. Whatever the case, his social standing seems to have been maintained - in 1864, three years before his death, he was made a Churchwarden of Woodchester's new parish church, and the following year, when his son Thomas Wathen Dunn was married, he witnessed the certificate and was referred to as a 'gentleman'. After Thomas died in 1867 Grace continued to live at their home, Selsley Lodge, taking an interest in her step-children (she had no children with Thomas) and her nephews and nieces. She died in the Vicarage in Penzance, the home of her nephew John Hunt, in 1885.

We do not know why the Dunn family insisted on the religious symbolism of the three-sided pyramid and the circle. Woodchester was certainly a centre of religious fervour in the middle of the 19th century. Before William Leigh began his new mansion he had founded a Catholic monastery in Woodchester, with buildings (demolished in 1970) by Charles Hansom, brother of architect Joseph Hansom, who gave his name to the Hansom cab even though he did not invent it. As the Dunns were buried in the Anglican churchyard it is unlikely they followed Leigh into the arms of Rome, but they may have been influenced by the local atmosphere of sanctity - an atmosphere that stretches back at least as far as the worshippers of the Roman gods.

IN THE PRIVATE garden of the Prince of Wales at **Highgrove** near Tetbury is a mysterious pyramid of ferns. It is particularly mysterious because we have not been able to see it - a polite request to Clarence House was just as politely turned down. The pyramid was designed by Bristol-based landscapers Julian and Isobel Bannerman, who have become garden purveyors to the gentry and the almost-crowned heads of Europe. Their clients include Lord Rothschild, John Paul Getty and Lord Lloyd Webber, their commissions such delectable spots as Waddesdon Manor, Houghton Hall, Leeds Castle, Hampton Court and the Castle of Mey.

Now the holders of a Royal Warrant as suppliers of garden extravaganzas to the Prince of Wales (Julian Bannerman refers to him as 'Principe') they have provided several buildings and other structures for Highgrove, but only the one pyramid. The official photographs show it in two states - during construction and planted. It stands ten feet high and is the Cestius-pyramid shape (see page 2). The basic construction resembles an aluminium greenhouse, but instead of glass it uses rigid wire mesh. The interior is packed with compost (Highgrove's own organic compost, of course) into which are planted hart's-tongue ferns, with their bright green, glossy leaves sprouting luxuriantly and contrasting with the softer green of moss. We are told that the autumnal contrast between the carpet of sere brown and orange leaves and the glow of the fern pyramid 'knocks you for six'. We must take the word of others for it; we have not seen the effect.

THE WORCESTER LODGE at **Badminton**, on the other hand, is extremely public. To say it is a lodge to the park is like saying that St Pancras Station is a wayside halt. It is the lodge *in excelsis*, beautifully placed in the landscape, superbly designed and finely executed. And it has two pyramids.

Worcester Lodge, as approached from Badminton House in Gloucestershire, with its two pyramidal wings - William Kent's architectural masterpiece

137

The entrance side of Worcester Lodge

The Lodge is the masterwork of William Kent. Kent was always at his best designing on this sort of scale - often, when working in greater dimensions, he lost something of the raw energy that characterises his best buildings. This one has energy in abundance. The effect is like a musical composition - like the opening to Handel's *Zadok the Priest*, perhaps. From outside the park you approach the Lodge through a huge semicircle of grass, enclosed by walls that end in small octagonal pavilions. The walls are given rhythm with buttresses topped by low pyramid caps and on each side by a false, pedimented gateway. As the walls near the Lodge the tension grows. At each side of the main block are cubic extensions, topped by the pyramids. The bases of the cubes are rough with rustication, providing a heavy foundation for the smoothness of the pyramids. Ball finials sit at each corner of the pyramids, as if holding them in place against a tendency to soar away. This was not the first time Kent had designed pyramids for an entrance lodge - they had also appeared in his sketch for the gateway to Holkham Hall, but they were struck out as frivolous by his client Thomas Coke. They also resemble the pyramid-topped temples he designed for Chatsworth (see page 9).

Each of the cubes is separated from the main block by a length of wall that is subtly higher than the rest of the curve of walling. Above the short wall hangs one of the prow-like balconies of the central pavilion.

And what a pavilion! The lower storey is weighty with rustication - more the sort of thing you might expect from a prison entrance than from the introduction to a ducal demesne. But through it punches the great entrance arch, with grass and sky beyond. Apparently floating above the hefty base is a smooth upper storey - perfectly proportioned, with a great window in the centre of each main facade that mirrors the arch below and adds to the lightness. Over it is an octagon with a shallow Palladian dome. Tying the dome to the arches is a heavy triple keystone, carrying aloft the coat of arms of Kent's patron, Charles Noel Somerset, the 4th Duke of Beaufort. The great room, lit by the large arched windows, is full of Kent's exuberant decorative plasterwork, showing the four seasons.

The 4th Duke succeeded to the Badminton estate in 1745 on the death of his brother. Mrs Delany, actress and singer, wrote that the 3rd Duke's death 'is not to be lamented, he was unhealthy in his constitution and unhappy in his circumstances' - a reference to the acrimonious divorce from his duchess, Frances Scudamore, for her adultery. His brother the 3rd Duke had inherited the title when he was seven. His tastes were artistic; on the Grand Tour, aged 19, he commissioned the Grand Ducal workshops in Florence to make for him what is now the world's most expensive piece of furniture, the Badminton Cabinet. It is made of ebony, with lots of gilded bronze figures by Ticciati and, best of all, inlaid panels of precious stones - pietra dura work - by Baccio Cappelli. It reputedly took 30 craftsmen to construct it; among the stone they used are red and green jasper, amethyst quartz, agate and lapis lazuli. The Cabinet, which is 12 feet 6 inches high and 7 feet six inches wide, was owned by successive Dukes of Beaufort until they sold it to pay death duties in 1990. It made £8.5 million at auction - campaigners failed to save it for the nation and it went to the United States. In 2004 it was sold again (it was too big for the new owner's house) and this time fetched £19 million.

The 3rd Duke began to develop the house at Badminton, too, with the help of James Gibbs. When Charles Noel Somerset succeeded as 4th Duke, Gibbs was ousted in favour of William Kent. Kent added domes to the house and designed some of the interior decoration. He also grappled with the park, which had been rigidly landscaped in the 17th century with long, straight avenues - in fact, the ducal influence was so great that neighbouring landowners extended his tree-lined rides across their own estates, so for miles around all roads apparently led to the front door of Badminton. The Third Duke had asked Charles Bridgeman to soften this regimentation, but he largely failed - and so did Kent. The park is still divided in a Euclidean way, and Kent's buildings, especially Worcester Lodge, make the most of the geometry.

Charles Noel Somerset died in 1756 after 11 years as 4th Duke of Beaufort. He had been lucky not to have been imprisoned after the Young Pretender's 1745 uprising - he supported the Stuart cause and plotted with the French. In fact, the Duke seems to have liked being in opposition to authority - he fell out with Walpole because of the Prime Minister's support for King George II in the royal spat with his heir, Frederick, Prince of Wales. The Duke was described as 'a man of sense, spirit and activity, unblameable in his morals, but questionable in his political capacity.' As a patron of Kent, though, he was generous and loyal - for the Worcester Lodge appears to have been one of Kent's final works, constructed faithfully to his designs after his death. Kent died in April 1748 'by slow increase of his distemper suddenly over powerd & tended to a Mortification in his bowels & feet especially inflamed'. He was 63.

SAINTS HAD A place in the birth of Ralph Allen, whose pyramid mausoleum at **Claverton** in Somerset followed on our tour. He was born in the Cornish village of St Colomb Major in 1693; his mother was from St Blazey and his father was an innkeeper at St Austell. It might be stretching the point to say that saintliness was part of Allen's character, but he seems to have been a kind man and a solid friend, whose wealth was spent in helping others. Alexander Pope, who corresponded with him, wrote, in his *Epilogue to the Satires* of 1738,

> Let low-born Allen, with an awkward shame,
> Do good by stealth, and blush to find it fame.
> Virtue may choose the high or low degree,
> 'Tis just alike to virtue, and to me.

The suggestion that, despite his fortune, Ralph Allen remained socially awkward and self-conscious of his wealth, fits with his life's pattern.

There was undoubtedly a good brain behind the modest demeanour. When he was 11 he was working with his grandmother in the newly-established post office at St Columb. By the time he was 14 he was running it himself - and the same year he was appointed to a more-important postal job at Exeter. By the age of 19 he was working in the postal hub of Bath. In 1712 he was appointed as Bath's deputy postmaster. His business nous attracted some of the local bigwigs, including General Wade, who came to Bath in 1715 to keep the Jacobites there under his thumb. His association with the town as a resident (and from 1722 to 1768 as its MP) was a great help to Ralph Allen. It appears that Allen acted as an informer for Wade - and there was even a rumour, now discredited, that Allen married Wade's illegitimate daughter.

With Wade's backing Allen was able to undertake his first ambitious project. In 1720 he paid £6,000 for the right to run the 'cross-posts' - the postal deliveries that ran not along the main coach roads that radiated from London, but cross-country. The system was already established, but it was neither well run nor

*Ralph Allen's
mausoleum at
Claverton near
Bath*

particularly lucrative; Allen's bid of £6,000 was a third more than it was bringing in. But he was confident of his abilities to make the system efficient and rewarding. He was right; the contract was renewed every seven years until he died, and soon came to yield profits of £12,000 a year.

Allen rapidly became a man of substance. In 1725 he was made treasurer of the scheme promoting plans to make the River Avon navigable between Bath and Bristol. In the same year he was made a freeman of Bath and a councillor. He bought a house near Bath Abbey (adjacent to General Wade) where he moved with his wife Elizabeth, daughter of a London merchant. Their only child, a son George, no doubt named after Wade, died in infancy that year. Now a major figure in the town, Allen felt the need of a country house. But he was canny; he was not going to cut himself off from business. He bought land from his wife's brother where he could build a house - but which, much more importantly, could be quarried for stone.

This was the age of Bath's greatest architecture, and Allen was the man to supply the stone for the crescents, terraces and circuses that were springing up, many of them designed by Allen's friend John Wood and his son, also John. Allen's Coombe Down Quarries, a mile and a half outside Bath, were famous: in 1753 Thomas Boddley wrote that 'The City of Bath is greatly improved within these few Years, in its buildings; the new Houses are strong, large and commodious; built with Free-Stone, conveyed

Prior Park, Ralph Allen's mansion, with his stone-moving 'admirable Machine' in the foreground

from a neighbouring Hill. The Quarries belong to RALPH ALLEN, Esq.; and the Stone is brought from them to the River Avon, near Bath, by an admirable Machine, which runs down the Hill near two Miles, by Grooves placed in the Ground, without Horses or any other Help, than one man to guide it; who also by a particular Spring, can stop it in the swiftly Part of the Motion. The Stone may be transported from Bath, by Water, to almost any Part of England.'

The 'admirable Machine' was not Allen's invention, but showed his eye for innovation; 'Mr Allen had the good fortune to meet with a person whose natural Genius for Mechanicks enabled him to improve on the original, whereby Block Stone came to be delivered to the Avon side for seven shillings and Six-pence a Tun, of twenty Cubical Feet, which was half a Crown a Tun cheaper than it had been sold for.' To make the work even more efficient, Allen had John Wood design 'two small towns' near the quarries for the workmen, who would otherwise have lost time 'in going between their Habitation in or about the City and the quarries'.

Yet it was not all plain sailing for Allen. He wanted to get Bath stone to be used throughout the kingdom, and especially in London. He was up against powerful opposition from the architects and builders who favoured Portland stone. They included Sir Christopher Wren, who oversaw the Portland quarries, and Hawksmoor. John Wood wrote that 'The introduction of Free Stone into London, met with opposition; some of the Opponents maliciously comparing it to Cheshire Cheeses, liable to breed Maggots that would soon devour it'. What he saw as London arrogance spurred Allen into action; 'Reflections cast upon the free Stone of Bath brought him to a Resolution to exhibit it in a Seat which he had determined to build for himself near his Works, to much greater advantage and in much greater variety of uses than it had ever appeared in any other structure.'

Allen's 'Seat' was Prior Park, designed by the elder John Wood as an advertisement for Bath stone. A school since 1830, it is a fine Palladian mansion at the summit of a hill overlooking the city. Below it in the gardens, which are in the care of the National Trust, is the famous Palladian Bridge, very like the example at Stowe but in a finer setting. There is also a newly-rediscovered cascade, similar to, though not as long as, that at Stanway (see page 123). Allen moved into Prior Park in 1741 with his second wife, another Elizabeth - the first Mrs Allen had died in 1736. There they entertained a wide range of friends, including Pope, William Pitt the elder, and the Princess Amelia, daughter of King George II. General Wade was always there, as a statue in Roman armour on the terrace. The novelist Henry Fielding was another regular, and he wrote Ralph Allen into his most famous book, *Tom Jones*. Allen appears as Squire Allworthy: '. . . who might well be called the favourite of both nature and fortune; for both of these seem to have contended which should bless and enrich him most. In this contention, nature may seem to some to have come off victorious, as she bestowed on him many gifts, while fortune had only one gift in her power; but in pouring forth this, she was so very profuse, that others perhaps may think this single endowment to have been more than equivalent to all the various blessings which he enjoyed from nature. From the former of these, he derived an agreeable person, a sound constitution, a solid understanding, and a benevolent heart; by the latter, he was decreed to the inheritance of one of the largest estates in the county.'

Benevolent Allen certainly was - he helped both financially and practically with the building of Bath General Hospital, he served on philanthropic committees and, it was said, he gave away upwards of £1,000 each year to charitable causes. In 1748 he bought Claverton Manor (now demolished) as a smaller house for his old age. The last years of his life were painful with (ironically) stones in his urinary tract. He died on 29 June 1764. He expressed a desire to be buried at Claverton. It is likely that his wish to have a pyramidal mausoleum came from Freemasonry. Certainly his friend John Wood the elder was an active Freemason; there is deep Masonic symbolism behind both the layout and the detailing of new Bath that he designed. Wood also specifically linked the chapel at Prior Park to the origins of Freemasonry; he would build it, he wrote, 'in the manner in which King Solomon finished the inside of his Temple of Jerusalem'. Wood had died in 1754, and perhaps Allen was not so close to the younger Wood. So the pyramid was not designed by him but by Robert Parsons, a stone-mason who hade worked for the elder Wood. His skill was not as an architect but as a sculptor, but he noted in his commonplace book that on 28 June 1764, the day before Allen's death, he went to see the great man and showed him designs for a memorial - it is on this statement that Parsons (who later became a Baptist Minister, while retaining his work as a mason) is credited with the pyramid.

It is not a sophisticated design; the pyramid sits rather uncomfortably on the arcaded base, and the mouldings on the arches are simplistic. The elder John Wood would have done a better job. It is though, quite handsome, and beautifully situated in the churchyard at Claverton. The inside of the pyramid is striking for its cat's-cradle of iron tie bars that hold the sloping stones in place. Beneath them is the tomb itself with its simple inscription. Really, though, Ralph Allen's monuments are elsewhere - in the pages of *Tom Jones*, in the mansion and garden of Prior Park and, above all, in the glowing, honey-coloured walls of the city of Bath which his stone helped to build and beautify.

The cat's-cradle of iron tie bars inside the Allen pyramid

'WE MUST EXPRESS an opinion that nowhere but in the Church of England, and only there among its priests, could such a state of moral indifference be found.'

'The part of Dorsetshire to which he alluded consisted of two villages . . . though the living [was] worth £750 a year, there had never been a resident clergyman there. Now, if the Catholic religion had increased there, let him not hear it said that it was owing to the encroaching spirit of that religion, but let it be attributed to the real cause - the want of efficient discharge of clerical duties on the spot by a resident clergyman.'

Fact or fiction? The first of these quotations is from *The Warden* by Anthony Trollope, the story of supposed corruption in the ranks of the Church of England by the innocent and amiable Mr Septimus Harding. It is taken from the editorial in *The Jupiter* written by the campaigning journalist Tom Towers. The second quotation is from *The Times*, in March 1829, reporting a speech in the House of Lords by the Marquess of Lansdown. Trollope's tale of Anglican clergy failing to perform their pastoral duties properly was mining a vein of reality that was prominent in the first half of the 19th century - and Lansdown's criticism of the supposedly non-resident rector was just one example. The 'Dorsetshire' villages on which the Marquess bent his criticism were **Spetisbury** (at the time often spelled Spettisbury) and Charlton Marshall, just south of Blandford Forum. And the 'absent' cleric was the Reverend Thomas Rackett MA.

There was a wedding about to take place in St John's church in Spetisbury when we arrived to see the pyramid in the churchyard. Young men in beige frock coats greeted long-lost uncles, and fashionable girls hugged well-dressed Dorset housewives. All of them ignored the pyramid - a tricky feat, as it is directly outside the south door of the church where they were congregating. The Spetisbury pyramid, like that at Woodchester (see Page 134), is trihedral - three-sided - an eminently suitable plan for a Trinitarian rector. On its east face it carries a long inscription, beginning:

TO

the

Memory of

DOROTHY

the Wife of the Rev'd

THOMAS RACKETT

Rector of Spetisbury & Charlton,

whose happiness was uniformly

promoted by her during an union

of more than Fifty Years

So this was initially Thomas's tribute to his wife, whose antecedents are rehearsed - daughter of James Tattersall, Rector of Streatham and St Paul's Covent Garden (where the Racketts were married by Dorothy's brother John) and of Dorothy de Chair, James's first wife. Dorothy Rackett died in 1835 (not 1833 as the pyramid's inscription says), aged 81; Thomas outlived her by more than five years, dying in 1840, and the pyramid became his memorial, too.

Thomas Rackett was in many ways typical of the well-educated 18th-century incumbent. While the Church of England slumbered in comfortable and well-endowed indolence, Rackett was always busy - though not too often with his parochial duties. His was a privileged existence. At the age of 14 he had impressed David Garrick by reciting the actor's *Ode on Dedicating a Building,*

Wedding guests at Spetisbury in Dorset beside the three-sided pyramid to Thomas Rackett and his wife

and erecting a Statue to Shakespeare, written in 1769 for the great Shakespeare Jubilee and beginning rather lamely with

> To what blest genius of the isle
> Shall Gratitude her tribute pay,
> Decree the festive day,
> Erect the statue, and devote the pile?

Thomas was painted by George Romney in mid-declaration, wearing a red velvet coat and waistcoat, with ochre breeches. He became a life-long friend of Garrick and was executor of Mrs Garrick's will.

Rackett was wealthy, not only from the generous tithes that came with the living at Spetisbury but also with money from his own family and from Dorothy's father. The couple maintained a London house throughout their lives, from where Thomas kept up his friendships with a wide range of friends, including the artist Paul Sandby (who taught him to draw; a picture by Rackett of Spetisbury church and rectory is in the church), the actress Mrs Siddons, the doctor and naturalist William Maton (a former pupil of Rackett's and Queen Charlotte's physician), Thomas Cavallop, a pioneer of electricity and the Misses Davies, virtuosi of the glass harmonica who were favoured by CPE Bach.

Much of Rackett's time was spent in pursuing his wide interests. Botany and conchology, magnetism and chemistry, the processing of salt and the eradication of dry rot in the navy's vessels, heraldry, gas lighting, perpetual motion and music, Greek coins and Dorset barrows, speleology and dog-stealing were among the subjects in which he was interested. He published several learned papers, especially on botanical and antiquarian topics. He lived a comfortable life, both in London and Spetisbury, with Dorothy and their only surviving child, Dorothea.

Rackett's comfort was shattered by the Marquess of Lansdown's attack on his supposed absenteeism from his parish, which began with a communication to the Bishop of Bristol in late November 1828. The Bishop could not ignore the charges of neglect and wrote to Rackett 'It has been stated to me, though perhaps not altogether upon such authority as I can depend, that there is a great complaint amongst your parishioners at Charlton & Spettisbury, that you are never at home, and that your Curate lives at Blandford, that all the children attend at a large Meeting house as there is no Church School in the Parish, & that many converts are made to the Nunnery & Catholic Chapel. I shall be happy to receive a letter from you on these subjects. By your Parochial returns there was some doubt as to residence.' Rackett must have replied immediately, for ten days later the Bishop responded 'I am very happy to find that you are able to refute so satisfactorily many of the insinuations . . . Permit me to suggest the propriety of making every exertion to counteract the baleful influence of the Roman Catholic Religion in your neighbourhood and of course encouraging the children of Dissenters as much as possible to attend your church.'

The Bishop's happiness did not last long. On 29 January 1829 the Bishop wrote again: 'It is with regret that I feel myself compelled to inform you that complaints are again transmitted to me to which I must request your serious attention. It is alleged in a letter which I have recently received "That you scarcely ever reside, that there is no church school & that a large Catholic Church is now building in your parish" etc.' Rackett's immediate reply has not survived among his papers, but there is a draft of a letter to the Bishop written after the report in *The Times* of Lansdown's House of Lords speech.

He is forthright. 'I positively assert that I have resided in my rectorial house at Spettisbury every year during the last 40 years, although I will readily admit that some circumstances of a private domestic nature have at various times during that period occasioned my temporary absence beyond that allowed by Law. Such circumstances were always stated to your Lordship's predecessors and never on any occasion found to be unreasonable. My Curate who could not be placed in the Parsonage House occupied by myself has always resided a mile and a half from my Parish.' He goes on to say that while the Convent of Augustinian Nuns is enlarging its chapel, 'the number of families in S. is 108 out of which 5 or 3 of the families are connected with the Convent, and were always so. There remains then 2 families and 6 individuals who have been induced to embrace the C. religion. So much for the increase of Catholics in Spettisbury . . . I deny therefore the whole of the charge, I deny that I have been for 30 years resident in London. I deny that the number of Catholic proselytes has been owing to the Rector's abandonment of his duty and I trust that the charge of negligence and abandonment of duty cannot in any shape be proved against him.' That was the last that we hear of charges against Thomas Rackett; the Bishop wrote sharply to Lord Lansdown and the Rector was left in peace.

Even after Dorothy's death, in his old age, Thomas remained cheerful, delighting in his granddaughter and playing the piano while he was still able. On his death the inscription on the pyramid was extended - as presumably had always been intended - to hymn his virtues:

*The Rev'd
Thomas Rackett*

'. . . during nearly LX years his diligence and eminent Talents were not confined to the exercise of ordinary Parochial duties they extended themselves to the Promotion and Cultivation of the various Useful Arts which soften the asperity of human nature and of those Sciences which fill the mind with the most exalted Ideas of the Goodness of our Creator'.

It sounds a little like special pleading of the extenuating circumstances that took him away so much from those 'ordinary Parochial duties' which he plainly found dull. Most of the weddings at Spetisbury were carried out by one of the succession of curates who ministered to the parish while the Racketts pursued their interests in London - a far cry from today, when the Rector of Spetisbury also looks after St Mary's in Blandford Forum as well as the church at Charlton Marshall, and is a permanent resident in the area. No doubt the villagers waiting for the bride and groom by Thomas and Dorothy Rackett's pyramid were grateful.

FOR ALMOST 200 years the name of Mowlem was synonymous with large-scale building and civil engineering projects. As far back as 1823 signboards with 'Mowlem' on them were around the streets of London as paviours replaced the muddy surfaces with hard granite sets. Only in 2006 did the Mowlem company lose its identity, becoming a subsidiary of Carillion plc.

The story of John Mowlem, the father of the firm, began in a dilapidated cottage in the Dorset town of **Swanage** in 1788 and ended with a pyramid in the cemetery of the same town in 1868. In those 80 years Mowlem had progressed from the poor boy who with his father and three of his brothers worked in the local quarries, to be the chairman of a large company and a generous local benefactor. He worked initially at Tilly Whim quarries on the Isle of Purbeck, where limestone was hewn for work on the Napoleonic War effort. John may have been inspired by Henry Manwell, the brother of his future wife Susannah, to seek work elsewhere; Henry had already gone from Purbeck to better jobs in Portsmouth and London. John Mowlem moved first to the Isle of Wight, where his work at Norris Castle attracted the notice of the architect James Wyatt (see page 62). Wyatt recommended Mowlem to Henry Westmacott, a sculptural mason, younger brother of the more famous Sir Richard Westmacott. Henry Westmacott did much work for Wyatt, including repairs to the pyramid of the mausoleum at Cobham in Kent (see page 62).

Mowlem worked conscientiously for Westmacott and eventually, in 1815 become his London foreman. But he did not like him. Mowlem wrote, '. . . his imperious spirit could never meet me freely and manly. He always appeared above his business, except in giving a receipt for money. I would only copy him in two things, cleanliness and punctuality. Very soon after I left him he gave up his business, which he need not have done if he had been liberal enough to have given me enough to live on.' And later he noted that, 'I was his foreman for about seven years. But he was a shabby master . . . I remained with him for beggarly wages knowing that I should be better off one day.'

In 1812 John Mowlem had married Susannah Manwell at St George's, Hanover Square, and it was St George's that gave him his first independent job, of paving the roads of the parish. In 1823 he set up the firm of John Mowlem and Company to undertake the work, and gradually built up the paving business, despite the opposition of rival firms. Mowlem's capacity for hard work and his ability always to be on top of the detail of a contract meant that by 1838 his annual turnover was more than £12,000.

Contractor John Mowlem's pyramid at Swanage, Dorset

The following year he began his most important contract up to that time, the repaving of Blackfriars Bridge. For the work he used 'narrow cubes' - the specially-shaped granite setts that made his name. He knew that this innovation would put him in a strong position to outdo his rivals: 'Although this is the devil's own battle to fight, I will stick here; for if the job is completed well, all will be well afterwards . . .I will have a large share of the Metropolis', he wrote. His ambition for 'a large share' depended on an ample and constant supply of the right sort of granite. He had already been working with the quarries in Guernsey, and in November 1839 Mowlem moved to the island, leaving the London business in the hands of 'my two young men', Susannah's sister's son, George Burt, and Burt's brother-in-law Joseph Freeman. Mowlem bought 'a field, all good blue granite, about an English acre, in the NE part of the Island . . . I have an excellent prospect with a head of stone about 60 feet long and 16 feet high. I am sure of success for I remain in this bleak hill all day, where I am determined to remain . . . until I have completed the job, or at least quarried the stone.' He stayed in Guernsey, battling with seemingly endless rain, until June 1840, producing enough granite to complete the Blackfriars contract, and with it to demonstrate his company's skills to the metropolis. New contracts came quickly - for the parishes St Clement Danes and St Martin's among them. The firm diversified; among the contracts was one for Nelson's tomb in the crypt of St Paul's Cathedral.

By 1845 Mowlem was ready to retire. In January the firm officially became Mowlem, Burt and Freeman. George Burt was soon the dominant partner and it was he who developed Mowlem into one of Britain's greatest contracting companies, with Billingsgate fish market, Smithfield fruit market, Queen Victoria Street and the Imperial Institute among their jobs in George's lifetime. The front of Buckingham Palace, Admiralty Arch, docks in London and Southampton, power stations (including Battersea), the Second World War Mulberry harbours, the NatWest Tower in the City of London and the Docklands Light Railway followed down the years.

John Mowlem was not inactive in his retirement. He not only kept a close involvement with the firm but also bought property in Swanage, which he helped to develop into a thriving town. He constructed its first pier, erected a monument to 'a great naval battle fought with the Danes in Swanage Bay by Alfred the Great AD 877' on the seafront and another (now demolished) to 'Albert the Good' on Court Hill, as well as the former Mowlem Institute 'for the benefit and mutual improvement of the working classes'. George Burt continued Mowlem's benefactions to Swanage, including the erection of bits of old London buildings that his firm had removed or replaced. They included the ornate Wellington Clock Tower originally at London Bridge, and the front of Swanage Town Hall, built in the City of London as the Mercers' Hall.

Mowlem's happy retirement was not to last long. In November 1849 his wife Susannah died. He wrote in his diary: 'My poor wife departed this life, I hope and trust for a better world, on Monday morning, November 12, at ¼ 4 am. It was a sad and awful thing to witness the wife of my youth die . . . Her last words to me were, "Mowlem, carry me about the room, will you?" I said, "No, my dear, I cannot." "Why?" said she. "Because I shall hurt you." "Oh," she said, and appeared disappointed. "And is there not one of you can do anything for me?" I said, "What can we do?" She then took her handkerchief carefully and wiped her face (which was getting cold) as carefully as she ever did in her life. Her eye then appeared to lose its brightness and her breath got more and more short until she sunk into the arms of death.'

Susannah was buried in the churchyard at Kingston, five miles west of Swanage, probably because the Swanage graveyard was too full for the pyramid monument Mowlem had planned. He was a Freemason, so his choice of a pyramid was dictated by his interest in the Craft. He commissioned the Guernsey mason Henry Bisson to prepare the monument. It took him a while. Not until August the following year could Mowlem note in his diary 'This morning I find the vessel, Cobbing master, in the Bay here from Guernsey with my poor Susannah's monument in 85 packing cases, also Henry Bisson and his wife'. Subsequent entries show the interest he took in its erection: 'Commenced with the plinth today and fixed one corner. It looks beautiful.' 'At Kingston all day, fixing granite.' 'This day the top piece of my poor Susan's monument is fixed. It is perfect in my opinion, beautifully worked, and will look well after 1000 years. Paid Henry Bisson for his time in fixing the monument and expenses back to Guernsey, £10. This is liberal indeed but he would like a little more.'

Five years later the pyramid, its silvery granite firmly inscribed 'JOHN MOWLEM'S VAULT', was on the move. When a new cemetery opened at Northbrook in Swanage, John Mowlem had Susannah's remains, complete with pyramid, moved there from Kingston. It crowns the highest point of the (now-closed) cemetery. Mowlem lived another 13 years, dying on 8 March 1868, and was buried beneath the pyramid (which curiously dates his wife's death 11, not 12 November). He was 79, and the couple had no children. In many ways he had remained a rough diamond. Only after his retirement did he manage a thorough wash each morning in cold water ('I have been too busy through the whole of my life to indulge in this sort of cleanliness') and discovered hot baths only late in life. Described as 'too fond of money to gamble', he became a magistrate but found his fellows on the bench 'a set of old ladies'.

Thomas Hardy's 1876 comic novel *The Hand of Ethelberta* was written in Swanage, the town in which Mowlem was born and died, and which he had largely pulled up by its boot-straps. Hardy called it 'Knollsea', writing that it 'had recently begun to attract notice in the world. It had this year undergone visitation from a score of professional gentlemen and their wives, a minor canon, three marine painters, seven young ladies with books in their hands, and nine-and-thirty babies.' He also has a nod to Mowlem's memory; 'Everybody in the parish who was not a boatman was a quarrier, unless he were the gentleman who owned half the property and had been a quarryman'. Not bad for someone who began as a child labourer on the Isle of Purbeck.

One of the inscriptions on the Mowlem monument

*The Geo-Needle
at Exmouth
marks the World
Heritage Site of
the Jurassic Coast*

IT IS NOT often that we have a time and a place for the origins of a pyramid, but there is precision in the case of **Exmouth** - 13 December 2001, Helsinki.   UNESCO's World Heritage Committee met that day to decide whether a 95-mile stretch of coastline, from Exmouth to Studland Bay, north-east of Swanage, should be designated as a World Heritage Site. The case put to them was overwhelming. The role of the coastline in shaping how we understand the structure of the earth was vital, and remains very important. When what is now called the Jurassic Coast was nominated to UNESCO it was described as 'a crucible of earth science investigations for 300 years.' Since John Ray wrote, in 1673, of how important Lyme Bay was for the study of fossils (even though their significance was not then understood), geologists have been drawn to this part of England's coast. In succession came other scientific pioneers - James Hutton, William Smith, William Buckland, Adam Sedgwick, Roderick Murchison, Charles Lyell . . .

What did they come to see, and what convinced the sages of UNESCO to inscribe the Jurassic Coast as Great Britain's first and only natural World Heritage Site, putting it on a list that includes Australia's Great Barrier Reef, the Giant Panda reserves in Sichuan Province, China, the Galápagos Islands, Sumatra's Tropical Rainforest, Russia's Lake Baikal and the Grand Canyon?

From Orcombe Point, where the pyramid stands, around Lyme Bay, along Chesil Beach to the Isle of Portland, then past Lulworth Cove and St Aldhelm's Head and into Swanage Bay, then finally to Old Harry Rocks, the 98 miles of coastline present a journey of 185 million years through geological time. Nowhere else on earth is the story of the rocks beneath us laid out so elegantly and so accessibly. Virtually all of the Mesozoic geological age, from the Triassic, through the Jurassic to the Cretaceous, are laid out - rocks between 66 million and 251 million years old. Over the millennia the rocks have tilted, so that the oldest are the red sandstone cliffs of the Triassic period around Exmouth and Sidmouth; as you move east they become younger.

From these Mesozoic rocks come very important fossils. Fossil dinosaur footprints have been found in quarries near Swanage - the quarries in which John Mowlem was working in the earliest years of the 19th century (see page 146). Fossils of plants, animals and insects are regularly discovered in the rocks - including trees from a late Jurassic forest, around 140 million years old, in Portland and Purbeck. On the coast near Lyme Regis Mary Anning, most famous of the fossil hunters of the 19th century, discovered, with her brother Joseph, some of the earliest fossils of ichthyosaurs, and she found the first compete plesiosaur fossil. Some of her most important finds are now in the Sedgwick Museum of Earth Sciences in Cambridge. The coast also has textbook examples of raised beaches and the remains of landslides. Chesil Beach is one of the world's best and most-studied barrier beaches, and behind it is one of Europe's most important saltwater lagoons.

All this was more than enough to convince the UNESCO Committee, and the 'Dorset and East Devon Coast World Heritage Site' was officially called into being. The local councils, very proud of their new asset, looked for ways of marking their success. By September 2002 plans were well advanced, and were brought to Devon County Council for approval. The proposal, approved in full council, was for 'a site marker at Orcombe Point', and was to take the form of 'the geoneedle site marker . . . a unique representation of the World Heritage Site's varying geology.' The site they chose is ideal - on top of the red sandstone cliffs, overlooking the sea and the estuary of the Exe. Paths below take visitors on a geological adventure through time, while from the Geoneedle itself there are views to the east along the coast.

Plans must have been almost complete by the time the County Council provided their rubber stamp, for, less than a month later, on 3 October 2002, the Geoneedle pyramid was unveiled amid great celebrations by the Prince of Wales. The design of the pyramid is imaginative. It is constructed of the stones found along the Jurassic coast. The main structure is of Portland stone of three types - from the bottom, Basebed, Whitebed and Roach Red. The point of the pyramid is of stainless steel. Let into the western side is a strip of the other stones of the coast, from the west to the east, the oldest to the youngest. They are Red Sandstone, White Lias, Blue Lias, Ham Hill Stone, Forest Marble, Portland Stone, Purbeck Marble and Beer Stone; the colours vary markedly from browny-red, through off-white, blue, yellow, grey and almost black. The Geoneedle was designed by Michael Fairfax, a sculptor who studied at Newport College of Art and lives in Somerset.

A board sets the Geoneedle in its historical and geological context, but most visitors spend their time not thinking deeply about strata and fossil remains, but enjoying the distant views from the headland. As for us, we were looking south-south-west, towards Torquay, where a reminder of wartime was waiting.

*Mary Anning,
19th-century
fossil hunter
on the
Jurassic Coast*

The Home Guard memorial at Torquay

TORQUAY IS FAMOUS as being the location of *Fawlty Towers*. There are still Torquay hotels that resemble that famous establishment (we stayed in one that had no teaspoons at breakfast time) but another famous BBC comedy was in our minds. *Dad's Army* introduced some popular catchphrases to the language - 'Stupid boy', 'We're doomed' and 'Don't panic Mr Mainwaring' among them - and larger-than-life characters: Walker the spiv, the effete Sgt Wilson and the bumptious Captain Mainwaring himself. But behind the clowning and the ridiculous situations in which the Walmington-on-Sea Home Guard unit found itself, there was a real, and often tragic, story. It was to mark the determination, heroism and sacrifice of members of the Home Guard that on 11 August 2005 a granite pyramid was placed on Torquay's Corbyn Head - the first such outdoor memorial to Britain's 'volunteer army'. Its shape reflects that of the so-called 'Dragons' Teeth' or anti-tank 'pimples' that were strewn across the countryside to slow down any Nazi panzer invasion.

The impetus for the memorial came from the Turning Point Heritage Trust, which helps to preserve the wartime heritage of Britain. Its founder, Peter Foreman, a Torquay resident, said, 'The project was inspired by the sacrifice of a few, but is dedicated to all those members of the Home Guard who lost their lives on active service'. The stone was donated by Plymouth and South West Co-operative Funeral Services.

The Home Guard was largely made up of men who were either too young or too old to fight. Some of them were very young - 16 or 17 - and lied about their age to join. In all, as the pyramid records, 1206 Home Guard members lost their lives during the war. And the worst disaster, and the reason for the siting of the memorial here, was at Corbyn Head. The whole of Torbay was an intensive military training area, and consequently the target for heavy enemy bombing. More than 40 times the Luftwaffe dropped explosives in the area; 14,000 houses were destroyed and 168 people died. The Torquay Home Guard was in the front line.

On 11 August 1944 nine members of the Home Guard were on exercise at Corbyn Head. Members of the nearby Brixham Battery were there, too, as observers, and one of them, Home Guard Lieutenant Gorrell, agreed to act as Safety Officer for the exercise. There were two 4.7-inch gun emplacements on the headland, and the guns were to fire across Torbay at targets being towed by vessels about 3,000 yards away. Shortly after firing began, Gun 2 misfired, then smoke and flames burst out of the emplacement. It is not clear what happened; a Court of Enquiry could find no definite cause of the accident, though it may have been a faulty breech safety mechanism.

The results of the accident were all too clear. Lieutenant Gorrell rushed from the emplacement, calling for help. The gun floor was ablaze, and there was live ammunition around. The men were badly burned, and two were already obviously dead. Eventually the flames were quenched. Three men were killed on the site of the explosion, and three more died in Torbay Hospital shortly afterwards. Five of the dead were Home Guard members, the other was an Army Regimental Sergeant Major. There were also three serious injuries.

One man who had a very lucky escape, Gordon Rendle, was at the pyramid's unveiling ceremony in 2005. He recalled, 'I narrowly escaped with my life but I lost close friends. I had been in there but I went out to check the ammunition so I survived. I carried my friend George from the gun to the first aid post but he was dead before we left the gun.' Gordon Rendle was only 16 at the time, and his friends were also under 18. The dead men's funeral, with full military honours, was held on 15 August 1944, and Gordon was a pallbearer. Large crowds watched the flag-draped coffins carried on two gun carriages to the Heroes' Corner of Torquay Cemetery, while two lorries packed with wreaths followed.

The names of the six men who died at Corbyn Head are inscribed on the pyramid. Three other Torquay Home Guards were killed by enemy action, two at the Barton Gas Works in June 1942 and one at the Palace Hotel the following October. At the unveiling Gordon Rendle said, 'It has taken a long time to get this memorial and those of us who have been campaigning are all delighted at the outcome. It will be good to go to Corbyn Head and see a memorial to those good friends.'

ELIZABETH HOWARD IS a mystery. According to the inscription on her pyramid in the churchyard at **Berry Pomeroy**, just outside Totnes, she is 'interred in a vault beneath'. Yet according to all the sources, she is buried, with her husband, in the churchyard of Old St Pancras in London - a Midland Railway cutting destroyed the graves in 1868. The parish registers clearly give her burial, though her age is given as 38, not her real age of 33. Perhaps she was reburied in London. And what was she doing in Berry Pomeroy? Who were her family? And how did she meet her husband?

That husband was Edward Howard, third son, as the pyramid inscription says, 'of the late Henry Howard of Glossop in the County of Derby Esq.' That means that he was part of the great Howard family, the Dukes of Norfolk - his eldest brother Bernard became the 12th Duke in 1815 on the death of his cousin. What the inscription is silent about is Edward's great scientific eminence.

As a third son Edward Howard might have been expected to join the army. Edward decided otherwise. There is no evidence as to why he chose a scientific career, though several members of the extended Howard clan had scientific interests - four Dukes of Norfolk were Fellows of the Royal Society, and two other family members, Charles Howard, brother of the 5th and 6th Dukes, and Philip Howard, a member of a junior branch of the family, were serious scientists. Like many of the Catholic Howards, Edward was schooled abroad from the age of nine, at the English College at Douai, near Lille in northern France. In 1788, aged 14, he returned to England, but there seems to be no record of his continued education. He must, however, have been well taught, especially in chemistry, to which he devoted his life.

His first important scientific breakthrough was the result of an accident. He was trying to synthesise hydrochloric acid to find a supposed element known as 'murium'. What he discovered instead was mercury fulminate - a highly-explosive chemical compound. Once he had found it, he experimented with it, twice injuring himself: 'I once poured 6 drams of concentrated sulphuric acid upon 50 grains of the powder. An explosion nearly at the instant of contact was effected. I was wounded severely and most of my apparatus destroyed', he wrote. His discovery was first published in 1800, the year after he had been admitted as a Fellow of the Royal Society. He investigated the chemical composition of mercury fulminate with care, but could not come to any firm conclusion - 'The affinities I have brought into play are

Edward Howard

complicated, and the constitutions of the substances I have to deal with, not fully known.'

Nevertheless, the explosive effects of mercury fulminate were obvious, and Howard worked closely with weapons manufacturers to see if it had practical applications. The explosion was too violent for pistols and sporting guns and caused them to split. On a larger scale, trials at the Royal Military Academy in Woolwich with pieces of ordnance and with shells, mines and grenades, and in mines for rock blasting, seemed to show that its power was too great to be harnessed. Only after Howard's death was it realized that small amounts of mercury fulminate were ideal for use in detonators, which could then set off larger amounts of gunpowder.

As soon as Howard's discovery was public knowledge he was widely praised, both in Britain and abroad. On 1 December 1800 he was awarded the Copley Medal, the Royal Society's highest honour, whose other winners include Mendeleev, Faraday, Darwin, Davy, Pasteur, Sedgwick, Bohr, Planck and Hawking. The Royal Society's president was Sir Joseph Banks, who spoke in praise of Howard's work, and who was to be instrumental in taking his studies into another field.

Banks knew that European chemists were interested in researching the origins of meteorites. The current theory was that these highly-metallic rocks were produced when lightning struck the ground. An alternative idea was that they were the ejecta of volcanoes, which accounted for observations that they fell from the sky. From the 1790s, though, the idea had been gaining ground that meteorites were extraterrestrial - and probably from the moon. At the time that Banks suggested Howard took an interest in the subject, there were a few well-known specimens he could work on - from India, Italy and Bohemia, as well as one that fell on Wold Newton in East Yorkshire.

Howard analysed the components of each of the stones, showing that all of them contained nickel in higher quantities that was ever found naturally on earth; that the pyrites within the meteorites were magnetic and gave off hydrogen sulphide when tested with acid: and that the small, grey-green globules they contained were a new mineral species. Although Howard was cautious about committing himself immediately, it was clear from his work that meteorites were indeed not from Earth - and later scientists, basing their work on Howard's pioneering efforts, have proved that to be true. In his honour special types of meteorites, originating from the surface of the asteroid called 4 Vesta, have been named Howardites.

It seems a long way from research into extraterrestrial objects to ways of better refining sugar, but that was where Howard's interest turned next. It is possible that the interest came through his wife Elizabeth's family. Edward married Elizabeth Maycock at St Leonard's Church in Shoreditch on 12 July 1804 - the marriage ceremony seems to have been very quiet, and witnessed not by family members but by strangers. The east end of London was at that time a centre of sugar production and Edward may have been living in the parish and already engaged in his research when he met Elizabeth.

In the early 19th century sugar production had hardly changed for generations. Raw sugar, in the form of barrels that contained a sticky brown mass containing many unusable impurities, came to London from the West Indies. The sugar was dissolved in hot water to clear out the rubbish, then clarified with either lime and egg-white or with fresh bulls' blood, known as 'spice'. When the

The pyramid to Elizabeth Howard at Berry Pomeroy, Devon

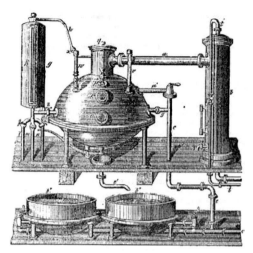

Edward Howard's sugar refining equipment

liquid was clear it was boiled in open pans over fires until the sugar crystallised. It was highly inefficient, as well as being dangerous - sugar houses often burned down, and insurance premiums were ruinous.

When Howard examined the process he saw that the first thing to do was to remove the impurities from the raw sugar before refining began. So he developed a new process that leached the pure sugar syrup, in a saturated solution, from all the unwanted extras. He then gave it a final clarification by adding, not blood, but aluminium hydroxide - which came to be known in the trade as 'Howard's Finings'. He invented a system of multiple filter units in a configuration that became a standard for the chemical industry in general. He then replaced the open fires and pans with a steam-heated boiler fitted with a vacuum pump. The sugar was boiled at lower temperatures under reduced pressure; temperature and pressure were constantly gauged. Howard also invented a way of taking samples from the vessel without opening it, using a piston and tube. His designs were made on a large scale in 1813, in collaboration with Birmingham engineers Watt and Boulton. They were an immediate success, revolutionising the industry.

With profit margins at least 20 per cent higher with the new equipment, Howard could name his price for his technology. Sir Joseph Banks write to a correspondent, 'Our friend Edward Howard has made a most valuable improvement in the art of refining sugar, and has at last prevailed upon a sugar boiler to erect works for performing the process, which answers so extremely well, that £40,000 has been offered for the patent and refused.' Instead of selling outright, Howard licensed his development, at the rate of half-a-crown (12½ pence) for every hundredweight of refined sugar that was produced. It was a shrewd move. The annual income it produced rose from £23,000 in the first year to £60,000 in 1816.

That was the year Edward Howard died, aged just 42. The source of his great income also killed him. He was said to have had an apoplexy or brain hemorrhage after spending many hours in the steam-heated drying room of a sugar refinery. Six years earlier, Elizabeth had died in Totnes. The Howards were probably staying at Berry Pomeroy Castle ('Britain's most haunted castle') for the good of Elizabeth's health. Their host was Edward Seymour, Duke of Somerset, a fellow scientist and Fellow of the Royal Society. The inscription on Elizabeth's pyramid says 'She supported with patience the suffering of a lingering and pulmonary Consumption and died at Totnes with pious resignation on the 4th of December 1810 in her 33rd Year.' When she died there were three infant children - Edward Giles, who was then four, three-year old Elizabeth and two-year-old Julia. What arrangements Edward Howard, while he was still alive, made for his children is not known, but his will, made in 1816, leaves them in the guardianship of his brother Bernard (the future 12th Duke of Norfolk) and his nephew Henry Charles Howard. The family name and the wealth of their father stood them in good stead. Both the girls married aristocrats, and Edward Giles, who died at the age of 35, was an army captain. His son Edward Henry was in the Life Guards, but later joined the Catholic priesthood, finishing as His Eminence Cardinal Howard, Bishop of Frascati.

How did Elizabeth fit into this high-powered family? Was the marriage not approved of by the Howards - hence the quiet wedding? Her family is not mentioned in Edward's will, and she died intestate. As the marriage took place in a Church of England building and she was buried in an Anglican churchyard - whether at Berry Pomeroy or at St Pancras - she was presumably not a Catholic. Despite his Douai schooling, perhaps Edward was indifferent to his Catholicism (what would his eminent Cardinal grandson have thought?); was he indifferent, too, to the lady herself? Are the words on her pyramid, that it was 'erected . . . to perpetuate the memory and record the conjugal and maternal Piety of his sincerely beloved wife' just Edward going through the motions of grief? We cannot know - nowhere in his writings does he give us any glimpse of his true feelings. The opposite may be true - perhaps the quiet, Anglican marriage was forced on him because his family did not approve of Elizabeth's class or religion, but he loved her deeply. The end of the inscription reads, 'Comfort ye my children. Her warfare is accomplished. MAY SHE REST IN PEACE.' Elizabeth Howard was, it seems, not involved with her husband's scientific career; only her pyramid remains as her memorial.

ODD PLACE NAMES are not unusual in Cornwall - think of Come-to-Good, Playing Place and Indian Queens, for example. For a short time in the 17th century there was another, Penny-come-quick. The place itself is still there, but now we know it as the more-prosaic **Falmouth**. And even Penny-come-quick (which in Cornish is nothing to do with speculation but means 'the head of a narrow valley') was not its first name; that was Smithwick. The transformation of Smithwick to Falmouth is closely bound up with the story of the Killigrew family of Arwenack Manor, whose last family member built a fine granite pyramid that now stands by the harbour and near the National Maritime Museum.

The Killigrews were a lawless lot. In the 15th century Thomas Killigrew was attacking French ships. In the following century Queen Elizabeth made John Killigrew governor of the newly-built Pendennis Castle but he still carried on the piracy - both he and his son John were imprisoned for looting a Spanish ship. Still, the younger John was knighted by the Queen and even became Chairman of the Commissioners for Piracy in Cornwall. That put him in an excellent position when his mother Elizabeth and his wife Mary were also implicated in piracy. Elizabeth apparently organised the ransacking of a stricken Spanish ship in 1582, while Mary helped dispose of the stolen goods. Lady Mary was charged before Sir John's court; while everyone else who took part in the raid was hanged, she was acquitted.

The third John Killigrew was a gambler and a conman. Twice he seems to have 'sold' Pendennis Castle, once to the Spanish. He ended up in prison. Fortunately, the family genes seem to have been more benign with his successor, again called John. He worked hard for Cornwall, even though his wife Jane was implicated in plundering a Dutch ship and carried on an affair with a soldier in Pendennis Castle; much of John's inheritance went on his long divorce. When Sir Walter Ralegh, staying at Arwenack, suggested that the mouth of the River Fal and the inland estuary called the Carrick Roads were the ideal place for a new port, Sir John (the fourth of the name) set about transforming Smithwick into Penny-come-Quick. In 1613 it had only ten houses, but he put forward a plan to build another 150 over the next 30 years. Progress was made; in 1652 it replaced Penryn as a main port - one of the biggest in England - despite the fact that Sir John's successor, Sir Peter Killigrew, was a Royalist during the

The peripatetic
Killigrew pyramid
at Falmouth

Commonwealth. He burned down the family home of Arwenack Manor rather than letting it fall into Parliamentary hands, and helped defend Pendennis for more than five months.

The restored King Charles II rewarded Sir Peter with a new charter, changing the port's name to Falmouth and giving permission to build new quays. Sir Peter also rebuilt Arwenack Manor, built Falmouth church (with its Royalist dedication to King Charles the Martyr), and may have laid out the area called The Grove, perhaps as a visual pun on his name - 'kelli' is Cornish for a grove. The Grove was an ambitious piece of landscaping, with three double avenues of elm trees, each 1200 feet long radiating out above the harbour. When the Killigrews were no longer at Arwenack one of the avenues was used in the 18th century as a rope walk, where Mr Deeble twisted hemp strands into ropes for the ships below.

Sir Peter Killgrew had two sons and two daughters. His younger son, Peter, was born in August 1680 - and died in November. The elder son, George Killigrew, had no male heirs, and he seems to have reverted to the ancient Killigrew habits - questionable companions and lots of drink. He was killed in a tavern brawl in Penryn in 1687, after taking exception to remarks by a fellow-drinker about hiss piratical great-grandmother. Sir Peter's elder daughter, Frances, only had girls. It was left to the other daughter, Ann, to try to carry on the family line. She married a Staffordshire man, Martin Lister, who was serving at Pendennis Castle. Sir Peter entailed the estate to Martin, who took the additional name of Killigrew.

It was a forlorn hope. Ann died before she had children so Martin was the last of the Killigrews. He tried to preserve the family's sway over Falmouth's affairs - in 1714 he bought a Congregational chapel and presented it as a Town Hall. But the influence was waning; there were constant arguments between Killigrew and an ungrateful corporation about the income he claimed from the quays built by his wife's ancestors and from the town market.

In the early 1730s, several years after Ann had died, Martin was planning a pyramid in The Grove. His reason for doing so is not known; he was particularly insistent that it was not a personal memorial; he wrote to his steward, 'I have already Charged you in the most Special manner . . . that there be no inscription about the pyramid or the whole Grove. No, not so much as the Date of the Year: Hoping that it may remain a beautiful embellishment to the Harbour, Long, Long after my desiring to be Forgott as if I had never been.' He also wrote to his builder, John Ragland, 'Without having any foolish Vanity Exposed, I may tell you that in having this projection Carried into Execution as it ought and I hope will be, I pretend to Insist that from the sheltered position and Durableness of the stone (Manual Violence Excepted) the thing may stand a beauty to the harbour without Limitation of Time and You and Your posterity have the honour of the Architecture'.

It is a substantial structure, 40 feet high and its base 14 feet square. Constructed of silvery granite from Constantine, it cost £455 1s 11½d and may originally have been intended to be painted. Despite its substance, though, it has not been still. In 1836 houses were built to form Grove Place, and the pyramid was in the way; it was moved to the top of the Rope Walk - one of the former Grove avenues. It stayed there until 1871, when it was threatened by the construction of a railway line. Its second move was to its present site, a green space near the harbour where there was formerly a semaphore station. Two bottles were hidden inside when it was rebuilt - an official one, containing a history of the pyramid, placed by the Resident Agent, the Manor Bailiff and the builder; and an unofficial one, with a list of the workmen's names and some coins.

Despite Martin Lister Killigrew's desire to be forgotten, his pyramid has ensured that, even without an inscription, his name has been remembered. And there was another legacy from him, too - a disputed will that, like the case of Jarndyce and Jarndyce in Dickens' *Bleak House*, dragged on for years. It was still being fought over while the Victorian workmen were hiding their sur-reptitious bottle. The money available to the heirs had more than halved over a century and a half. The case was eventually settled in 1886, 143 years after Killigrew's death, when £220 was dis-tributed among the 14 recognised heirs, including an Australian captain, who must have been delighted to receive all of £14 7s 9d.

A REMOTE CORNISH beach seems an unlikely place for industrial espionage and big-company rivalry. **Porthcurno**, at the foot of Cornwall, a couple of miles southeast of Land's End, is a magical place, where the sunlight shimmers from the blue sea, and the rocks tumble to sandy beaches. Yet its very tranquility and remoteness, sticking far out into the Atlantic, made it an ideal spot for the fledgling Victorian telecommunications industry. Its only fame before the 19th century was from the nearby Logan Rock, a huge boulder of granite that, as William Mason wrote in his tedious poem *Caractacus*,

> . . . poised by magic, rests its central weight
> On yonder pointed rock: firm as it seems,
> Such is the strange and virtuous property,
> It moves obsequious to the gentlest touch . . .

The local geologist Dr William Borlase stated firmly 'it is morally impossible that any lever, or indeed force, however applied in a mechanical way, can remove it from its present situation'. This was a challenge that Lt Hugh Goldsmith (nephew of the poet Oliver Goldsmith) and his fellow sailors on *HMS Nimble* couldn't let pass. In April 1824, with ropes and crowbars, they strained to dislodge the rock - and finally tumbled it into a gully. Local out-rage at the loss of tourist revenue forced them to re-instate it; it was back, balancing (though not like before, grumbled the locals), on 2 November. The restoration took 13 capstans, sever-al fathoms of chain and more than 60 men, and cost £130 8s 6d.

After that, Porthcurno slumbered again for almost 50 years, until, almost by accident, it became what today would be called a 'communications hub'. Telegraphing was the wonder of the age, and in 1869 John Pender founded a company to cash in by laying a submarine cable from England as part of a chain that linked to India. His first idea was to have the British end at Falmouth - his company was called the Falmouth, Gibraltar and Malta Telegraph Company - but a change was made to Porthcurno, almost at the last minute. The gently-shelving, sandy beach was the ideal place to bring the cable ashore. Pender's cable was laid to Carcavellos in Portugal, and the first message was transmitted from a hut near the beach on 8 June 1870. A second cable joined Porthcurno to Vigo in Spain three years later, and another, less ambitious, to the Isles of Scilly in 1878. Despite its international links, though, Porthcurno remained an isolated place; messages that sped along the wire were transcribed as telegrams at Porthcurno, then taken by horse and cart to Penzance.

The Logan Stone near Porthcurno

In 1880 came the development that had, indirectly, brought us to Porthcurno. A new cable was laid to Brest - for the first time giving Britain a transatlantic link, along the cable from France to Cape Breton in Nova Scotia, and then on to Cape Cod. The cable came ashore not on the gentle beach at Porthcurno, but straight from the sea up a sheer cliff face, into which a deep groove had to be cut to carry it. The cable ended in a small hut on the cliff top - on the site now occupied by a brilliant white pyramid. The hut - and the cable - were owned by La Compagnie Française du Télégraphe de Paris à New York. It soon came to be known after the initials of one of its directors, M Pouyer-Quertier, as the PQ Company. This was convenient; the company's neighbours (now merged into the Eastern Telegraph Company) below on the beach, were telegraphically known as PK.

Communications to Penzance improved with the provision of telegraph lines from the town to Porthcurno - though they were vulnerable. A huge blizzard in 1891 brought down the wires and the poles. Staff volunteered to walk with the telegrams. They sent a telegram back to Porthcurno saying they had arrived; because of the snow it had to be sent by a different route - and reached Porthcurno via Malta, New York and Brest.

In 1918 another cable was laid to the PQ hut at the top of the cliff. But by this time new wonders were around. In January 1901 Marconi sent a wireless message from the Isle of Wight to the Lizard. Within a year he had wirelessly communicated across the Atlantic. This, understandably, worried the telegraphers. They set up a covert espionage system to listen in to Marconi's experiments. Yet they still continued to lay cables from Porthcurno - to Gibraltar, to Madeira, to the Azores. By now the cliff-top cable hut and the cable terminals on the beach were all in the ownership of the Eastern Telegraph Company. Their spying on the Marconi Company showed them that competition would not work, so in 1928 the two merged to form Imperial and International Communications Limited - now Cable and Wireless.

The cliff-top cables had already, in 1919, been diverted on to the beach. The hut became a holiday cottage, while in the bay below the new company expanded its operations, with extra accommodation for the growing number of workers and facilities that included a theatre. During the Second World War local tin miners were drafted in to dig tunnels in the cliffs to protect the equipment and its operators from enemy action. The tunnels now hold the fascinating Porthcurno Museum of Submarine Telegraphy.

After the war much of the coastline was given to the National Trust - and that included the now-dilapidated hut. To improve the look of the area the Trust demolished the hut in the early 1960s - an action that had unintended consequences. Local boatmen had used the old building as a navigation mark, and they were vocal in their complaints. So the National Trust built an alternative - the small white pyramid that is easily visible from the sea (like the white navigation pyramids at Holy Island (see page 182), Porthgain (see page 221) and The Swellies (see page 225). It stands in exactly the same place as the hut it replaced. To keep the history of the spot alive, the Trust attached a plaque to the pyramid, which reads:

THE NATIONAL TRUST
ON THIS SPOT STOOD THE WOODEN HUT HOUSING THE END OF THE SUBMARINE TELEGRAPH CABLE LAID FROM BREST IN 1880 BY C.S. FARADAY, FOR LA COMPAGNIE FRANCAISE DU TELEGRAPHE DE PARIS A NEW YORK.

Porthcurno's cable pyramid (also depicted on the cover)

THE CABLE LINKED ENGLAND WITH THE AMERICAN CONTINENT VIA THE COMPANY'S TRANSATLANTIC CABLE FROM BREST LAID THE PREVIOUS YEAR. IN 1919 THE CABLE END WAS MOVED TO THE EASTERN TELEGRAPH'S HUT LOWER DOWN THE CLIFF NEAR PORTHCURNO, WHERE IT REMAINED IN OPERATION UNTIL 1962. THE EASTERN TELEGRAPH COMPANY FORMED IN 1870 PLAYED A KEY PART IN COMMUNICATIONS WITH INDIA. IT OPERATED THE CABLE LAID BY BRUNEL'S STEAMSHIP THE GREAT EASTERN FROM BOMBAY TO SUEZ, AND THENCE VIA MALTA TO JOIN WITH THE FALMOUTH, GIBRALTAR AND MALTA TELEGRAPH COMPANY'S CABLE TO PORTHCURNO. THIS PLAQUE WAS GIVEN BY JO GUY AND HER BROTHER AND SISTER.

IT IS 28 miles from Land's End to the nearest point of the **Isles of Scilly** ('and that is quite near enough' say the Scillonians) for our next pyramid. In 1834 those miles were crossed by a man who was to transform the islands from places of poverty to comparative wealth with methods that were a mixture of the paternal and the paternalistic. He was the new Lord Proprietor of the Isles of Scilly, Augustus Smith.

Scilly was in a bad state. In 1818 there had been famine on the off islands (St Mary's is the main island - all the others are off islands). The absentee landlord, the Duke of Leeds, had done little for his tenants. When the Duke relinquished his tenancy of the Islands they reverted to their owner, the Duchy of Cornwall, and it was from the Duchy that Augustus Smith took a 99-year lease (for £20,000) for the whole archipelago. His friends considered it an eccentric move - he was a Hertfordshire landowner, without knowledge of the sea-faring ways of the islanders. Yet in many ways he was the ideal man for the post of Lord Proprietor.

He had already shown in his dealings with the authorities around his home at Ashlyns Hall near Berkhamsted in Hertfordshire that he was a firm liberal, who would stand no nonsense. He had definite ideas on education (he was an Harrovian himself) and on farming. He had dealt with tenantry problems on his property in Ireland, and was unafraid of being unpopular. So when he came to Scilly he threw himself into island life with gusto - though not always with tact. As local author J G Uren wrote in *Scilly and the Scillonians* of 1907, 'To say that Mr Smith was received with open arms would be to do violence with the truth. The people had been left too long to their own devices . . . to take kindly to a new master who, as they soon discovered, was determined to play the part of the proverbial new broom.'

Mixing his metaphors, Uren reports that 'Mr Smith soon found that the pruning hook would have to be applied with no unsparing hand . . . The first thing to be done was to weed out the surplus population, which had become congested through the stay-at-home proclivities of the younger generation. They wanted more elbow room.' Smith realised that the islands could only support a certain number of people, and there had to be some way of thinning out the 'stay-at-home' children. So he sent the boys off to sea and packed the girls off to the mainland to work in shops or as housemaids. This made him some enemies, but eventually the islanders began to see that his reforms were good for Scilly. He encouraged the boatmen, collaborating with Trinity House to ensure that there was work for them piloting ships past the treacherous Western Rocks. He paid for the construction of

Augustus Smith, 'Emperor' of Scilly

a new pier on St Mary's. He encouraged the farmers to build up their farms and rebuild the houses - though he put a strict ban on building a second house on any farm for a younger generation, a policy that still restricts Scillonians. He built or restored churches on the islands, and meted out justice as the local magistrate.

In his education policy Smith was particularly enlightened. He decided that every child on the islands would be educated, and he ensured that there were schools to receive them. To help pay for this (the first compulsory education in Britain) he levied the parents one penny each week; they were charged two pence if the children didn't show up. Scholars were taught sums, English and a foreign language. The boys were also taught navigation and carpentry, and the girls, crafts and needlework - useful skills if they were to be sent off the islands.

Augustus decided that he would live not on St Mary's, where the bulk of the islands' population was based, but on neighbouring **Tresco**. He built a comfortable, if rambling, house beside the ruins of the former Benedictine Priory of St Nicholas, calling his new home Tresco Abbey. Around it he laid out a very special garden, still maintained by his successors. With many sub-tropical and exotic plants that cannot be grown elsewhere in the British Isles, and a 'Valhalla' of figureheads from ships wrecked off Scilly, it is one the world's great gardens.

In 1847 Smith hosted Queen Victoria and Prince Albert (only, it must be said, because the Royal Yacht *Victoria and Albert* was becalmed in fog *en route* to Balmoral) when they came ashore at St Mary's. It was an uncomfortable occasion. Victoria's seasickness did not make her very communicative, though she made pleasant references to her lack of height when she visited Star Castle above the harbour - she needed a chair to be able to see over the walls. Albert was, apparently, thunderous. Not only had his voyage been interrupted, but he had to deal with Mr Smith. He knew of Smith because Albert was Lord Warden of the Duchy of Cornwall - and the Duchy was currently in dispute about a new, modern lease that would have seen Smith with a more secure future. The Prince also disapproved of Smith's progressive ideas, which he thought smacked of advanced liberalism. So, combined with a near accident when the Queen and Prince were being driven around, the visit was not an unclouded success.

The remains of St Nicholas Priory amid the luxurious growth in the gardens at Tresco Abbey

'Emperor' Smith, as he was frequently known (though probably not to his face), fought hard for Scilly against the royal and governmental authorities who were either indifferent or downright obstructive. He was tough. As Mr Uren wrote, 'Mr Smith was to Scilly what the Czar is to Russia - he was an autocrat. It is true, the iron hand was hidden under a silken glove, but, nevertheless, there was the hand, and it knew how to strike when the occasion demanded. Not that Mr Smith was by any means a tyrant. On the contrary, all his dealings with the tenantry were conceived in a most liberal spirit, and he was respected and beloved by every man on the Islands.' It may have been, of course, that only those who agreed with him were allowed to stay on the islands. Opposition, said Uren, 'spelt ostracism and deportation; the man or woman became a pariah; no one dared shelter them or to give them a meal's meat, and thus a decree of banishment was just as effectual as the ukase of the Czar sentencing some unhappy Pole or Finn to the Steppes of Siberia.'

There is no doubt that Augustus Smith was, on balance, good for the Isles of Scilly, but his death on 31 July 1872 must have been a relief for some of his less amenable 'subjects'. It took place not in Scilly but in Plymouth - ironically at the Duke of Cornwall

'Emperor' Smith of the Isles of Scilly is commemorated with this rough pyramid on Tresco

Hotel. Oddly, he decided to be buried off the islands, too, at St Buryan in Cornwall, and at 6.00am. It seems he was trying to avoid a big funeral - but it happened anyway, with boats swarming from Scilly for the service.

His rather modest tomb is by the tower of St Buryan church. There is a memorial to him in the Old Town churchyard on St Mary's, but the best is a cyclopean pyramid on a high point of Tresco, on the fringes of his famous garden. It is beautifully sited;

the view over the harbour at New Grimsby on Tresco and of the neighbouring island of Bryher is almost Caribbean. For boats out at sea it provides an excellent navigational marker. It is said that Smith sketched a design himself, a few days before his death. As a prominent Freemason (he was Grand Master of the Cornish Freemasons when he died) he may have been influenced by the Brotherhood's supposed Egyptian origins. The simple marble plaque recording his 39 years as 'Lord Proprietor of these Islands' has been joined over the years by others for his successors - his nephew Captain Thomas Algernon Dorrien-Smith, who developed Scilly's flower industry, Thomas's son Arthur and grandson Thomas. Augustus Smith had no legitimate children, though there were at least two illegitimate children with his mistress Mary Pender, who were remembered generously in his will.

We visited Old Town Churchyard on **St Mary's**, the main island of Scilly, looking for the grave of the actress Mrs Cargill, who was drowned off the Gilstone, to the west of the main islands, in 1784 and has links with the pyramid in Duddingston near Edinburgh (see page 237). We could find no trace of her, though a new plaque to her memory, and all who perished in the wreck of the *Nancy*, was unveiled in 2008. We did, though, stumble on another pyramid - a tiny one, no more than two feet high. It has inscriptions on three faces - the earliest of 1888 and the latest 1952.

The three inscriptions commemorate a brother and two sisters, all members of the Edwards family, long-established in Scilly but originally from Dorset. Many of them were shipwrights, and ships seem to have been in the blood of the first of the siblings to be commemorated - 'John Edwards who died at Constantinople Sept 21st 1888 Aged 27 years.' The census of 1881 shows him, at the age of 20, living away from the family farm on St Mary's, in lodgings at Phillack near Hayle in Cornwall. In Hayle was the great engineering firm of Harvey and Company, which began as copper smelters but branched into shipbuilding. We do not know what John was doing in Constantinople in 1888 or how he met his death; but he became a fitter of ship's engines and was probably working there.

The pyramid may have been put up immediately after his death - or it may have been placed there later by John Edwards senior to commemorate both his son and his second daughter, Ethel. She is commemorated on the pyramid as 'Ethel Harriet the beloved wife of G Gilbert Uren, who died at Shanghai August 8th 1889. Aged 25 years.' So John Edwards senior (who lived until 1907) had lost both a son and a daughter, both in their twenties, within a year of each other - and his wife Clara had already died, in 1874.

Ethel Edwards was married in 1888 to George Gilbert Uren. The Uren family was from Cornwall - Gilbert's father was John G Uren, postmaster of Penzance and author of *Scilly and the Scillonians* (see page 161). Gilbert Uren and Ethel must have travelled to Shanghai soon after their marriage. We do not know why, or anything about Gilbert's work; there had been British traders in the Chinese city from the 1840s, and many of them lived in a separate enclave called the International Settlement. Collectively they were known as the Shanghighlanders. Were the Urens part of this group? Ethel had a son late in 1888 - he was named John G Uren after his grandfather. Within a year she was dead. Gilbert Uren outlived her by more than 60 years; he died, in Bournemouth, in 1954. Young John G eventually moved to

The small pyramid to three members of the Edwards family in Old Town Churchyard, St Mary's Isles of Scilly

Canada, where he changed the family name from Uren to Wren. He married Blanche Banfield, a member of another prominent Scilly family. After working in Chicago, they moved to Florida, where John died in 1975.

The third of the Edwards siblings commemorated by the pyramid is, according to the inscription, 'CMJ Ridyard. Died Feb. 10th 1952. Aged 98. Abide with me'. Clara M Jordan Edwards married William Robert Ridyard in October 1887. The Ridyards came from Birkenhead. William's father, Robert, was the manager of a salvage company and a diver, who worked for the famous diving company Siebe and Gorman, inventors of specialised diving equipment. Robert Ridyard was well-known in the profession for his work on the wreck of the *Hamilla Mitchell* in 1869; the ship sank at the mouth of the Yang-Tse-Kiang on its way to Shanghai with £50,000 and 100 chests of Mexican gold dollars aboard. Ridyard and his partner Penk brought up the money from 160 feet down - at the limits of current diving techniques. It is said that they were attacked by Chinese pirates as they undertook the salvage operation.

William Ridyard did not follow his father into the risky business of diving, but was, like John Edwards, an engine fitter; he may have met Clara though her brother. William died in 1897, leaving Clara with three young children. She survived another 55 years. The pyramid is the only memorial to a Ridyard in Old Town churchyard - but we know that there was, in fact, another Ridyard buried there. He was William Ridyard, named after his father. Like his father, he died in 1897. He was less than a year old.

'KNILLIAN' IS NOT an adjective that springs readily to the lips. The *Oxford English Dictionary* is ignorant of it. Yet every five years it in **St Ives** it causes great excitement.

On St James's Day, 25 July, in years ending in one and in six, the Cornish townsfolk climb from the seashore to the top of Vorvas Hill, gather round a pyramid, and watch ten white-dressed girls dance and sing to the accompaniment of a fiddle. They have done this since 1801 - even in the darkest days of two World Wars. For their efforts the girls receive 50 pence each and the fiddler twice as much. This spectacle is the Knillian Games, as much anticipated in St Ives as are the Olympics in other places. And the man who set it all in place more than two centuries ago was John Knill, who built the pyramid as his mausoleum, but did not, eventually, rest there.

'Johannes Knill', as the pyramid's inscription calls him, was a Cornishman, born at Callington on the River Tamar on New Year's Day 1733. After being an articled clerk to a Penzance solicitor and working for a London attorney, he began a career as a collector of customs at St Ives. His advancement there was through the influence of the 1st Earl of Buckinghamshire; in his turn, Knill might have influenced the 2nd Earl. Knill's pyramid at St Ives is dated 1782, eleven years before the Earl's pyramid at Blickling Hall in Norfolk (see page 53). Knill collected customs at St Ives for more than 20 years. His expertise was widely acknowledged, and part of his life was spent advising and working in Jamaica, where he seems to have made a lot of his money. He was an eminently respectable man - probably. There were stories that, despite his official position, he was not above joining his fellow townsmen in looting from wrecks and in smuggling contraband; it is even rumoured that the pyramid was built as a daymark for the smugglers.

The five-yearly Knillian celebrations take place around 'The Steeple', John Knill's three-sided pyramid on the hill above St Ives in Cornwall

He became a barrister at Grays Inn and a magistrate and was elected Mayor of St Ives in 1767. He eventually came to spend more time at Grays Inn than in St Ives; he apparently finished a short daily pub crawl at Dolly's Chop House in Queen's Head Passage off Paternoster Row near St Paul's Cathedral, a favourite haunt, too, of literary figures including Fielding and Smollett. He refused all invitations to dine elsewhere. His social circle was wide, and included both John Wesley and the engineer John Smeaton, as well as the architect John Wood junior, designer of Bath's Royal Crescent, who like his father was probably a Freemason (see page 141). Knill certainly was - he founded the Ship Lodge in St Ives on 16 July 1765, and was its first Worshipful Master. John Wood designed the pyramid for Knill. Built of fine silvery granite that hardly weathers and that sparkles in the light reflected from the sea, it is three-sided and 50 feet high. It was put up in 1782. Inside, with access from the now-blocked door, is a small stone room containing an empty granite sarcophagus.

Why did John Knill build such a monument? First, of course, as his mausoleum, because, he said, he 'abhorred the practice of burial within the body of the Church'. And in his will a passage that suggests that there had been some mutterings about his eccentricities gives his other justifications: 'I think it informatory here to give some reason for having built the aforesaid Mausoleum, which doubtless will appear to Mankind in general as an unpardonably vainglorious act in an ordinary individual. I am afraid I cannot repel this charge but it may perhaps mitigate my offence if I possibly acknowledge my motives; if not, I kiss the Rod and pray my Survivors to forgive me . . . Be it known then that during a residence of upwards of twenty years at Saint Ives where I was Collector of the Customs and served all Offices within the Borough from Constable to Mayor, it was my unremitting endeavour to render all possible service to the Town in general and to every individual inhabitant . . . It is natural to love those whom you have had opportunity of serving and I profess I have a real affection for Saint Ives and its inhabitants in whose memory I have an ardent desire to continue a little longer perhaps than the usual time those do of whom there is no ostensible memorial, and my vanity prompted me to erect a Mausoleum.'

For many people a 'vainglorious' pyramid would probably have been enough, especially when it is carved with one's coat of arms, painted in full colour, and motto, 'Nil Desperandum' - 'Do not despair' - as well as the text 'RESURGAM' - 'I shall rise again'. But Knill wanted to do more for his fellows. His will decreed that his body 'should be sent to the Anatomical Lecturer' at the Hunterian Museum in Windmill Street for public dissection. Only his bones were to be buried; the burial was to be at St Andrew Holborn if he died within 30 miles of London - as he did.

It is, though, the Knillian Games that keep his memory fresh. The procession from St Ives to Vorvas Hill includes, as well as the white-clad girls (who are not to be older than 10 and the daughters of sailors, miners or tinners) and the fiddler, a number of others. The list is specified in Knill's deed of 29 May 1797, which sets up the event. They include the Trustees of the fund that pays for it - the Mayor, the Vicar and the local Customs Officer, each of whom is allowed two guests and for whom £10 is provided for a dinner afterwards at the George and Dragon Inn. Then there are two widows, whose job is to 'certify to the Trustees that the ceremonies have been duly performed'.

When they all reach Knill's pyramid - known locally as 'The Steeple' - they are met by a large crowd. At noon the girls join hands to dance around the monument to the sound of the fiddle. Knill specified 15 minutes of dancing (the widows and the Trustees usually join in), then everyone has to sing 'All People that on Earth do Dwell' and that traditional Cornish song 'And Shall Trelawney die?'. The Vicar gives the blessing and the procession sets off back down the hill. Later Knill's doles are paid out - the fees to the girls and the fiddler, £2 to both the widows - and the Trustees and guests enjoy their dinner.

The first Knillian took place in 1801, when John Knill was still alive. He was there, too, for the second five years later, and almost made a third, in 1811. He died, at Grays Inn, on 29 March that year, less than four months before his eccentric institution gathered in his favourite place once again.

THE STOCKDALE PYRAMID in **Tiverton** Cemetery has seen better days. Its style is like that of the Irish pyramids in Naas (see page 343) and Kinnitty (see page 351), with a large iron door (now firmly shut) that gave access to the burial chamber inside. The Tiverton example is not as tall as the Irish ones, nor so well constructed - many of the stone blocks have slipped and the whole structure is in a precarious state. More importantly, the main inscription is missing, leaving us with little information about its purpose.

The remaining plaque dedicates the pyramid to Henrietta, wife of George Edward Parish. Much of Henrietta's life was spent in London; George worked for the War Office and their children were born in the capital. By 1881, though, George was dead and Henrietta was living in Exeter on 'income derived from dividends'. She died in 1891, aged, as the inscription tells us, 73. Perhaps more importantly, though, we also learn from it that she was 'fourth daughter of the late F.W.L. Stockdale.'

The Stockdale family had a long history as civil servants in the East India Company. Henrietta's father, whose forenames were Frederick Wilton Litchfield, was Assistant to the Military Secretary of the Company. It was probably in the course of this work that George Parish came into his circle and married Henrietta. Ill-heath forced Frederick Stockdale, who was born in London in 1786, into early retirement. He used his generous pension to develop his antiquarian and artistic interests. His talents were good enough for him to have exhibited paintings at the Royal Academy. His interests turned first to the south-east; his first published work was *Etchings from original drawings of antiquities in the county of Kent* in 1810, which was followed seven years later by *A concise and topographical sketch of Hastings, Winchelsea and Rye*.

From the 1820s, though, he turned his attention to the West Country; he seems to have had south-west connections, though what they are is unclear. He published *Excursions in the county of Cornwall* in 1824, and *The Cornish Tourist* in 1834. Devon came into the picture in 1840, when he began researching a history of the county, but despite amassing a great deal of information (now in the Devon and Exeter Institute) he never published it. In the 1850s Frederick and his wife Harriet were living at 'Montrose' in Higher Union Street, Torquay, the household of his son William Colebrook Stockdale.

It was William Stockdale who built the pyramid in the Tiverton cemetery as a final resting place for himself and for the family - it is an irony of time that only Henrietta's name remains. William Stockdale was born in the village of Colebrook near Tiverton -

The Stockdale pyramid at Tiverton, Devon

hence his middle name - and he, too, was an artist, as was his elder brother Frederick; both are listed as 'landscape painter' in the 1851 census, and William as a 'British painter in watercolours ' in 1861. William's greatest artistic achievement, though, was his advice on the layout of the great landscape garden of Monserrate at Sintra in Portugal for textile magnate Francis Cook, later a Baronet and Visconde de Monserrate. The landscape was originally laid out by Gerard de Visme, whose own pyramid is in Wimbledon (see page 77), and was then adapted by William Beckford before falling into oblivion. Cook brought in Stockdale to advise on picturesque vistas and on the structure of the revived garden. He was responsible, with botanist William Nevill and gardener James Burt, for features like the Fern Valley, the Mexican Valley and the Perfumed Path in the Sintra garden.

William Stockdale married a Tiverton woman, Sophia Wills. Her father was a local wine merchant and mayor of the town. In 1901 William and Sophia were living not in Devon but at Francis Cook's home, Doughty House, on Richmond Hill. It is likely, though, that William had commissioned the pyramid in the later years of the nineteenth century. The cast-iron doors carry typical symbolism of the time - the inverted torch, signifying death, and the star, a sign of eternity. We do not know why William Colebrook Stockdale particularly chose a pyramid for his family monument, but it is, as local historian Mike Sampson has written, 'Tiverton's most curious, and least known, construction.' It deserves listing and preserving.

The pyramidal
pump at
Winkleigh in
Devon marks the
passing of the
Great Reform Bill
of 1832

THE BRITISH ARE not given to commemorating political events with monuments. They are much more interested in remembering people by erecting statues of them. Occasionally political ideals are enshrined in stone - like the column to British Liberty at Gibside in County Durham. Yet in the village of **Winkleigh**, deep in the heart of the north Devon there is a simple granite memorial - an elongated pyramid containing the village pump - that is a tangible reminder of the appreciation of local people for the passing of the Great Reform Bill of 1832.

Winkleigh may have always been a place of revolutionaries. It was owned by William the Conqueror's wife in the 11th century and in the mid-12th century was split between the Keynes family and the Tracys. They each built a castle in the village, probably because they took different sides in the civil war between King Henry I's nephew Stephen and Henry's only surviving legitimate child, Matilda. Later in the same century, Sir William de Tracy was one of the assassins of Archbishop Thomas Beckett - what is now All Saints Church may originally have been dedicated to Thomas. Winkleigh suffered badly in the time of the Black Death. In the Civil War, despite its Royalist sympathies, it was spared by Cromwell's army, which marched on to attack Torrington (see page 171) instead. After that excitement Winkleigh, which became a village of some size, seems to have been relatively quiet.

So what made the villagers want to mark the passing of the Great Reform Bill? There seems to have been nothing notably corrupt in the parliamentary dealings of the area - Winkleigh was neither a rotten borough nor in the pocket of the local landowner. Part of the impetus seems to have been the fact that more men were now given the vote by the Act - though they still had to be property owners. There were obviously enough of them to launch celebrations of the Bill's passing. The whole of north Devon seems to have been *en fete* in the summer of 1832 - the Reform Bill was given royal assent on 7 June that year.

Winkleigh's celebrations took a practical turn. The village pump needed replacing, so, just as in the 20th century coronations and royal jubilees were celebrated with bus shelters and playgrounds, Winkleigh had its Reform Bill pump. And very elegant it is, sitting to one side of the Square in the heart of the village. A small copper plaque on the back, above the doorway that gives access to the mechanism, says that it was 'Erected by permission of the Lord of the Manor' - the townsfolk were not yet completely out of the thrall of authority. And so that everyone remembers the reason for the new pump's building, the date, 1832, is carved in the front, and the names of the main proponents of the reform of parliament are distributed round the four sides of the pyramid.

In pride of place is the King, WILLIAM IV, who played a leading role in supporting the ministry of Lord Grey by agreeing to dissolve parliament when the Opposition threatened to defeat the Bill, and by threatening to create enough new peers to swamp the House of Lords with supporters of reform if it was likely to be defeated there. Below the king's name is that of GREY himself, the Whig earl who became Prime Minister in 1830 in succession to the Duke of Wellington. Grey was determined to get rid of what he saw as the unbalanced representation in parliament. It was a hard battle, during which he had to fight a crucial general election; it saw him returned with an increased reforming majority. Despite severe opposition from many quarters, he carried the day with the (sometimes reluctant) support of the king.

The others named on the pyramid pump are (on the back) RUSSELL - Lord John Russell, who introduced the Reform Bills (there were actually three - two were defeated in the Lords; the third was passed) into the House of Commons. On the eastern side is inscribed BROUGHAM. Henry Brougham was Lord Chancellor at the time of the Reform, having been reluctantly persuaded to go from the Commons to the Lords to help carry the Bill. On the opposite side is the name ALTHORP. John Charles Spencer, Viscount Althorp (later Earl Spencer) was the Leader of the House of Commons. It was Althorp who insisted that Brougham, who was something of a loose cannon in the Commons, should be sent to the Lords. Althorp was a poor speaker, which was why Russell introduced the Bills in the Commons, but his management of the chamber's business was adept, and he played a crucial part in the Bill's eventual passage.

Political praise on pyramidal parish pumps is all very well, but of no use unless the pump actually works. Fortunately the Winkleigh pump works very well. It is reputed never to have run dry, and during droughts in 1920 and 1976 it proved a lifeline to the village. It was restored in 1994 to celebrate the centenary of the parish council. It looks little different now from its state in the late 19th century, when it was photographed for a local postcard. Standing beside it in the picture is an old lady, Mrs Temperance Hunt, who died in 1902 at the age of 99. She would have been 30 when the pyramid pump was erected.

The pyramid at Great Torrington was put up in 1818 to mark the victory at Waterloo

PERHAPS THE WINKLEIGH villagers were inspired to put up their Reform Bill pump by the example, 14 years earlier, of the ladies of **Great Torrington**, 11 miles to the northwest. In 1818 they put up a similarly-shaped monument to something more conventional - a military victory.

When the Duke of Wellington finally defeated the forces of the resurgent Napoleon Bonaparte at Waterloo in 1815, there was general rejoicing throughout the land. Torrington was no exception, but here the day of feasting on roast ox and drinking bumpers to the Iron Duke was not the end of the story. The town was one of the few places that immediately set about putting up a permanent memorial; their pyramid had long been in place when the painter Benjamin Haydon asked in 1823, 'Would any other nation, any other Government in the world but ours, have passed by the glories of the Peninsula and Trafalgar, or have suffered such a mighty battle as that of Waterloo to lapse without one single pictorial remembrance of its glory?'

The ladies of Torrington were more forward-looking - or more patriotic - than the government. They got together to raise funds for a special monument; the suspicion is that they were driven by one particularly energetic and vociferous lady. We have no record of the means they used in their money-raising efforts, though the fact that it took them more than two years suggests that it was small-scale fundraising - perhaps teas and sales of work - rather than a list of large subscriptions from the county gentry.

According to Miss Scrutton, the local archivist, there is almost no evidence about the fundraising for, or the opening of, the monument. She had found no link between the battle and the town; no soldier from Torrington seems to have been involved in the fighting. There are no papers in the archives that describe the opening, and it was not, apparently, described in the few local newspapers of the day.

Once the ladies had their funds they looked for a site for a memorial. The one they chose, on the edge of the small town, is superb. It is on common land, criss-crossed by paths, on the slopes of the valley of the River Torridge. Far below, the river snakes through the gorge between heavily-wooded hills. Here, in a commanding position, they built their pyramid, tall and thin, using small blocks of local stone. It has blind gothic arches in the lower section.

The inscription they put on it was carved by the local monumental mason. It reads:

> ERECTED JUNE 1818
> TO COMMEMORATE
> THE BATTLE OF WATERLOO
> JUNE 1815
> PEACE TO THE
> SOULS OF THE
> HEROES!!!

The three exclamation marks suggest great civic excitement at the structure, as well as pride in Wellington's victory. So it is sad to relate that Torrington seems to have forgotten about its Waterloo monument. It celebrates its Civil War skirmish of 1646 each year with a 'Cavalier Week'. It is excited by its links with Henry Williamson's book *Tarka the Otter* and by the Tarka Trail. It points out its (somewhat obscure) links with Sir Joshua Reynolds (his niece lived here and modelled for him once) and with Dr Johnson, who stayed for a few days. But the Town Trail, even though it actually goes very near the Waterloo pyramid, makes no mention of it. Perhaps in 2015, if not before, Torrington will wake up to its special monument.

THE PYRAMID AT **Halswell** Park (pronounced Haswell) in Somerset is, apparently, dedicated to 'a pure nymph'. Whether that is appropriate to the succession of brides who today use the great house for their nuptials we have no means of knowing. The grounds they survey from the main rooms during their reception are particularly special.

We went to Halswell twice, each time following the narrow, high-banked Devon lanes from Junction 10 of the M5 near Bridgewater, through North Petherton and Huntstile to Goathurst. Our first visit was hard to organise; we had trouble finding out who actually owned the house and the estate, but we eventually tracked down Grahame Bond and his sister Janine, new owners, who readily gave us permission to look at the pyramid. Goathurst, a huddle of houses around the church, is at the gates of the drive up to the house. It was raining hard; as we rounded the curve of the drive the front of the large mansion seemed gloomy and depressed. We could see the pyramid to the right. No one was about. The rain sliced down as we took pictures, but everything seemed uninspiring - the house proved to be empty, the out-buildings ramshackle and the pyramid neglected and overgrown with creeper.

When we revisited some time later, it was a different story. The sun shone. Goathurst was full of flowers. And the estate was undergoing a transformation. Workmen, most of them Eastern European, were busy everywhere, repairing and restoring the Grade I listed building. They were transforming it, under the watchful gaze of English Heritage, for its new role as both home and wedding venue. As part of the work they had cleared away straggling trees around the pyramid, pulled away the creeper and cleaned it up.

The pyramid
wellhead at
Halswell near
Goathurst in
Somerset is
dedicated
'To a pure nymph'

Now it was possible to appreciate the structure properly. From a substantial stone plinth the pyramid rises in twelve steps to a finial in the shape of a griffin holding a shield (or, rather, the front half of a griffin; the back has disappeared). On one side is a small wooden door giving access to the interior, where there is a water tank; on the other side is a plaque, perhaps of slate, that used to carry an inscription. It is now so worn that none of it can be read, apart from isolated and uninformative words - Who, THAT. It is supposed once to have carried a poem, possibly by Alexander Pope, which included the words 'to a pure nymph'; the rest is apparently, unrecorded.

Who was responsible for the pyramid and the house? And who was the 'pure nymph'? The first of these questions is the easier to answer. From the end of the 13th century the Halswell family lived on the estate. They built a succession of houses, parts of which can still be identified in the present structure. Last of the Halswell line was Hugh Halswell; his daughter Jane married John Tynte, and the estate succeeded in the Tynte family until 1944. They became Kemeys-Tynte when Sir John Tynte, second baronet of Halswell, married Jane Kemeys of Cefn Mably in Glamorgan.

Halswell in 1791, at the time of Sir Charles Kemeys-Tynte

Most important of the Kemeys-Tyntes to the estate was Sir Charles Kemeys-Tynte, third son of John and Jane and fifth baronet. His oldest brother Sir Halswell had rebuilt much of the house, including the north range with its military-inspired carvings. His designer was the London surveyor William Taylor, who had carried out work at Longleat House. Either Sir Halswell (whose marriage was childless) or the next brother, the Rev'd Sir John (who died unmarried) laid out a formal garden around the house.

Sir Charles Kemeys-Tynte swept this away. Instead, he created a garden in the new, modern style, 'naturalising' the landscape in the manner of William Kent. He was a friend of Henry Hoare, who was creating the magnificent landscape at Stourhead at much the same time, and Charles would also have known what was happening at Stowe (see page 93). He created an irregular lake, added a cascade, planted picturesque clumps of trees and softened the bounds of the garden, merging it with the wide park. He also dotted the landscape with a wide variety of garden buildings - a stone circle called the Druid's Temple (broken up in the 1950s), two grottoes, a rotunda and a pleasure pavilion known as Robin Hood's Hut (repaired in the 1990s and now a holiday home for The Landmark Trust). There is, too, a Temple of Harmony, repaired and cared for by the Halswell Park Trust, which is working to save other structures.

The pyramid is the closest of these odd buildings to the house. As Halswell stands on the spring line, it has a functional purpose - the water tank collects the pure water welling up beneath it for use in the house. Its date is a puzzle. The official Grade II listing hedges its bets by saying merely 'C18'. Some experts date it to after 1768 when the estate was visited by inveterate traveller and diarist Arthur Young, who failed to mention it, though he wrote about some of the other buildings. Others, though, believe that it dates from the 1740s, and that the 'pure nymph' was a niece of Sir Charles - she died in 1744. The earlier date could well be possible, for the stepped pyramid form may have been influenced by Vanbrugh's pyramid at Stowe (see page 93), which was in place in the 1720s and had been removed by the 1760s. Different architects have been suggested - Thomas Wright (see pages 124, 358 and 367) who was probably responsible for some of the other park buildings or John Johnson, architect of a number of mostly minor country houses and County Surveyor for Essex.

The griffin emerging from a coronet on the top of the pyramid is the crest of the Kemeys. On the shield it holds are the arms of the Kemeys-Tyntes. The griffin surveys a landscape and a range of buildings that have felt the vagaries of fashion and of neglect - in the 19th century the house was seldom occupied. In the 20th it suffered a fire. In World War II it was occupied for a short time by St Hilda's School for Girls, evacuated from Southend. Then a prisoner of war camp was built in the grounds. After the war some of the house became flats, but the upkeep of both the house and the estate was a great drain on resources. Its future looked precarious - having survived so comparatively well, were the estate buildings to be lost? By the end of the 20th century the House was on English Heritage's *Buildings at Risk Register*. Then Grahame Bond's Dunster Holdings took over. The house and the pyramid are now transformed, and there is new impetus behind the restoration of the remaining buildings. The brides who now celebrate their wedding day at Halswell may know nothing of the 'pure nymph' of the pyramid, but they certainly appreciate the vision of both Sir Charles Kemeys-Tynte in the 18th century and of Grahame Bond in the 21st.

NONE OF ENGLAND'S three kings called Richard has had a good press. Richard I was an absentee king who spent time in captivity and left his kingdom to his brother John. Richard II, two centuries later, was a great patron of the arts but antagonised his nobles by his authoritarian ways - he was forced to abdicate and was eventually killed in Pontefract Castle. And Richard III is today best known through his portrayal as the prince-killing deformed monster of Shakespeare's play.

Seen through the prism of Tudor propaganda, Richard III is an out-and-out rotter - 'determined to prove a villain' right from the start. Sir Thomas More described him as 'malicious, wrathfull and envious' and as being 'litle of stature, evill featured of the limnes, croke backed, the left shulder much higher than the right, hard favoured of visage'. Most portraits of him, which date from after his death, show a shifty-looking man with a hump back. Yet is this the right view? The City of York thought otherwise in 1485; the city records of 23 August that year, the day after the Battle of **Bosworth**, note, 'King Richard late mercifully reigning upon us was thrugh grete treason of the duc of Northfolk and many othere that turned ayenst hyme, with many othre lordes and nobilles of this north parties, was pitiously slane and murdred to the grete hevynesse of this citie'.

Whatever the rights and wrongs of Richard's life, we know that it ended in a bloody way at the Battle of Bosworth Field and that the crown was found in a hawthorn tree on the battlefield. Or do we? The crown in the tree is very possible; the victorious Henry Tudor, who succeeded Richard as King Henry VII, used a hawthorn bush with a crown as one of his badges. But where was Bosworth Field? Here controversy rages. Several sites have been suggested. Most historians believe that Richard and Henry fought near Market Bosworth in Leicestershire, in marshy ground near a hill; the first accounts say it was the Battle of Redemore, or Reedmoor. But that leaves open a number of questions as to where the reedy marsh actually was - and there are other researchers who say that the site may have been in Warwickshire . . .

The most widely-held belief is that the battle was held on the site now occupied by the Bosworth Field Visitor Centre and Country Park at Sutton Cheney in Leicestershire. The Centre opened in 1974, the first of its kind in England. The principal sites of the battle (if it took place here) are marked with the standards of some of the main participants - Richard, Henry and Lord Stanley, whose switch of allegiance was crucial to the outcome of the battle. Richard is supposed to have placed his army on Ambion Hill, where the visitor centre stands, though this would have been a foolish military move. Ralph Holinshed, whose Chronicle was Shakespeare's source for Richard III, charmingly calls the hill 'Anna Beame'. It is just north-east of the site. Crown Hill, where the hawthorn tree is said to have been and where Henry Tudor was proclaimed king, is to the south.

The south of the site is now occupied by Ambion Wood; beside it is King Dick's Well, a spring surmounted by a stone pyramid. Here, it is claimed, Richard drank during the two-hour course of the battle - perhaps to give him the strength to shout one of Shakespeare's most famous lines - 'A horse! A horse! My Kingdom for a horse!' It is possible that he died near here, too, and it is not far from the place where the crown was found.

The pyramid was put up, as a metal plaque records, by Dr Samuel Parr in 1813. There is no doubting whose side Dr Parr and his successors were on. The metal plaque tells us that the

King Richard III

Did Richard III drink from the well below the pyramid on the battlefield of Bosworth?

pyramid 'is maintained by the Fellowship of the White Boar'. The white boar was the badge of Richard III and appears on his standard, fluttering in the distance. The Fellowship is now called the Richard III Society. And the Latin inscription above the water of the well itself, provided by Parr, says 'Richard III, King of England, slaked his thirst with water drawn from this well when engaged in most bitter and furious battle with Henry, Earl of Richmond, and before being deprived of both his life and his sceptre on the morning of 22 August AD 1485.'

The pyramid was restored, 'haec tempore diruta' - 'damaged as it was by the passage of time' - in 1964. It was for more than 150 years the only indication of the location (or possible location) of the battle. Now it is one of the few highlights of the battlefield trail that is followed by schoolchildren and visitors. If Richard III did drink here on 22 August 1485 the place is appropriate - Bosworth is poised between the south, where he seems to have been mostly disliked, and the north of England, where he was brought up and where, as the York aldermen attested, he was respected. Richard still divides opinion; for all the pro-Richard lobbyists - the Ricardians - most British people will continue to believe Shakespeare's blackening of his name.

The Suez Memorial at the National Arboretum at Alrewas in Staffordshire

THE 50TH ANNIVERSARY of the Suez Crisis alerted us to a new pyramid. Newspapers reported that at the National Memorial Arboretum at **Alrewas** in Staffordshire the Suez Veterans Association had unveiled a memorial to their comrades who served in Egypt between 1939 and 1956. The memorial was, inevitably, in the shape of an Egyptian pyramid.

The National Memorial Arboretum proved fertile ground for pyramids - there are three proper ones and another, truncated, one there. The Arboretum is in the National Forest, established in 1990. The idea for a memorial arboretum came from its founding director, David Childs. Inspired by the United States National Arboretum and by Arlington National Cemetery, he launched a public appeal in 1994 for money to purchase and run a site where there could be memorials to the people who fought and died in the wars of the 20th century, to remind future generation of their sacrifices. The site, between Lichfield and Burton-on-Trent at Alrewas (rhymes with walrus) in Staffordshire, totals 152 acres. The land, the site of a former gravel-extraction plant, was donated on a 999-year lease by Lafarge Aggregates. Tree-planting began in 1997 and the site was opened in 2001.

When we arrived the Arboretum was awash with police. They were there for an annual service to remember victims of crime - just one of the many memorial days that the Arboretum runs. Despite its name, there was not much evidence of trees - or, rather, the trees that were there were very young and did not make their presence known - and in the summer of 2007 many of them were damaged by flooding.

This lack of trees was appropriate for the Suez memorial pyramid. About three feet high, it is surrounded by sand; down one side of the sandy area is a strip filled with blue glass chippings, representing the Suez Canal. The memorial was unveiled on 13 March 2004, and was a focal point in May 2006 for commemoration of the 50th anniversary of the withdrawal from the Suez Canal after the ill-fated invasion.

Nearby is a truncated pyramid dedicated 'In recognition of all those who served in or supported the armed forces of the SULTANATE OF OMAN and in memory of those who died in that service'. Further away, across the lawns that will one day be glades amidst the thousands of trees of the Arboretum, are two taller, thinner pyramids, one commemorating a naval disaster, the other to friendships made in the 41 Club.

In the 41 Club garden there are 41 trees. This sounds like the start of a fairy tale, but the origins of the 41 Club are traced not to an enchanted castle once upon a time but to Liverpool in 1936. Members of the local Round Table Club - itself an offshoot of Rotary - found that, having reached the age of 41, when they were obliged by the rules to leave Round Table, they had nowhere to go to carry on their friendships. So they set up the first 41 Club. Although delayed by war, the idea spread, and today there are more than 900 41 Clubs throughout the world.

The pyramid in the centre of the 41 Club garden is three-sided, with circular plaques holding the symbols of Round Table and the 41 Club, as well as the garden's name. A plaque nearby says that it 'commemorates the huge achievement of the National Association of Round Tables of Great Britain and Ireland, in terms of Fundraising and Community Service, since the first Round Table Club was formed in Norwich, in 1927, by a young Rotarian, Louis Marchesi'. The funds for the pyramid, which was put up in 2003, were raised by a national appeal coordinated by the local 41 Club in Lichfield.

On 18 December 1941 a convoy of ships left Malta and headed towards the coast of Libya to intercept an Italian convoy that was carrying tanks, fuel and military equipment for the enemy to Tripoli. Leading the British ships was the Leander-class light cruiser *HMS Neptune*. Among the supporting destroyers was *HMS Kandahar*. Just after 1.00 am on 19 December, *Neptune* struck a mine, in a position a long way from land and in very deep water where mines were totally unexpected. Going astern to try to get away from the mine, it struck another and then a third. *Kandahar*, along with *HMS Lively*, came in to try to assist *Neptune* and tow her to safety. Then *Kandahar*, too, hit a mine. It was now after 3.00 am. The captain of *Neptune* signalled the other ships to keep away - then *Neptune* stuck a fourth mine, turned over and sank. *Kandahar*, by now partially submerged, signalled that the other ships should leave. At 4.00 am *HMS Jaguar*, sent from Malta to assist, came close to the ship. *Kandahar*'s crew jumped into the sea; 178 were rescued but 73 died. At dawn *Kandahar* sank.

Of *Neptune*'s crew of 763 men there was only a single survivor - Able Seaman Norman Walton. He lived to the age of 85, dying in 2005. The disaster was the Royal Navy's greatest loss of life in the whole of the Mediterranean during the war. Many of the ship's crew were New Zealanders and South Africans; for their countries this was the heaviest loss of life in a single incident.

The *Neptune* Association had long planned to raise a memorial to the events of 18 and 19 December 1941. Their seven-foot-high pyramid of Derbyshire stone was unveiled at the National Arboretum on 9 July 2005 to mark the 60th anniversary of the end of World War II. The cost of more than £20,000 was raised by appeal. The names of everyone who lost their life on *Neptune* and *Kandahar* are listed on a bronze plaque, and there is a map and a history of the disaster, as well as plaques showing the badges of the two ships.

The memorials in the National Arboretum are in a curious mixture of styles, many of which, though obviously sincerely meant, lack subtlety or artistic integrity. The *Neptune* and *Kandahar* pyramid is certainly one of the most poignant and satisfying - another tribute to the power of the shape of the pyramid.

A truncated pyramid marks the service of forces of Sultanate of Oman'

Two pyramids at the National Memorial Arboretum - to the crews of the ships Kandahar and Neptune (front) and to the 41 Club

Tour 5

NORTH AND WEST ENGLAND

IT WAS A wet start. Not that the weather at the start of our tour of North and West England was unaccommodating. It was just that, by coincidence, five of the first six pyramids were connected with water.

We walked from **Bishop Auckland**'s stately market square and through The Batts, a grassed area beside the River Wear. The wall of Auckland Castle, seat of the Bishops of Durham, curved uphill. We followed, on the lookout for the pyramid. We knew it was in the castle's High Park, but not its exact location.

It was the horses that drew our attention to it. A dozen sturdy brown and white animals were grazing in a field to our right, just as the park wall ended. In the middle of them was a stone pyramid about 12 feet high on a low plinth.

The pyramid is set on top of a ridge above the castle, and is now surrounded by short-cropped grass. It serves no apparent purpose, except for the horses to scratch themselves on it. When it was built in the 18th century, though, it played a vital role in ensuring that the Bishop of Durham could take a bath.

Beneath the pyramid, and now inaccessible because the outlet has been blocked, is a reservoir for storing cold water taken from a spring a little way to the north. The water used to be channelled down the hill and eventually into the castle; the details of just how that happened are unclear. In the grassy hillside south of the pyramid is an indentation that indicates where the channel flowed - though it seems to stop where the hillside becomes steeper.

Hanging in the entrance hall to Auckland Castle is an estate map drawn in the 1770s by Jeremiah Dixon, later the surveyor of the Mason-Dixon Line between Pennsylvania and Maryland. It shows High Park and marks a square labelled 'The Reservoir' at the exact spot where the pyramid is set. It is likely that the pyramid was in situ by this date - indeed, its design, with the heavy rustication, in the manner of Vanbrugh, suggests that it is earlier. It may have been built at the very end of the 17th century or the beginning of the 18th. The map shows that southward from it ran a gap in the woodland; the gap corresponds to the position of the former channel.

Which of Their Graces the Bishops of Durham was responsible for the pyramid? There is no helpful inscription to tell us. There may once have been an indication on the cistern (like the pyramid a listed building, though it has been added to with modern bricks and corrugated iron), but all that remains today is a single carved stone with the letter D (presumably for 'Dunelm' - Durham). It lies between two other, grooved stones, one of which has the remains of a hasp still attached. They were once on the edges of the cistern. A wooden cover fitted into the grooves and was secured by the hasp.

Assuming the date of a decade or so either side of 1700 is correct, the pyramid would fall within the episcopacy of Nathaniel Crewe, one of the Church of England's longest-ever-serving bishops. He held the see of Durham from 1674 to 1722 - a remarkable 48 years. He had previously been Bishop of Oxford. He

OPPOSITE:
The episcopal
pyramid at
Auckland Castle,
Bishop Auckland,
Co Durham

179

became 3rd Baron Crewe in 1697 on the death of his brother, but his temporal title was as nothing to his spiritual one.

Lord Crewe, like all the Bishops of Durham from Walcher in the 11th century to Van Mildert in 1836, was ruler of his own land. The steward to Bishop Antony Beck, who held the see from 1284 to 1310 (and was also the only Englishman to be Latin Patriarch of Jerusalem), wrote that 'There are two kings in England, namely the Lord King of England, wearing a crown in sign of his regality and the Lord Bishop of Durham wearing a mitre in place of a crown, in sign of his regality in the diocese of Durham.' This was no mere flattery; it was literally true. The holder of the see of Durham was known as the Prince Bishop, and the land over which he held sway was the County Palatinate of Durham. He held all the powers of the king - he could raise an army, hold his own parliament, appoint judges, make laws, issue charters, levy taxes and mint coinage. Auckland Castle still contains a Throne Room, from where the Prince Bishops would wield their very extensive powers.

Lord Crewe was not only a man with the rights of a king; he was also very wealthy - W H Auden, a frequent visitor to the north-east, wrote about the Crewes' extensive land-ownership in *The Dog Beneath the Skin*. Crewe was a generous local benefactor, and set up charities to help poor people in the diocese. He also spent lavishly on his own accommodation, including Auckland Castle. So it would be entirely in keeping that he wanted to improve the water supply to the castle, and had the pyramid and cistern constructed.

The Harelaw springhead pyramid, Co Durham

AT FIRST SIGHT the little pyramid at **Harelaw** in County Durham seems to have served much the same purpose as Bishop Crewe's more sophisticated version at Bishop Auckland. It marks the place where a spring gushes out of the ground, only for the water to disappear again into a boggy area nearby.

The pyramid was hard to find. Harelaw is a dour former mining village that stretches along the B6168 three miles west of Stanley. It links seamlessly with Annfield Plain to the south - continual rows of gritstone terraced houses, later council housing in grimy red brick, and a few shops and industrial units. The official English Heritage listing said that the pyramid - known as Harelaw Watering Place - was on the west side of North Road. Not obviously, it wasn't. We wandered the length of North Road and enquired of the inevitable dog-walker, who knew nothing. Eventually a man working in his garden set us on the right route: 'Take the black path through there,' he said, indicating a narrow band of cinders winding between the brick houses. 'You'll find it.'

A man in a junkyard was attacking a car panel with a sledge-hammer and manic enthusiasm. This did not look promising. But the pyramid was close by. Its immediate surroundings contrast with the scrubland around it; it is set in a neatly landscaped area complete with specimen evergreens, clipped bushes and mown grass. The rougher area alongside is part of Harelaw Heath and home to a wide variety of wild flowers.

It is an oasis of quiet beauty in a rather unprepossessing area. The pyramid is tiny - no more than three feet high - and rather mysterious. From beneath a roughly-curved stone lintel, remarkably-clear water bubbles out. There is a hole in the lintel to which a chain and cup may have once been attached - though that is by no means certain.

In fact, not much is definite about the origins and dating of the pyramid. The listing (it is Grade II listed) says, 'Spring Head. Possibly C17.' But is it? Not according to the local historian John Milburn. 'It was put up around 1930,' he said. 'The whole area was given over to troughs of water where horses from the adjacent waggonway could drink - that's why it's called Harelaw Watering Place.' He also told us that he knew a local resident remembered helping her father in the 1920s to take working horses owned by the local council from nearby Stobb House to the troughs.

The Harelaw Waggonway served the nearby Lily Colliery at Flint Hill, just north of the village. Horse-drawn wagons, laden with coal, would trundle past on wooden sleepers. It linked with the more famous Tanfield Railway, built in 1725. Causey Arch on the line of the Tanfield Railway is the world's oldest railway bridge. It is 105 ft long and 80 feet high. The remains at Harelaw are less spectacular - only the line of the Waggonway is still visible, now used as a cycle track that links local schools and businesses and connects with a network of other local cycleways, many of them also along old railway lines.

There are now plans to redevelop the area around the tiny spring, to make it more accessible and more attractive. The pyramid, whatever its age, should remain to tell something of the story of the area's long industrial history.

IT WAS DISMAL weather when we arrived in **Monkseaton** Community High School, a little inland from the coast between Tynemouth and Whitley Bay. It had taken a more-than-usual amount of detective work to find the pyramid here. We first came across a reference to it in a website for the then Department for Education and Skills. It mentioned a language-teaching seminar taking place in a glass pyramid in a school in England. And that was it. An e-mail to the DfES did not get us much further - they were unable to disclose the whereabouts of the school. There was an indication, though, that it was a specialist language college, so the next step was to look for the colleges on the net. There are 216 of them, so we were getting warmer. Then it was just a matter of trawling though the schools' sites to find what we were looking for. It was a good job that Monkseaton comes only halfway down the alphabetical list; we may have given up before getting down as far as York . . .

Once we'd found it, a call to the Head, Dr Paul Kelley, confirmed that they did indeed have a glass pyramid, the school's pride and joy. And, yes, we were welcome to visit - just make arrangements with the caretaker, John Frain. So here we were,

The pyramid at
Monkseaton
Community High
School glows
at night

*Inside the
pyramid at
Monkseaton
Community High
School*

under leaden skies, driving though the dreary monotony of brick houses that make up Monkseaton (a place so devoid of architectural merit that it has no separate entry in *The Buildings of England*) to the sprawling school.

First impressions were not good. It was hard to find where the school's entrance might be, and the buildings looked in desperate need of having some money spent on them - and in 2009 they were replaced. We eventually located Mr Frain, who unlocked what seemed to us an insignificant door and led us through drab corridors. Where was the pyramid? At last, he unlocked another door and light flooded down on us. We'd arrived.

Actually, it looked rather as if the pyramid had arrived, craned down from above to cover what must have once been an internal courtyard. It is impressive. It is similar to the entrances to the Parkhead Forge Shopping Centre in Glasgow (see page 276) - a grid of metal struts that leaps up to a point above the centre of the building. The impression is slightly marred by the lumpen squares suspended from it to carry the climate control and lighting systems. Mr Frain told us that at night the pyramid glows, suspended over the rest of the low, spreading building.

The pyramid was added in 1996 to the original building, which was constructed in the 1970s - as was obvious from both its design and its state. As the school's foreign languages centre it fulfills Monkseaton Community High's specialist role. Beneath the blue and gold flag of the EU and the flags of several of its member states, students can work at a battery of computers, consult books, chat in foreign languages - the pyramid has good acoustics, so there is a pleasant hum rather than a babel even when they are in full voice.

The school is part of a Europe-wide network of schools, the Students Across Europe Language Network. Inside the pyramid the school's 900 students can take part in video-conferencing with their partner schools in France, Germany and Spain, can surf the internet, e-mail and undertake research for their work. There are also links with more than a hundred local primary schools; their pupils come to Monkseaton to get their first taste of modern languages. The centre is open to the local community, too, and hosts lectures, seminars and workshops.

Paul Kelley believes that the pyramid, along with other modifications to the school environment, has had a marked effect on the motivation of the school's students. 'It's a fantastic, airy place,' he says. 'It's been a great inspiration for all the children.' He adds that where once the students couldn't get out of the school fast enough when the bell rang at the end of the day, now they stay around to play or study. Another mark of the power of pyramids, perhaps.

ST CUTHBERT FOUND **Lindisfarne** too much of a metropolis when he was abbot of the monastic community there, and took himself off to the distant island of Inner Farne to commune with God. To most people, though, Lindisfarne - known also as Holy Island since Norman times - is remote enough. As Bede wrote in AD 731 in his *Ecclesiastical History*, 'As the tide ebbs and flows, this place is surrounded by sea twice a day like an island, and twice a day the sand dries and joins it to the mainland'. This semi-island was chosen as his base by St Aidan who arrived from Iona in 635 at the request of King Oswald, whose seat was at nearby Bamburgh.

The daymark pyramid on Emmanuel Head, Holy Island

The surrounding sea has always held many dangers, though not for Cuthbert, who would stand praying in it for hours with the water to his chin, while the curious seals came and nuzzled him. He died in Inner Farne in 687. A century later disaster struck this peaceful coast. In 793, says *The Anglo-Saxon Chronicle*, 'came dreadful forewarnings over the land of the Northumbrians . . . there were immense sheets of light rushing through the air, and whirlwinds, and fiery dragons flying across the firmament. These tremendous tokens were soon followed by a great famine; and not long after, on the sixth day before the ides of January of the same year, the harrowing inroads of heathen men made lamentable havoc in the church of God in Holy-island, by rapine and slaughter.' The Vikings had come.

More and more harried by the invaders, the monks finally fled in 875, taking with them Cuthbert's coffin. After a hundred and twenty years of wandering they settled at Durham in 995; from there, after the Norman conquest, they re-established a Priory on Holy Island. But the waters were not yet safe. Wrecks were frequent, and many souls perished within sight of the Priory, which was dissolved by King Henry VIII in 1537. In the following century, Robert Rugg, who commanded the garrison at Lindisfarne Castle, noted that the local people had not quite followed the monks' lead in praying for the souls of the mariners: 'The common people there do pray for ships which they see in danger. They all sit down upon their knees and hold up their hands and say very devotedly, "Lord send her to us, God send her to us." You seeing them upon their knees, and their hands joined, do think that they are praying for your safety; but their minds are far from that. They pray, not to God to save you, or send you to port, but to send you to them by shipwreck, that they may get the spoil of her. And to show that this is their meaning if the ship come well to port, they get up in anger crying "the Devil stick her, she is away from us".'

Despite the dangers of the coast off Holy Island nothing was done to stem the appalling loss of life (as many as 700 in some years) until the start of the19th century. Between 1801 and 1810 Trinity House in Newcastle began to build beacons and lighthouses to warn shipping of the treacherous coast. One of the first was the next pyramid on our list - the daymark on Holy Island's Emmanuel Head.

Although 500,000 visitors cross the causeway to Lindisfarne each year, few of them venture to the north-east corner of the island. The 'sights' - Priory, Castle, Visitor Centre, cafés - are all on the southern edge. But head north out of the car park and you are immediately into a landscape of empty fields and, eventually, grass-covered dunes, where, as Natural England notices warn, pirri-pirri bur (*acaena novae-zelandiae*) grows - a nasty and tenacious bur that is thought to have come to Britain in the wool of imported sheep.

Avoiding the antipodean menace, we crossed the dunes to the pyramid. It was one of those structures that seem to be near and yet are really quite some distance away. Although it looks small, it is actually about 35 feet high, and brilliant white. It stands on a low cliff at the edge of the sea, and is visible from a great distance out to sea. Its purpose is to ensure that incoming boats make the harbour at Holy Island safely; there had previously been many instances of navigators mistaking other, smaller headlands for Emmanuel Head, turning west and ending up on the rocks.

The Emmanuel Head pyramid is said to be one of Britain's earliest daymarks - though there are certainly some earlier, including the red-and-white striped example on St Martin's in the Isles of Scilly, which dates from the late 17th century. There are other pyramidal navigation marks at Porthgain (see page 221) and Menai (see page 225). The Holy Island mark was certainly effective in reducing wrecks - along with better regulation of pilots by Trinity House, which from 1808 had a statutory right to licence them.

Although the pyramid at Emmanuel Head is the most prominent in the Holy Island area, there are two more examples to the south. They are rather taller and thinner and are set on Guile Point, an almost-inaccessible area of waterlogged sand and shingle that is part of the mainland. They were constructed perhaps a decade later than their northern neighbour. Sited 122 yards apart on a shingle spit called Old Law, they are known as East Old Law, 70 feet high, and its even bigger brother West Old Law, an 83-foot giant.

Their construction was a miracle in itself. Such was the nature of the site that everything - materials and workmen - had to be brought in by small boat. In good weather a flotilla of craft would leave South Shields harbour and sail north, landing bricks, mortar and ironwork, as well as the navvies, on the spit; in the frequent bad weather they stayed away. Eventually the pyramids grew higher, and were each tipped with an iron pole carrying aloft a warning triangle - now lost.

East Old Law and West Old Law, daymarks on the mainland coast overlooking Holy Island

These two pyramids may have had a distinguished designer - John Dobson, the great Newcastle architect, who was responsible for the city's Grey Street, one of Europe's greatest urban experiences. He worked as architect for Trinity House in Newcastle during the time they were being built. If they are by Dobson, they are his least known works, but they have a presence on this magical coast that is ethereal and moving.

IN THE TIDES of history that washed over **Corbridge** in the Tyne valley for more than two millennia, its two pyramids are insignificant pebbles. They have nothing to do with the Romans, who first built a fort here around AD 90, three decades before Hadrian began his wall. The fort guarded the bridge where Dere Street crossed the Tyne, and lay astride another Roman road, Stanegate. The remains of the fourth fort on the site and the supply town into which it developed lie just west of the present-day town. But although wealthy Romans built themselves pyramid monuments (see page 2), there are none in Corbridge.

Nor were the pyramids constructed by Danes or Scots, though both nations sacked the town. Saxons built the first church in Corbridge and used Roman stones, including a complete Roman archway. Two defensive pele towers, from the 13th and 14th centuries and also constructed with Roman stonework, are

*The Duke of
Northumberland's
pant of 1815
at Corbridge,
Northumberland*

reminders of continuing unsettled times. It was only after Scotland and England were unified that relative peace descended on Corbridge, and it became a centre for the surrounding villages and a staging post on the route north.

In the 18th century it came under the control of the Percy family, successively Earls then Dukes of Northumberland. It was the 2nd Duke who 'beautified' Corbridge in the first quarter of the 19th century with two additions to its marketplace - a market cross in 1814 and a pyramidal water fountain - locally known as a 'pant' - the following year. The cross, of cast iron, is marked with the stiff-tailed lion that is the Percy Crest. It displaced a medieval cross which disappeared for more than a century before being rediscovered at St Mary's Roman Catholic Cathedral in Newcastle in 1974. It was returned to Corbridge and is now in the churchyard.

The pyramid pant is a handsome structure, the pyramid sitting on top of a sturdy stone plinth and capped with a stone ball surmounted with an iron cross. An iron plaque records that it was 'Erected by Hugh Percy Duke of Northumberland Anno MDCC-CXV'. In front is a stone trough - now used as a planter - and above it a long-disused tap. Access to the plumbing was by a wooden trap-door on the opposite side. On each side of the trough are shaped stones designed to protect it from the wheels of carts; they are of different sizes and look like an afterthought, perhaps as damage was noticed.

Henry Percy seems to have been a generous man and well-loved - except possibly by his first wife. His father was Sir Hugh Smithson, who married the Earl of Northumberland's daughter. He eventually succeeded to the title, changing the family name to Percy in 1750. Hugh became 1st Duke of Northumberland (of the third creation) in 1766. Henry, then known as Earl Percy, went to Eton and Cambridge and then joined the Infantry. He served with distinction in Europe and especially in the American War of Independence until he fell out with the General in command, Lord Howe; the last straw was a consignment of hay that Howe demanded Percy send him. Percy resigned and returned to Britain.

He served as a Member of Parliament and when his father died in 1786 he entered the House of Lords as the Duke, remaining politically active. At home in Northumberland he looked after his business interests; as well as his estates, cultivated mostly by tenant farmers, he had interest in many coal mines. They made him one of England's wealthiest men, with an annual income of more than £80,000. His wealth did not buy him domestic bliss, though. His first marraige, to Lady Anne Stuart, daughter of the third Earl of Bute, lasted for almost 15 years but was childless. He divorced her by Act of Parliament in 1779, citing her 'criminal conversation' (a euphemism for adultery) with a member of Trinity College, Cambridge. Northumberland's second marriage, to his sister-in-law Frances Burrell, was more blessed; the couple had three sons and two daughters.

It would be appropriate to think that on his death in 1817 the people of Corbridge gathered to remember the Duke by the cross and the pyramid that he put up for them, as he was buried far away in the family vault in Westminster Abbey.

FORTY-FIVE YEARS after the 2nd Duke of Northumberland breathed his last, another death was marked in Corbridge. The deceased was George Lowrey - a man less eminent than the Duke though, it could be argued, more valuable. George was a surgeon and general practitioner who lived on Watling Street in the town and was the Treasurer of the Corbridge Library and Newsroom. George and his wife Sybella are remembered by a small stone pyramid on a plinth near the south door of St Andrew's Church.

Their life had its tragedies. A tombstone next to the pyramid details the deaths of three of their children - John at six months old in 1838, Thomas, at 12 years, in 1846, and George, who reached 20, in 1853. It seems likely that the elder George had invested many of his hopes in young George, who was awarded an exhibition at Newcastle upon Tyne College of Medicine in the year he died. He was already in the city two years earlier; he is noted in the 1851 census as living with a fellow student and two servants in a house owned by a washerwoman.

George the elder, who studied at Edinburgh University, was retired by 1861 and his household had shrunk further. There was a daughter, Isabella, who was 24 but was away with her aunt and uncle in Bellingham at the time of the census. Isabella's brother, called John after his deceased brother, was 21 and seems not to be noted by the census. George and Sybella, whose home formerly housed two servants as well as a surgeon's assistant, were now down to just one servant.

When George Lowrey died in October 1862, was it Sybella who decided to mark his passing with a pyramid? And was she influenced by the Duke's pyramidal fountain? Certainly the form of the monument is very similar, except that, while the fountain is surmounted by a sober ball and cross, the Lowrey monument breaks out into a Gothic finial that seems to have strayed from the Percy tomb in Beverley Minster. Sybella survived George for more than 8 years. Although it is not a major monument, their pyramid reminds us of life in an upper-middle-class family in mid-Victorian Corbridge - a comfortable existence with a sense of public duty, but underscored with the tragedy of the loss of several children - typical for the time.

George and Sybella Lowrey are rememberd by this pyramid in the churchyard at Corbridge

IN THE 17TH century William Blackett's mines in Allendale were among the most productive in Britain. As coal was hewn from the rock and transported to Newcastle and, by sea, to London, money rolled in to Blackett's bank. He rose up the social scale as a result - he was Mayor of Newcastle five times and, from 1673, MP for the city. He was colloquially known as 'King of Newcastle'. The year he was elected MP the real king, Charles II, created him Baronet Blackett of Newcastle. The baronetcy is said to have been awarded by the king in recognition of Blackett's support during the Civil War.

The Blackett family intermarried with the best of northern society, and had seats in various places, including Wallington Hall and Aydon Castle in Northumberland and Newby Hall in Yorkshire, as well as town houses in London and Newcastle. Yet despite judicious marriages, the family was never raised to the peerage - they remained, and still remain, baronets.

In 1830 the Blacketts, in the shape of Sir Edward, 6th Baronet, settled at **Matfen**, north-west of Newcastle. Their impressive house was the result of a compromise - Blackett commissioned architect Thomas Rickman to design it, but fell out with him when Rickman refused to design in anything but the Gothic style. So Blackett, who wanted an Elizabethan-style structure, took over as his own architect. The result is a comfortable, spreading building, with large, mullioned bay windows and shaped gables. Yet inside Rickman's views prevail, especially in the vast hall with its huge Gothic window and hammerbeam roof; it resembles the

Matfen Hall and the pyramid marking the entrance to the mechanism for regulating the lake water

assembly hall of one of the great 19th-century public schools - or perhaps a very grand railway station.

On the lawn in front of the house is Matfen's pyramid. Unlike the house, which is built of sandstone from Chollerford, it seems to be built of limestone, and may be linked not to the present Matfen Hall but to an earlier house on the site that is now hidden within the later structure. The pyramid sits isolated amid a sea of green grass, apparently not related to anything else. It certainly seems to have puzzled the official English Heritage listers. 'Well or pant, and drinking trough. Early C19. Ashlar. The pant is a low pyramid about 3 feet high with the spout on the east side. Beside it a large stone trough set into the ground.'

This was written in 1986. Since then, things have moved on. The structure is plainly not a 'pant' - the Northumbrian word for a public water fountain; and if there was a spout on the eastern side in the 1980s no evidence now exists, not even a hole where it might have been. And the 'drinking trough', which must have been earth-filled when the listers saw it, has since been excavated and turns out to be the walls and low parapet of steps down into the space beneath the pyramid.

So what was this for? It seems to have been part of a compli-cated subterranean water-control mechanism for the Matfen lake. From beneath the pyramid the gardener could control the level of the lake's water with the judicious manipulation of sluice gates that allowed water to enter or leave. The pyramid, which conve-niently marks the location of this mechanical 'plant room', may be 18th rather than 19th century; the changes brought about by Sir Edward Blackett's development of the estate have robbed it of its original context in the landscape.

Today the pyramid stands beside the 18-hole Matfen Golf Course and keeps company with the restored hall, now an impressive country house hotel run by the present baronet, Sir

Hugh Blackett, and Lady Blackett. They returned to Matfen in the early 1990s when the hall, which had been a Leonard Cheshire Home for 30 years, came back into their direct control. Now visitors can take tea in the conservatory and dinner in the library, sleep in a four-poster bed and, if the fancy takes them, marry in the great Gothic hall. They can enjoy an 'ice shower' in the spa then a pint of beer in the Keeper's Lodge pub. Or they can sit in comfort to take afternoon tea by a fireplace intended for Buckingham Palace - it was specially carved by Sir Francis Chantrey in 1830 but the king forgot to pay for it . . .

NO PROBLEMS ABOUT paying at the next stop on the search - across the country at **Wigton** in Cumbria. On the contrary - in the 1870s George Moore spent £12,000 (at least £750,000 in modern terms) on the memorial to his wife in the centre of Wigton's Market Place. It was money well spent; it is a handsome structure, and incorporates sculptures that are among the greatest works of art in the country.

Until local boy Melvyn Bragg became famous, George Moore was Wigton's most illustrious son. He was born in the village of Mealgate, four miles south west of the town, in 1806. At the age of 12 he was apprenticed, despite his father's initial opposition, to Messenger's drapery business in Wigton. When his apprenticeship was over he left for London with, legend says, just half-a-crown in his pocket. At first he earned his living as a successful wrestler, but he was eventually taken on by Flint, Ray, Nicholson & Co, a large textiles company - it helped that Mr Ray was a Cumberland man. George was so good at the trade that by the age of 26, having in the meantime worked for another firm, he was made a partner in a third, the lace manufacturers Groucock, Copestake and Co. It was Moore who made the firm the country's biggest, with factories in Glasgow, Nottingham and Manchester, as well as in France and the United States. As a result he became very rich.

His riches did not go to his head. He became Sheriff of Cumberland in 1871, but generally shunned public office; he paid a fine rather than become Sheriff of the City of London, and adamantly refused to enter Parliament. Instead, he applied his time and money to philanthropy. As his memorial in Carlisle Cathedral notes, 'He was not born to wealth, but by ability and industry he gained it, and he ever used it . . . for the furtherance of all good works'. Among the roll-call of charities he helped found or support - all of them redolent of their Victorian date - were The Female Mission among Fallen Women, The Royal Hospital for Incurables, The Commercial Travellers' Orphan School, The Field Lane Ragged Schools, The Little Boys' Home and The Reformatory for Thieves at Brixton. The French Government gave him the Grand Croix of the Legion d'Honneur to recognise his work in helping distribute funds, collected in Britain, to starving Parisians after the capitulation of Paris in 1871 at the end of the Franco-Prussian War.

Moore died in November 1876. He was knocked down in Carlisle by two runaway horses on his way to speak to a meeting of the Nurses' Institution. He expired at the Grey Goat Inn - the same place that he had spent his last night in Cumberland in 1825 before leaving for fame and fortune in London.

Amid all his beneficial works - which were celebrated by *Self Help* guru Samuel Smiles in one of his biographies - Moore was also happily married, though childless. His wife Eliza Flint Ray was the daughter of his first London boss, ten years old when he

George Moore

Panels by Pre-Raphaelite sculptor Thomas Woolner adorn the pyramid to Eliza Moore at Wigton, Cumbria

first knew her. To mark her death in December 1858 he commissioned a memorial in the centre of the Market Place in Wigton. The site was not empty. Until 1805 it was occupied by a wooden market cross; this was burned in the town's jubilant celebrations after Nelson's Trafalgar victory. Its replacement, a gas lamp and a pump, made way for Moore's tribute to Eliza.

It was not put in place until 1872, but for his £12,000 Moore received a substantial structure. From a seventeen-foot square base, with four drinking fountains set into it and (restored) railings around it, rises a tall plinth, holding aloft a gilded pyramid crowned with a knop and a cross. As its gold leaf and pink Shap granite glitter in the sunshine it resembles a fragment of a Russian Orthodox cathedral. For its design George Moore did not choose the northern architect Anthony Salvin who had designed his own substantial house, Whitehall, at Mealsgate in 1861. He turned instead to a lesser architect, though one with an extensive London practice. He was J T Knowles, Senior, whose *chef d'oevre* is the Grosvenor Hotel by London's Victoria Station, designed in conjunction with his son J T Knowles, Junior (later Sir James).

Knowles provided the structure, but it was left to a genius to provide the best parts of what Wigton people call 'The Fountain'. Moore commissioned the Pre-Raphaelite sculptor Thomas Woolner to provide four square reliefs, one for each face, showing four of the scriptural Acts of Mercy. Cast in bronze, they are beautifully modelled and crisply detailed. They are classically-influenced - the Elgin Marbles come immediately to mind - but within the constraints imposed by the style they are full of human feeling - anguish, compassion, wonder, gratitude. The contrast between the draped and the naked figures is particularly striking, especially in the panel depicting *Feeding the Hungry*, where the starving people face the compassionate food-bearers. Here the central figure is modelled on Amy, Woolner's wife. Along with the other panels, *Visiting the Afflicted*, *Clothing the Naked* and *Instructing the Ignorant*, it was shown at the Royal Academy in 1872, before being taken to Wigton for the Fountain. Woolner was also the sculptor of the gilded portrait head of Eliza Moore that appears in each of the four gables on the monument.

In 1848 Thomas Woolner became a founder of the Pre-Raphaelite Brotherhood - the only member who was a sculptor. They all believed that truth to nature was important in their work. Unfortunately, mid-Victorian England was not ready for such truthfulness in sculpture, so in 1852 Woolner emigrated to Australia; his embarkation from Gravesend for the other side of the world gave Ford Madox Brown the inspiration for one of his most famous paintings, *The Last of England*. The painting shows Woolner and his wife on the deck of a crowded steamer, gazing for the last time on the White Cliffs of Dover.

Woolner intended to become a gold miner, but found the work hard and not lucrative, so he turned back to sculpture. He opened a studio in Melbourne, where he successfully specialised in portrait medallions. Returning to England in 1854 he found his style was more acceptable, and he quickly became one of the most respected of Victorian figure sculptors. When he died in 1892 *The Times* obituarist wrote of Woolner that 'In life, as in art, he was the uncompromising foe of sham, of claptrap and of superficiality.'

However great the work he provided for Wigton's Fountain, it is often unregarded. The local authority has restored it in recent years but there are some questions to which we shall never know the answers. How did the second Mrs Moore, whom George married in 1861, react to this grandiose monument to her predecessor? Did she avert her face every time her carriage was driven through Wigton? And on George's accidental death in 1876 what did she think of his last request to be buried beside Eliza? She was perhaps a very forgiving and understanding woman.

Feeding the Hungry from the Wigton pyramid; the central figure is Amy Woolner, the sculptor's wife

*Penrith Beacon,
known to
Wordsworth*

IT COULD BE the ultimate trivia quiz question - 'Which poet was frightened by a northern pyramid?' It would stump most pub quiz teams - except possibly those in the pubs of **Penrith**. There the older quizzers, downing their pints, would murmur, 'Eh, lad, it were that William Wordsworth, used to stay with his granny at Arnison's shop, and went to school at t'Tudor Coffee Room!'

All this sounds unlikely, but it is essentially true. Wordsworth's grandparents, William and Dorothy Cookson, ran a drapers, that was later to become Arnison's, in the centre of Penrith. Here young Wordsworth and his sister Dorothy came to spend holidays when they were small. It was not a happy household. William's grandparents were busy with the shop and had little time for the young children. Their uncles, Christopher and William, were not inclined to entertain them. At home in Cockermouth William and Dorothy were allowed to run free; in Penrith they were kept firmly in place, by both harsh physical discipline and by incessant sermons on wickedness. William later recalled that when he was four he lay awake, terrified that God, who was good, allowed evil to be abroad in the world.

During one protracted stay William and Dorothy went to the school that was run in what is now the Tudor Coffee Room. One of their schoolfellows was Mary Hutchinson, later to marry William. The school was run by Anne Birkhead, who each May Day encouraged her pupils to wander round the countryside garlanding the local wells and springs. This was much more to young William's liking than the harsh regime of the Cooksons, and it is small wonder that he escaped the dour household whenever he could. As he wrote in *The Prelude*,

> O'er paths and fields
> In all that neighbourhood, through narrow lanes
> Of eglantine, and through the shady woods,
> And o'er the Border Beacon, and the waste
> Of naked pools, and common crags that lay
> Exposed on the bare felt, were scattered love,
> The spirit of pleasure, and youth's golden gleam.

The Border Beacon - or Penrith Beacon - was to play a major part in one of the 'visions' that enlivened the young poet. North-east of the town, and dominating it, is the high sandstone Beacon Hill, now heavily wooded but clear in Wordsworth's day. A climb from Beacon Edge Road winds through the trees and reaches a clearing, 937 feet above sea level. From here there are majestic views over the plain of the Rivers Eamont and Lowther. Ullswater gleams in the distance, backed and surrounded by the great Lake District fells. Crowning the hill is the Beacon itself, built in 1719 and repaired in 1780. Hewn from the surrounding rock, its red walls are scarred with nearly three centuries of graffiti.

The site had been used for earlier beacons - probably as far back as the Armada, like the site at Compton Wynyates (see page 121), or even earlier, when it warned of raids by the Scots. In its current form it played an important part in the 1745 rebellion, warning the locals of the nearness of Prince Charles Edward Stuart's army. The fire was lit inside the barred windows. The door on the eastern side gave access to the fire chamber. It is similar in construction and use to Ashurst's Beacon (see page 197), 75 miles due south and part of the same early-warning system.

To young Wordsworth it must always have been part of his memories of visiting Penrith. But it became an important part of his poetic education when he was just five. *The Prelude* records the time:

> While I was yet an urchin, one who scarce
> Could hold a bridle, with ambitious hopes
> I mounted, and we rode towards the hills.
> We were a pair of horsemen: honest James
> Was with me, my encourager and guide.
> We had not travelled long ere some mischance
> Disjoined me from my comrade.

Lost and alone, the little boy comes to the foot of the beacon hill, to a place where he knows that in the past

> A man, the murderer of his wife, was hung
> In irons.

This frightening, Gothic image is intensified by his surroundings:

> . . .reascending the bare slope I saw
> A naked pool that lay beneath the hills,
> The beacon on the summit, and more near
> A girl who bore a pitcher on her head
> And seemed with difficult steps to force her way
> Against the blowing wind.

Looking back on this experience 30 years later in the first draft of The Prelude of 1815, Wordsworth acknowledged that it was 'an ordinary sight', but it was a formative moment for him. Another 35 years on, in his 1850 revision, he underlines its importance:

> . . . I should need
> Colours and words that are unknown to man
> To paint the visionary dreariness
> Which, while I looked all round for my lost guide,
> Invested moorland waste and naked pool,
> The beacon crowning the lone eminence,
> The female and her garments vexed and tossed
> By the strong wind. When, in the blessed hours
> Of early love, the loved one at my side,
> I roamed, in daily presence of this scene,
> Upon the naked pool and dreary crags,
> And on the melancholy beacon, fell
> A spirit of pleasure and youth's golden gleam.

'THE NORTH OF England has produced many great men, but none greater than John Taylor'. 'John Who?' we asked on seeing this sentence on a website during our research. In fact, John Taylor was only a footnote to the information we discovered about the next pyramid, at Heversham near Kendal. Usefully for us, he linked Penrith, where he worked for a time, and the pleasant village of **Heversham**, where he was baptised. And Taylor's claim to fame? He is the only man not born in the United States to have been President of the Church of Jesus Christ of Latter-day Saints - the Mormons.

It's a long way - physically and probably spiritually - from the Mormons' Salt Lake City headquarters to the churchyard at Heversham. East of the church is a small plinth-based pyramid, not in good condition, which poses something of a mystery. It has inscriptions on all four sides, though two of them are broken and parts of the text are missing.

When was the pyramid put up? The inscription with the earliest date seems very simple. 'Behind this cold Memorial,' it says, 'lie the Remains of Henrietta Lawson, as a Wife and Mother affectionate, and to the needy bountiful. She died Novr 1825 Aged 55.' Henrietta was born around 1770. Her father was Andrew Ronaldson, a tacksman - a man who rented a piece of land then sub-let it to smaller tenants - from Blairhall between Alloa and

The mysterious pyramid at Heversham, Cumbria

Dunfermline. She married the Reverend Doctor George Lawson in St Andrew's church in Edinburgh on 19 October 1798. The year before, George had been appointed vicar of Heversham - the advowson was (and is) in the hands of Trinity College, Cambridge; unsurprisingly, George Lawson was formerly a Fellow of the College.

Henrietta's maiden surname became a family Christian name in succeeding generations. She and George had at least three children; two of the sons became clergymen, but the family began to slide down the social scale; a grandson had lengthy periods of unemployment, and a great-grandson was sent to prison. The inscription to Henrietta on the pyramid is straightforward - but why is there no date in November for her death? In fact, there is only one accurate date on the whole edifice.

There is another mystery - the identity of the next person commemorated on the pyramid. The carefully-chiselled text says, 'In memory of JOHN YOUNG ESQr the oldest Son of Col JAMES YOUNG and many years a beloved inmate of the VICARAGE. His Death in 1836 at the Age of 27 was sudden as a warning to others to be equally ready.' This may have meant a great deal to the grieving family and friends of young John Young. Unfortunately, it leaves us with very little to go on. We don't know who Col James Young was. We have no idea why John was 'a beloved inmate of the Vicarage', though he could have been a pupil - or even a master - at Heversham Grammar School who boarded at the Vicarage. Or was he the son of one of Lawson's sisters (though why not say so in the inscription if he was?). Nor do we know what caused his early death.

On the eastern side of the pyramid the language changes from English to Latin. The stone is broken so that we have only part of the text: 'Inter arbores aliis profuturas quas AD 1800 . . . hic jacet qu . . . GEOR . . .' Fortunately, the inscription had been noted before it was damaged, and we can fill in the missing parts. 'GEOR' was George Lawson, and he was 'plus quadruginta annis Vicarii' - vicar for more than 40 years. He died, it states, 'A.D. 1842 Aetis 77'. But as well as commemorating his death, the inscription points out the trees among which he is buried - 'inter arbores'. The trees - two chestnut trees by the churchyard gate and the great beech beside the pyramid - remain. George Lawson planted the trees - though maybe not in 1800, as the text says. A tradition says that they were perhaps planted to celebrate the victory at Waterloo in 1815, but local historian Roger Bingham believes that they commemorate an event nearer home. Just four days before the Waterloo victory, the vicarage was awarded 663 acres of land under the terms of the Heversham Enclosure Act of 1804.

The land should have brought Lawson a very healthy rental income; but unfortunately he determined to farm it himself. It was perhaps inevitable that he lost a great deal of money in the enterprise. To help pay his debts, his daughter Tamar turned the vicarage (it is now the Blue Bell Inn, just down the hill from the church) into a 'seminary' - a girls' boarding school. In the 1841 census returns she is described, at the age of 40, as a governess. Along with her were another governess and three servants. Between them they taught and cared for sixteen girls aged between 11 and 15. If Tamar was running her little school in 1836 then John Young would have been part of the establishment, too - what part did he play in relation to the young ladies?

The final Heversham mystery concerns the fourth inscription on the pyramid. Broken at the top, it leaves us with this fragment:

' . . . .Vicar . . . is Parish . . . died near Pau in France June 20th 1888 Aged 87 years'. Despite the unusual accuracy of the date, we have not managed to find who this dweller-on-the-continent was. It was not Tamar; although she was born in 1801 and so would be the right age, she died in Kendal in 1875. Was it a twin brother or sister? Or a cousin? Heversham has not yet given up all its secrets.

LOGICALLY, HIGH BENTHAM should be in Lancashire. It is only 17½ miles from Morecambe on Lancashire's west coast. In fact, it is Yorkshire's most westerly town - a massive 96½ miles from Bridlington on the county's east coast. A mile south west of the town and you cross the Lancashire border; a quarter of a mile further on is Clearbeck House at **High Tatham**, where Peter Osborne - sculptor, gardener, theologian - has created one of England's great small gardens.

Clearbeck is not the obvious place for a garden. The site is exposed and boggy, and required a great deal of work with a digger to sculpt it in to shape. There are, though, magnificent views; the garden is in rolling landscape between the secret grandeur of the Forest of Bowland and the open expanses of the Yorkshire Dales, not far from the heights of Ingleborough and Great Whernside. Working with the grain of the landscape, Peter Osborne has created a garden of water and grass, trees and sculpture, with varying levels and hidden corners - as Alexander Pope wrote:

> Let not each beauty everywhere be spied,
> Where half the skill is decently to hide.
> He gains all points, who pleasingly confounds,
> Surprises, varies and conceals the bounds.

Osborne's garden is perhaps more metaphysical than Augustan; it might even be seen as paradisal - the Paradise of Eden and the original enclosed paradise gardens of the Persians. When we arrived it certainly seemed as if we had come when angels were on a visit, too - the sun shone and from the groves music sounded. It wasn't musical angels, though; it was Lancaster's Haffner Orchestra on a day out, playing in ensembles and raising funds for their concerts.

Clearbeck garden has surprises at every corner. A turf maze with finely-balanced mobiles at its edge invites contemplative walking. Logs disguised as giant pencils lean against the door of a potting shed. And at the heart of the garden is the pyramid. It is the focal point of the garden-within-a-garden, the Garden of Life and Death.

About 12 feet high and almost completely covered in ivy, the pyramid is where you pass though death into a perfect life beyond. Peter Osborne has written: 'The Pyramid Garden is symbolic in colour, form and feature as well as in its planting. A short Valley of Shadow leads to the tomb-like grotto of the pyramid interior, where bones, fossils and grave fragments form a "memento mori". Passing through this you emerge into light at the little pool, which is a transition between Death and Life. Seen thus the water is a baptism leading to the Life Garden beyond, though looking back the other way it may remind you of Caron crossing the Styx in Böcklin's *Island of the Dead*, which was one of the inspirations of the garden. In the Garden of Life the light, colour, form and planting are all opposite to those in the Valley and pyramid, and tell not only of life but also of everlasting life.'

*Giant 'pencils'
in the garden
at Clearbeck*

The Clearbeck pyramid from the Life Garden

Böcklin's painting, which also inspired a symphonic poem by Rachmaninov, a horror film starring Boris Karloff and a novel by Roger Zelazny, is disturbing and, oddly, both claustrophobic and spacious. Clearbeck does not compete on the effect of spaciousness, but within a small compass has the same unsettling effect. The subtle use of appropriate plants helps - even people ignorant of names of plants cannot help but notice that the transition from one area to another is marked by changes in planting.

In the Valley there are plants with black or purple foliage amid the grasping ivies. Inside the pyramid, within the central, bone-strewn space, are more ivies - *Dark Night* and *Pedata* - as well as the *Ice Plant*, to make us think of the fate of fire-stealing Prometheus; chained to a rock, his liver was forever pecked by an eagle, and each drop of spilt blood formed an ice plant. Leaving the pyramid, the water of baptism is marked by *gypsophila* Baby's Breath, representing Moses in the bulrushes, while the golden conifer is *Arbor Vitae*, the tree of Life. Elsewhere in the garden the subtle language of plants adds its own commentary; balm represents sympathy, daisies are innocence, snowdrops are hope, lilies modesty and mint, virtue.

Dispensing drinks to music-loving visitors to the open day, Peter Osborne told us of the unromantic origins of the pyramid. 'It was a coal bunker, which we demolished, and we used the foundations for the pyramid. We made a circular, conical structure out of breeze blocks, then used strings from the apex to get the angles for the pyramid, which again we built of blocks. Then the whole surface was covered with a mixture of peat, cement, and cow dung, to encourage the ivy to grow up it.'

Compact though it is, Clearbeck is a garden of big ideas. It has affinities with Ian Hamilton Finlay's Little Sparta garden at Dunsyre (see page 246), but is easier to comprehend and is without the profusion of jostling ideas that characterise the Scottish garden. Peter Osborne's pyramid is thought-provoking and fascinating - one of the best and most picturesque of the modern pyramids.

NEXT CAME 'THE Beetle'. Not a strange Lancastrian version of one of the *coleoptera* in the shape of a pyramid, but the local name for the more-formally-known Ashurst's Beacon. It crowns a hill just north of the new town of **Skelmersdale** - the most westerly of the hills of Lancashire before they peter into the great coastal plain that stretches to the Mersey. From the Beacon there are stupendous views in all directions. Given good weather you can see as far as Liverpool and the mountains of Snowdonia, to the Isle of Man and Lake District fells, to the Dales of Yorkshire and to the Peak District. There are not many British locations from where you can see four National Parks - the remark of Gwendoline Fairfax in *The Importance of Being Earnest* when told that a neighbouring hill affords a view of five counties comes irresistibly to mind; 'I don't think I should like that; I hate crowds'.

It is no surprise, therefore, that the hilltop was chosen as the ideal spot for one of the chain of beacons that were the early warning systems of the past. It was probably in use for centuries - it was certainly prepared to give warning of the landing of the Spanish Armada in 1588, like the beacon at Penrith to the north

The Beetle or Ashurst's Beacon on the hills above Skelmersdale, Merseyside

197

(see page 192) and the one at Compton Wynyates in Warwickshire (see page 121). The structure in place now, though, was built in 1798 in anticipation of a Napoleonic invasion.

It is an elegant building, planned with some care. On a low plinth sits a cube of sandstone, once accessible through a doorway on the south side that is now blocked by a massive sheet of iron. On the other three sides are window openings (also now closed, this time with stone) that have well-detailed surrounds and heavy keystones, typical of a late-18th-century date. They must once, like the Penrith beacon, have had iron grilles so that the burning wood of the beacon fire would be visible. Topping the cube, on its own low plinth, is a tall, beautifully-built pyramid, which not only marks the location of the beacon but also acts, it is said, as a daymark for shipping in the Irish Sea.

So much for the Beacon, but who was Ashurst? If the 1798 date is correct for the current structure, the most likely candidate is Sir William Ashhurst (the double 'h' seems to have been optional at the time), born in 1725. He was a member of the long-established Ashhurst family who owned land in the area from the end of the 13th century. Sound Puritans, they fought on the Parliamentary side in the Civil War, and later had estates in Oxfordshire as well as in Lancashire. Sir William was born at Ashurst Hall, down the hill from the beacon. After education at Charterhouse he became a barrister, practising for 16 years; he was also Auditor of the Duchy of Lancaster (a royal appointment) and a counsel for the Commissioners of Excise.

In 1770 he became a judge of the King's Bench. His duties as an Assize judge sometimes took him back to Lancashire, so he must have kept his links with the area, even though his elder brother had sold the local estates in 1751. He seems to have been a hard-liner as a judge; it is said that a higher proportion of criminals was sentenced to death in his courts than in the courts of his contemporary judges. Ashhurst was criticised in his time not for his severity but for his 'passive indolence and inertness', his 'apathy and inattention'. His manner was described as 'confused and embarrassed, and he seemed to shrink from the eye of every one who approached him'. When serving with fellow judges he often would pass no opinion on a case, allowing the others to speak. When he did express a view, his judgments were coloured by his high Protestant ethics - he hated immorality, drunkenness, duelling and gambling. He retired from the Bench in 1799, and died in 1807.

Without a Bonapartean invasion Ashurst's Beacon remained unlit, and gradually decayed for more than a century. Thomas Meadows, who edited the *Wigan Observer*, bought the land and the Beacon in the 1920s and paid for the structure to be repaired. Such was public appreciation of the local landscape that when electricity pylons were striding across the country in the 1930s, the electricity company put the cables underground to avoid spoiling the view from the Beacon. By 1940 the beacon had again deteriorated and was on the point of collapse. Repairs were again undertaken by Mr Meadows, perhaps there were thoughts that in the event of a German invasion - a real possibility at the time - it could be brought into use. Meadows died in 1956; in 1962 his widow Florence donated the land and the Beacon to Wigan Corporation. The inscription on the Beacon noted that Thomas Meadows' desire 'was that this land should forever remain a beauty spot for the enjoyment of the people of Wigan'. It is now the centrepiece of Beacon Country Park.

THOMAS TELFORD. GEORGE and Robert Stephenson. Isambard Kingdom Brunel. We know the names and works of the great engineers and contractors of the 19th century. Or do we? The career of another, William Mackenzie, born in 1794, is largely unknown to the public, but his achievements were as solid as those of his contemporaries and the fortune he amassed was as great. A Lancastrian, he was born in Nelson and died in **Liverpool** - where his grave is marked by a pyramid. Yet his life was spent as much abroad as in Britain, securing and overseeing contracts throughout Europe.

Mackenzie's father Alexander is described as a 'contractor', too, but it seems more likely that he began as a navvy, working on the Forth and Clyde Canal. He later helped to organise labour on the Leeds and Liverpool canal. William started as an apprentice weaver in Blackburn, but soon became a lock-carver on the Leeds and Liverpool. Later he helped build the Edinburgh and Glasgow and the Gloucester and Berkeley canals before becoming the resident engineer on Telford's Mythe Bridge at Tewkesbury, and then on the huge excavations on the Birmingham canal.

William Mackenzie

Canals seemed destined to be his life, but in 1832 he successfully put in a tender for a tunnel on the Liverpool and Manchester railway, and subsequently worked on other lines in England and Scotland. The canals did not entirely slip from his grasp, though; in the 1830s and 1840s he worked on, for example, the Manchester and Sheffield Junction canal and the Shannon navigation. But in 1840 came his big break; with the engineer Thomas Brassey he began working on railways in France, first on the Paris to Rouen line and then in other areas, including the routes from Rouen to Dieppe, Abbéville to Boulogne and Orléans to Bordeaux. The first railway line in Spain, from Mataro to Barcelona, was built by Mackenzie and Brassey.

Mackenzie's diary turned up in 1988. It is the only one of any of the great engineers' journals to survive. Short on human detail - though we learn of his somewhat short temper and of his being prone to painful boils - it charts his obsessive journeying across the continent and at home. Between 1843 and 1846 he spent 1088 days out of 1461 in France alone. It is not surprising that eventually he bought an apartment in Paris, as well as a grand home in Liverpool.

For a man of such energy and drive, Mackenzie's end was sad. In the late 1840s, a time of political unrest on the continent and of financial crises at home, the partnership with Brassey was wound up, at the end with some acrimony. In January 1848 he discovered severe problems with his left foot, which had been troublesome for some years. He wrote to a friend, 'I perceived my foot much inflamed & near my small toe . . . a sort of hard seg where the shoe pressed upon was a large white lump - I sent for the Doctor he pronounced it gangrene he was right.' Mackenzie (though not his doctor) thought it had developed as a result of a long coach journey with freezing feet. Bathing and poulticing the affected area gave some relief, and Mackenzie set off again on his journeys; between April 1848 and November 1849 he travelled 20,000 miles to 160 destinations, including 14 Channel crossings.

That November did not start well. On the sixth, his diary records, 'Mr and Mrs Brassey, I and Meg [Mrs Mackenzie], Murton and Neumann dined at Café de Paris we had stinking Oysters could not eat them - Mrs Brassey got into one of her sulk moods made herself ridiculous she prophesied the [that] my life was short Brasseys were & Lockes were as bad I feel she is either insane or most Horribly spitefully wicked.' But Mrs Brassey was

The pyramid to Victorian railway contractor William Mackenzie in Liverpool

right. On 18 November he writes 'My feet are very sore'; on 19 he has to go to a meeting in his slippers; from 20 to 26 he is confined to bed. On 27 November he signs contracts for more French railway works, though he is probably still in bed. Then on 29 November another hand, probably Meg's, writes 'Mr Mackenzie taken suddenly speechless & lost use of his right Hand. Dr Burnett bled him copiously.' By 1 December he resumes the diary, though his writing is much shakier. Worse is to follow; the gangrene returns. He is virtually housebound in Paris for six months. Three doctors are treating him, but can do little; they amputate first his toes then, in stages, the rest of his foot. He can now get out in a wheelchair, and returns to Liverpool, but the fight has gone. He dies on 19 October 1851.

William Mackenzie was buried in the graveyard of St Andrew's Presbyterian Church in Rodney Street in Liverpool, where he had worshipped for many years. The church is still there, though it was gutted by fire in 1983. Seventeen years after his death his brother Edward, who inherited the bulk of William's fortune, paid for the construction of the pyramid over the grave. It is of grey granite, in the shape of the pyramid of Cestius (see page 2), with a blind entrance porch surmounted by the Mackenzie cost of arms in bronze, once surrounded by bronze laurel leaves. Below is an inscription carved on a pink granite slab. Unfortunately, the churchyard is railed and locked, and the inscription is too worn to see at a distance. The pyramid is sufficiently substantial to form a fitting monument to a great man.

But the story does not quite end there. Mackenzie's pyramid has attracted odd legends, none of which has anything to do with reality. The most persistent seems to be that, as was supposed to have been the case with Mad Jack Fuller at Brightling in Sussex (see page 68), the pyramid contains a body sitting upright at a table, this time with a Royal Flush of poker cards in his hand. The story is that the man - variously named as William McKenzie, William James Alastair McKenzie, James William McKenzie and even Tom McKenzie (but never William Mackenzie) - was an inveterate gambler, a tycoon who gained much of his wealth at the poker table.

And that's not all. Rodney Street is said to be haunted by him, a shadowy figure in top hat and cape who passes through the locked railings around the graveyard and fades into the pyramid. A Dr Harland was supposed to have seen 'McKenzie' in 1871 - the ghost's face was lit up as if with an internal fire, and his eyes were black and lifeless. Harland expired almost immediately, but managed to tell his friend to ask a local millionaire, Ralph Brocklebank, about the ghost. Brocklebank was a shipping magnate and Chairman of the Mersey Dock and Harbour Board from 1863 to 1869.

The garbled story that Brocklebank supposedly related is decidedly odd. He had known the ghost, whom he called James McKenzie, in life. McKenzie, he said, backed the early railways (almost right) but was also a body-snatcher, digging up new corpses and shipping them from Liverpool docks to Scottish medical schools, pickled in barrels. One night McKenzie played poker with a Mr Madison - who turned out to be the devil. McKenzie sold his soul in return for a winning streak, and asked to be buried above ground to escape Satan's clutches. The tale ends with Brocklebank hinting that his own riches might have come from a meeting with the same Mr Madison . . .

It is very curious that a life of such apparent probity and good Protestant hard work as William Mackenzie lived should be forgotten, yet his name should, after a fashion, live on in a tenacious Liverpool legend.

Mackenzie's coat of arms on his pyramid in Liverpool

St John's
Cathedral in
Salford, with the
pyramid designed
by Janet
Fitzsimmons
in 1992

SALFORD HAS LONG suffered as the almost-invisible neighbouring city to Manchester. It has never been clear where one stopped and the other started; Salford was seen as the grubbier side of its brother settlement, the place where L S Lowry attended Art School and painted his grim scenes of mills and blackened churches.

One of those Salford churches was St John's - the Roman Catholic Cathedral of the Diocese of Salford since 1851. The building of the church was an act of faith in itself. Until it was built, many of the Salford Catholics had crossed the River Irwell to worship in St Mary's Church in Manchester's Mulberry Street, but in 1835 part of that church's roof collapsed. Though the Salford worshippers had already been raising funds for a new church of their own - 'pennies from the poor and guineas from the gentry' - the disaster acted as a spur to their efforts. With hard work they had enough money to buy a plot of land in 1840; but just as they were about to start building, along came the Manchester and Leeds Railway, which offered them a good price for the land, vital to its progress. The parishioners then had more funds for another, better site, and they found one in Chapel Street.

Matthew Hadfield was chosen as the designer. He was from the Sheffield architects Weightman, Hadfield and Goldie, a staunch Catholic firm, with a long list of Catholic churches to their credit. St John's is not an original work, but a patchwork stitched together from sources - and, it seems not from first-hand experience of the sources but from a book, *Architectural Parallels* by Edward Sharpe. Hadfield combined, with a great deal of success, elements from three great parish churches - Selby Abbey and Howden Minster, both in Yorkshire, and Newark in Nottinghamshire, which provided the pattern for the tower and spire.

The church cost £18,000 (around £11 million at today's prices) and despite the generous giving of the faithful it plunged the Catholics of Salford into a debt that was not discharged until near the end of the century. But it was money well spent. The church was opened in August 1848 with support from the Salford authorities, who provided a celebratory banquet. There was a small anti-Catholic protest, but the protestors' views were soon swept away by the inexorability of Catholic Emancipation, recognised in law in 1829. This led in 1850 to the re-establishment of the Roman Catholic hierarchy, with 13 sees and an archdiocese in Westminster. St John's Church was immediately elevated to the status of the cathedral of the new Diocese of Salford. Cardinal Wiseman, Cardinal Archbishop of Westminster, came to Salford to consecrate William Turner as the diocese's first bishop in the new cathedral.

St John's suffered some indignities over the years - severe storm damage to the spire in 1881, the rebuilding of tottering turrets in 1919, and the removal of 60 feet from the top of the spire, which was out of perpendicular. Fortunately, money was raised to rebuild the spire in 1938. War damage from the 1940s was repaired in the early 50s, but when the building was found to be extensively infested with dry rot in 1969 there were mutterings about the need for demolition. Fortunately, the cathedral was spared, and £80,000 repaired it again.

By the 1970s the surroundings were looking decidedly grim, but a grant to clean the building in 1972 seemed to act as a catalyst for the area. Like much of the city, it has become more attractive and welcoming - in 1992 the immediate area around St

John's was given a £400,000 facelift. To the east of the cathedral a new public square and gardens were laid out, with railings, benches - and a pyramid.

It is a work of classical formality, a narrow pyramid on four ball feet, resting on a square plinth set on an octagonal base - a total height of around 11½ feet. It is inscribed 'St John's Square 1992'. Around it, defining the Square, are decorative metal screens and seats. All these, including the pyramid, were designed by Janet Fitzsimmons. The pyramid cost £12,000 and the whole project was financed by money from the government's Urban Programme. Unsurprisingly, there was much local muttering at the expense; letters to the newspapers described it as 'a monstrosity' and called for the money to be given to the cathedral's drop-in centre to help people who were homeless. Despite these criticisms, the scheme went ahead, and it still provides an oasis where local office workers can eat their sandwiches in the summer and where local skateboarders can hone their skills.

Janet Fitzsimmons was a landscape officer with Salford City Council in 1992, and a member of the landscaping team that undertook the urban regeneration of 1992. For the pyramid she specified not fine limestone but Florentine aggregate, a type of concrete mix that takes a high polish to resemble stone. It was specially cast by Forticrete Architectural Masonry of Bootle. The pyramid shape was chosen to imitate the spire of Hadfield's cathedral. And after all the aggravation over the aggregate pyramid, it is good to report both that in 1993 it came second in the annual Street Design competition run by *Local Government News*, and that, despite a little graffiti, and more severe vandalism that meant it had to undergo repairs in 1999, the pyramid still provides the focal point for an attractive urban space.

Detail from the Salford pyramid

NOT FAR AWAY, in **Manchester**'s Oxford Road, was one of the oddest of our pyramids. We came across it on the website of a Pennsylvania State University student called Jeremy R Cooke, who was studying in Manchester. He provided a picture and the text: 'This funky-looking pyramid thing was not on our tour, but we pass it all the time on our way to class. It's ugly, but it looked lonely, so I took a picture of it.' Obviously a man after our own heart; we had to go and see.

The pyramid is just opposite the Royal Eye Hospital. It is a simple construction, of slatted boards covered with mesh. A small door gives access to the interior. The pyramid covers a pit, in which electrical equipment hums quietly to itself. A broken sign attached to the north side proclaims 'Whitworth Park', which is an open space with a fine art gallery just down the road. 'Barry Horne' has been spray-painted over the pyramid by someone - probably Barry Horne.

This is a utilitarian solution to the problem of covering essential equipment that needs to be sited on a wide pavement; the pyramid was a good idea, but the execution is not up there with the best pyramids.

A pyramid that covers electrical equipment on Manchester's Oxford Road

The Cooperative Bank's blue, poo-powered pyramid in Stockport

FROM ONE OF Britain's most insignificant pyramids to the biggest - and one with both a curse and a hidden secret. Prosaically known as The Cooperative Bank, but recognised by thousands of motorists speeding through the heart of **Stockport** on the M60 as the Blue Pyramid, it dominates this stretch of the Mersey valley. Indeed, the area is now known as 'The Valley of the Kings' - Stockport people have a sense of humour.

The pyramid is 130 feet tall, and its blue glass sides rise through 10 floors before breaking to provide a platform for the superstructure - first, a mostly-solid blue section in two parts, convenient for the sign proclaiming 'The Cooperative Bank', then a transparent pointed cap. The building was designed by Michael Hyde and Associates, a practice that has offices in Manchester and Sheffield. It won the contract in a design-and-tender competition run by Stockport Council in 1987. The developers were Provincial and City Properties of Wilmslow, and management contractors Rush and Tomkins were appointed to undertake the construction. There were to be five distinctive buildings on the site - hence an early name for the structure, Pyramid 1.

The curse of the Stockport pyramid struck not long after work got underway in September 1989. The steelwork was almost completed when in April 1990 Rush and Tomkins collapsed, a victim of the recession of the late 1980s. They owed £300 million. Work stopped. It was another year before new finance, this time from the Cooperative Bank, and a new contractor, Ballast and Nedam, were in place, and work resumed. Did all now go according to the new plan? Not entirely. In September 1991 the main electrical contractor went into receivership. Nevertheless, the project was completed on the new schedule, by March 1992, only 15 months later than originally planned.

So all ended happily? Not quite. Despite the undoubted prestige that would come from occupying so distinctive a building, its 104,000 square feet of space remained entirely unlet for nearly four years - while the Cooperative Bank continued to pay the bills. At last, in 1995, the bank decided to move in itself. Even this was not the end of what many people began to see as a pharaonic malaise over the site; other buildings in the development, too, remained unlet for years, and in the late 1990s plans to put a cinema and leisure complex on the site collapsed.

Now, though, all seems to be going well in the Blue Pyramid. The Cooperative Bank has 800 call centre staff hard at work there, including 250 working for its internet banking subsidiary Smile, launched in 1999. They take around 10,000 calls a day, and make another 2,500 outgoing calls.

And the secret at the heart of the pyramid? The Cooperative Bank is noted for its espousal of green energy: it plants thousands of trees in community woodlands in the north west of England. It recycles all the waste it can, and takes almost all its electricity from renewable sources. One of these sources is used directly to power the pyramid - sewage. And not just any sewage - sewage from the residents and visitors in Bournemouth. Raw sewage is fermented at Bournemouth treatment works to produce methane, which is then compressed and burned to create electricity, which is sold to Scottish and Southern Energy for transmission to Stockport. This replaces an earlier source, methane from a landfill site in St Helens on Merseyside. The Pyramid has helped to reduce the Cooperative Bank's carbon dioxide emission levels by 77 per cent, and sulphur dioxide by 82 per cent. As Smile's website tells visitors, the call-centre staff 'work in a poo-powered pyramid'. So its smiles all round.

The Stockport pyramid in the 'Valley of the Kings'

IF STOCKPORT'S PYRAMID is Britain's biggest, the one at **Biddulph Grange** in north Staffordshire may be the most vulnerable - or at least was so until 1986. Its vulnerability comes from the material used in its construction - it is made of clipped yew.

From 1923 until the mid-1980s Biddulph Grange was a hospital - but a hospital with a garden unlike any other for which the National Health Service was responsible. It is one of the most eclectic Victorian gardens, full of exotic surprises and unexpected delights; not something that hospital administrators expect to have to deal with. Yet they coped with it very well, despite the attempts of local vandals to destroy it. Soon after we first visited, in the mid-1970s, the ornate Chinese Temple was burned out. Over the years some of the layout was simplified, and the yew of the pyramid grew in shapes perhaps not originally intended. By the middle of the 1980s the garden was on the critical list; it needed a transfusion of enthusiasm and cash to save it.

The National Trust recognised the garden's unique style and its needs. When the hospital closed, a public appeal launched in

1986 allowed the Trust to acquire the garden in 1989, and restoration began; such was the interest in the work that when the Trust opened the garden to the public in the early 1990s there were very large crowds of visitors. What they saw was work in progress, bringing the garden back to something approaching the vision of its founders.

The garden's original owner James Bateman inherited a large fortune from his father's interests in banking, coal mining and iron-founding. James, though, was more interested in the discovery and cultivation of orchids. Born in Bury in Lancashire, he grew up at Knypersley Hall, two miles from Biddulph, and even while at Oxford he pursued his interest in orchids. When he was 22 he employed a collector to discover new species in Demerara, and was industrious in cultivating at Manchester's Natural History

Museum specimens received from Guatemala. He wrote extensively on the subject - especially a sumptuously-illustrated (and very bulky) volume called *Orchidaceae of Mexico and Guatemala*, of which only 125 hand-coloured copies were printed, and his *Monograph of Odontoglossums*. In 1838 he married another keen horticulturalist, Maria Egerton-Warburton, and they moved to Biddulph Grange in 1840. After extending the existing house (a fairly modest vicarage) they turned their attention to the garden.

Gardens need structure as well as plants, and the man they turned to for help was a painter, Edward Cooke. Cooke was widely-travelled (including a visit to Egypt) and fascinated by nature; in 1872 he published a book called *Entwicklungsgeschichte* - grotesque animals - full of his own inventions of nightmare, Frankenstein-like combinations of different animal parts into new forms. Ruskin described Cooke as 'full of accurate and valuable knowledge in natural history with which he is always overflowing at the wrong times'. Cooke also had a wide knowledge of plants, especially ferns. It may have been a common interest in that subject that brought Bateman and Cooke together.

Their discussions about Biddulph Grange must have been fascinating. Who came up with the novel concept of a world-encompassing garden, which brings together Italy, China, Egypt and other locations? Did Cooke influence the Batemans, or were they both brimming with ideas? It doesn't really matter - the result is sensational.

The bones of the garden are laid out in what was boggy ground south of the Grange. Two areas of water were created, and paths serpentine around them. Some of the gardens within the ambit of the paths are conventional; many are not. China, for example, has a delicate temple, reflected in still water, with upswept roofs ending in dragons with bells suspended from their mouths. A pretty Chinese bridge crosses the water, while nearby a stone frog watches over this hidden space. A 'Great Wall', complete with watch tower, forms the boundary. Not far away, a huge gilded buffalo peers from its own Chinese stable. Other oddities in the garden include The Stumpery, where stumps of trees are planted upside down in the earth, their roots exposed. But the greatest of the garden features is what Bateman and Cooke called 'Egypt'.

The formal way to approach Egypt is through beech hedges into the forecourt. Two pairs of stone sphinxes, with more-than-usually blank expressions, line the path to the stone gateway, which is carved with a winged solar disc, now restored to its original red, blue and gold. The archaeological accuracy of these elements may have been assisted by Joseph Bonomi, Egyptologist and architect of the Egyptian-style Temple Mills in Leeds (see page 16), who was a friend of Cooke's (see Blickling, page 53). The rest of the structure is made of carefully-clipped yew, including the surmounting pyramid. By the 1970s the pyramid had ceased to be clipped in the lines of its Nile-side originals; it was instead more like a lopped-off version of the Cestius pyramid in Rome (see page 2). Clever restoration work in the 1990s involved growing new, small yews in boxes and training them to the proper shape, so that when the rest of the structure was repaired and re-trimmed, the pyramid could crown it once again.

Once the visitor has crossed the forecourt, passed the enigmatic sphinxes and entered the dark doorway beneath the glowing solar disc, what delights or horrors await? In a *coup de theatre* Bateman and Cooke have placed an ugly stone statue of the Ape of Thoth. It sits hunched, hands on knees, wearing a cloak of leaves and a fearsome expression. It is lit from above - but the light is not

The Biddulph pyramid in the 1970s

natural; a piece of ruby-coloured glass forms the skylight and bathes the Ape in blood. This was no doubt Cooke's idea. Thoth was the ibis-headed god of the Egyptians, among whose many attributes was being the guardian of the Eye of Horus and father of all science - including, appropriately in this garden, botany.

The ape - or baboon - was sacred to Thoth, who once disguised himself as the animal. There may also be a link with Freemasonry. By the late Pharaonic period, when the Greeks ruled in Egypt, Thoth was known particularly as the god of magic, and his name was never to be spoken. Thoth was identified by the Greeks with Hermes, and in one of the transmogrifications that such beliefs seem to attract, Thoth became associated with Hermes Trismegistus, the mythic founder of Freemasonry (see page 5).

We do not know if this burden of imagery was in the minds of Bateman and Cooke when they commissioned Waterhouse Hawkins, who also created the life-size dinosaurs in the grounds of the Crystal Palace in Sydenham, to sculpt the Ape. Perhaps they just wanted something startling at this point in the progress around the garden. And it is certainly startling if you approach not from the main Egyptian forecourt but along the Pinetum and through what appears to be a half-timbered Cheshire cottage, with the date 1859 large on its beamed façade. To enter this Hansel-and-Gretel house, and see the Ape, faintly glowing in the darkness behind, and then to walk to it, turn through 90 degrees and emerge in the Egyptian temple, is a psychedelic experience.

HENGIST THE SAXON is said to have built the first castle at **Tong** in Shropshire. As Geoffrey of Monmouth's *History of the Kings of Britain* tells us, Hengist went to King Vortigern and asked for land to build a fortress - 'as much land as can be encircled by a single thong.' The thong Hengist produced was a very long strip of leather carefully cut from the complete hide of a bull. 'With this thong he marked out a certain precipitous site which he had chosen with the greatest possible cunning. Inside the space which he had measured he began to build his fortress. Once this was completed, it took its name from the thong'. Thong became Tong - so the story goes. Hengist's much-rebuilt castle passed through a succession of owners, including William the Conqueror's cousin Hugh de Montgomery, and others, more exotically-named, including Adelicia de Belmeis and Sir Fulke de Pembrugge. After many years in the Vernon family it was sold, eventually passing to the Dukes of Kingston-upon-Hull. The ducal family sold Tong in 1760. The purchaser ane his son - both called George Durant - were the oddest people to have owned it.

The second son of a Worcester clergyman, George went to St Edmund Hall in Oxford, and it seems to have been in the Long Vac that on a visit home he captivated the second wife of the patron of his father's living. She was Elizabeth, Lady Lyttleton, who did not get on with her husband. Sir George Lyttleton lived in London, his wife at Hagley Hall, under the beady eye of her husband's brother, the Dean of Exeter. The Dean wrote to another brother that as soon as young George Durant came home, 'her Ladyship spent the whole day and evening, except mealtimes, at the Parsonage, and at last invited herself to dinner there . . . every attention that could be shewn to the greatest guest that ever entered the house was shewed to the parson and his family, and all kinds of neglect to everybody else and downright rudeness to me on every occasion'. Not only this; young Durant 'was admitted to a private audience with the lady in her closet . . . all the town talk of it, and 'tis generally said her Ladyship was caught abed with the young man'. Sir George clearly could not allow this. He forbad Durant's visits to Hagley Hall and threatened his wife with disgrace, virtually imprisoning her at Hagley, where, the Dean noted, 'she has been confined to bed with an eruption of the erysipelas kind, but not in danger of her life'.

Elizabeth was thus dealt with, but clearly George must be removed, too. In 1757 Lyttleton found him a job as a clerk in the Government Pay Office. By the next year he had become a Deputy Paymaster General and was sent to the West Indies with a naval expedition. He saw the ships of war in action in Martinique and Guadeloupe between November 1758 and March 1759, writing a fascinating journal of his experiences: he noted floggings on board, which he called 'the utmost torture; nor were these violent strokes, every one of which sunk onto their Flesh, the worst of their punishment, for their backs were afterwards bathed in brine to prevent a Mortification & stanch the Blood'. During military action on the ship he noted that 'Death has been Familiar and Horror prevailed . . . most of the men that were kill'd in action & hurried overboard with little or no ballast, had rose again & were now swimming on the surface of the Water. The Quarter Deck was absolutely steeped in blood & gore'.

Durant later accompanied the Navy to Cuba. In 1761 he was paid £250 a year. Within four years he was worth at least £300,000 and could buy his new estate in Tong. This wealth came from his dealing with military funds. Sums of money were paid into his hands and he had to pay them out again as part of his duties. As was common, he bought coin at a cheap rate and then charged the government a higher rate for selling it back to them. An even more profitable way to make money was in his dealings with prize money. Before the attack on Havana on 5 June 1762 the commanders of the British forces agreed on the distribution of any spoils. As the amount captured was around £3 million, there was a great deal to distribute. The Admiral and the General each received more than £120,000, and even ordinary seamen and infantrymen received almost £5.00 each (more than £600 today). One of Durant's jobs was to see to the distribution. There were 12,000 men who could have been paid; of them fewer than 1,000 had been killed in action. But another 9,000 died of sickness, leaving only around 2,000 alive to claim. And with so few to pay the money to, there was a fat surplus for Durant to keep.

The local Shropshire gentry must have regarded Durant as a *parvenu* when he came to Tong in the early 1760s - but that was unlikely to have worried him. He had plans. The castle was old, inconvenient and unfitted to his new status. He and his 18-year-old bride Maria, Quaker heiress to the Beaufoy vinegar brewery in Lambeth, had the castle pulled down, and in 1764 commissioned a new house. George Durant may have been his own architect, but the house is usually credited to Lancelot 'Capability' Brown. Architecture was not Brown's strong suit, though he did a considerable amount. Tong Castle (Durant kept the name) was a showy Gothick pile; imagine the Archbishop of York's Bishopthorpe Palace with Wren's Tom Tower in Oxford stuck in the centre. It was not great architecture. Sold by a later Durant in 1855, it was inhabited until 1909 and then partly dismantled in 1913. Its coup de grace was given in 1954, when the ruins were blown up as part of a Territorial Army exercise. An embankment of the M54 motorway now sits on the site.

George Durant's son, also George, commissioned the two pyr-

Tong Castle - carved on the surviving gateway, now part of the entrance to the Villiers factory at Wolverhampton

209

amids on the estate. If George senior was acquisitive and careless of county gossip, George junior was a full-blown eccentric. Much of his eccentricity manifested itself in building projects, but he also seems to have exercised an informal *droit de seigneur* in Tong. He had 14 children by his first wife Marianne (whom he divorced and then pursued in a single-minded law suit) and six by his second, Celeste. But he also acknowledged 32 illegitimate children in the village - an average of one in every house.

George junior's two pyramids in the area speak volumes about his interests. The first we came to is just over the border in Staffordshire, at **Bishop's Wood** - the nearest village to the oak tree where Charles II hid after the battle of Worcester. After some searching we found the pyramid in the garden of a house that belonged to the second dog-walker we asked for directions. It was a pigsty - not any utilitarian sty, but a pyramid in the best British tradition, built of rubble stone with some parts, including the point, made of better-quality, tooled stone. It is about eight feet high. On the side that contains the low entrance for the animals there is a carved inscription: 'TO PLEASE THE PIGS'. This cheerful message suggests that for all his eccentricities, George Durant was essentially a charming man. Adjacent to the pyramid for pigs is another of his animal structures; what appears to be a tiny Gothic chapel, complete with crow-step gables and blank window tracery, is really a cowshed, with another Durant inscription, 'RANDZ DE VACHE' - perhaps cod French for 'the cow's ranch'.

The other Durant pyramid is a bigger affair, but no less individual. It stands in the farmyard at Vauxhall Farm, not far from **Tong** village. Usually known as the Egyptian Aviary, it is getting on for 20 feet high. It was built for the Vauxhall Farm hens, which accounts for the protruding perches that break the line of the pyramid. Ornamental holes give access for the fowl, and a fancy top, like the cap of the Palace of Westminster's clock tower, may have been intended to provide a pinnacle for the rooster. Apart from the stone plinth, perches and cap, the structure is of brick - red for the body, black for the quoins and the corbels that hold up the perches. With some of them now yellow with lichen, the whole edifice has an air not so much of Westminster, more of an avian Keble College, Oxford.

George Durant's penchant for texts was once visible here, in a variety of pithy thoughts carved in the stonework - now they have been weathered away. One, indeed, proclaimed it EGYPTIAN AVIARY. Others included hen-related messages such as SCRAT BEFORE YOU PECK and AB OVO, as well as BETTER COME OUT OF THE WAY LOVE. Other texts were more general: LIVE AND LET LIVE, HONESTY IS THE BEST POLICY, TRIAL BY JURY and, ominously, TRANSPORTATION. Did Durant have an agenda here? It is also said that some of the bricks were carved with emblems that represented the local area, though the only one that was known about was a lizard, a reference to Lizard Hill, north west of Tong.

Nothing became George Durant junior's life like the leaving of it. Another of his buildings was put up on Tong Knoll, north of the village - a celebration of a victory in court against his first wife Marianne. His sons so hated this reminder of how he had treated their mother that they blew it up with two barrels of gunpowder, in an explosion that shook the village and rocked Tong Castle, just at the moment George breathed his last. Let us hope that, even if his sons did not appreciate him, the pigs of Bishop's Wood and the hens of Vauxhall Farm spared a thought for their dotty benefactor.

'To please the pigs' - George Durant junior's pyramidal pig-sty in Bishop's Wood, Staffordshire

The pyramid at Astley, Worcestershire

WE KNEW THE next place with a pyramid from its vineyard. **Astley** does a good line in fine white wines from its five acres of vines. Astley itself is a tiny village in the hills northwest of Worcester, not far from the canal town of Stourport. Its claims to fame are that it once held a Benedictine priory, now long gone; and that two well-known people had connections with it. They were the hymn writer Frances Ridley Havergal and Prime Minister Stanley Baldwin.

Francis Havergal was born in Astley rectory in 1836. Always delicate, she was educated by her father, who was himself a hymnodist and composer. In adulthood she continued to live with her parents or with her married sisters in Bewdley and Stourport. The excitement of her life seems to have been her appearances as contralto soloist with Kidderminster Philharmonic Society - one can envisage her in oratorios by Mendelssohn and Spohr. She also wrote for the *Church of England Magazine*, contributing verse and short stories. She wrote the words of 71 English hymns, and one in French. Eight were included in editions of *Hymns Ancient and Modern*, but only one, *Take my life and let it be*, written at Astley, is regularly sung today, while *Who is on the Lord's side?* gets an occasional airing. Frances died in 1879 at Mumbles, Swansea and is buried at the west end of Astley Church.

Baldwin was born in 1867 just north of Stourport, where his family's wrought iron and tinplate factory operated. Two of his mother's sisters were married to artists - one to Edward Burne-Jones and another to Ambrose Poynter. Rudyard Kipling was his cousin. Throughout his political career Baldwin was often in the area; from the age of 25 he first rented and later owned Astley Hall. He was Prime Minister three times between 1923 and 1937, dealing with crises such as the General Strike of 1926 and the Abdication of King Edward VIII in 1936. When he retired in May 1937 he returned to the village; he was made Earl Baldwin of Bewdley on 8 June that year. After his death ten years later a national appeal to raise a memorial to him failed to make enough money; Winston Churchill, annoyed at the lack of support, contributed the final sum himself. The monument is beside the road from Astley to Stourport.

Astley's pyramid is to neither Francis Havergal nor Stanley Baldwin. In fact, we have little idea who is commemorated. There was once an inscription, but the sandstone has been worn away over the years, and only ghosts of the words remain. It is possible to make out something that might be JAMES, followed by another name that may begin with K . . . Only the word 'died' is clear, and there may be the date 1704. It seems that the pyramid is not to one of the Blount family, lords of the local manor, whose brightly-coloured effigies have lain in prayer in the church since Tudor times. Nor is it to their successors the Cookes and the Winfords - a marble monument of 1702 to Sir Thomas Winford can be found inside the church. Whoever James K was seems likely to remain a mystery. And there's one other mystery at Astley. A watercolour of the church, painted in the 1780s for Dr Nash's *History of Worcestershire* by the artist Thomas Burney (cousin of the novelist Fanny Burney) does not show the pyramid. Was it not there? Was it out of sight, elsewhere in the churchyard? Or did Burney ignore it for artistic reasons?

CLIFFORD IN HEREFORDSHIRE is border country. A couple of miles north of Hay-on-Wye, it was described in the Herefordshire *Shell Guide* of 1955 as 'Thinly populated Welsh countryside . . . redeemed by the wide, meandering Wye.' In fact the village is beautifully set in rolling hills, and there is a wooden toll-bridge to take you across the river from Whitney as you approach it. Clifford is one of the biggest parishes in England; until 1853 it extended to 10,500 acres - even now it is 6,500 acres, the size of Ashdown Forest. What remains of Clifford Castle - dramatic ruins perched on a cliff over the ford across the Wye - was built around 1250. The powerful Clifford family took their name from the earlier castle; the best-known member was Rosamund. At Clifford she met King Henry II and became his mistress. He built a very private retreat, Rosamund's Bower, for them near Woodstock Palace in Oxfordshire, destroyed when Blenheim Palace was built, despite Vanbrugh's plea to keep it.

In the 19th century the Reverend Francis Kilvert was a regular visitor from his parish at Clyro, two miles down the valley, to Clifford Priory, a Victorian country house, owned by the Allen family. He described it in his *Journal* as 'certainly one of the nicest most comfortable houses in this part of the country'. At the Priory Kilvert watched an eclipse of the moon, flirted at a ball, enjoyed dinner, played croquet. Sometimes, too, he was invited to preach at St Mary's Church, across the fields from the Priory. To the south of the church, he would have seen the pyramid, on a pedestal, to Thomas Wheeler. Despite the loss of its apex, the pyramid is a listed structure which is 'a good example of stone masonry and enhances the setting of the church'.

The inscription is rather worn, but it is clear that the pyramid is 'IN MEMORY OF THOMAS WHEELER FORMERLY OF BURFORD IN THE . . .' where? The first thought was that it was Burford in the county of Oxfordshire, but while there were undoubtedly Wheelers there, engaged in the wool trade, we cannot link this Thomas with them. A more likely possibility is that the inscription refers to Burford in Shropshire, about 30 miles from Clifford. Thomas is described as 'OF THIS PARISH GENTLEMAN.' A possible Thomas Wheeler was married in Burford in October 1776, and it may have been him, though it is not clear if he was a 'gentleman'.

The plinth has a shield with the arms of Wheeler (a chevron between three leopards' faces) alongside an unknown and rather odd coat of arms, with a bird above and a gate below. The crest of an eagle rising from a coronet is that of the Wheelers. This suggests that Thomas Wheeler was part of a collateral branch of the Wheler family from near Worcester, who still use the coat of arms. They are descended from the 1st Baronet, Sir William Wheler. He was MP for Queenborough on the Isle of Sheppey from 1660, the year the baronetcy was created. His wife Elizabeth was the Royal Laundress.

How Thomas Wheeler came to be in Clifford remains lost in time. He may have been the "Thomas Wheeler of Hay" who was in the local militia during the Napoleonic threat; his wife may have been the Mrs Wheeler who held the tithes of Clifford at around the same time. We do not know for certain. It is curious that we have considerably more information about Fair Rosamund of the 12th century that we do about the early 19th-century Wheelers. There was one final quirk to Clifford - until 2004 the village boasted a Calvinistic Methodist church, built in 1827. One of the stops on our next journey was at another such chapel with its own small pyramid (see page 222). But before that there were other Welsh pyramids, old and new, to explore.

'Thomas Wheeler of this parish gentleman' is honoured by this monument at Clifford,

Tour 6

WALES

IT IS A brave village that takes on the conservation of its historic buildings as a labour of love. Too often structures are lost if they cease to be commercially viable or become of no use to the community. Not at **Cross Ash**, twenty miles south-south-east of Clifford in Herefordshire - where we had visited our last English pyramid - and just in Wales. A unique trust - the Village Alive Trust - has been set up in this part of Monmouthshire. It brings the community together to find out from its members which local buildings they feel are important, and then they find the funds to restore them.

Having renovated the local church at Llangattock Lingoed, the parishioners, led by their new deacon, Dr Jean Prosser, decided to look for new projects. They restored a large well-house near Cross Ash, then moved into the heart of the village, where a second, pyramid-topped well-house claimed their attention. Set at a field edge near the village crossroads, the well-house covers a spring of clear water, and probably dates from the 18th century. As the Village Alive Trust's plaque on the restored building notes, it 'supplied the village of Cross Ash until it was replaced by mains water. The spring still provides water to a nearby house'.

It is constructed with courses of quite narrow local stones, which form a hollow cube over the well before rising to the point of the pyramid. A doorway, now blocked, leads to the basin within. The restoration work was carried out by local craftsmen - and indeed the whole project is about as local as it is possible to get. It was the villagers who decided that the well-house merited restoration, and it is they who run the Trust.

Money for the restoration came from the Welsh Assembly and from the European Union, with additional help coming from the Welsh Development Agency. The Trust is also supported by local government, by other charities and by grant-giving bodies. Unlike many building preservation trusts Village Alive does not see restoration as a means to increase the value of a building that can then be sold for profit to finance the next project. All the buildings it rescues - and there are others, like a cider mill and a 17th-century barn on their list - remain in their original ownership. As the Society for the Protection of Ancient Buildings noted, the Village Alive Trust's approach to saving their local heritage 'offers a solution to be tried elsewhere, not just in Monmouthshire'.

The restored Cross Ash wellhead

FIVE YEARS HAVE past; five summers, with the length
Of five long winters! And again I hear
These waters, rolling from their mountain-springs
With a soft inland murmur. . . Once again I see
These hedge-rows, hardly hedge-rows, little lines
Of sportive wood run wild; these pastoral farms,
Green to the very door; and wreaths of smoke
Sent up, in silence, from among the trees.
We were a few miles further south on the border between Wales and England, in that almost-English corner of the Principality that

OPPOSITE:
The slate pyramid to Benjamion Wyatt at Llandegai (see page 227)

The ruined church at Chapel Hill near Tintern, with the pyramid to ironmaster Richard White

borders the Bristol Channel. Wordsworth had been here before us; his *Lines composed a few miles above Tintern Abbey, on revisiting the banks of the Wye during a tour. July 13, 1798* tell of his second visit, this time with Dorothy, 'my dear, dear Sister', and the emotions that this beautiful pastoral landscape evoked.

But was it entirely peaceful and pastoral? The pyramid we had come to see, at **Chapel Hill**, overlooking the ruins of Tintern Abbey, led to a different story.

The cobbled lane climbed steeply up the hillside to the churchyard of St Mary's. The church had been abandoned in 1972; the congregation moved away and the building was burned out in 1977, leaving a dank and rather sorry ruin that feels neglected, though members of the church at Tintern Parva have regular working parties to keep down the worst of the vegetation. It is a sharp contrast to the mown lawns and well-kept stonework of that other, nearby, ruin, Tintern Abbey.

Still, the views - abbey and river, woods and fields - are magnificent. It was certainly a fine place to be buried under a pyramid, as was Richard White in 1765. Set on a panelled base with a finely carved top, the pyramid is tall and slim, like the pyramids at, for example, Clifford in Herefordshire (see page 213) and Astley in Worcestershire (see page 212).

Generations of Welsh rain and wind had scrubbed away the inscription. Fortunately, an early-20th-century historian had recorded it, so that we know it read:

Richard White Son of George White of New Weir
In the County of Hereford, Gent. Died Oct. 30, 1765,
Aged 67 years.

Richard seems to have been the only White to have been buried at Chapel Hill - and the reason he is here is that he was the local industrialist.

Long before industrial production turned the valleys of south Wales to coal-producing, slag-heap-scarred grimness, and the coastal areas around Port Talbot and Newport into the heart of steel-making Britain, the Wye Valley was the powerhouse of iron production. The monks of Tintern Abbey probably produced iron, and certainly by the reign of Elizabeth I iron was smelted here and wire was produced; in the reign of Charles I annual profits were more than £175.

Some time around the beginning of the 18th century the wireworks at Tintern were taken over by Richard White. As his tomb says, he was a 'Gent.' and did not get involved in the dirty end of the business. But he knew the industry at first hand; his father George owned the ironworks at New Weir at Whitchurch in Shropshire.

The wire was actually made by skilled German and Swedish workers, who lived all around the area. An early 19th-century observer described the method; 'A large beam was erected across the building in which were affixed as many seats (in the form of large wood scales) as there were men employed, who were fastened in them by means of a girdle that went round their bodies.

'Between them stood a piece of iron filled with holes of different bores for reducing the wire to the various sizes. When the iron to be worked was heated the beam was put in motion by means of a water wheel that moved it, with the workmen in their seats, regularly backwards and forwards, who, with a large pair of tongs, passed and repassed the iron through the holes till by force they reduced it to the sizes required.'

Richard White was succeeded at the Tintern wireworks by his nephew Edward Jordan, but by 1775 the business was out of the family's hands. The work went on, however. William Gilpin was there in 1770, when Edward Jordan still was in charge at the wireworks. In his *Observations on the River Wye* Gilpin wrote, 'The country around Tintern-abbey hath been described as a solitary tranquil silence; but its immediate environs only are meant. Within half a mile of it are carried on great iron works, which introduce noise and bustle into these regions of tranquillity.'

In 1781 Admiral The Hon John Byng noted in his journal that if you were visiting Tintern Abbey you should 'spread your table in the ruins; and possibly a Welch Harper may be obtained from Chepstow'.

And then in 1798 Wordsworth came, for the second time, to
　　. . . these steep woods and lofty cliffs
　　And this green pastoral landscape . . .
Many learned papers have been written on what Wordsworth actually saw, and where he saw it. How close was he to the forges and the ironworks? Were the
　　　　　　　. . . wreaths of smoke
　　Sent up, in silence, from among the trees
coming from the industrial-scale burning of charcoal in the woodlands - a vital component for the smelting process - rather from cosy domestic hearths? In short, was Wordsworth's idyll a piece of Romantic self-delusion?

Today the ironworks are long abandoned, and visitors to Chapel Hill can view the wonders of Tintern Abbey in harmony with nature, their ears unassailed by the clangour of the wireworks and their nostrils unsullied by smoke from the charcoal and the forges. And Richard White, once master of the industry here, can sleep undisturbed beneath his hillside pyramid.

NEXT, WE NEEDED street signs to find our way round the intricacies of inner **Cardiff**. With them, we should have found the striking modern pyramid more easily. As it was, we circled Cathays Park and the City Hall a couple of times before we found the right spot.

We parked in a side street and walked over the railway to the junction of Ocean Way and Tyndall Street. We wanted street signs? Here they were in profusion, in the middle of the round-about - among them our pyramid, made of triangular warning signs. There was a sphere of circular signs, an up-ended cube of all types of squares, a cylinder of directional arrows and a cone of speed limits - topped, of course, by a cone.

This may have looked like the results of a fun night out for Trafnidiaeth Cymru - Transport Wales: 'Come on, boys, let's build something interesting with all those boring traffic signs we have to deal with every day!' Sadly, it wasn't them.

The pyramid of triangles and all the other shaped sculptures were part of a great investment in public art in Cardiff. They were commissioned by the Cardiff Bay Development Corporation in 1990. Funds were raised by a small levy on incoming business-es that were developing sites in Cardiff Bay. Altogether getting on for seventy pieces of public art have been produced. The project was coordinated by Cardiff Bay Art Trust.

The roundabouts have proved a popular place for some of the art (as they were in Scotland at Livingston - see page 247). Collectively the roundabout sculptures are called the Gateway pieces and act as an introduction to the Cardiff Bay area.

The road sign sculptures at Ocean Way were commissioned from Paris-born sculptor Pierre Vivant, who has studios both in his home city and in Oxford. The whole work has an official title - *Landmarks* - but it's not usually called that by locals, even by locals who are being polite. There was much criticism when the sign-sculptures were installed, of the 'Call that art? My five-year-old could do better' and 'They paid HOW much?' variety. Now, though, they are well-loved, and even the severest critics find them a useful, well, landmark - 'Turn right at the roundabout with the weird road sign sculptures . . .'.

Pierre Vivant's road-sign pyramid on Ocean Way, Cardiff

Pierre Vivant likes working with the trappings of traffic; one of his most famous pieces is his *Traffic Light Tree* near London's Canary Wharf estate. Made of 75 traffic lights on a single stem (and, of course, set on a roundabout) it stands where a lime tree failed to flourish. It changes its colours manically, though it does not usually confuse passing motorists or cause accidents.

Like the *Traffic Light Tree*, Vivant's Welsh road sign pyramid and the other geometrical shapes certainly live up to their billing as public art, adding a touch of frivolity to the otherwise rather dull infrastructure of the Cardiff Bay area. In 1998 Welsh MEP Glenys Kinnock wrote that 'We want those who visit Cardiff to remember Cardiff. Public art represents a real statement about a shared history and a shared culture. Public art is in no way elitist - it can touch those who may not otherwise volunteer to troop round a gallery or museum.' Certainly not elitist, the *Landmark* sculptures have attracted the expected level of vandalism - some of the triangles are missing from the pyramid, for example. But it still lifts the heart as you drive past on your way to your meeting, your rendezvous or your assignation.

FOR US IT was Abertawe - or **Swansea** as the English know it. We parked near the banks of the River Tawe, within sight of the next pyramid.

Parc Tawe Centre is much like any city-centre shopping and leisure area developed in the late 1980s and early 1990s. The same shops line its malls as you'll find elsewhere - Toys 'R' Us, Homebase, Staples, JBB Sports, Mothercare World . . . And there's a ten-screen cinema and a Megabowl. So what makes Parc Tawe different - and where does the pyramid fit in?

In fact, the pyramid and its contents are the difference, for this is Plantasia, 1,600 square metres of tropical fantasy, full of heat-loving plants and animals, all set within an elongated pyramidal glass hothouse. Visitors can spend an intensive morning hitting the shops, enjoy lunch at any one of the many fast food outlets and then unwind in somewhere so unlike the rest of Swansea - and indeed Northern Europe - that it's as if you've been teleported to another planet.

And it's not just one single tropical environment you experience. You might expect the rainforest - all bananas, tree ferns and lianas. But then there's the humid climate, where the humidity is kept at 85 per cent, and the tropical zone where a cascade drops

Plantasia in Swansea is housed in a pyramid designed by Percy Thomas

into the central pond. In season, tropical butterflies, so brilliantly-coloured that they seem to be lit from inside, flit in their graceful dance around the humid zone. Harsher is the arid zone, which mimics parts of the earth that have less than 25 centimetres of rain in a year - many of them very much less. Here there are the dense-skinned plants that have adapted themselves to store what moisture they can find - prickly cactus chief among them.

This may sound worthy, but dull. Actually, it's great fun, partly because the form of the pyramid allows different levels from which the plants can be viewed. There are the animals to look at, too - chief among them a colony of Cotton-top Tamarin monkeys from the Columbian rain forests, which can be watched from a tree-top high walkway. Add to that insects, reptiles and fish - including piranhas (in their own aquarium tank!) - and birds, and it's a recipe for a good afternoon out.

This pyramidal pleasure palace was the idea of an enlightened bureaucrat at Swansea City Council. It is said, perhaps unsurprisingly, to be the first in Europe - there can't be a lot of competition for a combined shopping centre and hothouse. The pyramid cost £7 million to construct and fit out, and in 1990 it won a bronze medal and an Architecture award from The Royal Institute of British Architects (RIBA) for its designers, Cardiff-based Percy Thomas Architects.

Sir Percy Thomas, founder of the firm in the second decade of the 20th century, was one of the Principality's most famous architects. Starting as a conventional neo-Baroque architect in the 1900s, Percy Thomas developed a style for his biggest work, Swansea Guildhall, that was a combination of strict classical planning with the look of cubist-style white boxes - though this was probably because the city fathers balked at the cost of the columns and decoration he had intended. Only in the immensely tall tower, oddly decorated with the sculpted prows of longboats, did he get his way. Its interior is best known for the Brangwyn Hall, with its startlingly-colourful murals by another Welshman, Sir Frank Brangwyn.

Percy Thomas's most famous building is probably the Temple of Peace and Health in Cardiff's Cathays Park - it's very satisfying, like a fragment left over from Swansea Guildhall. It was built in the late 1930s as a World War I memorial to promote the well-being of everyone.

A knighthood and the Presidency of the RIBA (twice), as well as its Gold Medal in 1939, five years after the completion of the Swansea Guildhall, were among Percy Thomas's rewards. More importantly, perhaps, his practice continued, with buildings around the country (Clifton Cathedral in Bristol, finished in 1973, and the Wales Millennium Centre of 2004, for example). Now part of the Capita group, the firm is still designing, though Sir Percy's classical-meets-modernist style is no longer used.

Plantasia is a successful building, and much loved by local people - it gets more than 90,000 vistors a year - so there was a great outcry in 2003 when new owners of the whole complex suggested that it should be demolished and moved elsewhere to make way for a new car park. Local councillors sprang to its defence; Cllr Davies said, 'I am amazed that people are even asking questions about it. Plantasia is not for sale. Plantasia is very dear to the heart of the people of Swansea. We think it is the best botanical garden in Wales.'

Fortunately, the threat has retreated, and the Cotton-tops, piranhas, tarantulas, frogs, lizards, butterflies and all their friends, animal and human, are safe for now.

SMOKE BELCHES INTO the still air from the burning of limestone. Horses and carts creak through the valley to the sea, laden with grey slate or granite, shining dully in the mist. And bricks by the thousand - the hundred thousand - are kiln-fired and stacked here, ready for transport. A horse-drawn tramway takes the strain, and steam engines chug away in the background. All around are shouts and singing, curses and laughter.

Where are we? Perhaps in the heart of the south Wales industrial belt, where long terraces wind along the hillsides and the sun is permanently obscured, when the rain's not falling, by a dense smog of mist and smoke.

No. We're on the Pembrokeshire coast, inside the National Park, standing by a whitewashed pyramid and looking out along the jagged rocks of the spectacular shoreline. Gulls cry overhead and the sea susurrates far below us. No sound of industry now, but a century ago the tiny harbour at **Porthgain** was crammed with ships, up to twenty each day, transporting the slate, granite and bricks produced here out to the rest of the British Isles.

The Porthgain pyramid is a white navigation marker, to help all those ships make their way safely in and out of the narrow harbour entrance. (see also Holy Island, page 182 and Menai, page 225). It is on the southern headland; its northern counterpart is a cone. A quirk of landownership means that, whilst the pyramid is owned (and re-whitewashed) by Pembrokeshire Coast National Park Authority, the cone is ministered to by the National Trust.

Both markers are about 22 feet high and were built in the early 1870s. The cliffs on which they stand are made of very hard igneous rock, but behind them is much softer, sedimentary rock. The eternal niggling of the sea through hard rock eventually let it reach the softer rocks and the cleft in which Porthgain harbour developed was created. The geology of the area - slate intruding into granite, with clay suitable for brick making around the granite's edges, contributed to its 19th-century wealth.

For some entrepreneurs, though, the facts of geology had to be embroidered. John Davies from Narbeth, for example, tempted investors to buy shares in his quarries by being more than a little economical with the geological truth. In fact, the slate at Porthgain was never top-quality - better in large slabs suitable for gravestones and gateposts rather than for splitting into roofing tiles. Just occasionally, though, it was chosen for prestigious jobs; University College Bangor used Porthgain slates on its roof - and its use there caused a long-term rumpus with the north Wales slate quarries, like those at Bethesda (see page 227).

The evidence of industry is all around in Porthgain. A row of small stone quarrymen's cottages is dwarfed by the great bulk of the hillisde of Ty Mawr, by the machinery shed built in 1890 and, alongside the harbour, by huge brick-built hoppers. Crushed stone was stored in them, graded into different sizes, and ships could sail directly beneath them for loading.

The hoppers were built in the very early 20th century, when the tiny harbour was enlarged. But the writing was already on the wall for Porthgain. The harbour was just too small, and too remote from the main railway system. Access, despite the pyramid and the cone up on the headlands, was too hard. By the end of World War I Porthgain probably knew its days were numbered. A last, rather desperate attempt to make the harbour even bigger in 1930 was doomed. Industry stopped here in 1931.

Now Porthgain is one of Pembrokeshire Coast National Park's most individual villages. The industrial remains are in a conservation area, and there is a thriving artistic colony. The heart of the

The pyramidal daymark at Porthgain on the Pembrokeshire coast

village today - and probably always was - the Sloop Inn. It was founded in 1743, long before the quarries opened. It is still there, long after the quarries have closed. Surviving for more than 260 years suggests that it is as durable as the granite cliffs beneath which it huddles.

THE STRONG DRINK taken at the Sloop is unlikely to have met the approval of Lewis Evan, to whom our next pyramid was dedicated. Evan was an early Calvinistic Methodist preacher, who was frequently imprisoned for his beliefs. His pyramid is in the remote mid-Wales village of **Adfa** near Llanllugan in Montgomeryshire, nine miles north west of Newtown.

We were challenged as soon as left our car in the village.

'Are you Mr Fury?' asked a small, very Welsh woman.

'Er - no. Why?'

'Oh, sorry. I was waiting to meet Mr Fury. He's coming to look at the Chapel House.'

'We're here to look at the pyramid to Lewis Evan.'

Her face lit up. It seemed that not many people wanted to know about Lewis Evan - and perhaps even fewer about his pyramid. Mrs Ruth Jones, chief steward of the Lewis Evan Memorial Chapel, decided we were worth consideration, and took us under her wing.

First, she tried to sort out our ideas about Calvinistic Methodism. It started when George Whitefield (see page 133), once John Wesley's right-hand-man, parted company with him in 1741 when they had a difference of theology about predestination and free will (perhaps fortunately there wasn't time for Mrs Jones to go into too much detail here). Whitefield's followers split into three (it was a very schismatic time). The Whitefield Methodists soon faded away. Whitefield himself became chaplain to the Countess of Huntingdon. The Countess of Huntingdon's Connexion (see also page 369)mn still flourishes in England. The third strand was kindled in Wales, first by Whitefield's own preaching, and then by native preachers. Welsh Calvinistic Methodism was formalised only in 1823. It is now part of the Presbyterian Church of Wales.

The Adfa chapel building is white-painted and solidly late Georgian, with round-headed windows at its eastern end. To the west, the secular use of the adjoining Chapel House is marked by rectangular, segment-headed windows. The weather-battered west wall is hung from top to bottom in Welsh slate. The other walls are whitewashed (and suffering from rather too much rain) and the woodwork is painted green.

It was built in 1770 as the Gerizim Chapel, named after the holy mountain in the Promised Land from which Joshua read the Law to the assembled Israelites. It was enlarged in 1820, and remained in use until 1995 when, as Ruth Jones told us, 'A terrible storm took off part of the roof and we couldn't use it'. Restoration took two years, but now it has reopened to serve its small congregation.

But where was the pyramid? It sat by the south wall of the chapel, surrounded by a low, ornate, green-painted rail. Sadly, it was a bit of a disappointment as a pyramid, but interesting historically. Its tall white plinth supports a rudimentary banded pyramid topped by a leafy finial. It has an inscription in Welsh. The English translation, also carved on the plinth for others to understand, reads:

*Preacher
Lewis Evan's
pyramid-topped
monument at
the Calvinistic
Methodist Chapel
at Adfa*

In memory of LEWIS EVAN Llanllugan
The first Preacher in connection with the Calvinistic
Methodists in North Wales
Born in 1719 a. d. Died in 1792 a. d.
He had trial of cruel mockings and scourgings
yea moreover of bonds and imprisonment.

Lewis Evan was a weaver in Llanllugan. At the age of 18 he
heard the fiery local preacher Howell Harris speak in Trefeglwys,
and was converted. Almost immediately he began his career as a
Methodist 'exhorter' - not an easy job, as his memorial notes. He
was imprisoned several times - first at Dolgellau for preaching
illegally at Bala in 1745. He was regularly heckled and mocked.
Beatings were frequent. Despite this, however, he remained
steadfast and, according to eyewitnesses, cheerful.

He lived long enough to see the chapel at Adfa built, when he
was 71. Until then the Calvinistic Methodists of the area had
worshipped in local farmhouses. Evan was buried in Llanlluggan
churchyard; only a fragment of his gravestone remains.

Inside the Lewis Evan Memorial Chapel at Adfa

Now the Adfa chapel, reopened after its restoration in 1997, is his memorial, and Mrs Jones is one who helps to keep his memory alive. 'Would you like to see inside?' she asked. She led us through the arched doorway. It was a surprise - first because the chapel is orientated in an unexpected way. Instead of pews arranged in rows facing one of the short walls, they are curved to face the long south wall, where the tall pulpit, approached from each side by steps with fearsome spikes on the posts, dominates the space. This may sound rather grim, but it is actually very attractive. The walls are painted in soft lemon, and the elaborate ceiling rose is picked out in other citrus hues. Over the windows to each side of the pulpit are text scrolls - GWYN EU BYD Y TANGNEFEDDWYR and NI A EWYLLYSIEM WELED YR IESU. Ruth Jones kindly translated for us - 'Blessed are the peacemakers' and 'Sir, we desire to see Jesus'.

She said that it was a struggle to keep the chapel going. 'Adfa is a very small village. We are getting a few new houses, but the young ones moving in are not interested. They'd rather wash their cars on Sunday.' As she finished speaking, a car drew up outside. The long-awaited Mr Fury had arrived. We left Mrs Jones ushering him through the door of the Chapel House, hoping he would take it as a tenant. She was probably hoping, too, that he would help swell the congregation of the chapel dedicated to the cheerful Lewis Evan.

OUR ROUTE NOW took us into the heart of north Wales - to the slate-grey town of **Dolgellau**. We had found a website reference to the Dolgellau Town Trail, and to 'Dolgellau's own pyramid, a pyramid to local bard and schoolteacher Dafydd Ionawr (1750 -1827)'. And that was it, except for another site that indicated that the poet's pyramid was in the Old Cemetery in Marian Road.

It took several circuits of Dolgellau town centre before we located Marian Road. The cemetery was at the end of it, overlooking the rugby pitches and the Afon Wnion. At its far end was the pyramid, a handsome, though perhaps rather severe, stone construction.

It is clearly inscribed in the band above the plinth with the words 'BEDD DAFYDD IONAWR' - Dafydd Ionawr's grave. Further illumination comes from two other inscriptions, in Welsh and Latin. In translation, both tell us that he died on 12 May 1827 at the age on 77; the Latin also says that he was 'BARDI CHRISTIANI MERVINIENSIS' - a Christian bard from Merioneth. The other information on the pyramid is that it was placed there by Rev J Jones of Ynysfaig.

What had Dafydd Ionawr done to merit his pyramid? He was born - as plain David Richards - near Tywyn on the west cost of Wales, and was at school there. He was probably taught there by the local curate, Evan Evans, one of the most renowned Welsh poets of the time, whose bardic name was Ieuan Brydydd Hir. Dafydd went on to school in Ystradmeurig near Aberystwyth, where another poet and scholar, Edward Richard, taught him.

Young David is said to have been gifted at mathematics and the classics, and after he had left Ystradmeurig he worked at a school in Wrexham for a time before going up to Jesus College, Oxford. A glittering academic career seemed to beckon, but he was apparently unhappy in Oxford, and stayed only a term. He went back to teaching, first at Oswestry and then at Carmarthen. In 1779 he applied to the Bishop of Llandaff to admit him to holy orders;

the bishop refused because there was a suspicion that David Richards was tainted with religious 'enthusiasm'.

He returned to teaching. In 1790 he went back to Tywyn as master of the free school. All this time he had been writing poetry, and in 1793 he published *Cywydd y Drindod*, under the bardic name of Dafydd Ionawr - Ionawr means 'January'. Running to more than 300 pages, this is the longest cywydd ever written. This complicated poetic form was devised in the 14th century by Wales's best-known poet Dafydd ap Gwilym. It employs cynghanedd (harmony), a very involved system of alliteration and internal rhyme.

The subject of *Cywydd y Drindod* is the Holy Trinity - and its author had trouble selling it. He tried to sign up subscribers to help him publish it, but with little success. Still, his fame slowly grew, and he followed up the work with a series of others, while he continued to teach. In 1794 he moved to Dolgellau, and was in charge of the school there from 1800 to 1807. He seems also to have been in charge of the new Merionethshire Gaol in the town, which was built in 1811.

In 1798 his father died, and Dafydd, who had never married, entered into a rather odd arrangement with the family of his relative and friend Thomas Jones. Dafydd gave all his inheritance to Jones, on condition that they took him in and looked after him. Thomas Jones founded the first bank in Dolgellau, and Dafydd's gift probably helped its success. Thomas's wealthy son John Jones was a well-known patron of the Welsh arts and a regular adjudicator in eisteddfodau. It was John Jones who championed Dafydd Ionawr's work and paid for a new edition of the poet's collected works in 1851. He is the 'Rev J Jones' who in 1834 paid for the pyramid to the poet.

THE SWELLIES. WHAT else would you call one of the most turbulent stretches of water on the Welsh coast? And swell it certainly does, as the incoming tide pushing north up the **Menai Strait** and between the massive piers of Robert Stephenson's great Britannia Bridge of 1850 meets an equally powerful flow southward from Bangor that slides purposefully beneath the suspended roadway of Thomas Telford's magnificent 1826 Menai Bridge. Add the narrowness of the channel to the mix and dot it with submerged and barely-visible rocks that set up whirlpools, and you have perfect conditions for tricky navigation.

Certainly writer and broadcaster Libby Purves found it a challenge as she circumnavigated Britain with her husband Paul Heiney and their children, then aged five and three, in a 30-foot boat, the *Grace O'Malley*. It was her account of the voyage, *One Summer's Grace*, which alerted us to the pyramid that helps intrepid navigators brave the Swellies.

Fortunately, Libby and Paul had the help of the pilot for the Straits, who told them just when to run The Swellies - there is sufficient depth of slack water 20 minutes before high tide at Caernarfon to get through without hitting the rocks - and provided cheering information, like the fact that at least one yacht a week is wrecked in the Strait.

The pyramid - tall and white-painted, sitting right on the mainland waterline not far from the Britannia Bridge and near the island called Gored Goch - helps navigators avoid tragedy. With the water moving at anything up to eight knots, they have to keep their wits about them; there are sandbanks as well as the rocks and the whirlpool. The white pyramid is what vessels coming

The life of poet Dafydd Ionawr - David Richards - is honoured by this pyramid at Dolgellau

*A yacht passes
the navigation
pyramid marking
The Swellies in
the Menai Strait*

under Britannia Bridge must aim for, altering course when they are opposite; coming from the Menai Bridge direction, it is again a target and a signal to shift direction. Experienced sailors can make the traverse of the Swellies by just one change of course; less-skilful navigators will need to tack more often.

It was the whirlpool at The Swellies - in Welsh 'Pwll Ceris' - that gave rise in part to one of the earliest railway publicity stunts and helped Anglesey's nascent tourism industry. In 1860 one of the villagers - either the blacksmith or the tailor - of the already-cumbersomely-named Llanfair Pwyllgwyngyll decided to call the railway station Llanfairpwllgwyngyllgogerychwyrndrobwllllantysiliogogogoch. Unsurprisingly, this was the longest name on the entire United Kingdom railway system, and people began to come - and continue to come - to see it and buy a very long platform ticket to prove it. The name is 58 letters long (or 51 if you are Welsh as the lls and the chs count as single consonants) and means 'the church of St. Mary in the hollow of white hazel trees near the fierce whirlpool by St. Tysilio's of the red cave'. The central part of this sesquipedalian extravaganza, 'gogerychwyrndrobwll' is the fierce whirlpool section, and refers to The Swellies.

WE HAD ALREADY come across the architect James Wyatt as the designer of one of the best pyramidal structures in the country, the Darnley mausoleum at Cobham in Kent (see page 62). Now we were heading for another Wyatt pyramid, a memorial to James's elder brother Benjamin and his wife at **Llandegai**, just around the top of Wales near Bangor.

Many of the people commemorated with slate gravestones in St Tegai's churchyard worked for the owner of the massive slate quarries that still scar the Snowdonia hinterland. At the edge of the churchyard is the slate pyramid to Benjamin Wyatt - appropriately slate, as Wyatt was for many years Land Agent to the landowner, Richard Pennant - Lord Penrhyn.

Wyatt took up his post in 1785, when he was 40. He had previously worked as a road surveyor in Staffordshire, but had also had some training in architecture as part of the family firm, with his uncle William Wyatt. His elder brother Samuel got Benjamin the Penrhyn appointment. Samuel was at that time rebuilding Penrhyn Castle, just north of Llandegai. Samuel's work at Penrhyn was largely replaced early in the 19th century by the present neo-Norman fantasy now in the care of the National Trust.

An 18th-century Land Agent was an important figure. Directly responsible to the estate owner, he was in effect the boss of the place and director of all operations. In Wyatt's case, he had an enlightened and ambitious master. Lord Penrhyn was keen to develop his lands in North Wales. When he inherited the estate it consisted of little more than a derelict castle at Penrhyn and acres of bare mountains. He was already a wealthy man, with sugar plantations in the West Indies and salt works in Cheshire, but he looked for new ways of making his land work for him.

He found a few local slate workers in the valleys of the Snowdon massif, who were producing about 1000 tonnes of slate a year. With Benjamin Wyatt's help, Lord Penrhyn transformed a cottage industry into a huge industrial operation. Within a few years the new Bethesda quarry on the slopes of Elider Fawr was shipping 12,000 tonnes a year just to London - no doubt helped by Samuel Wyatt's advocacy of Penrhyn slate to

A slate pyramid at Llandegai marks the burial place of Benjamin Wyatt, 'brother of the late James Wyatt, His Majesty's Surveyor General'

his clients, not just for roofs but also for lavatory seats, shelves and window sills. In a shrewd business move, the Wyatts cornered the best of the slate for themselves; Lord Penrhyn made an agreement to supply four Liverpool merchants with slates, but excepted from the deal 'all such slates as Samuel Wyatt or James Wyatt of London shall or may want within business respectively'.

Benjamin Wyatt's work made sure the slate reached its new markets. He designed the first railway in the area - a horse-tramway with a gauge of just under two feet, which ran $6\frac{1}{4}$ miles from Bethesda to Port Penrhyn. The port, just east of Bangor on the northern edge of the Penrhyn Castle estate, was another of Wyatt's developments. He laid out the breakwaters and designed the inn and harbour offices. He was the architect of workers' cottages at Bethesda and of the inn at another estate village, Capel Curig. He laid out miles of roads through the mountains. He also built a sea-bathing pavilion and a Gothic villa for the Penrhyns.

Benjamin Wyatt's architecture is not particularly polished. His architect brothers, Samuel and James, Benjamin's own son Lewis Wyatt and his nephews Benjamin Dean Wyatt (designer of the Theatre Royal Drury Lane) and James (later Sir James Wyatville, rebuilder of Windsor Castle) were more accomplished. But Benjamin had a profound impact on the look of buildings throughout Britain and abroad: it was largely through his efforts that Welsh slate became the preferred roofing material for most buildings.

He lived at a house called Lime Grove in Bangor, with his wife Sarah and their four children. It was a privileged life. The Wyatts were gentry - they even had a butler - and the family was respected throughout the area. Sarah was a distant cousin of Dr Johnson, and occasionally Benjamin met the great writer and lexicographer on his visits to London.

It was to Sarah that the pyramid was raised by Benjamin, when she died in 1813. The inscription to her tells us a great deal about the Wyatt family pride. It says:

> Within this TOMB Are Deposited the Mortal Remains of
> SARAH Wife of BENJAMIN WYATT Of LIME GROVE
> in this Parish ESQ Formerly of Weedon in the CO: of
> STAFFORD AND Brother of the late JAMES WYATT
> His Majesty's Surveyor General.

Not much about Sarah, but a great deal of restrained boasting about the family's connections. James was the star of the dynasty, and was worth trumpeting before the Llandegai locals.

When Benjamin died five years later a longer inscription was added. It is full of conventional Georgian phraseology, but still allows something of the man to shine through:

> HERE Also lieth Entombed the Body of the Said
> BENJAMIN WYATT, who, for Upwards of Thirty Years
> was Chief Agent to The PENRHYN ESTATES in this
> COUNTY Distinguished by an Able, Faithful and
> Honourable Discharge of His Stewardship by that
> Solidity of Judgement, Strictness of Integrity, Modesty of
> Deportment, Benevolence of Heart and Complacency
> Of Temper, which Entitle a Man to Esteem and
> Reverence, By that Humility which Marks the True
> Servant of Christ, and by That Piety which Alone can
> Sustain the Hope of Everlasting Life. He died Jany: 5 1818
> AGED 73 years.

It is entirely appropriate that having done so much for the slate industry in Wales he has a slate pyramid for his last resting place - and that pride of place should go in his inscription to the dominant forces in his life - the Wyatt family and the Penrhyn Estates.

INSCRIPTIONS, TOO, AT **Clocaenog,** south-west of Ruthin. The vast Clocaenog forest - 500 hectares of coniferous planting - sprawls across the hills, providing one of the last strongholds of red squirrels in Wales. At its eastern edge, near the village of Clocaenog, is a hill called Llys y Frenhines, part of an area known as Pincinllys. And on the top of the hill was our next pyramid.

Lettering by Eric Gill is a feature of the Clocaenog pyramid

Despite Wales's reputation of mountains, this was the only pyramid in Wales to which we had to walk any distance. Fortunately the uphill path through the forest was well worn, and presented no difficulties. Before long we were out of the forest and on top of Llys y Frenhines. It is not particularly high - less than 1500 feet - but it's certainly well placed. We could see the huge sweep of the Clwydian range, and, to the south, the Berwyn massif. North west was Moel Famau, which was nearly the site of another pyramid. In 1810 a monster pyramid that would have towered 150 feet above the 1818 foot summit of the hill was begun there. It was intended to mark the Golden Jubilee of the reign of King George III. Work was started, but never completed, thanks to storm damage on the very exposed summit.

So the Clocaenog pyramid is left in the area to represent the genre. It is a rather rough-and-ready affair, of random stone that may once have formed part of a cairn. In form it is like the pyramids at Skelmersdale (see page 197) and Penrith (see page 192). It was built in 1830, as the inscription on the eastern face says:

'AS A MEMORIAL OF HIS HAVING COMPLETED
THE LARGE RANGE OF MOUNTAIN
PLANTATIONS WHICH IN PART SKIRT THE BASE
OF THE HILL WILLIAM, SECOND LORD BAGOT,
ERECTED THIS PILE OF STONES IN THE YEAR 1830.'

Lord Bagot, who owned nearby Pool Park, as well as the family's main base at Blithfield at Bagot's Bromley in Staffordshire, was a keen natural scientist. He was a member of the Linnean Society, the Zoological Society and the Horticultural Society, as well as a Fellow of the Society of Antiquaries and a Doctor of Laws. And, of course, he was for many years a Member of Parliament.

The trees around Llys y Frenhines had been sacrificed to the battle against Napoleon - in much the same way as iron railings were torn from the fronts of houses and public buildings in World War II. They were also harvested for the oak bark that played a vital role in leather tanning. Bagot's new plantings, which were mainly of oak, though peppered also with larch, spruce and Scots pine, helped to replace the losses, as well as being a source of profit; as early as 1810 it was said that his plantations in the Vale of Clywd were worth £50,000 - getting on for £2.5 million today.

Bagot's Welsh plantings survived until another war had them felled - the Great War and its aftermath saw the oaks, larches, pines and spruce disappear. Only in 1930 did trees reappear - as the second of the inscription plaques, on the northern face of the pyramid's plinth says:

LORD BAGOT'S PLANTATIONS WERE FELLED
DURING AND AFTER THE GREAT WAR, 1914-18.
THE FORESTRY COMMISSIONERS BEGAN TO
PLANT COLCAENOG FOREST IN 1930.
1934 R. L. ROBINSON, CHAIRMAN

What makes this rather pedestrian inscription much more interesting, and worth the climb to the top of the hill, is that it is in beautiful hand-cut letters by the greatest British carver of the 20th century, the eccentric genius Eric Gill.

In 1934 Gill was at the height of his powers and of his fame. He was sculpting the famous statue of *Prospero and Ariel* that stands over the front door of Broadcasting House in London. He was also designing print typefaces - *Gill Sans* is his most famous. Probably the job for the Forestry Commissioners in an obscure forest in North Wales was a very minor work. Yet Gill carried it out with his usual scrupulous care. The letters are very finely cut,

Eric Gill's inscription on the Clocaenog pyramid

but clearly done by hand rather than mechanically using a template. The 1830 inscription is very pedestrian its execution. Gill's work a century later breathes craftsmanship. It is certainly worth the effort it takes to reach it, and a fine finish to the Welsh pyramids.

Tour 7

SCOTLAND - EAST

SCOTLAND'S PYRAMIDS BEGIN in the village of **Stow**, eight miles north of Galashiels. Stow lies beside the Gala Water in what was once known as Wedale, the vale of woe. Renowned in the Middle Ages for the (to our thinking, unlikely) possession of a fragmentary figure of the Virgin Mary brought from Jerusalem by King Arthur, Stow was one of the homes of the Bishop of St Andrews, and later a centre for textiles.

All we knew of the pyramid was a reference in the database of the Royal Commission on the Ancient and Historical Monuments of Scotland (RCAHMS) to 'a 3.0m high pyramid of mortared stone' on the site of an ancient burial ground. The pyramid 'bears a plaque inscribed "here rest two generations of Rutherfords Lairds of Bowland 1697-1752 W.S. 1912" '. There was also a grid reference, but the site was in the middle of a wood full of game-birds. We were directed by villagers to the home of the game-keeper. There was no answer at his door, but as we were coming away he drove up in his Land Rover and agreed to take us to the pyramid.

He was Adrian Walton, once a miner in the South Yorkshire pits. When the coal industry collapsed he followed his lifetime love of the outdoors and became a keeper - now he was head keeper to the Bowland estate, and very proud of his birds. He drove on a bumpy track through the woodland - the partridge scuttled away as we approached - until we reached the small, fern-filled clearing where the pyramid stands. Built of roughly-coursed and mortared stone, it is surrounded by mountain ash trees and by firs - an eerie, rather dank place.

The inscription is on a black marble plaque; the RCAHMS transcription is nearly accurate - except for the initials WS, which are really WR, for William Ramsey, who owned the estate from the 1880s. But there is another error, made by Ramsey himself - the name of the family at Bowland was not Rutherford but Rutherfurd - and their story takes us back and forth across the Atlantic to the British colonies in America, and to the decks of a warship in the Battle of Trafalgar.

The Rutherfurds of Bowland, the estate on the edge of Stow village, were a junior branch of the Clan Rutherfurd - itself part of the larger Rutherford clan. In the 17th century Robert Rutherfurd married a wealthy widow, Anne Pringle. Anne's father was Sir John Murray of Philiphaugh, an estate about six miles south of Stow. The marriage was to have a marked effect on later generations; it was through the Murray family that the Rutherfurds began their long and not always happy relationship with America.

Robert and Anne Rutherfurd's son James married Isabella Simpson, an even wealthier woman. James and Isabella Rutherfurd had ten children; oddly, two were called Anne and both Annes married men called Schaw; both the Schaws and the Rutherfurds were distantly related to Sir Walter Scott. James Rutherfurd's third son, John, provides the American link.

OPPOSITE:
The dykestone
pyramid in the
garden at Fintry
(see page 250)

233

In 1739 young John Rutherfurd - he was 15 years old - was taken by his cousin James Murray to Carolina. James Murray had been in America since 1735, first in Charles Town and then in Wilmington, where he first opened a store and then went into agriculture. Murray returned to Britain in 1738, where he was asked to look after young 'Johnnie' Rutherfurd. Johnnie returned to Carolina with James Murray, who was a generation older than him, the following year. After working as James's clerk for around a decade, he found himself a government post, as receiver-general of quit-rents. This meant he had to collect the rents from tenants of crown property and remit them to the Treasury in London; he made money on the interest from them.

Unfortunately, John Rutherfurd was not very good at his job - he was either too easy-going or just lazy. The fact that he was rather deaf did not help him, either. He was suspended from his duty, but reinstated on appeal to the Treasury - though he had to return to Britain to make his appeal. Back in North Carolina, he became a farmer, introducing new methods of agriculture on his estate. He called his plantation Bowland after his ancestral lands in Scotland. He also had a town house in Wilmington, where he was a town commissioner. His other business activities included running a tar house. An advertisement in the *Edinburgh Evening Courant* of 19 September 1752, offers for sale 'BY JOHN RUTHERFURD . . . a parcel of fine thick TAR, in Barrels, running from 70 to 90 Scots Pints, fit for smearing of Sheep'. There are also 'a considerable Quantity of Pitch and Turpentine, and Deer Skins in the Hair'.

In 1754 married a widow, Frances Johnston. In fact, she was twice widowed; her second husband had been Gabriel Johnston, Governor of North Carolina. This in theory should have made her another woman of wealth - but there were problems. Governor Johnston's salary was far in arrears, and Frances, as executrix, was pursuing the payments. Her new husband, John Rutherfurd, took up the case, but it was still not settled on Frances's death in 1768. John was already in debt to his former mentor, James Murray. Murray pressed John to repay his debts; eventually he had to hand over all his property - almost 7,000 acres of land, valued at £4,300.

Rutherfurd soon bounced back. Using money that had been left in trust for his children by his wife, he bought a new estate, Hunthill (named after another former Rutherfurd Scottish estate, just south of Jedburgh), 'on which,' his relation Janet Schaw wrote, 'he has a vast number of negroes employed in various works. He makes a great deal of tar and turpentine, but his grand work is a sawmill, the finest I ever met with.'

From Miss Schaw we know a great deal about the Rutherfurds this time. She was the author of a narrative description of a journey from Scotland to North Carolina, via the West Indies, from 1774 to 1775. She was visiting two of her brothers - Alexander in Antigua and Robert in Carolina. With her on the voyage were three children - the daughter and two sons of her cousin, John Rutherfurd of Wilmington. They had been born in North Carolina, and sent in 1767 to Scotland for their education. At the time of the voyage Fanny was 18, young John was 11 and William Gordon was just nine.

Janet Schaw delivered her charges safely to their father - but the unrest in Wilmington, with the pro-independence rebels threatening the loyal British subjects like Rutherfurd and his fellow plantation owners, made the place unsafe. Fanny, John and William Rutherfurd were eventually taken aboard a British

An edition of Janet Schaw's Narrative *telling of her journey to Carolina with the three Rutherfurd children*

JOURNAL

OF A

LADY OF QUALITY;

Being the *Narrative* of a

Journey from

SCOTLAND

to the *West Indies, North Carolina,*

and *Portugal,* in the years

1774 to 1776.

frigate, the *Cruizer*, and returned to Britain. Two years later the American War of Independence broke out in earnest. John Rutherfurd senior was fiercely loyal to the crown and did 'everything within his power to suppress the distractions in North Carolina, before the arrival of his Majesty's troops'. He also had both his sons join the British forces - that was one of the charges brought against him by the American victors, when in 1781 he was deprived of his estates and his possessions. The following year, almost penniless and a broken man, he sailed for England, but died at Cork en route, aged 60.

The sons who were placed in the forces prospered. John junior joined the Army as an Engineer, eventually rising to become Surveyor-General of Gibraltar. He spent some years attempting, unsuccessfully, to have the North Carolina estates restored. He died in 1813 and was buried at sea. His brother William had a distinguished career in the Royal Navy. Known to the family as 'Little Billie', he first went to sea in 1788 when he was 23 - a decade older than most officer recruits. Patronage helped his rise, but so did his undoubted abilities; as a lieutenant he fought bravely in the West Indies, especially at the storming of the forts on Martinique, where he won promotion.

By 1796 he was a Post Captain, and when the Treaty of Amiens, which suspended hostilities between France and Britain, broke down in 1803, he was made Captain of the 74-gun HMS *Swiftsure*. He made several voyages to the West Indies and also took part in the blockade of the French coast. In 1805 he joined Nelson's fleet at Cadiz, and was present at the Battle of Trafalgar. *Swiftsure* was at the rear of the line, and because of damage to her hull was late joining the battle. Nevertheless her intervention proved decisive in several skirmishes, and her crew helped to rescue many survivors from damaged ships. After the battle William was rewarded, but without sufficient seniority as a Captain he did not receive promotion to Admiral, which would have given him a secure pension. Instead he was made Governor of Greenwich Hospital and a Companion of the Order of the Bath. He died in 1818 after some years of illness and was buried in St Margaret's Church, Westminster.

By the beginning of the 19th century the Bowland estate in Scotland had passed out of Rutherfurd hands - first to the Pringles, who were distantly related, then to the Walker family. Later it was bought by William Ramsey, who erected the pyramid to the former Rutherfurd owners - though it is not clear why he chose the particular dates he inscribed on the plaque.

Gamekeeper Adrian Walton is now one of the few people who visit the hidden pyramid at Bowland. He says he enjoys seeing it as he makes his rounds; it reminds him of the long continuity of care that he and his predecessors have given to the estate in the vale of woe.

THE GATE TO **Gosford House** was stuck. It had taken us a while to find it, driving several times up and down the road between Gosford Bay on the Firth of Forth and the snaking park wall. The park was due to open to the public at 2.00 pm - but there was a power cut and the electrically-operated grille on the gatehouse was inoperable.

Behind the gate was Jo Duguid, who was trying to open up. We explained that we were due to meet the Earl and Countess of Wemyss and March to see their pyramid. 'OK,' said Jo, sliding through a narrow pedestrian gate that didn't depend on a motor to open it. 'If you'll give me a lift, I'll take you the back way.' As we bumped along an unsurfaced track through woodland, Jo told us that she was South African and had married a chap from Aberlady, the village at the entrance to Gosford House. She worked for the Earl and Countess in several capacities - 'Everything!' she said.

We had been told about Gosford when we were visiting the pyramid at Stanway House in Gloucestershire (see page 123). Lord Neidpath, who is restoring the water garden at Stanway, succeeded his father, who died in December 2008, as the 13th Earl of Wemyss. We arrived in the car park at the south end of the Wemyss' palatial house, and were met by Lady Wemyss. She was the second wife of the 12th Earl. He moved into the house in the early 1950s despite its having been fire-damaged during military requisition in the war. (The Earl, born in 1912, succeeded to the title in 1937; he lived to be 96.) Lady Wemyss introduced us to him. He was sitting comfortably in an antique wicker Bath-chair, and was insistent that we visit the interior of the house while the Countess made ready to take us to the mausoleum.

Gosford House (not to be confused with *Gosford Park* of the feature film) was designed by Robert Adam in 1790, but not completed until 1800. It was much altered and extended by Glasgow architect William Young in 1891. Young's tour-de-force, and the main show-room in the house, is the Marble Hall - a confection of white-and-rose Derbyshire alabaster columns that reaches the full height of the building and holds a magnificent double staircase. It makes the word 'imposing' seem inadequate. It's reminiscent of the grand entrance to a late-Victorian town hall, or an exclusive bank. And it rather overwhelms the great paintings on its walls, which include works by Rubens, Botticelli and Murillo, mostly gathered by the 10th Earl.

We followed the Countess in her converted golf buggy in a straight line across the lawns and back into the woodland. She pulled up in a glade, and we parked beside her. 'The mausoleum's up here,' she said. 'We've been clearing the way to it, and we discovered that the avenue leading to it is exactly a Scots chain in width.' A Scots chain, we later found, is 24.71 yards - just over eight feet more than a standard imperial chain.

Ahead was a pair of tall stone gate piers topped with Grecian statues. Two rather inadequate wooden gates hung from them - 'There were huge bronze gates here originally - long since gone,'

Gosford House mausoleum for the 7th Earl of Wemyss

Lady Wemyss explained. They would have excitingly concealed what is now easily visible beyond - the mausoleum.

It is a piece of perfect geometry - a tall, square base with a stringcourse a few feet below the top. Above this base is the pyramid - totally plain and massively impressive. It is in the tradition of the mausoleum at Cobham (see page 62), but, where that has refinement and elegant detailing, here is elementalism and - almost - brutality. The effect is mitigated slightly by the four Doric porticos, only one of which is functional.

Lady Wemyss produced the key for the great door. It was the original, stamped with 'MEASOLEUM'. The door swung open to reveal the interior.

Within the square of the external plan, the inside is octagonal, and lined with coffin niches so that it resembles a giant's wine cellar. Above the niches soars an octagonal vault, tapering into the apex of the pyramid.

Only one of the niches is occupied - and that is one more than the mausoleum at Cobham. It holds the remains of the 7th Earl of Wemyss, Francis Charteris. It was Francis who bought the Gosford estate 'to be nearer the golf'. But it was not golf that inspired the building of the mausoleum; it was Freemasonry.

Several Earls of Wemyss have served as Grand Master Masons of Scotland - the first was James, the 5th Earl, who was Grand Master from 1743 to 1744. The occupant of the mausoleum, the 7th Earl, was master from 1747 to 1748 as The Hon Francis Charteris of Amisfield before his succession to the earldom. The 8th Earl, as Lord Elcho, was Master from 1786 to 1788. Finally, there was another Francis, Lord Elcho, later 9th Earl of Wemyss and March, who was Grand Master from 1827 to 1830.

Lady Wemyss was keen to count the niches and measure the interior of the mausoleum. There are 12 niches in the main rows, and four rows of 13 in the subsidiary rows - these are significant Masonic numbers, and make 64 in all - 4x4x4. There are doubtless other numerological tricks that are being played here, too. More importantly, perhaps, is the pyramidal form of the structure itself, linking the mausoleum with Freemasonry's supposed Egyptian origins.

There was evidently a master hand behind the design of the mausoleum - but who was it? The traditional attribution is to Robert Adam, working on the house in the 1790s. The date of the mausoleum has not been accurately established, but it was certainly here by 1796, when James Ramsay, who landscaped the park, was busy organising the planting around it. There is just the possibility that he was responsible for designing the building, too.

Lady Wemyss locked the mausoleum's door, climbed back into her golf buggy and we followed in her tracks once again. She gave us a cheery wave as she left us back at the car park. The power was back on, and we were able to leave the estate in the approved manner by the gate on to the road by Gosford Bay.

BODYSNATCHERS, SHIPWRECK, AN actress, a Professor of Greek, a Commissioner of Excise and a failed judge, several illegitimate children, rhubarb, a famous hotel and a meeting of world statesmen - Agatha Christie would have made a best-seller from them. They are all connected with the next pyramid we visited.

Duddingston, now a suburb of Edinburgh, was once a village on the edge of Holyrood Park, below Arthur's Seat. It was on Duddingston Loch that The Reverend Robert Walker went skating - an activity immortalised in Henry Raeburn's famous

Key to the Gosforth 'Measoleum'

The Haldane
pyramid at
Duddingston kirk
has links with a
story of scandal
and shipwreck

painting of him. Duddingston church, partly dating from the 12th century, is the oldest Scottish kirk still in regular use. At its entrance is a two-storey watch tower, now called the Session House, from which kirk elders could keep an eye on the grave-yard in the years when the resurrectionists were digging up newly-buried bodies to sell to the medical schools (or murdering people for the same purpose, in the case of Burke and Hare). Sir Walter Scott was an elder of Duddingston Kirk from 1808, and wrote part of *The Heart of Midlothian* in the manse garden.

Alongside the church is the pyramid we had come to visit. It has been rather battered over the years, but the inscription still remains legible. It reads 'Captain John Haldane in his last Will bequeathed these words: "Two hundred pounds sterling towards erecting a Monument to the memory of my deceased Grandfather Patrick Haldane Esq. of Gleneagles whose body is interred at his own request in Sir Alex. Dick, Bart's vault at Duddingstone, this being the only tribute in my power to bestow to the Memory of the Best of Parents and Worthiest of Men".'

Who was Patrick Haldane that he should be remembered so affectionately by his grandson that £200 (about £17,500 in mod-ern terms) was available for this monument? An early Scottish biographer wrote of Patrick's youth, 'From the pregnancy of his parts, very sanguine were the expectations of his friends'. The Haldane family were Lairds of Gleneagles, and Patrick, second son of John, 14th Laird, had a conventional upper-class Scottish education, graduating as a Master of Arts at the University of St Andrews in 1701 at the age of 18.

After four years of studying law privately, he returned to St Andrews as, oddly it seems today, Professor of Greek, at the age of just 22. His election to the chair was not without problems, but this did not stop him taking another post in 1707, this time as Professor of Ecclesiastical History, which he held until 1711. Patrick then went to the University of Leiden to resume his legal studies. He returned to Scotland in 1715 as an Advocate, and was elected Provost of St Andrews.

So far, so good. But then came his false move. He accepted an appointment as one of the Commissioners who were given the job of organising the removal assets and estates from Scottish landowners who had supported the Old Pretender during the 1715 Rising. His actions, which were characterised as 'harsh and intemperate', caused outrage amongst much of the Scottish estab-lishment. Thereafter his career was dogged by opposition.

He was for a short time an MP, for Cupar, and in 1721 was nominated as a judge of the Court of Session. The Faculty of Advocates and Clerks, remembering his work as a Commissioner, petitioned against him, and despite the support of the monarch, he failed to be appointed, after several years of law cases. Eventually he became Solicitor-General.

As well as being disappointed in his legal career, Patrick Haldane had private griefs as well. He had become the 16th Laird of Gleneagles in 1755 on the death of his brother Mungo. Patrick placed all his hopes for reviving the estate's fortunes on his son George, who after a career in the Army, finishing as a Brigadier-General, was appointed Governor of Jamaica early in 1759. Patrick's hopes were not to be fulfilled; George died on 26 July 1759, without legitimate children. Not only that, he left enor-mous debts, too - so much that Patrick was forced to sell the Gleneagles estate to his half-brother Robert to pay them off.

In 1768, when Patrick was 84, his daughter Margaret died, also without heirs. With the end of all his hopes and with his health failing, he moved to Duddingston, where he lived in the manse, a guest of the Minister, William Bennett, who had been George Haldane's tutor. Here Patrick became a close friend of the eminent Edinburgh surgeon Sir Alexander Dick. Among Dick's other claims to fame was that he introduced rhubarb into Britain, as a medicine. But even Dick's medication and care did not save Patrick; he died on 10 January 1769.

The Duddingston pyramid was not raised until after the death of Captain John Haldane, who was Patrick's grandson, in 1784. Although Brigadier-General George Haldane died unmarried and without heirs, he had a long liaison with a Yorkshire woman, Frances Pool, whose father was vicar of Strensall, near York. Frances bore him two children, John and Henry.

Illegitimacy does not seem to have been a particular burden to the two boys. Henry became a Lieutenant Colonel in the Royal Engineers, but the family's penchant for not making the best of things caught up with him; he had a large family and no income, and spent his final years living on charity from his friends. John - known to the family as Jack - became a Captain in the East India Company, and he was dogged by perhaps even worse misfortune. He spent much time in India, taking to drink and at one point being, according to a contemporary chronicler 'once cast away when mate of an Indiaman, losing everything he possessed.'

Later, John Haldane was given command of the East India Company's ship *Fairford*; it caught fire in Bombay on its maiden voyage, in June 1783. The Company's Governor, feeling sorry for Haldane (now nicknamed 'Calamity Haldane') and wanting to help, fitted out another ship, the *Nancy*, for him. It set sail for England. On board was an actress and opera singer, Mrs Ann Cargill. Born Ann Brown, she had made her Covent Garden debut in 1771, aged 11 and subsequently appeared in operas by Thomas Arne and in plays by Sheridan and Allan Ramsay (see Penicuik, page 244), as well as making a great impression as Miranda in *The Tempest*. She also appeared regularly as Polly Peachum in *The Beggar's Opera* - and once, in a 1781 travesty production, as the hero Macheath. 'She hit off the gayety of manner, easy deportment and degagé air of Macheath with singular and wonderful success,' wrote a reviewer in the *Morning Chronicle*. She eloped twice before she was 21 and then, in 1763, she became besotted with John Haldane. Amid great scandal she left the London stage to sail with him on *Fairford* to India, where she was a great success on the stage - her benefit performance in Calcutta, where she 'played all her applauded opera characters at immense prices', raised an astonishing 12,000 rupees. She was now accompanying Haldane back to England, at the urgent request of the government. With her came her fortune.

The voyage of the *Nancy* went well until 4 March 1784. In terrific winter storms the ship struck rocks twice in the Isles of Scilly, first, as The Rev'd Mr Troutbeck's history of Scilly wrote, 'upon a rock called Gilstone, where Sir Clowdisley Shovell was lost in 1707 and was afterwards driven with the tide upon the island of Rosevere'. Captain Scott from Hartlepool, whose ship was stranded on the island of St Mary's on its way from London to Cork, led the islanders in a rescue attempt. By the time they got there, everyone on board the Nancy was dead. Some of the bodies were buried on Rosevere, more were lost in the sea, but they brought back, for burial in Old Town (see page 164), the corpses of two men, and of Mrs Cargill, 'floating in her shift, and her infant in her arms'. It seems likely that the child was John Haldane's.

The wreck of the Nancy on the Gilstone in the Isles of Scilly, from the relief sculpture on the Duddingston pyramid

The wreck of the *Nancy* is depicted on the pyramid at Duddingston, in a marble bas relief sculpted by William Gowan of Edinburgh. Huge waves overwhelm the ship, while a small boat battles bravely alongside it. There is no inscription that commemorates the tale - though it is possible that two grooves on one side of the pyramid once held plaques. As for the *Nancy* herself, its wreck was identified by divers off the Gilstone in the summer of 2007; the rupees have not yet been recovered.

Despite the misfortunes of the 18th-century Haldanes, the family survived, having some notable members in its ranks. They include a noted evangelist, James Alexander Haldane, a physiologist, John Scott Haldane, and a novelist, Elizabeth Haldane. More famous than them, perhaps, was the first Viscount Haldane, whose reforms in the first decade of the 20th century, when he was Secretary of State for War, laid the foundations of the modern army. The biologist J B S Haldane and author Naomi Mitchinson are also family members.

There are still Haldanes at Gleneagles. In 2005 the current Laird, Martin Haldane, objected when the British government put his estate at risk from protestors during a meeting of the G8 nations' leaders. They refused to make it clear that the meeting was at the Gleneagles Hotel, not on the Gleneagles estate. It's a battle of nomenclature that the Haldanes have carried on since the hotel was opened in 1924.

Appropriately, perhaps, the motto in the Haldane family coat of arms is 'Suffer'.

FROM DUDDINGSTON WE drove round the base of Arthur's Seat and eventually on to Princes Street, heading west. Just off Queensferry Road is **Dean** Village. After 800 years as a centre for grain milling, and a short heyday as a spa, Dean declined into poverty in the late 19th century. The late 20th rediscovered the area, so close to the centre of Edinburgh, and the workers cottages, mills and warehouses are now very desirable homes. Pleasant walks beside the Water of Leith and the Dean Gallery, which shows modern art, including many works gifted by the sculptor Sir Eduardo Paolozzi, add to Dean's attractions.

Dean Cemetery, in the heart of the village, was opened in 1845 on the site of a demolished 17th-century house. It soon became one of the most fashionable places to be buried in the city. At the western end of the shaded walks through the grounds stands the pyramid we had come to see - a beautifully-crisp pink granite memorial to Sophia Rutherfurd.

Sophia was the wife of Andrew Rutherfurd, Lord Advocate of Scotland from 1839 to 1841, and again from 1846, and later Rector of Glasgow University. The Rutherfurds were very prominent in Edinburgh society. Sophia, from an Irish landowning family in Co Donegal, was a noted hostess, both at the couple's Edinburgh home at 9 St Colme Street, on the edge of the New Town and part of the prestigious Moray Estate, and later at Lauriston Castle, a mile or so north-west of Dean.

Andrew Rutherfurd was created Lord Rutherfurd in 1851, when he was appointed a Senator of the College of Justice and a Privy Counsellor. He was responsible for drawing up the Acts of Parliament that regulated marriage in Scotland. The previous lax laws, which were, he said, 'a disgrace to any semi-barbarous nation', allowed 'hasty, ill-assorted and bigamous unions' of the type that were famously arranged at Gretna Green. He also sorted out Scottish inheritance law, and proposed the repeal of the

William Playfair's
granite pyramid
to his friends
Andrew and
Sophia Rutherfurd
in the cemetery
in Dean village,
Edinburgh

Corn Laws. He was the Rector of Glasgow University and was no mean scholar; he read Greek as most people would read a newspaper, and a friend said that Rutherfurd and Mr Gladstone were the only two people he had even known who were able to 'conquer the difficulty of obsolete Italian dialects' - though whether there was much call for that skill in mid-19th-century Edinburgh may be doubted.

All this is eminently respectable, and the Rutherfurds counted much of the aristocracy and intelligentsia among their friends. But there was a darker secret behind the façade - they were not really Rutherfurds at all.

Andrew's father was the Reverend William Greenfield. He was a minister at Edinburgh's High Kirk - St Giles's Cathedral - and an acquaintance of Robert Burns. Burns wrote of him, 'Mr Greenfield is of a superior order. The bleedings of humanity, the generous resolve, a manly disregard of the paltry subjects of vanity, virgin modesty, the truest taste, and a very sound judgement, characterise him . . . and as a companion, his good sense, his joyous hilarity, his sweetness of manners and modesty, are most engagingly charming.'

The hilarious and charming Mr Greenfield became Moderator of the General Assembly of the Church of Scotland in 1796. In the same year the University of Edinburgh made him an honorary Doctor of Divinity. Two years later he was in disgrace.

To supplement his modest clergy stipend he took university students as lodgers in his manse. Some time in 1798 he was discovered 'indulging in unnatural lusts with some of these youths'. There was no public scandal; the matter was hushed up to preserve the good name of the Church and because the young men involved were from respectable families. Greenfield had his degrees rescinded and was sent into 'exile' in the north of England, where he changed his name to that of his wife - Rutherfurd (she was probably related to the Bowland estate Rutherfurds (see page 233). He supported himself by writing literary criticism - ironically, as he has become the subject of literary scholarship himself in the 20th century, in works such as *William Greenfield: gender and the transmission of literary culture* and *The "Equivocal Gender" of Professor William Greenfield*.

We can imagine what the tabloid newspapers of today would have made of such a 'juicy' story. Yet at the end of the 18th century, hardly a whisper seems to have escaped. Certainly it had no effect on the careers of either of his sons - Andrew the lawyer and his brother James, who became an army officer.

Among the friends of Lord and Lady Rutherfurd was Edinburgh architect William Playfair. Playfair is credited with emphasising the classical nature of Edinburgh, which earned its title as 'the Athens of the North'. He designed many of the great early 19th-century Edinburgh landmarks, including the National Gallery of Scotland and the Royal Scottish Academy on The Mound, St Stephen's Church in St Vincent Street and the City Observatory on Calton Hill, where Charles Piazzi Smyth (see page 23) was later in charge. Playfair designed for the Rutherfurds; among his work was the interior decoration of their house in St Colme Street, and the creation of an Italian Garden at Lauriston Castle.

When Sophia Rutherfurd died in 1852 it was inevitable that Lord Rutherfurd should turn to Playfair to design a monument. Together they chose the pyramid as the form, and Peterhead granite, a favourite Victorian monumental stone, as the material. The pyramid sits at the front of the Rutherfurds' plot, and was once surrounded by railings.

Carved on the front is Sophia Francesca's name, and below it, inset into the front of the pyramid, is a fine bronze plaque. The inscription to Andrew Rutherford's dearest wife apologises to her for erecting a monument against her wishes. Above it is a double portrait of Andrew and Sophia by the Aberdeen-born sculptor John Steell, who was also responsible for the statue of Sir Walter Scott on the Scott Memorial on Princes Street and for Edinburgh's Albert Memorial in Charlotte Square, for which he was knighted.

The pyramid later served as a memorial to Lord Rutherfurd himself, who died, after some months of severe illness, at home in St Colme Street. Near his grave are those of many of his friends, including Lord Jeffrey, editor of the Edinburgh Review, and the lawyer and writer Lord Cockburn. Cockburn's intimacy with Rutherfurd enabled him to poke fun at him. In one letter he wrote, 'For God's sake, Andrew, take care of your eyes.

John Steell's portraits of Andrew and Sophia Rutherfurd on their pyramid in Dean Cemetery

Severe Students too are very apt to suffer sorely from their bowels . . . Do call at Alexander the druggist's shop in Dundee and ask for the Idler's pill, or the Scholar's belly salve, or the Sedentary man's doup plaster, or the Student's windy cordial, or the Philosopher's clearer, or the Lawyer's delightful pocket companion, or the Judge's rectifier, or Vacance Powder - or anything else that will keep you as well and make you walk as stately as during the idleness of last winter.'

The nearest of the Rutherfurds' cemetery neighbours, though, is William Playfair himself. His relationship with the Rutherfurds was very close - he was really part of their extended family, and Sophia seems to have served as Playfair's manager, both promoting his architectural practice and dealing with his domestic arrangements, down to hiring housemaids - 'an awful business', he called it. Playfair, who died in 1857, a year after Andrew, left the residue of his estate to Andrew and Sophia's nephew, also called Andrew, the son of Andrew's brother, Major James Rutherfurd.

The Dean Cemetery pyramid opened a door on to high society in early- and mid-19th-century Edinburgh. The next pyramid brought us very much down to earth.

THOUSANDS OF PEOPLE visit Rosslyn Chapel (see page 243) every year, thanks to the success of Dan Brown's book *The Da Vinci Code*, which links it to the Knights Templar and to the Holy Grail. Not far away is the Roslin Institute, where Dolly, the world's first cloned mammal, was developed. Neither of these spots was our next goal, though. We were headed for nearby **Bilston Glen**.

In 2002 Hills Electrical and Mechanical Engineering plc commissioned a new regional centre for the Edinburgh area. Not for them the boring standard office block. They wanted a statement - especially because, as boss David Hill said, 'There are three of our competitors on the same industrial estate. They're bigger than us, with larger office blocks. We didn't need as much office space, but we did want something that was both cost-effective and impressive.'

The Hills pyramid is certainly bold - a £500,000, grey-clad, three-storey Euclidean solid with a quarter segment removed to allow the light to flood into the interior. It is a slightly incongruous sight beside the fairly nondescript Dryden Road, named after the nearby Dryden Tower, a tall folly tower overlooking the wooded glen of the Bilston Burn.

'I hadn't visited our pyramid for a couple of years until last month,' David Hill said. 'It seemed to be dark and brooding. But it certainly makes a point!'

As we were taking photographs a man emerged from the pyramid. It was Martin Meehan, Regional Centre Manager, come to see what we were doing. He betrayed little surprise when we told him that we were researching pyramids in the British Isles, as if it was something that happened every day. He invited us inside his pride and joy. Unfortunately, in 2008 the Hills company failed, and was bought by rivals Southern Electric Contracting for £1.

Despite its eye-catching external appearance, the interior is, sadly, much like any office block. There are a few interestingly-sloping walls, but otherwise it's rectangular rooms, corporate furniture, computers. No soaring vistas into the apex of the pyramid. Not even any Egyptian prints on the walls. It is, perhaps, a missed trick, though presumably the building works well as offices.

The former Hills Electrical and Mechanical Engineering's pyramid office block at Bilston Glen

The Clerk Mausoleum in the old kirkyard at Penicuik dates from 1683

THE TOWN OF **Penicuik** has been a papermaking centre for more than 300 years - and has had the patronage of the Clerk family for more than 350 years. Most of the town was laid out about 1770 by Sir James Clerk. He was just one of the remarkable - and still surviving - Clerk family. Its luminaries also include John Clerk, Sir James's brother, an eminent naval tactician who greatly influenced Nelson, and the 19th-century physicist James Maxwell Clerk, who was renowned for his experiments in electromagnetism.

Sir James's Penicuik street plan survives, though few of his buildings can still be seen. The old town that he largely did away with was clustered around the parish church of St Mungo, with its holy well. Sir James replaced the church with a new one in 1771 and the tower of the Old Kirk was left to become a picturesque ruin. Attached to it are several mausoleum enclosures, which culminate in a pyramid-topped structure that is a monument built by James' grandfather - Sir John, the first Baronet (a baronetcy of Nova Scotia) - in memory of his first wife, Elizabeth Henderson.

It is the second-oldest pyramid in Scotland, after the Greenock well head (see page 272); Elizabeth died in 1683. The structure consists of a tall and massively-built stone base surmounted by a striking pyramid. Inside there is a finely-built chamber with a stone barrel vault. Where the pyramid joins the base there is a beard of bushes and young trees. On the top there was once an urn inscribed with Elizabeth's initials, EH.

Why did Clerk choose this form of monument? The Clerk family was well-educated, and at this date that meant classically-educated. It seems likely that Sir John wanted to build a version of a classical tomb. There are ancient examples in Syria of the pyramid-topped type that he chose, but it's very unlikely that he knew them. Nor is he likely to have known of the Roman tombs they inspired, or the Indian cemetery drawn by Vanbrugh (see page 7). Perhaps the idea came from his wife, who was the granddaughter of the Scots poet Sir William Drummond. Clerk may have had the run of Drummond's renowned library at Hawthornden and come across his inspiration there. There are possible sources for the mausoleum in John Evelyn's translation of Roland Freart's *Parallel of the Antient Architecture with the Modern* (see page 6).

Elizabeth Henderson was by all accounts a talented woman, with a particular gift for music. She passed her artistic genes to her son, Sir John, the second Baronet. After a fairly conventional education at the local grammar school and at the University of Glasgow, John spread his wings and travelled, as so many Scots of his age did, (see, for example Patrick Haldane, page 238) to Leiden to study law. There he met the Dutch physician and philosopher Herman Boerhaave. John then travelled through Germany to Italy. His mother had already seen that he was proficient in music - 'Before I came to Leyden . . . I play'd tolerably well on the Harpsechord and since I was 7 years of age I touched the Violon a little', he wrote.

In Rome he met Bernardo Pasquini, 'a most skilful composer and performer on the Organ and Harpse, and Archangelo Corelli, whom I believe no man has ever equalled for the violin'. Clerk had composition lessons from Corelli; his own surviving compositions are a violin sonata in the style of Corelli and five cantatas, some to texts by Boerhaave, including the politically-charged *Leo Scotiae Irritatus* - 'The Lion of Scotland angered'. It deals with the unlikely subject of the Darien Scheme, a Scottish attempt to develop trade with Panama. The Scheme was a failure because the Spanish and the English harried the Scottish merchant ships. John Clerk was a Freemason, and the musical structure of *Leo Scotiae Irritatus* is full of Masonic symbolism - 33 bars representing the degrees of The Ancient and Accepted Scottish Rite of Freemasonry, for example, and another section of 27 bars - three times three times three - that represents the perfect cube of the Holy of Holies in the Temple of Solomon.

Sir John was also an architect and a friend of Scottish architect William Adam - father of the more-famous Robert Adam. In 1723 Sir John 'not only finished my design for the House of Mavisbank, under the correction of Mr Adams [sic] but laid the foundation.' Mavisbank, at Loanhead, is a large villa in the Palladian style, and was one of the most influential of Scottish houses throughout the Georgian period. A lunatic asylum in the 19th century, it was gutted by fire in the 20th and now is in the early stages of restoration.

The polymathic Sir John was also, like his great-grandfather Drummond, a poet, and both he and his son James were friends of the poet and bookseller, (and early in his career wig-maker) Allan Ramsay. Ramsay's collections of old Scottish and English songs, augmented by his own poems, and especially his pastoral drama *The Gentle Shepherd*, brought him fame and highly-placed friends. John and James Clerk were among his particular friends, and there was a portrait of Ramsay at Penicuik House, the

'The Albano Gate', reconstructed from Freart's Parallel of the Antient Architecture

*The pertuse
Ramsay pyramid
at Penicuik*

Palladian mansion (like Mavisbank ruined by fire in the 20th century) built by James.

Such was the esteem in which the Clerks held Ramsay that when he died at the beginning of 1757 Sir James, who had succeeded his father as 3rd Baronet in 1755, determined to commemorate him in the park at Penicuik.

What he chose to build is extraordinary. It is a tall, thin pyramid on a square base with an arch running through it. The pyramid is pierced by three oval holes of diminishing size. It is built of honey-coloured stone and is beautifully set in farmland in Cauldshoulders Park above the wooded valley of the River Esk, on the opposite bank from Penicuik House.

Inscribed inside the archway in Brobdingnagian letters is a partially-worn inscription that begins ALANO RAMSAY POETAE and ends with MONUMENTUM INSCRIBI . . . D. JACOBUS CLERK ANNO MDCCLIX.

If we don't know where the first Sir John had his inspiration for the mausoleum in the churchyard, we have even less idea about the inspiration of this structure built by his grandson. It has a distant cousinship to the Pyramid Gate at Castle Howard in North Yorkshire (see page 28), with its triumphal arch base. But this pyramid is thinner and taller. And those holes! What do they mean? There are some precedents - windows in French buildings of the late 17th century, for example - but nothing approaching this brutalist punching right through an apparently solid structure. It is so different from the urbanity of Penicuik House's Palladian perfection. Perhaps its roughness in some way mirrors the character of Allan Ramsay.

LITTLE SPARTA, DEEP in the Pentlands Hills near **Dunsyre**, is a unique and poetic garden. Developed since 1966 by the artist and poet Ian Hamilton Finlay, it is a garden for philosophers and thinkers as well as for plant and landscape enthusiasts. Divided into compartments that flow into each other, the garden is enlivened with a myriad objects that reflect the thoughts of its creator.

Certain obsessions quickly become apparent. At the entrance gate (reached after a long climb through cow-infested pasture from the parking space on the nearby road) is a bronze plaque showing a machine gun. This is a reminder of Finlay's battle with the Sheriff Officer of Strathclyde in 1983 who came to seize some of his artworks to pay a disputed debt of £500 for rates on what the council said was an art gallery and Finlay said was a garden temple.

The battle was symptomatic of the younger Finlay, who was a determined (some say pugnacious) man. Born in the Bahamas but raised in Scotland, he left school at 13, spent a year at Glasgow School of Art and worked both in a commercial art studio and as a copywriter. He was in the Royal Army Service Corps during the war.

Military artefacts and references abound throughout the Little Sparta garden. Outside the modest house where Ian Hamilton Finlay lived (he died in 2006) is a sign saying 'Achtung! Minen'. There are signposts to the Siegfried Line and the Maginot Line. Carvings of warships contend with turrets holding machine guns. What appear to be two urns on classical gate piers turn out to be oversized hand grenades cast in concrete.

In one of the more philosophical - not to say calmer - parts of the garden is the pyramid we had come to see. It's in a wooded glade, set out as a funerary walk. Small classical columns, some

*Ian Hamilton
Finlay's Little
Sparta pyramid is
inscribed with the
dates of German
Romantic artist
Caspar David
Friedrich*

of them broken, are placed to aid contemplation of an Ozymandean type.

The pyramid is small - perhaps three feet high. Its five rows of carefully-fitted ashlar blocks, and its cap, are made of a shelly limestone. Carved on one face are the dates 1774-1840; nothing else. What do they signify?

These are the birth and death dates of Caspar David Friedrich, the German Romantic painter whose mysterious landscapes are full of the deepest allegorical and religious meaning. By linking the traditional *memento mori* imagery of the pyramid and the poetic imagination of a great painter of empty, often disturbing landscapes, Finlay was underlining the brevity and isolation of life.

For all its imagination, interesting vistas and, indeed, sense of fun, Little Sparta failed to move us. It is perhaps too quirky for its own good, and one needs to be fully tuned to Ian Hamilton Finlay's psyche to appreciate it fully. Or perhaps we were just in too much of a hurry to see our next pyramid to have time to sit and take in its subtlety.

LIVINGSTON, DUE NORTH of Little Sparta across the Pentland Hills, is not subtle. It is a 'New Town' - officially so, as it was set up under the 1946 New Towns Act, which also saw Cumbernauld (see page 249) and Milton Keynes (see page 89) on the drawing board. Like many new towns, there was already the nucleus of a settlement here - Livingston village, a tiny agricultural settlement until the 1850s, when shale was found in the area in large quantities. From 1857 until 1962 the shale was exploited ruthlessly, at first under the direction of Dr James Young. He patented a method of extracting the oil from the shale to obtain

David Wilson's dykestone pyramid on a roundabout in Livingston

kerogen, which he used to make oil for lighting and lubrication.

When the internal combustion engine arrived, processed kerogen could be used instead of petroleum. It was only in the 1960s that the cheap price of petroleum made kerogen extraction uneconomical and the Livingston shale quarries closed - at around the time that work on Livingston New Town was just getting underway.

The town's layout is dominated by roundabouts, earning Livingston its nickname of 'Roundabout City'. We had been told of a pyramid on one of these many roundabouts, 'definitely on the A899'. We left the M8 at Junction 3 and travelled the full length of the A899. We negotiated three roundabouts, some of which contained sculptural forms, but no pyramid. We turned round and went back north. No, we definitely hadn't missed it.

In search of enlightenment, we ended up at Craigshill Fire Station. Craigshill (and its Fire Station) were among the first parts of Livingston to be built, in the 1960s, and it showed in the boxiness of the houses and the rather regimented layout. The firemen were in the middle of a meal - plenty of calories on each plate - but were happy to stop to consider our strange request to find a lost pyramid; it probably made a change from cats stuck up trees. After much discussion and argument ('Oh, it's no' there Jock'. 'Down Howden way?' 'Och aye, that's a bus shelter!') they agreed that it was in Deans, and pointed us in the right direction.

The irony of this was that the pyramid, and other sculptures on roundabouts in the town, were intended to make navigation easier by providing landmarks. The pyramid is built, like the other sculptures, of dyke (or walling) stone and copper to the designs of artist David Wilson (see also Perth, page 255). It is called *Chrysalis*, and it is designed to reflect the town's transformation from a simple agricultural backwater to a modern, vibrant settlement.

David Wilson, who studied at Duncan of Jordanstone College of Art and Design in Dundee (see also Stan Bonnar's pyramid at Dundee, page 259), has written that 'my passion for art has always been outside the gallery system . . . I became aware that if the environments we live in and pass through are respected and treated as if they really matter, then the greater public will have a more positive response to those surroundings.' Nearly all his works have used dyke stone, and his Livingston sculptures have won the Drystone Walling Association of Great Britain's 'Pinnacle Award' for innovative design and inspirational use of stone.

The first of David Wilson's artworks in Livingston went up in 1995. The commission was one of the last acts carried out by Livingston Development Corporation, then at the end of its 30-year existence. It decided that what Livingston needed was landmarks. The cynical might say that they also wanted to ensure that their budgets were spent before West Lothian District Council took over from them. As one local journalist wrote of the sculptures, 'Love 'em or hate 'em, you can't deny that they've put Livi on the map'.

APPROACHING FROM THE south along the A73, **Cumbernauld** looks quite impressive. It is set on a ridge and the massing of the buildings gives a slight (very slight!) impression of an Italian hill town. Dominating the centre of this vision is a greened-copper pyramid - the roof of St Mungo's Parish Church.

This was our second New Town of the day. As we drew nearer, the vision disintegrated into a confusing mass of distributor roads, roundabouts and grey cubes. The main cube is the town's shopping centre, modelled, it seems, on the inside of a 1960s transistor radio. Square concrete columns hold aloft weather-streaked concrete boxes, linked by flights of odorous concrete stairways. Cumbernauld is often called 'a rabbit warren on stilts', and recently won 'The Carbuncle Award' as the most unattractive Scottish town from the business magazine *Unlimited*. On the other hand, it has been voted Britain's fourth-happiest place . . .

This seemed an unlikely location for a decent pyramid, but St Mungo's Church, opposite the shopping centre, surprised us. A Grade B listed building since February 2000, it was designed by Scottish architect Alan Reiach and constructed between 1962 and 1964. It has a square plan, over which the pyramid squats, with its second pyramid floating above as a fleche. The top of the larger pyramid is glazed, allowing light to flood into the timber-lined sanctuary.

Attached to the church is a range of halls, deliberately kept lower and subservient to the drama of the pyramid roof. The iron cross, fashioned from simple I-section girders, is included in the listed building status. The walls are built of a grey brick with a slight purple tinge, which in some lights can appear brown.

The church is approached from St Mungo's Way by a flight of steps. North Lanarkshire Council has tried to make the vista attractive with flowerbeds, though the lamp standards add little to the effect - they are too fussy and traditional to sit well with the modernity of the church. There are now plans to redevelop the centre of Cumbernauld, with St Mungo's church as its focal point.

Alan Reiach studied at Edinburgh College of Art and was a pupil of Sir Robert Lorimer. His architectural style was formed by his travels in the United States, Northern Europe and Russia in 1935. He met Frank Lloyd Wright and two Scandinavian architects - the Swede Erik Gunnar Asplund and Alvar Aalto from Finland. Reiach absorbed from them the pure geometry of Modern Movement architecture and a freedom of organic expression that softened the starkness of some early 20th-century buildings.

In the years after his continental experiences Reiach undertook an important photographic study of Scottish vernacular buildings, which resulted in a seminal book, *Building Scotland*, published in 1942. The book inspired Scottish architects to look at the simple buildings of their own country as a way forward for their architecture. Alan Reiach worked for the Clyde Valley Planning Authority

St Mungo's Church, Cumbernauld, designed by Alan Reiach

from 1944 to 1946, at a time when it was beginning to plan what eventually became Cumbernauld New Town. In 1949 he established his own practice in Edinburgh, later joining with Eric Hall as Reiach and Hall. Among his many buildings is the Appleton Tower of the early 1960s in Edinburgh's Crichton Street, part of Edinburgh University. The tower, one of Edinburgh's biggest structures, was featured as one of Britain's most hated buildings in Channel 4 television's *Demolition* series.

FINTRY IS TUCKED in the valley of the Endrick Water below the Campsie Fells. It is a very rural area - yet it is only 12½ crow-flight miles north of the centre of Glasgow. On the south side of the rather ordinary village street is a remarkable garden - with a fine pyramid.

Dun Ard house is modern and comfortable, but it is not a grand mansion. Yet its garden, developed from the early 1990s onwards, is one of the most exciting gardens to have been created in Britain in recent years. We were welcomed by one of its originators, Niall Manning, who moved here from Paisley with Alastair Morton. They were both determined to put their ideas for a new garden into practice.

Their inspiration has been taken from years of visiting some of the world's major gardens, and from a deep knowledge of plants. From the house a long straight avenue climbs directly towards the steep fells to the south. Off this central axis is a series of garden 'rooms', each with a different character - some, like the smooth, high-beech-hedge-surrounded lawn with a rectangular mirror pool and the area of pleached hornbeams are formal - others are wilder, with waving grasses or areas of underplanted woodland.

As the garden, which is open by appointment, merges into the wilder woods of the Fells, there are two highlights - the Circle, where a low wall has beech and bamboo around it, and the Pyramid, which is sited where a burn, tumbling down the hillside, enters the garden. In fact, it enters through the pyramid, for there is a tall rectangular slot through it; the water is channeled through the slot and falls into a small pool below. The base on which the pyramid stands was constructed, as a terracotta block says, by Corinthian Stonemasons. Next to it are Niall and Alastair's initials and the date 1999.

The pyramid itself is remarkable. Six feet high, it is built of red sandstone from Locharbriggs quarry near Dumfries - and is built without mortar. It is a dry-stone-wall *tour de force*, and is the work of waller Irwin Campbell. It was Irwin who alerted us to the Dun Ard pyramid, when we asked him about his pyramid at the Smith Art Gallery & Museum in Stirling (see page 254). Niall Manning told us that Irwin was determined to get the joints in the pyramid as perfect as possible, and that the precision of the internal walls of the slot caused much thought and planning. The base of the slot, over which the water runs, is of polished Caithness slate.

There is another drystone, unmortared pyramid in Scotland - on the hillside above Balmoral (see page 260) - but Niall did not cite it as an inspiration at Dun Ard. Instead, he named three sources. One was the pyramidal ice-house at Le Désert de Retz, the extraordinary late-18th-century garden at St Germain-en-Laye, just north of Versailles and west of Paris. It has the same basic form, of a pyramid sitting on a low base, though at Dun Ard the scale is smaller. The second was James Scanlon's pyramids at Sneem in southern Ireland (see page 321) - of which Niall and Alastair had seen pictures - the use of smaller coursed stones and the idea of piercing the pyramid came from there. The third inspiration was the pyramidal well head at Greenock (see page 272) - Scotland's oldest pyramid - water and pyramid combined. This fusion of ideas has resulted in one of the best of Scotland's modern pyramids - and one of which Niall and Alastair are very proud.

The slotted pyramid in the garden at Dun Ard, Fintry

IT PAYS TO advertise. And few advertising gimmicks can have lasted as long as the one thought up in 1863 by William Drummond of **Stirling**.

Drummond was part of the Stirling Tract Enterprise, started by his half-brother Peter in 1848. Their father, also William, was a successful land surveyor and seed merchant - 'a man of industry and integrity' as a contemporary described him. He passed both his business acumen and his strict religious views on to his eleven sons and four daughters, but it was Peter in particular who united the two strands he had inherited.

The Tract Enterprise began in 1848 when Peter was 50, and his father had been dead for almost a quarter of a century. Peter was incensed by the way local people treated the grounds of the ruined Cambuskenneth Abbey just across the river from Stirling. Each Sunday they would go and picnic there, play games and generally behave in what Drummond considered an unbecoming manner for a sacred place, especially on the Sabbath.

As Peter's biographer wrote, 'What lay in the well of his thought came up in the bucket of his speech', and he wasn't a man to keep quiet. His answer to this outbreak of immorality was to write a leaflet - a tract called *The Sabbath* - berating these feckless and un-Christian people. His words must have hit the mood of the times, for within a month his first edition of 10,000 copies was sold out. Further tracts had similar success, and Peter Drummond found that he had a new business on his hands. His publishing company, the Stirling Observer Press, continued to print religious works - and in the form of the Drummond Trust it still exists, 'Giving

*The Star Pyramid,
Stirling*

*William (left) and
Peter Drummond*

financial assistance for publications of sound Christian doctrine and outreach' as its website says.

While Peter oversaw his new publishing empire, William, who was seven years his senior, appears to have carried on the seeds business, but to have been involved in the publishing business, too. He became one of Stirling's most prominent and generous businessmen. Among his benefactions to the city was the extensive Valley Cemetery, immediately below the esplanade of Stirling Castle. The cemetery surrounds a rocky outcrop known as Ladies' Rock, from which medieval women would watch tournaments and enjoy the landscape views.

The Valley Cemetery was conceived as much as a tribute to Scottish Presbyterianism as a place for burial. Drummond peppered it with statues of Protestant divines, including John Knox. There is also an elaborate monument - sculpted figures of a girl and a young woman watched by a guardian angel, all enclosed by a cast-iron domed temple - to Margaret Wilson. She is described as 'Virgin Martyr of the Ocean Wave', and was drowned in the Solway in the 1680s after refusing to give up her allegiance to the Scottish Covenant (see also page 296). The Covenant was the national declaration by the Presbyterians to keep the Kirk free from any taint of Catholicism, including the Anglican church.

Having nailed his colours firmly to the mast of the Scottish faith, William Drummond then commissioned local sculptor William Barclay to design a structure that would be both a monument to the heroism of the Scottish Covenanters and an advertisement for the Stirling Tract Enterprise - the Star Pyramid at the edge of Valley Cemetery.

The Star Pyramid is finely positioned - it sits on a knoll and is elevated on a deep base of three steps, so that when you approach from below it dominates the view. It is built of blocks of hammered stone, beautifully fitted together and with very sharp edges. It is a classic pyramid shape - but what gives it its special interest is the abundance of chiselled texts and sculpture that adorn it.

The name Star Pyramid comes from the stars that appear in roundels on each side. Above them are an elongated object that is possibly intended to be either an appropriately-Scottish thistle or the Rod of Jesse (in this context it is unlikely to be that Catholic emblem of the Virgin Mary, the lily), and, in the pyramid's apex, a crown of eternity. Below the pedestal are stone spheres inscribed with lines of latitude and longitude, symbolising God's sway over the world (and, perhaps, that of the tract-publishing company, too?).

On one of the sphere-capped entrance piers to the pyramid is carved SALEM ROCK. In the same script on the topmost step of each face of the plinth are carved texts - ROCK OF AGES, COVENANT REST, THRONE OF RIGHT, UNION BANNER - with references to specific texts below them. Above the inscriptions are white marble open Bibles, the most obvious symbol of the Drummonds' enterprise. The words on them are uncompromising: Word of God; Light and Truth; Law of God; Book of Life.

In the centre of the side overlooking the cemetery is a circular plaque with an inscription - and this is where WIlliam Drummond's advertising ploy has failed. The text has almost worn away, leaving a few odd words at the top, and the remains of a pious thought at the base, finishing ' . . . dew impearled, at dawn on healing wings ascend TO GLORIOUS GOD ENTHRONED WITH CHRIST IN GOD. GOD ALL IN ALL'.

As with many a good pyramid, the Star has attracted a local legend. It is not the most imaginative - like Mad Jack Fuller's pyramid at Brightling (see page 68) and William Mackenzie's in Liverpool (see page 199), it is reputed to contain a local eccentric (presumably a Drummond), sitting upright at a feast-laden table. There were certainly eccentrics throughout Stirling's history - in 1656 rival ministers in the town, who could not agree on the form of worship to be used, built a wall across the Church of the Holy Rude, not far from the pyramid, so their two congregations could worship separately. The wall was removed only in 1936.

In fact, there is something inside the Star Pyramid, but it is not human. Just before the last stones were placed in 1863, William Drummond deposited a copy of the Bible and of the Scottish Covenant (probably both published by the family firm) in a niche, which was then sealed. William himself is buried in the Valley Cemetery nearby, in an austerely-plain tomb.

A PLANNING APPLICATION notice on the internet alerted us to Stirling's other pyramid. It was for 'Erection of a stone pyramid to house signage at The Smith Museum, 49 Albert Place, Stirling.' Submitted in February 2003, it was 'Approved with condition' - though there was no note of what the condition was. That was the only clue. A call to the Museum confirmed that, indeed, the pyramid had been built, and it holds information about The Stirling Smith, as it's known locally.

The Smith is not very far from the Star Pyramid - descend the ridge that holds the castle, back to the Kings Park on the plain of the River Forth and it's just wide of the city centre. It is a severe classical building, with a Doric portico fronting a more utilitarian shed - a bit like an early railway station. It sits low and comfortable amid handsome Victorian villas. Its collection is a wonderfully-eclectic mix of the artistic, the intriguing and the mundane - works by Scottish artists, archaeological remains, stained glass, furniture, the world's oldest curling stone . . . There are plans to re-display the collection - though any rearrangement should not be allowed to spoil the quirky air of the present arrangements.

And is the pyramid quirky? Perhaps it is. Like the pyramid at Fintry (see page 250) it was built by master waller - or drystone dyker as they are known in Scotland - Irwin Campbell. Campbell is an authority on the broch - the Iron Age round towers, unique to Scotland, which were first built around 500 BC. These cooling-tower-shaped structures were all built with drystone walling techniques, and to prove it Irwin has built part of one, using only the tools and techniques that the early builders would have. The result, at Strathyre, 20 miles north-west of Stirling, is a section of a double broch wall 2.5 metres high, built between 2004 and 2006. Irwin believes the work proves that building a full-size broch would have needed a massive community effort - and that suggests they were built when times were stable. Brochs were status symbols, not fortresses.

For The Stirling Smith, the job was somewhat simpler. The Gallery had a modest supply of stone handy, and asked Irwin for his advice on how to build their sign. 'I came up with the idea of the panel set into the pyramid,' he said. 'We constructed a polystyrene template for the most difficult parts, and when the keystone was set we sawed away the template. Each stone is now pushing against its neighbour, so it's very strong.' The cap, with its 2003 date, is of Yorkshire limestone. The pyramid is quite narrow, with a rectangular footprint.

Irwin Campbell's pyramid at The Smith, Stirling

The information on the circular panels set into the pyramid tells visitors about the biodiversity of Allie's Garden behind the main building, and about the history of the King's Garden. What we liked best, though, was the sign propped up against it. Children had obviously been misbehaving, with no proper respect for the work of art that Irwin had created. The sign - the only one we have seen anywhere in Britain or Ireland - reads 'PLEASE DO NOT CLIMB ON THE PYRAMID'.

'THERE ARE PYRAMIDS at **Dunfermline** Bus Station,' wrote Mrs Walls in response to a plea from us in her local paper for information about local examples.

This seemed so unlikely we had to go and see. We knew a few things about Dunfermline - it has the ruins of an abbey founded by St Margaret of Scotland, and eight kings are buried in the town. It's the birthplace of the ill-fated King Charles 1 and also of Andrew Carnegie, who became the world's richest man - the Bill Gates of his day - and a notable philanthropist. And that was about it. Were we about to discover hidden depths to the place?

We parked to the north of the city centre, beside - of course - Carnegie Drive. The bus station, with its adjoining multi-storey car park, was a short walk way. It is a typical 1980s structure (it was opened in November 1984), box-like and built of reinforced concrete blocks speckled with those brownish, pebble-dashed rectangular panels that architects of the period used as a way of relieving the monotony of their structures. But where were Mrs Walls' pyramids?

On the side that held the bus bays there were some strange sculptural decorations of cast concrete - rows of canted, fluted triangles that look like pale, oversized pasta. Had Mrs Walls led us astray? We looked around - and there at our feet were the pyramids!

Jammed between the walls of the bus station and multi-storey car park building and the columns holding up the bus shelters is a row of pyramidal structures, each around four feet high. They are faced with smoothed cobbles, which make an effective contrast to the sharp lines of the rest of the building. Their purpose is obvious - to prevent the strip of land being used for, well, anything at all. No standing, sitting or sunbathing. No skateboarding or rollerblading. No cycling, running or playing hopscotch. In fact, nothing.

The question is, were they part of the original design of the architects from Fife Regional Council and included in the £2.7 million cost of the spanking new bus station? Or were they added later when a design flaw was discovered, perhaps as part of the 1997 £50,000 facelift, which also saw £3,000 being spent on CCTV cameras?

Neither the Dunfermline Carnegie Library (what else?) nor Fife Council's planning department (who really should have known) was able to tell us. We're just grateful that Mrs Walls had her wits about her and spotted these rather endearing pyramids for us.

CARNEGIE TURNED UP again, albeit tangentially, in connection with the next group of pyramids. From Dunfermline we headed north up the M90 to **Perth**. They are in Perth's attractive riverside park and form part of the Perth Sculpture Trail. They were designed by someone whose work we had already met - David Wilson, who designed the Livingston pyramid (see page 247).

'There are pyramids at Dunfermline Bus Station,' wrote Mrs Walls

Wilson was commissioned to produce three 'waymarkers' for the Trail. He wanted to base his work on the beauty of the natural surroundings and to offer visitors something which they could quietly contemplate as they walked. But he also needed to make them, as the brief required, relevant to Perth.

In his researches for a theme he came across the work of Patrick Geddes. Geddes, who was born in 1854 in Ballater, not far from Balmoral, moved to Perth when he was three, and was a student at Perth Academy. He went to study mining at London's Royal School of Mines, but quickly came under the influence of the biologist Thomas Huxley, and switched disciplines - not for the last time in his career.

After running an experimental zoological station in Aberdeen for a while, he joined a scientific expedition to Mexico, where an illness affected his eyesight. Back in Britain, no longer able to use a microscope for his biological studies, he started to study humans; he became a social scientist. From there it was short step to seeking to improve living conditions for the poorest people, and to the elements of town planning that created good communities. He set up new student flats in Edinburgh in the late 1880s, as well as the Outlook Tower, an experiment in educating tenants of the inner city.

From 1889 Geddes was professor of Botany at Dundee University, but continued to develop his social theories, mixing observations from the animal kingdom, ideas from the study of geography and philosophy from Plato, as well as a dash of anarchism. From 1900 he was in London, helping to found the Sociological Society and exhibiting his ideas on town planning. He spent ten years from 1914 in India, working on town planning in Bombay (now Mumbai) before settling in Montpellier, honing his ideas on how life can be reinvigorated. He had already planned the Hebrew University in Jerusalem, and in 1925 drew up the blueprint for the new city of Tel Aviv. He was knighted in 1932, the year he died.

In 1905 Geddes published a report for the Dunfermline Carnegie Trust (that's where the link is) called *City Development: a Study of Parks, Gardens and Culture Institutes*. He would no doubt have been pleased that a century later a park in Perth became home to sculptures inspired by his work. David Wilson was particularly intrigued by passages from Geddes' book *The World Without and The World Within*. Geddes contrasts the perception of the outer world of our actions with the inner world of our thoughts and imaginations, and shows how in the contemplation of nature we can come to understand the cycle of life and death.

This gave Wilson the stimulus he sought. His three sculptures consist of dyking-stone pyramids, capped with black granite and bronze. Collectively known, with a bow to Geddes, *Outwith Within* each is about four feet high. They are called Seed, Bud and Leaf. The Seed, which is on an island in the River Tay, has been damaged by vandals and has lost its metal cap; it represents that which seems dry and dull, but is full of potential life; the Bud is the symbol of regeneration, and the Leaf is the burgeoning of all plant life.

Wilson's work is far more than a worthy attempt to interest the public in modern sculpture. It fits beautifully into the landscape of the riverside park - in many ways the sculptures are reminiscent of another sculptural group, *The Way the Fairies Went* at Sneem in Co Kerry (see page 321). As Wilson has written, his Perth sculptures are 'an incredible affirmation of renewal and the power of life over death'.

DEATH WAS TO the fore at **Strathkinness** in Fife. A letter from David Smith in St Andrews had alerted us to a pyramid we had not come across, in woodland to the south of the village, a couple of miles outside St Andrews.

A winding path through woodland led us to a small clearing with a five-foot-high pyramid of irregular stone. We were on Magus Muir, and this was the spot where an archbishop was murdered.

James Sharp was born in 1618, and educated at Aberdeen University. By the age of 30 he had already forged links with St Andrews as a Regent - a don - at the university. He was also a convinced Presbyterian minister and a member of the Covenanters, who were pledged to protect the Scottish Presbyterian system from the wishes of the English to impose bishops on the Scots (see page 253). He spent time in prison under Cromwell for his views, and was the author of a justification of Presbyterianism, *A true representation of the rise, progresse and state of the present divisions of the Church of Scotland.*

An eloquent speaker and diplomat, Sharp was a natural choice to be sent from the Covenanters, who at that time formed the government in Scotland, to negotiate with the English. He was in London in 1657 and again in 1660. Sharp seems to have been involved in the negotiations to restore Charles II to the throne in England, although his letters to Scotland imply that he wanted to be home: 'I weary much of my imployment here now, and long absence from my charge, finding I can do no good here, to the stemming of that current for prelacy.' He had to stay, finally returning to his parish at Crail on the Fife coast in August 1660, three months after the Restoration.

In his claims to be trying to 'stemming that current', Sharp was dissembling. Becoming a prelate of the church was on his own horizon. In late 1660 he abandoned his Covenanter colleagues and the Presbyterian church and in December 1661 he was consecrated as Archbishop of St Andrews and Primate of Scotland.

Not surprisingly, his former co-religionists regarded him as a traitor. He did not help himself by the severity with which he immediately attempted to repress the Covenanters throughout Scotland. He became a figure of hate. In 1668 there was an assassination attempt, when James Mitchell fired at him, missing by inches. Mitchell was apprehended six years later and executed in 1678; he was hailed as a martyr and his death inflamed the Covenanters even more against Sharp. As Sir Walter Scott wrote in *The Minstrelsy of the Scottish Border*, 'It was well known, that James Sharp, Archbishop of St Andrews, was regarded by the rigid Presbyterians, not only as a renegade, who had turned back from the spiritual plough, but as the principal author of the rigours exercised against their sect'.

It was inevitable that Sharp's enemies would eventually catch up with him. It happened on 3 May 1679 - by accident. A group of Covenanters was given a tip-off that Sharp's agent for repression, William Carmichael (or Carstares - there are different versions) was travelling across Magus Muir on that day, and they set an ambush. But it was not Carmichael who came. It was the Archbishop himself, travelling in his coach with his daughter Isabella.

The Covenanters fired their pistols at the carriage, bringing it to a halt. Then one of them, John Balfour of Kinloch, dragged Sharp out, calling him 'Judas' and 'Murderer'. Isabella and Sharp's servants pleaded for his life, but Balfour fired his blunderbuss at close range into the Archbishop. Believing that he was dead, the

Archbishop Sharp was killed on the spot marked by this pyramid at Magus Muir near St Andrews

OPPOSITE:
Seed (top), Bud and Leaf by David Wilson in Perth

257

Archbishop Sharp

Covenanters turned to leave, but one of them overheard Isabella calling her servants to help her father, who was still alive. Balfour returned. He kicked off Sharp's hat and then applied his boot to the Archbishop's head with such force that the brains were exposed - though some sources say he used his broadsword to finish the job.

Balfour then had Sharp's pockets searched. They found a mandate from King Charles authorising Sharp to undertake further repression. They also discovered a purse containing two pistol bullets, a ball of multi-coloured silk and, even more puzzlingly, a small piece of parchment, about half an inch across, with two long words on it. No one could read them - they seemed to be in a script resembling Hebrew or Chaldean. The Covenanters believed these were magic charms, proof against gunfire, which was why Sharp had survived the blunderbuss shot.

Not far from the pyramid later erected on the spot where Sharp fell is a grave to five men who were implicated in the murder, though there is some doubt as to whether they were among the nine murderers. They were captured at the Battle of Bothwell Brig, south of Glasgow (see page 279), in June 1679, where the Presbyterians fought the English army. The English victory marked the effective end of the Covenanters' power. The five men, Thomas Brown, James Wood, Andrew Sword, John Weddell and John Clyde, were charged with the Archbishop's murder and were hanged in chains at Magus Muir on 25 November 1679.

Only two of the men who were definitely known to have been among the assassins were caught and executed. David Hackston of Rathillot, Balfour of Kinloch's brother-in-law, was identified as the leader. He was captured after the Battle of Airds Moss (see page 281). He was sentenced to death and his right hand was cut off and publicly displayed in Cupar as a warning. The other man, Andrew Guillan, was hanged, drawn and quartered in St Andrews. His head was displayed in Cupar, and his body was hung in chains at Magus Muir.

The Magus Muir pyramid to Sharp, which is a scheduled Ancient Monument, carries a Latin inscription which translates as 'Near this place James Sharp, Archbishop of St Andrews, was slain by savage enemies in the presence of his pleading daughter AD 1679.' It is not, though, his only memorial; there is a much grander one in Holy Trinity Church in St Andrews. A sumptuous, even overblown, black and white marble monument, put up by his brother, includes dowsed torches, a figure of the Archbishop at prayer, another of him being crowned as a martyr by an angel, and a bas relief of his murder. The inscription speaks of him as 'a most pious prelate, a most prudent senator and a most holy martyr'. At his funeral service the sermon was preached by Bishop Patterson, the inventor of the thumbscrew. Although Sharp is supposedly buried beneath the monument, his bones were not there when it was opened in 1849. It is likely that the Covenanters had removed them.

Archbishop James Sharp was notorious in his own lifetime, and his death was one of the causes of the dreadful repression of the Covenanters in the following decades (see page 279). His name still lives on in St Andrews. Each year he is one of the figures represented in the city's Kate Kennedy procession, a medieval tradition resurrected in the 1920s. Sharp is portrayed in his coach in the show. And it is said that on dark nights a similar, though ghostly, vehicle passes through St Andrews' streets - in absolute silence.

*Dundee's Formica
pyramid by
Stan Bonnar*

UNLIKELY AS IT seems, there is a link between Archbishop
Sharp and the location of the next pyramid on the list through
William Topaz McGonagall, Poet and Tragedian. In his poem *The
Village of Tayport and its Surroundings* he advises his readers:

>Do not forget to visit the old Tower,
>Where Archbishop Sharp spent many an hour,
>Viewing the beautiful scenery for miles away
>Along the banks o'the Silvery Tay.

As a native of **Dundee**, McGonagall was loud in his praise for his
city:

>Oh, Bonnie Dundee! I will sing in thy praise
>A few true but simple lays,
>Regarding some of your beauties of the present day -
>And virtually speaking, there's none can them gainsay.

The poet's words were running through our heads as we crossed
the 'Silvery Tay'. We tried to negotiate the one-way system on to
Westport, but failed. A University student set us on the right
track, and we found the place.

All the pyramids of Britain and Ireland are unique - but this has
two special claims. It is the only pyramid that sits above a disused
Victorian gentlemen's toilet, and it is the only one made mainly
of Formica. About ten feet high, the pyramid looks as if it is

formed from marble slabs, but touch it and examine the joints closely, and it reveals the material of which it is constructed.

Information about this pyramid came in an e-mail from Ian of Dundee. He said that the pyramid was designed by Stan Bonnar who, like him, was a student at Dundee's Duncan of Jordanstone College of Art, part of the University of Dundee ('Twas in the 5th day of October, in the year of 1853, / That the University College was opened in Dundee . . .'). But Ian had lost touch with Stan, who was last heard of in the Carlisle area.

There was information about him from Axis Arts, including a CV. Stan has taught at Glasgow School of Art and at Darlington College, and has exhibited his work around the world. But there was no contact address, and Axis Arts said they were trying to re-establish connection with him. Other information we gleaned told us of a very jolly set of sculptures, *The Witty Parade of Hippos*, made in 1972 for the paddling pool in Riverside Park, Glenrothes, and four standing, naked figures called *The Community* in Whitevale Street, Glasgow. There is also the tantalising information that Stan is 'Currently involved in film work with his son, Mark Bonnar'. Mark is a well-known actor, with appearances ranging from roles at the Royal Shakespeare Company to television's *Holby City*. Mark's bother Vini is a professional drummer.

None of this brought us any nearer to finding out why Stan had chosen a pyramid for Dundee. The project was part of Dundee's public art programme, started in 1982 as the Blackness Public Arts Programme. It includes work by David Wilson (see pages 247 and 255). The project's website has details of many of the sculptures it has commissioned - but, of course, no mention of Stan's pyramid. So all we could do was enjoy the incongruity of a Formica pyramid beside the road near the University of Dundee, and to ponder the images set into it - among them a Celtic cross and a fish. We should have liked to have asked Stan Bonnar about the significance of these Christian symbols, and about the angular steel sculptures surrounding the pyramid - were they part of his original concept, or were they added later by another artist?

These questions remain, but we had to leave. As the Poet and Tragedian wrote:

> Farewell! 'Farewell! To the bonnie banks o' the Silvery Tay . . .
> Which I will remember when I am far away.

THE APPROACH TO **Balmoral** from Braemar along the valley of the River Dee had us craning our necks to look at the heights above for signs of Prince Albert's Cairn. A couple of contenders appeared on bluffs among the trees - the Princess Royal's Cairn and Princess Alice's Cairn - but they were not the genuine pyramid we had come to see.

We knew that Prince Albert's Cairn differed from these other, conical cairns. As Diane Eddy, Administration Secretary at Balmoral told us, 'His cairn is indeed a proper pyramid. It is 35 feet in height and made of granite. This is the only pyramid on Balmoral Estate.' With such a pedigree and recommendation, how could we miss it out of our tour?

Armed with permission from the Estate, we set off from the gates of Balmoral Castle to climb Creag-an-Lurachain, an outrider of the great Lochnagar massif. Keeping a wary eye out for the Old Man of Lochnagar (as chronicled by the Prince of Wales) we climbed steadily on a rough track through pinewoods. Suddenly the trees gave way to open heath. In front of us was the pyramid

OPPOSITE;
Prince Albert's
pyramid at
Balmoral
(see also page vi)

- and coming round its flank was a party of pony trekkers. The riders were an American family and were led by Fiona Stuart on her pony, Quarry.

'Gosh!' she exclaimed. 'I've been coming up here for ten years, and it's the first time I've ever seen anyone here.' Albert's pyramid was obviously not the place for general recreation. Given its origins, that is not surprising.

There was a long tradition at Balmoral of the Royal Family building cairns. It started in autumn 1852. Victoria and Albert bought the Balmoral Estate that year, having leased it since 1848. Queen Victoria's *Highland Journal* for Monday 11 October noted,

> It was nearly eleven o'clock before we could go to the top of Craig Gowan to see the cairn built, which was to commemorate our taking possession of this dear place . . . We set off with all the children, ladies, gentle men, and a few of the servants . . . to the highest point on Craig Gowan; where were assembled all the ser-vants and tenants, with their wives and children and old relations. I laid the first stone, after which Albert laid one, then the children, according to their ages. All the ladies and gentlemen placed one; then everyone came forward at once, each person carrying a stone and plac-ing it on the cairn. It took, I am sure, an hour's build-ing; and whist it was going on, some merry reels were danced . . . At last, when the cairn, which is, I think, seven or eight feet high, was nearly completed, Albert climbed up to the top of it, and placed the last stone: after which three cheers were given. It was a gay, pretty and touching sight; and I felt almost inclined to cry. The view was so beautiful over the dear hills; the day so fine; the whole so *gemüthlich*. May God bless this place, and allow us yet to see it and enjoy it for many a long year!

Ten years later the Queen was on Creag-an-Lurachain at the founding of another cairn - but this time the circumstances were anything but *gemüthlich*. Victoria's wish for 'many a long year' had not been fulfilled for Albert. His death from typhoid on 14 December 1861 was a devastating blow to her. A few months earlier Albert had said to her 'I do not cling to life. You do; but I set no store by it. If I knew that those I love were well cared for, I should be quite ready to die tomorrow. I am sure, if I had a severe illness, I should give up at once, I should not struggle for life.' He was 42 when he died, and Victoria went into the deep-est mourning.

It was as part of her grieving that Prince Albert's Cairn was constructed. She chose a pyramid, rather than a simpler cairn, as the most fitting funerary monument. The site was very care-fully chosen - it has a commanding view up and down the Dee valley, and can be seen from most parts of the 24,000-acre Balmoral Estate. The tale that it was the place that Albert shot his last stag can be discounted - it would be too much of a coin-cidence that the feat was achieved in so perfect a spot for his memorial.

On 21 August 1862 Victoria ascended Creag-an-Lurachain in a pony carriage, accompanied by the six of her children ('my poor six orphans', as she called them) who were in Britain at the time. On reaching the summit they each put a stone in place on the fourth course of the granite blocks of the new monument. The stones were inscribed with their initials and with those of

The shape of Prince Albert's pyramid is matched by these topiary versions at Easter Balmoral

their siblings who were not present.

The initials are: AEA - Prince Alfred Ernest Albert, later Duke of Edinburgh; AMM - Princess Alice Mary Maud, Grand Duchess of Hesse: VAML - Victoria Adelaide Mary Louise, Princess Royal, Crown Princess of Germany and Prussia (and mother of Kaiser Wilhelm); BMVF - Beatrice Mary Victoria Feodore, later Princess Henry of Battenberg; LCA - Princess Louise Caroline Alberta, later Marchioness of Lorne; HAV - Helena Augusta Victoria, later Princess Christian of Schleswig-Holstein; LGDA - Prince Leopold George Duncan Albert, later Duke of Albany; AWPA - Prince Arthur William Patrick Albert, later Duke of Connaught and Strathearne; and AE - Albert Edward, Prince of Wales. The final stone is inscribed for the Queen, VR.

On the valley side of the finished pyramid is an inscription:
TO THE BELOVED MEMORY OF ALBERT, THE
GREAT AND GOOD, PRINCE CONSORT, ERECTED
BY HIS BROKEN-HEARTED WIDOW VICTORIA R.
21st AUGUST 1862.

There is also an appropriate verse from chapter 4 of the *Book of Wisdom*, chosen by the Princess Royal: 'He being made perfect in a short time, fulfilled a long time, for his soul pleased the Lord, therefore hastened He to take him away from among the wicked.'

Prince Albert's Cairn is beautifully constructed of 34 courses of quite small granite blocks. It is said that there is no mortar used in its construction. Despite its sad origins, the cairn is an exhilarating place to stand, with its far-reaching views of the Grampians and with the lush valley of the Dee far below. And the walk back down was exhilarating, too, following another path that Fiona Stuart recommended. It took us past Princess Beatrice's Cairn, which marked her marriage to Prince Henry of Battenburg in 1885 and brought us out into Easter Balmoral, where a tenant has created topiary pyramids in his garden to match Albert's granite version on the hill above.

NOW IT WAS time for the most northerly of our British pyramids - and one that is well hidden. The route took us over one of Britain's highest roads, from Cockbridge to Tomintoul, then up to Inverness and across the bridge into the Black Isle. Just south of Conon Bridge at the western end of the Isle is **Kinkell** Castle, home to artist Gerald Laing.

Laing was famous in the 1960s as one of the leaders of Pop Art. His most famous work of this period is the 1962 work *Brigitte Bardot*. His Pop Art phase, influenced especially by newspaper photographs, lasted only three years.

From 1965, now in America, he produced abstract works, many of them cut out of metal, gaining a wide reputation as a minimalist artist. In 1969 he left America behind and after a long search for a suitable property in Britain bought Kinkell Castle. It provided him with both a restoration project and with space to work. From the early 1970s his artistic work changed again, moving away from abstraction to creating figurative sculptures, many cast in bronze in his own foundry at Kinkell. At first these figures were angular, like *An American Girl*, a cast of which is in the garden at Kinkell. Later projects, including the frieze of the *Wise and Foolish Virgins* on the Standard Life Assurance building in Edinburgh's George Street, and the Highland Clearances Memorial at Helmsdale are more naturalistic.

The most public of Laing's later sculptures is the new Mercat Cross in Inverness, unveiled in 2003. The following year Laing

Gerald Laing's ivy-covered pyramid and his sculpture An American Girl at Kinkell Castle

startled the art world by returning to his Pop Art roots with cartoon-like paintings based on the infamous pictures from Iraq's Abu Ghraib jail of American soldiers abusing Iraqi prisoners. In 2008 he was again in the news for his Pop Art canvases showing stars like Amy Winehouse and Pete Docherty.

All this seemed far away when we visited Gerald Laing at Kinkell. The castle is a typical tower house of about 1590, painted an earth yellow. Laing spent many years restoring it as accurately as possible, demolishing an 18th-century extension in the process. On the lawn in front of the castle, near the *American Girl*, is a curiously-shaped bush - the pyramid we had come to see.

This is one of Laing's abstract sculptures, a split pyramid of concrete with an elongated top section like the blades of a pair of short shears - in all, about 15 feet high. It dates from the early 1970s, and is a response to the landscape of the Scottish Highlands. Now it is virtually covered with ivy, softening the starkness of its outline and forming a shape akin to the alien in *The Quatermass Experiment*.

We asked Gerald Laing why he had allowed the ivy to take over the pyramid. 'I like it,' he replied laconically. 'It makes an interesting shape.'

Inside his studio, Gerald Laing showed us what the pyramid looked like before it became a horticultural specimen. A steel maquette about four feet high showed the clean angles of the pyramid and its extraordinary appendages. It looked even more alien than its big brother in the garden.

This was the most northerly point of our Scottish journey. It was time to turn south and make our way down the western side of the country - with pyramids in wilderness and in cities, with tales of heroism, adventure and bloodshed. In fact, another typical pyramid adventure.

The maquette for Laing's Kinkell pyramid

Tour 8

SCOTLAND - WEST

THERE WAS NO sign of the Loch Ness Monster as we drove south west down the Great Glen. Not long after we had passed through Fort Augustus at the foot of Loch Ness we came to **Invergarry**, a village of solid 19th-century estate cottages built for the Ellice family of Glengarry Castle. A little further south, at the narrowest part of Loch Oich, stands Tobar-nan-Ceanu - the Well of the Heads. Its site is marked by a tall pyramid standing on a plinth, marking a bloody chapter in Highland history.

On 25 September 1663 there was an assassination. Alexander MacDonald, the Chief of the Clan Keppoch, and his brother Ranald were murdered by seven assailants in a feud ostensibly about a parcel of land claimed by another of the clan, Alexander MacDougall MacDonald of Inverlair. In reality the antagonism between the two branches of the clan went back many years - to at least 1431, when a MacDonald ancestor had had part of his estate confiscated. It is thought that MacDonald of Inverlair was incited to the murder by other members of the clan, who thought that the Chief was introducing reforms that threatened their way of life.

Whatever the cause, vengeance was clearly called for. But it was slow in coming. Two years passed, and the MacDonalds of Keppoch did nothing. Finally the MacDonald bard, Ian Lom - Bald John - appealed to Lord MacDonald, Chief of Glengarry, to take action. MacDonald refused, so Ian Lom wrote to Sir James MacDonald of Sleat, but he was reluctant to interfere. Fired by the righteousness of his cause, Ian Lom went to Sir James' castle at Duntulm. On his arrival a curious, allusive conversation took place:

'Where do you come from?' asked Sir James.

'From Laodicea,' replied Ian.

'Are they hot or cold in that place?' enquired Sir James, clearly knowing the reference in the *Book of the Revelation* to the church in Laodicea - 'You are neither cold nor hot. I wish that you were one or the other, but since you are neither, but only lukewarm, I will spew you out of my mouth'.

'Abel is cold and his blood is crying out in vain for vengeance', retorted Ian Lom, now in the Old Testament. 'Cain is hot and red-handed and hundreds are lukewarm as the black goat's milk.'

Sir James MacDonald took the point. He applied for permission - 'Letters of Fire and Sword' - from the Privy Council to pursue and apprehend the assassins, who were named as 'Allan MacDonald, eldest son of the Tutor of Keppoch, his brother Daniel Gorm, Alexander MacDougall MacDonald in Inverlair in the Brae of Lochaber, John Roy MacDougall MacDonald brother to the said Alexander, Donald Orie MacCoull there, Dugall MacCoull in Tallie, Patrick Dunbar there'. They were arraigned, in the document issued on 29 July 1665, for 'giving the said Alexander 33 great wounds and the said MacDonald his brother 28 wounds of which they immediately died upon the place'.

Once the legal assent for the pursuit was given, things moved swiftly. What in the Wild West would be known as a posse, of 50

The Well of the
Seven Heads,
Invergarry

OPPOSITE:
Kilmuir, near
Dunvegan, Isle of
Skye: the Fraser
pyramid, seen by
Dr Johnson
(see page 268)

The top of the Well of theSeven Heads - a fist holds the seven heads and the dagger that severed them

men, was put under the command of Sir James MacDonald of Sleat's brother Archibald, called An Ciaran Mabach, the Warrior Poet. They were led to Inverlair, in Glen Spean, by Ian Lom, and surprised the murderers there. They set fire to the building and flushed their enemies out. Bitter fighting followed, but Archibald's men won the day. All seven of the men named in the indictment were slain.

What happened then was, if anything, even more gruesome. Ian Lom severed their heads and wrapped them in his plaid to bear them away. He headed north to Invergarry Castle to show them to Lord MacDonald - but first he stopped at the well beside Loch Oich to wash off the blood. On reaching the castle he flung them down in the great hall at Lord MacDonald's feet.

The heads were later taken to Edinburgh, where they were 'affixit to the gallowes standing on the Gallowlie between Edinburgh and Leith' before being buried nearby. More than two centuries later the mound where the burial supposedly took place was excavated - and seven skulls were unearthed.

The Invergarry pyramid, which commemorates the gory events of the late 17th century, was put up only in 1812 by Colonel MacDonald of Glengarry. On top of the monument are carved the seven heads that were washed by Ian Lom in the well. They are held in a mailed fist which also grasps a dagger. The heads appear, too, in the modern railings that separate the monument from the road. Steps down the side of the monument allow access to the well itself - or rather, to a tunnel leading under the road to the site of the well, for the road has been widened, the monument moved and the well covered. It is still possible, nevertheless, to imagine Ian Lom with his grisly bundle, bending to wash the blood-spattered heads in the water. Some authorities think that his actions had their origins in ancient Celtic beliefs in the magical properties both of wells and of the severed heads of enemies.

Colonel Macdonald was keen that his inscription should be understood by all who pass by. It is carved into the pyramid's plinth in four languages - English, French, Latin and Gaelic. The words were written by the early-19th-century Celtic scholar Ewen MacLachlan - but unfortunately, his facts are incorrect. He says, 'The heads of the seven murderers were presented at the feet of the noble Chief in Glengarry Castle after having been washed in this spring and ever since that event which took place early in the sixteenth century has been known by the name of "Tobar-nan-Ceann" The Well of the Heads' - making his dates out by around 150 years. And his prose, though it might sound fine in Gaelic, becomes pedestrian in English and French - it lacks the immediacy of Ian Lom's own poem on the subject, *Murt Na Ceapaich*. More fitting, perhaps, is the link between the events of 1665 around the shores of Loch Oich and one of the most famous of the Scottish Regiments, the Cameron Highlanders. They wore the Keppoch MacDonald tartan - the same that Ian Lom used to carry the seven heads to the well.

LOCH CORUISK ON the Isle of Skye - 'That Dread Lake' as Sir Walter Scott described it - is difficult to access. There is a long trail, a round trip of more than 16 miles on foot from the Sligachan Hotel, where the Dunvegan road leaves the route from Broadford to Portree. There's a shorter walking route, starting near Kirkibost on the road down to Elgol - but that involves the tricky traverse of the fearsome Bad Step, a spine of rock with wide gaps and a 30-foot drop into the sea for the unwary. The easiest way is

*Captain Maryon's
memorial near
Loch Coruisk, in
the Black Cuillin,
Isle of Skye*

to continue to Elgol and take one of the boats that regularly cross
Loch Scavaig into the heart of the Cuillin mountains, from where
it's a short walk to Coruisk.

That is the theory. In practice it can be more difficult. We drove
to Elgol through a monsoon-like downpour - torrents from the
hills crossed the narrow road, and the wind tried to blow us off
track. The rain had stopped by the next morning but the wind
still blew. Would the boats sail? Not that day. We stayed a second
night. Any better? The sun shone, but still the wind blew. We
waited in the harbour at Elgol. At 11.00 am the final decision
came - there would be no boats that day, either. We could stay no
longer; Loch Coruisk had to remain unvisited. So we never saw
the pyramid on the nearby slopes, between Sgurr Hain and Sgurr
na Stri, that is a memorial to Captain A J Maryon, who died there
in 1946.

Maryon's story up until then is largely unknown. It is likely that
he came from an Essex family - he was probably the Arthur James
Maryon who was born in Epping in 1908. He was the only son of
elderly parents. There are no further details of his life until 1945,
when he was on a troopship returning from India. He had been a
member of the General Headquarters of India Command, working for the Commander in Chief - Field Marshal Auchinleck from
1943, Field Marshal Wavell before that. On the ship he met Staff
Captain Myles Morrison, a Scottish civil engineer seven years
older than him, who had been working as Royal Engineer for the
Army in India - though it is likely that they knew each other in
India, too. Myles Morrison was a great character, and he and
Maryon were soon talking. Morrison asked what Maryon was
planning to do when he returned home. 'Have a mountaineering
holiday in Skye,' he replied. A great mountaineer himself, the
reply delighted Morrison, and the two became friends.

The friendship was short-lived. In July 1946 Capt Maryon set off alone from the Sligachan Hotel to climb in the Cuillin. He never returned. The search parties that went to look for him failed to discover the body. When Myles Morrison heard about the search he was convinced that they were looking in the wrong places. Maryon would not be found where accidents were likely to happen, like the foot of precipices; he was too good and careful a climber for that. So the search was widened - but it was two years before the body was found. It is likely that Maryon had had an attack of malaria, which he had contracted in India, and had died as a result. His remains were taken for burial in Portree, but there seems to be no memorial to him there.

With no family to mourn him, Maryon might have been forgotten without the determination of Myles Morrison. Over a period of years he spent 30 days constructing a pyramid in tribute to Maryon, bringing together large stones with the help of his friend the Glasgow architect Fred Wylie. It was Wylie who designed the lettering for the small plaque attached to the foot of the pyramid. The inscription reads 'Erected in the memory of Staff Captain A. J. Maryon G.H.Q. India Command who met his death here in July 1946. He lay on this spot for nearly two years and now rests in Portree. This cairn was built by his friend Myles Morrison ex staff captain R.E. who served with him in the 1939-45 war.'

Morrison died, aged over 90, in 1992. Into his old age he remained a climber and an inveterate traveller. He was always proud to have remembered his friend Maryon, and to have provided a fitting memorial in such a remote and awesome place. We still plan to go and pay our respects to them both - when the weather allows.

DR JOHNSON FAMOUSLY said that 'the noblest prospect which a Scotchman ever sees, is the high road that leads him to England.' Yet he at last, in 1785, submitted to Boswell's repeated requests to visit Scotland. Boswell and Johnson had mentioned the proposed tour to Voltaire the previous year. Boswell wrote, 'I mentioned our design to Voltaire. He looked at me, as if I had talked of going to the North Pole, and said, "You do not insist on my accompanying you?" "No, sir." "Then I am very willing you should go".' The two men set out in August to make their way to the Hebrides.

By September they were in the Isle of Skye. They spent a week as guests of the McLeods at Dunvegan Castle, leaving on 21 September. Johnson liked Dunvegan - 'Our entertainment here was in so elegant a style, and reminded my fellow-traveller so much of England, that he became quite joyous', wrote Boswell. On the day they left they passed the parish church of Durinish - otherwise **Kilmuir**. Boswell noted, 'The churchyard is not enclosed, but a pretty murmuring brook runs along one side of it. In it is a pyramid erected to the memory of Thomas Lord Lovat, by his son, Lord Simon, who suffered on Towerhill. It is of free-stone and, I suppose, about thirty feet high.'

A thirty-foot pyramid! We retraced our steps from Elgol to Broadford then travelled west, through Sligachan from where Capt Maryon (see page 267) had set out, with its tremendous views of the Cuillin. Then still west, descending almost to sea-level until the twin flat-topped summits of McLeod's Tables came into view and we knew we were almost there.

Approaching Dunvegan, we stopped to enquire in the Tourist Information Office. Trish Garron was on duty. 'Can you tell us where the old churchyard is, please?'

'Old churchyard?'

'Where the Fraser pyramid is.'

'Pyramid?'

This was not going well. We dug out the map. 'Is there a big monument where it's marked "Cemys", just here?' we asked, pointing to a spot about a quarter of a mile from where we stood.

'I'm afraid I don't know,' Trish replied, obviously both embarrassed by her lack of local knowledge and puzzled by the odd request.

'Don't worry, we'll go and look,' we said.

The sky had been threatening rain as we drove west, and the summits of McLeod's Tables were shrouded in mist as we walked the short uphill distance to the cemetery. The first few spots of rain began to fall. But the pyramid was there, now within a stone-walled enclosure near the ruins of the old Durinish Parish Church.

Boswell was wrong about its height - 15 feet would have been nearer the mark. But it is still an impressive monument. On the slope of the pyramid is a much-weathered and patched coat of arms sculpted in white marble, and on the plinth a long marble inscription. These were apparently the other way round when Boswell saw them and were transposed in a 19th-century restoration. The inscription, which was recorded by Boswell, begins:

> This pyramid was erected by SIMON LORD FRASER of LOVAT, in honour of Lord THOMAS his Father, a Peer of Scotland, and Chief of the great and ancient clan of the FRASERS. Being attacked for his birthright by the family of ATHOLL, then in power and favour with KING WILLIAM, yet, by the valour and fidelity of his clan, and the assistance of the CAMPBELLS, the old friends and allies of his family, he defended his birthright with such greatness and fermety of soul, and such valour and activity, that he was an honour to his name, and a good pattern to all brave Chiefs of clans. He died in the month of May, 1699, in the 63d year of his age, in Dunvegan, the house of the LAIRD of MAC LEOD, whose sister he had married.

A dutiful and loving son paying a tribute to a beloved father. Note the 'soft' words - honour, fidelity, fermety, pattern . . . What could better express the gentle nature of Simon, Lord Fraser of Lovat and his love for his amiable father?

Unfortunately, Simon was by no means such a paragon as the inscription implies. His father Thomas, 10th Lord Fraser of Lovat, succeeded his cousin Hugh, 9th Lord. Hugh had no male heirs, but his daughter Amelia opposed the new Lord, and assumed the title of Lady Lovat. Thomas and his heir Simon were roused to action. They hatched a plot for Simon to force Amelia to elope with him; she was engaged to a cousin, Alexander Fraser. Thomas and Simon seized Alexander and showed him a gibbet, saying they would hang him if he did not relinquish Amelia. Alexander and Amelia were forced to yield, but though she was taken by Simon, she soon returned to her mother, so Thomas and Simon violently seized her estates instead. In 1689 Simon was tried *in absentia* for his crimes and sentenced to death. He was also attainted - which meant that he and his heirs were disinherited.

That did not stop Simon. When his father died in 1699 he styled himself 11th Lord Fraser of Lovat, and made a move against Amelia's widowed mother - also Amelia. He raped and abducted her and forced her to marry him. Her outraged family, the powerful Atholls, prosecuted him. He escaped to France, but was, again *in absentia*, outlawed. He joined the court of the Old

The Fraser pyramid at Kilmuir (see also page 264)

Pretender near Paris in 1702 - the same year in which the Scottish Court of Session supported the younger Amelia's claims to her father's title and estate.

The Jacobites sent Simon back to Scotland in secret, to assess and stir up support for an invasion. He did not have much success, and seems to have become a double agent, telling the government about the Jacobite plans. Out of spite, he also tried to implicate the Duke of Atholl in the Pretender's plans. When Simon retuned to Paris the Jacobites imprisoned him in the castle of Angoulême. He was there for ten years, escaping to England only in 1714.

Disillusioned with the Jacobites, he toed the British line during the 1715 Rising. As a reward his sentences of outlawry and death were revoked, and he was given the lands of a cousin, Fraser of Fraserdale, who had backed the wrong side in the attempted rebellion. This was not enough for Simon. He continued to try to vote in the Scottish parliament, and finally, in 1729, by now in his 50s, he succeeded. The Court of Session changed its decision of 1702 and at last declared that he *was* Lord Fraser of Lovat - or would be if the title was not under attainder. Such legal niceties did not worry Simon. As far as he was concerned he had always been, and always would be, the 11th Lord Fraser of Lovat.

Once his law suits were out of the way he might have enjoyed his estates. But Simon was not known as 'the Fox' and 'the most devious man in Scotland' for nothing. He continued, as he had throughout his life, to play high-stakes games with both the Jacobites and anti-Jacobites. He had become a Catholic when he first fled to France (though this may have been through expediency rather than conviction - he raised his children as Protestants) but he professed attachment to the British Crown, while still keeping his links with the Pretender.

The 1745 Rising was a moment for him to choose - and he chose the wrong side. He threw in his lot with Prince Charles Edward Stewart, and sent his son, the Master of Lovat, and the Fraser clan to fight for him. After the Young Pretender's final defeat at Culloden - where the Master arrived too late to fight - on 16 April 1746, Simon retreated into the Highlands and was eventually found hiding on an island in Loch Morar. He was taken to the Tower of London. After a five-day trial in Westminster Hall he was sentenced to death.

He was the last person to be executed on Tower Hill. By now Simon, Lord Fraser of Lovat was almost 80, and huge. On his way to the block an old woman jeered at him, saying, 'You'll get that nasty head of yours chopped off, you ugly old Scotch dog!' His reply, owned at the time as being a witty one, given the circumstances, was 'I believe I shall, you ugly old English bitch.' When he was on the platform for the execution, he gave the headsman 10 guineas and ran his finger along the axe to try its sharpness, commenting that he believed it would do. He read the inscription on the coffin awaiting his body, quoted both Horace and Ovid and said farewell to his friends. He loosened his collar for the executioner, prayed for half a minute, then signalled that the axe should fall. The execution took place on 9 April 1747.

Less than 20 years later Johnson and Boswell were looking at the monument Simon had erected to his father's memory. Did they ponder the tumultuous life and death of Lord Lovat, whose story must have been well known to them? No. Johnson read through the inscription, then commented that it was 'poor stuff, such as Lord Lovat's butler might have written.'

The decaying Fraser arms on the Kilmuir pyramid

WE FOLLOWED IN Johnson's wake to Mull, taking Caledonian Macbrain ferries from Armadale to Mallaig and from Kilchoan on Ardnamurchan to **Tobermory**. Johnson and Boswell had sailed from Coll:

> Between six and seven we hauled our anchor, and set sail with a fair breeze; and, after a pleasant voyage, we got safely and agreeably into the harbour of Tobermorie, before the wind rose, which it always has done, for some days, about noon.
> Tobermorie is an excellent harbour. An island lies before it, and it is surrounded by a hilly theatre. The island is too low, otherwise this would be quite a secure port; but, the island not being a sufficient protection, some storms blow very hard here. Not long ago, fifteen vessels were blown from their moorings. There are sometimes sixty or seventy sail here: to-day there were twelve or fourteen vessels. To see such a fleet was the next thing to seeing a town.

When Johnson and Boswell were there, Tobermory was tiny - it expanded only after 1786, when the British Society for Extending the Fisheries and Improving the Sea Coast of the Kingdom chose it as an ideal site for a herring-fishing harbour. The building of the harbour and town began in 1788. As a fishing port it was not a success, but soon it attracted tourists visiting the Highlands. Mendelssohn came, *en route* to Staffa and the *Hebrides Overture*. Queen Victoria and Prince Albert came - and then visitors by the thousand. Few of them would have climbed the hill behind the town to find the origins of its name. Tobermory is a version of Tobar Mhoire, meaning 'Well of Mary'. Exactly where the well, which was said to have curative properties, was located is a matter of dispute. There was a chapel of St Mary, now very ruined; the most likely place for the well was a little way to the south.

Despite that, a new, pyramidal structure, labelled 'Tobarmhurie St Mary's Well' was built in a different spot in 1902 to mark the Coronation of King Edward VII. Surmounted by a Celtic cross, it sits in a rather suburban area of upper Tobermory, with bungalows for company. Its surroundings had recently been improved when we visited - previous reports spoke of its being almost obliterated by hedges. The irregular blocks that make up the pyramid had been re-pointed very severely. Unlike most drinking fountains more than a century old, the Coronation Well of Mary still boasts both a tap and a chained cup for passers-by.

Neither the pyramid nor other aspects of Tobermory's history - like the fact it was Britain's most-important centre of anti-submarine training in World War II - are likely to impress the many families that stroll along the harbourside. They are scanning the brightly-painted houses - Scotland's answer to Copenhagen's Nyhavn - for signs of Miss Hoolie, PC Plum, and Edie McCredie. For, as any under-six will tell you, Tobermory is where the children's television hit series *Balamory* was set and filmed. Understandably taking full advantage of the interest from young families, many of the townspeople of Tobermory are happy to play up to the expectations of their visitors. There's a *What's the Story in Balamory* leaflet that takes them round the town to see the buildings used for filming. You can even stay in Miss Hoolie's house and take a ride on the preserved railway that appears in the series. What would Dr Johnson have made of it all?

The Well of Mary commemorates the 1902 coronation

*Greenock - town
of towers*

IS SAN GIMIGNANO ever called 'the **Greenock** of the South'? Probably not - but then, Greenock is rarely eulogised as 'the San Gimignano of the North'. Yet there are similarities, for, like the Italian World Heritage Site, Greenock is a town of towers.

There's the tower of St George's Church in George Square, built in 1871 - a handsome structure of turrets and a small dome. It may have been influenced by the 1854 spire of St Luke's in nearby Nelson Street - a version of the tower and spire of London's St Vedast Foster Lane, which was probably designed by Hawksmoor. St Luke's may in turn have been built to vie with the 146-foot spire (after Gibb's St Martin-in-the-Fields) of the Mid Kirk, built in 1787. They are all fine works. But they - and Greenock's other towers, are dwarfed by the 245 feet of the tower on the town's Municipal Buildings.

Civic pride rarely comes taller than this. Indeed, it is probably hubris. Greenock's tower - inevitably the Victoria Tower - is just a little taller than the tower on Glasgow's City Chambers. Could inter-council rivalry ever have had a more solid form? Greenock's tower was finished in 1886, to designs by architects Hugh and David Barclay. Their design for the whole Municipal Buildings was the winner of an architectural competition - but it was never completed. A local businessman refused to sell his property to the Corporation so part of the façade, intended for the site he owned, could not be built.

One Greenock monument must regard these towers as parvenus. On the plateau above the town is Well Park - and in Well Park is the well itself, with Scotland's oldest pyramid. Its surroundings have changed greatly since John Schaw married Helen Houston in 1629. The well-head, with its pyramid top and short columns, was probably put up to mark the event - the date, and their initials, are still visible on stone shields at either side of the pyramid.

The son of this John Schaw - or Shaw, as the family later spelled it - another John, was a Royalist in the Civil War, and was knighted by King Charles II at the Battle of Worcester on 3 September 1651. Charles's brother, as King James VII and II, made Sir John a Baronet in 1687. The family had had earlier dealings with royalty; the Schaws were hereditary cup-bearers to the kings of Scotland, and their coat of arms has three cups on it. A charter of 1589 gives 'Johnne schaw of grenok' leave 'to Erect and bild one parroche kirk vpoun his awin heretage' so that people do not have to make a long journey 'having ane greit river to pas over' in winter, but have 'better comoditie to convene to goddis sruice on the sabboth day and rest according to goddis intitutioun'. The charter was 'Gevin under or privie will AT halyruidhous the auchtene day of Nouember The yeir of god Jm vc fourscoir nine yeiris' by King James VI.

These Schaws were ancestors of the Janet Schaw who looked after the Rutherfurd children of Bowland on their American trip (see page 234) and of the Rutherfurds commemorated in Dean Cemetery in Edinburgh (see page 240). For his new wife John Schaw rebuilt the family mansion in what is now Well Park - a handsome residence with wonderful views over the mouth of the River Clyde. The centre of the site it occupied is now marked by Greenock's war memorial, for the house, which had become the estate office of the Greenock Estate, was demolished in 1886. By then the former garden of the mansion house was already in public ownership; Sir Michael Shaw-Stewart gave it to the town in 1851. The well, which was once the mansion's main water sup-

ply (necessary even though Greenock is 'the wettest town in Scotland'), is almost the only remnant of the site's past - apart from some ornate gate piers that lead to the 'Terraces on the Brae Fell' overlooking the town.

The well head is, after Compton Pike (see page 121), the oldest pyramid in Britain and Ireland - older even than the Clerk mausoleum at Penicuik (see page 244), which is more than 50 years younger. Its form is both practical - the pyramid protects the well from the weather and the columns allow access for drawing the water - and decorative. There was obviously an architectural hand at work here, but what were the influences? Had he seen other well heads in the same style, or did he strike out on his own? One possible influence is from Bologna in Italy.

There, in the churchyard of San Francesco, is a series of lawyers' memorials that have much the same shape - a square base and short columns that hold up a pyramidal roof. It is possible that one of the Schaws had seen the tombs, or had heard of them. More likely, though, that the link to Bologna, like that to San Gimignano, is purely accidental.

IN THE CURIOUS way that seems to link many of our pyramid journeys, our next stop was no more than half a mile away from the studio where the interior scenes of *Balamory* (see Tobermory, page 271) were filmed. We were, though at the opposite end of the educational spectrum - at West of Scotland Science Park in Maryhill Road in **Glasgow**.

The Science Park was constructed on what was formerly the 92-acre Garscube estate of the Campbell family. The University of Glasgow bought it in 1948 when they needed more space for student halls of residence to cope with a projected expansion. They demolished the Campbells' early 19th-century villa and, after some delay, started to commission new buildings.

One of the earliest results was Wolfson Hall, an accommodation block crowned with an impressive copper pyramid. It is named after Sir Isaac Wolfson, the son of a Russian Jewish joiner who emigrated to Glasgow. Isaac Wolfson, born in 1897, was brought up in the tough Gorbals area of the city, and made a fortune from his mail-order business, Great Universal Stores. In 1955 he founded the philanthropic Wolfson Foundation which gives generous grants to support education and health.

For the new Hall the University authorities commissioned the architect George Grenfell-Baines' practice, Grenfell Baines and Hargreaves. Preston-born Grenfell-Baines was, like Alan Reiach (see page 249) influenced early in his career by Alvar Aalto. His

Wolfson Hall,
West of Scotland
Science Park,
Glasgow

practice expanded during World War 2, designing factories and runways. He was the only architect from the north of England to be invited to design a building at the Festival of Britain in 1951; his *Power and Production* pavilion (see also page 76) was a high-tech work and included the largest sheet of glass in the world.

Grenfell Baines and Hargreaves won the closed competition to design Wolfson Hall in 1959, though construction did not begin until 1963. It was the company's last big commission before it transformed into what remains one of the UK's biggest multi-disciplinary design companies, Building Design Partnership. George Grenfell-Baines steered the company throughout the 1960s, and retired in 1974. He became Professor of Architecture at Sheffield University. He was knighted in 1978 and died, aged 95, in 2003.

The Wolfson Hall pyramid is still in excellent condition, but the podium on which it stands, made of weather-boarded concrete and grey brick, has worn less well. The building is now surrounded by the high-tech structures of the Science Park. It still stands out, though, thanks to Grenfell-Baines' pyramid, which forms the park's focal point.

'WITHOUT AN ORIGINAL there can be no imitation' as the Grossmith's *Diary of a Nobody* succinctly puts it. And it may be that without Wolfson Hall our next pyramid, only five miles to the south near the centre of Glasgow, might not have existed.

Anderston Kelvingrove Church of Scotland on Argyle Street is crowned by a green copper pyramid over the church hall that must have been influenced by Wolfson Hall. There is the same ribbed construction, a range of similar windows near the base of the pyramid, and the same relationship between the pyramid and the podium. The date is 1970 to 1972 - a decade after its more northerly neighbour.

Who was responsible? The architects were Honeyman, Jack and Robertson, a local Glasgow firm. Both James Honeyman, who was born in 1890, and William Jack, 22 years his junior, worked on factory design during World War II, as had George Grenfell-Baines, designer of Wolfson Hall. Their joint practice was on hold during hostilities, but after the war they took Honeyman's brother-in-law George Robertson into the firm. When Honeyman and Jack were made Associates of the Royal Institute of British Architects on 29 November 1949, one of their sponsors was Basil Spence (see page 98).

Honeyman, Jack and Robertson were decent but not inspired architects, whose other works in Glasgow include two more churches - St Matthew, Bell Drive, North Kelvinside, of 1950, and St Mark, Kinfauns Drive in Maryhill (1955) - as well as the impressive Ladywell housing scheme in the city centre. The sub-Wolfson pyramid on Anderston Kelvingrove Church is a good way of closing the view down Elderslie Street, and provides a contrast to the great blocks of the Anderston Housing scheme, started in 1965. It also has a very 1960s concrete campanile, with a severely-angled top and emphatically-vertical ribs. It no longer holds the bells.

The Church of Scotland in this area has an unconventional history. Part of Anderston Kelvingrove Church's congregation began in St Peter's Church in Oswald Street, built in 1836. Exactly a century later, the worshippers having left and moved to Anderston, the church building became a zoo, with lions replacing the Christians. It boasted among its other attractions a mynah bird with a strong Glaswegian accent (though nothing is recorded of its vocabulary).

Anderston Kelvingrove Church of Scotland, Argyll Street, Glasgow

There are signs that the Anderston area is recovering from a rather grim past. Once a settlement outside Glasgow, it began as a planned village called Anderson Town after James Anderson of Stobcross House. Its original inhabitants were weavers, and as the industrial revolution took over in Scotland, Anderson's Town - soon shortened to the more convenient Anderston - became a centre for the cotton industry. To serve the weavers, and the many Irish immigrants who soon flocked there, the grocer Thomas Lipton opened his first shop here, in Stobcross Road.

In the mid-20th century the Finneston Crane, a well-known local landmark 175 high, was installed beside the Clyde to install boilers and engines in ships, but soon the shipbuilding industry declined. The motor car became king and the cohesion of the area was severed by the construction of the M8 motorway and the dual carriageway of the A814. The associated underpasses and fly-overs, together with ill-advised underground shopping areas and concrete tower blocks, led to social problems, including Scotland's largest red light district.

Now the area is smartening up, with new housing, hotels and offices - a change fuelled by the city's emergence as an important financial centre. And in the midst of the changes sits the Anderston Kelvingrove Church pyramid - a landmark in the changes being wrought in Glasgow.

BIG CHANGES, TOO, at Parkhead on the eastern edge of Glasgow - as well as lots of pyramids and a link to the world's largest glacier.

To many people **Parkhead** means only one thing - Celtic Park, home to Celtic Football Club. The massive 60,830-seat stadium, with its inevitable green-and-white-striped outer walls, dominates the area. Because of its location it is often just known as 'Parkhead' (when it's not being called 'Paradise'). It was perhaps fortunate that Celtic were not playing at home - and especially not against Rangers in an 'Old Firm' match - when we were in the area. Barely a quarter of a mile away is what we were making for - Parkhead Forge.

As a destination for east-side Glaswegians, The Forge runs Celtic Park a close second. It is one of the city's largest shopping complexes, with more than 400,000 square feet of retail space, 70 or so stores and a ten-screen multiplex cinema, as well as the usual complement of fast-food outlets, including a super-sized McDonalds. Internally it has little to distinguish it from any other shopping mall area anywhere in the country - it is really just a collection of rectangular structures pushed together. From the outside, though, it is an Egyptologist's fantasy - or, more probably, nightmare.

The entrances to the main shopping mall are marked at each end with large glass pyramids, the northern one also forming part of the cinema's entrance. They are impressive and their generous floor space does help to moderate the crowding that often occurs at the entrances to busy shopping areas. The height of their impressive internal structure also relieves the slightly claustrophobic atmosphere of the mall's main drag - even if they do get unbearably hot when the sun beats down.

It does not stop there, however. All along the sides are pyramid-shaped additions, jostling with each other like calving icebergs. Even the walkways from the 1800-space car park and the shopping trolley stands are covered with pyramids.

The architects responsible for this fantasy were Scott,

The multi-pyramided Forge Shopping Centre at Parkhill, Glasgow

Brownrigg & Turner, who designed The Forge in 1985. It was opened in 1988. Pyramid designs were in the air in the early 1980s, though few of them were realized. Scott, Brownrigg & Turner, who also designed the BBC's White City building in London, may have been influenced by Britain's biggest modern pyramid, in Stockport (see page 204), which was built in the early 80s. It is a pity that, presumably in the interests of economy, the Egyptian theme was not continued inside, in the manner of some 1930s cinemas. It would have been fun to see shop fronts with lotus columns and sphinxes guarding the entrance to the ASDA supermarket.

Such thoughts lead to another - if it's called The Forge, why pyramids at all? Why not a theme based on the name - exposed girders with prominent rivets, huge chains, a fire motif . . .? Perhaps the memory of the closing of the real forge in the 1970s was too recent and too painful.

In its heyday, Parkhead Forge was the largest steelworks in Scotland. It was 25 acres in extent and employed 20,000 men. It was founded around 1837 by Reoch Brothers and Company, and was bought in 1841 by pioneer shipyard owner Robert Napier to make iron plates and other forgings. Napier was instrumental in establishing Glasgow as a shipbuilding centre; he built some of the earliest iron-clad warships, pioneered steam-powered transatlantic liners with Samuel Cunard, and built the world's first train-carrying ferry.

William Beardmore became Napier's partner in the 1860s, and his son, also William, joined the company, aged 15, in 1872. In 1886 young WIlliam took over the company, renaming it William Beardmore & Co. The company continued to make armour plating, and in the run up to World War 1 increasingly turned to the manufacture of armaments. The company built battleships, submarines, and later tanks and aircraft. Beardmore was made a baronet in 1914 and became Lord Invernairn in 1921. He died in 1936, but, although his company has vanished, his name lives on - in Antarctica.

In 1908 William Beardmore sponsored the *Nimrod* expedition to the Antarctic by Ernest Shackleton. Shackleton was employed at the time by Beardmore as his personal assistant. The aim of the expedition was to reach the South Pole. It failed, though the expedition did show that the way they went was a possible approach to their goal - and it was the route the ill-fated Captain Scott expedition used four years later.

Shackleton set out for the Pole from his winter camp on 31 October 1908. He had not set a definite route, but as he traversed the sea ice of the Ross Ice Barrier towards the land he saw ahead of him the lip of a huge glacier that offered a way on to the Antarctic massif. It was a 9,000-foot climb, and a 120-mile journey, but Shackleton and his team found that the glacier was indeed a gateway to the Pole; when forced to turn back, he was less than 85 miles from the Pole. In honour of his patron he named it the Beardmore Glacier. It is the largest in the world.

'IN THE MIDDLE of nowhere'. That's how **Muirkirk** was described to us. Harsh? Of course - if it implies that the place is backward and dull. Yet it has a certain accuracy - there are few villages around it, and Muirkirk is distant from other centres of population. Glasgow, from which we approached, is 30 miles away. Ayr, the nearest sizeable settlement, is 26 miles west. There is a good road from Edinburgh to Ayr - so good, in fact, that people whizz by Muirkirk without stopping.

It is worth a halt, though. It was the first place in Scotland to be lit by gaslight (and one of the last to have its own local gasworks). Two poets, both friends of Burns, came from Muirkirk. They were John Lapraik, a farmer and eventual bankrupt, and Isabel 'Tibby' Pagan, whose colourful life included keeping a private drinking club and the illegal distillation of whisky. John Loudon McAdam, who developed the road-surfacing method that bears his name, ran the tar works here. Liverpool football manager Bill Shankly was born nearby. The area, though scarred by a long history of coal mining and iron-working, is still starkly beautiful ('a district rude and bleak' as it was described in 1837). Dark hills surround it, and to the west is windswept moorland and bog, white with cottongrass and shining with emerald green patches of moss. This is Covenanter country.

The Muirkirk pyramid is modern - so modern that it sits in the awkwardly- and oxymoronically-named - 'Heritage lay-by' in the village centre, beside the A70. It commemorates three local Covenanters who were all shot in the neighbourhood by the government forces, and whose names still resonate in the area today.

The history of the Covenanters is confusing in the extreme - as factional and religious disputes usually are. Its origins lie deep in the rise of Presbyterian Protestantism in Scotland, and the rejection of anything that could be seen as 'popery'. The first of a series of covenants drawn up to cement anti-Catholic feeling in the country dates from 1580 and was signed by King James VI in 1581. Later, James's son Charles I, reigning from London, tried to impose the English prayer book on the Scots. It was too Catholic for the tastes of many of the Presbyterians, who vowed to fight it. An assembly in Edinburgh drew up the National Covenant, adopted on 28 February 1638, from which the Covenanters take their name. The Scottish Parliament adopted the Covenant in 1640.

Muirkirk's modern pyramid commemorates the local Covenanter martyrs

It brought a great divide between the forces aligned to the Presbyterian church and those who supported the monarchy. The Covenanters sent an army to fight alongside the English Parliamentary forces, then showing their muscle against the king. In the Scottish Civil War that followed, the Covenanters defeated the Royalists. Charles I was captured and handed to the Parliamentarians.

There was no trust between many of the Covenanters and Cromwell's Parliamentarians, however. After the execution of Charles I in 1649 the Covenanters, denied the opportunity to have the final word in how Scotland was governed, changed sides and supported Charles II, who swore to uphold the Covenant and was crowned at Scone in 1650. But the Covenanters' army was defeated by Cromwell's New Model Army, which then occupied Scotland.

Discouraged and oppressed, the Covenanters expected a new deal when Charles II was restored to the throne in 1660. They were to be bitterly disappointed. Not only did Charles reject the Covenant; he also insisted on imposing an episcopal hierarchy on the Scottish church. Ministers who refused to accept the jurisdiction of the bishops were thrown out of office. These 'outed' ministers, and everyone who supported them, became rebels. Their secret meetings for worship - the conventicles - were attacked. There were swingeing fines for not attending the established church.

Despite this persecution, they stuck to their beliefs. In 1669 the authorities offered what was called an 'Indulgence' to outed ministers. They were allowed back into their livings on stringent conditions. Some returned, but the hard-liners despised them for it. The Covenanters were split, as the government had intended. A further Indulgence followed in 1672, but as well as the carrot came more stick. Any minister who preached out of doors or not in a recognised kirk was committing a capital offence.

Patience with the extreme Covenanters of the south-west of Scotland ran out in 1687. Government troops, many of them Highlanders with Catholic sympathies, were sent in. This 'Highland Host' showed no quarter to the Covenanters, who were utterly defeated at the Battle of Bothwell Brig.

Yet opposition from them still continued, as a form of guerilla warfare. Richard Cameron (see page 281) was one of their leaders. Another was James Renwick from Moniaive. In 1684 his *Apologetical Declaration* told his Covenanter followers that everyone who was against them was a fair target for violent action. The government reacted swiftly. They introduced a countermeasure, the *Abjuration Oath*. Anyone who refused to take it could be killed without trial.

What followed was known as the 'Killing Time'. It lasted from 1684 to 1688; most of the killing happened in 1685. Men and women were hunted down and summarily executed. Among them were the three Muirkirk Covenanters commemorated in the Heritage Lay-by pyramid - William Adam, John Smith and John Brown, all killed within the space of four months in 1685.

Smith was the first of them to die. Not much is known of his story. In February 1685 the government officers hunting the Covenanters discovered him in a field near Lesmahagow church. He was questioned about his adherence to his beliefs - would he take the Abjuration Oath? Receiving no satisfactory answer, the officers shot him through the head. His body was taken to Muirkirk, where it was buried in the kirkyard.

The next victim, William Adam, was possibly the wrong man. He worked for the Campbell family at Upper Wellwood farm just outside Muirkirk. The Campbells were well known to the government troops and were arrested several times. They were in hiding when the government soldiers came looking for them. William Adam was engaged to a servant from a nearby farm, and had arranged to meet her in a secluded place, not far from Upper Wellwood. He arrived first, and as he waited he read his Bible. Suddenly the dragoons arrived. William jumped up in alarm. Some sources say he was shot immediately, others that he started to run away and was brought down as he fled. Did the soldiers assume that as a Bible-reader he must be a Covenanter? Or did they think he was one of the Campbells? It seems that no questions were asked. WIlliam Adam was buried where he fell. The grave is inscribed 'Here lyes William Adam, who was shot in this place by Cap. Dalzeal and his party, for his adherence to the Word of God and Scotland's Covenanted Work of Reformation, March 1685.'

The best-known of the Muirkirk Martyrs is John Brown of Priesthill. He made a living partly as a farmer on his land at Priesthill, deep in the hills to the north east of Muirkrik, and partly as a carrier. He was a firm Covenanter, always ready to give evidence of his beliefs; it was said that if he had not had a speech impediment he would have been a fiery preacher. For many years he refused to go to the kirk as the law required. When he was 55, in 1682, he married. Isobel bore him two children; she and the infants witnessed his death. In 1685 Brown was 'shopped' to the authorities by the curate of Muirkirk for non-attendance at divine worship. John Graham of Claverhouse rode over from Lesmahagow on 1 May with a troop of soldiers. They found Brown cutting peat. Claverhouse immediately put the test question to him - would Brown reject the *Apologetical Declaration* and recognise the king's right to be the head of the church? Brown's reply was forthright - and, reports say, when speaking his mind to Claverhouse, his stammer vanished. He acknowledged Christ, not the king. He knew it was his death sentence. Claverhouse told him to kneel to say his prayers before he was shot, in front of his wife and children. Brown's prayers, spoken out loud, were long. Three times Claverhouse told him to hurry; he was supposed to be praying, not preaching.

At last he finished, and told Claverhouse he was ready to die. The firing squad hesitated; they probably did not want to carry out an execution before the man's family. Exasperated, Claverhouse himself killed Brown with a shot from his pistol. Callously, he then asked Isobel what she thought of her husband now. Her reply was heroic; 'I aye thocht meikle o' him, but noo fair more than iver' (I always thought a lot of him, but now far more than ever). Brown was buried where he fell, and a monument stands over his grave.

As for Claverhouse, he was raised to the peerage as Viscount Dundee (*Bonnie Dundee* of the famous folksong). In 1689 he brought together an army of Highlanders to fight for the deposed James VII & II against the new King William. On 29 July the two armies met at the Pass of Killiecrankie north of Pitlochry. Although vastly outnumbered, Dundee's 2,000 or so Highlanders inflicted a defeat on the government troops. In the fighting, Dundee was killed; without their leader, the rebellion was unsustainable, and their triumph was short-lived.

FROM MUIRKIRK WE travelled three miles west, beyond
Upper and Nether Wellwood, to **Airds Moss**. A walk of about
¾ mile from the A70 brought us to Cameron's Stone - a grave slab
surrounded by railings - and the pyramidal monument to the battle. Once again we were on Covenanter martyrs' ground. To
understand the significance of the Battle of Airds Moss, we had to
dig a little more into Covenanter history.

After the assassination of Archbishop Sharp in 1679 (see page
257) the south-west of Scotland provided a bolt hole for the assassins. David Hackston of Rathillot and John Balfour of Kinloch,
the chief of them, fomented rebellion among the local
Covenanters. News of the threat to law and order reached John
Graham of Claverhouse (see page 280). With a band of soldiers
he met some of the Covenanters in a skirmish at Drumclog,
between Strathaven and Kilmarnock; Hackston and Balfour were
among them. Claverhouse's force was routed.

This minor victory was a great boost to the confidence of the
Covenanters. They gathered hundreds of extra supporters and,
hubristically, marched on Glasgow. The Glaswegians withstood
the advance, and the Covenanters withdrew to work out their
next move. This hesitation proved their undoing. It allowed time
for the doctrinal differences between the different sects among
them to burst out. What had been a threatening army became an
argumentative rabble.

At this point another army arrived. It was the English, sent for
by the Edinburgh government. They joined forces with Scottish
troops, all under the command of the Duke of Monmouth. On
24 June 1679 the loyalists met the Covenanters at Bothwell Brig
- just next to the place where today there sits Junction 5 of the
M74. It was always a foregone conclusion. The Covenanters
were still at odds with each other and lacked both the command
structure and the numbers to be an effective fighting machine.
Only David Hackston and his 300 men from the Galloway area
left the field with any honour, but they, too, were defeated.
Hackston survived this major battle, only to be captured at Airds
Moss.

The end for the Covenanters? It looked like it - until events
took another dramatic turn. On to the scene came Richard
Cameron, brought up in Falkland and one of the most extreme of
the Covenanters. Cameron was in Rotterdam from May to
October 1679 to be ordained at the Scots Kirk there, so he was
not in the country when the Battle of Bothwell Brig was fought.
On his return he began his preaching around Annan in
Dumfriesshire and soon gathered around him a group of loyal and
fanatical followers who were dubbed the Cameronians. Only
they, he believed, knew and could carry out God's commands.

Such a man was unlikely to hide his light under a bushel. He
sowed the seeds of his destruction with the *Sanquhar Declaration*.
On 22 June 1680 he entered the small town of Sanquhar with an
armed escort of twenty men. At the Mercat Cross in the town-
centre he asked his brother Michael to read out the Cameronians'
credo, which declared that:

> Although we be for government and governors, such as
> the Word of God and our covenant allows; yet we . . .
> disown Charles Stuart, that has been reigning, or rather
> tyrannising, as we may say, on the throne of Britain these
> years bygone, as having any right, title to, or interest in,
> the said Crown of Scotland for government, as forfeited,
> several years since, by his perjury and breach of
> covenant both to God and His Kirk . . . As also we . . .
> declare a war with such a tyrant and usurper, and all the

*The site of the
Battle of Airds
Moss is marked
by a whitewashed
pyramid*

men of his practices, as enemies to our Lord Jesus Christ, and His cause and covenants; and against all such as have strengthened him, sided with, or anywise acknowledged him in his tyranny, civil or ecclesiastic.

Having nailed their colours firmly to the mast, the Cameronians then nailed the Declaration to the cross and rode away, their challenge to the established order still ringing in the ears of the inhabitants of Sanquhar.

Richard Cameron continued his firebrand preaching - but the end came on 20 July 1680. He had been preaching at Muirkirk the day before, and spent a restless night at Nether Wellwood Farm. He went out in the darkness crying out 'Poor auld bleeding Scotland! Who shall now haud up thy heid?' - as if he knew that he would not live to do the work himself.

In the morning thick mist gave the Cameronians illusory security from the searches of their enemies. They went out into the wilderness of Airds Moss to pray. But they had been tracked by government troops, who silently surrounded the praying men.

Despite the sudden and unexpected attack, the Cameronians fought fiercely. Richard Cameron, in the thick of the battle, cried out 'Lord, spare the green and take the ripe.' He was killed, along with his brother Michael and seven other Cameronians. Richard - called 'The Lion of the Covenant' - was just 32. His head and his hands were severed from his body and taken to Edinburgh, where they were shown to Richard's father, a prisoner in the Tolbooth, He kissed them and said, 'They are my dear son's. Good is the will of the Lord. He has never wronged me or mine.' The head and hands were placed on Edinburgh's Netherbow gateway.

David Hackston of Rathillot, one of the murderers of Archbishop Sharp at Magus Muir (see page 257), who was captured at Airds Moss, was dragged through Edinburgh's streets upside down on a hurdle before, at the Mercat Cross, his hands were cut off (they were dispatched to Cupar). Then he was hanged, but cut down and disembowelled and his body was quartered. The parts were distributed around Scotland - to St Andrews, and other quarters to Burntisland, to Leith and to Glasgow - as a dreadful warning to those planning insurrection.

Cameron and his followers who died at Airds Moss are buried where they fell. The pyramid memorial records their names - 'the Rev Richard Cameron, Michael Cameron, John Gemmel, John Hamilton, James Grey, Robert Dick, Captain John Fowler, Thomas Watson, Robert Paterson'. On the railed-in gravestone nearby is the inscription:

Here lies the corpse of that famous and faithful preacher of the Gospel, the Rev Richard Cameron, with the corpses of several others, who were conquered by the bloody enemies of Truth and Righteousness.

Halt, curious passenger, come and read,
Our souls triumph with Christ our Glorious Head.
In self-defence, we murdered here do ly,
To witness 'gainst this nation's perjury.

Despite Cameron's death - or maybe because of it - the Cameronians continued the fight. 'Do you uphold the Sanquhar Declaration?' became a test question from the government forces to suspected adherents, and persecution continued for years. Cameronian-inspired United Societies were established to take up the cause - by 1683 there were 80 of them, with 7,000 members. They were prime targets during the Killing Time. Their influence was felt in the Scottish Kirk throughout the 18th century, and they eventually became part of the Free Church of Scotland in the 19th century.

IN THE KIRKYARD at **Kirkmichael**, three miles east of Maybole, there was more Covenanter history.

The squat pyramid on its tall base was put up in 1829, but it incorporates an older stone, the gravestone to Covenanter Gilbert McAdam, who came from Dalmellington. In 1685 McAdam - whose brother was the great-grandfather of the road-surface pioneer John Loudon McAdam (see page 278) - was arrested and questioned in Dumfries about his religious views. He was probably asked to take the Abjuration Oath (see page 279). On this occasion he was severely cautioned and set free.

The next time he was arrested he was not so lucky. Again refusing the Oath, he was expelled from the country and sent across the Atlantic to the colonies - probably to New Jersey. That might have been the end of his dissenting - but Gilbert was a determined man. Within a few months he had managed to make his way back to Scotland, where he continued his Covenanting agitation, organising military training in Carrick. In the early hours of a Sunday morning in Kirkmichael, his luck ran out. He was at a prayer meeting in a local house when the troops stormed in. McAdam tried to escape through a window, but was shot in the attempt.

He was buried in the churchyard, and the gravestone was carved with an inscription telling how 'the Laird of Colzean and Ballochmyl' was the chief of his persecutors. This was Sir Archibald Kennedy of Culzean Castle, a few miles away on the coast. Sir Archibald is supposed to have fired the fatal shot. Known to posterity as 'Wicked Sir Archibald', his soul is reputed to have been taken to hell by a 'muckle devil' on his death in 1710.

At some time in the half-century after the gravestone was put in place, someone came along and chiselled away the words 'Laird of Colzean and Ballochmyl'. It was 'Old Mortality' who chiselled them back in again. 'Old Mortality' was the nickname of Robert Paterson, a stonemason from Hawick who spent most of his life wandering from grave to grave of the Covenanter martyrs, repairing or providing stones for their graves. He was born in 1715 and took up both stone-work and Cameronian beliefs (see page 281) in early youth. As he grew older he did less and less paid work and more of his self-imposed gravestone task. In 1758 he left his wife and children and began to wander around the hills, searching for graves where his work was needed. He did not return home for 40 years.

In the 1780s he met Walter Scott in the churchyard at Dunnottar near Stonehaven. More than 30 years later Scott wrote: 'An old man was seated upon the monument of the slaughtered Presbyterians, and busily employed in deepening, with his chisel, the letters of the inscription, which, announcing, in scriptural language, the promised blessings of futurity to be the lot of the slain, anathematized the murderers with corresponding violence . . . Although I had never seen the old man before, yet from the singularity of his employment, and the style of his equipage, I had no difficulty in recognising a religious itinerant whom I had often heard talked of, and who was known in various parts of Scotland by the title of Old Mortality.'

Scott used the character of Robert Paterson (whom he called Peter Pattieson) as narrator of one of his best novels, *Old Mortality*. The story deals with the Covenanters and includes one of the murderers of Archbishop Sharp (see page 257) as a character and the Battle of Bothwell Brig (see page 258) among its episodes. Scott published *Old Mortality* under the ludicrous pseudonym of Jedediah Cleishbotham of Gandercleuch, in 1816.

Monument to Gilbert McAdam at Kirkmichael

HERE·LYES·GILBERT·
M°ADAM·UHO·UAS·
SHOT·IN·THIS·PARISH·
BY·THE·LAIRD·OF·CO
LZEAN·AND·BALOCHIL
FOR·HIS·ADHERANCE·TO
THE·UORD·OF·GOD·AND
SCOTLANDS·COVENAN
TED·UORK·OF·REFORM
1685   ATION

*The orginal
inscription
marking Gilbert
McAdam's burial
was recut by
Old Mortality*

Fifteen years earlier, Paterson had died in abject poverty, aged 86, at Bankhead of Caerlaverock.

Old Mortality had been dead more than a quarter of a century when McAdam's original stone was incorporated in the present, pyramid-topped memorial. With its Greek-style decoration it is absolutely typical of its date. There are two inscriptions; one reads: 'Erected A.D. 1829 by a publick contribution of a few well disposed people as a testimony of their adherence to these truths and approbation of that cause in which the martyr suffered'. The other details the inscription on the back of the old stone, which is now hidden in the pyramid's plinth. It says; 'This stone belongs to Gilbert McAdam who lies here, son to William McAdam and Bessie Follirtoun'.

THE TEN MILES southwest from Kirkmichael to **Old Dailly** outside Girvan were once coal mining country, though all the scars are long healed. The parish of Dailly has no sea coast, but as an historical anomaly it includes the impressive granite bulk of Ailsa Craig, the conical island ten miles off the Ayrshire coast. The parish is now centred on Dailly, but the next pyramid lies in the churchyard at Old Dailly, just south of the ruined church that was abandoned in 1695 when the congregation moved further up the valley of the Water of Girvan. The Pre-Raphaelite artist William Bell Scott is buried at Old Dailly, and there is a plaque to him not far from the pyramid.

The Old Dailly pyramid is another Covenanters memorial. The inscription - which, like that on Gilbert McAdam's stone at Kirkmichael (see page 283), seems to be the original, reads:

> HERE LIES the corpse of JOHN SEMPLE who was shot
> by Kilkerran at command of Cornet James Douglas
> Also here lies THOMAS McCLORGAN who was shot
> uncertain by whom for their adherence to the word of
> GOD and the covenanted work of Reformation 1685

The inscription is on the plinth that supports a small, grey-painted pyramid.

John Semple was a quiet, unassuming and harmless local farmer who lived at Eldington. He was, though, a man of strong principle, and refused to go to any church that had a minister who belonged to the episcopal church. And, as one of his biographers perhaps rather naively put it, 'being given to hospitality, and of a compassionate nature, he did sometimes harbour those poor people who were then hunted for their lives.' Or maybe it was Semple who was naïve. It was, of course, inevitable, that his actions should come to the attention of the authorities.

In April 1685 Alexander Fergusson of Kilkerran, a landowner who lived not far from Eldington, laid accusations against Semple at the local barracks. He then, under cover of darkness, guided troops led by Cornet Douglas to Semple's farm. Around midnight they took up positions around the house. Semple heard their footsteps and their whispers, and guessed what was happening. He decided to try to effect an escape through a small side window. As he was climbing out he was shot by several of the troopers.

There is even less information about Thomas McClorgan. As the inscription says, his assassin was not known even when he was buried at Old Dailly - and he was killed more than ten miles north of the village, at Drumellan, north east of Maybole.

In contrast to the Covenanters, Cornet Douglas had a long and prosperous career. The son of William Douglas of Castle Morton in Dumfriesshire - and a member of the great Douglas clan that

includes the Marquesses of Queensberry and the Earls of Mar - he was party to the killing of a number of other Covenanters, including 'The Covenanters' Prophet', Aleaxander Peden, whose body he tried to hang, even though it had been buried for 40 days. Douglas subsequently became Colonel of the Scots Footguards and fought at the Battle of Malplaquet in 1709. In the same year he became Brigadier of one of the three Scottish Brigades in the Netherlands Army, set up in 1585 to help the Dutch against the Spanish. Douglas died in 1726, aged 71.

Although not a major monument, the Old Dailly pyramid - and other nearby Covenanters' graves - are kept in good order and are regularly visited by descendents following in the footsteps of the men and women who suffered in the 'Killing Time'.

JOHN LOUDON MCADAM, distant relative of Gilbert McAdam of Kirkmichael (see page 283), manager of the tar works at Muirkirk (see page 278) and road-surfacing pioneer, nearly lost his life at the age of six in **Carsphairn**. His childhood home, the now-ruinous Lagwyne Mansion, just by the village, caught fire in 1762. As a friend wrote to James Boswell, who knew the family, 'With great difficulty the children's lives were preserved by their leaping naked out of windows two storeys high. Not a single paper nor piece of furniture could be saved from the flames'.

Carsphairn is the biggest and least-populated parish in Dumfries and Galloway. Although the main A713 from Ayr to New Galloway runs beside it, the hamlet feels remote. It must have been even more so when Covenanter Roger Dunn was killed here in 1689. He - as well as Gilbert McAdam and McAdam's son James - have memorials in the kirkyard. It is often suggested that

Carsphairn's war memorial above the Water of Deugh

Gilbert McAdam is buried in Carsphairn, but it is more likely that his grave is at Kirkmichael (see page 283). In the church the Covenanting and imprisoned minister, John Semple - not the same John Semple who is commemorated in the Old Dailly pyramid (see page 284) - is remembered.

But Carsphairn's pyramid remembers more distant, though more modern, conflict. It is the village's memorial to the men of Carsphairn who died in World War I. The site, a low mound on the edge of the village, is beautifully chosen. To the south west are the slopes of the Rhinns of Kells. At its foot flows the Water of Deugh. Northwards are the heights of Cairnsmore of Carsphairn. Here, on a stone base, local workmen erected a pyramid of local stone, of a variety of sizes, topped by a larger stone inscribed 1914-1918 and, over that, a taller upright with the chi-rho symbol and the words 'Pro Patria'. It bears a striking similarity - probably unwittingly - to the memorial to Augustus Smith on distant Tresco in the Isles of Scilly (see page 163), built more than 30 years earlier, and also to the explosion memorial of 1918 at Chilwell (see page 113).

Thirteen men from Carsphairn died in the War. They are listed, democratically, in alphabetical order - four Privates and a Gunner, two Lance Corporals (one, C H Buck, won the Military Medal), a Sergeant, a Lieutenant and three Captains. Two of the Captains - A K and A D H Clark-Kennedy - must have been brothers, one in the King's Own Scottish Borderers and the other in the Royal Scots Fusiliers. The Clark-Kennedys were from nearby Knockgray; the family included some notable ancestors, including one who captured a French flag at the Battle of Waterloo. Another Clark-Kennedy, Colonel William Hew Clark-Kennedy, unveiled the war memorial in 1923. He had won the Victoria Cross for actions near Wancourt in France, during the Arras Offensive, on 27 and 28 August 1918. Although he was severely wounded, he refused medical help for more than five hours and remained at his post until his men were safe. He was also awarded the Distinguished Service Order and Bar, the Croix de Guerre and was made a Companion of the Order of St Michael and St George.

A quarter of a century after the unveiling, a plaque was added to the Carsphairn memorial for the three local men who died in World War II.

PARTS OF THE old Mercat Cross of **Sanquhar**, to which Richard Cameron (see Airds Moss, page 281) nailed the Sanquhar Declaration, are built into the walls of the manse of St Ninian's Baptist Church in the town. In the High Street, on the spot where the cross once stood, is a granite obelisk marking the events of 22 June 1680 (see page 281) and the second *Sanquhar Declaration*, made in 1685 by James Renwick, author of the *Apologetical Declaration* (see page 279).

It was a relief to us to turn from the dreadful events of Covenanter history for a while and look in St Bride's Parish Church graveyard off Church Road for a much more peaceful pyramid. We could not miss it - it's by far the biggest monument there - a tall, thin pyramid, reminiscent of the pyramid at Lusk in Co Dublin (see page 363). Like that one, it is topped by an urn. As a 19th-century writer put it, the pyramid 'is at once the largest and most eminent sepulchral erection in Sanquhar Kirkyard; it stands close to the footpath . . . and cannot fail to arrest the attention of every visitor to the ancient field of graves.'

It is a memorial to James Abbot Hamilton. Hamilton is an ancient Scottish name. A John Hamilton was Archbishop of St Andrews before the Reformation; Richard Hamilton was burned at the stake as a Protestant martyr in 1528. And the ill-used husband of Lord Nelson's mistress, Emma, was a Hamilton.

James Abbot Hamilton did not fly as high - or sink as low - as these namesakes, but he was a man of substance in Sanquhar. Born in 1770, he married Jane Thomson, carrying her on his horse, like *Young Lochinvar*, from her home at Glenim to his own house.

Sanquhar people had developed textile skills (Sanquhar knitted gloves are still famous) so James began a carpet business in 1798 at Crawick, immediately north of the town. The enterprise grew, until by 1830 there was a large mill, with more than 50 looms making durable and well-regarded carpets. Hamilton's works had an international reputation - many thousand square yards of carpeting were exported from Sanquhar to Chile, for example.

James did not live to see the greatest extent of his business. Elected Provost of Sanquhar in 1812, he died in 1815, aged 45, having also been Captain of the Nithsdale Volunteers and Local Militia Corps, raised in 1803 to fight off the threat of a

Napoleonic invasion. The pyramid to his memory was put up in 1816, 'Erected by a few friends as a mark of their highest esteem'.

Jane outlived him by 38 years, dying in 1853. She is also commemorated on the pyramid, as are 'four children, who died in infancy'. Mentioned separately are two other children - Jane, who lived to be 64 and died in 1867, and, more poignantly, James and Jane's eldest son Robert, who died in the West Indies in 1827, aged just 29. Was he following the family trade and undertaking a selling trip? Or had he joined the military, and was stationed in the Caribbean?

Another family of Hamiltons is also commemorated on the pyramid. John Hamilton was born in 1801 so he could be another son of James and Jane. He is described only as 'formerly merchant in Glasgow, who died at Crawick Cottage on 16th January 1876' - which suggests that he was not directly involved in the carpet business. He may have been one of the Hamiltons who, apparently, fell out over the running of the factory, causing it to fail in the 1860s and put many workers out of a job.

John's wife was Marion Crichton, a member of the former Sanquhar lords. James Crichton, a 16th-century traveller, swordsman and scholar, who was nicknamed 'The Admirable' Crichton, was of the same family. His adventurous life ended in a street brawl in Mantua in 1582. He was killed by Prince Vincenzo di Gonzaga, later the patron of both Monteverdi and Rubens, who had been Crichton's pupil. Crichton was only 22. According to the author of *Lives of Remarkable Youth of Both Sexes*, a moral guide published in 1830 and dedicated to the future Queen Victoria, he possessed an 'extraordinary conjunction of mental and physical power.' Gonzaga, on the other hand, 'was a man of strong passions, and of a darkly revengeful nature.' The cause of the quarrel seems to have been a woman.

James Crichton's appellation 'Admirable' became a proverbial phrase and was used by J M Barrie as the title of a play. The Crichtons bankrupted themselves with a hugely lavish party in 1617 for King James VI and I. Among the extravagances they laid on was a torch to light the king to bed, which burned IOUs that the king had given them for loans totalling £30,000 - getting on for £4 million in today's values.

Marion Crichton, who was 11 years her husband's junior, predeceased him by two years. James and Janet, their two children, whose names are the last on the pyramid, 'died in infancy, and are interred in Glasgow Necropolis.' It would be fitting if they were in the Necropolis' Egyptian Vaults - but perhaps that would be too much of a coincidence.

The Crichtons have their own pyramid tomb in the churchyard. It was probably once topped, like the Hamilton's, with an urn, and was erected by John Crichton of Crichton Hall, who died in 1834 - the Crichton name was placed on it only in 1874. John Crichton was, like his father James, Town Clerk of Sanquhar.

John's brother James was more adventurous; a physician, he went to China in his youth and made a fortune. He came back to Sanquhar in 1808, when he was 43, and two years later married Elizabeth Grierson, whose father was Sir Robert Grierson, fifth Baronet of Lag. Unlike his turbulent and unpleasant ancestor (see Lockenkit, page 296) this Grierson of Lag seems to have been inoffensive - and his daughter Elizabeth did good works. When her husband James Crichton died in 1823 she used his fortune on charitable works, as he decreed in his will. They included found-

Pyramid to the Crichtons at Sanquhar

ing, in 1839, the Crichton Institution for Lunatics in Dumfries. Despite its name, this was a forward-looking and enlightened place, treating the patients with kindness and pioneering different types of therapies, including occupational and art therapy. It also had the world's first hospital magazine, written by the patients; provocatively called *New Moon Magazine* it was published from 1844 to 1937. The Institution, now the Crichton Royal Hospital, is still serving the local community.

There is a yet another pyramid in Sanquhar churchyard - to another related family. Like a short version of the Hamilton pyramid, complete with urn, it was put up by Thomas Thomson in memory of his wife's parents and of four of his own children who died in infancy. A fanciful coat of arms, that includes an anchor, a stag's head, a cross crosslet and a crescent moon, is carefully labelled 'Thomson's Arms' and is displayed on the pyramid with the date 1807. No trace of the original colouring is now left.

'Robert Lorimer and Agnes Galt, his spouse' are the first names on the finely-cut inscription on the plinth. Lorimer was a well-to-do farmer from Connelbush, a mile up the Nith valley from Sanquhar. It was their daughter Janet who married Thomas Thomson. Janet and Thomas lost Robert, John, James and Janet in infancy; only two children survived. They were another James, and Jane who married Provost James Hamilton and is commemorated on the Hamilton pyramid.

James Thomson was a farmer and a banker. He had inherited some property in Sanquhar so he was considered a rich man, but the high life he lived as a result did not last. He became bankrupt in 1830, with liabilities of more than £6,000. His two surviving sons, John and James, learned the lesson of their father's profligacy too well. Both were merchants in Glasgow and spent so little they amassed great fortunes. They would often revisit the Thomson farm at Glenim, deep in the hills about ten miles east of Sanquhar; they would sit on the opposite hillside, munching sandwiches, then return to Glasgow. When John, who outlived James, died, Sanquhar hoped for a windfall. All they received was a £100 donation to the local Nursing Association, because the brothers felt that the people of the town had been unfair to their father at the time of his bankruptcy.

The three pyramids in Sanquhar churchyard, to three inter-related families, form a unique group. Did they copy each other - or was there, perhaps, an ambitious stonemason in the town who persuaded them to spend their money in this way? It is a pity he wasn't around to provide one for Abraham Crichton, whose ghost was said to haunt the kirkyard. Another of Sanquhar's wealthy men, he too managed to avoid paying people by declaring bankruptcy. In 1745 he tried to pull down the unused church at Kirkbride, but the day he went with his men to carry out the work his horse, frightened by a flash of lightning, bolted. Abraham fell off, but he caught his foot in the stirrup and was dragged for several miles. After his body was buried at Sanquhar there were regular reports of a haunting. Eventually the minister performed a long exorcism, sitting for several nights in the kirkyard with a Bible and (just to be sure) a sword. And to make doubly certain that Abraham stayed put, his tombstone was chained down. In the 1860s a descendant, Charlie Crichton, was asked where he wanted to be buried. 'Juist tak me up an clap me in Abraham's bosom,' he replied. 'He was the best Crichton amang us, and he rose in the first resurrection.'

Sanquhar's third pyramid, to the Thomsons

Old Mortality and his donkey at Balmaclellan (above) and the Grierson pyramid in Balmaclellan churchyard (right)

THE MOST PROMINENT monument at **Balmaclellan** is not a pyramid but a life-size sculpture of Old Mortality (see page 283), who once lived in the village. His wife ran a school here for some time. In the kirkyard there is the grave of a Covenanter, Robert Grierson, shot at Moniaive in 1685 (see page 297). But although it was a Grierson monument that brought us to Balmaclellan, it was not this one.

The pyramid on the edge of the church grounds, overlooking the Ken valley, is to Elizabeth Gordon, the wife of Adam Grierson of Burnfoot, and their infant son. It is an elegant, thin pyramid, like the ones at Sanquhar (see page 286). Like them it seems once to have had an urn on the top. It sits inside a railed Grierson enclosure, with other memorials huggermugger beside it.

This rather disorderly arrangement seems to reflect the very confusing Grierson family. Exactly how - and how far back - these Griersons were related to Covenanter Grierson, or to the Covenanters' persecutor Grierson of Lag (see page 307), is hidden within the tangled undergrowth of the family tree. Certainly, the family members named on the pyramid lived in a less bloody time, but they had their own sorrows.

Adam Grierson was a merchant in Glasgow, though he came from nearer at hand; Burnfoot is a couple of miles east of Carsphairn (see page 285). He seems to have been one of three (or possibly four) brothers; the others were all farmers and landowners. Adam married Elizabeth Gordon, whose father was a vintner, on 15 August 1813 in Dumfries. Their marriage was destined to be short-lived. Elizabeth died in childbirth less than 18 months later, on 28 January 1815. The couple's son, named James, died three days after his mother.

Elizabeth and James are named twice on the pyramid - on the original inscription on the base of the pedestal, and again on a marble plaque inset into the pyramid at a later date. The plaque adds further information - not only the dates of death of Elizabeth and young James, but also that Adam died, aged 67, on 30 March 1843. By then he was back at Burnfoot. His brother, James Grierson of Nunwood (near Dumfries) and James's wife, another Elizabeth, are also named. James died in 1832 and Elizabeth in 1841.

The Griersons commemorated on the Balmaclellan pyramid are surrounded by memorials to dozens of others. Nearly all of them seem to have lived and worked around this corner of Scotland; only one, 'David Grierson, late of Jamaica' seems to have had a spirit of adventure - and he ended his days back in Castle Douglas. This was one part of the Grierson family tree that seems to have been very firmly rooted in its native soil.

IT TOOK TWO attempts to reach the pyramidal Covenanters' monument at **Auchencloy**. It is in the eastern part of the Galloway Forest Park and more than three miles from a metalled road. Our first attempt, on the advice of a Forestry Commission officer, was to take the forest track called the Raiders Road and park at Barney Water. We then walked a long way up the track - but there was no sign at all of the monument - just trees or clear-felled land.

Our second attempt seemed destined to end in failure, too; another track we were told to try proved impassable by car. Eventually we realised that the only way to reach our target was to park by the Raiders Road north west of Barney Water, and follow the track that went nearest to the monument. That meant wading, knee-deep, across the Black Water of Dee. Once across, we followed the track for a mile and a half until, away to the left of the track, the monument appeared; if there had not been a recent clearance of trees we might have missed it again.

In this remote spot four Covenanters were killed by Claverhouse (see page 280) and his men on 18 December 1684.

The remote pyramid at Auchencloy is another memorial to Covenanters where they died

They were led by 'Black' James MacMichael, one of the most fearsome and quarrelsome of the Covenanters. He had fought alongside Cameron at Airds Moss (see page 281), and had been instrumental in ambushing government troops in a ravine near Dalry. John Grier (or Grierson), Robert Fergusson and Robert Stuart all fell with Black James at Auchencloy.

The story of how they came to be there that day in December 1684 begins a week earlier in Carsphairn, a few miles to the north. On 11 December a party headed by Black James murdered the Minister of Carsphairn, Peter Peirson, at the door of his Manse. Although Peirson was described as 'a surly, ill-natured man, and horribly severe' who was not only serving the episcopal church but may have even had papistical leanings, the cold-blooded nature of the way MacMichael shot him was disapproved of by many of the Covenanters.

Five days later Black James was once again in the thick of the conflict. This time he was leading a party of more than 100 Covenanters that stormed the Tolbooth in Kirkcudbright - a place described by Claverhouse as 'the most irregular place in the kingdom'. MacMichael's men killed the sentry and released all the prisoners, leading them in procession from the town, accompanied by the beating of the town drum. Claverhouse, who was nearby, set off in pursuit with his men.

Many of MacMichael's men scattered quickly, but a sizeable group was tracked down to Auchencloy. Among the hills near the Black Water of Dee they believed they were safe, but Claverhouse received a tip-off and surprised them in their camp. Two of the company immediately escaped, but the rest were forced to fight a bitter skirmish. At its height Claverhouse came face to face with Black James. They fought with swords, neither giving way. Claverhouse felt he had met his match and called out for help; MacMichael taunted him with the words 'You dare not abide the issue of a single combat; and had your helmet been like mine, a soft bonnet, your carcase had ere this found its bed on the heath!'. Claverhouse was saved from this fate when a dragoon crept up behind MacMichael and split his head open with a single blow of his sword.

The Covenanters seem then to have lost heart. Two men, Smith and Hunter, were captured and taken to Kirkcudbright, where they were tried and hanged. John Grier, Robert Fergusson and Robert Stuart were killed and buried alongside Black James MacMichael at Auchencloy. Fergusson's gravestone still exists a little way from the monument. Curiously, an image of his gravestone also appears on the Scott Monument in Edinburgh's Princes Street; on the north-east buttress there is a carving of Old Mortality (see page 283) who is depicted with the stone bearing the words 'FERGUSON shot at the water of Dee 18 Dec 1684.'

The present pyramidal memorial at Auchencloy was put up in the 1830s after a conventicle was held on the spot. A collection was taken on the day, and more money was raised from selling copies of the sermon preached that day by the Rev'd R Jeffrey of Girthon, near Gatehouse of Fleet. His text for the sermon was from the *Book of Daniel*, and included the words 'Be it known unto thee, O king, that we will not serve thy gods, nor worship the golden image which thou hast set up' - words that must have resonated as much with his 19th-century Presbyterian congregation as it would have with Black James MacMichael and his fellow Covenanters as they fought the imposition of the king's ways of worship and church structure in the Killing Time.

Old Mortality with the gravestone to Robert Fergusson, carved on the Scott Monument in Edinburgh

The three-sided pyramid at Kirroughtree marks the 50th anniversary of Galloway Forest Park

WE HAD THOUGHT we had found all the Scottish pyramids that we were likely to unearth - until another four came along. Over dinner at an Outdoor Writers and Photographers Guild weekend in Gatehouse of Fleet there was a discussion of our pyramid search (they were all very polite!) and the following day the first of the new ones came to light.

'We've found another for you,' announced David Ramshaw, who had been out on a mountain-biking day. 'It's at **Kirroughtree** in the Galloway Forest Park.'

'A proper pyramid?' we asked. We'd been misled before.

'Certainly. Though I think it's got three sides rather than four.'

'We've had those before - they count. We'd better go and see.'

Kirroughtree Forest is just east of Newton Stewart. It is part of the huge Galloway Forest Park - at 300 square miles Britain's largest. We had already been to the visitor centre there, but now we made our way to it again, turning north off the A75 at Palnure. From the visitor centre car park we followed the track through the forest, gently climbing through pine trees.

This is prime mountain-biking country - some bikers say it's the best in the UK. There are three waymarked courses, which crisscrossed our track as we climbed. The blue is the easiest - though confusingly (for us) labelled 'moderate'. The red-marked route is 'difficult' and the black is 'severe'. On the black course is what the bikers love best - a really difficult descent, in this case along a ridged and often slippery granite slab nearly 200 yards long and 30 yards wide and then down the steep end of its spine. This is known throughout the mountain bike world as 'McMoab'. There's also 'Hissing Sid', a winding descent that can catch out even experienced riders.

A few mountain bikers were whizzing through the forest and crossing our path as we ascended, but it was not busy, even though it was Sunday morning. When we reached the summit and found the pyramid, we had it all to ourselves.

It is in a magnificent setting. The pyramid is surrounded on three sides by the forest, while to the east the land falls steeply away to the valley of the Palnure Burn, which joins the River Cree a little to the south and then empties into Wigtown Bay. The trees in the valley were wearing their late-autumn colours, and the sun shone fitfully from behind fast-moving clouds. The heights of Cairnsmore of Fleet across the valley were capped with mist.

A fine place for a pyramid, then - but why was it here?

The adjacent signboard made it all clear. It commemorates the 50th anniversary, in 1997, of the creation of Galloway Forest Park in 1947 - then known as Glentrool Forest Park. That explained the capstone, which is carved with both dates. One mystery solved. But the pyramid contains a secret - or rather, more than 80 secrets. Entombed within it are many time capsules, simple tubular canisters prepared by 80 or so local community groups, from schools to clubs of retired people. Each holds whatever the groups' members decided they wanted to preserve to tell future generations about themselves - pictures, text, objects.

As the sign says, 'At some time in the future, someone may decide to open our Time Capsule and investigate its contents. It is hoped that the wide range of objects and regalia they find will give them an interesting and enlightening glimpse into the life of the Forest Park and the world around us as it was in 1997. Until that time, we hope that this Commemorative Cairn will be an appropriate monument to the achievements of the generations of people who have been involved in the creation and growth of The Galloway Forest Park.'

KIRROUGHTREE WAS THE start of our Dumfries and Galloway pyramids. More were to come. At a talk that evening we had learned of another three - one to more Covenanters, one to a scientific pioneer and the third to a local huntsman.

We worked our way from west to east. First was a pyramid on a ridge north of **Ringford**, about five miles from Kirkcudbright. Marked in the Landranger map as 'Obelisk' but very definitely a pyramid, if a slightly etiolated one, this is a monument to James Beaumont Neilson.

And who was Neilson? As a centenary booklet published by The West of Scotland Iron and Steel Institute in 1928 tells us, he was 'Inventor of THE HOT BLAST'. 'Of what?' was the obvious question. Neilson's invention was important in the history of iron smelting. In essence, what he discovered was that, contrary to the popular belief of ironworkers that only by introducing cold air - the colder the better - into the smelting furnace would decent iron be produced, the opposite was true. He heated the blast of air, with remarkable results that revolutionised the industry. Scotland had hitherto been unable to smelt except by first coking its inferior-grade coal. Neilson proved that the coal, uncoked, made very good iron with his hot blast method. And it worked just as well with the inferior coals and anthracites of Wales.

It took some time for him to be allowed to experiment with furnaces; 'a strong prejudice was felt against any meddling with the furnace, and a kind of superstitious dread of any change', he said. When at last, in 1829, he was allowed to try his method at the Clyde Iron Works in Glasgow, it proved an instant success. Neilson immediately patented the idea, the patent being granted on 18 February 1829.

As soon as Neilson's discovery was taken up, there was a dramatic improvement in the Scottish iron trade. In 1829 the total output of pig iron was 29,000 tons. By 1845 it had risen to 475,000 tons, and within another few years it was over a million tons. Add to that its rapid introduction around the world, from the USA to India, and it is obvious that Neilson's patent was very lucrative - users of the hot blast method had to pay a shilling a ton for the privilege. The selling price of iron was around £2 10 shillings, so Neilson's premium was about two per cent.

James Neilson was undoubtedly both a clever inventor and a shrewd businessman. For many years he worked for the Glasgow Gas Works, eventually becoming its Manager and Chief Engineer. His inventive mind was also turned to gas; he invented the popular swallow-tail gas burner. He was elected a member of the Royal Society in 1846. In 1863 he was the subject of a chapter in *Industrial Biography* by Samuel Smiles, the author of *Self Help*. In 1851 Neilson bought an estate at Queenshill in what was then known as the Stewartry of Kirkcudbrightshire, moving there from his house in Glasgow's Great Western Road.

From Queenshill 'he continued,' as the Iron and Steel Institute's booklet tells us, 'to be active in every good work - whether it was agricultural improvement, railway extensions, or the moral and social good of those about him . . . he was quiet, reflective and unassuming, kind-hearted, and fond of harmless mirth and social intercourse. He was a strict Presbyterian, with perhaps a little too much of the Puritan in his character; severe and exacting in all questions of truth and honour.'

Neilson died on 18 January 1865, and is buried in a small mausoleum in Tongland churchyard. It was not until the 1928 centenary of his invention that the pyramid was put on the hillside above Queenshill. It is inscribed with the simple words 'NEILSON HOT BLAST 1828.'

'NEILSON HOT BLAST 1828' is carved in his memorial pyramid near Ringford

NEILSON'S SCIENTIFIC GENIUS had provided a respite from the blood and thunder of the Covenanters' history, but it did not last. Not much further east, towards Crocketford, on Bloodmyre Moss, we were back among them.

Set deep in a pine forest called Craigadam Woodlands, not far from **Lochenkit** Loch, a memorial of grey granite is set on a small rise in a clearing. The weather was grey, too, as we walked up the hill. In the mist the monument looked particularly forbidding. On top of the plinth sits a narrow, rather rough pyramid, similar to the monument at Auchencloy. It is crowned with a forbidding symbol - a clenched fist with the index finger raised to point to the skies.

This resembles something that a mid-20th-century totalitarian government might have erected to urge the proletariat on to greater effort in the latest five-year plan, but it was actually put up in 1843, 'erected,' as the inscription says, 'by subscription after sermons here by Messrs McLachlan and McGill'.

The subject of their preaching was the death of four Covenanters who died here in the 'Killing Time'. The monument names them as William Heron of Glencairn and Galloway men John Gordon, William Stewart and John Wallace, and it tells us that they 'were found out and shot dead here on 2 March 1685 by Captain Bruce for their adherence to Scotland's Covenanted reformation.'

With four other men, including Edward Gordon, Alexander McCubine and Robert Grierson, they were surprised at this place by troopers. The incident forms an episode in R M Ballantyne's book about the period, *Hunted and Harried*: Quentin Dick and Ramblin' Peter are in Galloway:

' . . . they were passing over a wide moorland region one afternoon when a man suddenly appeared before them, as if he had dropped from the clouds, and held out his hand.

"What! McCubine, can that be you?" exclaimed Quentin, grasping the proffered hand. "Man, I am glad to see ye. What brings ye here?"

McCubine explained that he and his friend Gordon, with four comrades, were hiding in the Moss to avoid a party of dragoons who were pursuing them. "Grierson of Lagg is with them, and Captain Bruce is in command," he said, "so we may expect no mercy if they catch us." . . . Refusing to delay for even half an hour, the two friends [Quentin and Peter] hurried away. They had scarcely left, and the six hunted men were still standing on the road where they had bidden them God-speed, when Bruce with his dragoons suddenly appeared -- surprised and captured them all. With the brutal promptitude peculiar to that well-named "killing-time," four of them were drawn up on the road and instantly shot, and buried where they fell, by Lochenkit Moor, where a monument now marks their resting place.'

Captain Bruce of Earlshall had almost five years earlier played a leading part in the Battle of Airds Moss (see page 258) and continued to persecute the Covenanters. He was with Robert Grierson of Lag. Two Robert Griersons on opposite sides in the story have caused some confusion in the sources. This Grierson, who in 1685 was just 30, was laird of Lag Castle near Dunscore in Dumfriesshire and one of the most virulent of the persecutors of the Covenanters. He was responsible for the deaths of the Solway Martyrs, two women who were tied to a stake in Wigtown Bay and left to drown as the tide roared in (see Stirling, page 253). He also invented other cruel ways of killing Covenanters, including putting them in barrels full of spikes and then having

them rolled down a hill. Despite (or possibly because of) his activities he reaped many honours; he was given a baronetcy and married the sister of a duke. Unlike his victims, Grierson of Lag - also called both 'Auld Lag' and 'The Persecutor', and described by a contemporary as 'a great persecutor, a great swearer, a great whorer, blasphemer, drunkard, liar and cheat, and yet out of hell' - died peacefully in his bed, aged 88.

The other Robert Grierson was a Covenanter. Along with another man whose name is now unknown he was captured at the place where the monument now stands. It is not clear why the two were not shot dead like the other four Covenanters; instead, Grierson and his companion were sent for trial and then exiled, probably to the West Indies. Grierson may have come back to Scotland - someone of his name was shot as a Covenanter near Moniaive a little later and is buried in the churchyard at Balmaclellan (see page 290).

The four men who were shot were buried on the moor. Their grave is just down the hill from the monument - a red slab set on a low plinth within a walled enclosure. The inscription on the

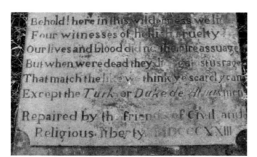

*The inscription on
the martyrs' grave
at Lochenkit*

stone, which seems to have been set up not long after the events it describes, records how the four men were 'found out and shot dead upon the place by Captain Bruce and Captain Lag for their adhering to the word of GOD, CHRIST'S Kingly Government in his House and the Covenanated work of reformation against Tyranny, Perjury & Prelacy.'

Beneath the inscription is a verse that reads:

> Behold! Here in this wilderness we lie
> Four witnesses of hellish cruelty
> Our lives and blood did not their ire assuage
> But when were dead they did against us rage
> That match the like we think ye scarcly can
> Except the Turk or Duke de Alvas men.

There is real anger here - comparing the viciousness of Bruce and Grierson of Lag with the infamous Duke of Alba's troops (Alba terrorised the Low Countries in the late 16th century) would still have had great resonance in the 1680s.

This brutality was, if anything, even more manifest when Bruce and Grierson of Lag dealt with the other Covenanters. Having shot Heron, Stewart, Wallace and John Gordon where they were found, they took McCubine and Edward Gordon, with Robert Grierson and the unnamed man, to Bridge of Urr, where Grierson of Lag asked them to swear the Abjuration Oath (see page 279). They refused. Robert Grierson and his companion were then taken away for trial and deportation, but McCubine and Edward Gordon were dealt with differently. Although Captain Bruce argued that they should be tried, too, Grierson of Lag would have none of it. The two men were taken to Hallhill, west of the village of Irongray, and hanged on an oak tree. McCubine was asked if he wanted to send a message to his wife and children. 'I leave her and the two babies upon the Lord and to his promise; "A Father to the fatherless and a judge of the widows is God in His holy habitation".'

As a footnote to what can be seen, on both sides, as a form of religious mania, we could not leave the Crocketford area without remembering the Buchanites, who settled in the town of Crocketford in 1787 after being expelled from both Irvine and Closeburn, near Dumfries. They were followers of the deluded Elspeth Buchan, who in 1783 declared herself a prophet - and immortal. Her followers were a strange bunch; their worship is said to have included orgies in the woods. Mother Buchan disproved her own prophecy by dying in 1791. The last Buchanite died in 1846, having been disappointed that Mother Buchan had not been resurrected five years earlier, on the half-centenary of her death.

THE STORY OF John Corbet, who is commemorated with a pyramid at **Tinwald**, north east of Dumfries, links the persecutions of Claverhouse, the horror of a dark prison, a fever-ridden trans-Atlantic sea voyage and the possibility of near-slavery in New Jersey. The monument was 'erected in 1844 by the voluntary contributions of a number of the grateful admirers of the faith and constancy of the honoured confessors and martyrs of the reformed Scottish Presbyterian Church'. The main inscription says that Corbet 'endured persecution and bonds for adherence to the Covenanted Reformation in Scotland'.

We do not know how Corbet came to be captured by Claverhouse's troops in 1684, but there is evidence that he was first imprisoned in Edinburgh. In May 1685, however, along with many other Covenanter prisoners, he was moved to Burntisland.

There the captives were asked to swear allegiance to the established church. Everyone who refused - 122 men, including Corbet, and 45 women - was taken to Dunnottar Castle near Stonehaven.

The reason for these actions was the fear of an invasion from the Low Countries, led by the 9th Earl of Argyll. Argyll had escaped from custody after being found guilty of high treason for refusing to swear the Test Act, which required holders of public office to affirm they were members of the Established Church. The Earl believed that the new king, James VII and II, was about to try to re-establish the Catholic religion in England and Scotland. Argyll wanted to ensure that Protestantism was protected but the government forces thought that if his invasion came, the Covenanters would join his cause. In the event, the invasion, under Argyll's confusing banner 'For God and Religion against Poperie, Tyrrany, Arbitrary Government, and Erastianisme', did arrive in Scotland, but fizzled out in ignominy. The Earl was captured trying to cross the Clyde. He was imprisoned in Edinburgh Castle and executed on 30 June 1685.

The Covenanters in Dunnottar Castle knew nothing of this. All 167 of them were thrown into a room only 55 feet long by 15 feet wide, lit by two small, barred windows. There were so many people in such a small space that they could not sit; many died where they stood. They were made to pay for small amounts of water. After a time there were changes; the women were put in a separate room, while some of the men were incarcerated in an even more horrible, unlit chamber. Some who tried to escape were quickly recaptured and tortured.

It was only after Argyll's arrest and execution that the survivors were liberated from Dunnottar Castle. They were taken to Leith, where some of them, broken by their experiences, took the Oath of Allegiance and were set free. For the others, including John Corbet, there was an alternative - shipping across the sea to what was then called East Jersey.

The voyage was organised by George Scott, Laird of Pitlochie near Auchtermuchty in Fife. He was influenced in his desire to set up a colony in America by his conversations with the Quaker William Penn. Scott was authorised to take the Covenanters on board the 350-ton ship *Henry and Francis*. He was offered 500 acres of land in East Jersey if he did so - and would pay a penalty of 500 marks if they were not there by September 1686. The ship set sail on 5 September 1685, with 125 people aboard, many of them survivors of the Dunnottar prison.

Not far off Land's End, fever, incubated in the former prisoners, was rife. George Scott and his wife died - in fact, there were not enough of the crew left to sail the ship without help from the prisoners. Bodies were thrown into the sea each day, and the ship sprang a leak several times. Yet despite the help of the prisoners, the captain, with the connivance of Scott's son-in-law John Johnston, continued to persecute them, refusing to let them worship on board.

After 15 weeks at sea the boat made land at Perth Amboy in East Jersey, in the middle of December 1685. At that point Johnston tried to charge the former prisoners £5 each for the voyage - or have them sign an agreement to act as indentured servants - virtually unpaid slaves - for four years. Not surprisingly, they refused - and their refusal was eventually upheld in the Jersey courts.

Many of the former Dunnottar prisoners settled in America, but a number, including John Corbet, returned to Scotland. He

John Corbet's adventurous life is marked at Tinwald

Pyramid at
Tinwald to Colin
Campbell, aged
19 days

came back as early as 1687; on 4 April that year James VII and II promulgated the Declaration of Indulgence. The Declaration removed the requirement for people to worship according to established religion, and allowed them to go to chapels or meetings instead. There is no information about the last 20 years of Corbet's life. He died on 17 March 1706, aged 65. His tombstone, on the north side of Tinwald church, includes the words:

Banisht I was for Covenanted cause
And none complyance with their wicked laues
God whom I servd, made me their firme to stand
Brought back again unto my native land'

John Corbet's pyramid is not the only one in Tinwald kirkyard. On the other side of the church is a smaller, simpler example. And the life it commemorates was totally unlike that of the covenanters. The inscription reads 'In beloved memory of Colin Campbell who died May 16 1877 aged 19 days'. Little Colin's life was too short to make any mark on history - but his is one of the most poignant of all the pyramids in Britain.

ANNANDALE, NORTH OF the eastern reach of the Solway Firth, is hunting country. Or rather, it was. For more than 150 years the Dumfriesshire Hunt galloped over the fields, jumped the hedges and kept down the foxes. All this ended in October 2002 when the hunt was disbanded, a result of the ban on hunting introduced by the Scottish Parliament the previous year. The last straw for the hunt was when it was banned from riding over the 20,000-acre estate of Sir Rupert Buchanan-Jardine. Though a keen hunt supporter, Sir Rupert felt he could not risk the prosecution he might face if an illegal hunt took place on his land.

Had Joe Graham, who is remembered on our final Scottish pyramid at **Dalton**, heard of the ban and the disbandment he would have been perplexed and horrified. He was responsible for the formation of the Dumfriesshire Hunt in 1848, and remained its driving force for the next 32 years.

Joe Graham was born in Caldewgate, just across the River Caldew from Carlisle, in 1813. He trained as a weaver, but horsemanship and hunting were his first loves, and he managed to buy, very cheaply, an old horse that proved to be a remarkable jumper. It may have been Blood Royal, which later won the Caledonian Hunt Cup at Ayr Races for Graham. With his fine horse, Joe was out following the hounds whenever he could, and soon came to the attention of a local landowner, Colonel Thomas Salkeld of Holm Hill, near Dalston. Impressed with the weaver's keenness, Salkeld offered him the job of running his kennels and taking charge of his staghounds.

At the end of the 1848 season Joe Graham took the Salkeld hounds to hunt in Dumfriesshire. He was so successful over the three days that, at a dinner in the Blue Bell Hotel in Lockerbie, local huntsmen got up a subscription and asked him to hunt in Dumfriesshire permanently. The Dumfriesshire Hunt was established, with kennels initially in the yard of the Blue Bell. Lord Drumlanrig, later the 7th Marquess of Queensberry, was the first Master.

Joe was a character as well as a fine horseman. Out hunting five days in each fortnight, he was not above swearing at the huntsmen - even the aristocracy, if he thought they were being stupid or unsporting. He said, 'Don't swear in the hunting field if you can help it, but if you can't, give it them hot and strong and to the point.'

Despite his language, Joe - 'Old Joe' as he was universally known towards the end of his life - was a valued member of the community. 'He was a fearless rider', his obituary in the *Dumfries and Galloway Standard* on 10 June 1893 said, 'and took great pride in his field, which included many dashing horsemen. But old age came creeping on with stealthy step, and the veteran huntsman, who had often been seen in the saddle at hunt steeple-chases, retired from the pursuit of the fox to the more peaceful life of a cultivator of the soil.' When he died he was buried in Annan cemetery and his remains 'were accompanied to their last resting place by a large number of county gentlemen connected with the Hunt'.

The county gentlemen also subscribed generously to a monument to Old Joe. It stands on Almagill Hill not far from Dalton, overlooking the land over which he hunted for so many years. A tall pyramid built of stone quarried nearby, it is missing its top stones, but the circular bronze plaque with a picture of a huntsman blowing his horn by a fox's lair while three hounds race towards him is still crisp. Below it, on a granite slab are inscribed the words:

> In memory of Joe Graham, for many years huntsman of the Dumfriesshire fox hounds, who died in
> 1893 at the age of 80.
> 'And now he has gone far, far away,
> We shall ne'er hear his voice in the morning.'

This appropriate quotation is from the song *Do ye ken John Peel*, one of the most famous of hunting songs; it may be doubly appropriate, as Joe Graham very probably did know the famous Peel. A contemporary of Joe's, Peel lived in Caldbeck, not too far away from Graham's early haunts.

Joe also had another hold on sporting history. In 1886 one of the huntsmen entered a horse named Old Joe after Graham in a prestigious race. It won, at odds on 25 to 1. The race was the Grand National. Joe Graham must have been very pleased - though there may have been some gentle ribbing about it in the pub at Newton Stewart, where he had retired.

The view from Joe Graham's pyramid takes in large tracts of south-west Scotland, with its bloody history. Now another country awaited us - the island of Ireland, with plenty more pyramids to discover.

Huntsman Joe Graham's pyramid near Dalton

Tour 9

IRELAND

ARRIVING BY FERRY into Larne - the start of our Irish journey - would not be described as one of the great sea approaches of the world, but within a few minutes of docking we were on the beautiful Antrim coast road. This was a scenic route to the first planned stop on our Irish pyramid tour, Garvagh in Co Londonderry (see page 304), but hardly five miles from the port we jammed on the brakes. 'There's a pyramid!'

A three-sided pyramid about six feet high, proudly labelled **'Carnfunnock** Country Park', it sits beside the main road. Above the wording is the coat of arms of Larne Council. The Council took ownership of the Carnfunnock estate in 1957, but it was another 33 years before the country park opened. The pyramid was constructed as an easy-to-spot marker at the entrance and was in place by the time HRH The Duchess of Kent officially opened the park in 1990.

Today Carnfunnock offers something for everyone - a hornbeam maze in the shape of Northern Ireland (we were tempted to see political symbolism here, but resisted), a golf course, miniature railway, tug of war, bouncy castle, camping and caravan site . . . There are also several gardens, including a wildlife garden and a walled garden that holds 13 modern sundials, much praised by the British Sundial Society. Waymarked trails take visitors around the gardens, along the seashore, through woodland and to some of the park's historical features, including a Norman castle motte, an18th-century icehouse and three 19th-century lime kilns.

The estate has had a long and sometimes tempestuous history. The name Carnfunnock means 'the place of the hooded crow'. The Norman castle was built to defend the coast from Scottish pirates, and the area stayed in conflict for several centuries. By the early 17th century only the motte remained, and James Schaw from Greenock (see page 272) built another so-called castle - really a country 'plantation' house called Ballygally Castle - nearby in 1625. It is said to be Ulster's only 17th-century building still used as a residence, and the most haunted hotel in Ireland; the spirit of James Schaw's wife Isabella, pushed from a window by her husband for giving birth to a girl instead of a boy, manifests itself in shrieks and eerie light.

The Carnfunnock estate was leased in 1823 by the Agnew family, who built their own house, Cairncastle Lodge. In 1865 they sold it to James Chaine, one of Larne's most enthusiastic developers. Chaine developed Larne harbour, extended the railway to the pierhead and set up the Larne and Stranraer Steamboat Company to offer a ferry service to Scotland on the paddle steamer *Princess Louise*. He also encouraged transatlantic liners to call at Larne, to the benefit of the local economy - and to enable Irish emigration to America. He was MP for Larne from 1874 until his death at the age of 44 in 1885. The pencil-like round tower at the entrance to Larne harbour is a memorial to him; there are rumours that he is buried inside it, standing up, dressed in his yachting clothes.

OPPOSITE:
The Malone
mausoleum
at Kilbixy,
Co Westmeath
(see page 354)

*A pyramid marks
the entrance to
Carnfunnock
Country Park*

Carnfunnock passed to Chaine's son, who in 1937 sold it to Sir Thomas Dixon. Sir Thomas and his wife Edith lived at Cairndhu House, built by the Agnews on the estate. They were great local benefactors, and in 1947, three years before Sir Thomas's death, they gave Cairndhu House and 162 acres of land to the Northern Ireland Hospitals Authority. It remained a hospital until 1968 when there were funding problems and it closed. After standing empty for almost 10 years the house was bought by property developer and entrepreneur Diljit Singh Rana - Baron Rana of Malone since 2004. He had plans to turn the listed building into a luxury hotel, but he hit problems; in 2003 he was compelled by Northern Ireland's Department of the Environment to repair the building under the Province's first Urgent Works Notice. If he had not complied, the government would have compulsorily repaired the building and sent Rana the bill. In October 2005 the planning application from his company Andras House to develop Cairndhu with an extension was refused because it would 'detract from its character and setting and result in loss of architectural integrity'. In 2006 the estate was sold again, many of Cairndhu's architectural features having been listed in the meantime. The Cairndhu saga continues, while, mostly oblivious to the negotiations, local people flock to Carnfunnock Country Park to enjoy its delights - with the pyramid as its herald.

THE PYRAMID AT **Garvagh** is eerie. Set on the edge of the 600-acre Garvagh Forest, near the centre of the small town of Garvagh, it is densely surrounded by trees in a dank, still, overgrown glade. It is impressive in size - 21 feet high on an 18-foot-square base. It stands on a low, 21-foot-square platform, badly infested with weeds. Like many Irish pyramids, it is well built, of good-quality ashlar and with sharp edges. Yet it has an atmosphere of neglect and menace.

It was intended as a final resting place for George Canning, 1st Baron Garvagh. Lord Garvagh is thought to have been impressed by the pyramids when on a visit to Egypt; this may be true, but it is equally possible that he was more swayed by the fashion of the time and by the precepts of the Freemasons. His cousin and namesake, the George Canning who was Foreign Secretary twice and briefly (from April to August 1827) Prime Minister, was a prominent Mason.

The two George Cannings led very different lives, though they were both born in Garvagh. The future Prime Minister's father (another George) died on his son's first birthday; he had already been disinherited by his own father for marrying a beautiful but penniless Irish woman, Mary Costello. The widowed Mary, to the horror of the Cannings, became an actress to support young George. It was a life of travelling and insecurity from which he was rescued by his uncle, the merchant banker Stratford Canning. Stratford sent George to Eton, where he shone, and he went on to Oxford. He read for the Bar, but Parliament beckoned. With the help of William Pitt he was elected as an MP in July 1793. His career blossomed. After six years in opposition with Pitt, from 1801 to 1807, he returned in triumph as Foreign Secretary, though his frustration with the conduct of the war against Napoleon led to a duel with Castlereagh, Secretary for War, in which Canning was wounded. Further years in opposition followed, but he was eventually Foreign Secretary again from 1822 to 1827, when he was at last appointed Prime Minister (despite an attack on him by Lord Grey who said that Canning was unfit for so high an office because his mother had been an actress). Canning's elevation was too late. He was already ill with a chill caught at the funeral of the Duke of York at Windsor in January that year; he died at Chiswick House on 8 August, having been Prime Minister for just 116 days - the shortest British premiership.

His cousin George, the future Lord Garvagh, led a somewhat less public life, although he was an MP for 14 years, from 1806 to 1812 for Sligo, and then for Petersfield. There must have been confusion in the lobbies of the House with two George Cannings voting. As befitted his station in life, he was also Lord Lieutenant for Co Londonderry and Colonel of the Londonderry Militia. He was born in 1778, son of Paul Canning. His great-grandfather George Canning Senior had married Abigail Stratford of Baltinglass (see page 331). Paul Canning inherited the Garvagh estate after his elder brother was disinherited, and was succeeded by George of the pyramid in 1794. George may have gone to Eton like his Canning relations - his cousin, another Stratford Canning, who became Viscount Stratford de Redcliffe and was British Ambassador to Constantinople, was two years older than him and was at Eton. George went on to Christchurch, Oxford, like his namesake, though some years after the future Prime Minister, who was eight years his senior.

Thereafter he lived the life of an Irish landowner with mild parliamentary duties - rather like a character in one of Trollope's *Palliser* novels. He sat on the Bench, commanded the militia, gave land for a new schoolhouse in Garvagh town and built himself a new home, Garvagh House, now demolished. In 1810 he was elected as a Fellow of the Royal Society, being described by his proposers as 'a gentleman well informed in various branches of Natural Science'. He was also a Fellow of the Society of Antiquaries. He was married twice - first, in 1803, to Lady Charlotte Stewart, daughter of the Marquess of Londonderry. After less than a year Charlotte died. Twenty years later George married again. His second wife, and the mother of his children, was Rosabelle Charlotte Isabella Bonham of Titness Park in Berkshire. She was the great-granddaughter of the slave-trader Samuel Bonham, whose pyramid monument is found at Orsett in Essex (see page 60). Her father Henry Bonham was the great-great-great-great-grandfather of Camilla, Duchess of Cornwall.

George Canning, Lord Garvagh, planned to be buried in his pyramid at Garvagh, Co Londonderry

George Canning was raised to the peerage as Baron Garvagh on 28 October 1818. Like many of the aristocracy he travelled widely - his visit to the pyramids was probably undertaken at this time, and from there he is said to have imported a number of huge crows for the park at Garvagh. The crows there today, still of great size, are their descendants. A journey undertaken to France in 1840 proved to be his last. He died at a hotel at Châlons-sur-Marne (now Châlons-en-Champagne) east of Paris in August 1840; Rosabelle survived him by 51 years. He was to have been laid to rest in the Garvagh pyramid - but as was often the case (see Cobham, page 62, Gosford, page 235) this did not happen and he was buried elsewhere. The door into the pyramid is sealed and the vault is empty. Only the monstrous crows now call mournfully for the 1st Baron Garvagh in the forest that bears his name.

AT **DESERTCREAT** IN Co Tyrone we failed to answer an intriguing question - what was a prominent Northern Irish Quaker family doing having a grand pyramidal memorial in a Church of Ireland graveyard? It was hard enough finding where the pyramid was - the scant references we had were to 'Lindesayville', which turned out to be a row of cottages across the Killymoon River from Desertcreat, south of Cookstown. The Lindesays were the owners of the nearby Loughry estate. Robert Lindesay was a friend of Jonathan Swift (see page 358), who came to stay at Loughry; the house is now subsumed into Loughry College, which specialises in food technology. Nearby, on Tollyhogue Fort, the Kings of Ulster were crowned for more than 500 years.

Impressive though this was, we needed to know about the pyramid. The Ulster Architectural Heritage Society's list of buildings around Dungannon and Cookstown came to the rescue. It describes the structure as 'a most sophisticated Egyptian-style mausoleum of C 1830, built by Thomas Greer of Tullylagan house'. There was even a picture - but it did not tell us much; we could see a square base, but the pyramid structure on top was smothered in ivy.

When we arrived in Desertcreat in the late afternoon, it proved to be a quiet corner of County Tyrone, with the river flowing nearby, tall trees rustling above and little sign of the sparse local population. The church, set in a wide churchyard, is a simple early-19th-century box with lancet windows, but it replaced an earlier structure - many of the headstones around it are from the 18th century. There is a plain burial vault of about 1790 - but dominating the site is the Greer mausoleum.

It has been restored and cleared of ivy since the Architectural Heritage Society was there. Now it is possible to see clearly that the mausoleum is one of those hybrid pyramid-cum-obelisk confections that we had met elsewhere - at Staverton in Gloucestershire (see page 127) and at Cheshunt in Hertfordshire (see page 84), for example. Above the almost-cubic base is a heavy stepped cornice topped by the pyramid. In front of it, above the entrance, is a stone sarcophagus, like the ones at Cobham in Kent (see page 62). Iron doors are firmly closed in a doorway with slightly splayed jambs - called a Vitruvian entrance. Stylistically the 1830s date is spot on. But who was it built for?

The best candidate among the Greer family is Thomas - known to family historians as Thomas Greer III. He lived at Tullylagan Manor, which he commissioned in the late 1820s. The house is in a stripped-down style like the pyramid, with reminiscences of

The mausoleum of the Greers, Desertcreat, Co Tyrone

Greek architecture. The mausoleum may well have been built while Thomas was alive - he died in February 1840. The stone for both the mausoleum and the house came from Greer's own quarry on the estate.

The Greers have a complex pedigree. They have amended the family name many times - variations include Grier and even Greves. They are descended from another variant, the Griersons. The family's fortunes seem to have been founded by William Grierson of Lag in Dumfriesshire, who was knighted by King James VI and 1 in 1608. Sir William's great-grandson was the feared Robert Grierson of Lag (see page 296), numbered in a *Scotland on Sunday* survey as among the country's 'Twelve worst baddies - Scotland depraved'. His exploits in the Killing Time in Galloway did not bring glory to the family, and may have been good reasons for the collateral branches to rename themselves. The fifth son of Sir William Grierson, Sir James, was the founder of the Ulster branch of the family. James's son Henry moved to the Province in the 1660s, possibly to escape intolerance of his membership of the Society of Friends, which he had recently joined. Despite the Quaker pacifism, the family was not immune from violence; Henry's son Thomas was shot at the door of his house in Redford, Co Tyrone, in 1689, in the crossfire between skirmishing Irish rebels and English infantry.

Around the beginning of the 18th century the Greer family (the spelling seems now to have settled down) became involved in the linen trade. Their history is well documented in thousands of family papers in Northern Ireland's Public Record Office. Thomas Greer II (father of the mausoleum builder and great-nephew of the stray-bullet taker in 1689) seems to have been the most dynamic member of the family business. He was closely associated with other Quakers in the industry. Some of them, indeed, were his relations - among them the Hancocks, the Christys and the Bells; prison reformer Elizabeth Fry was a distant relative through the Bells. They were also related to a branch of the Lowry family of Co Tyrone (see page 309). Thomas, despite his Quaker principles, sometimes seems to have been at odds with the other linen manufacturers. He originally rented his bleaching green at Tullylagan (then known as New Hamborough) from Wakefield, Pratt and Miers, and later bought the property from them. Mr Wakefield and Mr Bell then went into partnership with Greer, but it did not last long. After a series of disputes the partnership foundered and Greer thereafter went his own, very successful way.

Thomas II died at the family house at Rhone Hill near Dungannon in 1803 aged 78, when Thomas III was 41 and also involved in the linen business. The younger Thomas married a Yorkshire woman, Elizabeth Jackson. Her family included her cousin Andrew Jackson, seventh President of the United States, and a younger relative Thomas, who became better known as General Stonewall Jackson. Thomas and Elizabeth Greer seem to have lived as much as country gentry as business people - their eldest son, yet another Thomas (IV) was a JP, as was his brother Alfred (though Alfred seems to have tried - and failed - to be a businessman, managing a vinegar works in Dublin). Thomas IV's son Frederick served in the Royal Navy before retiring to Tullylagan; he was last Greer to be buried in the pyramid mausoleum at Desertcreat. The next generation, in the form of Thomas, Frederick's son, was a noted lepidopterist. He amassed at least 10,000 mounted specimens of moths. He was also a leading figure in the Orange Order, a member of the B-Specials and a daring motorcyclist; born in 1875, he was still racing in competitions in 1949, his 74th year. In World War II he was distinguished as being the oldest dispatch rider in the Home Guard.

At what stage did the Greers stop being Quakers and take up membership of the Church of Ireland? If the mausoleum is that of Thomas Greer III the likelihood is that it was his decision. Did it cause friction with his father, a staunch Quaker? Or did the family view it as a pragmatic act - the rich businessmen becoming part of the ruling class and therefore of the established church? The family motto is *Memor Esto* - a translation of the Greek word *gregoreo* (presumably intended as a distant pun on the family name). It means 'Be Watchful'; just what the Greers had been with their judicious changes of name and religious affinity as their social standing rose through the 18th and 19th centuries.

CASTLE COOLE, ON the outskirts of Enniskillen, is one of Ireland's greatest houses. The family seat of the Earls of Belmore, and now in the care of the National Trust, the silver-grey mansion was designed in chaste neo-Greek style by James Wyatt. It sits in green parkland, undisturbed by ornamental gardens or other structures. The building speaks of wealth and security of position, of the Irish Ascendancy and of a long and distinguished aristocratic lineage.

Appearances are deceptive. The builder of Castle Coole had been a member of the peerage - Baron Belmore (the title comes from a mountain near Castle Coole) in the Peerage of Ireland - for just seven years before he began his new house. Throughout its building he was chronically short of money to pay the workmen. And his family, the Lowry Corrys, was descended, four generations back, from Scottish merchants who had moved to Ulster when land was cheap and there was money to be made. It was through the Corry family, who bought the Castle Coole estate in 1656, that the Eniskillen land came to the family. But it was the Lowrys who provided the link with the family's pyramid mausoleum more than 30 miles away at Caledon, near Armagh.

John Lowry was the second generation in Ireland. In 1700 his son Robert Lowry bought the townland of Aghenis, just on the edge of **Caledon**, and in the adjacent parish of Aghaloo. It was at Aghaloo, now part of Caledon village, that the family put down its roots, and where its members were buried. In 1733 John Lowry's grandson Galbraith (Gilly) married Sarah (Sally), daughter of Colonel John Corry of Castle Coole. A series of deaths in the Corry family without any male heirs eventually brought the whole of the Corry lands to Sarah and her new husband. To succeed to the property, which included Castle Coole, they changed their name to Lowry Corry.

Sally and Gilly's only son was christened Armar after his mother's brother-in-law, Margetson Armar. He succeeded to the estate on his father's death in 1769. Armar and his mother had the pyramid at Caledon constructed in the style of Vanbrugh to mark Gilly's death. There is no obvious reason why they chose a pyramid, other than that English aristocrats were making it fashionable. Vanbrugh's pyramids at Castle Howard (see page 28) and Stowe (see page 93) had been built 40 years earlier. In Ireland, though, this is the earliest of the smooth-sided pyramids. Only the step pyramids at The Neale (see page 317) and Killiney (see page 337) are earlier.

The Caledon pyramid may have influenced Armar's second wife's father to choose the pyramid form when he came to build his own mausoleum. He was John Hobart, 2nd Earl of Buckinghamshire, who commissioned the pyramid at Blickling in Norfolk (see page 53). Armar's first wife, Lady Margaret Butler, was descended from three kings - Henry VII of England, Robert the Bruce of Scotland and Brian Boroimhe (Brian Boru) of Ireland. She died in 1776; her death was caused by catching a cold, in the aftermath of measles, when she gave her coat to a poor woman.

Amar's second marriage, to Henrietta Hobart in 1780, was engineered for political reasons; her father, Buckinghamshire, was at that point Lord Lieutenant of Ireland and well placed to help Armar's political career. Buckinghamshire jokingly wrote of Armar that 'He is universally esteemed, acknowledged to be generous without profusion, honourable upon the most correct line. He is rather well in his figure. His age is 23, and in addition to these capital points his nose resembles mine.'

The Lowry Corry family had their pyramid mausoleum at Caledon, Co Tyrone

Unfortunately, though Armar Lowry Corry and the Earl got on well, no one had thought to consult the young lady. Her marriage, at 17, to Armar at Dublin Castle by the Bishop of Killaloe, was the start of a period of domestic strife. Henrietta hated her new husband - and she made her hatred apparent in public as well in private. Within a year of their marriage, and coinciding with his elevation to the peerage as Baron Belmore, Armar had had enough. He told Buckinghamshire's private secretary of 'his determined resolution of being separated from Lady Belmore so soon as she shall be recovered from her lying in'. At first Henrietta objected to the separation, but was eventually persuaded. By this time she had given birth; Armar reached an agreement that Henrietta would have her child with her for five years. But in fact, as soon as his wife left, he took the child away from her. He paid her maintenance of £1000 a year - to be paid in Irish pounds, worth 8 per cent less than Sterling.

Lord and Lady Belmore formally separated in June 1781. After five years living in Paris and two more in England, Henrietta fell in love with Lord Ancram and became pregnant with his child. She asked for a divorce, but Armar refused. Only when she disported herself with her new lover so blatantly that Armar was becoming a laughing-stock did he consent. The divorce, which needed an Act of the Irish Parliament and cost Armar £4,187, became absolute in March 1793. The following month Henrietta married Lord Ancram.

Sometime in the midst of this protracted unhappiness, Armar Lowry Corry, who became Viscount Belmore in December 1789, built the pyramid at Caledon. In it he interred his parents and the heart of his first wife Margaret - she was buried in Dublin. He also sought solace from two women who lived on the Castle Coole estate; one bore him a daughter and a son, the other, who was the daughter of his coachman, another son. All three children were acknowledged as his.

After his divorce from Henrietta, Armar married for a third time, in 1794. His wife was Mary Caldwell, daughter of a friend. She was 39 and he was 54. Significantly, they married in Bath - for it was in the spa town that, after Armar's death, Mary, as Dowager Lady Belmore, resided. She was a large and familiar figure in the Pump Room and at the gaming tables. She appears in Dickens' *The Pickwick Papers* as Lady Snufanuph; Angelo Bantam, Master of Ceremonies at Bath, when asked 'Anybody here?' replies:

> 'Anybody! The ELITE of Ba-ath. Mr Pickwick, so you see the old lady in the gauze turban? '
> 'The fat old lady?' inquired Mr Pickwick innocently.
> 'Hush, my dear sir - nobody's fat or old in Ba-ath. That's the Dowager Lady Snufanuph.'
> 'Is it, indeed?' said Mr Pickwick.
> 'No less a person, I assure you,' said the Master of Ceremonies.

Armar Lowry Corry received another bump up the peerage in 1797, becoming Earl of Belmore - a United Kingdom peerage this time. He died in 1802 and was buried in the Caledon pyramid. He had spent more than £70,000 on building Castle Coole, and left his heir, Somerset, with debts of more than £130,000. Somerset, who in 1800 had married Juliana, daughter of the Earl of Carrick, set about selling land and property to help reduce the debt, especially after 1815, when a depression hit the country in the wake of the Napoleonic Wars.

Nevertheless, the 2nd Earl was a great traveller. In August 1816 he took his wife and his two sons, along with assorted retainers, on a long journey around the Mediterranean. With them went Lieutenant Corry, the Earl's illegitimate half-brother, and two-year-old Juliana Brooke, the Earl's illegitimate daughter, whose mother was Lady Brooke, wife of a neighbour. There seems to have been no difficulty in this period with acknowledging children born the wrong side of the blanket; Lady Belmore must have been a very accommodating woman. Juliana Broooke lived only to the age of 21. She is interred in the pyramid at Caledon.

Among the party's adventures was time spent at the Pyramids, and Somerset set about excavating with enthusiasm - but it was the Countess, digging just once, who discovered the greatest treasure, a black granite funerary boat that once held the remains of Mutemwia, mother of Amenhotep III. It is now in the British Museum.

In 1829 Somerset was appointed Governor of Jamaica, but this was an unhappy period and he resigned the post in 1832. In 1839 he suffered a debilitating stroke; he died in 1841 and was laid to rest at Caledon. His son, another Armar, succeeded as 3rd Earl of Belmore, but lived for only another four years. He was the last of the family known to have been buried in the pyramid. The 4th Earl, Somerset Lowry Corry, had a distinguished political career, including time as Governor of New South Wales from 1868 to 1872; the Sydney suburb of Belmore is named after him.

Both the 4th Earl's sons succeeded to the title as 5th and 6th Earls. They were unmarried and lived at Castle Coole - even during World War II when the park was requisitioned by the Military - with their four spinster sisters to whom the 5th Earl never spoke. The 5th Earl died in February 1948 and the 6th in March 1949. A distant cousin succeeded as 7th Earl. Hit with two successive demands for death duties, he arranged with the government that Castle Coole would be handed to the National Trust to help meet the bill. The family retains most of the contents and the right to live in part of the building.

CLUES TO THE existence of pyramids come from many sources, but once they pop up it is not usually too hard to track down the structure. In the case of the **Drumkeeran** pyramid, though, it proved extremely elusive. The only reference we had was in *Mausolea Hibernica*, an attractive, slim volume by Maurice and Michael Craig. It has fine line drawings of a number of pyramids - Baltinglass (see page 331), Castlerickard (see page 358), Kilbixy (see page 354) and Arklow (see page 334). The introduction mentions four others; Kilcooley (see page 329), Naas (see page 343), Kinnity (see page 351) and 'Drumkeerin, Co. Leitrim (a stepped pyramid)'.

Why had this one escaped us? It soon became clear - this was virtually the only reference we could find anywhere to a pyramid at Drumkeerin. And Drumkeerin itself proved elusive. In a way often found in Ireland, the place had different spellings - it was more often Drumkeeran than Drumkeerin. There are also at least two Drumkeerans, 30 miles apart - one in Co Fermanagh and one in Co Leitrim, and it is not always clear which one is meant.

Calls to the Representative Church Body in Dublin provided some information and the library at Ballinamore more. But it was Eileen Hewston, who researches graveyards both on the Indian sub-continent and in Ireland, who at last confirmed the existence of the pyramid at the Drumkeeran near Lough Allen. Once we knew it was really there, we made arrangements with parishioner Morag Harris of the Church of Ireland parish of Innismagrath to get us into the usually-locked churchyard.

The stepped pyramid, at Inismagrath church in Drumkeeran is probably to members of the Cullen family

Morag said that she believed that the pyramid - a massive, low stepped pyramid with heavy bronze chains supported by elaborately-cast columns - was a memorial to the Palmer family. She told us there were five Palmer brothers who built a row of houses in Drumkeeran, all identical, to live in; she now occupies one of them. The Palmers ran the local ironworks and brickworks. An earlier Palmer had been High Sheriff of Leitrim.

The Palmers were certainly involved in the building of the church in 1828, on the hill above Drumkeeran - the parish is called Innismagrath. It is a typical grey-stone church to the standardised style of the Board of First Fruits - a grant-giving body, equivalent to Queen Anne's Bounty in England, which funded hundreds of new Church of Ireland churches from 1711 to the 1820s; at least some of its funding came from taxing the income of newly-ordained Church of Ireland clergymen, which hardly seems fair. Myross church (see page 325) is another Board of First Fruits church. Most, like Drumkeeran, are a simple rectangular box with an adjoining, pinnacled tower.

But is it the Palmers who are commemorated by the pyramid? Probably not, though they were closely associated with the family that is likely to have had it built, the Cullens. The Cullens were a prominent family with houses near Manorhamilton in Co Leitrim. As there is no inscription on the outside of the pyramid, and as the doorway has been sealed for almost a century, we cannot be certain it was for them. Judging by the style of the pyra-

The Cullen pyramid at Drumkeeran

mid - and more particularly by the heaviness of the moulding on the chain-supporting columns - its date is probably in the second half of the 19th century. The most likely candidates for the first occupants are Francis Nisbett Cullen, who settled at Corry on the shores of Lough Allen east of Innismagrath and who died in 1864, and his sister Anna who died in 1869. Three members of the next generation - Capt Edmond Willoughby Cullen, Capt Richard Francis Cullen and Arthur Patrick, who died aged 30 in 1882, are also known to have been buried at Innismagrath.

Francis Cullen had married, in 1838, his second cousin Marianne Louisa Palmer. His was not the only Cullen marriage with a Palmer; another of Francis's second cousins, the Rev'd Cairncross Thomas Cullen, married his cousin, Jane Palmer - whose father Henry had married Catherine Cullen . . .

Who were these Cullens, so closely related to the Palmers? The family claims to be descended from an ancient Irish family called O'Culliean which (in the time of King Charles I) was given extensive lands in Co Leitrim. The family never rose above the ranks of the country gentry; the sons served as clergymen or army officers. From family member Kate Cullen, who died in 1913, we have a glimpse of the 19th-century family.

Kate, cousin of the eccentric Rev'd Cairncross Thomas Cullen, wrote a memoir of her life. The Catherine Cullen who married Henry Palmer was Kate's aunt. Henry was a Captain in the Prince of Wales's Fencibles, and Catherine Cullen eloped with him, using a ladder to climb over a wall. Kate noted in her memoir:

> A horse provided with a pillion was waiting with the lover, and, seated behind him, she rode 27 miles to Boyle, where they were married, by a dis-frocked parson; but the Revd. Carney [Cairncross Cullen, Catherine's father] followed them and married them over again himself.

Despite his two marriage ceremonies, Captain Henry Palmer did not turn out well. Kate Cullen's father did not approve of his brother-in-law, calling him 'the little grey man'. He once had to pay a tailor's bill after Henry was arrested for debt. Taking her cue from her father, Kate described Henry as 'a worthless man, selfish, always in an impecunious condition, hiding from his creditors and evading them.'

Kate was dead by the time the Cullen's Drumkeeran pyramid played a small part in Irish history. During the Irish Civil War in the 1920s a number of IRA fighters holed up in the pyramid for several months, being supplied with goods by local people and causing a fire in the church one night when they were trying to get warm. Once they were ejected the pyramid was sealed, and has remained so ever since, with the Cullens (and possibly some Palmers) securely within.

ACROSS THE ROAD from the churchyard in Drumkeeran is a white-painted cast iron signpost. It points through a tangle of weeds and its legend reads:

UAIGH NA BhFRANCACH
GRAVE OF HUMBERT'S
FRENCH SOLDIERS WHO
DIED ON MARCH TO
BALLINAMUCK 1798 AD

The sign is a direct link to the next of the Irish pyramids, outside **Castlebar** in Co Mayo, and the bloody history of the French-backed Irish uprising against British rule that flared and was extinguished in the late summer of 1798.

The monument at French Hill near Castlebar that honours 'the gallant French soldiers who died for the liberty of Ireland'

The town of Castlebar today is hardly an epicentre of history. Yet for a few days at the end of the 18th century, its name was a badge of shame to the British Army and the town itself fêted an invading power. The impulse that began the story goes back to 1791, when disaffected Irish nationalists founded the Society of United Irishmen. The Society - Wolf Tone was one of its founders - submitted its demands to the British rulers; they included an Irish parliament that represented the people of the island, a vote for everyone, both Catholic and Protestant, and the right to sit in the Irish parliament.

At first the United Irishmen were successful. The British, horrified by the events in France since the 1789 revolution there, wanted to avoid a similar event in Ireland, and agreed to many of the demands. There was no progress on allowing Catholics to sit in parliament, however, and in 1793, when Britain went to war with revolutionary France, all progress ceased. The following year the Society of United Irishmen was proscribed.

The Society's reaction could have been predicted; its members espoused outright revolution, seeking French backing for their plans. The French cared little for the Irish, but were keen to attack Britain, so they gave their support. The first attempt, to land 15,000 French troops at Bantry Bay, was foiled by a combination of bad weather and inept seamanship - though it did have one effect, that of dividing Irish opinion, with many Irishmen joining the British army while others joined the ranks of the United Irishmen. The Society was increasingly persecuted from that time, and there was growing unrest.

An attempted uprising in May 1798 lacked firm coordination

and was soon crushed, but in August the French were again ready to help. An invasion force, commanded by Général Humbert, arrived off the west coast of Ireland on 22 August. Humbert and 1060 men were put ashore at Killala in Co Mayo. The landing was greeted with great joy by many of the locals, who flocked to the cause, but it remained a pitifully small force against 100,000 British troops in Ireland.

The British commanders expected Humbert to send his men in an arc north through Ulster, but he gambled with a march due east. After a number of minor skirmishes his men marched through the night on 26 August and arrived in Castlebar at 6.00 am. The town was guarded by General Lake and 6,000 men; the French and Irish in all comprised less than half that number. The first attack was repelled by British artillery, but the French regrouped and advanced. This was too much for most of the British, who threw down their weapons and fled - some not stopping until they reached Athlone, more than 40 miles away. So sudden and precipitate was their flight that the battle of Castlebar has always been known as 'The Castlebar Races.'

It was not all success for the French, though. Buoyed by the sight of the fleeing English, a group of French soldiers gave chase to three of them. They followed them a few miles to the south. Near Belcarra they lost them. The English had hidden beneath a bridge and as the French crossed it five of them were shot dead. It is to their memory that a stone pyramid was erected nearby, on what is now known as French Hill. It took some time for the pyramid to be placed there - it was built only in 1876. The inscription, obviously intended to antagonise the British who were then still entrenched in Irish rule, reads:

> In grateful remembrance of the gallant French soldiers who died for the freedom of Ireland on the 27th August, 1798. "They shall be remembered for ever".

After the victory, Humbert was treated as a hero in Castlebar, where a celebratory dinner was held in the Linen Hall. Humbert promulgated the 'Republic of Connaught' and issued edicts. He dated them in full accord with the French revolutionary calendar: the month was named as 'Fructidor, sixth Year of the French Republic, One and Indivisible'. Humbert made his headquarters in what is now the Humbert Inn; today it is marked, like many places in the town where events of 27 August 1798 happened, with a plaque.

His stay in Castlebar was not prolonged, though. The march east continued, constantly harried by British troops under the command of Lord Cornwallis. They reached Drumkeeran (see page 311) on 6 September and Ballinamuck two days later. By that time exhausted and dispirited, the French met the British in a pitched battle. It was over in less than half an hour, with the surrender of Humbert, along with his 96 fellow officers and 746 men. They were treated honourably as prisoners of war, being sent to Dublin and then deported to France. Humbert went on to serve in Germany and Switzerland, as well as in San Domingo - now Haiti - from where he was sent home and cashiered for siding with bandits. He eventually settled in New Orleans and died in 1823. And his Irish supporters in the events of 1798? They were all butchered by the British at Ballinamuck.

CO MAYO'S NORTHERN coast. In a narrow strip of land between the slopes of the mountain now called Man an Cheo and the precipitous cliffs that rise 370 feet from the sea, farmers are fighting a losing battle. Climate change has altered the way they

The Linen Hall in Castlebar, where Humbert's celebratory dinner was held in August 1798

Ceide Fields Visitor Centre pyramid, Co Mayo, with the outline of a prehistoric hut circle

farm - no longer can they maintain their fertile fields, grow their simple crops and tend their animals. Soon they will have to abandon their farms and move elsewhere to scratch a living. Has global warming caught up with even this corner of Ireland, where it rains for seven days in every ten?

No. The date is somewhere around 5000 years ago. The climate has certainly changed; but it is a change to colder weather - around five degrees colder in a very short space of time. What had been a mild and equable weather system is now wet - relentlessly wet. And wet ground means the inexorable advance of the moss. The farmers move away as the ground becomes saturated. Over the millennia successive layers of moss decay and form beds of sodden peat over the farms and homesteads of the neolithic farmers - beds more than 13 feet deep in some places.

Fast forward to the 1930s. Local teacher Patrick Caulfield notices that as his neighbours dig peat above the cliffs, every so often they will come across deeply-buried stones, apparently laid in regular lines. He alerts the archeologists to his discovery. Eventually, under the leadership of his son Dr Seamus Caulfield, a systematic examination of the site - five square miles of it - is undertaken. It is impractical to dig the whole site, so the archeologists follow the method of local farmers searching for the submerged trees called bog oak - they probe the yielding peat with metal poles until they strike stones, then mark the places with white bamboo poles. Soon they have mapped a whole complexity of field patterns and houses far below the current land surface.

The site is called **Céide Fields** - céide (say *cage-uh*) means a hill with a flat top, so these are the fields below it. The archaeologists realised that here was a major neolithic discovery, a monument as well preserved and as important as Skara Brae in Orkney, as Italica in Spain, as Persepolis in Iran or as Pompeii.

Eventually the authorities, having informally allowed visitors to the site to see progress, decided that it was time to make better provision for the public. A new visitor centre was planned by Ireland's Office of Works. The resulting building was in the shape of a pyramid - perhaps an irony, for the great Egyptian pyramids were not started until half a millennium after Céide Fields was abandoned.

The lead architect for the Office of Works was Mary McKenna. She wrote that the pyramid shape was the result of a wide-ranging discussion with colleagues. It was only after the pyramid was finished that she realised that the design mirrored the idea of the 'magic mountain' that symbolically links earth and heaven (see page 1) - an idea that seems to have been present as much in the neolithic past as in more recent history. She refers especially to the pointed mountain of Croagh Patrick, the holy place of pilgrimage in the south of Co Mayo.

The entrance to the Ceide Fields Visitor Centre

Approaching the pyramid along the coast road, whether in the sunshine or the rain, is an inspiring journey. Suddenly, out of the bog, rises a square, turfed mound, from which come sloping slate walls and a glass observation tower that rises to a point. It is impressively primeval - an impression emphasised by the main approach to the entrance, through a sunken, stone-lined circular courtyard reminiscent of some of the tombs and enclosures that have been unearthed on the site, as well as of some of Ireland's spectacular hill-top ring forts.

Inside the pyramid are displays that explain the geology, archaeology and natural history of the Céide Fields site, but somehow they seem subsidiary to other aspects of the buildings. The first is a huge pine tree, 5000 years old and dragged from the bog, that rises like a totem from the slate floor and up through a circular gallery to the top-lit apex of the pyramid. The second is the spectacular view from the external viewing gallery below the summit - both over the ancient mysteries of the partially-exposed stone-age landscape and, looking northwards, over the sea towards Co Donegal.

Fascinating guided tours take visitors around the site. They are vital to understand exactly what you are seeing, and as they are led by the archaeologists themselves they are interesting and accurate. They also provide stunning views of the pyramid, which was opened, to much acclaim, in 1993. Among its many awards are the Triennial Gold Medal of the Royal Institute of Irish Architects in 1994 and the Europa Nostra Architectural and Natural Heritage Diploma in 1996. In 1995 it was named as the *Sunday Times* Irish Building of the Year. But it has not been all praise. One writer described Ireland's largest pyramid as 'a great big glass pyramid-style thing'. It is 'hideous, horrible, awful, manky, terrible, rotten, ugly . . . [and] looks about as attractive as a warthog with elephantiasis' - though he does concede that 'inside, it's got some pretty good audio-visual presentations'.

While few people (except us!) would visit Céide Fields solely for its pyramid, this seems unduly harsh. The pyramid is a means to an end - that of allowing visitors a glimpse into a far distant past that has been almost miraculously preserved. It does its job with great efficiency and elegance.

FIFTY MILES SOUTH of Céide Fields is a pyramid that has also had the assistance of Ireland's Office of Works - though only to stabilise and preserve it. **The Neale**, south of Ballinrobe, is a village with an often-turbulent history. At about the time when the neolithic settlers were leaving their threatened farms at Céide Fields, this part of Co Mayo was a battleground between warring tribes. One legend says that Slainge, king of the Celtic Fir Bolg tribe, died at The Neale in a fierce battle with warriors from

Scandinavia. He was buried under a large cairn here, made of the same number of stones as the number of Scandinavian soldiers they had killed. Better authorities, though, say that Slainge died at the place now called Slane on the banks of the River Boyne, west of Drogheda.

At The Neale, thousands of years after Slainge, another battle took place, between the peasant tenants of the land and the absentee, often English, landlords. Despite the ravages of the Great Famine of 1845 to 1859, when the potato blight destroyed nearly all the subsistence crop, landlords increased rents without regard to the tenants' ability to pay. In some places the people took to violence, destroying property and even killing the land agents. In this part of Mayo, however, where much of the land was owned by Lord Erne, there was a different tactic. Encouraged by the parish priest of The Neale, Father John O'Malley, locals used a form of non-violent protest against the agent and against anyone who worked with him. Charles Stewart Parnell, who took up this 'ostracisation', urged them to take action against anyone who took over a farm from an evicted tenant: 'You must shun him on the roadside when you meet him, you must shun him on the street of the town, you must shun him in the shop, you must shun him in the fairgreen and in the marketplace and even in the place of worship.' This was a powerful weapon, and it proved particularly useful against Lord Erne's agent, whose name was Captain Charles Cunningham Boycott. Father O'Malley was the man who coined the verb 'to boycott' for such action.

When Boycott was being 'boycotted' the pyramid at The Neale had already been in place for almost 150 years. It owes its origins to a childless marriage and to the influence of one of Ireland's greatest patrons of the arts. The Browne family came to Co Mayo in Tudor times - the first to settle in The Neale was John Browne, a mapmaker and agent of Sir Francis Walsingham, Elizabeth I's spymaster. Browne was the first Sheriff of the new county of Mayo in 1583, and was given almost 4,000 acres of land at The Neale. The times were unsettled, though; in 1588 he was killed during an insurrection by the Bourkes of Mayo.

The family persevered at The Neale, and John Browne's grandson, also John, was made a Baronet of Nova Scotia by King Charles I in 1635. The Brownes seem not to have used the title for nearly a century - it was probably politically inexpedient to do

The step pyramid at The Neale once had a lead statue of Apollo on its summit

so. They were apparently Catholic throughout this time; the 3rd baronet, another John Browne, fought on the side of King James VII & II. He was captured at the siege of Derry in 1698 during the Glorious Revolution. It was this John Browne who unwittingly caused another conflict, this time a duel of 1748 which his grandson Sir John, the 5th baronet and the first to use the title, fought against Robert Miller of Kilmaine, the next village east from The Neale.

Sir John wanted to join the Tory 'True Blue Club' in Kilmaine. By this time the Browne family was impeccably Protestant. Sir John's father had agreed under Ireland's Penal Laws to embrace Protestantism; had he not, he would have lost the family estates. The rules of the Club said that no one could join if their grandfather was a Catholic. Sir John's grandfather was a Catholic - so Sir John was blackballed. Robert Miller, an official and past-president of the Club, wrote to Browne and told him, politely, that this was not a move against him, just a way of stopping the Club getting too big. But Sir John took it as a personal insult and challenged Miller to a duel. On 21 January 1748 they met. Negotiations broke down, and Browne strode away and fired two shots at Miller, who managed to return fire. Browne's homemade bullet hit Miller in the stomach and he died of his wound five days later. Sir John then vanished from the scene, but in January 1749 gave himself up to the authorities. He was tried for murder but was found guilty only of manslaughter - to the great rejoicing of local people. He was sentenced to six months imprisonment and was branded on his hand.

It was in honour of Sir John's son George, 6th baronet, that the pyramid at The Neale was created. George Browne, who succeeded to the baronetcy in 1762, had continued the family tradition by serving as Sheriff of Co Mayo in 1747 and as a JP. He married twice - but neither marriage produced a son and heir. He died in 1765 and was succeeded by his brother John, the 7th baronet. To commemorate the life of his brother, the new Sir John, who was made Baron Kilmaine in 1789, built the pyramid.

He may have been influenced in choosing the shape by the advice of his brother-in-law, James Caulfeild, 1st Earl of Charlemont. Caulfeild was the most enlightened patron of the arts in 18th-century Ireland. At the age of 18 he had taken the obligatory Grand Tour - but his Tour was unusually extended, both in time and in distance. He was away nine years; five were spent in absorbing the art and culture of Italy, but his journeying also took him to Turkey, Greece and Egypt. On his return to Ireland his step-father offered him an estate on the coast north of Dublin, which Caulfeild named Marino. Here he commissioned from William Chambers, whom he had met in Rome, one of the world's most perfect classical buildings, The Casino. Like an exquisite watch, whose serene casing hides myriad subtly-interconnecting parts, The Casino is a tribute to both Caulfeild's patronage and Chambers' ingenuity and taste.

The Marino estate was landscaped by Matthew Peters, who had previously worked at Stowe. The influences of Caulfeild's Egyptian experiences and of Peters' knowledge of the now-vanished pyramid at Stowe (see page 93) come together in the Earl's suggestion to his sister's husband, Sir John Browne, that the pyramid shape would be a suitable monument to his late brother. Caulfield is said to have provided the plan for the structure. There may have been expediency in the suggestion, too; the pyramid was built on top of a large cairn - possibly even that of Slainge (see

The Casino at Marino, Dublin - designed by Sir William Chambers for James Caulfeild, Earl of Charlemont, brother-in-law of the builder of the pyramid at The Neale

page 317) - which offered a basic shape and may have dictated its 30-foot height. Like many follies in Britain and Ireland the pyramid has attracted the story that Lord Kilmaine started the construction to relieve local poverty, paying people to gather the loose stones from the surrounding fields to build the structure. The nine steps of the pyramid, restored to pristine condition in 1990 by the Office of Works, were originally surmounted by a lead statue of Apollo, which was later replaced by a weather vane that helped a 19th-century Lord Kilmaine in his meteorological observations.

On a plaque built in to the pyramid is an inscription:

TEMPLVM FORTITVDINIS MEMORIAE
DILECTISSIMI FRATRIS GEORGII BROWNE ARMI.
HVISQVE PATRIAE QUONDAM
DECUS & TUTAMEN VIXIT AD 1750

This is all quite clear - the pyramid is a 'Temple of Fortitude'. George is a 'dearest brother', as well as an 'ornament and a safeguard to his country'. But what of the date? If George died in 1762, it cannot have been erected in 1750; even a misreading or mis-carving for 1760 is wrong. At around the time of the pyramid's building Lord Kilmaine was also constructing other follies on his estate - a sophisticated Doric temple with an impressive groined subvault, and a stone monument to house 'The Gods of The Neale', an ancient stone slab incised with representations of a human being and two animals. The slab had been found on the estate in 1739. The Gods are also known as 'The Gods of Welcome'; na Ffeale is the Irish for 'of welcome' and was the origin of the name of the village. Perhaps in the construction of these various works, which seems to have gone on into the 1770s, the correct date of George's death was misplaced.

The Two Mile Inn Hotel, Limerick

ED MYERS OF **Limerick**'s local radio station, presenter of *Limerick Today*, 'the most listened-to show in the mid-west', alerted us to the pyramid in his city. The Two Mile Inn Hotel on Ennis Road, north east of the centre, was built in the 1970s. The prominent Limerick architects John and Nuala Kernan were responsible for the design; they also designed the innovative yurt-shaped church of Christ the King in the Limerick suburb of Shahbooly, and were instrumental in founding the University of Limerick's School of Architecture.

Now part of the Dunne Group of Hotels, most of the Two Mile Inn building is typically 1970s - utilitarian, single-storey, low and spreading. But the climax is a tall, tile-clad pyramid with a glazed apex, its structural steels protruding beyond the low windows to anchor it to the ground. It is an early prototype of some of the leisure centres, like Bexhill (see page 67) and Southsea (see page 109) that were built in the 1980s.

The pyramid works well as a way of signposting the existence of the hotel. It is less successful inside, where it forms the reception area. It is spacious and reasonably light because of the glazed point, but it rather dominates the low sofas and tables, which seem somewhat adrift in a large volume of nothingness, despite the million-euro refurbishment a few years ago. Receptionist Patricia said that as a place of work it can be very cold in the winter as all the heat rises up, but all her colleagues agree that it is 'a nice feature'.

The hotel has formerly had a Pyramid Restaurant - which oddly wasn't in the pyramid but in a subsidiary structure - but this is now Thady's Restaurant, and is partnered by Thady O'Neill's Bar. They are both named from the hero of an old Irish ballad who abandons his girl then returns to her:

> He said it was better his fate to go roaming
> But what would be gold to the joy I could feel
> If he should come back to me tender and loving
> Still poor but my own darling Thady O'Neill.

IF YOU ARE to encounter fairies anywhere it Ireland, it may well be on the Ring of Kerry. Not among the traffic-clogged roads in summer, though; they are unlikely to lift you into an ethereal land inhabited by nymphs and sprites, but rather to take you to a circle of hell full of tourist coaches and caravans, aimless pedestrians and, when we were there, some of the most severe road works to be found in western Europe. Still, the scenery is magnificent, if you have time to take your eyes off the (probably now-improved) road.

Having battled through, we were relieved to reach **Sneem**. Sneem, too, is busy. It consists of two village greens that spread either side of a narrow bridge over Abha na Snadhma - Sneem River. Near the bridge is St Michael's Catholic Church. Beyond it are the fairies - and the pyramids. There is a sign, with an incised Egyptian figure, that tells you that you have arrived at 'The Pyramids Built by FÁS 1987'. To reinforce the message, you will just have passed a statue of Isis, donated to the village by the Egyptian Ambassador to Ireland.

This seems very clear. But what you get is not so straightforward. The first structure you come to is not a pyramid but a cone. Then there's a three-sided pyramid, a more squat pyramid pierced with a circular hole and with a slit in the apex, and, on the edge of the site, a pyramid sliced in two.

The origin of these works goes back to Sneem's winning the Irish Tidy Towns Award in 1987. As its prize, the Arts Council of Ireland provided £5,000 for a sculpture. Sneem already had a reputation as a place for new sculpture, with works in various places around the two greens. So when the chosen artist, James Scanlon, visited the town he felt that the greens 'looked a little like a mantelpiece that was already full'. He abandoned his first idea, for 20-foot steel columns with glass prisms, and wandered round looking for a site and for inspiration. The area he came upon was, he says, 'ludicrous. It was just rocks and bottomless bog . . . like a piece of scar tissue.' He decided that it would be good to try to heal the scar.

In some ways Scanlon was an odd choice for the project. Although he trained as a sculptor in the late 1970s, he made his name as a stained glass artist. He has produced large glass installations in Ireland, and undertaken commissions in Britain and Japan, as well as exhibiting in New York and Poland. But he is a Kerry man so he was awarded the commission in Sneem - and his pyramid structures incorporate stained glass panels.

A stone stile that was already on the site gave him his first inspiration, to use traditional stone walls as the basis of his work. To help with the project he was offered a team of about 20 local people, who were sent by FÁS - Foras Áiseanna Saothair, the Irish National Training and Employment Authority. Their skills in stone-laying were tested and their particular aptitudes were noted. While he was contemplating the exact form that his sculptures should take, Scanlon visited Staigue Fort. A few miles west of Sneem, Staigue is one of Ireland's largest and best-preserved prehistoric ring forts. Its massive walls, made from undressed and unmortared stone, made a deep impression on him. He determined to use the technique in his Sneem commission.

The Pyramids marker at Sneem - next to a cone by James Scanlon

Two of the pyramids at Sneem, Co Kerry

Half-pyramid and St Michael's Church, Sneem

The result is both primeval and modern. The pyramids grow from the boggy landscape - now with more vegetation than when Scanlon first came across it - as if they are elemental forces. The pyramid shape is ancient, but here he has given them a modern twist; the three-sided version is pierced by irregular windows, glazed with fragments of coloured glass. The half-pyramid is supported on a wooden framework like a tepee. And the largest of the pyramids, the one pierced with the circular hole, has its upper section slightly overhanging, like the eaves of a house. The cumulative effect is like the early monastic beehive-shaped huts on Skellig Michael, the World Heritage Site twelve miles out into the Atlantic off the coast of the Ring of Kerry.

Sneem people, inevitably, nick-named the scheme *The Pyramids* - but Scanlon wanted to call it *Sligh na Síoga, The Way the Fairies Went*. His inspiration came from his boyhood in Co Kerry, when he would help make haycocks in the fields. 'You would have a little whirlwind, the *síodh-ghaoth*. It comes into a meadow, knocks the tops off the cocks of hay, goes on to the next field and does the same to damage it . . . it is very irritating, the *síodh-ghaoth*, the fairy wind.' With local names in Sneem including the Fairy Fort, Scanlon decided that his structures would be permanent haycocks, tempting the fairies round and through them. But when he

*The finest of
James Scanlon's
Sneem pyramids*

told the local committee who oversaw the project there was much sucking of teeth. Eventually Father Murphy, the chairman, said, 'Look, James, sure, we'll call it *The Pyramids*. There's only two pyramids. There's pyramids in Egypt and there's pyramids in Sneem, and we'll leave it at that.' So *The Pyramids* they have stayed, even if Fr Murphy's knowledge of pyramids was somewhat limited.

There was a curious twist to the story of James Scanlon's work at Sneem. One day he happened to mention to Fr Murphy that he was related to a former Bishop of Kerry, Bishop Mangan. The priest told him that Mangan, Scanlon's great-great uncle, had once been parish priest at Sneem. In 1913 the then Fr Mangan had assisted a poor family that had been evicted by their landlord. Mangan offered them a piece of land in the village to build a new house. It was on the same land that, 74 years later, James Scanlon chose to build his fairy pyramids.

THE SEARCH FOR Irish pyramids took us east from Sneem, then south round Bantry Bay and down to **Ballydehob**, a few miles inland from Ireland's most south-westerly point, Mizen Head. This part of West Cork was particularly hit by the potato famine of the 1840s; the local population was almost halved. Now the area is more prosperous. It is said that Ballydehob has more pubs per head of the population than anywhere else in Ireland ('one on each corner and two in between'). One of them is called *The Irish Whip* after the nickname of world wrestling champion Danno Mahony, a Ballydehob man who is commemorated by a statue in the village for his winning of the championship in 1935.

The landscape attracts eminent visitors - former UK Prime Minister Tony Blair among them - and residents. Actor Jeremy Irons has restored a typical medieval tower house nearby. And

Michael Bulfin's sculptural pyramid called Our Shining Future Emerges at Ballydehob has been overtaken with vegetation

like other places in the area, Ballydehob is a centre for craftsmen and for sculptors. We had been told by local resident Cathy Cook about a pyramid near Ballydehob. At first we thought it was part of the *Sky Garden* at Liss Ard just beyond Skibbereen, an ambitious project to create a contemplative, ecological landscape garden. But enquiries showed that the intended pyramid there, which would have been carved out of the landscape and contain internal passages and staircases, was never built. So we enquired further.

The Ballydehob pyramid is a much smaller affair, part of the West Cork Sculpture Trail. It sits beside a lay-by east of Ballydehob, at Skeaghanore. We pondered it. What was it meant to be? Fortunately, West Cork Arts Centre in Skibbereen came to our rescue. They provided a booklet called *Living Landscape '91* that detailed the exhibits in the Centre's fifth *Living Landscape* exhibition. Our pyramid was exhibit number 5, a sculpture called *Our Shining Future Emerges*.

Not any more, it doesn't. It is not an impressive sight. There seems to be a weed-covered hillock topped with a small, slightly-askew metal pyramid. Some of the weeds poke up between a tumble of boulders. The slopes of the hillock appear to be slightly shaped. It is only by reference to the illustration in *Living Landscapes '91* that it makes sense.

The metal point is really only part of the picture. The sculptor, Michael Bulfin, planned the pyramid to be a turf structure, its angles like those of the Egyptian pyramids, with the more acute metal cap sitting on top. Up one side is a tumble of rocks. The symbolism seems to be that the metal is 'our shining future', the turf pyramid the dullness of our previous existence and the rocks the hard road by which we attain the future.

Michael Bulfin, who was born at Birr in Co Offaly in 1939, is one of Ireland's leading sculptors - a long-serving chairman of the Sculptors' Society of Ireland. He represented the country at the Paris Biennale in 1971, founded the Project Arts Centre in Dublin and has sculpture throughout Ireland, including at Lough Boora Parklands (see page 352). He's also the uncle of Ireland's Eurovision winner and candidate for the Irish Presidency, Dana.

The Ballydehob pyramid may not be one of Bulfin's best or most prominent works, but in a land where rain and mist ensure that vegetation is never short of water, it would merit a little more upkeep - or even the importation of a few sheep to crop the sloping turf below the 'shining future' pyramid.

THE ROAD SOUTH to **Myross** from the N71 east of Skibbereen, is a delight. It winds over undulating countryside with views across Glandore Harbour down to Union Hall, then on past the tiny Lough Cluhir and along a causeway over Blind Harbour. On a bluff overlooking the sea, with nothing except a few close-offshore islets until landfall at Cape Finisterre 600 miles to the south, are the remains of Myross church, surrounded by its former churchyard. Of all the pyramids we visited in Britain and Ireland the O'Donovan pyramid at Myross ranks alongside the transatlantic cable pyramid at Porthcurno in Cornwall (see page 159) as being the most beautifully sited.

Myross church has been abandoned for a long time; even in 1699 it was noted as being ruinous, and the minister was told that he had to have services in his own house until the parishioners had decided where they wanted a new chapel to be sited. It took them until 1826, when the Board of First Fruits (a Church of Ireland building fund, established mainly at the instance of Jonathan Swift, who spent time in Myross) gave a grant of £830 for a new building. The churchyard, though, remained the place of burial for the parish until the new church was founded, and so became the last resting place in 1778 of Daniel (or Donal) O'Donovan and, 34 years later, of his second wife Jane.

The O'Donovan pyramid on the far south-west coast of Co Cork

The original O'Donovans (the name means a descendent of the dark brown one - whether the hair or the face was brown remains a mystery) were one of Ireland's ancient families. They were kings in Limerick before being forced by war to move to Cork in the 12th century. They remained powerful for centuries, with their main powerbase at Castledonovan in Drimoleague, about ten miles north-west of Myross. As Catholics they were on the losing side in the wars against Cromwell and William III; but they managed to retain some of their lands after the Treaty of Limerick ended the Williamite war in 1691. Their main residence was moved to Bawnlahan in Myross parish, just west of Union Hall.

By the beginning of the 18th century they seem to have settled into the role of country gentry, marrying into other Irish gentlemen's families and sending the younger sons off to the Army or, occasionally, the Church. They called successive eldest sons Donal or, as they became more anglicised, Daniel. The Daniel O'Donovan whose pyramid is at Myross was the son of Richard O'Donovan and his wife Elizabeth. She was the daughter of the Knight of Kerry. Daniel became the Clan Chief, called 'The O'Donovan', on the death of his father, whose older brothers predeceased him. Daniel was first married when he was 18 to Anne Kearney of Garretstown. It is not clear how long they were married, but there were no children of the union.

It was to be another 42 years, in 1763, before Daniel married again, aged 60. His wife was Jane Becher, 45 year his junior. She came from Hollybrook, a house north of Skibbereen. Her family was originally from Kent, and they were given 14,000 acres of land in Co Cork by Elizabeth I. Captain Becher, the jockey after whom Becher's Brook on the Grand National Course at Aintree is named, is part of the family, too. In 1836 he won the first, unofficial Grand National; in 1839, during the first proper running of the race, he fell off at the brook, remaining submerged while the rest of the field thundered over him. He emerged to exclaim that he hadn't known water without whiskey in it tasted so foul.

The marriage of Daniel O'Donovan and 15-year-old Jane Becher seems to have been a love-match - or at least, he was besotted with her. He changed the name of his house from Bawnlahan to Castle Jane. And she bore him four children before his death in 1778, the eldest son, breaking with tradition, being christened Richard after his grandfather. The direct O'Donovan line faltered with Daniel and Jane's children. Richard, a general in Spain and Flanders in the Napoleonic wars, died in 1829 without having had children. His brother John was killed in action in Jamaica in 1796. Of the two daughters, Helen's marriage was childless and Jane died unmarried. So the succession went to General Richard's fourth cousin, Morgan O'Donovan.

Curiously, today The O'Donovan lives not at Bawnlahan (which soon reverted to its original name) but at Jane's family home of Hollybrook. The house passed from the Bechers to the Morgans. Rebuilt in the Arts and Crafts style in 1903 (and with the addition of a fashionable Japanese garden) by Lt Col and Mrs Morgan, Hollybrook eventually went in 1950 to Mrs Morgan's niece Cornelia. Cornelia had married Morgan O'Donovan in 1917. On inheriting Hollybrook they moved there. It is now the home of The O'Donovan, their son Daniel.

Although Jane would no longer recognise the house, she may have been pleased to know that her family home has, after more than a century, come back to her descendents. She outlived her husband by more than 30 years; she seems to have cherished his memory and eventually was united with him at the pyramid in Myross, their 'tomb by the sounding sea.'

OF ALL THE small pyramids in the whole of Britain and Ireland, the one at Boyne Crescent, just north of **Cork** city centre, is probably the most used. Large modern structures like Ceide Fields (see page 315) or Fantasy Island at Ingoldmells (see page 50) may have more visitors, and offices like the Co-operative Bank pyramid at Stockport (see page 204) or leisure centres like Bletchley (see page 90), Bexhill (see page 67) and Bedford (see page 85) may have more people working or playing there - but at only seven feet high, this one takes the prize for usefulness.

Ask any of the boys (no girls were in sight) who were out and about on the grass in the centre of the Crescent what the use of the pyramid was, and the answer would have been obvious. It's a place to hang out, it acts as an over-sized goal post for impromptu, though very serious, games of football, it's a castle, a mountain, a ramp for the skateboard - and above all, it's just right for leaning against. Occasionally, though, it's a place to vent your frustration or your love of vandalism; it is not quite in the condition that the artist left it when it was put up in 1996.

It was commissioned for Cork's public art scheme to be part of the Cork Sculpture Trail. It cost £20,000 and was paid for out of the Department of the Environment's *Per Cent for Art* scheme. The scheme, which has operated in Ireland under different names since 1978, is designed to encourage public art throughout the country: it is, says the government publicity, 'a great opportunity for collaboration between artist and community. Public art needs to have been developed and created with local ownership in mind.'

Julie Kelleher was chosen for the commission. She was born in Tralee in 1957 and studied sculpture at Crawford School of Art in Cork and mixed media studies at the National College of Art and Design in Dublin. She has been particularly associated with a series of touring art exhibitions for schools, producing artworks that are rooted in identifiable localities or that resonate with particular groups of people. For the Boyne Crescent sculpture she took the trouble to consult widely with local people to find out both what sort of piece they would like and where they wanted it sited.

The result is a three-sided pyramid called *Pyre - Fire - Heart - Hearth*. It sits towards one end of the attractive central area of the crescent, amid trees. The main structure is concrete with metal edges and it is covered with square tiles of riven slate. Let in to the slate are brass plaques that illustrate the title of the work - someone using bellows, a chair, a disc and circle that can be interpreted as the sun or as the hearth. It is simple and attractive, and provides a good focal point for the area.

It has not always been popular. In July 2001 Cork County Borough Council received a report on the pyramid. Apparently there had been complaints from some local residents that it was in a bad condition and attracted undesirables - a few people expressed similar sentiments to us when we visited more recently. The Council report noted under the heading *Condition* that 12 tiles were missing at the base, there was a small amount of leaching of concrete at some joints, and that one side was going slightly green with algae. Otherwise, it said 'the structure is in good condition'. Even better, two long-term residents of Boyne Crescent attested that 'there is no problem with anti-social behaviour with or around the pyramid'.

The Council was presented with a choice. It could have the missing tiles replaced at a cost of IR£1,000; or the pyramid could be removed. That would cost IR£2,000. A third possibility was the relocation of the pyramid, but as that would 'entail demolition and total rebuilding costs approaching those of the original commission' - that is, another IR£20,000 - that wasn't likely to happen. The recommendation from Council officials, which was adopted by the Council, was that there should be full restoration, which as the cheapest option was hardly surprising.

It is not clear if this happened. If it did, it was not particularly effective, for there are more missing tiles. This is a pity, but it does not make the pyramid any less attractive to the boys who play around it every day. And as a community focus it has another purpose, too. Buried inside it are personal time capsules created by local residents in 1996. They were celebrating the positive contribution the new pyramid makes to Boyne Crescent's urban landscape.

OUR INTRODUCTION TO **Kilcooley** Abbey was odder than any other in Ireland. We had arranged to meet the estate's owner, Peter Ponsonby, at the front of the 18th-century mansion - 'I'll be putting in some fence posts,' he said. It was raining as we drove from the gates along a sweeping carriageway, with a glimpse of the medieval abbey that gave its name to the later residence. As we rounded a bend the house came into view - but no Mr Ponsonby. We parked - but before we reached the front door there was a furious knocking on a window in a wing of the house. Peering through the grimy glass (the whole building had a *Satis House* air) was a woman who seemed angry. Gesticulating wildly, she gestured for us to be gone. We bellowed 'Mr Ponsonby? Pyramid?' like a battlecry, and eventually got our message across. 'Are you the English people?' she shouted. 'It's that way.'

Only a little unnerved, we turned the car and headed back to the abbey. The pyramid was easy to find, squatting among the ruins like an alien craft attempting to be at one with its surroundings by camouflaging itself with a covering of the same stone as the abbey. It is tall - around 25 feet high - and of typically-18th century proportions, based on the pyramid of Cestius (see page 2). It sits beside a gable of the abbey, the gothic window contrasting attractively with the slopes of the pyramid.

By the time the pyramid was built from the rubble lying around the site, the abbey had been in ruins for more than two hundred years. It was founded in 1182 by Donagh O'Brien, who was King of Munster. A Cistercian house, with around 20 monks and a similar number of lay brothers, it was founded from Jerpoint Abbey, 20 miles south east. As well as farming the surrounding lands, the brothers catered for pilgrims on their way to the holy site of the

Rock of Cashel, 20 miles to the south west. Armed men attacked the abbey in 1445, and burned most of it down; it was reconstructed - with the addition of a tower - but it was to survive less than a century. The last abbot, Thomas Shortal, surrendered Kilcooley to King Henry VIII's commissioners on 8 April 1540; he was given a comfortable pension for his acquiescence.

Monastic properties were frequently awarded by the king to a courtier - in this case to James Butler, 9th Earl of Ormonde and 2nd Earl of Ossory. The Butlers (who had been given the title 'Chief Butler of Ireland' by King Henry II in 1171) already had connections with Kilcooley - Pierce Fitzjames Oge Butler, who died in 1526, is buried there, as is his grandfather, also Pierce. The Butler family kept Kilcooley until 1636, when James Butler, Ist Duke of Ormonde, sold the estate to Sir Jerome Alexander - though that was not the end of their involvement with the inhabitants of the Abbey. Sir Jerome Alexander's daughter Elizabeth married Sir William Barker, and they set up home in the ruins of the Cistercian buildings, adapting and rebuilding as necessary.

Their descendant, Sir William the 4th baronet, inherited Kilcooley in 1770. He must have found the adapted medieval buildings uncomfortable because he was responsible for building the new mansion. It survived intact until 1839, when it was badly burned. The butler, Ashby, set fire to it by stuffing mounds of paper up a chimney and lighting it. He had just been dismissed for fathering an illegitimate child. A later butler redeemed the good name of his office by scaring away a gang of raiders during the Irish Civil War. He had ascended to the roof to play the Last Post on a bugle.

Sir William Barker seems to have viewed the abbey ruins as a garden ornament, just as the Aislabies at Studley Royal in North Yorkshire (see page 46) saw the larger ruins of Fountains Abbey. Sir William's portrait was painted with a view of the abbey's east end in the background. It was through Sir William that the Kilcooley estate came to the Ponsonby family. Having no heirs of his own, he willed the estate to his nephew, the grandly-named Chambré Brabazon Ponsonby.

'Chum' Ponsonby, as he was known in the family (both the Chambré and the Brabazon were family names - the family were the Earls of Bessborough), was the son of Mary Barker, Sir William's sister. Mary was Chum's father's third wife. She was responsible for organising the building of the so-called Famine Wall around the estate during a particularly savage time in the Great Famine. Selling her jewellery to pay for the structure, she organised bands of starving people to build what is the longest of such walls in Ireland. It was seen as a moral duty of the aristocracy to help the poor, but it was frowned on to dole out money; poor people had to be given work to maintain their self-respect.

Perhaps the most famous member of the Ponsonby clan was Chum's half sister, Sarah. It was through Sarah that the Butlers return to the story. As an unhappy child, she was sent away to live with her godmother, the delicate Lady Fownes. Sir William Fownes made unwanted advances, seeing young Sarah as a suitable replacement for his ailing wife. Twice Sarah 'eloped', dressed as a boy, with her friend Eleanor Butler, daughter of the 17th Earl of Ormonde, who was also miserable at home. Brought back in disgrace both times, Sarah was eventually helped by Sir William Barker to set up home in Wales with Lady Eleanor, 17 years her senior. They moved to a picturesque house, Plas Newydd, in Llangollen, where they lived with the help a single maid. They became known as 'The Ladies of Llangollen' and were the objects of great curiosity to society. They corresponded with Queen Charlotte, counted the Duke of Wellington a friend, were visited by literary figures including Wordsworth, Sir Walter Scott and Thomas de Quincey and became much loved in the Welsh hills, despite the 'tantalisingly ambiguous nature of their relationship' and suspicions that they were spies or men in drag. Lady Eleanor died, aged 90, in 1829, and Sarah Ponsonby two years later.

When Sir William Barker, the 4th and last Baronet, died in 1818, Chum Ponsonby inherited. He changed his name to the even more grand Chambré Brabazon Ponsonby-Barker; the additional surname lasted only one more generation, the family once again becoming the plainer Ponsonby, though Chambré's eldest son styled himself plain William Barker. William was a gentleman of old fashioned principles - although a strict Protestant evangelical, he sometimes used the Kilcooley maids as hot water bottles, citing King David as his model for doing so. Once, offended by the rankness of the maid's body, he sprinkled her, in the darkness, with what he believed was perfume. In the morning he found it was ink.

And which of these Barkers, Ponsonbys or Ponsonby-Barkers was responsible for the pyramid at Kilcooley? There is no inscription on it, so it is unclear. Stylistically it would seem to have been constructed some time in the very late 18th century, so it may have been built by either Sir William Barker the 3rd Baronet or his son the 4th. An alternative theory is that the builder was the maid-hugging William Barker, who was a Freemason and started an Orange Lodge at Kilcooley. Whichever of them it was, there are unlikely to be more of the Ponsonby family interred there. For the first time since the Duke of Ormonde sold it to Sir Jerome Alexander, the Kilcooley estate has been on the market, and was sold in 2006. Fortunately, the pyramid, as part of the medieval ruins of Kilcooley Abbey, is listed by the Office of Works, and will be protected.

Sir William Barker, 4th Baronet, with the ruins of Kilcooley Abbey in the background

LIKE THE PONSONBY family, the Stratfords of **Baltinglass** had their pyramidal mausoleum in the grounds of a ruined Cistercian abbey. But where the Ponsonbys were, on the whole, rational and sober, the Stratfords were argumentative, choleric and devious.

The monument - an amalgam of classicism with the merest hint of Egyptian in the sloping walls and curving cornice on the base, below the emphatically Egyptian pyramid - would appear to show the elements of good taste. Its setting beside the chancel of the abbey church is picturesque (even if the mausoleum does occupy the space of one of the south transept's former altars). There was a good eye at work here - but whose eye? Or perhaps a better question, whose mausoleum? The generally-accepted date for the structure is 1832. According to Lewis's 1837 *Topographical Dictionary of Ireland*, 'over the remains of his deceased ancestors the present earl, in 1832, erected a massive mausoleum of granite, terminating in a pyramidal spire'.

The earl was Benjamin O'Neale Stratford, 4th Earl of Aldborough. The Stratfords were originally Warwickshire gentry who claimed descent from one of William the Conqueror's barons. They reached Ireland during Cromwell's Irish Wars. They settled first in Co Tipperary but soon acquired lands around Baltinglass and, not far away, at Belan near Moone in Co Kildare. Their lands were once held by Queen Elizabeth's godson Sir John Harrington, inventor of the water closet. John Stratford, who

Argumentative Stratfords were laid to rest in a pyramidal mausoleum attached to the ruined abbey

was born in 1698, was the founder of the family's fortunes - or misfortunes. High Sheriff for, successively, Kildare, Wicklow and Wexford, John was raised to the Irish peerage in 1763 as Baron Baltinglass, having been MP for the town since 1721. In July 1776 he was further ennobled as Viscount Aldborough of Belan and, less than a year later, as Viscount Amiens (on account of his supposed French ancestry) and 1st Earl of Aldborough.

John's wife Martha (who had impeccable Protestant credentials as the daughter of the Chaplain to King William III at the Battle of Boyne) bore him 19 children; the ones who survived infancy spent most of their lives quarrelling. The eldest son Edward succeeded as 2nd Earl. This Lord Aldborough was cultured; he had a town house (variously known as Stratford House and as Aldborough House) designed for him by Robert Adam, just off Oxford Street in London, and another palatial town residence, also Aldborough House, in Dublin. He was a friend of the painter Thomas Gainsborough. But he also spent time in prison in Dublin because he insulted the Irish Lord Chancellor, Lord Clare. Lady

Aldborough (Anne Henniker, his second wife) joined him in Newgate, and in his will he described her as 'living and sleeping with me in prison and room about sixteen by fourteen feet without furniture, bed or bedding until we had them supplied'. He praised her 'innocency, complacency, ingenuity and every feminine accomplishment and compassion, integrity, cheerfulness, ableness, modest upright gentleness, goodness, meekness, temperance, and tender affection.'

It was as well he had such a paragon to support him, for the rest of his family hated him, especially his 'ingrate brothers' John, Paul and Benjamin. They argued particularly about which of them should be MP for Baltinglass - all of them eventually held the office. They quarrelled, too, about money; as a result, Edward decided to tie up the family estates as far as possible in legal red tape so that on his death the brothers inherited as little as possible. In his will he left them just one shilling each 'because they . . . have repaid earliest attention, care and affection with the utmost ingratitude, undermining my character and fortune, doing me all the possible acts of unkindness and uniformity opposite my interests, attacking my Borough which they have, for many years and at enormous expense to each, endeavoured to wrest from me by violence, fraud, threat, mob assault and every species of baseness and injustice'.

The earl's brother Paul was a clergyman, whom Edward accused of defrauding their sister Lady Hannah. A parsimonious parson, 'Holy Paul' passed his last years in prison for debt, rather than pay what he owed to his niece's family. But the 2nd Earl's greatest bile was reserved for John and Benjamin, described by a contemporary as 'two of the most slippery customers I have the displeasure to be acquainted with'. Both of them succeeded Edward as earl, but, as he had threatened, Edward left the bulk of his property to their nephew John, son of their sister Amelia. There were problems with the will - in fact, he left 50 wills, and there were legal arguments about which was his final word on the matter of his inheritance.

John Stratford became 3rd Earl of Aldborough in 1802. He was notably eccentric. Newly-arrived guests would be asked 'When are you leaving?' and he often dined in private on fruit which he 'scrumped' from his own garden. His wife was a granddaughter of the Duke of Hamilton; he seems to have been estranged from her early in the marriage. Despite her lineage she was considered coarse and fast. She dallied with the future Duke of Wellington (dumping him from her carriage far from home when tired of him) and was rude to King Louis Philippe of France. She lived to be more than 90, never telling anyone her age; the Duchess of Sutherland, being told of the invention of a new calculating machine, wished that it would 'calculate two things, first Lady Aldborough's age and secondly, whether the Tories will ever come back to power'.

John was the last of his family to live at Belan House. When he died in 1823 without male heirs, his brother Benjamin O'Neale Stratford succeeded as 4th Earl and moved to Stratford Lodge at Baltinglass. Intended as a lawyer, he left his legal studies to join the army, becoming an officer in the 7th Dragoons. He served with his regiment in the Seven Years' War, but found time to fight several duels. It was probably Benjamin who was responsible for building the pyramid mausoleum at Baltinglass to commemorate his family - or presumably those parts of it that he had not fallen out with. It may, though, have been John, who enriched the gardens of Belan House with follies.

Among those with whom Benjamin was at loggerheads was his son Mason Gerard Stratford, who succeeded him as 5th Earl in 1833. Mason seems to have been a bigamist. At least two of his three wives were alive and married to him at the same time. He was also penurious, writing in a letter from Carlsbad to a London newspaper, 'My father left me for twenty years without one shilling of allowance. I had a large family, seven infant children dependent on me, myself dependent only on credit, payable at his demise, to support them.' It is not surprising that when Mason died in 1849 the inheritance was disputed. One of his wives, calling herself Mary, Countess of Aldborough, petitioned the Committee of Privileges for recognition of her son Henry as 6th Earl. Eventually, in 1854, she lost, and the son of Mason Gerard by his lawful wife, Cornelia Tandy, was confirmed as a peer. This son, Benjamin, 6th and last Earl of Aldborough, was just as odd as his predecessors. After a brief army career he became a recluse at Stratford Lodge. Most of his life was spent trying to build the world's biggest hot air balloon at Baltinglass. He lost heart when, before its inaugural flight, it was destroyed by fire. He moved to the continent, living free in a house at Leghorn (Livorno) owned by Thomas Holloway, purvey of quack medicines and founder of Royal Holloway College. In return for the manufacturer's hospitality, the Earl gave his name to advertising *Holloway's Pills*. He appeared in newspaper advertisements for the *Pills*, which he claimed had cured him of a disorder of liver and stomach. At one point he appeared in a pantomime, singing in praise of the medicine:

Whoever would be free from earthly ills

Will take, each night and morn, six of these pills.

and dancing at the same time.

Holloway's Pills were not efficacious for the 6th Earl very long. He died at Alicante on 19 December 1875 at the age of 67, intestate and unmarried. He was not interred in the family pyramid at Baltinglass - indeed, it is not clear who was. The interior, with its niches for the coffins, is now completely empty and the door has vanished. It is a glory departed - perhaps a fitting monument for such an extraordinary family.

THE OLD KILBRIDE cemetery at **Arklow** on the Wicklow coast is a spooky place. Local tradition says that at night ghostly wails and hideous groans emanate from its graves. Legend says that someone was once buried alive there. These stories may be a convenient fiction put about by people who did not want their activities in the graveyard examined too closely - it is said that in the 1920s the Black and Tans searched there for IRA weapons (see also Drumkeeran, page 311). Yet even in the daylight the graveyard gives off an air of dank oppression; it feels wise not to linger.

Chief among the monuments in Kilbride is the Wicklow mausoleum - a tall structure, around 20 feet high. It is much more akin to the Egyptian originals than to the Cestius pyramid (see page 2) and rests on a square base about four feet high. The site is attractive - on a wooded eminence, with the Irish Sea in the background. From one face a carved sarcophagus with an inscription protrudes. Below it is an arched opening (now blocked) into the hollow interior and burial chamber. It is a smart piece of work in the local granite, now fully cleaned and restored, at a cost of 28,000 euros, to something like its pristine glory after decades of vandalism.

The spooky Howard pyramid at Arklow, Co Wicklow

The pyramid's architect was Simon Vierpyl, a London sculptor who had trained under the great Peter Scheemakers. He was brought to Ireland in 1756, when he was around 30, by Lord Charlemont (see The Neale, page 317) and his tutor the Rev'd Edward Murphy. They had met in Rome, where Murphy had commissioned Vierpyl to make terracotta copies of statues and busts of Roman emperors in the Capitoline Museum. Vierpyl's architectural experience was very limited, but he did work closely with Sir William Chambers on the Casino at Marino (see page 319) - and certainly the Arklow pyramid is both sculptural and architectural.

The church at Arklow is no longer there, but the pyramid's inscription was put up in memory of one of the people buried inside the now-vanished former structure: 'Within the walls of the adjoining Church lie interred the Remains of M Dorothea Howard otherwise Hafels Relict of John Howard Esq Who Departed this Life at Shelton in December 1684 to Whose Memory and that of their Descendants and as a place of Burial for his Family Ralph Viscount Wicklow has caused this Monument to be Erected in the year of our Lord 1786'.

The Howards of Wicklow are part of the extensive Howard clan that also includes the Dukes of Norfolk as well as the pyramid-building Earls of Carlisle in Yorkshire (see Castle Howard, page 28) and Elizabeth Howard whose pyramid is in Berry Pomeroy in Devon (see page 153). It is possible that the Castle Howard pyramids had an influence on the Arklow mausoleum - it has similarities to the Castle Howard Great Pyramid (confusingly, there is also a Castle Howard in Ireland, owned by a branch of the Wicklow Howards). Already by the late 17th century, however, the different branches of the family were widely separated geographically and probably had little connection with each other. The Irish line was begun by Dorothea Howard, to whom the pyramid is dedicated. She was born Dorothea Hassels and was married in England in the 1630s to John Howard. John died in 1643, aged just 27, and Dorothea moved to Ireland, where she married her cousin Robert Hassels. With her she brought her son, Ralph Howard, who trained as a doctor and became President of the College of Physicians in Ireland in 1674. He married Jane Sotheby and bought the family estate of Shelton Abbey from the Duke of Ormonde in 1697.

Ralph and Jane Howard had three sons and three daughters. The daughters all married well (two to baronets and one to a bishop). The eldest son Hugh was a minor portrait painter, an art collector and artistic adviser (commonly nicknamed 'The Oracle') to the gentry. He died, without heirs, in 1738, worth £40,000. His younger brother, Robert, was left to carry on the line. He rose to become Bishop of Elphin in 1729. The third brother, William, who became an MP, had died two years earlier. Bishop Howard's eldest son Ralph was an MP, too, and an Irish Privy Councillor. In 1776 he was elevated to the Irish peerage as Baron Clonmore; nine years later he became Viscount Wicklow; the Arklow pyramid may have been erected to celebrate this elevation and to mark the family that had brought him to such esteem.

There may be another influence at work in his choice of a pyramid. Viscount Wicklow's family had close links with the Earls of Darnley. In 1766 the Viscount's niece Mary had married John Bligh, the 3rd Earl of Darnley. The Darnley Mausoleum in Kent (see page 62), designed in 1783, was under construction when Lord Wicklow planned his own. The families' ties were strengthened in 1792 when Wicklow's fourth son John married the 1st Earl of Darnley's niece.

The Ist Lord Wicklow enjoyed his eminence for almost exactly four years. On his death in 1789 he was succeeded by his son Robert. Then a curious, though not unique, thing happened. In 1793 Robert's mother, Anne Forward from Castle Forward, the widow of the 1st Viscount, was created a Countess in her own right, as Countess of Wicklow. The 6,000-acre estate she brought to the marriage with Ralph Howard, added to his own 20,000 acres, made the Howards one of the biggest landowners in the east of Ireland. When Anne died in 1807, Robert, 2nd Viscount Wicklow, became 2nd Earl of Wicklow, even though there had never been a 1st Earl. Unmarried, he was followed as Earl by his brother William, then by William's son, William Forward Howard, the 4th Earl.

Then the succession falters. William Forward Howard had seven daughters (who lived in a specially-built wing of the family home, Shelton Abbey, known as 'The Nunnery') but no son. The heir presumptive to the earldom had been his brother the Hon and Rev'd Francis Howard, Vicar of Swords near Dublin - but Francis had died before the earl. The vicar had married twice. A son by his first wife, William George Howard, died in 1864 apparently without children. So when the 4th Earl died in 1869, the Rev'd Francis's only surviving son Charles Howard asserted his right to be 5th Earl of Wicklow. Suddenly, a challenger appeared - claimed to be the infant son of William George Howard. William George had married Ellen Richardson when he was deep in debt and in hiding from bailiffs. In 1864 he was in seclusion in Ireland when Ellen, she claimed, gave birth to a son. If legitimate, the son would have a prior claim to be the 5th Earl.

It was up to the House of Lords to decide to whom the Writ of Peerage should be issued. A trial was held in the House in 1870 to decide between the two claimants. Ellen Howard had given birth without the outside assistance of a midwife or a doctor, so there was no-one except her landlady and her landlady's sister, both her close friends, to testify to the birth. There was also evidence that Ellen had never been pregnant and that around the time of the supposed birth she had visited a workhouse in Liverpool, from where she had taken away a baby. The whole scenario seems to have been arranged by one of the landlady's friends, Mr Buadenave - but he had conveniently disappeared.

The Lord Chancellor and his fellow peers judged firmly in favour of Charles Howard, declaring him rightful Earl of Wicklow. The witnesses for Ellen and her son were, they said, guilty of conspiracy and perjury. The earldom of Wicklow was safe - though it was to last a little more than a century more.

The last of the line was the 8th Earl, William Cecil James Philip John Paul Howard, who became an Anglican clergyman and then converted to Roman Catholicism. He was known to his many friends as Billy. Those friends included the author Evelyn Waugh, who wrote in his diary in 1924 that everything Billy told him about Ireland proved unreliable. Billy was buried at Kilbride cemetery in 1979 - though apparently not in the pyramid.

The very last of the Howards of Wicklow was Lady Katherine Howard, Billy's cousin. In 1979 she set up the Katherine Howard Foundation to help support projects and initiatives in disadvantaged communities. Lady Katherine died in 1990, but the Fund continues its public work - a tradition of service foreshadowed by a long line of her ancestors, many of them entombed in the family pyramid at Arklow, who served as High Sheriffs, Members of Parliament and senior clergy from the 17th century onwards.

'MORE THAN ONCE it has been my lot to witness the tourist on board the Holyhead packet, coming to Ireland for the first time,' wrote the Rev'd Jon O'Rourke in 1902, 'straining his eyes towards the coast, when the rising sun gave a faint blue outline of the Wicklow mountains, and assured him that he had actually and really before him "The Holy Hills of Ireland".' The view of **Killiney** Bay from the sea is still wonderful. Wooded hills, studded with large mansions, fringe the coast. Above them the bulk of Killiney Hill is crowned with a cone known, inaccurately, as The Obelisk, while below it are a smaller cone and the Wishing Steps - a pyramid similar to the Browne monument at The Neale (see page 317).

The view from the summit of Killiney Hill is equally good; 'unrivalled for beauty - the sublime it has not' says O'Rourke. Like Llandudno Bay, it is often compared with the Bay of Naples (though the compliment is seldom reciprocated) and the late-19th-century builders and speculators of the area obviously thought the same, calling their roads Capri, Sorrento, Monte Alverno. It is said that, on a clear day, you can see the Mountains of Mourne and, exceptionally, Snowdonia, far to the east across the Irish Sea. It was certainly a good place to build a landmark, and The Obelisk is certainly that. It is a tall, white-painted cone set on two almost-cubic lower storeys, one with a niche for a bench and the upper one with windows from which to view the bay and the sea.

Like the Famine Wall at Kilcooley (see page 329) it had its origins in Irish poverty. The winter of 1741 to 1742 was exception-

The Mount Mapas cone, known as 'The Obelisk', at Killiney, adjacent to the step pyramid

ally harsh, and there was severe distress. As the inscription on The Obelisk states, 'LAST year being hard with the POOR the walls about these HILLS and THIS erected by JOHN MAPAS Esq. June 1742'. By providing paid employment Mapas helped alleviate the worst effects of the crisis - and it gave him something to show off to his friends. John Mapas seems to have inherited some of his philanthropy from his grandmother, whose will left one shilling to each of the poor on her estate at Rochestown, near Killiney Hill, and from his father, Christopher, a man of 'the most worthy and honest character, and of unknown charity'. The family, originally from Co Louth, were prominent Catholics but managed to retain their estates and their station in life after the Williamite wars.

The small cone on the hillside below The Obelisk was probably also erected by John Mapas - it has a plaque on it saying 'Mount Mapas'. But is the pyramid one of his philanthropic structures, too? It is not clear. On the top cube is a date, 1852. Is this the original date? It seems unlikely - the pyramid was restored in the mid-19th century, when the flight of small steps to the top was added to make the ascent easier. It may well be that the original pyramid was part of Mapas's job creation scheme.

The Obelisk, cone and pyramid were once the private property of the Mapas family and their successors, but in 1887 they, along with the whole estate, were purchased with public funds from Robert Warren, who had earlier repaired The Obelisk and probably provided the pyramid with its extra steps. The land became part of a public park, opened by Prince Albert Victor, to commemorate the Golden Jubilee of his mother Queen Victoria. It was called, inevitably, Victoria Park. After being made accessible to the public, the pyramid acquired its special name - the Wishing Steps. The legend soon developed that if you walk once round each of the six layers of the pyramid, any wish you then make while standing on the top will come true. It is something that residents of the exclusive houses by the Bay (they include singers Bono and Enya) and the Dublin commuters who live in the smart houses of nearby Dalkey may not need to try - they seem to have had their wishes granted already.

Step pyramid at Killiney - the Wishing Steps

FOR MANY HIGH-CLASS young ladies of the early 19th-century throughout the British Isles, their wishes had to remain unfulfilled when the most eligible bachelor of his day met an untimely death at **Ballybrack**, just a mile inland from Killiney.

George John Frederick Sackville, the 4th Duke of Dorset, was in Ireland with his mother, the Dowager Duchess Arabella. With them was the Duchess's second husband, Viscount (later Earl) Whitworth, who was Viceroy of Ireland from 1813 to 1817. George Sackville's father, the 3rd Duke, had died in 1799 when his heir was just five. He had been Lord Lieutenant of Ireland and British Ambassador to France, but seems to have been more interested in cricket. A contemporary poem describes him:

> He firmly stands with bat upright
> And strikes with his athletic might.
> Sends forth the ball across the mead,
> And scores six notches for the deed.

He made cricketing history when his 77 for Kent against Hambledon in 1774 was part of the first-recorded 100 partnership, and he very nearly led the first English team to tour abroad. Unfortunately it only got as far as Dover; he had chosen to take his players to France in 1789.

The 3rd Duke's widow, Arabella, was the stepdaughter of the Earl of Liverpool. She brought £140,000 to her marriage. She devoted herself to caring for the Duke's estates, especially at Knole in Kent, during his long last illness. Left with a small child, on her remarriage she continued to run the ducal estates for young George until he came of age on 15 November 1814. Less than three months after the celebrations, he was dead.

His life had been one of great promise. He was at Harrow at the same time as Lord Byron. Byron's poem of 1805 (when the Duke was just 12) called *To the Duke of Dorset* warns him against pride in his rank ('let not this seduce thy soul') but foretells great things:

> A glorious and a long career pursue,
> As first in Rank, the first in Talent too . . .
> The Guardian Seraph who directs thy fate
> Will leave thee glorious, as he found thee great.

From Harrow, the young Duke went to Christ Church College, Oxford, but his academic career was cut short by the loss of an eye after an accident in a game of real tennis. It was not long after this that he went to Ireland with his mother to join his stepfather. On 14 February 1815 George went out hunting on the heath with Viscount Whitworth and with Viscount Powerscourt, who was four years older than the Duke. All went well until they came to a wall. Dorset was in the lead and urged his horse over; what he did not know was that there was a steep drop on the other side. He plunged over, landing on his chest. He died from his injuries, 'preserving his ducal dignity to the end'. It was said that, had he lived, he would have succeeded his stepfather as Viceroy.

The spot where the Duke died, below the wall over which he urged his horse in his final act, was marked soon afterwards by a pyramidal monument to his memory. It is now in the grounds of St Columba's Marianist Community in Church Avenue in Ballybrack. The very worn inscription reads

> THIS PILE WAS RAISED
> TO MARK THE FATAL SPOT
> WHERE AT THE AGE OF 21
> GEORGE JOHN FREDERICK
> The 4th Duke of Dorset
> Accidentally lost his life
> 14th Febry 1813

The spot where the 21-year-old 4th Duke of Dorset died is marked by a pyramid at Ballybrack

The date is incorrect - the accident happened in 1815, but, as another plaque on the rear of the pyramid, hemmed in by the hillside and dank bushes, says, 'The inscription on this monument was recut in 1905 by his kinswoman Olivia, wife of Lord Ardilaun.' Olivia was the wife of Sir Arthur Guinness, 2nd baronet and the first (and last) Lord Ardilaun. Born Olivia Hedges-White, she traced her kinship to the young Duke of Dorset's great-grandmother, who was a member of the Hedges family. Olivia (or her stonemason) must have misread the original inscription.

In form, the monument is one of the pyramid-cum-obelisk structures, like that at Desertcreat (see page 306). As often, there may have been Masonic influences at work here - the 2nd Duke of Dorset was certainly a Mason: in 1733, during his Grand Tour, he founded the English Lodge in Florence. He also picked up an opera singer there as his mistress, and later promoted a season of Italian opera in London as a showcase for her (apparently meagre) talents. The 2nd Duke's brother was Grand Master of the Irish Masonic Lodge from 1751.

Our visit to the Marianist Community at Ballybrack was assisted by Brother Fred Rech SM and Father Michael Reaume SM, who were keen to tell us the story of the Duke. Their house was once the Powerscourt family's hunting lodge; next door was Dorset Lodge. It was easy to imagine the distress in the two houses as the body of the young Duke was carried back to his home. His mother, the Dowager Duchess, would be grief-stricken - we know that Lord Whitworth, her husband, took three months' leave of absence to accompany her and the Duke's body back to the family estate at Knole.

There are two curious literary footnotes to the 4th Duke's death. The long direct male descent of the Sackville family ended with him; Knole and most of the estates went to his two sisters. Only the younger sister had children; she married Earl de la Warr, who changed his family name to Sackville. This change of descent from the male to the female lane, it has been suggested, gave Virginia Wolfe the idea for the change of sex of the long-lived protagonist of her novel *Orlando*; Orlando starts as a man in the reign of Elizabeth I and finishes as a young woman in the 1920s. Virginia Wolfe was lover of Vita Sackville-West, a member of Duke of Dorset's family,

The other bookish footnote is from a few years earlier. In Max Beerbohm's 1911 novel *Zuleika Dobson* he chose the title Duke of Dorset for his main male character - an extremely eligible bachelor who leads the undergraduates of Oxford in their devotion to the pulchritudinous Miss Dobson. He is the paragon of aristocracy - handsome, generous, immensely rich and extremely clever. 'At Eton he had been called "Peacock," and this nick-name had followed him up to Oxford. It was not wholly apposite, however. For, whereas the peacock is a fool even among birds, the Duke had already taken (besides a particularly brilliant First in Mods) the Stanhope, the Newdigate, the Lothian, and the Gaisford Prize for Greek Verse.' He is on his way to 'a particularly brilliant First in the schools'. He is a prince of the Holy Roman Empire and a Knight of the Garter (an honour given to him after an outstanding off-the-cuff speech in the House of Lords). Yet the life of this Duke of Dorset ('the 14th'), like that of the real 4th Duke, comes to an abrupt end. He drowns himself for love of Zuleika in the River Isis, in his Garter robes: 'Full on the river lay the mantle outspread. Then it, too, went under. A great roll of water marked the spot. The plumed hat floated.' Beerbohm does not take us beyond the 14th Duke's watery grave; perhaps, like the 4th Duke's, his short life is commemorated somewhere by a granite pyramid.

LARCH HILL, ON the edge of the Dublin mountains just south of the city's peripheral motorway, was where the first European larch trees were planted in Ireland. The grand mansion on the site was built in the late 18th century for an Irish Judge, known as Counsellor Calbeck. He once remarked in court that although he had to sentence a bigamist to seven years' transportation, 'If I had my own will, I would certainly give you a more severe fate - I would sentence you to seven years imprisonment in the same house with your two wives.' Larch Hill was later owned by a succession of wealthy businessmen until in 1907 it became a military sanatorium, which closed in 1920. It was bought by an American, who lived there with his mother until the mid 1930s; he sold it to a bookmaker, John Coffey, whose rocky financial affairs led to the estate's being taken by his bank.

The headquarters of Scouting Ireland at Larch Hill south of Dublin

So Larch Hill was on the market in 1937 - just as the Chief Scout of Ireland, Professor Wheelan, was leading the search for a national campsite for the Irish Scouts. It was then Wheelan's casting vote as chairman of Catholic Scouting Ireland's National Executive that chose Larch Hill over the other front runner, Santry Demesne, north of Dublin. The Scouts paid £3,500 for the 88-acre estate, and the site was officially opened with an appropriately-outdoor Mass on 4 June 1938. Since then Larch Hill has played an important role both in hosting scouts from all over the world and in training scout leaders.

Until the mid-1970s the original Larch Hill House was used for both accommodation and office space, but in 1972 the scouts had a hostel built and the old mansion was demolished. By the 1990s, though, it became obvious that the Irish Scouts needed a proper headquarters building. They commissioned Paul Martin of architects Collins Maher Martin of Dublin to come up with a design. He was the obvious choice as architect, having been an International Commissioner for the Scouts. The design he produced is an impressive slate and glass pyramid that stands on the site of the former house. Its shape is designed to reflect the shape of the mountains, as well as that mainstay of scouting, a tent - the laminated wood frames that protrude below the slate cladding are like a series of guy ropes holding the structure steady against the wind.

The pyramid was built between 2000 and 2002; the Scouts newsletter reported 'Special precautions will be put in place during the construction process to keep Beavers, Cubs and Scouts out of the construction area' - a wise move, as scouts are trained to be adventurous. As well as offices, the new building contains a multi-purpose hall called, inevitably, the Millennium Room. There is also a museum full of scout badges and mementos of World Scout Jamborees. Pride of place in the new building goes to a bust of the founder and first National Secretary of the Catholic Boy Scouts of Ireland, Father Tom Farrell. Fr. Tom, 'a boy at heart', began the organisation in November 1926. He was then a curate at Dublin's Pro-Cathedral, and by all accounts a wonderfully-approachable man. He was greatly missed when he died in 1940.

Fr Tom's legacy lives on at Larch Hill in the many scouts who attend camps and courses there. But they were by no means the first to use the site for outdoor purposes. Not far from the pyramid are the remains of a prehistoric portal tomb, made of large slabs of granite that may have been dislodged in the 1800s during a local earthquake. And, more recently, bookmaker John Coffey reputedly buried his racehorse *Fast Pam* in the grounds - somewhere near the campfire circle where today's scouts cook their sausages.

NAAS IS UNIQUE. Nowhere else in the British Isles are there two large pyramids in such close proximity. They are little-documented. We came across a reference to them first in Section 2.9 of Naas Town Council's 1999 *Development Plan*; objective CE8 aims to 'preserve the Church of Ireland cemetery and extension on the Dublin Road including the surrounding wall, caretaker's cottage and two pyramid tombs.' We could find no further information, so when we arrived in Naas we went to the Dublin Road cemetery that was marked on the street plan. There were no pyramids there. Someone tending a grave suggested we try the 'old' cemetery on the opposite side of the road, a little further out of the town. This turned out to be the now-disused Maudlins cemetery; inside are two 25-foot stone pyramids to members of the Burgh family.

Delving into the history of the Burghs is fraught with difficulty - the family spread so widely and under so many different variations of the Burgh name that it is like trying to trace the spores of the world's largest organism, the giant fungus of Oregon. The Burghs can trace their origins back to the Emperor Charlemagne, and to Baldwin de Burgh, King of Jerusalem in the 12th century. Odo, Bishop of Bayeux, who commissioned the Tapestry, was an ancestor. One of the most enduring of the Burgh first names, Walter, entered the family in the second half of the 13th century with Walter, Earl of Ulster, father of Richard, 'The Red Earl'. The Red Earl's son John married Elizabeth de Clare, founder of Clare College in Cambridge. Over the centuries the different branches of the de Burghs multiplied and so did the family name, mutating into Bourke and Burke - statesman Edmund Burke was a family member, as were the founder of Burke's Peerage and former Irish President Mary Robinson; it is even possible that the body snatcher and murderer William Burke, confederate of Hare, was a scion of the house.

The Burghs to whom the twin pyramids of Naas were erected are part of the branch that settled at the Oldtown demesne on the western edge of Naas in the early 18th century. Thomas Burgh of

Twin peaks - the two pyramids in the disused Maudlins cemetery in Naas, Co Kildare

Oldtown, born in 1670, was one of Ireland's greatest military engineers and a fine architect. As Surveyor-General for Ireland he was responsible for designing the finest room in Ireland, the Long Room of his library (now the Old Library) at Trinity College in Dublin, where the Book of Kells is kept. Thomas bought the Oldtown estate, where he built one of Ireland's earliest Palladian villas. Both he and his son, also Thomas, were MPs for Naas; three generations later another Thomas applied in 1844 to the Chief Herald of Ireland to change the family name by restoring the 'de'.

Since then, one branch of the family has been 'de Burgh' - a name adopted by one of the family's most celebrated sons, singer Chris de Burgh (whose mother was a de Burgh; he took her name professionally). Chris de Burgh's daughter also has a claim to fame - as Miss World 2003.

Surveyor-General Burgh had a daughter, Elizabeth. She married Ignatius Hussey of Donore, three miles north-west of Naas. Ignatius seems to have been a bit of a lad in his youth - in 1709 he appeared as a defendant in a court case in England. Richard Gomeldon Esq claimed that Hussey (described as 'Gentleman') and Patrick Segrave (significantly not a gentleman), while they were all drunk together, conspired to defraud him in a game of Passage - a game with three dice where the aim is to throw a double over ten. Marriage to Elizabeth seems to have steadied Ignatius - or perhaps it was the influence of her father, who seems to have insisted that Ignatius added Burgh to his name on marriage. It may, though, have been their son Walter Hussey Burgh who added the name, when he inherited property from one of the Burghs of Drumkeen. This Walter married into another branch of the Burgh family - his wife was his cousin Anne Burgh of Bert House, north of Athy.

Walter Hussey Burgh inherited his grandfather's strength of character. Called to the Irish Bar in 1769 - the same year as he was elected MP for Athy - he rapidly became both one of the country's top advocates and a prominent politician. He was a member of the 'Monks of the Screw', a club that was 'partly political and partly convivial' and had links to Freemasonry. A passionate free-trader, he was for a time leader of the government party in the Irish House of Commons, but resigned when the government showed no signs of accepting Irish free trade. His most famous speech, made in November 1779, included the words, 'Talk not to me of peace; Ireland is not in a state of peace; it is mothered in war. England has sown her laws like dragon's teeth, and they have sprung up as armed men.' The Marquess of Wellesley rated Burgh's oratory as being superior to that of Pitt, Fox or Burke. He was known as 'Silver-tongued Burgh.' In 1783 Walter Hussey Burgh was appointed Chief Baron of the Exchequer, and the writ was made out for his ennoblement as Baron Brittas and Earl of Castleconnell. But before he took his seat in the Irish House of Lords, he was struck down by jail fever, a form of typhus, which he caught while inspecting Armagh prison. He died just 40 years old. A versifier of the time wrote:

> With sublime Burgh sweet Nature's voice lies dead,
> With his expression's softest tones have fled;
> Persuasive sensibility must mourn,
> Whilst heavenly language weeps around his urn;
> Harmonious speech and every charm of sense
> Laments the music of his eloquence.

Walter was succeeded at Donore (where he had built a new brick mansion) by his son the Rev'd John Hussey Burgh - who followed family tradition by marrying another Burgh, his cousin Mary, also from Bert House. One of the Rev'd John's proudest claims was that his wife, mother, grandmother and great-grandmother were all Burghs. John and Mary's son Walter Hussey Burgh could claim another generation on top of his father's boast. This Walter, who died in 1862, was High Sheriff of Co Kildare in 1839, and seems to have sold off most of the Burgh property in Co Kildare and Co Clare, though he held on to Donore. And, hacking through the undergrowth of Burghs, we at last get to the Naas pyramids.

The anonymous pyramid at Naas

Of the two pyramids, only one has an inscription. It is not obvious - it is hidden away round the back, visible only from a narrow strip of land between the pyramid and the cemetery wall. From it we know that it was built 'To the memory of Elizabeth Jane Hussey Burgh, otherwise Fitzgerald'. Elizabeth Jane Fitzgerald of Shepperton, Co Clare, married Walter Hussey Burgh as his first wife, and had borne him, as her inscription says, 'one son and seven infant daughters to mourn their irreparable loss' when she died on 7 February 1834, aged just 33. She was obviously unwell before her death - the inscription says 'Approaching dissolution held no terrors for her, who died in the blessed hope of eternal life'. She was, of course, 'eminently distinguished by unaffected humility, exemplary piety and Christian charity'. The pyramid was erected by her husband, '(who best knew her worth and revered her virtues) as a monument to her departed worth and as a resting place for himself and family in future'. Walter Hussey Burgh goes on to describe himself proudly as 'grandson to the late celebrated patriot Walter Hussey Burgh, Lord Chief Baron of His Majesty's Court of Exchequer in Ireland and member of the Irish House of Commons for Trinity College Dublin.'

The Burgh coat of arms (said to have been designed by Richard the Lionheart, who drew a cross with the blood of a Saracen on a shield, saying 'These, knight, be thine arms for ever') are carved in a panel on the front of the pyramid, above the sealed iron door. So it is clear to whom this pyramid belonged. But whose was the other? There is no visible inscription, and the panel on the front is bare. Yet the two pyramids are very similar, and of a typical design of the Irish midlands - instead of being constructed of courses of rectangular ashlar blocks, the edges of the pyramid are 'tumbled-in'. This elaborate and laborious process is also seen in the pyramids at Castlerickard (see page 358) and at Kinnity (see page 351). The interiors of the pyramids are of brick, visible through the rusted doors of the second.

So who is commemorated by the second Naas pyramid? Was it another Burgh? If so, why a new pyramid? Or was it a friend or neighbour, emulating the Burghs? Unless further evidence turns up, we may never know. On our two visits to Maudlins cemetery, several years after the promulgation of the Naas Council Development Plan, nothing seemed to have been done to care for the pyramids; they are becoming overgrown with ivy and some of the stones are loose. They need conserving - especially as the Burgh's house at Donore, sold by the younger Walter Hussey Burgh, is now a ruin and the Oldtown demesne, seat of the parallel branch, was sold in 1999. After an attempt to make it into a public park, it is now disappearing under housing as Naas expands rapidly, thanks to its recent motorway link to Dublin. These distinctive twin pyramids are the only surviving Burgh link with Naas.

'THERE IS APPARENTLY,' we were told by a correspondent, 'a rather fine example, built of granite, in the grounds of **Gilltown** House (near Kilcullen), former home of the Borrowes family. This is now a stud owned by the Aga Khan and . . . a difficult place to get into.' This did not sound encouraging, but a pyramid we had not previously come across was worth investigating. In the end, it proved very easy - a phone call to the Stud and an arrangement to meet the very helpful Stud Groom, John Garrett. He picked us up at the entrance in his Land Rover and drove us through the immaculate grounds. We passed a life-size

The arms of the Burgh family from one of the Naas pyramids

The Borrowes mausoleum at Gillown near Kilcullen is now on the Aga Khan's stud

statue of the Aga Khan's famous but ill-fated horse Shergar, Derby-winner and victim of kidnap and slaughter, probably by the IRA. Eventually we drove across open fields to the wooded enclosure that holds the pyramid.

Of genuine Egyptian shape, it stands on a low base and has a sunken doorway with appropriately-sloping sides. There is no exterior inscription, but there is a coat of arms carved into the granite - and it is similar to the one on Elizabeth Jane Hussey Burgh's pyramid at Naas (see page 343). The golden shield with a red cross is differenced here with five silver stars and a golden lion on a red square in the top corner - the colours are shown by conventional heraldic hatching.

The pyramid is a mausoleum for the Borrowes (sometimes Burrowes) family - and the Borrowes are yet another part of the huge Burgh clan, Burgh in this case transmogrifying to Borough and thence to Borrowes. The Borrowes were baronets from Gilltown. Their ancestor Henry Borrowes, a lineal descendant of the medieval de Burghs, came to Ireland from Devon in the mid-16th century, and by the end of the century he owned the Gilltown estate. It was his son Erasmus (named after his grandfather) who was created 1st Baronet. The honour was badgered out of Charles I in 1645 by Erasmus. He claimed that with unrest in Ireland in the early 1640s he had lost most of his income from his farms and from his property. He said his income was £1,200 but his debts were £11,932 2s. King Charles may have given out the baronetcy to shut him up, though the baronetcy patent, delivered in February 1646, diplomatically says it is 'for his many good and faithful services in this Kingdom both in War and Peace'.

Sir Erasmus had one surviving son, Sir Walter, who married Lady Eleanor Fitzgerald, a daughter of the Earl of Kildare. So the third of the trio of names by which future baronets were known - Erasmus, Walter and Kildare - was set. Walter's son, Sir Kildare, married a Dixon, so that name was tagged on, too. Sir Kildare's grandson, Sir Kildare Dixon Borrowes, was the 5th baronet, and it seems to have been him or his son Erasmus, 6th baronet, who built the pyramid. Because the structure was broken into and vandalised in the 1970s there is no complete record of who was interred there; all we have are three small plaques. They are to Robert Burrowes, who died in June 1850 and his wife Charlotte who died seven years later. With them was the Honourable Louisa Katherine Borrowes, who died in 1877.

Robert Borrowes was the 5th baronet's sixth son. He married Charlotte just before Christmas 1804; she was a Madden from Co Monaghan. Her ancestors included 'Premium' Madden, a writer whose forward-looking *Memoir of the Twentieth Century* was published in 1728. It was so controversial that nearly all the 1000 copies were pulped on government orders - only five are known to have survived. 'Premium' gained his nickname from prizes awarded to students at Trinity College, Dublin. Charlotte's father Samuel was of a different cut. He gambled away most of the family's fortune, and contrived to burn down the family home, Hilton Park, in 1803, the year before Charlotte's marriage; she was probably glad to move to Gilltown.

Louisa Katherine Borrowes was Robert and Charlotte's daughter-in-law. She married their only son, Robert Higginson Borrowes. Louisa was a Browne, great-granddaughter of John, 1st Baron Kilmaine, who built the pyramid at The Neale (see page 317). There is another interesting pyramidal link between the Borrowes and a landed Irish family. Robert Borrowes (Louisa's father-in-law) had an elder brother, William. He was a banker, in partnership with Stratford Canning (see Garvagh, page 304). Stratford Canning brought up the future Prime Minister George Canning, and when Stratford died in 1787 Robert Borrowes was named as the legal guardian of George, then just 17. It was George's cousin, the 1st Baron Garvagh, who built the pyramid at the town that gave him his title. There may be other links, too, especially through Freemasonry - successive Borrowes baronets were particularly involved in their local and national Lodges.

It is possible that the pyramid was not built by Sir Kildare Dixon Borrowes, 5th Baronet, but by Robert Higginson Borrowes, who had a new house at Gilltown built for him to designs by the Scottish architect David Bryce. As well as country houses, Bryce also designed Edinburgh's Fettes College and Bank of Scotland buildings. If Robert was the patron of the pyramid, it may be an as-yet-unrecognised work by Bryce. If it is, it has fared better than Gilltown House, which was burned down by Irish rebels in the years before World War I. The main branch of the Borrowes had usually lived not at Gilltown but at another family residence, Barretstown Castle at Ballymore Eustace.

The last Kildare Dixon Borrowes - 10th Baronet - had no children and when he died in 1924 he was succeeded by his brother Eustace. No one followed Eustace - his son Kildare Henry Borrowes had died in the Battle of Jutland on 31 May 1916, serving as a midshipman on HMS *Queen Mary*. He was just 16. The only other possible heir was already dead. He was Eustace's half-brother Walter; he had drowned in a submarine on 23 January 1915.

MUCH OF THE rock underlying the Irish midlands is limestone. Around 370 million years ago the British Isles were part of a great landmass just north of the equator. Here, for around 45 million years, tiny sea creatures, mostly crinoids, lived and died. Their shells sank to the seabed and were covered with clay and sand. In the slowly-grinding aeons of geological time, the crinoidal mud compacted to form limestone as the landmass drifted north.

The Irish blue limestone is some of the most prized, and one of the main centres for its working is around the town of **Stradbally** in Co Laois, where McKeon Stone's eight-acre site is full of skilled men who have years of experience in working the stone. When Laois County Council organised a sculpture symposium in 1994 to promote public art in the county, they went to McKeon's for sponsorship. An open competition was held for the first pieces of modern sculpture to find a permanent home in the county as part of the Laois Sculpture Trail.

McKeon Stone donated blue limestone and six artists were chosen. They included Dave Lambert, who was commissioned for a work in Stradbally itself. His *Lost* consists of a curved bench, a shallow font-like bowl - and a pyramid. It stands in Stradbally's Court House Square, just off the wide main street. Its setting is very similar to the pyramid at Boyne Crescent in Cork (see page 327), on a grassed area surrounded by young trees. It is considerably smaller than the photographs suggest. The pyramid is not much more than six feet high, and between the bench and the bowl there is barely room to squeeze a pair of junior-sized knees.

Still, it is an attractive work - and is obviously a place where the young people of the town congregate. There was a plastic drink bottle floating in the shallow pool, and evidence of snacks being consumed around it. The pyramid is in two parts, separated by a narrow space, and the two parts are of slightly different heights. It is the texture and colour of the stone that makes an impression. The limestone has a definite blue cast and the texture given by the tiny sea creatures is clear. Dave Lambert has sculpted circles of different sizes into the rock's surface. They give it an ancient, weathered look, as if primitive man had carved cup-and-ring marks on it thousands of years ago. The edges of the pyramid are criss-crossed with chisel marks. The limestone's adamantine strength gives the three pieces of the sculpture - pyramid, bowl and bench - a sense of unchanging permanence. They are a good advertisement for the local area's industry and an attractive work of art - thanks to the death of the millions of microscopic inhabitants of tropical seas so many millennia ago.

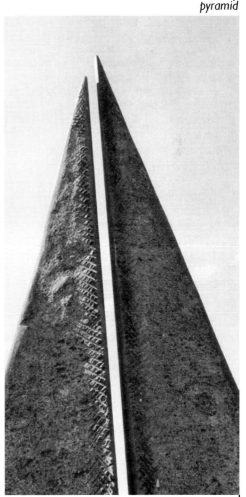

*The Bernards'
pyramid
mausoleum at
Kinnitty, Co Offaly,
was designed by
Lt Col Richard
Wellesley Bernard*

DRUIDS ONCE GATHERED at the foot of Knocknamon, the conical hill that looms over the village of **Kinnitty** on the western fringe of the attractive Slieve Bloom Mountains. Beltane fires were lit on the summit of Knocknamon. According to some sources, Kinnitty is built at an intersection of important leylines. No wonder, then, that in AD 557 St Finan Cam from Munster was instructed by his master St Brendan to found a monastery at Kinnitty as a Christian counterblast to paganism. Finan set up a high cross at Kinnitty. Its 11-foot-high, 10th-century successor still exists, carved with the crucifixion and Adam and Eve, as well as with stylised birds.

The cross stands in the grounds of Kinnitty Castle Hotel. The Castle dates from only 1928 - it was built after its predecessor was burned down by Irish Republicans in 1922. Its new form mirrors the old, which was constructed in 1811 to designs by John and George Richard Pain, English pupils of John Nash. The old house was commissioned by Lady Catherine Henrietta Bernard. She was the daughter of the 3rd Earl of Donoughmore, and the wife of Colonel Thomas Bernard. In Lady Catherine's day Kinnitty Castle was called Castle Bernard - a name it had had since the Bernard family bought it from the Winters in the 1760s. Catherine Bernard's elder sister Anna Louisa had married the Very Rev'd Thomas John de Burgh of Oldtown in Naas. The twin pyramids at Naas (see page 343) may have inspired the pyramid in Kinnitty - or they may have been influenced by it.

The Kinnitty pyramid is, along with Arklow (see page 334), the most famous of the Irish pyramids. Indeed, it is frequently but wrongly described as 'the only one of its kind in Ireland'. It was constructed by Lt Col Richard Wellesley Bernard, brother of Col Thomas. The Wellesley name suggests an earlier alliance with the family that later included the Duke of Wellington. Richard Bernard, who trained as an architect and engineer, had a military career. He was one of many Irish officers who served the Emperors of Austria in the Imperial Austrian Army. He later served with the British Army in the Crimea - his wife Ellen was the widow of a fellow officer killed at Sevastopol - then in the King's County Rifles. Like his brother Thomas he also worked for some of the Viceroys of Ireland. More importantly, though, he saw service in Egypt and seems to have been impressed by the pyramids.

On his return to Castle Bernard, therefore, he set about constructing his family's 30-foot-high mausoleum in pyramidal form. Work began in 1830 and was completed in 1834 - the same year that Elizabeth Jane Hussey Burgh was buried in one of the Naas pyramids. Its form is very similar to them, with the ashlar blocks laid in diagonal courses. Did the Burghs ask Richard Bernard to design their pyramids? Or did one family copy from the other? The Kinnitty pyramid has a pointed, gothic arch, not a straight-headed doorway, as its opening, but it is supplied with iron doors like the Naas pyramids. Scored on to the doors are more diagonal lines, continuing the angle of the mortar joints of the structure.

The pyramid is sealed, but we know there are steps down from the door to the burial chamber, eight feet below ground level. There are six burials recorded; the first was Margaret, sister to Col Thomas and Lt Col Richard Bernard, who died in 1842. She was followed by Col Thomas himself in the following year, and by Thomas's wife Lady Catherine, in 1844. Other burials were Col Thomas's and Lady Catherine's nephew Thomas Scrope Wellesley Bernard, who died in 1882 and Ellen Georgina, wife of Richard,

The iron doors that lead to the interior of the pyramid at Kinnitty

the pyramid's builder, in 1907. By then Castle Bernard was occupied by Thomas Scrope Wellesley Bernard's sister Marguerite Adeline and her husband Capt Caulfield French. They died in successive months in 1910. The estate then went to Thomas SW Bernard's four daughters. After the Castle's fiery destruction and subsequent restoration, it was sold to Arthur George Marcus Douglas de la Poer Beresford, 6th Baron Lord Decies, who in turn sold it to the Irish state in 1951. After many years as an operating base of the Forestry Department, it became an hotel in 1994.

The sixth occupant of the pyramid is Major Scrope Bernard, who died in 1857 - the Scrope name came from the Irish branch of an old Yorkshire family. Scrope was a younger son of Col Thomas and Lady Catherine Bernard - and thus a nephew of the Earl of Donoughmore. The governess to the Earl's family suddenly announced to them that she was in fact the Duchess Caramonte Manfredonice, a member of the Sicilian aristocracy. She told them the secret of why she had had to flee her fine home on the Italian island and find menial employment in Co Tipperary. Instead of laughing her out of court, the Earl and his family accepted her story. She was given special apartments in their house, Knocklofty near Clonmel, and she was looked on as at least the Earl's equal. Along came Scrope Bernard, who was smitten by her (or by her exalted position - it seems she was very plain) and married her. Inevitably, she turned out to be a fake, and once unmasked rapidly removed herself from King's County, with at least some of Scrope Bernard's property.

LOOK AT **LOUGH Boora** in Co Offaly on the Irish Ordnance Survey's Discovery Series map 54 and it does not seem a promising area. Just a few miles north of the hill-surrounded Kinnity (see page 351), the landscape could not be more different. The map shows no contours, just many square miles of flat land, crossed with 'industrial railway' lines. This is peat country, where the Bord na Móna - the Irish Peat Board - has dug and milled peat commercially since 1946. The Bord's work was not the first time peat had been dug on the site. Systematic cutting began a century earlier, when local man Kieran Farrelly stripped layers and dried the peat, which he then sold to the British Army as bedding for the horses; it was first used in the Crimea. This prosperous business lasted until 1903, when the factory was flooded and forced to close. The area was drained and a peat-fuelled power station - the forerunner of the modern ones - was set up to drive peat-cutting machines. The peat that wasn't used to fuel the power station was shipped along the Grand Canal for sale in Dublin.

Bord na Móna owns altogether around 80,000 hectares - almost 200,000 acres - of Irish bog-land that has already had its peat extracted and is now out of commercial production. The problem of what to do with this so-called 'cutaway' land has been hard to address; some areas have been planted with trees, and others left to nature to colonise with low-level plants and scrub. At Lough Boora, though, a number of Bord workers got together to form the Lough Boora Parklands Group, whose aim was to find environmentally-sustainable ways of using the cutaway land. They have developed angling, bird-watching and walking areas, and places to relax and watch the world go by.

Eileen MacDonough's step pyramid at Lough Boora, Co Offaly

And, as in many areas in Ireland, they have developed a liking for public sculpture. In 2002 there was a Lough Boora International Sculpture Symposium, which brought seven Irish and international artists to Lough Boora. They created eight sculptures for specific sites. Among them was Irish sculptor Eileen MacDonough, whose work is a step pyramid 18 feet high with sides 24 feet long. It is made of stones that were exposed by the removal of the blanket bog, and is put together without mortar. Working with Belgian artist Marc Wouters (and with the help of a JCB), Eileen MacDonough completed the pyramid within 21 days. She has written that 'The pyramid is one of the most stable structures and has resonance with previous times and cultures' - even, perhaps, with the other Irish step pyramids at The Neale (see page 317) and Killiney (see page 337).

Most of Co Sligo-born MacDonough's work is on a large scale, and she has a fascination with geometry. As well as the pyramid, she has sculpted large spheres, triangles and icosahedrons. She has public sculpture throughout Ireland, including at Dublin, Cork, Waterford, Limerick and Tullamore, as well as in Tokyo and in India. She was a founder-member of the Sculptors' Society of Ireland, like Michael Bulfin, sculptor of the pyramid at Ballydehob (see page 323) who also has work at Lough Boora.

The Lough Boora pyramid sits close to the Boora Lake amidst grassland. It is monumental in its simplicity. The varied colours of the long-buried stones provide a changing kaleidoscope in the rapidly-passing weather. On our visit there was an addition to Eileen MacDonough's work - on the top stone were three (empty) Polish beer bottles. From the summit it is possible to see many of the other sculptures that now have a place at Lough Boora, including Michael Bulfin's *Sky Train*, developed from old peat-cutting transport; *Tree in a Sculpture* by Japanese sculptor Naomi Seki; *Lough Boora Triangle* by Jorn Ronnau from Denmark and *60 Degrees* by Irishman Kevin O'Dwyer.

The efforts of the Lough Boora Parklands promoters are beginning to pay off, and there are more and more visitors to the site - an encouraging sign as Bord na Móna is looking to the area as a possible model for work at the rest of its huge cutaway estate. Yet it is unlikely that this rather desolate, windswept landscape will ever attract huge numbers - even with the fascination of a varied collection of modern sculptures to explore.

The Malone mausoleum and Kilbixy Church, Co Westmeath (see also page 302)

THE MALONE MAUSOLEUM at **Kilbixy** is Ireland's best example of a pyramid-topped burial vault. It was probably influenced by James Wyatt's 1783 Darnley Mausoleum at Cobham in Kent (see page 62). The Kilbixy mausoleum, though, is much plainer and more severely-Grecian in style. An 18-foot-square cube of local limestone has sheer walls on two sides, relieved only by simple pilasters. Affixed to the west side is a cast-metal achievement of arms. On the east side is a recess for the tall entrance doors, which are flanked by two fluted Doric columns. Above the simple entablature the pilasters are extended into cubes at each corner, with three rising steps between them - and above soars an elegant pyramid.

We do not know the name of the designer of the mausoleum and its adjoining, cardboard-gothick church. Nor do we have a precise date. Although the earliest of the Malone family to be interred in the vault died in 1776, it is hardly likely to be so early; the church was built in 1798, and sometime between then and around 1820 is more likely. There are at least four family members in the mausoleum. Their burial vault is below ground level, while on the entrance level the space is flanked by three recessed niches, each containing a black marble sarcophagus. Above is an impressive cross-vault supporting the pyramid.

It is most likely that the mausoleum was built for Richard Malone. It is his coat of arms on the building, and his date of death - 1816 - would fit with the style. Of all the family, Richard was the most closely connected with Kilbixy. He had the present church built, on the site of what in the Middle Ages was a thriving town. Richard is one of four Malones beneath the pyramid. He trained as a lawyer at the Inner Temple in London, and practised at the Irish Bar until 1776 when he inherited the wealth of his uncle, Anthony Malone. Richard was the Member of Parliament for Banagher in the Irish House of Commons from 1783 to 1785, when he was elevated to the House of Lords as Baron Sunderlin. His title comes from the name of a lough a few miles south of Kilbixy and his nearby seat of Baronstown.

Lord and Lady Sunderlin were part of the fashionable social circle both in Ireland and in the north of England. They had a house on the shores of Derwentwater in the Lake District. There they knew the Wordsworths and Southey. In a letter from Keswick in 1815 Southey described a great bonfire on the summit of Skiddaw to celebrate victory at Waterloo; 'The weather served for our bonfire, and never, I believe, was such an assemblage upon such a spot. To my utter astonishment, Lord Sunderlin rode up, and Lady S, who had endeavoured to dissuade me from going as a thing too dangerous, joined the walking party. Wordsworth, with his wife, sister and eldest boy, came over on purpose. James Boswell arrived that morning at the Sunderlins . . .' Coleridge, who was also on Skiddaw for the celebrations, wrote to an acquaintance, 'Have you heard, my dear Sir, of the rejoicings we have had on top of our great mountain Skiddaw . . . Wordsworth & Southey & their families ascended, besides a very large party of ladies & gentlemen among whom were Lord and Lady Sunderlin, the former seventy-six & the latter upwards of sixty years old.'

Lord and Lady Sunderlin had no heir, and the title became extinct when he was entombed in the mausoleum in 1817. Alongside him was the man whose fortune had enabled him to live so pleasant a life, his uncle Anthony Malone. Anthony was a lawyer and an Irish parliamentarian. Early in his legal practice he was already earning around £3,000 a year; his oratory in court served him well in the House of Commons, too; he was described as 'a man of the finest intellect that any country ever produced'. The Bishop of Armagh said Malone was 'the most considerable Man here, and the most usefull to the Government . . . the most independent and the least importunate of Favours'. His independence sometimes caused him to be out of favour with the Viceroys of Ireland, but such was his integrity that he was appointed Chancellor of the Exchequer for Ireland from 1757 to 1761. This was despite his being a partner in a short-lived bank, Malone, Clements and Gore, which opened for business in July 1758 and collapsed in November the same year. Malone continued in parliament until his death in Dublin in 1776. He was a friend of Samuel Johnson, and he probably commissioned the portrait of the Doctor by Sir Joshua Reynolds that was bequeathed to his younger nephew Edmond. The bulk of his estates were left in his will to his other nephew Richard, 'in the utmost confidence that they will be settled and continue in the male line of the family and branches of it, according to priority of birth and seniority of age'. His confidence was ill-founded; when Richard, Lord Sunderlin, died childless the succession became a source of heated dispute in the family.

Of the remaining two Malones in the Kilbixy mausoleum, both were called Edmond. The elder was the brother of Anthony Malone and like him a barrister and politician. His career seems to have been the epitome of what was expected for a well-brought-up gentleman in late 18th-century Ireland; he had a good private law practice, was MP in the Irish House for Askeaton in Co Limerick and then for Granard, Co Longford. On the death of his wife he went back to London, where he had read for the Bar, and served as a judge in the Court of Common Pleas and in Chancery. He died in 1774. His two sons were Richard, the future Lord Sunderlin, and Edmond, the most important member of the family to be interred at Kilbixy.

The younger Edmond Malone was the foremost Shakespearean scholar of the late 18th century - and it was he who first established a chronology for the plays. He was also assiduous in collecting biographical facts about Shakespeare (though his long-term appropriation of some of Stratford-upon-Avon town council's records suggests a rather overbearing manner). His almost forensic analysis of Shakespeare's life led him to refute many of the legends that the Bard's life had accreted. He also applied his mind to other literary areas - he was one of the people who showed that Thomas Chatterton's supposedly-medieval 'Rowley' poems were a fake, and he exposed the Shakespearean forgeries (including a whole 'rediscovered' play, *Vortigern and Rowena*) of William Henry Ireland.

He edited all Shakespeare's plays and brought out new editions of both them and of the prose works of Dryden - though not without criticism from his contemporaries. He was mocked by judge and writer George Hardinge, who had also edited Dryden, in two books - *The Essence of Malone* and *Another Essence of Malone - the 'Beauties' of Shakspeare's Editor*. Malone was shaken by the criticism, and virtually stopped his literary work. He was in any case well off, having received an annuity of £1000 a year from his uncle Anthony, the former Chancellor of the Exchequer.

Much of Edmond Malone's life was spent in London, where his acquaintance among the literary and artistic set was very wide. He was a friend of Johnson and of Reynolds - and was instrumental in having them both commemorated in St Paul's Cathedral. He knew Edmund Burke, Edward Gibbon, Dr Charles Burney, Joseph Banks and Charles James Fox. James Boswell was another friend and Malone spent a great deal of time helping him write and edit both his *Tour to the Hebrides* (see Skye, page 268) and his *Life of Johnson*. Boswell commented that, despite twice proposing marriage to different ladies, Malone was rejected because of his 'Irish stare'. Malone was also closely acquainted with Horace Walpole, George Canning (see Garvagh, page 304) Oliver Goldsmith and Lord Charlemont (see The Neale, page 317).

In his last years he returned to Shakespearean scholarship and his new edition was ready for the press when he was taken ill. As James Boswell's son wrote in his obituary in the *Gentleman's Magazine* 'In his last illness he was soothed by the tender and unremitting attentions of his brother, Lord Sunderlin, and his youngest sister . . . He left no directions about his funeral; but his Brother, who was anxious, with affectionate solicitude, to execute every wish he had formed, having inferred from something that dropt from him, that it was his desire to be buried among his ancestors in Ireland, his remains were conveyed to that country, and interred at the family seat of Baronston [sic], in the county of Westmeath.' The Latin memorial inscription inside the pyramid was written by Malone's friend the Bishop of Meath, Dr O'Beirne. 'He displayed great skill as a critic of Shakespeare's plays, revealing hidden meanings . . . he was endowed with an enlightened mind and showed much versatility in his learning.'

It is not clear from Boswell Junior's description if Edmond Malone's original place of interment, in 1812, was in the mausoleum at Kilbixy or elsewhere on the estate. If the mausoleum

The cast metal coat of arms of Lord Sunderlin on the Malone mausoleum at Kilbixy

was constructed for Lord Sunderlin, then Edmond, his father and his uncle would have been moved later. So it may be fanciful to imagine London society braving the voyage to Dublin and travelling on to the remoteness of Kilbixy, and literary giants forming the cortege as it wound slowly to stand beneath the great pyramid of the mausoleum in the June sunshine to honour Edmond Malone. Probably most of them stayed safely at home anyway. Lord Sunderlin created one memorial to his brother by presenting his papers to Oxford's Bodleian Library. Yet the Kilbixy pyramid is an equally fine memorial to him and to his noteworthy family.

THE REFERENCES FOR the gateway at **Bracklyn** House, north of Killucan in Co Westmeath, about 20 miles east of Kilbixy, were intriguing and confusing. There was what *The Buildings of Ireland* calls 'a fantastic neo-mannerist composition of rocks and arches - a grotto-cum-grand-gateway' with 'a pyramidal-shaped bellcote.' Photographs taken on the axis of the gateway show what appears to be a pyramid over the central arch. It was worth investigating.

The gateway was built in 1821 as a herald to the Bracklyn estate (sometimes called Bracklyn Castle). It was built for Thomas James Fetherstonhaugh not long after he married. His wife was Lady Eleanor Howard, daughter of the 3rd Earl of Wicklow (see Arklow, page 334). The Fetherstonhaugh family (sometimes confusingly just called Fetherston, including in Thomas James's own will) were mostly stolid, unremarkable landowners. They trace their ancestry in Ireland back to Cuthbert Fetherston, originally with properties in Cumberland and County Durham, who fought on the royalist side at the Battle of Worcester in 1651 and fled to Ireland immediately afterwards. He was related to the royalist commander Sir Timothy Fetherstonhaugh who was beheaded at Chester the same year. Cuthbert settled at Phillipstown in the north of Co Louth. His second son Thomas carried the standard of the town of Enniskillen at the Battle of the Boyne. Thomas

Gateway to Bracklyn House, Co Westmeath

James Fetherstonhaugh, builder of the gateway, was the great-great-great grandson of Cuthbert.

The house where Thomas and Lady Eleanor lived is a plain, elegant Georgian box, with absolutely no frills. It was built by Thomas's father James around the time of Thomas's birth in 1790. Thomas rebelled against this buttoned-up classicism with his riotous 1821 gateway, as well as with an eccentric mausoleum in a similar style some years later.

When we arrived at the gateway we discovered that the description of a 'pyramidal-shaped bellcote' was inaccurate. There is a bellcote, but it is not really a pyramid - just tall gables. There are, though, low pyramid roofs over the rooms to each side of the archway and a few pyramid finals. The architect of the gateway - if there was one - is not known. The building is constructed of water-weathered limestone, interspersed with boulders. The effect is very similar to some of the garden buildings designed by Thomas Wright (see Stanway, page 124 and Tollymore, page 367). Wright cannot have been the designer; he died in 1786. Thomas James Fetherstonhaugh may, though, have owned a copy of Wright's influential *Universal Architecture*, which gives designs for arbours and grottoes, and handed it to his builder. There is another possible influence, too. William Kent's great Worcester Lodge at Badminton Park in Gloucestershire (see page 137) may be a long way away both geographically and in its Palladian style - but it has much of the same spirit of bravado and panache as the Bracklyn gateway.

Thomas Fetherstonhaugh had more than 30 years to enjoy driving in and out of his fancy gateway before his death in 1853. His will bequeathed Bracklyn to his son Howard, named from Lady Eleanor's family; he also left 'my four-wheeled carriages and carriage horses if any also Diamonds' to Howard, and his two-wheel carriage to his daughter Emily. He left a town house in London, just off Grosvenor Square, in Upper Brook Street. Lady Eleanor survived her husband by another 32 years, dying in 1885 aged 94. Her last years must have been blighted by a curious mystery - the assassination of her son Howard in a shooting. No more information has come to light about the circumstances of his death.

'SWIFTE' SAYS THE only inscription on the three-sided pyramid (the only one in Ireland) in the churchyard at **Castlerickard** in Co Meath. But which Swift - with or without a final 'e'? In the absence of a date, we can only surmise which of the family built the pyramid from its appearance and from external sources. Like the twin pyramids at Naas (see page 343) and Kinnitty (see page 351) the Castlerickard pyramid is constructed of diamond-shaped stones laid in diagonal courses - but here there is a finer workmanship and crisper edges. The stones are centred on the lozenge that is carved with the family name. This would seem to point to an early 19th-century date for the pyramid construction. So who was responsible?

There have been Swifts in Ireland (the 'e' seems always to have been optional) since the early 17th century, but the branch at Castlerickard owes its origins to the arrival in Ireland of five sons of the Rev'd Thomas Swift, rector of Goodrich in Herefordshire. Thomas had helped to conceal Charles II after the defeat of the Battle of Worcester, and had given his life savings, sewn for security into his waistcoat, to the king's cause. The first of his sons to settle in Ireland was Godwin (his great grandfather had married a Godwin) and he was followed by his brothers - Dryden (the poet John Dryden was a distant cousin), William, Jonathan and Adam.

'SWIFTE' is the only inscription on this three-sided pyramid at Castlerickard in Co Meath

They all settled, initially, in Dublin. Godwin Swift, a lawyer, became Attorney-General to the Duke of Ormonde for the County Palatine of Tipperary. He grew very wealthy in the role - he was, his nephew wrote, 'a little too dexterous in the subtle parts of the law'. Ormonde rewarded Godwin Swift with land at what became Swift's Heath, Castlerickard.

Godwin's younger brother Jonathan, a Dublin solicitor, married Abigail Herrick, of the same family as the poet Robert Herrick; but the marriage, according to his son, 'was on both sides very indiscreet'. Abigail 'brought her husband little or no fortune' - he died after only 15 months of marriage, leaving her almost penniless and with an infant daughter, Jane. She was also two months pregnant; there is some doubt as to whether the child was her husband's. The child, a son, named after Jonathan, was born on 30 November 1667. He grew up to be the great satirist and Dean of St Patrick's Cathedral in Dublin, Jonathan Swift.

Young Jonathan Swift had a very strange childhood. According to his testimony he was stolen by his nurse when a baby and taken to Cumbria. He stayed there almost three years, being well looked after and carefully taught by the nurse - it sounds as if

Author Jonathan Swift. The most famous of the Swift family, he was buried not at Castlerickard but at St Patrick's Cathedral in Dublin, where he was Dean.

Abigail connived at the 'kidnapping'. When he was returned, his mother rapidly decamped with young Jane to her old home in Leicestershire, shunting Jonathan off to his uncle Godwin in Castlerickard. Godwin seems to have taken little trouble with him; there were many cousins around, for Godwin married four times and had 15 children, but seems to have been cold and undemonstrative - perhaps he doubted the true identity of Jonathan's father. Jonathan wrote of his uncle that 'he gave me the education of a dog' - despite the fact that Godwin sent him, with his cousin Thomas, to the prestigious Kilkenny School, 'the Eton of Ireland', where the future dramatist William Congreve (see page 96) was among his school contemporaries. There was, though, some affection in the Swift family; Godwin's eldest son Willoughby befriended Jonathan. When Jonathan was at Trinity College, Dublin (where his career was notoriously rackety) he was saved from penury and depression by the gift of a large sum of money from Willoughby, then a merchant in Lisbon. Jonathan was also helped by his uncle William.

The rise of Jonathan Swift as an important literary figure, and his parallel rise through the hierarchy of the church to his eminence as Dean of St Patrick's, must have been watched with both admiration and surprise by the family in Castlerickard. The first biography of Dean Swift was written by his cousin Deane Swift - a fact that has caused untold confusion. Far from being named in honour of his illustrious cousin's position, Deane was only eight years younger than Jonathan. His name, which was often used in the family, came from his mother, Godwin Swift's third wife Hannah Deane. Their marriage scandalised some of the family, for Hannah's father was General Deane, one of the Parliamentarians who signed the death warrant of King Charles I.

The story of the Swifts at Castlerickard now becomes even more convoluted, with cousins marrying left, right and centre, even across different generations. Deane Swift's half-brother Godwin (a son by his father's second wife Katherine) had, inevitably, an eldest son called Godwin. *His* son was also Godwin - the Rev'd Godwin Swift (or Swifte) of Swift's Heath. He married his cousin, Sophia Jane Swifte, in 1803 - even though her long-term admirer, the poet Walter Savage Landor, begged her not to agree to the marriage. Landor called Sophia Jane 'Ianthe' and wrote several poems to her over their long association, including the much-anthologised *Ianthe's Question*:

> 'Do you remember me? or are you proud?'
> Lightly advancing thro' her star-trimm'd crowd,
> Ianthe said, and look'd into my eyes.
> 'A yes, a yes to both: for Memory
> Where you but once have been must ever be,
> And at your voice Pride from his throne must rise.'

Godwin Swift died in 1815 and was probably the builder of the pyramid in the churchyard at Castlerickard. Sophia Jane remarried; her new husband was the Comte Lepelettier de Molandé. When she died, at Versailles in 1851, her body was brought back to Castlerickard and interred alongside her first husband's, beneath the pyramid.

None of the other Swifts attained the fame of their cousin, the author of *Gulliver's Travels*, but there were some who shone with lesser light - Theophilus Swift, for instance, son of Deane Swift the biographer. He was, like so many of the family, a lawyer, and 'saw everything whimsically, many things erroneously, and nothing like another person.' He said, 'I seldom deliberate: my feelings are my only guide. They have never deceived me.' He defended 'The London Monster', a Welshman called Rhynwick Williams who had gone round London attacking more than 50 innocent women with knives. Sometimes the knives were strapped to Williams' knee and he attacked the women from behind; sometimes there was a sharp spike hidden in a small bouquet he invited them to smell. Theophilus's defence was spirited, but, given the horror that the crimes had aroused, it was inevitable that Williams was convicted and imprisoned in Newgate Prison in Dublin, even though it is questionable whether he was really guilty.

Not long after, Theophilus Swift was in Newgate himself, convicted of libel against the Fellows of Trinity College, Dublin. He had taken against them because his son, Deane, had not managed to distinguish himself in his examinations. This was, in his father's opinion, despite Deane's being 'the cleverest lad in all Ireland'. The Trinty Fellows were required to be unmarried, but, Swift wrote of them, 'notwithstanding their solemn oath, several of these fellows and clergymen . . . forgetful of morality, common decency, and good example, had actually taken to themselves each one woman, at least, who went by the name of Miss Such-a-one, but who, in fact, had in many instances undergone . . . the ceremony and consummation of marriage.' The Fellows' could not let this calumny pass. A libel action was brought in the court of the King's Bench. Even Theophilus's barrister said the case was indefensible, and Theophilus duly lost. His 12-month sentence was enlivened when Theophilus sued one of his main persecutors among the Fellows for libel on him. Theophilus won, the libeller was convicted, and he and the Fellow ended up sharing a cell in the gaol.

Theophilus's younger son Edmond was in charge of the Crown Jewels as Keeper of the Regalia at the Tower of London - he lived into his hundredth year. His cousin Godwin Meade Pratt Swifte (the terminal 'e' had now become a fixture) was perhaps a less stable character. In the mid-19th century he announced to a no-doubt startled world that he was 'the inventor of the aerial chariot'. A prototype flying machine, it was 'made in the shape of a boat, extremely light, with one wheel in front and two behind, and having two wings' - a sort of ethereal Bath chair. The wings were shaped to resemble those that propel birds and were, he assured readers of *The Engineer*, capable of enabling the chariot to 'float on the air for several miles, perhaps at 50 or 60 feet.' There is no record of Swifte's invention ever taking off.

How many of the Swift family lie beneath the pyramid in the now-disused churchyard at Castlerickard? There is no record. Certainly not Dean Jonathan, who was buried in splendour in his own cathedral. Probably the only occupants are the Rev'd Godwin Swift and his wife Sophia Jane, the muse of Landor. They now lie unnamed under the handsome, trihedral pyramid simply marked 'SWIFTE'.

THE DUBLIN RESIDENTIAL suburb of **Glasnevin** is probably best known for being the home of the Irish National Botanic Gardens, of one of the capital's major cemeteries and of Ireland's largest theatre, The Mahoney Hall in The Helix Arts Centre. In the 18th century Jonathan Swift (see page 359) lived here - and it is now the home of two of Ireland's largest pyramids.

It was a chance encounter on Killiney Hill that drew our attention to one of them. We asked directions to the Killiney pyramid (see page 337) from Peter Hamilton - who also mentioned the Met Éireann building in Glasnevin as a pyramid we should see. It

proved to be a large office block along the lines of the Co-operative Bank in Stockport (see page 204) - though it was built in 1979, ten years before the design of the Bank. The Met Office moved to Glasnevin Hill - formerly Washerwoman's Hill - from O'Connell Street in Dublin city centre.

Met Éireann - it changed its name from the Meteorological Service in 1996 - had its pyramid designed by Derry architect Liam McCormack, better known for a series of Catholic churches in Ireland and elsewhere. Originally the building was finished with sheets of limestone that soon began to slip down the sloping sides. They were replaced by the modern grey cladding; this is a pity, as the limestone was handsome and sparkled when the sun shone. The greyness of the building now matches the sometimes-grey weather of Ireland's 'soft days' often predicted from here. The top few storeys of the pyramid are recessed so that there is a fourth-floor terrace where meteorological instruments can be used and which provides a good base for the satellite dishes to receive the data coming in from the nine manned observing stations and the many automated stations around Ireland.

The Met Office pyramid - 'Millibar Mansions', some have named it - is a curiously alien presence in suburban Dublin. More than anything, with its metal-framed windows and recessed balconies, it resembles the superstructure of a large ship - a tanker rather than a cruise liner - that has somehow lost its way from Dublin docks a couple of miles south east, and sailed inland, coming to rest, like Noah's Ark on Mount Ararat, on top of Glasnevin Hill.

JUST ROUND THE corner from the Met Éireann pyramid - over the Tolka River and opposite the Botanic Gardens - is Glasnevin's other pyramid. This is the Church of Our Lady of Dolours, often known as 'the New Woodener' or 'the Wigwam'. The last name is self-evident - but why 'New Woodener'? This goes back to the previous church on this site. A timber-built church stood originally in Berkeley Road, a short distance to the south, beyond the Royal Canal. It was dismantled and moved to the site beside the Tolka, on Botanic Avenue. Unsurprisingly, it was known as 'the Woodener'. So when in 1972 the much-loved church was demolished and replaced by a pyramid, it became known as 'the New Woodener'.

The new church is an emphatic statement of faith. Steel-framed and clad in slate, it is designed to look as if a slice has been taken away from the complete pyramid and the two halves rejoined. This provides a vertical, glazed section that faces west. From the outside this is a dramatic coup; from the inside it provides a flood of light on to the east wall and the altar, its source invisible as you enter. Its form is identical to Bedford's Oasis leisure centre (see page 85), which uses the same split pyramid technique to illuminate the interior space.

The interior decoration is deliberately kept subsidiary to the drama of the roof. Only the coloured crucifix over the altar draws the eye. There are a few other attractive details, including the use made of the low-level glazing below the roof line, and the Stations of the Cross that are etched into the glass of the windows.

On the side of the church by the river there is a lower area that gives access to the meeting rooms below the pyramid. This gave the architects a problem - how to dispose of the rain running off the large area of the pyramid's roof without intruding ugly gutters and downpipes. The answer, used on all four sides of the building but particularly striking here, was ingenious. From the eaves hang bundles of chains - eight in each bundle - that are anchored at the base in a square concrete trough. The water from the roof flows down the chains into a drainage hole below the anchorage point and is taken to the drains via a concrete pipe.

Clever though the details are, it is the bulk of the church, its sharp outline as seen from beside the river or from inside the Botanic Gardens, that sticks in the mind. Of the two Glasnevin pyramids it is certainly the more inspiring.

LUSK, A FEW miles north of Dublin city centre and three miles from the coast, is a quiet dormitory town. It is made special only by its 100-foot-high, 10th-century round tower on the site of the monastery founded here by St Maccullin, a native of Lusk, in about AD 455. Unlike most of Ireland's round towers, this one is not free-standing but was incorporated into a later, more-conventional tower in 1480. The rest of the church - which was confiscated from the Catholics in 1538 - fell into disuse because there were very few Protestants in Lusk to look after it. It was finally abandoned when the roof blew off in a severe storm in 1839. By then the Catholics had had their own church for 30 years. It stood on the Green at Lusk, and it was here that Father Peter Tyrrell, commemorated by an elongated pyramid outside its 1922 successor, was the parish priest.

Tyrrell served at Lusk for just two years, from 1841 - but they were years of great political turmoil in Ireland. Under the leadership of the charismatic Daniel O'Connell the Irish Catholics were seeking freedom from what they saw as the oppression of the English government. In 1829, after considerable agitation, the Emancipation Bill had been passed by Parliament. This at last allowed Catholics to take seats in the House of Commons and in the House of Lords (despite Lord Eldon's dire warning that 'if ever a Roman Catholic was permitted to form part of the legislature of

Our Lady of Dolours - 'The New Woodener' - at Glasnevin is opposite the National Botanic Gardens

Father Peter Tyrrell of the Loyal National Repeal Association is commemorated by this elongated pyramid at Lusk, north of Dublin

this country, from that moment the sun of Great Britain would set') and to hold civil and military office.

Although the Emancipation Bill became law, it was imperfectly implemented. In Ireland, Catholics were still ignored in many areas of public life. O'Connell and his associates began to agitate for a repeal of the Act of Union of 1807, which had abolished the Irish parliament. They wanted Ireland to be an independent kingdom under the British crown. The movement for repeal spawned a plethora of associations, many of which amalgamated in 1840 into the Loyal National Repeal Association. Large sums were subscribed to the cause, which had branches in Ireland and the United States.

Father Peter Tyrrell was one of the leading members of the Association nationally, working closely with O'Connell. He had studied at the Irish College in Paris and did missionary work in Rouen before working in Stratford, east London. Illness forced him to return to Ireland, where he worked as a chaplain in Dublin. Eventually he became the curate of St Audoen's, Dublin's only-remaining medieval church, before being made parish priest at Lusk at the age of 49.

Tyrrell's role in the Loyal National Repeal Association seems to have been little different from that of other priests throughout Ireland. There were huge rallies all around the country, usually on Sunday mornings, where Tyrrell and his colleagues would celebrate mass before the political speeches began. He would occasionally make speeches, but reports suggest that they were neither inflammatory nor particularly stirring.

The biggest of the rallies was held in 1843 on the Feast of the Assumption of the Blessed Virgin Mary - 15 August - at the Hill of Tara. It is a place deep in the history of Ireland as the scene of the crowning of the Irish kings. It had greater resonance for the Repealers as the place where 400 Irish men, rebelling against the English forces, were killed during the uprising of 1798 (see page 313). The estimates of the number of people at the 15 August rally vary from 100,000 to 1.5 million. The scale of the movement frightened the government, so when an even-larger rally was planned at Clontarf, immediately north of Dublin, for 8 October, the authorities acted. On the evening of 7 October they banned the event. Many people believed that the ban was left so late because the government wanted to provoke the Repeal supporters into violence that would have damaged their cause.

The ploy did not work. O'Connell immediately sent messengers out urging supporters not to come to Clontarf. So well organized were the Repealers that there was no disturbance. None the less, arrests were made. Nine men, including Daniel O'Connell and Fr Tyrrell, whose involvement may have been greater than usual because of the nearness of Lusk to Clontarf, were charged with 'unlawfully, maliciously and seditiously contriving, intending and devising to raise and create discontent and disaffection amongst the liege subjects of our said lady the Queen, and to excite the said liege subjects to hatred and contempt of the government and constitution of this realm.' They were given bail while the legal processes were undertaken, including a review by a Grand Jury on 8 November, which led to the scheduling of a full trial on 16 January 1844.

Only eight defendants were brought before the Queen's Bench in Dublin that day. Fr Tyrrell had died on 14 October 1843, 'from illness produced by his prosecution and exertions for liberty', as the inscription on his pyramid memorial puts it. The remaining Repealers faced the longest indictment ever seen, with 11 counts including conspiracy. Each day O'Connell was accompanied to the court by a large crowd, including the Lord Mayor of Dublin and the Catholic Aldermen in their full robes. Their support did little good. On 12 February the jury - which included no Catholics - deliberated for six hours before finding the defendants guilty. Legal arguments delayed sentence until 30 May. O'Connell was given 12 months in prison and a fine of £2,000. He was also required to give bonds for £10,000 to keep the peace for the next seven years. The other 'conspirators' (except Tyrrell's fellow clergyman Fr Tierney) were sent to prison for nine months and fined £50. They were allowed to choose their own prison.

The incarceration of the leaders of the Loyal National Repeal Association only served to fuel the movement. Subscriptions soared and support grew. On 4 July a debate on the legality of the verdict against O'Connell and his fellows began in the House of Lords in London. It made legal history as the first case in which all the peers except those specifically appointed as law lords withdrew from proceedings. The Irish court's verdict was overturned on 4 September. Lord John Russell said, 'The trial was not a trial by a fair jury, but one put elaborately together for the purpose of conviction, and charged by a judge who did not allow any evidence or consideration in favour of the traversers to come fairly before his mind.'

O'Connell was released from gaol and paraded through the streets of Dublin, preceded by an Irish harper. It was a moment of triumph that was short-lived. He was already ill. Obstacles began to appear in the path of the Repealers - including a virtual ban from Rome on priests taking part in any political agitation. And all paled into insignificance two years later when the Potato Famine began. O'Connell died in May 1847 at the age of 71, in Genoa, where he had gone for his health. His heart was buried in Rome, and his body in the cemetery at Glasnevin.

The pyramid at Lusk to Fr Tyrrell was erected by members of the Loyal National Repeal Association of Ireland. Of grey granite, it lies in that no-man's-land between pyramid and obelisk. It is topped with an urn surmounted with a cross. How deeply Fr Tyrrell was involved in the Repeal movement is open to question - was he just implicated because he was close by as the Clontarf rally was being planned, or was he really a fervent adherent of the cause? Whatever the truth, it was probably as much politics as grief that led to the erection of the monument, with its inscription describing the priest as 'a Martyr for Ireland', while the legal process to try the remaining defendants was still underway.

THE CONNECTION BETWEEN the origins of the universe and the shape of the Milky Way, the Titanic and a Northern Irish pyramid may not seem obvious, yet there is a link. At **Tollymore,** a few miles inland from Newcastle in Co Down, is a collection of wayward structures collectively known as 'Lord Limerick's Follies'. Among them is a small pyramid raised on a high base supported by diminutive flying buttresses. It forms part of the wall round the Tollymore estate, once owned by Lord Limerick and now Tollymore Forest Park. The park is one of Ulster's major tourist attractions and was noted by the *Sunday Times* as one of the United Kingdom's best picnic sites.

The Lord Limerick responsible was James Hamilton. He succeeded his father to the Tollymore estate in 1701 at the age of 11. After graduating from Oxford he became MP for Dundalk, where

Pyramid-topped turret, probably by Thomas Wright, on the wall surrounding Tollymore Forest Park

his family had other property. Over succeeding years he rebuilt the town and opened a successful linen factory. In 1719 he was created Viscount Limerick and he seems to have set about immediately transforming the park at Tollymore into one of the most admired 'naturalistic' landscapes in Ireland, enclosing the former deer park and planting thousands of trees. It was trees from his Tollymore forests that supplied the oak used by Harland and Wolfe in Belfast for the panelling in the great state rooms of the Titanic.

Limerick was created Earl of Clanbrassil in 1728, and by 1750 he decided to rebuild his house at Tollymore. He turned for advice to a friend, Thomas Wright (see Bracklyn, page 357 and Stanway, page 124). Wright was introduced to the Earl through his links with the second Earl of Scarborough, Richard Lumley. Wright was born in Byers Green, just north of Bishop Auckland in Co Durham and only a dozen miles from Lord Scarborough's Lumley Castle. Wright became known to Scarborough as a mathematician, scientific instrument maker and teacher of navigation.

He came before a wider public with the publication of his book on navigation, *Clavis Pannautici*, which, with Lord Scarborough's help, was adopted by the Admiralty. Its success, and Wright's ability as a teacher, led to a lecture series in London, where he was known as 'The Wizard of Durham', and to a growing number of aristocratic private pupils. At the same time Wright developed his astronomical calculations. In 1742 he published a huge diagram, as big as a dining table, of how he thought the heavens were organized. In the same year he was offered the post of Professor of Navigation at the Imperial Academy in St Petersburg. As he asked for nearly twice the salary they offered, he stayed in London.

Wright was also giving thought to the shape of the Milky Way. His theories were propounded in *An Original Theory or New Hypothesis of the Universe*, which he published in 1750. In it he proposed that we see the Milky Way as we do because it is either the shape of a grindstone or of the spiral peel of a great orange. This idea had no immediate follow-up, though the German philosopher Kant saw a review of the book and wrote 'Mr Wright of Durham . . . first suggested to me to regard the fixed stars, not as a host scattered with no visible order, but as a system . . . distributed relatively to a plane drawn across the sky; and form[ing] a luminous path, which is called the Milky Way, by their denser crowding in that region'.

All Wright's astronomical interests were mixed up with his mystic beliefs in reincarnation and parallel universes. He believed the heavens contain many universes, all nested within each other like the layers of an onion. What Wright seems to have been attempting was the marriage of strict Newtonian scientific theory with his own unorthodox religious ideas and the tenets of Freemasonry, of which he was a member. His parallel career as an architect and landscape designer was also influenced by his mystical beliefs. He described his alternative universes as 'a group of Worlds, all Vallies, Lakes and River, adorn'd with Mountains, Woods and Lawns, Cascades and natural Fountains . . . all fertile islands, cover'd with Woods, perhaps upon a common Sea and filled with Grottoes and romantick with Groves and Wildernesses.' All this seems to be a detailed description of the sort of estate the Earl of Clanbrassil was laying out at Tollymore.

From 1746 to 1747 Wright was in Ireland, and stayed with the Earl at Tollymore. The new house that Clanbrassil and Wright designed between them was a relatively simple affair of two storeys, with a full-height bay window and wings. It underwent extensive alterations several times in the later 18th and 19th centuries, becoming, according to visitors, one of the most comfortable houses in Ireland. It was demolished in 1952, a few years after the estate was taken over by the Northern Ireland Ministry of Agriculture from the Clanbrassils' successors, the Earls of Roden.

It is likely that while Wright was at Tollymore he put forward ideas - and perhaps sketches - for the follies that not only line the park walls but can also be found throughout the park. But the estate maps are unclear about when they were actually built. It is

*Thomas Wright,
eccentric architect
and discoverer of
the Milky Way*

*Detail of the
Tollymore
pyramid, showing
the 'bap-stones'
from the River
Shimna*

possible that they were erected by the Earl's son, another James who, before his father's death in 1758, was known by his father's lesser title of Lord Limerick. He was actually given lessons in architecture by Thomas Wright, and it is possible that he oversaw the building of the pyramid and the other structures when he succeeded to the estate.

The follies are certainly in the Thomas Wright style, as put forward in his Universal Architecture, but they lack a little of the sophistication of buildings personally supervised by Wright. As well as some rather clumsy workmanship, they have some very local additions - bun-shaped stones, locally called 'bap-stones', which are placed symmetrically on the irregular stonework like cabochons on metalwork. The bap-stones came from the bed of the River Shimna, which flows through Tollymore demesne.

The little Tollymore pyramid is perhaps a minor facet of the joys of Tollymore, which attracts thousands of people every year. Thomas Wright's other buildings are perhaps more on their radar - especially the Clanbrassil Barn, constructed to look like a church and now with an interpretation centre upstairs and toilet facilities on the ground floor. There is also a series of ornate stone bridges across the Shimna, a stone Hermitage with views of the river and a gothic gateway. The other two follies along Lord Limerick's wall - a gateway with turrets crowned with cones, and a hexagonal tower containing a stone seat crowned with a taller spire, both of them decorated with bap-stones and both looking like part of Cinderella's castle - have more presence because they do not have to be seen against a backdrop of mature trees beside a busy road. But the small pyramid is a *jeu d'esprit* that is fully in keeping with the rich variety of all Ireland's pyramidal structures.

'The Hut' - a pyramid by Francisco de Asis Checa Romero in Spa Fields, Islington

And yet another . . .

This book had been written and designed when we were told of yet another pyramid - and as a modern take on an ancient shape we thought it worth its own addendum.

London's Spa Fields, between Clerkenwell and Islington, has been many things. According to a mid-19th-century writer, 'Spa Fields, or the Ducking-pond Fields, now intersected by streets of well-built houses, was the summer's evening resort of the towns-people, who came hither to witness the rude sports that were in vogue a century ago, such as duck-hunting, prize-fighting, bull-baiting, and others of an equally demoralising character.'

By the mid-18th century the springs that provided the spa water (which also gave their name to nearby Sadlers Wells) had been superseded by a genteel tea room called the Pantheon, surrounded by pleasant gardens. In 1779 this large, circular building was taken over by the Countess of Huntingdon's Connexion (see page 133 and 222) as a chapel - the Countess lived close by. The garden was transformed into a highly-profitable burial ground - it attracted customers because charges for burial there were considerably less than at the parish church. The original estimate was that there was space for just over 1,300 bodies. Once burials began, though, they continued, with numbers rising all the time.

Despite the continuous interments, Spa Fields still provided valuable open space - and it was here in 1816 that revolution was fermented. On 15 November around 20,000 supporters of the radical politician Thomas Spence met, with the intention of seizing power from the government. But the ringleaders had already been detained, and the meeting was dispersed. More serious was the second meeting, on 2 December, when the revolutionaries heard inflammatory speeches, then set off towards the city of London. They attacked the Royal Exchange (where a bystander was killed) and tried to take the Tower before they were stopped by troops.

The Pantheon Tea Room - later a chapel of the Countess of Huntingdon's Connexion - formerly in Spa Fields

Meanwhile, the burials went on. To cram them all in, even newly-buried corpses were dug up and either burned or dissolved in quicklime. Some were sold for dissection in the London hospitals. By the time the Spa Fields burial ground was closed in 1849, after 70 years' use, more than 80,000 people had been buried there. The chapel was eventually demolished - it was sited where the Church of Our Most Holy Redeemer, built in 1888, now stands - and in 1885 London County Council bought Spa Fields and turned it into a children's playground.

After more than a century it is still a playground - now with bright new climbing and swinging equipment, thanks to a regeneration scheme commissioned by Islington Council in 2004 from consultants Parklife. The scheme turned Spa Fields from a dangerous area back to a welcoming open space. In close consultation with the local community - especially the young people - the tired site was transformed. As well as the new play equipment there are shelters (some built by local teenagers), places where you can picnic - and that most essential of all park features, a hut.

This, though, is not just any hut. It's an architect-designed, copper-clad pyramidal hut - but a pyramid that's a bit eccentric. One of its sloping faces reaches the ground; the others are sent askew by short walls, two triangular, one trapezoid, so that the pyramid's point is off-centre. There are doors in the taller wall, leading to an interior with a small meeting room as well as storage space and a lavatory. It is lit from a tower of glass and mesh that thrusts through the pyramid.

The Hut (as it's known locally) has the same footprint as its predecessor, a run-of-the-mill park shed - itself on the site of the former furnace. The tower is intended as a reminder of Spa Fields' past as a cemetery and of the chimneys that vented the smoke and fumes as the bodies burned.

It's the work of a young architect - one who designed it in his year off after graduating from the Royal College of Art. Francisco de Asís Checa Romero was on a placement with Parklife when he came up with the pyramid. It's a very sensitive site; not only did the structure have to relate to the needs of the park, it had to pay attention to its neighbours - both the Victorian red-brick church and also one of the 20th-century's seminal buildings, the Finsbury Health Centre designed in 1938 by Berthold Lubetkin. The back of the health centre is only a dozen yards away from the pyramid. Romero hasn't imitated either of these neighbours, but made a statement of his own. He says that he was influenced in his choice of the pyramid shape by the symbolism of Nicholas Hawksmoor (see page 7) and by the American modernist architect John Hejduk's oddly-shaped buildings.

It has its practical merits; the steep roof makes it difficult for vandals to climb, for example, and mesh protects the glass from stone-throwers. Local people were trained to help in the construction of the pyramid, so they feel they own it. As a result, it has suffered little graffiti. All this came at a price, of course - the final bill was £270,000. It has not been universally admired, though; a blogger wrote in January 2009 that he thought that 'this is surely one of the most pointless constructions in the history of mankind; it's ugly, very poorly detailed, does not match nor fit in with anything surrounding it.' That has not been the judgement of the architectural press, who have praised Romero's design. And most of the park's users seem to like it. A practical pyramid that's also a statement and a decent piece of architecture - it's what so many of the pyramids in the British Isles have striven to achieve.

The Hut, showing its 'chimney', a reminder of the dark past of Spa Fields

BIBLIOGRAPHY

Aalen, FHA, Whelan, K and Stout, M (eds)	Atlas of the Irish Rural Landscape	Cork University Press	1977
Abrioux, Yves	Ian Hamilton Finlay - A Visual Primer	Reaktion Books	1994
Allen, Nic (ed)	Scottish Pioneers of the Greek Revival	Scottish Georgian Society	1984
Anthony, John	Renaissance Garden in Britain, The	Shire	1991
Archer, Percy	Historic Cheshunt	The Cheshunt Press	1923
Auden, WH and Isherwood, Christopher	Dog Beneath the Skin, The	Faber	1968
Baigent, Michael and Leigh, Richard	Temple and the Lodge, The	Jonathan Cape	1989
Ballantyne, R M	Hunted and Harried	James Nisbet & Co	1892
Balmori, Diana	Architecture, Landscape and the Intermediate Structure: Eighteenth Century Experiments in Mediation	Journal of the Society of Architectural Historians Vol 50 No 1	1991
Banham, Mary and Hillier, Bevis	Tonic to the Nation, A	Thames & Hudson	1976
Barbara Jones	Follies and Grottoes	Constable	1974
Barlow, N, Knox, T and Holmes, C	Follies of Europe	Garden Art Press	2008
Barnes, Richard	Norfolk: The Year of Public Sculpture	Frontier	2000
.. ..	Obelisk, The	Frontier Publishing	2004
Beazley, Elizabeth and Brett, Lionel	North Wales - A Shell Guide	Faber and Faber	1971
Beck-Friis, Johan	Protestant Cemetery in Rome, The	Allhems	1956
Bede (trans Sherley-Price. Leo)	A History of the English Church and People	Penguin Books	1968
.. .. (trans Webb, J F)	Lives of the Saints - Life of Cuthbert	Penguin Books	1965
Bell, Alan (editor)	Lord Cockburn - The Letters	John Donald Publishers Ltd	2005
Bence-Jones, Mark	Burke's Guide to Country Houses Volume 1 Ireland	Burke's Peerage Ltd	1978
Betjeman, John	Cornwall - A Shell Guide	Faber and Faber	1969
Birkbeck, John	Peter Drummond, Man of Conviction and Action	The Saint Andrew Press	1984
Blackwell, John	Gwaith Alun	R E Jones, Conwy	1909
Bond, James	Somerset Parks and Gardens - A Landscape History	Somerset Books	1998
Boswell, James	Journal of a Tour to the Hebrides	William Heinemann	1936
Bowdler, Roger	Mausoleum at Blickling, The	Apollo Magazine Vol 434 pp 11-14	1998
Bradley, Simon and Pevsner, Nikolaus	London 1: The City of London	Penguin Books	1999
Bradley, Simon and Pevsner, Nikolaus	London 6: Westminster	Yale	2003
Bragg, Melvyn	Soldier's Return, The	Hodder & Stoughton	1999
Bragg, Melvyn	Son of War, A	Hodder & Stoughton	2001
Breasted, James Henry	Oriental Exploration Fund of the University of Chicago - Second Preliminary Report of Egyptian Expedition	American Journal of Semitic Languages and Literatures Vol 25 No 1	1908
Brereton, John	Briefe and true relation of the discoverie of the North part of Virginia, A	Da Capo Press	1975
Brett, C E B	Buildings of County Antrim	Ulster Architectural Heritage Society	1997
.. ..	Buildings of County Armagh	Ulster Architectural Heritage Society	1999
Briggs, Asa (ed)	Dictionary of 20th Century World Biography, A	Oxford	1993
Brooke, David	William Mackenzie, International Railway Builder and Civil Engineer	The Newcomen Society	2004
.. .. (ed)	Diary of William Mackenzie	Thomas Telford	2000
Brooke, Melancthon W H L	The Great Pyramid of Gizeh: its riddle read, its secret metrology fully revealed	R Banks & Son	1908
Brown, Dan	Da Vinci Code, The	Bantam Press	2003
Brown, Ian et al	20th Century Defences in Britain	Council for British Archaeology	1996
Bruce, David	Sun Pictures - the Hill-Adamson calotypes	Studio Vista	1973

Brück, HA and MT	Peripatetic Astronomer, The	Adam Hilger	1988
Bryson, Bill	Shakespeare	Harper Press	2007
Bunbury, Turtle	Landed Gentry & Aristocracy of Co Kildare	Irish Family Names	2004
.. ..	Landed Gentry & Aristocracy of Co Wicklow Vol 1	Irish Family Names	2005
Campbell, Thomas	Essay on English Poetry, An	John Murray	1848
Cananagh, Terry	Public Sculpture of Liverpool	Liverpool University Press	1997
Carrott, Richard G	Egyptian Revival, The; Its Sources, Monuments and Meaning 1808 - 1858	University of California Press	1978
Casey, Christine	Dublin (The Buildings of Ireland)	Yale	2005
Casey, Christine and Rowan, Alistair	North Leinster (The Buildings of Ireland)	Penguin	1993
Casson, Hugh (ed)	Monuments (National Benzol Books)	Chatto and Windus	1963
Catling, Christopher and Merry, Alison	Gloucestershire and Hereford & Worcester - The New Shell Guide	Michael Joseph	1990
Causton, H Kent Staple	Howard Papers, The	Henry Kent Causton & Son	1862
Cherry, Bridget and Pevsner, Nikolaus	Devon (The Buildings of England)	Penguin Books	1991
.. ..	London 2: South (The Buildings of England)	Penguin Books	1994
.. ..	London 3: North West (The Buildings of England)	Penguin Books	1999
.. ..	London 4: North (The Buildings of England)	Penguin Books	1999
Chonaill, Muireean Ni (ed)	Laois Sculpture Trail	Laois County Council	1994
Clark, Lorna J (ed)	Letters of Sarah Harriet Burney	University of Georgia Press	1997
Clifton-Taylor, Alec	Pattern of English Building, The	Faber and Faber	1972
Colvin, Howard	Architecture and the After-Life	Yale University Press	1991
.. ..	Biographical Dictionary of British Architects 1600-1840 (Third Edition)	Yale University Press	1995
Connor, Patrick (ed)	Inspiration of Egypt, The	Brighton Borough Council	1983
Cooper, Glynis	Rosevear: A desert island story	Historic Occasions	2000
Cox, Ian	South Bank Exhibition, The	HM Stationery Office	1951
Craig, Maurice and Craig, Michael	Mausolea Hibernica	The Lilliput Press	1999
Craske, Matthew	Entombed Like an Egyptian	Journal of The Church Monuments Society Vol XV pp 71- 88	2000
Culbertson, J and Randall, T	Permanent Londoners	Robson Books	1991
Curl, James Stevens	Arts and Freemasonry, The	B T Batsford	1991
.. ..	Death and Architecture	Sutton Publishing	2002
.. ..	Egyptian Revival, The	George Allen & Unwin	1982
.. ..	Mausolea in Ulster	Ulster Architectural Heritage Society	1978
.. ..	Victorian Celebration of Death, The	Sutton Publishing	2000
Cussans, John Edwin	History of Hertfordshire, A	E P Publishing	1972
Darwin, Bernard et al	Oxford Dictionary of Quotations, The (2nd Edition)	Oxford University Press	1975
Davie, Michael (ed)	Diaries of Evelyn Waugh, The	Penguin Books	1979
Davies, Edwin and Howells, Brian (eds)	Pembrokeshire County History Vol 111 - Early Modern Pembrokeshire, 1536 - 1815	Pembrokeshire Historical Society	1987
De Breffny, B and ffolliott, R	Houses of Ireland, The	Thames & Hudson	1975
Dewar, H S L (ed)	Thomas Rackett Papers, The	Dorset Record Society	1965
Dick, The Rev'd C H	Highways and Byways in Galloway and Carrick	Macmillan & Co	1916
Dickerman, Lysander	On the etymology and synonyms of the word Pyramid	Proceedings of the American Oriental Society Vol 15	1893
Dietrich, William	Napoleon's Pyramids - a novel	Harper Collins	2007
Dixon, Roger and Muthesius, Stefan	Victorian Architecture	Thames & Hudson	1978
Dixon, W MacNeile and Grierson, HJC	English Parnassus, The	Oxford	1909
Dixon Hunt, John and Willis, Peter (eds)	Genius of the Place, The - The English Landscape Garden 1620 to 1820	Paul Elek	1975
Doak, A M and Young , A M (eds)	Glasgow at a glance	Hale	1977
Dooley, Terence	Decline of the Big House in Ireland, The	Wolfhound Press	2001
Downes, Kerry	Hawksmoor	Thames & Hudson	1969
Drysdale, William	Old Faces, Old Places and Old Stories of Stirling	Eneas Mackay	1898
Du Prey, Pierre de la Ruffiniere	Hawksmoor's London Churches	University of Chicago Press	2000
Eagle, Dorothy and Carnell, Hilary (eds)	Oxford Literary Guide to the British Isles, The	Oxford University Press	1977

Author	Title	Publisher	Year
Edwards Brian	Basil Spence 19097 - 1976	The Rutland Press, Edinburgh	1995
Edwards, Jack	Cheshunt in Hertfordshire	Cheshunt Urban District Council	1974
Elliott, Brent	Victorian Gardens	B T Batsford	1986
Elwin, Malcolm	Charles Reade, A Biography	Jonathan Cape	1931
Enge, Torsten Olaf and Schroer, Carl Friedrich	Garden Architecture in Europe 1450 - 1800	Benedikt Taschen	1990
Evans, Rosemary	Visitor's Guide to Northern Ireland, The	Moorland Publishing Co	1981
Eyres, Patrick, et al	Mr Aislabie's Gardens	New Arcadians	1981
Farmer, David Hugh	Oxford Dictionary of Saints, The	Oxford University Press	1979
Fedden, Robin and Joekes, Rosemary (ed)	National Trust Guide, The	Jonathan Cape	1973
Fielding, Henry	History of Tom Jones, The	Penguin Books	1985
Fiennes, Ranulph	Captain Scott	Hodder & Stoughton	2003
Finlay, Ross et al	Discovering Britain	Readers Digest	1982
Fleming, Laurence and Gore, Alan	English Garden, The	Michael Joseph	1979
Freart, Roland (transl Evelyn, John)	Parallel of the Antient Architecture with the Modern	Roycroft, Thomas	1664
Geddes, Patrick	City Development	St George Press	1904
.. ..	World Without and the World Within, The	St George Press	1905
Geoffrey of Monmouth trans. Thorpe, Lewis	History of the Kings of Britain, The	Penguin Books	1968
Gifford, John	Fife (The Buildings of Scotland)	Penguin	1988
.. ..	Highlands and Islands (The Buildings of Scotland)	Penguin	1992
.. ..	Perth and Kinross (The Buildings of Scotland)	Yale	2007
Gifford, John and Walker, Frank Arneil	Stirling and Central Scotland (The Buildings of Scotland)	Yale	2002
Gifford, John; McWilliam, Colin; Walker, David; Wilson, Christopher	Edinburgh (The Buildings of Scotland)	Penguin	1984
Girouard, Mark	Life in the English Country House	Penguin Books	1980
.. ..	Victorian Country House, The	Oxford	1971
Gloag, John	Victorian Taste	David and Charles	1972
Greaves, John	Pyramidographia	London	1646
Greenhill, Thomas	Nekrokedeia or The Art of Embalming	London	1705
Greenwod, Margaret et al	Rough Guide to Ireland, The	Rough Guides	2003
Grossmith, George and Weedon	Diary of a Nobody	Everyman	1963
Gunnis, Rupert	Dictionary of British Sculptors 1660-1851	The Abbey Library	1968
Guy, Alan J (ed)	George Durant's Journal of the Expedition to Martinique and Guadeloupe, October 1758-May 1759 in Military Miscellany 9	Sutton Publishing Ltd for Army Records Office	1996
Haldane, J Aylmer L	Haldanes of Gleneagles, The	William Blackwood & Sons	1929
Hannigan, Ken and Nolan, William (eds)	Wicklow History and Society	Geography Publications	1994
Hardy, Thomas	Hand of Ethelburta, The	Macmillan	1975
Harris, John	Georgian Country Houses	Country Life Books	1968
Harris, John and Lever, Jill	Illustrated Glossary of Architecture	Faber and Faber	1966
Harris , Lucian	Suffolk's Hindu Mystery	Country Life 16 Oct	2003
Harrison, Crystal	Ebley, Gloucestershire; Historical Notes and Memories	Privately printed	2004
Hart, Vaughan	Nicholas Hawksmoor	Yale University Press	2002
Hart, Vaughan	St Paul's Cathedral	Phaidon	1995
Harvey, Paul (ed)	Oxford Companion to English Literature	Oxford University Press	1937
Harwood, Elain	England - A Guide to Post-War Listed Buildings	Batsford	2003
Haslam, M J	Chilwell Story, The	RAOC Corps Gazette	2005
Haslam, Richard	Powys (The Buildings of England)	Penguin	1979
Hayden, Peter	Biddulph Grange, Staffordshire	National Trust/George Philip	1989
Headley, Gwyn and Meulenkamp, Wym	Follies - A Guide to Rogue Architecture in England, Scotland and Wales	Jonathan Cape	1986

.. ..	Follies, Grottoes and Garden Buildings	Aurum Press	1999
Heaton, H	Benjamin Gott and the Industrial Revolution in Yorkshire	The Economic History Review, Vol 3 No 1	1931
Hebbert, Antonia (ed)	Secret Britain	Automobile Association	1986
Heehan, Rosa	Story of Mayo, The	Mayo County Council	2003
Hewson, Eileen	Old Irish Graveyards County Leitrim Pt 1	Kabristan Archives	2007
Hickey, Elizabeth	Epitaph on Edmond Malone	Riocht na Midhe (Journal of the Meath Archaeological and Historical Society) Vol VII Pt 2	1982
Hickman, Douglas	Warwickshire - A Shell Guide	Faber and Faber	1979
Hill, Leonard, and Greenwood, M	Influence of Increased Barometric Pressure on Man, The - No 1	Proceedings of the Royal Society Series B	1906
Hinton, Jeanne	Communities	Eagle (IPS)	1993
Hobhouse, Penelope and Taylor, Patrick (eds)	Gardens of Europe, The	George Philip	1990
Hope, Thomas	Household Furniture and Interior Decoration	John Tirani & Co	1946
Howley, James	Follies and Garden Buildings of Ireland, The	Yale University Press	1993
Howse, Geoffrey	Fitzwilliam (Wentworth) Estates & The Wentworth Woodhouse Monuments, The	Trustees of the Fitzwilliam Wentworth Amenity Trust	2002
Hubbard, Edward	Clwyd (The Buildings of Wales)	Penguin	1986
Hudson. Kenneth	Fashionable Stone, The	Adams and Dart	1971
Humbert, Jean-Marcel and Price, Clifford (eds)	Imhotep Today - Egyptianising architecture	UCL Press	2003
Humver, Jean-Marcel; Pantazzi, Michael and Ziegler, Christiane	Egyptomania - Egypt in Western Art 1730 - 1930	National Gallery of Canada	1994
Hunt, John Dixon	William Kent Landscape Garden Designer	Zwemmer	1987
Hussey, Christopher	English Gardens and Landscapes 1700 - 1750	Country Life	1967
Hutchinson, Geoff	Fuller - The life and times of John Fuller of Brightling	Geoff Hutchinson	1988
Inglis-Jones, Elisabeth	Augustus Smith of Scilly	Faber & Faber	1969
Ingram, James (transl)	Anglo-Saxon Chronicle, The	J M Dent, Everyman Edition	1934
Jackson-Stops, Gervase	Arcadia under the Plough	Country Life 9 Feb	1989
.. ..	English Arcadia, An 1600 - 1990	The National Trust	1991
Jacques, David and van der Horst, Jan	Gardens of William and Mary, The	Christopher Helm	1988
Jardine, Lisa	On a Grander Scale: The Outstanding Career of Sir Christopher Wren	Harper Collins	2002
Jeffery, Paul	City Churches of Sir Christopher Wren, The	Hambledon Continuum	1996
Jellicoe, Ann and Mayne, Roger	Devon - A Shell Guide	Faber and Faber	1975
Jellicoe, Geoffrey and Susan, Goode, Patrick and Lancaster, Michael	Oxford Companion to Gardens, The	Oxford University Press	1986
Jencks, Charles	Garden of Cosmic Speculation, The	Frances Lincoln	2003
Keating, Michael	History of Spitalfields and its Communities	University of East London	1999
Ketcham, Diana	Désert de Retz, Le	The MIT Press	1997
Kurzer, Frederick	Life and Work of Edward Charles Howard	Annals of Science V56 pt 2	1999
Laing, Gerald	Kinkell - The Reconstruction of a Scottish Castle	Ardullie House	1984
Lambton, Lucinda	Beastly Buildings	The Atlantic Monthly Press	1985
Langdon-Davies, John (ed)	Richard III and the Princes in the Tower	Jonathan Cape	1965
Larn, Richard	Shipwrecks of the Isles of Scilly	Shipwreck & Marine	1999
.. .. (ed)	Ships, Shipwrecks and Maritime Incidents around the Isles of Scilly	Isles of Scilly Museum	1999
.. .. and Larn, Bridget	Shipwreck Index of the British Isles	Lloyd's Register	1995
Le Vay, Benedict	Eccentric Britain	Bradt Publications	2000
Lemmon, Kenneth	Wentworth Castle: A Forgotten Landscape	Garden History Vol 3 No 3	1975
Levine, Neil	Castle Howard and the Emergence of the Modern Architectural Subject	The Journal of the Society of Architectural Historians Vol 62 no 3	2003
Lewer, David (ed)	John Mowlem's Swanage	Dorset Publishing Co	1990
Lewis, Samuel	Topographical Dictionary of Ireland	S Lewis & Co	1837
Linstrum, Derek, and Friedman, Terry	Artist and the Yorkshire Country House, The	Harrogate Art Gallery	1975
Littell, E and Keenan, W	Lives of Remarkable Youth of Both Sexes	E Littell	1830

Author	Title	Publisher	Year
Little, Bryan	Catholic Churches since 1623	Robert Hale	1966
Livingstone, E A (ed)	Concise Oxford Dictionary of the Christian Church, The	Oxford	1977
Lloyd, Thomas, Orbach, Julian and Scourfield, Robert	Pembrokeshire (The Buildings of Wales)	Penguin	2004
Loeber, Rolf	Biographical Dictionary of Architects in Ireland 1600 - 1720	John Murray	1981
Loghlin, John and Margaret	St Margaret Clitherow's Church, Threshfield		nd
Loudon, John Claudius	Encyclopædia of Gardening, An	Longman	1822
.. ..	Encyclopædia of Cottage, Farm, and Villa Architecture and Furniture, An	Longman	1835
Mackenzie, Thomas B (ed)	Life of James Beaumont Neilson FRS	West of Scotland Iron and Steel Institute	1929
Maddison, John (ed)	Blickling Hall (guidebook)	National Trust	1987
Maitland, Sara and Matthews, Peter	Gardens of Illusion	Cassell & Co	2000
Malins, Edward and Bowe, Patrick	Irish Gardens and Demesnes from 1830	Barrie & Jenkins	1980
Marshall, H E	Our Island Race	Civitas reprint	2005
Marson, Peter	Belmore: The Lowry Corrys of Castle Coole	Ulster Historical Foundation	2007
Martin, Julie et al	Living places: urban renaissance in the South East: case studies	ODPM	2000
Martin, Peter	Edmond Malone, Shakespearean scholar	Cambridge University Press	1995
McCartney, James K	Ages of Darkness and Blood - A Guide to the Muirkirk Martyrs www.e-ayrshire.co.uk/local/sornweb/agesofdarkness.pdf		
McGonagall, William	Last Poetic Gems	David Winter & Son	1971
.. ..	More Poetic Gems	David Winter & Son	1966
McGuffie, T H	Deputy Paymaster's Fortune, A	Journal of the Society for Army Historical Research, Vol 32 pp 144-147	1954
McIntyre, Anthony	Shell Book of British Buildings, The	David & Charles	1984
MCLean, Lesley (ed)	Winkleigh Ways	Hedgerow Print	nd
McWilliam, Colin	Lothian (The Buildings of Scotland)	Penguin	1978
Meller, Hugh	London Cemeteries	Scolar Press	1994
Miller, Eric	Leckhampton Court; Manor House to Hospice	Matador	2002
Mitchell, W S	East Sussex - A Shell Guide	Faber and Faber	1978
Moor, Edward	Hindu Pantheon, The	Garland	1984
Moor, Edward	Suffolk Words and Phrases	David & Charles	1970
Morris F O	Series of Picturesque Views of the Seats of the Noblemen and Gentlemen of Great Britain and Ireland Vol 4	William Mackenzie	1889
Morris, Ralph	Cruising Anglesey & adjoining waters	North West Venturers Yacht Club	2003
Morrison, Eleanor M	Myles Morrison - A Charmed Life	The Pentland Press	1991
Mowl, Timothy	Gentlemen & Players	Sutton Publishing	2000
.. ..	Stylistic Cold Wars - Betjeman versus Pevsner	John Murray	2000
Mowl, Timothy	William Kent, Architect, Designer, Opportunist	Jonathan Cape	2006
and Earnshaw, Brian	Insular Rococo, An	Reaktion Books	1999
.. ..	Trumpet at a Distant Gate	Waterstone	1985
Murray, Colin (ed)	Living Landscape '91	West Cork Arts Centre	1991
Nairn, Ian and Pevsner, Nikolaus	Sussex (The Buildings of England)	Penguin Books	1965
National Trust Handbook 2003, The		National Trust	2002
Nash, T R	Collections for the History of Worcestershire	London	1781-99

From: 'References', Fasti Ecclesiae Anglicanae 1541-1857: volume 7: Ely, Norwich, Westminster and Worcester dioceses (1992), pp. VIII-IX. URL: http://www.british-history.ac.uk/report.aspx?compid=35226 Date accessed: 29 March 2009.

Author	Title	Publisher	Year
Neale, Freda D	Eminent Talents - A history of the Reverend Thomas Rackett	Freda D Neale	2000
Neely, W G	Kilcooley: Land and People in Tipperary	Slieveardagh Rural Development	2005
Newman, John	Glamorgan (The Buildings of Wales)	Penguin	1995
.. ..	Gwent/Monmouthshire (The Buildings of Wales)	Penguin	2000
.. ..	North East and North Kent (The Buildings of England)	Penguin	1969
.. ..	West Kent and The Weald (The Buildings of England)	Penguin	1969
.. .. and Pevsner, Nikolaus	Dorset (The Buildings of England)	Penguin	1972
Nicoll, Josephine and Allardyce	Holinshed's Chronicle as used in Shakespeare's Plays	J M Dent and Sons Lrd	1927
O'Donnell, Ruan	Exploring Wicklow's Past 1798 - 1805	Wicklow '98 Committee	1998
O'Regan, John (ed)	James Scanlon, Sneem	Gandon Editions	1995

O'Reilly, Seán	Casino at Marino, The	Office of Public Works	1991
Osborne, Harold (ed)	Oxford Companion to Art, The	Oxford University Press	1970
Pearson, Robert, Mitchell, Susan and Hunt, Candida (eds)	Ordnance Survey Guide to Gardens in Britain, The	Ordnance Survey and Country Life Books	1986
Pevsner, Nikolaus	Bedfordshire, Huntingdon & Peterborough (The Buildings of England)	Penguin Books	1968
.. ..	Berkshire (The Buildings of England)	Penguin Books	1966
.. ..	Cambridgeshire (The Buildings of England)	Penguin Books	1970
.. ..	Cumberland and Westmorland (The Buildings of England)	Penguin Books	1967
.. ..	Herefordshire (The Buildings of England)	Penguin Books	1963
.. ..	History of Building Types, A	Thames & Hudson	1976
.. ..	Leicestershire and Rutland (The Buildings of England)	Penguin Books	1960
.. ..	North-East Norfolk and Norwich (The Buildings of England)	Penguin Books	1962
.. ..	North Lancashire (The Buildings of England)	Penguin Books	1969
.. ..	North Somerset and Bristol (The Buildings of England)	Penguin Books	1958
.. ..	Shropshire (The Buildings of England)	Penguin Books	1958
.. ..	South and West Somerset (The Buildings of England)	Penguin Books	1958
.. ..	South Lancashire (The Buildings of England)	Penguin Books	1969
.. ..	Staffordshire (The Buildings of England)	Penguin Books	1974
.. ..	Worcestershire (The Buildings of England)	Penguin Books	1968
.. ..	Yorkshire The North Riding (The Buildings of England)	Penguin Books	1966
Pevsner, Nikolaus and Harris, John	Lincolnshire (The Buildings of England)	Penguin Books	1964
.. .. and Hubbard, Edward	Cheshire (The Buildings of England)	Penguin Books	1971
.. .. and Lang, S	Egyptian Revival, The Architectural Review CXIX	pp 242 - 254	1956
.. .. and Lloyd, David	Hampshire and the Isle of WIght (The Buildings of England)	Penguin Books	1967
.. .. and Neave, David	Yorkshire: York and the East Riding (The Buildings of England)	Penguin Books	1995
.. .. and Richmond, Ian, rev Grundy; McCrombie; Ryder; Welfare	Northumberland (The Buildings of England)	Penguin Books	1992
.. .. and Wedgwood, Alexandra	Warwickshire (The Buildings of England)	Penguin Books	1966
.. .. and Williamson, Elizabeth	Buckinghamshire (The Buildings of England)	Penguin Books	2000
.. .. and Wilson, Bill	Norfolk 1: Norwich and North-East (The Buildings of England)	Penguin Books	2000
.. ..	Norfolk 2: North-West and South (The Buildings of England)	Penguin Books	1999
.. .. rev Cherry, Bridget	Northamptonshire (The Buildings of England)	Penguin Books	1973
.. ..	Surrey (The Buildings of England)	Penguin Books	1971
.. ..	Wiltshire (The Buildings of England)	Penguin Books	1975
rev Radcliffe, Enid	Yorkshire West Riding (The Buildings of England)	Penguin Books	1967
.. ..	Cornwall (The Buildings of England)	Penguin Books	1970
.. ..	Suffolk (The Buildings of England)	Penguin Books	1974
rev Williamson, Elizabeth	Nottinghamshire (The Buildings of England)	Penguin Books	1979
rev Cherry, Bridget	Hertfordshire (The Buildings of England)	Penguin Books	1977
rev Radcliffe, Enid	Essex (The Buildings of England)	Penguin Books	1965
rev Williamson, Elizabeth	Derbyshire (The Buildings of England)	Penguin Books	1978
.. ..	Durham (The Buildings of England)	Penguin Books	1985
Ponsonby, Sir John	Ponsonby Family, The	The Medici Society	1929
Pope, Alexander	Collected Poems	Everyman	1965
Purves, Libby	One Summer's Grace	Coronet Books	1997
Pyle, Hilary	Sligo-Leitrim World of Kate Cullen 1832-1913	The Woodfield Press	1997

Author	Title	Publisher	Year
Reade, Charles	Cloister and the Hearth, The	James Nisbet & Co	1905
Reade, Charles L and The Rev J	Charles Reade, A Memoir	Chapman and Hall	1887
Rees, Vyvyan	South-West Wales: A Shell Guide	Faber and Faber	1976
Religious, A	Short Memoirs of the English Martyrs	J Whitehead	1885
Ridgeway, Christopher and Williams, Robert (eds)	Sir John Vanbrugh and Landscape Architecture in Baroque England	Sutton Publishing	2000
Robb, Peter A	Temple of Pan at Halswell Park, Somerset, The	Garden History Vol 5 No 3	1977
Robinson, John Martin	English Country Estate, The	Century/National Trust	1988
.. ..	Temples of Delight	The National Trust	1994
.. ..	Wyatts, The: An Architectural Dynasty	Oxford University Press	1979
Robinson, W R	Robinson's Guide to Richmond	W R Robinson	1833
Rogerson, Robert W K C	Jack Coia, His Life and Work	Robert Rogerson	1986
Rowan, Alistair	Garden Buildings	Country Life Books	1968
.. ..	North West Ulster (The Buildings of Ireland)	Penguin	1979
Sadie, Stanley	New Grove Dictionary of Opera, The	Grove	1992
.. .. and Tyrrell, John	New Grove Dictionary of Music and Musicians, The	Grove	2001
Sampson, Mike	History of Tiverton, A	Tiverton War Memorial Trust	2004
Sampson, R A	Thomas Wright's Theory of the Universe	The Observatory, No 344	1903
Scanlon, James	Sneem	Gandon Editions	1995
Scarfe, Norman	Suffolk - A Shell Guide	Faber and Faber	1976
Schaaf, Larry	Charles Piazzi Smyth's 1865 Conquest of the Great Pyramid	History of Photography, Vol 3 No 4	1979
.. ..	Origins of Photography	St Andrew's University Alumnus Chronicle	June 1985
Schul, Bill & Pettit, Ed	Psychic Power of Pyramids, The	Fawcett Publications Inc	1976
Schulz, Max F	The Circuit Walk of the Eighteenth-Century Landscape Garden and the Pilgrim's Circuitous Progress	Eighteenth Century Studies Vol 15 No 1	1981
Scott, Sir Walter	Old Mortality	Black	1871
.. ..	Minstrelsy of the Scottish Borders	EP Publishing	1975
Scott-Giles, C W	Looking at Heraldry	Phoenix House	1962
Scully, Vincent	Architecture: the natural and the manmade	St Martin's Press	1991
Sellar, W C and Yeatman, R J	1066 and all that	Methuen	1930
Semmell, Stuart	Reading the Tangible Past: British Tourism, Collecting, and Memory after Waterloo	Representations (University of California) No 69	2000
Service, Alastair	Architects of London, The	The Architectural Press	1979
Seymour, Susanne and Calvocoressi, Rupert	Landscape Parks and the Memorialisation of Empire: The Pierreponts' 'Naval Saescape' in Thoresby Park, Nottinghamshire during the French Wars, 1793-1815	Rural History (2007) Vol 18 no 1	2007
Shakespeare, William	Richard III	Cambridge University Press	1968
Sheeran, George	Landscape Gardens in West Yorkshire 1680 - 1880	Wakefield Historical Publications	1990
Sheppard, F W H (ed)	Survey of London Vol XXVII, Spitalfields and Mile End New Town	The Athlone Press University of London	1957
Sherburn, George (ed)	Correspondence of Alexander Pope, The	Oxford	1956
Sherwood, Jennifer and Pevsner, Nikolaus	Oxfordshire (The Buildings of England)	Penguin Books	1974
Simons, Rabbi Dr. Chaim	Seven Years at Carmel College, Reminiscences of a Pupil 1953-1960 www.geocities.com/CapitolHill/Senate/7854/carmelcollege03.html		2004
Sitwell, Sacheverell	British Architects and Craftsmen	Pan Books	1960
Smiles, Sam	Image of Antiquity, The	Yale University Press	1994
Smiles, Samuel	George Moore, Merchant and Philanthropist	George Routledge & Sons	1884
.. ..	Industrial Biography	John Murray	1863
Smith, Ruth	Achievements of Charles Jennens, The	Music and Letters Vol 70 No 2	1989
Smyth, Charles Piazzi	Great Pyramid, The; Its Secrets and Mysteries Revealed	Bell Publishing	1978
.. ..	Life and Work at the Great Pyramid	Edmonson and Douglas	1867
.. ..	Teneriffe - an Astronomer's Experiment	Lowell Reeve	1858
Somervell, D C (ed)	Selections from Wordsworth	J M Dent	1965
Stevens, Todd, and Cumming, Edward	Ghosts of Rosevear and the Wreck of the Nancy Packet	Todd Stevens and MIBEC Enterprises	2008
Stockholm, Johanne M	Garrick's Folly - The Stratford Jubilee of 1769	Methuen & Co	1964
Strong, Roy	Renaissance Garden in England, The	Thames & Hudson	1979

Strong, Roy, Binney, Marcus and Harris, John	Destruction of the Country House	Thames and Hudson	1974
Summerson, John	John Nash	George Allen & Unwin	1935
Symes, Michael	English Rococo Garden, The	Shire	1991
Tangye, Michael	Guide to the Old Church of St Mary the Virgin, Isles of Scilly	Privately printed	1995
Taylor, John	The Great Pyramid	London	1856
Thorndike, Joseph J, Junior	Magnificent Builders, The	Paul Elek	1978
Thorold, Henry	Staffordshire - A Shell Guide	Faber and Faber	1978
Timpson, John	Timpson's England	Jarrold	1987
Trollope, Anthony	Warden, The	Thomas Nelson & Sons	nd
Turnor, Reginald	James Wyatt 1746 - 1813	Art and Technics	1950
Tyack, Geoffrey	Victorian Architectural Correspondence, A	Architectural History Vol 22 pp 78-87	1979
Uglow, Jenny	Little History of British Gardening, A	Chatto and WIndus	2004
Verey, David	Gloucestershire - A Shell Guide	Faber and Faber	1970
.. ..	Gloucestershire: The Cotswolds (The Buildings of England)	Penguin Books	1970
.. ..	Gloucestershire: The Vale and the Forest of Dean (The Buildings of England)	Penguin Books	1970
.. ..	Herefordshire - A Shell Guide	Faber and Faber	1955
.. ..	Mid Wales - A Shell Guide	Faber and Faber	1960
Victoria, HM Queen	Leaves from the Journal of our Life in the Highlands	Webb and Bower	1983
Vitruvius, tr Morgan, Morris H	De Architectura - The Ten Books of Architecture	Dover Publications	1960
Wales, HRH The Prince of, and Lycett Green, Candida	Garden at Highgrove, The	Cassell	2000
Walker, Frank Arneil	Argyll and Bute (The Buildings of Scotland)	Penguin	2000
Walpole, Horace	History of the Modern Taste in Gardening, A	Pallas Editions	2004
.. ..	On Modern Gardening	Brentham Press	1975
Walton, R D	Dumfries & Galloway Highways and Byways - Guide to 200 Walks and Climbs	Robert Dinwiddie & Co	nd
Ware, Dora	Short Dictionary of British Architects, A	George Allen and Unwin	1967
Watkin, David	Thomas Hope, Designer and Patron in Regency London	Yale University Press	2008
Watkin, Bruce	Buckinghamshire - A Shell Guide	Faber and Faber	1981
.. ..	Surrey - A Shell Guide	Faber and Faber	1977
Wesley, John	John Wesley's Journal	Isaac Pitman & Sons	1905
Whistler, Laurence et al	Stowe: A Guide to the Gardens (3rd ed)	Privately Printed	1974
White, Colin (ed)	Nelson Companion, The	Alan Sutton Publishing Ltd	1997
Wilde, Oscar	Complete Works of Oscar Wilde	Collins	1967
Williams, Archibald	Romance of Modern Mechanism, The	Seely & Co	1907
Williamson, Elizabeth; Riches, Anne and Higgs, Malcolm	Glasgow	Penguin	1990
Wilson, Tom	Memorials of a Sanquhar Kirkyard	Robert G Mann	1912
Winpenny, David	Northumbria and Hadrian's Wall	AA Publishing	2006
Wittkower, Rudolph	Palladio and English Palladianism	Thames & Hudson	1974
Woolner, Amy	Thomas Woolner RA - His Life in Letters	Chapman & Hall	1917
Wordsworth, William ed de Selincourt, Ernest	Guide to the Lakes	Oxford	1977
Worple, Ken	Cemetery in the City, The	Comedia	1997
.. ..	Here comes the sun	Reaktion Books	2000
.. ..	Last Landscapes: The architecture of the cemetery in the West	Reaktion Books	2003
Wrathmell, Susan	Leeds - Pevsner Architectural Guides	Yale University Press	2005
Wyke, Terry, with Cocks, Harry	Public Sculpture of Greater Manchester	Liverpool University Press	2004
Yarwood, Doreen	Robert Adam	Aldine	1970
Yates, Jack and Thorold, Henry	Lincolnshire - A Shell Guide	Faber and Faber	1965
Young, Wayland and Elizabeth	London's Churches	Guild Publishing	1986
	Burke's Peerage	Harrison/Burke's	1914
	Burke's Landed Gentry	Shaw Publishing Co/Burke's	1937
	Exhibition Hall and Boathouse, Carmel College	Concrete Quarterly Oct-Dec, pp 2 to 4	1970
	Jerusalem Bible, The	Darton, Longman & Todd	1968
	Penrhyn Castle (Guidebook)	The National Trust	2004
	Titles and Forms of Address	Adam and Charles Black	1969

ACKNOWLEDGMENTS

The author is grateful to everyone who has helped with the research and travel for this book.
First and greatest thanks go to my wife Sheila, who undertook much of the research, arranged itineraries, read maps, drove, commented, proofread, corrected and supported throughout the six years that the book took to come to print. The faults that remain are all my own.

For general help thanks are due to:
Turtle Bunbury, Peter Burton, Cadw, Julie Freeman, Richard Taylor, Harland Walshaw.

Particular assistance has been given, knowingly or otherwise, by:
Adfa - Mrs Ruth Jones; **Anderston Kelvingrove Church** - The Rev'd Anthony Craig; **Arklow** - Graham Caswell, *Wicklow Today*, Deidre Burns, *Wicklow County Council*; **Athy** - Frank Taaffe; **Attleborough** - Moira Brown and Barbara, *Attleborough Public Library*; **Auchencloy** - Billy Maxwell, *Forestry Commission*; **Badsworth** - Sue Baker, *Local Studies Library, Wakefield*; **Ballybrack** - Anne McElheron and Graham Montgomery, *Dalkey Library*: Brother Fred Rech SM and Father Michael Reaume SM; **Ballydehob** - Margaret O'Regan, *West Cork Arts Centre*, Cathy Cook; **Balmoral** - Fiona Stewart and her pony Quarry, Diane Eddy, *Administration Secretary Balmoral Estate*; **Berry Pomeroy** - Phil Speirs; **Bexhill** - Julian Porter, *Bexhill Museum*, Adrian Gaylon, *Bexhill Leisure Centre*, Julie Baker, *Rother District Council*; **Bilston Glen** - David Hill and Martin Meehan, *Hills Electrical and Mechanical*; **Bishop Auckland** - Eileen Hall, *Bishop Auckland Town Hall*, Dan Gracey, *Smiths Gore*, Alan Anderson, *Auckland Castle*, Grace McCombie; **Bishop's Wood** - David and Karen Foster; Blackburn - Rob Howell, *Blackburn with Darwen Borough Council*; **Bletchley** - Sue Coker and Abdul, *Steel Construction Institute*, Jon Wright - *The Twentieth Century Society*; **Blickling** - Russell Sparkes, R C Watling, Mrs Val Bardsley, Patricia A E Fearns, Wendy Matthews; **Bolton-on-Swale** - Richard Stancliffe, Jackie Logan *York Castle Museum;* Bonchurch - David Booth, *Isle of Wight Council*; *Ventnor Heritage Museum;* **Bosworth** - Ian Horsford, Gill Steer, *Ripon Cathedral*; **Bowland** - Adrian Walton; **Cork** - Liz Meaney, *Cork Corporation*; **Bretton Park** - Professor Derek Linstrum, Charles Boot, *Garden History Society*, Glyn Headley, *The Folly Fellowship*, Richard Bell, *artist*; Carlisle - Stephen White, *Carlisle Library*; **Castle Howard** - Dr Christopher Ridgeway; **Castlerickard** - Frank McQuaid; **Ceide Fields** - Geoff Holland, Dr Gretta Byrne; Cerne Abbas - Frank Hamblin; **Chapel Hill** - Dr Madeleine Gray, *University of Wales, Newport*, C J Gibson, *Gwent Record Office*; **Chilwell** - Capt John Pasco, *Station Adjutant*; **Clearbeck** - Richard Osborne; **Clifford** - Glenys Parrington; **Clocaenog** - Nicola Samuel, *Denbighshire County Record Office*; **Cobham** - Philip Sharp, Alison Nailer; **Corbridge** - Michael Harris; **Cross Ash** - Dr Jean Prosser, *Village Alive Trust*, Mrs C Nash; **Crowle** - Mrs Andrew, Crowle Library, John Ramsden; **Cumbernauld** - Erin French, *North Lanarkshire Council*; **Dalton** - Neil Moffat, *Ewarts Library, Dumfries*; **Desertcreat** - Andrew McClelland, *Ulster Architectural Heritage Society*; **Dolgellau** - Robert Jones, *Dolgellau Library*; **Drumkeeran** - Eileen Hewson, *Kabristan Archives*, Mary Comfrey, *Ballinamore Library*, Dr Raymond Refaussé, *Representative Churches Board Library*, *Dublin*, Bernie Christie, Moraig Harris, Norman Kelly; **Duddingston** and Isles of Scilly - Richard Larne, Todd and Carmen Stevens, Ann Langton; **Dundee** - Ian, Cath Coultas, *Axis Arts*, Deborah Pemberton-Pigott, *University of Dundee*, Joanne Soroka, *Society of Scottish Artists*; **Dunfermline** - Mrs Walls; **Falmouth** - Carol Philp, *Falmouth Library*, Joanne Laing, *Cornish Studies Centre*; Enfield RSA - Ray Tuthill; **Farley Mount** - Beverley Morris, *Hampshire Record Office*; **Garvagh** - Josephine Dempsey; **Gilltown** - John Garrett, *Stud Groom*, Alan Norton, *Stud Personnel Manager*, Cathy Flynn and Nessa Dunlea, *Kilcullen Heritage Centre*, Ger McCarthy, Dr Alastair Disley; **Glasnevin** - Peter Hamilton; Glenlyon - Colin Wilson; **Goathurst** - Erica Adams, *Somerset Buildings Preservation Trust*, Grahame and Janine Bond, Russell Lillford, *Somerset County Council*; **Gosford** - The Earl and Countess of Wemyss and March, Jo Duguid; **Gosport** - Karen Sturdy; **Great Bealings** - Jonathan Peto; **Greenock** - Betty Hendry, *Watt Library*; **Hambleden** - Charles Gray; **Hampstead Norreys** - Pamela and Richard Betts; **Harelaw** - John Milburn; **Harrogate** - Nikki Stones, *Hornbeam Park*; Helston - Jenni Sheldon and Paul Phillips, *Helston Town Council*, Rolf Necke, *Kerrier District Council*, Bill Finlay, *Flambards*; **Heversham** - Judith and Martin Ellis, Peter Bingham; **Highgrove** - Amanda Foster, *Prince of Wales' Office, Clarence House*; **Introduction**: Diane Naylor, *Chatsworth;* Trisha Buckingham, Nick Cistone, *Bodleian Library, Oxford*; **Ipsden** - Helen McRobbie; **Isle of Skye** - John Phillips, *Countryside Ranger*, John McLeod; Kilberry - Elaine McFadden, *Bert House*; **Kilcooley** Abbey - Peter and Faith Ponsonby, John O'Gorman, *Thurles Library*, Peter Schermerhorn; **Killiney** - Peter Hamilton; **Kilmuir** - Trish Garron, *Dunvegan TIC*; **London, Spa Fields** - Richard Taylor; **Marylebone** - Tom McManus, *Site Manager*, Cheryl Francis, *School Administrator and Finance Officer, King Solomon Academy*; **Kinkell** Castle - Gerald Laing, Eric Angus; **Kinnitty** - James O'Carroll; **Kirroughtree** - David Ramshaw; **Leckhampton** - Eric Miller, Rob Marriott, *Weatherby's Stud Book Department*; Lewisham - Canon David Garlick, Julian Watson; **Limerick** - Ed Myers, *Limerick Today*, Patricia, *Receptionist, Two Mile Inn Hotel*; Lis Ard - Pat O'Mahoney, Margaret Newcombe; **Liverpool** - Carol Morgan, *Institution of Civil Engineers*; **Livingston** - Officers and Men, *Craighills Fire Station*; London - Leigh Hatts; Manchester UMIST - Liam Curtin, Cheryl Bowman, Alan Jones, *UMIST*; **Matfen** - Heidi Gaulton, *Matfen Hall Country House Hotel*; Mold - Merfyn Wyn Tomos, *Meirionydd Archivist*; **Monkseaton** - Huw Lewis, *The Journal, Newcastle*, Dr Paul Kelley, Barry Jennings and John Frain, *Monkseaton Community High School*; Moulton - Mr R H Vincent; **Muirkirk** - James Taylor; **Myross** - T Mulcahy, *Myross Wood Retreat House*; **Naas** - Nick Coy; **Nether Wallop** - Beverley Morris, *Hampshire Record Office*; **Nonington** - John Kings and Fritz Kleiner, *Bruderhof Community*; **Old Town, Scilly** - Carmen and Todd Stevens, Roger Banfield, David Teague; **Orsett** - John Whitworth; **Penicuick** - Sir Richard Clerk; **Perlethorpe** - Sheila Pool, Rowan McFarren, Andrew Poole, George Clarke; Pool, Cornwall - Colin French, *The Trevithick Society*; **St Leonards** - Christine Francis, *Burton's St Leonards Society*; **Salford** - Tim Ashworth, Patricia Nuttall, Salford Local History Library; **Scarborough** - Mike Stevenson, *Merlin Aquarium Projects*; **Sharow** - Richard Stansfield; **Skye** (Maryon) - Ralph Storer; **Southsea** - Heather J New; **Stanway** - Lord Neidpath; **Stirling** - Mary Craig, *Hill & Robb Solicitors*, Isobel, *Stirling Library*, Michael McGinnes (for Star Pyramid): Alison Shaw, *Drystone Walling Association* (for The Smith); **Stradbally** - Bridey Keenan, *Laois County Council*; **Strathkinness** - Jim Black, David Smith, **Studley Royal** - Ross and Anna Horsey; **Terrington** - Nigel Goodwill; **The Neale** - Dermot Keane, *Neale Heritage and Development Association Ltd*; Thorndon - Dave Lott, *Essex*

Ranger Service; **Tiverton** - Harland Walshaw, Sue Warren, *Mid-Devon Council*, ; **Tobermory** - Murdo MacDonald and Marina, *Argyll and Bute Council Archives*; **Tollymore** - Mark Parker, *Forestry Service Northern Ireland*; **Tong** - David de la Motte; Toombridge - Michael Lynn, *North Eastern Education and Library Board, Ballymena*, Karen Ledder, David Jordan, *Antrim Borough Council*; **Torrington** - Kate Garvey, *Torrington Library*, Miss Scrutton, *Archivist*; **Watford** - Peter Fox, *Emporio Home* (High Street): Joe Kovacik, Charles Lequesne, Les Capon (The Grove); **Welham** - Richard and Wendy Rhodes, John Wilmot, The Rev'd Ian Gemmell; **West Drayton** - William Pye; **Widford** - Anastasia Ward and Jillian, *Chelmsford Public Library*, The Rev'd Dave Robins; **Wimbledon** - Duncan Mirylees, *Surrey History Centre*, Elaine Bushell and Filomena Galuao, *Quinta de Monseratte, Portugal*; **Woodchester** - Derek Woodward, Barbara Warnes, Alan Fielder; **Wootton St Lawrence** - Ann Mitchell, *Basingstoke Reference Library*, Beverley Morris, *Hampshire Record Office*, Daphne Oliver-Bellasis; Winchester - Richard Farrington, *sculptor of Blade*.

Thanks also to the libraries in Annan, Athy, Attleborough, Ballinmore, Ballymena, Bishop Auckland, Broadford, Bury St Edmunds, Carlisle, Cumbernauld, Dalkey, Doncaster, Dumfries, Dundee, Dunfermline, Falmouth, Greenock, Helston, Institute of Advanced Architectural Studies, York, London Borough of Havering, Manorhamilton, Market Harborough, Naas, Penicuik, Portree, Ripon, Stirling, Thurles, Torrington, Ventnor, Wakefield and Watford.

♦ Places in **bold** appear in the book; the other places were investigated but not included.

Photograph and illustration acknowledgments

The majority of the photographs were taken by David Winpenny. ©

Grateful thanks to the following for permission to reproduce photographs, drawings and illustrations:

Page 7   Vanbrugh's drawing of Surat, India - © *Bodleian Library, Oxford*

Page 9   Kent's design for a hillside with pyramid temples - © *Devonshire Collection, Chatsworth. Reproduced by permission of Chatsworth Settlement*

Page 12   Blade, Winchester - © *Richard Farrington*

Page 25   Henry Jenkins - ©*York Castle Museum*

Page 85   Paternoster Square and Temple Bar from St Paul's Cathedral - © *Tom Winpenny*

Page 114   Aftermath of the 1918 explosion at Chilwell - *courtesy Capt John Pasco, Station Adjutant*

Page 181   Monkeseaton - *courtesy Monkseaton High School*

Page 199   William Mackenzie - © *Institution of Civil Engineers*

Page 267   Pyramid to Captain Maryon - © *Ralph Storer*

Page 281   Monument to the Battle of Airds Moss - © *Walter Baxter*

Back cover David Winpenny - © *Ben Winpenny*

The photographs on pages 35, 36, 54, 94 -96, 160 (and front cover) and 206 were taken by David Winpenny and are reproduced with the permission of The National Trust, on whose land the pyramids are found; *with thanks to Nikita Hooper, National Trust Picture Library*

♦ Every effort has been made to trace the copyright holders of other illustrations.
Apologies to anyone whose name is omitted or mis-spelled, or whose copyright has been unwittingly infringed.

INDEX